SUPERGIRL

VOLUME 5: THE HUNT FOR REACTRON

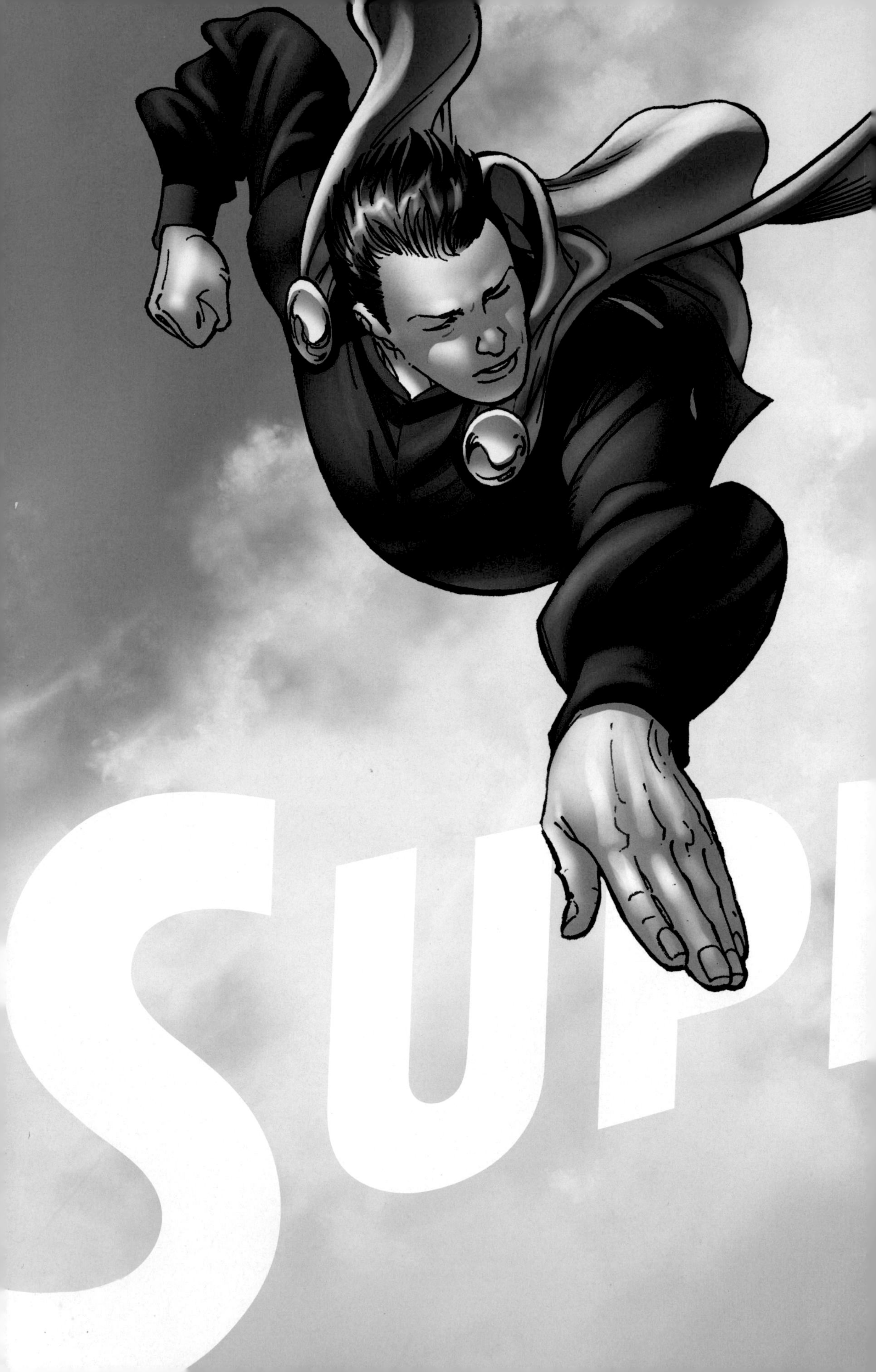
SUP

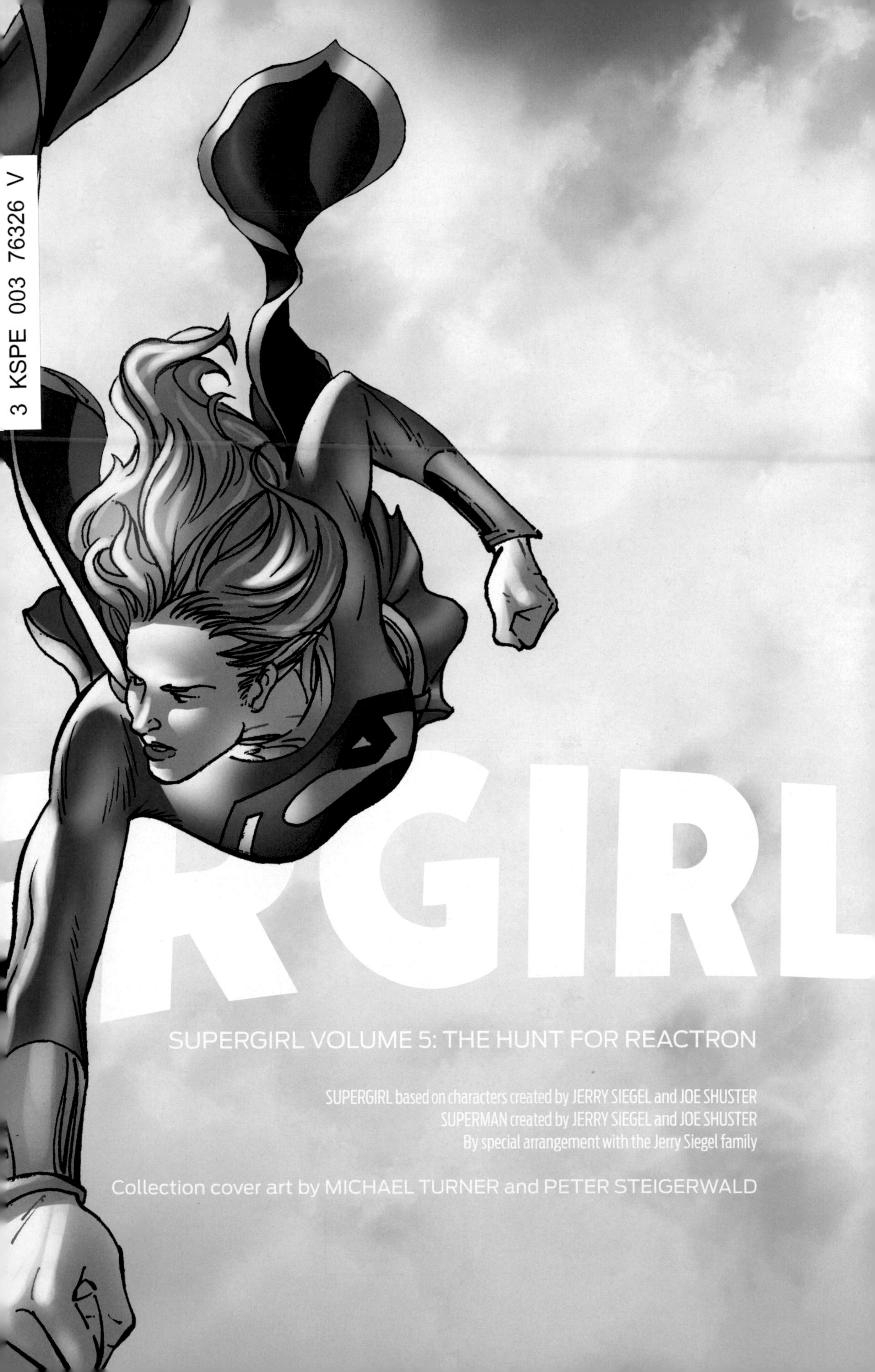

RGIRL

SUPERGIRL VOLUME 5: THE HUNT FOR REACTRON

SUPERGIRL based on characters created by JERRY SIEGEL and JOE SHUSTER
SUPERMAN created by JERRY SIEGEL and JOE SHUSTER
By special arrangement with the Jerry Siegel family

Collection cover art by MICHAEL TURNER and PETER STEIGERWALD

Matt Idelson Editor – Original Series
Wil Moss Assistant Editor – Original Series
Jeb Woodard Group Editor – Collected Editions
Eric Searleman Editor – Collected Edition
Steve Cook Design Director – Books
Monique Narboneta Publication Design

Bob Harras Senior VP – Editor-In-Chief, DC Comics
Pat McCallum Executive Editor, DC Comics

Dan DiDio Publisher
Jim Lee Publisher & Chief Creative Officer
Amit Desai Executive VP – Business & Marketing Strategy, Direct To Consumer & Global Franchise Management
Bobbie Chase VP & Executive Editor, Young Reader & Talent Development
Mark Chiarello Senior VP – Art, Design & Collected Editions
John Cunningham Senior VP – Sales & Trade Marketing
Briar Darden Vp – Business Affairs
Anne DePies Senior VP – Business Strategy, Finance & Administration
Don Falletti VP – Manufacturing Operations
Lawrence Ganem VP – Editorial Administration & Talent Relations
Alison Gill Senior VP – Manufacturing & Operations
Jason Greenberg VP – Business Strategy & Finance
Hank Kanalz Senior VP– Editorial Strategy & Administration
Jay Kogan Senior VP– Legal Affairs
Nick J. Napolitano VP – Manufacturing Administration
Lisette Osterloh VP – Digital Marketing & Events
Eddie Scannell VP – Consumer Marketing
Courtney Simmons Senior VP – Publicity & Communications
Jim (Ski) Sokolowski VP – Comic Book Specialty Sales & Trade Marketing
Nancy Spears VP – Mass, Book, Digital Sales & Trade Marketing
Michele R. Wells VP – Content Strategy

SUPERGIRL VOL. 5: THE HUNT FOR REACTRON

DC Comics, 2900 West Alameda Ave., Burbank, CA 91505
Printed by LSC Communications, Kendallville, IN, USA. 12/14/18. First Printing.
ISBN: 978-1-4012-8574-6

Library of Congress Cataloging-in-Publication Data is available.

PEFC Certified
This product is from sustainably managed forests and controlled sources
PEFC
PEFC/29-31-337
www.pefc.org

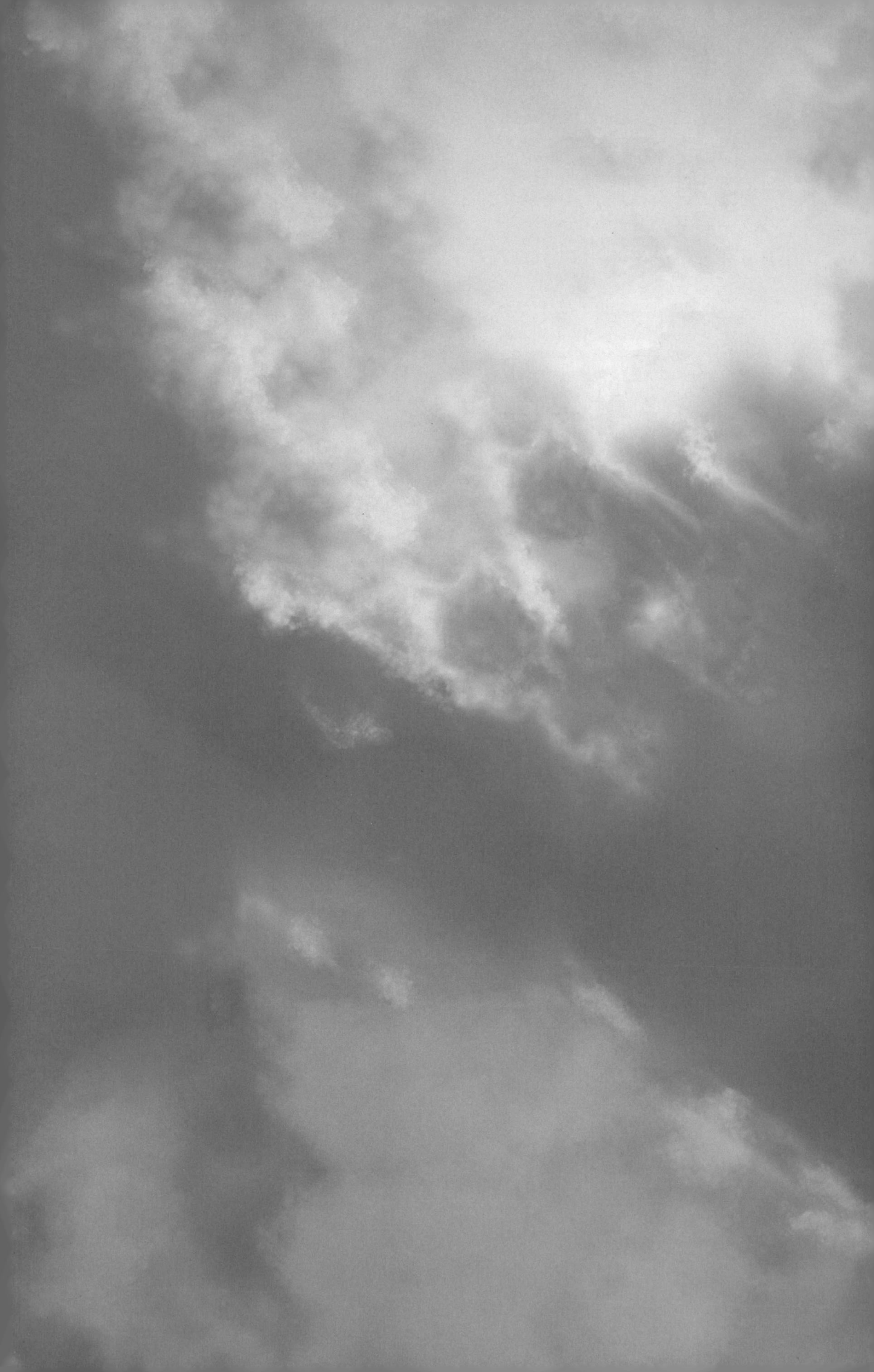

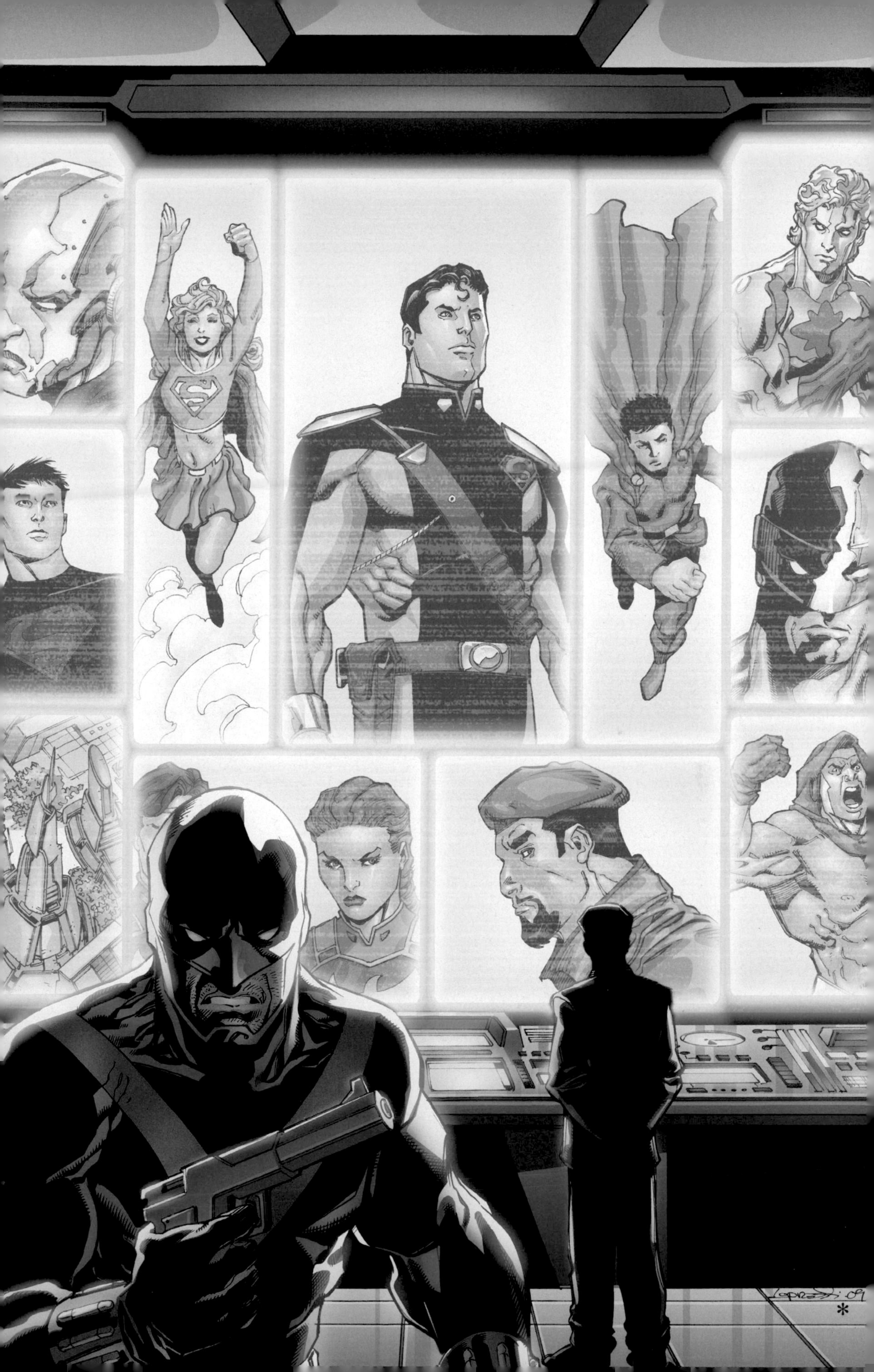

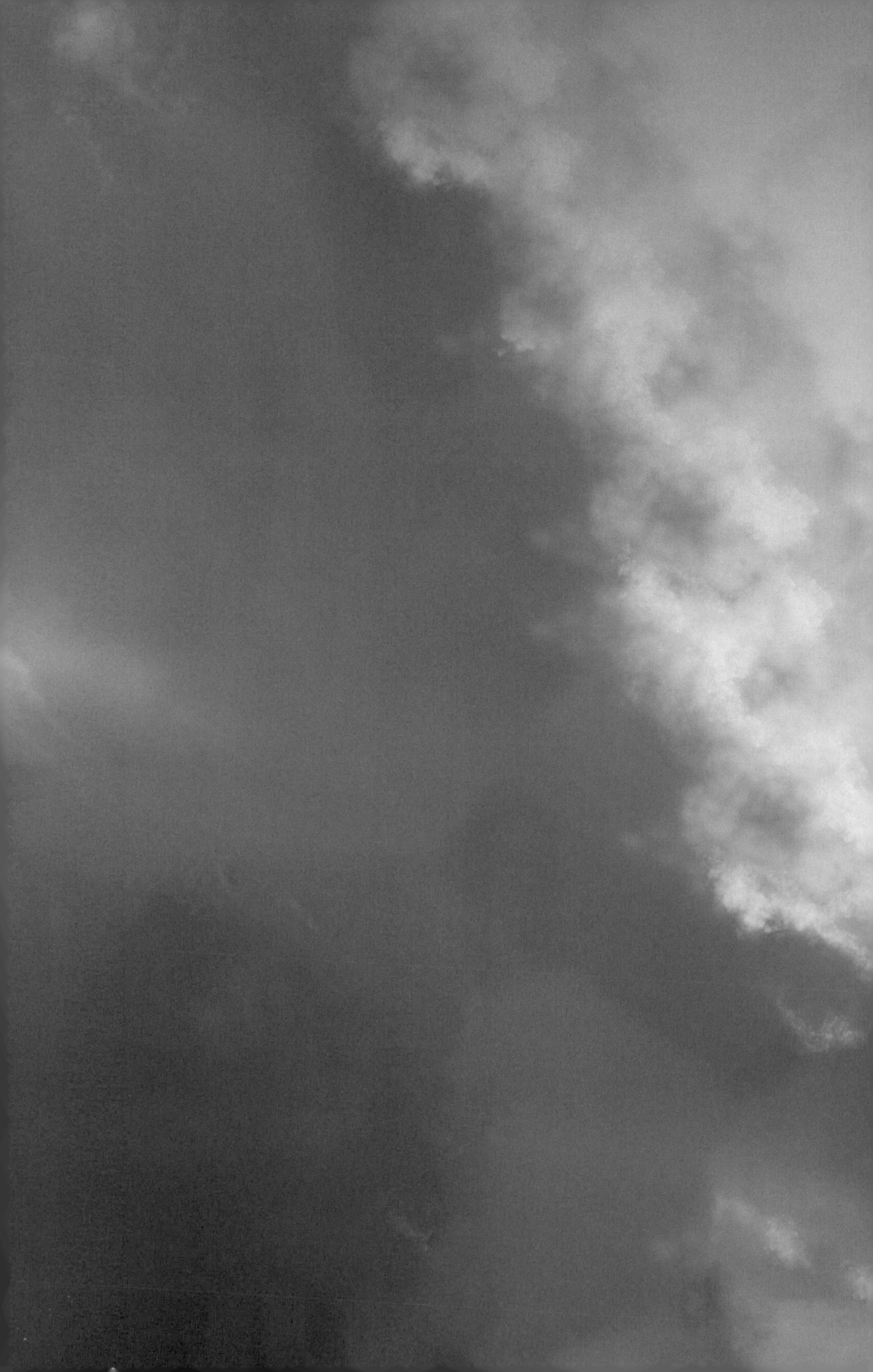

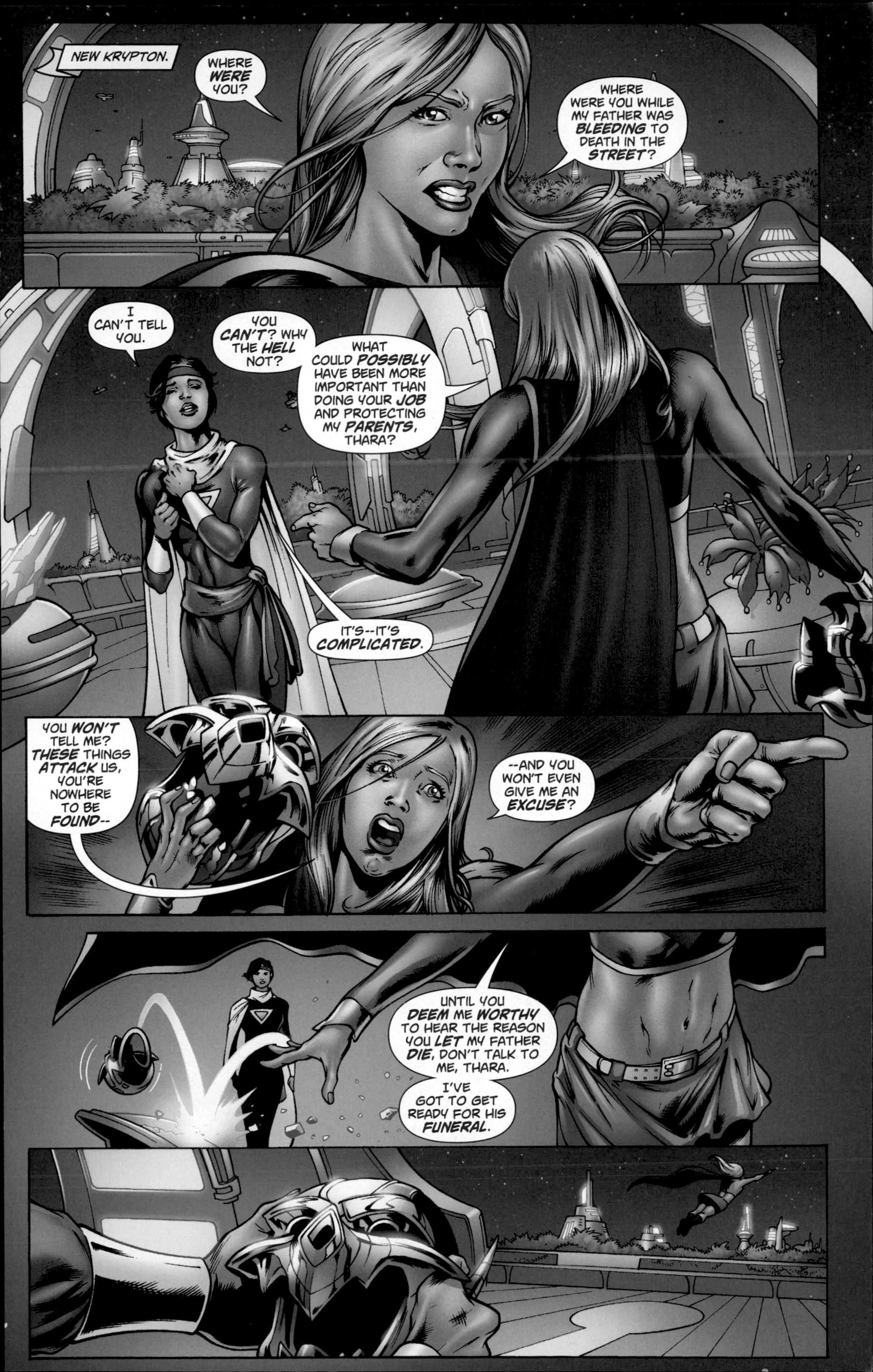
NEW KRYPTON.
WHERE WERE YOU?
WHERE WERE YOU WHILE MY FATHER WAS BLEEDING TO DEATH IN THE STREET?
I CAN'T TELL YOU.
YOU CAN'T? WHY THE HELL NOT?
WHAT COULD POSSIBLY HAVE BEEN MORE IMPORTANT THAN DOING YOUR JOB AND PROTECTING MY PARENTS, THARA?
IT'S--IT'S COMPLICATED.
YOU WON'T TELL ME? THESE THINGS ATTACK US, YOU'RE NOWHERE TO BE FOUND--
--AND YOU WON'T EVEN GIVE ME AN EXCUSE?
UNTIL YOU DEEM ME WORTHY TO HEAR THE REASON YOU LET MY FATHER DIE, DON'T TALK TO ME, THARA.
I'VE GOT TO GET READY FOR HIS FUNERAL.

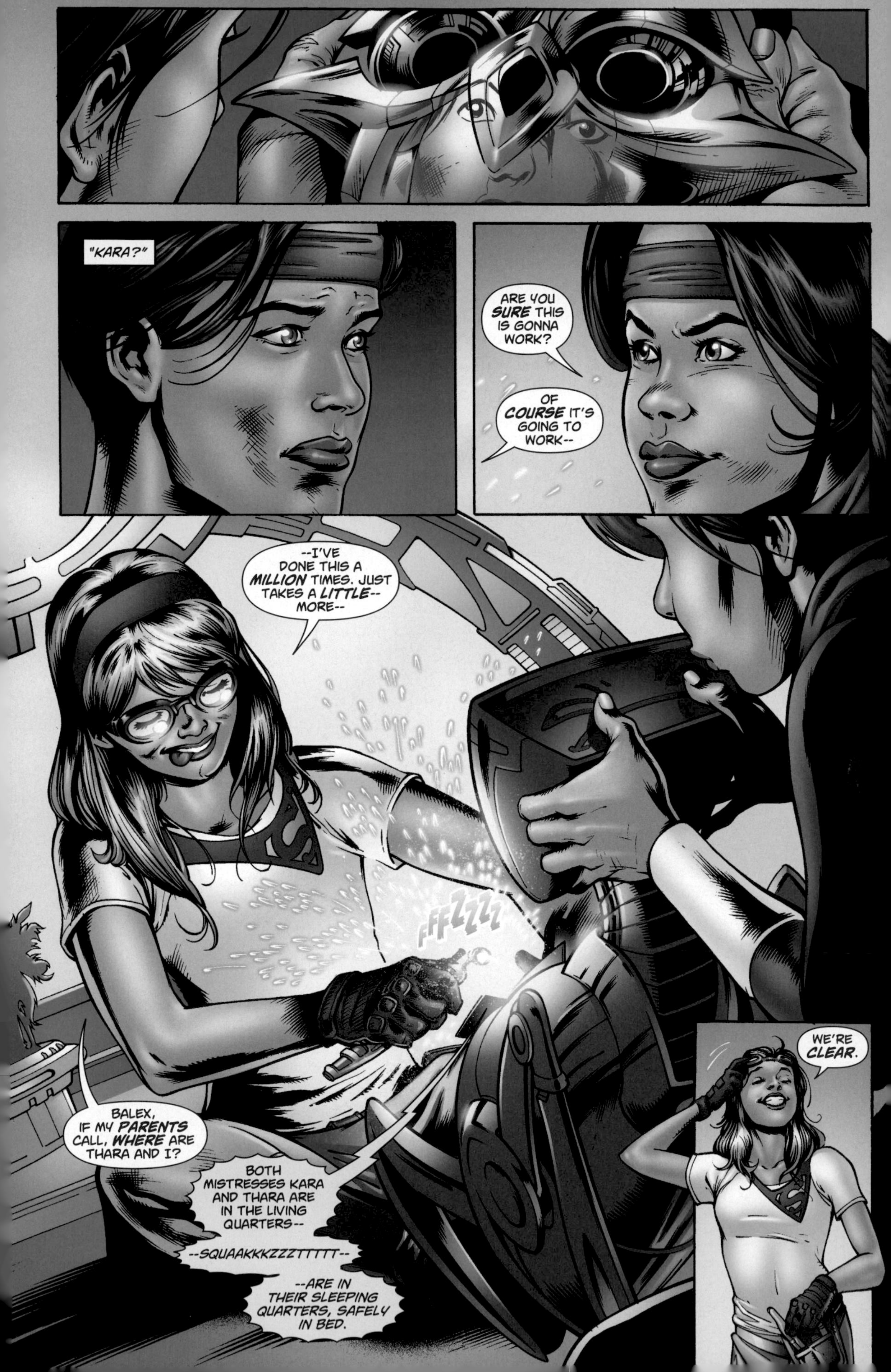
"KARA?"
ARE YOU SURE THIS IS GONNA WORK?
OF COURSE IT'S GOING TO WORK--
--I'VE DONE THIS A MILLION TIMES. JUST TAKES A LITTLE-- MORE--
FFZZZZ
BALEX, IF MY PARENTS CALL, WHERE ARE THARA AND I?
BOTH MISTRESSES KARA AND THARA ARE IN THE LIVING QUARTERS--
--SQUAAKKKZZZTTTTTT--
--ARE IN THEIR SLEEPING QUARTERS, SAFELY IN BED.
WE'RE CLEAR.

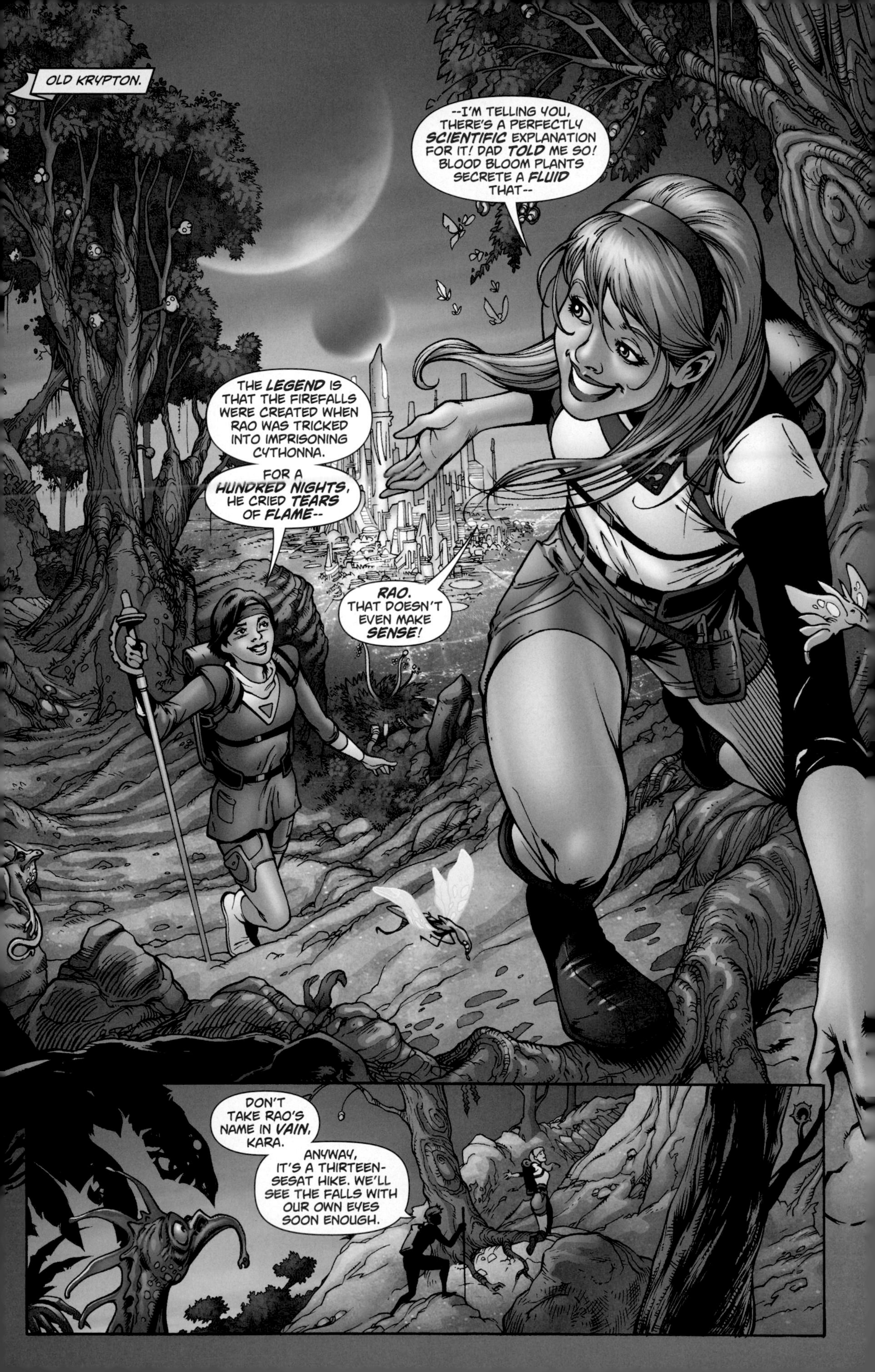
OLD KRYPTON.
--I'M TELLING YOU, THERE'S A PERFECTLY SCIENTIFIC EXPLANATION FOR IT! DAD TOLD ME SO! BLOOD BLOOM PLANTS SECRETE A FLUID THAT--
THE LEGEND IS THAT THE FIREFALLS WERE CREATED WHEN RAO WAS TRICKED INTO IMPRISONING CYTHONNA.
FOR A HUNDRED NIGHTS, HE CRIED TEARS OF FLAME--
RAO. THAT DOESN'T EVEN MAKE SENSE!
DON'T TAKE RAO'S NAME IN VAIN, KARA.
ANYWAY, IT'S A THIRTEEN-SESAT HIKE. WE'LL SEE THE FALLS WITH OUR OWN EYES SOON ENOUGH.

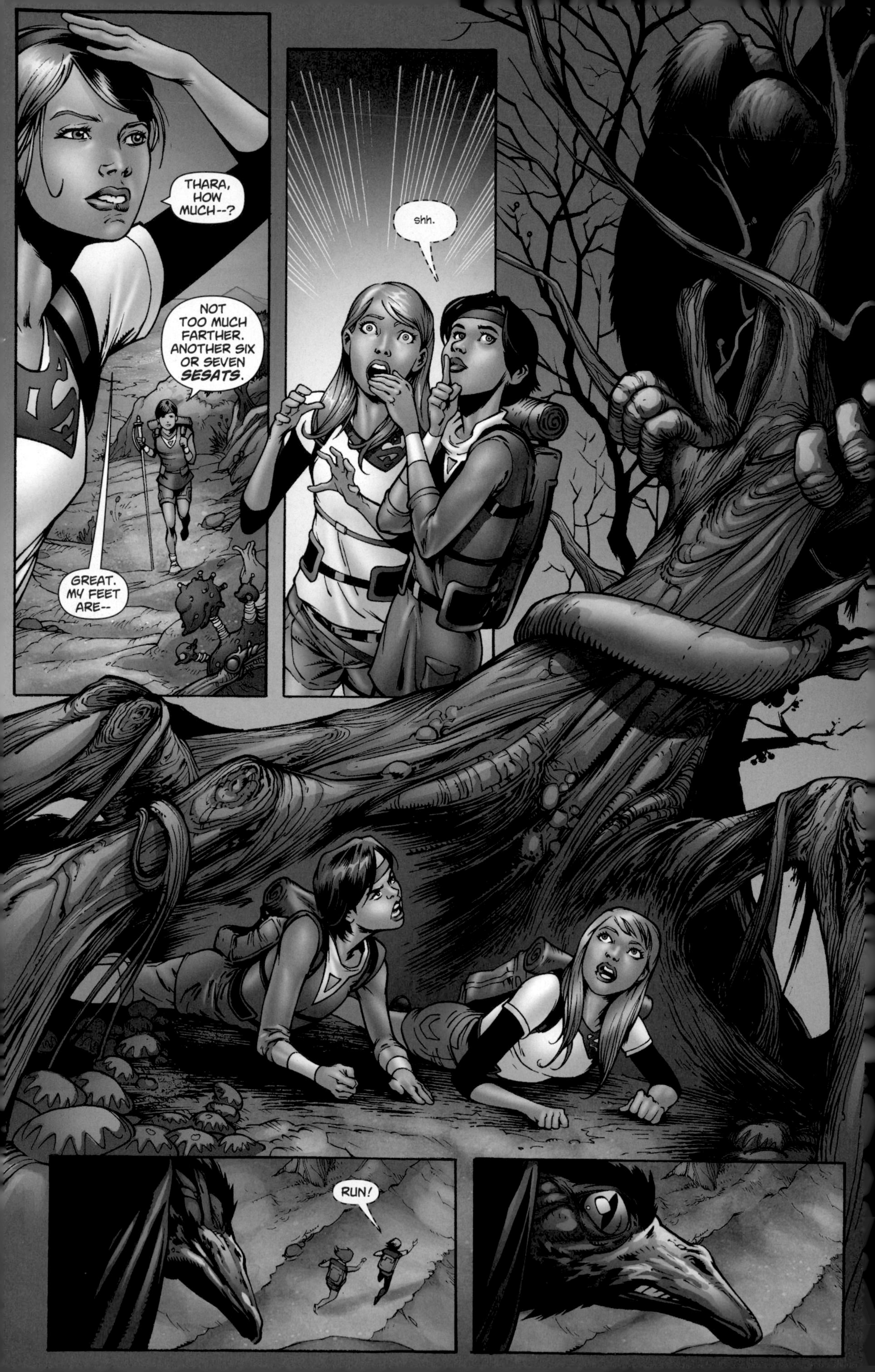
THARA, HOW MUCH--?
NOT TOO MUCH FARTHER. ANOTHER SIX OR SEVEN SESATS.
GREAT. MY FEET ARE--
shh.
RUN!

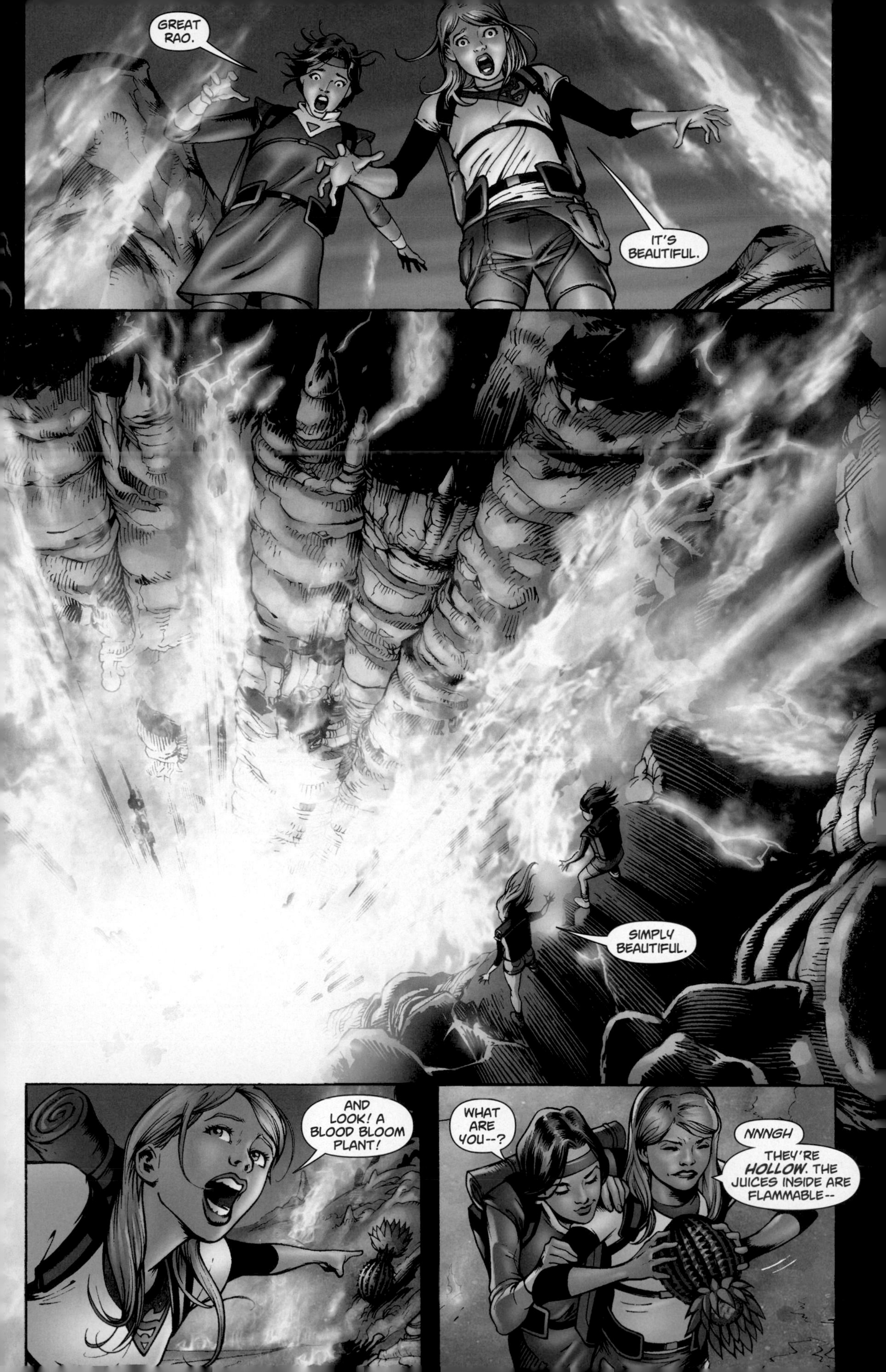
GREAT RAO.
IT'S BEAUTIFUL.
SIMPLY BEAUTIFUL.
AND LOOK! A BLOOD BLOOM PLANT!
WHAT ARE YOU--?
NNNGH
THEY'RE HOLLOW. THE JUICES INSIDE ARE FLAMMABLE--

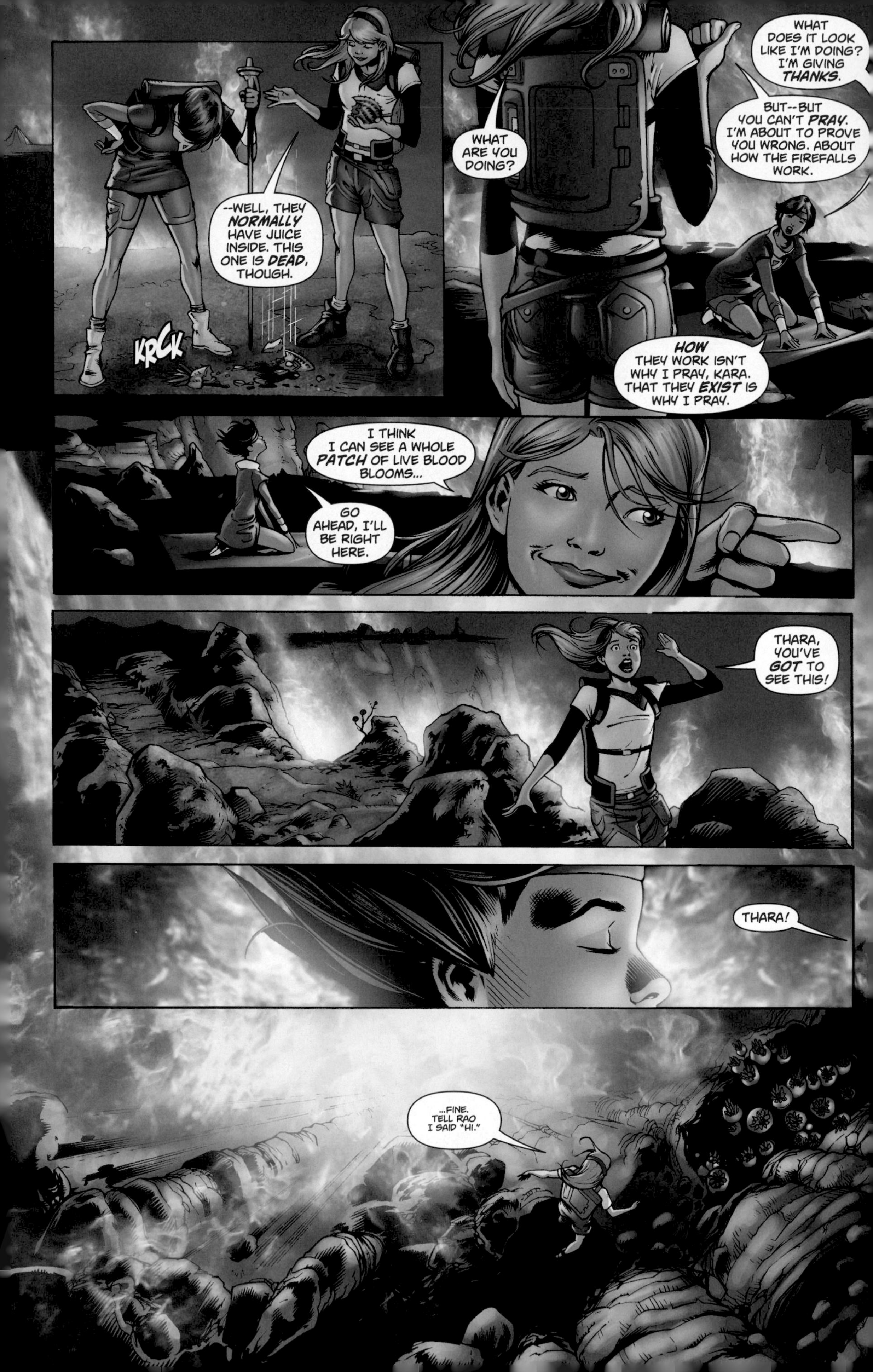
--WELL, THEY NORMALLY HAVE JUICE INSIDE. THIS ONE IS DEAD, THOUGH.
KRCK
WHAT ARE YOU DOING?
WHAT DOES IT LOOK LIKE I'M DOING? I'M GIVING THANKS.
BUT--BUT YOU CAN'T PRAY. I'M ABOUT TO PROVE YOU WRONG. ABOUT HOW THE FIREFALLS WORK.
HOW THEY WORK ISN'T WHY I PRAY, KARA. THAT THEY EXIST IS WHY I PRAY.
I THINK I CAN SEE A WHOLE PATCH OF LIVE BLOOD BLOOMS...
GO AHEAD, I'LL BE RIGHT HERE.
THARA, YOU'VE GOT TO SEE THIS!
THARA!
...FINE. TELL RAO I SAID "HI."

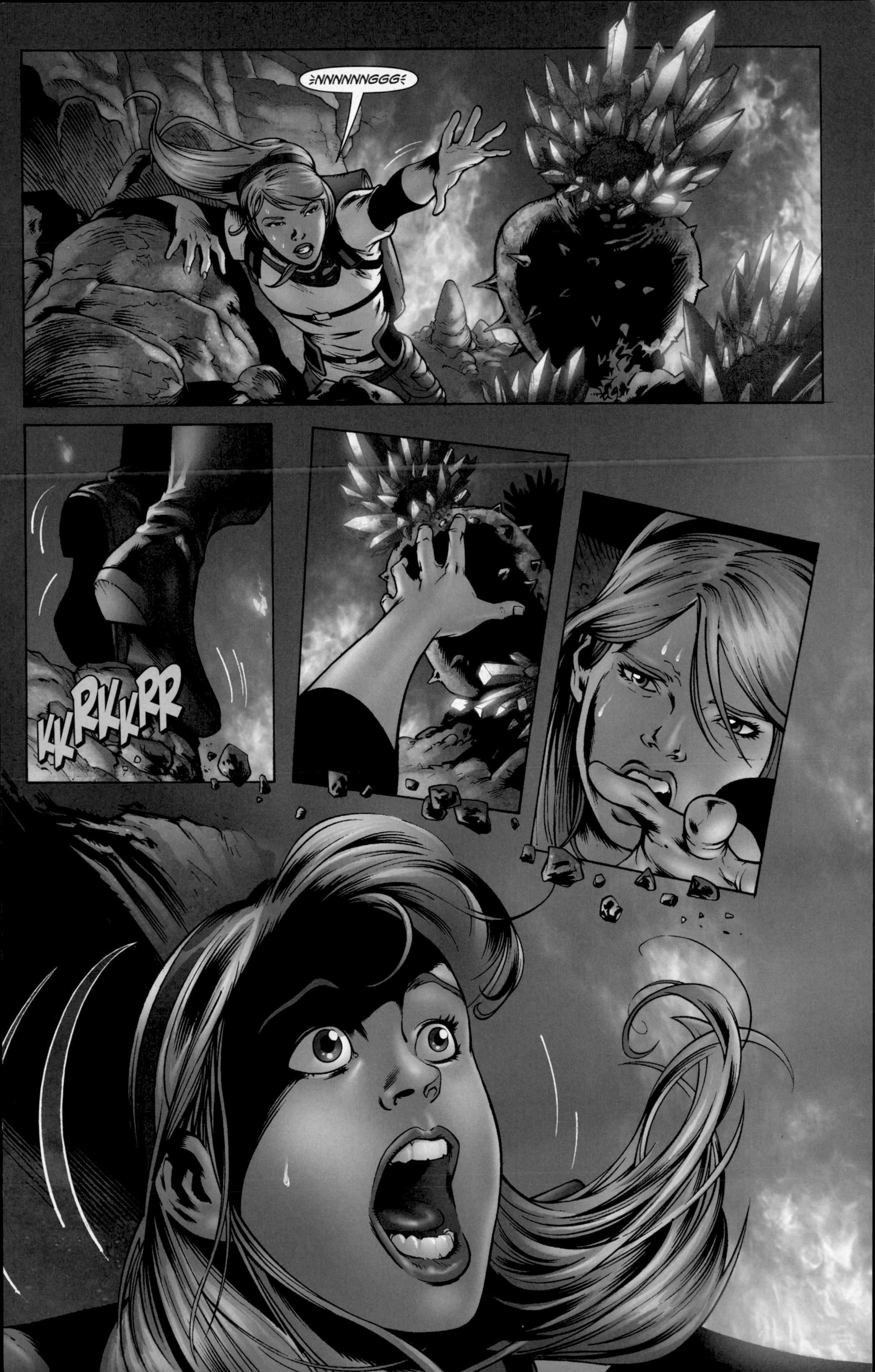
NNNNNNGGG
KKRKKRR

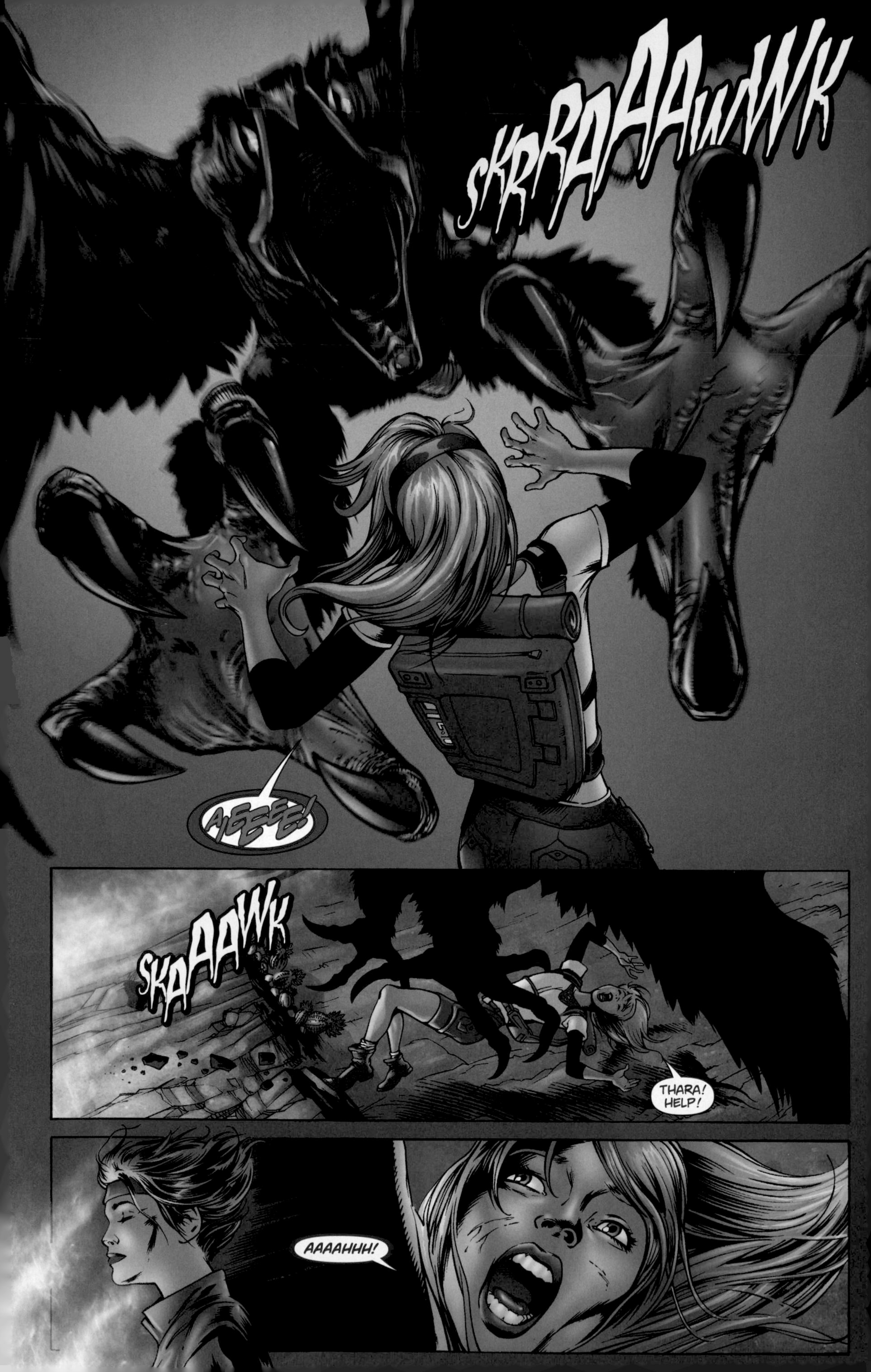
SKRAAAWWK
AIEEEE!
SKAAAWK
THARA! HELP!
AAAAHHH!

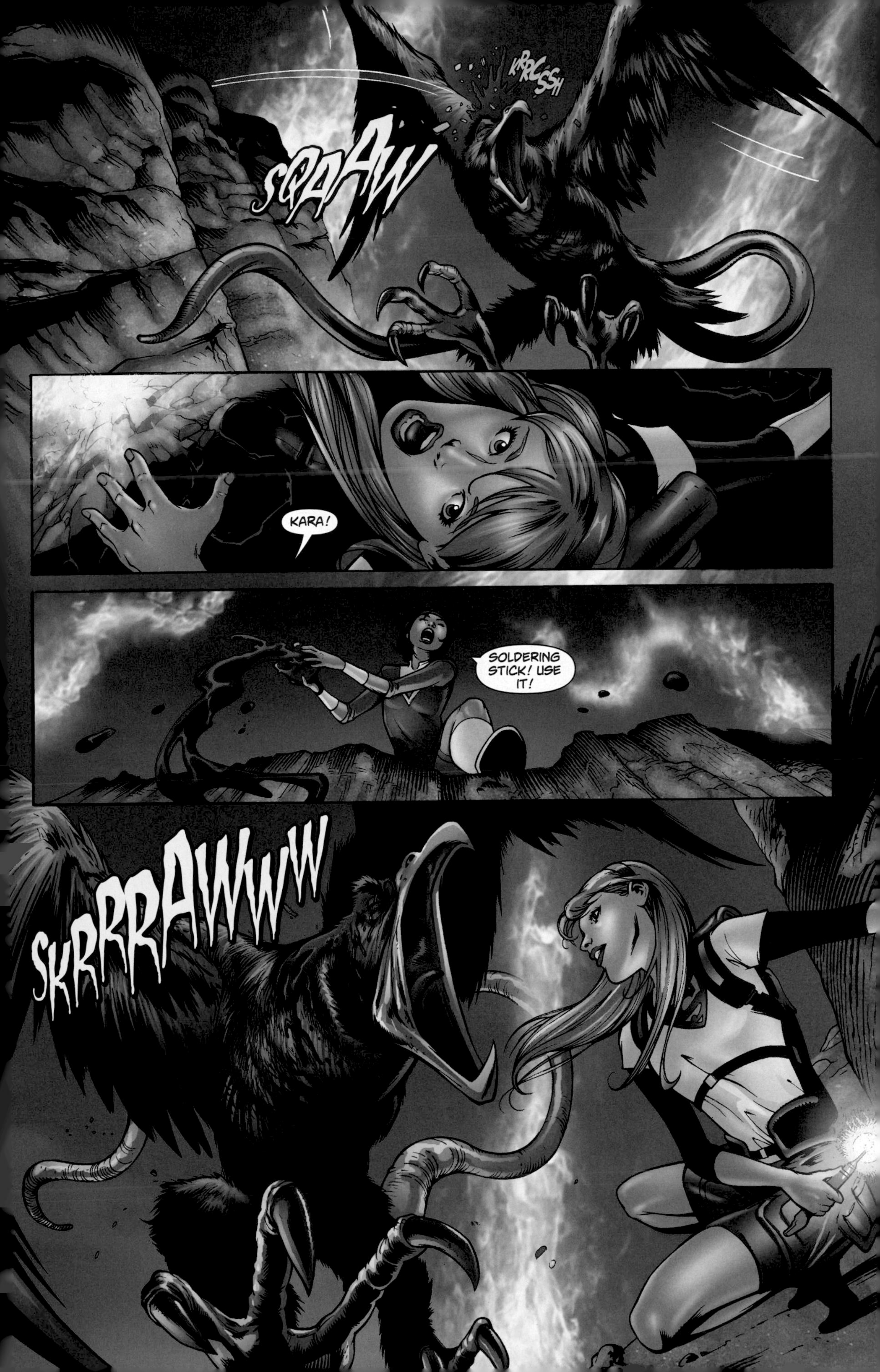
KRRCSSH
SQAAW
KARA!
SOLDERING STICK! USE IT!
SKRRRAWWW

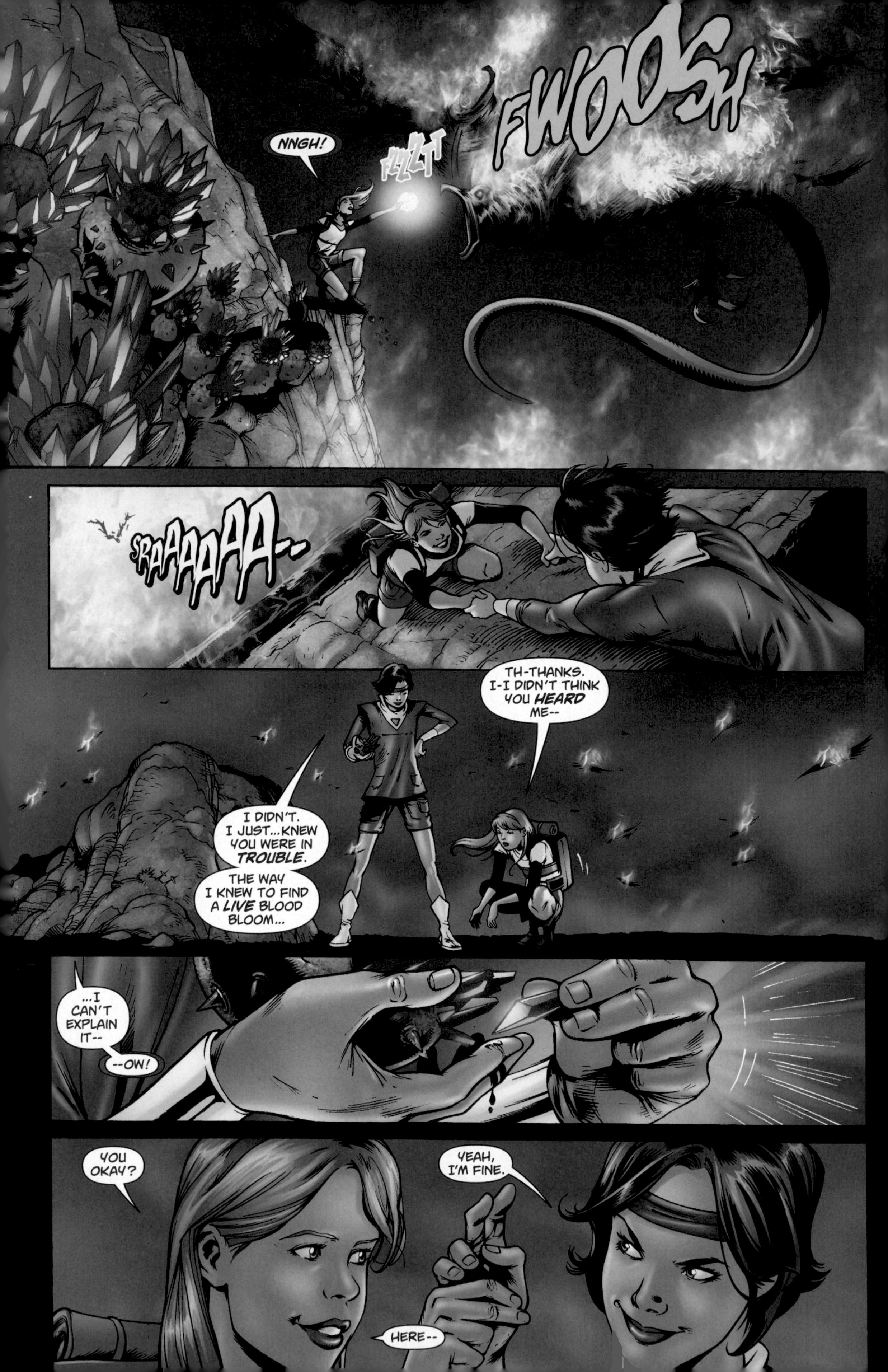
FWOOSH
NNGH!
FZZZT
SRAAAAAA--
TH-THANKS. I-I DIDN'T THINK YOU HEARD ME--
I DIDN'T. I JUST...KNEW YOU WERE IN TROUBLE.
THE WAY I KNEW TO FIND A LIVE BLOOD BLOOM...
...I CAN'T EXPLAIN IT--
--OW!
YOU OKAY?
YEAH, I'M FINE.
HERE--

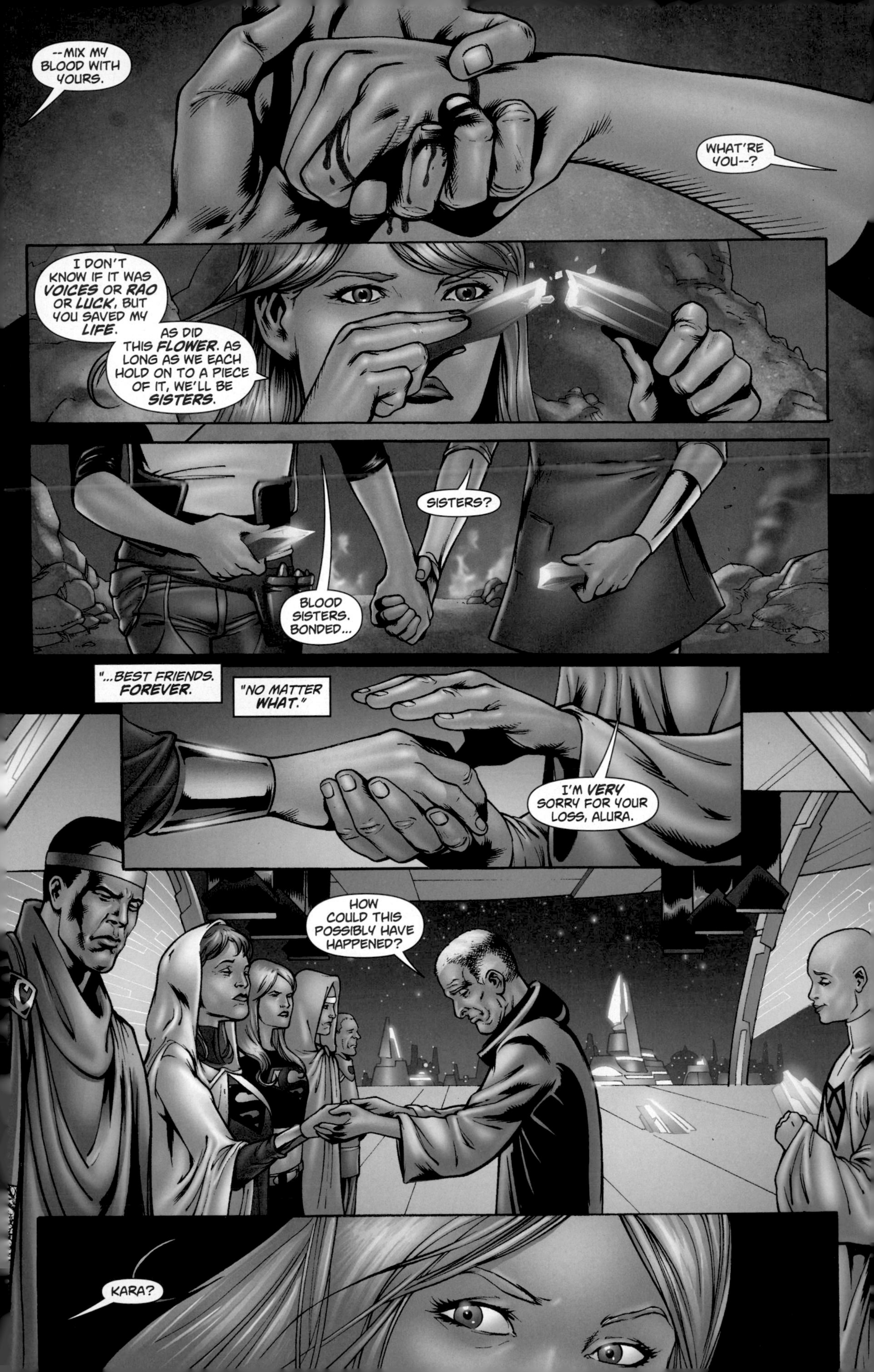
--MIX MY BLOOD WITH YOURS.
WHAT'RE YOU--?
I DON'T KNOW IF IT WAS VOICES OR RAO OR LUCK, BUT YOU SAVED MY LIFE.
AS DID THIS FLOWER. AS LONG AS WE EACH HOLD ON TO A PIECE OF IT, WE'LL BE SISTERS.
SISTERS?
BLOOD SISTERS. BONDED...
"...BEST FRIENDS. FOREVER.
"NO MATTER WHAT."
I'M VERY SORRY FOR YOUR LOSS, ALURA.
HOW COULD THIS POSSIBLY HAVE HAPPENED?
KARA?

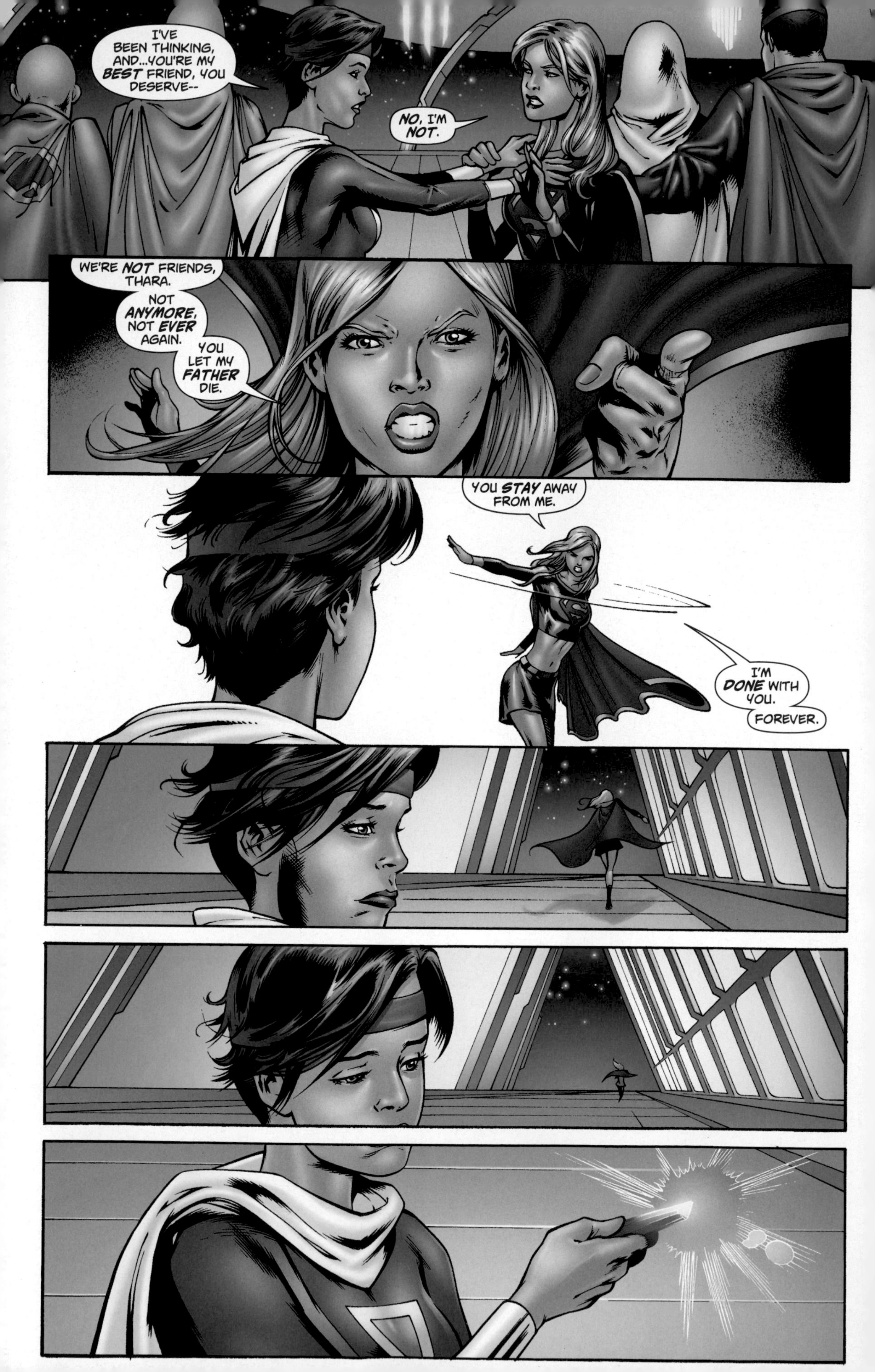
I'VE BEEN THINKING, AND...YOU'RE MY BEST FRIEND, YOU DESERVE--
NO, I'M NOT.
WE'RE NOT FRIENDS, THARA.
NOT ANYMORE, NOT EVER AGAIN.
YOU LET MY FATHER DIE.
YOU STAY AWAY FROM ME.
I'M DONE WITH YOU.
FOREVER.

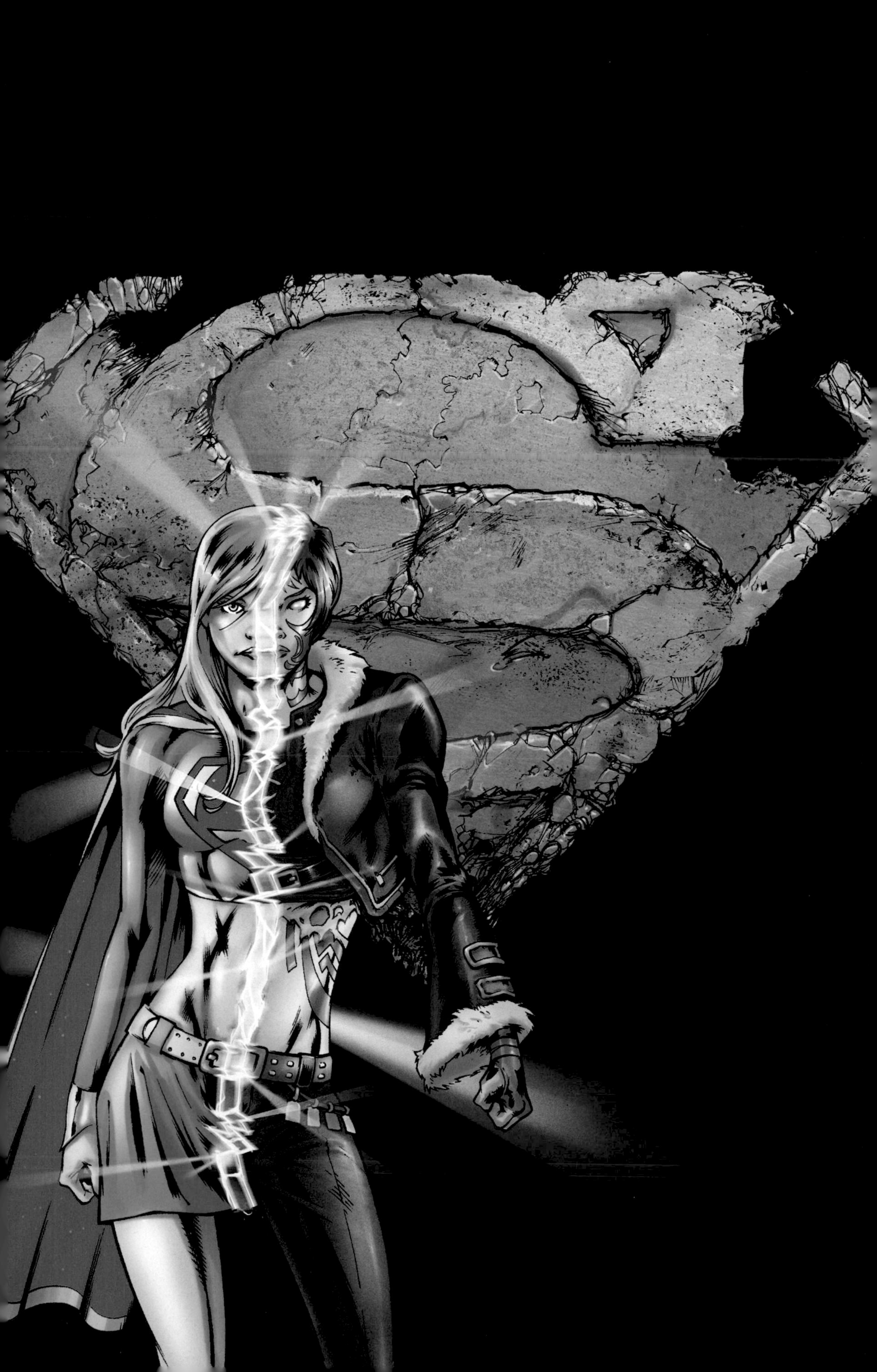

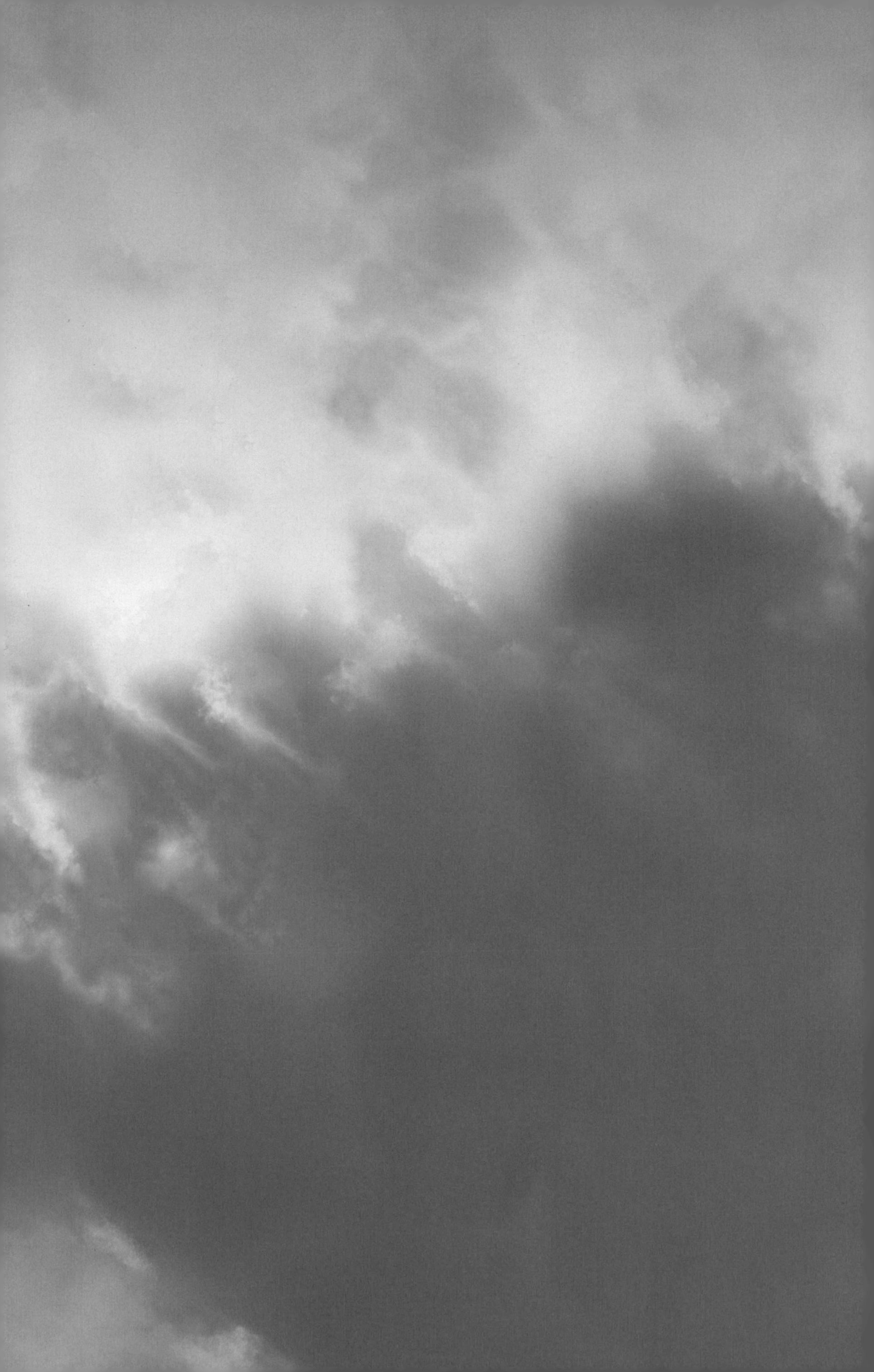

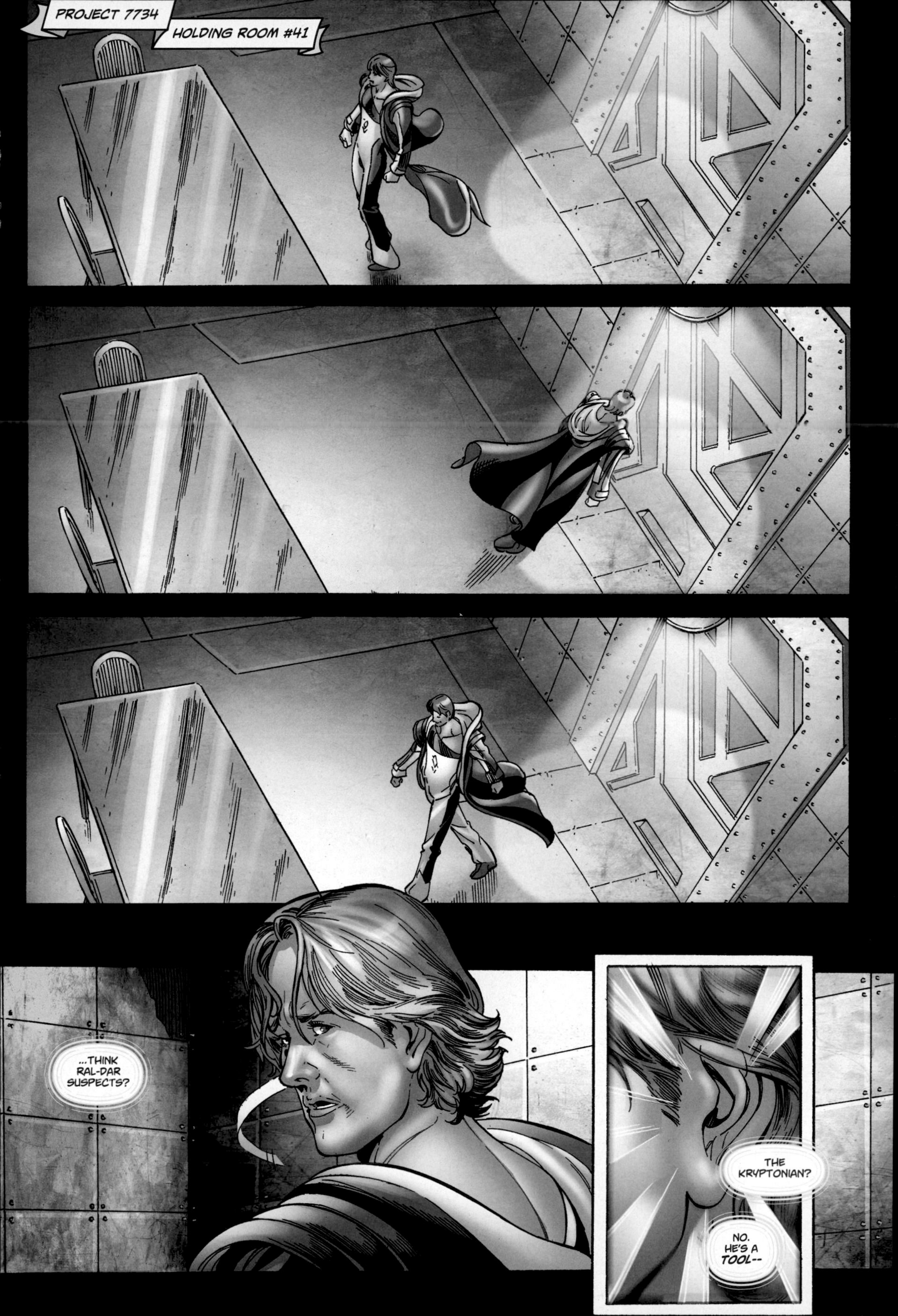
PROJECT 7734
HOLDING ROOM #41
...THINK RAL-DAR SUSPECTS?
THE KRYPTONIAN?
NO. HE'S A TOOL--

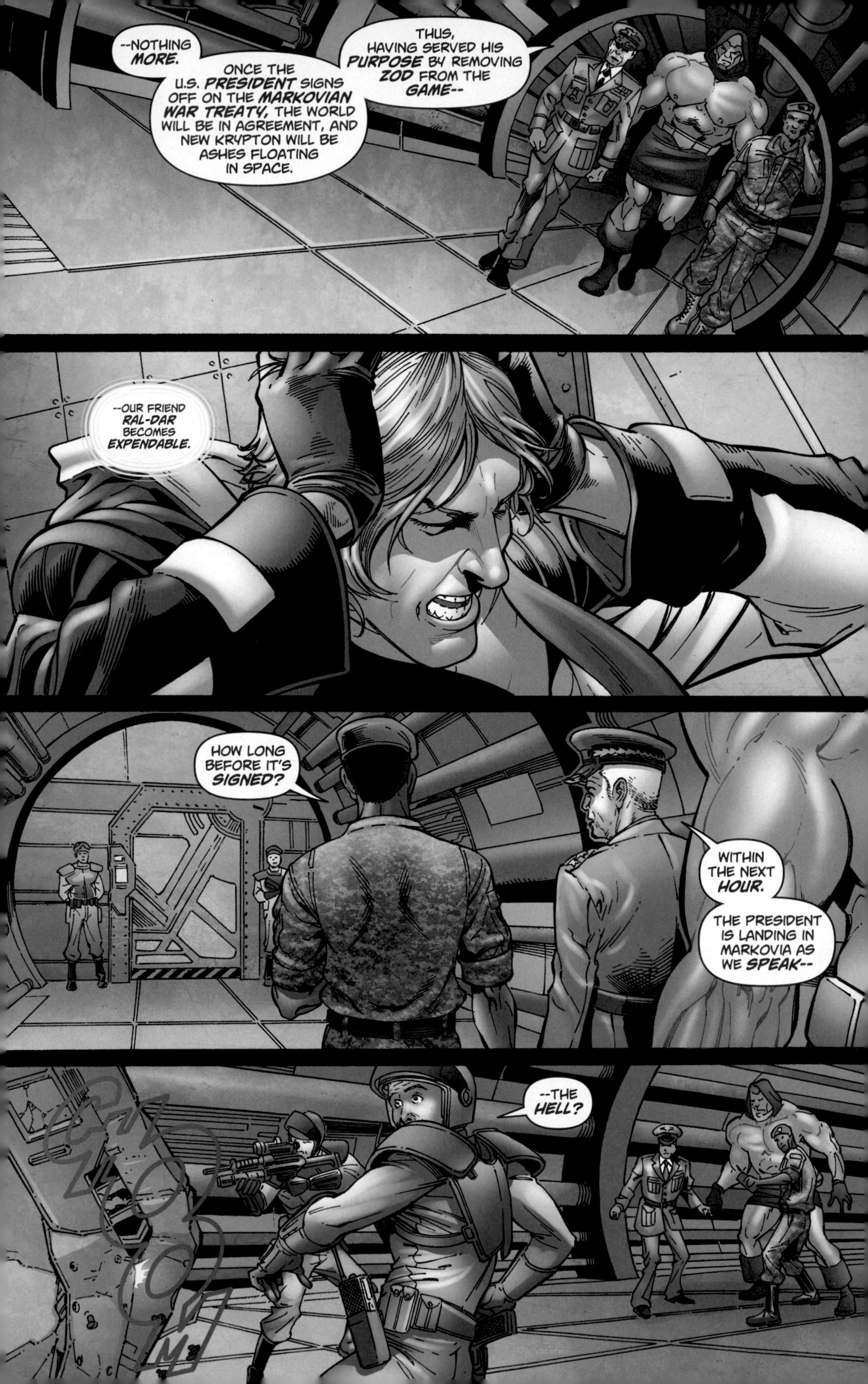
--NOTHING MORE.
ONCE THE U.S. PRESIDENT SIGNS OFF ON THE MARKOVIAN WAR TREATY, THE WORLD WILL BE IN AGREEMENT, AND NEW KRYPTON WILL BE ASHES FLOATING IN SPACE.
THUS, HAVING SERVED HIS PURPOSE BY REMOVING ZOD FROM THE GAME--
--OUR FRIEND RAL-DAR BECOMES EXPENDABLE.
HOW LONG BEFORE IT'S SIGNED?
WITHIN THE NEXT HOUR.
THE PRESIDENT IS LANDING IN MARKOVIA AS WE SPEAK--
--THE HELL?

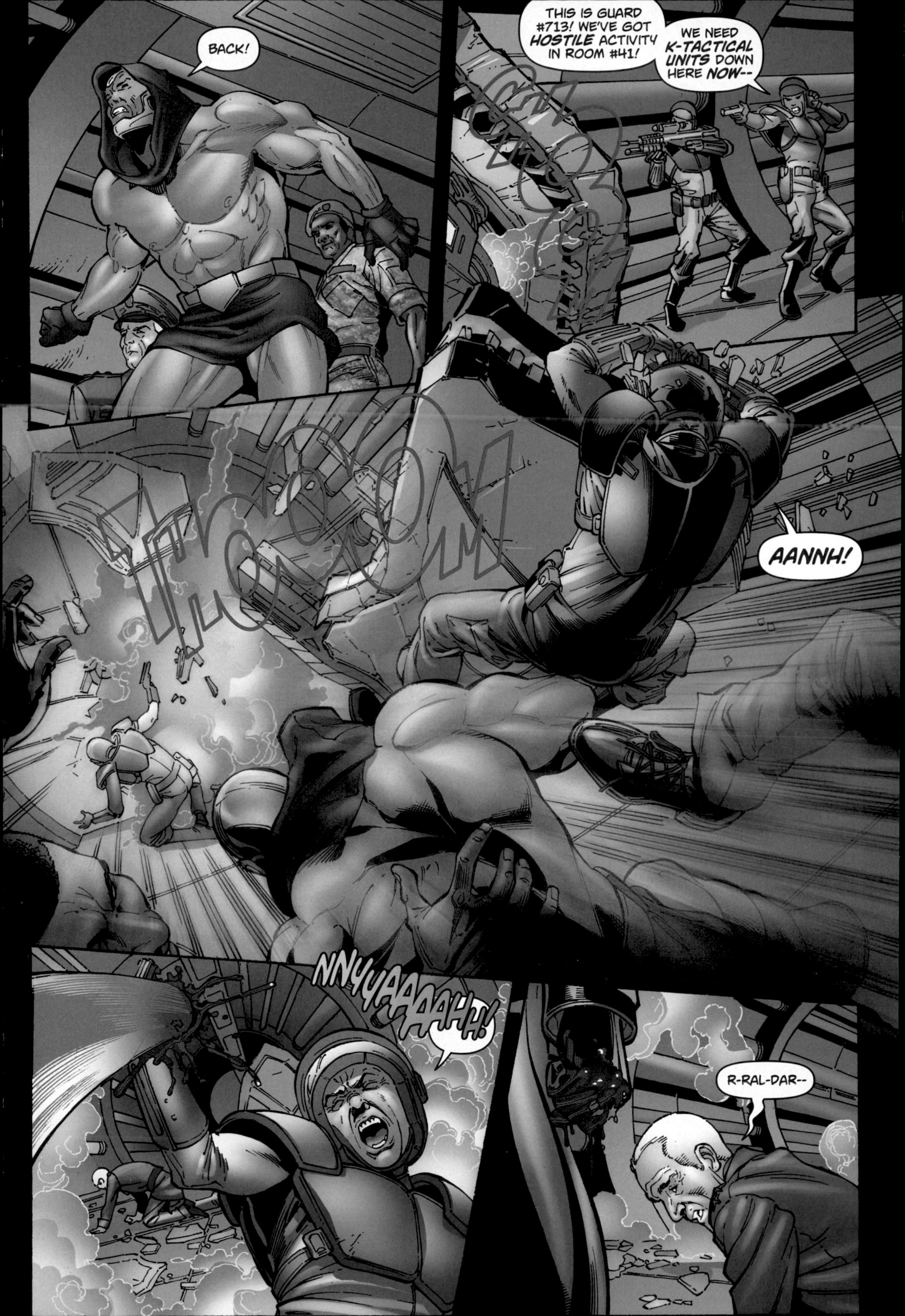
BACK!
THIS IS GUARD #713! WE'VE GOT HOSTILE ACTIVITY IN ROOM #41!
WE NEED K-TACTICAL UNITS DOWN HERE NOW--
THROOOM
AANNH!
NNYYAAAAAHH!
R-RAL-DAR--

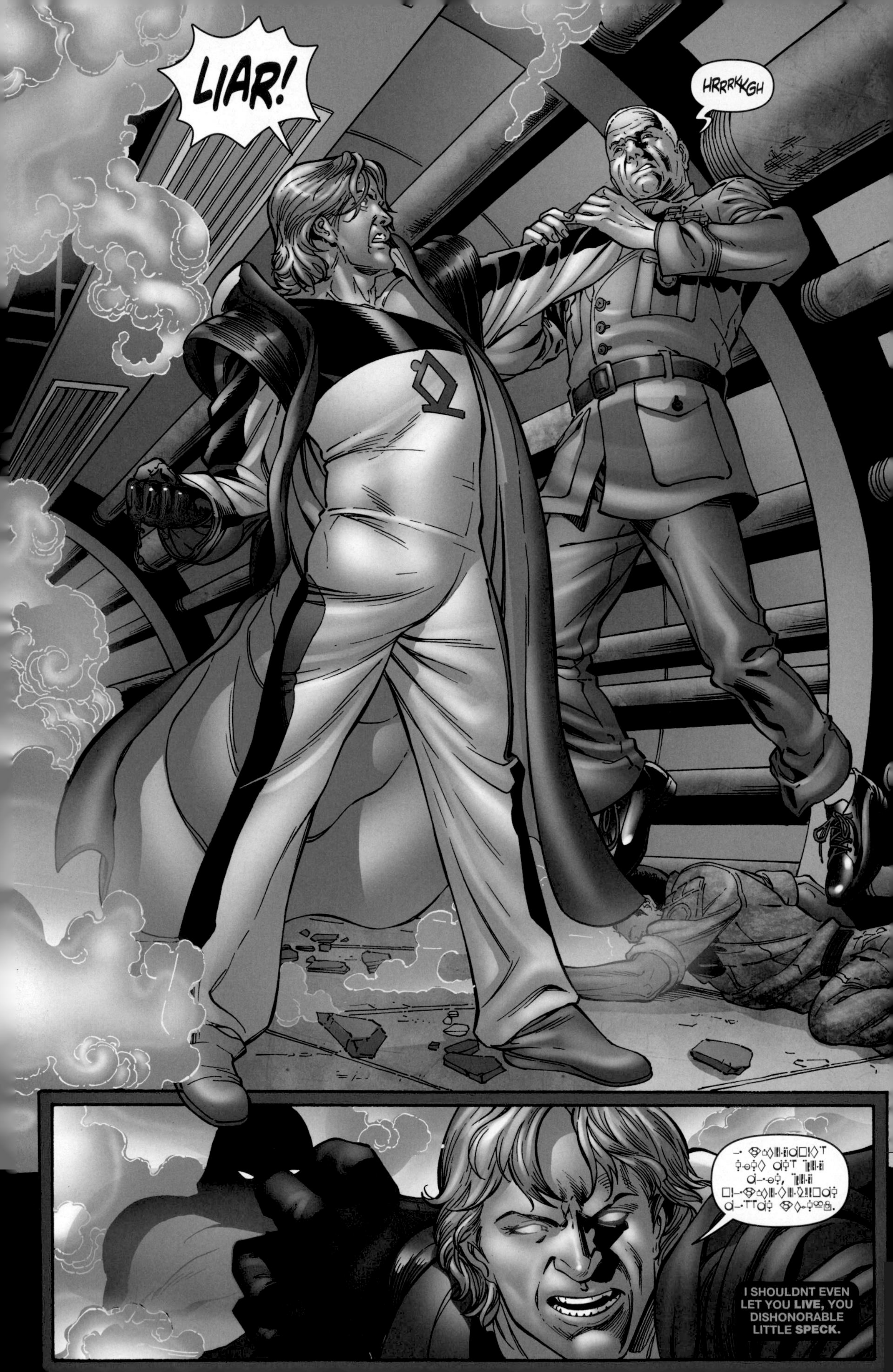
LIAR!
HRRRKKGH
I SHOULDNT EVEN LET YOU LIVE, YOU DISHONORABLE LITTLE SPECK.

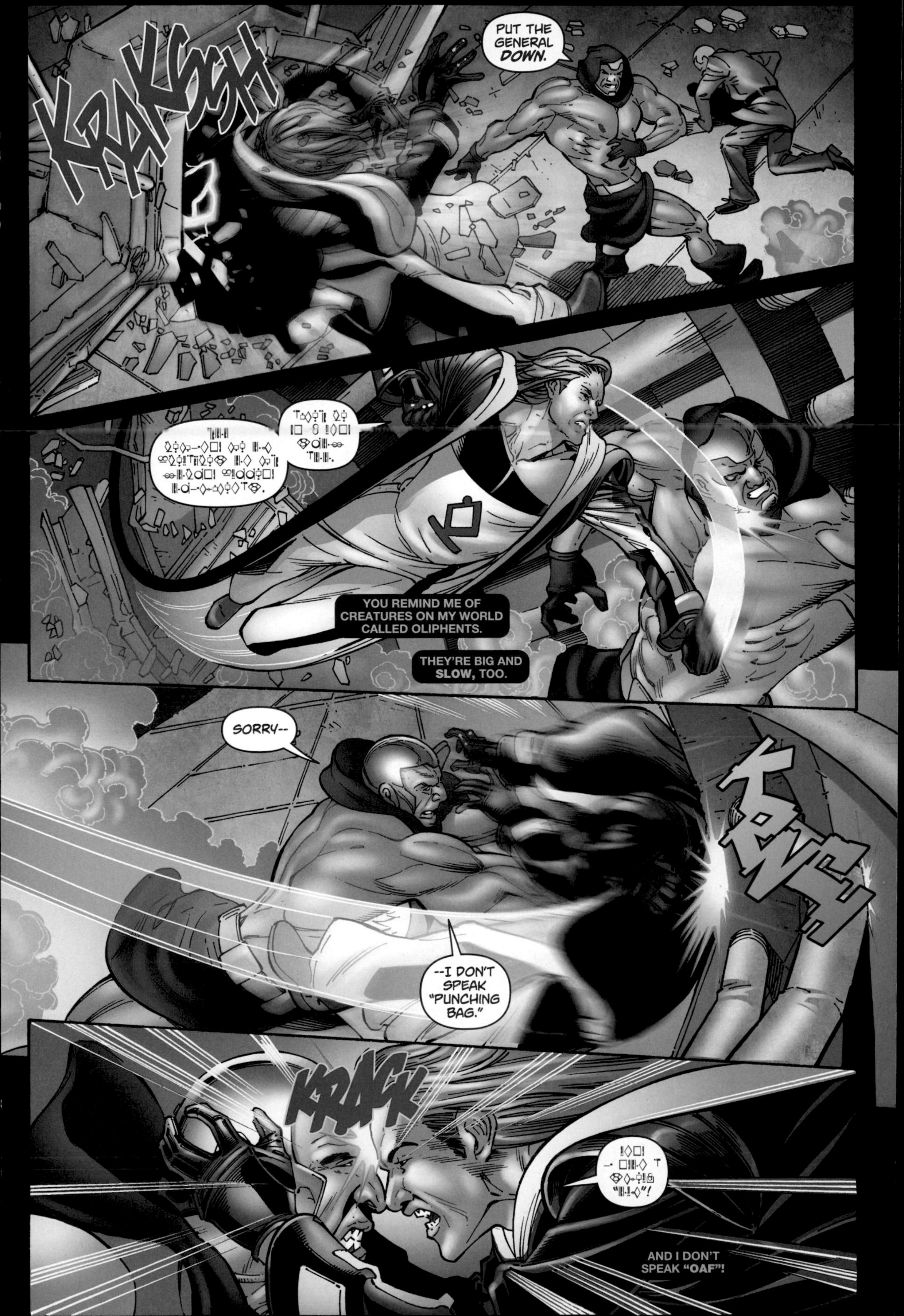

KRAKSSH
PUT THE GENERAL DOWN.
YOU REMIND ME OF CREATURES ON MY WORLD CALLED OLIPHENTS.
THEY'RE BIG AND SLOW, TOO.
SORRY--
--I DON'T SPEAK "PUNCHING BAG."
KRACK
AND I DON'T SPEAK "OAF"!

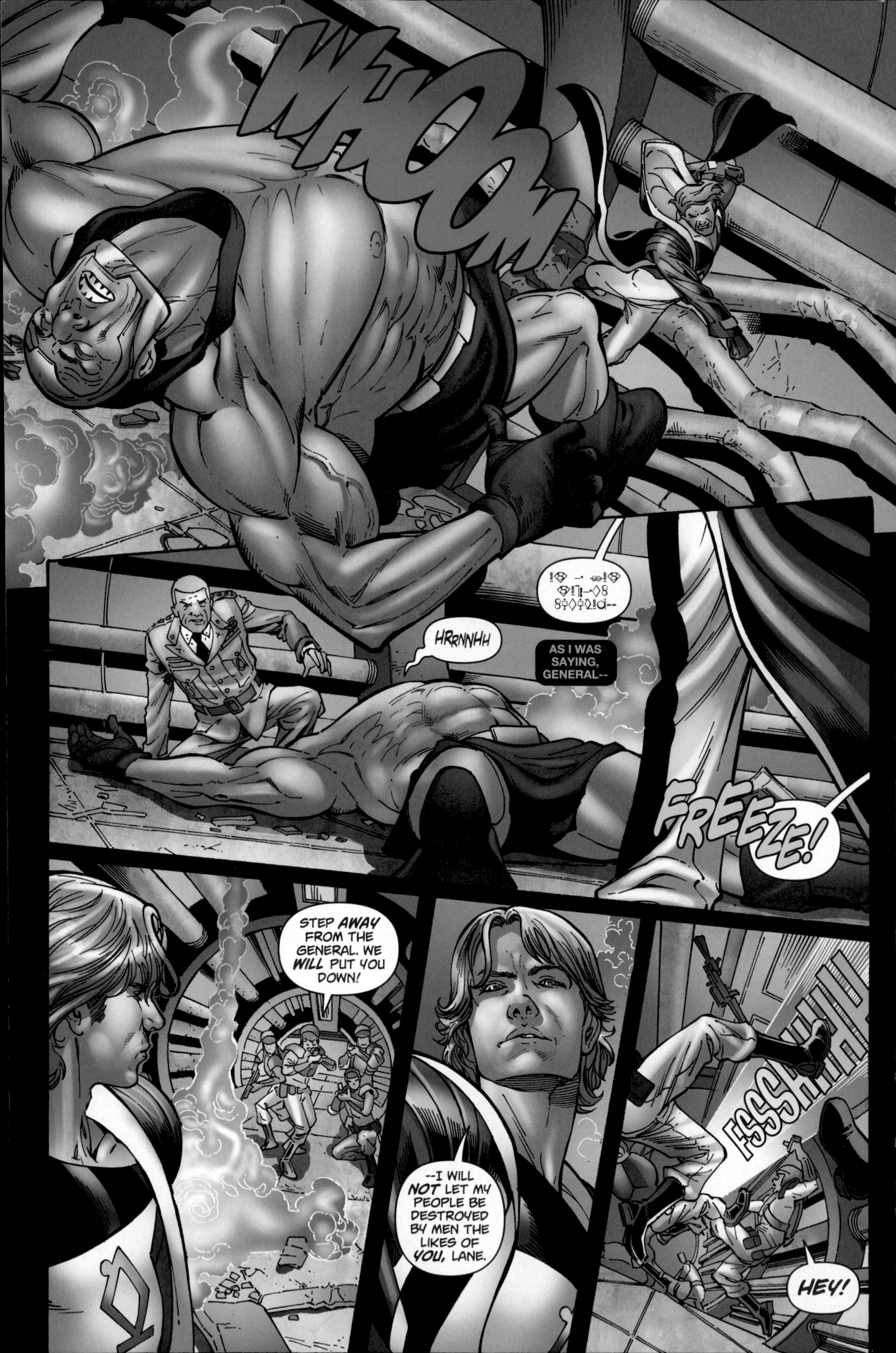
WHOOM
HRRNHH
AS I WAS SAYING, GENERAL--
FREEZE!
STEP AWAY FROM THE GENERAL. WE WILL PUT YOU DOWN!
--I WILL NOT LET MY PEOPLE BE DESTROYED BY MEN THE LIKES OF YOU, LANE.
FSSSHHH
HEY!

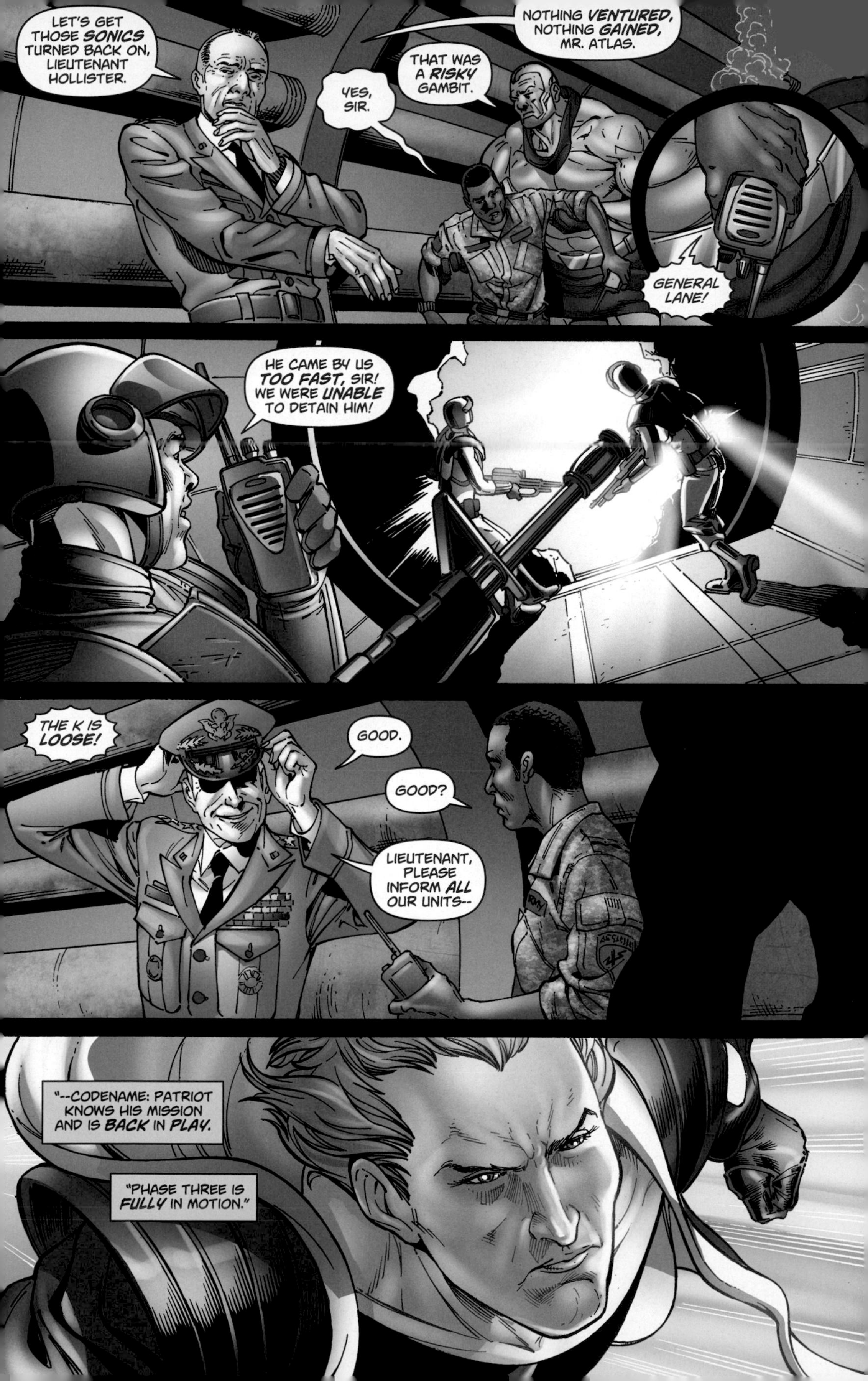
LET'S GET THOSE SONICS TURNED BACK ON, LIEUTENANT HOLLISTER.
NOTHING VENTURED, NOTHING GAINED, MR. ATLAS.
THAT WAS A RISKY GAMBIT.
YES, SIR.
GENERAL LANE!
HE CAME BY US TOO FAST, SIR! WE WERE UNABLE TO DETAIN HIM!
THE K IS LOOSE!
GOOD.
GOOD?
LIEUTENANT, PLEASE INFORM ALL OUR UNITS--
"--CODENAME: PATRIOT KNOWS HIS MISSION AND IS BACK IN PLAY.
"PHASE THREE IS FULLY IN MOTION."

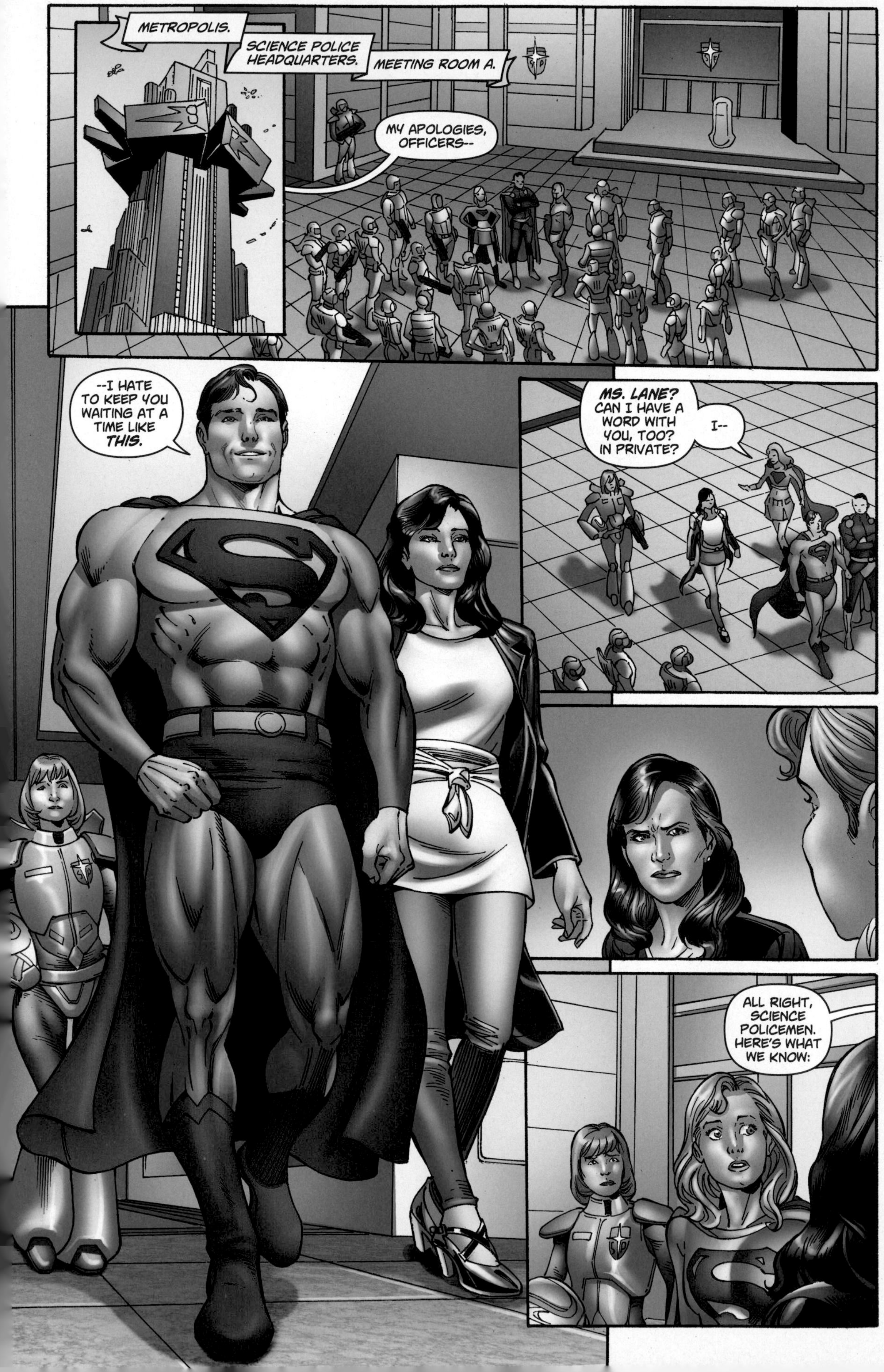
METROPOLIS.
SCIENCE POLICE HEADQUARTERS.
MEETING ROOM A.
MY APOLOGIES, OFFICERS--
--I HATE TO KEEP YOU WAITING AT A TIME LIKE THIS.
MS. LANE? CAN I HAVE A WORD WITH YOU, TOO? IN PRIVATE?
I--
ALL RIGHT, SCIENCE POLICEMEN. HERE'S WHAT WE KNOW:

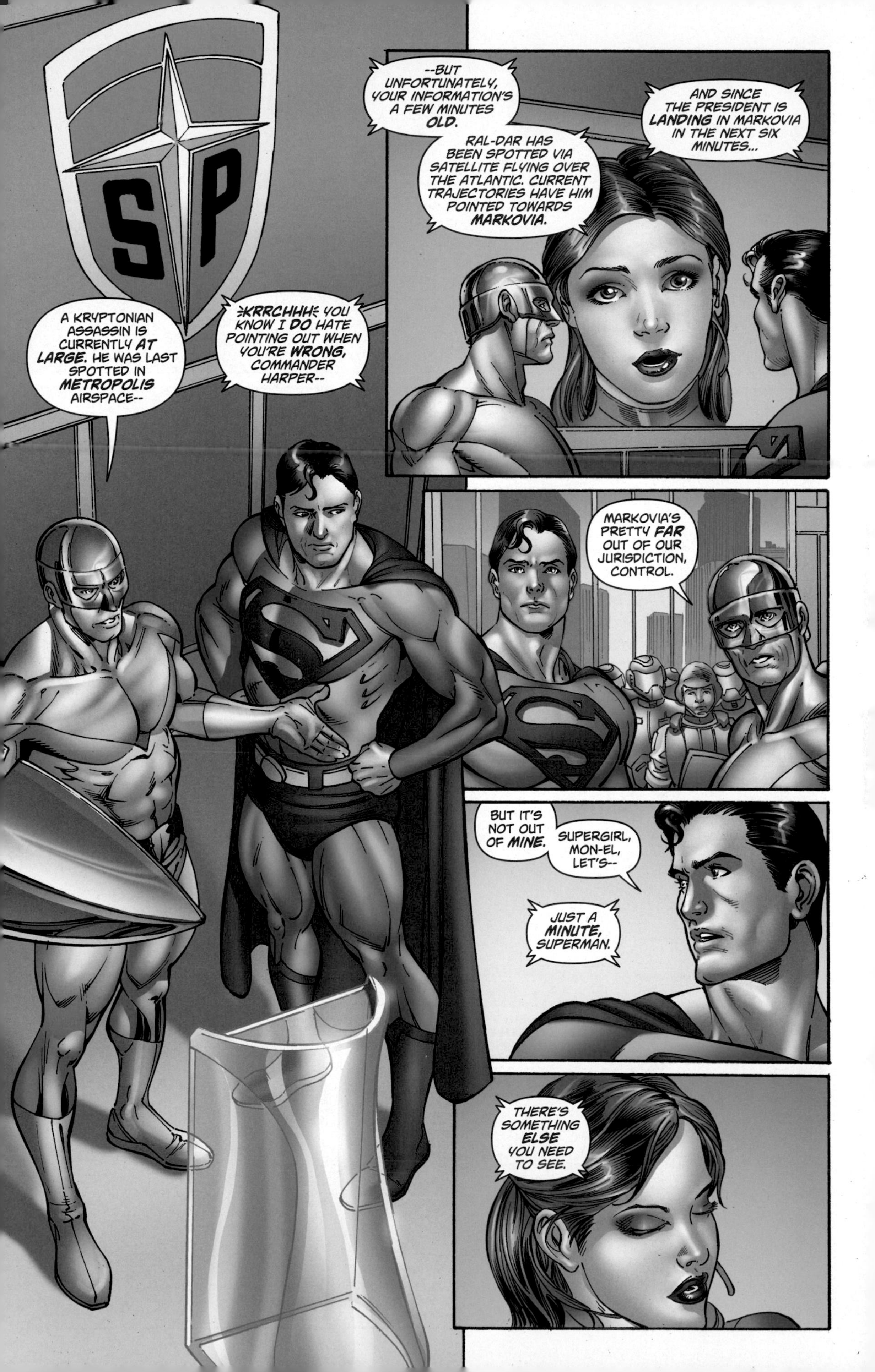
A KRYPTONIAN ASSASSIN IS CURRENTLY AT LARGE. HE WAS LAST SPOTTED IN METROPOLIS AIRSPACE--
KRRCHHH YOU KNOW I DO HATE POINTING OUT WHEN YOU'RE WRONG, COMMANDER HARPER--
--BUT UNFORTUNATELY, YOUR INFORMATION'S A FEW MINUTES OLD.
RAL-DAR HAS BEEN SPOTTED VIA SATELLITE FLYING OVER THE ATLANTIC. CURRENT TRAJECTORIES HAVE HIM POINTED TOWARDS MARKOVIA.
AND SINCE THE PRESIDENT IS LANDING IN MARKOVIA IN THE NEXT SIX MINUTES...
MARKOVIA'S PRETTY FAR OUT OF OUR JURISDICTION, CONTROL.
BUT IT'S NOT OUT OF MINE.
SUPERGIRL, MON-EL, LET'S--
JUST A MINUTE, SUPERMAN.
THERE'S SOMETHING ELSE YOU NEED TO SEE.

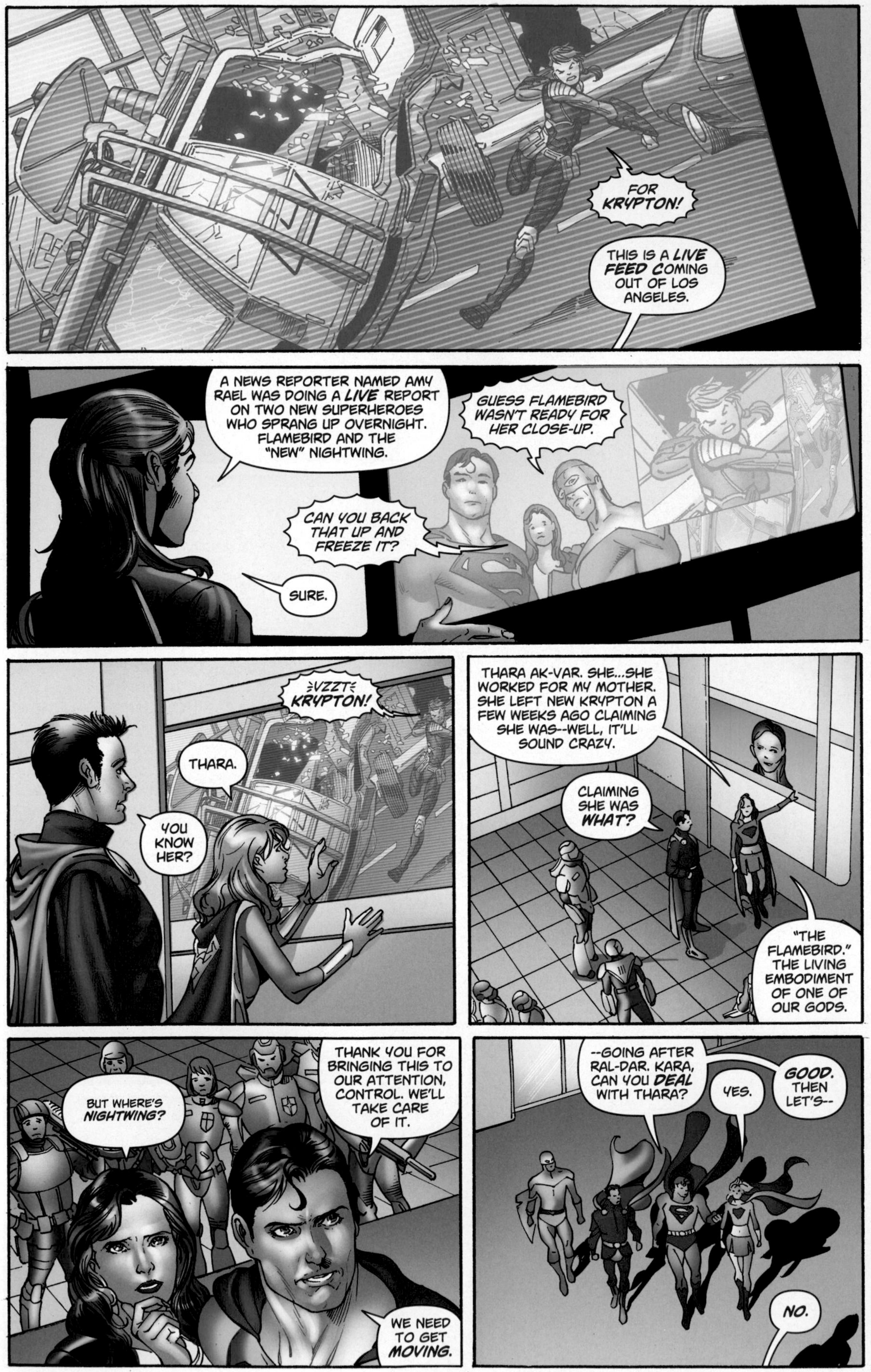
FOR KRYPTON!
THIS IS A LIVE FEED COMING OUT OF LOS ANGELES.
A NEWS REPORTER NAMED AMY RAEL WAS DOING A LIVE REPORT ON TWO NEW SUPERHEROES WHO SPRANG UP OVERNIGHT. FLAMEBIRD AND THE "NEW" NIGHTWING.
GUESS FLAMEBIRD WASN'T READY FOR HER CLOSE-UP.
CAN YOU BACK THAT UP AND FREEZE IT?
SURE.
VZZT KRYPTON!
THARA.
YOU KNOW HER?
THARA AK-VAR. SHE...SHE WORKED FOR MY MOTHER. SHE LEFT NEW KRYPTON A FEW WEEKS AGO CLAIMING SHE WAS--WELL, IT'LL SOUND CRAZY.
CLAIMING SHE WAS WHAT?
"THE FLAMEBIRD." THE LIVING EMBODIMENT OF ONE OF OUR GODS.
BUT WHERE'S NIGHTWING?
THANK YOU FOR BRINGING THIS TO OUR ATTENTION, CONTROL. WE'LL TAKE CARE OF IT.
WE NEED TO GET MOVING.
--GOING AFTER RAL-DAR. KARA, CAN YOU DEAL WITH THARA?
YES.
GOOD. THEN LET'S--
NO.

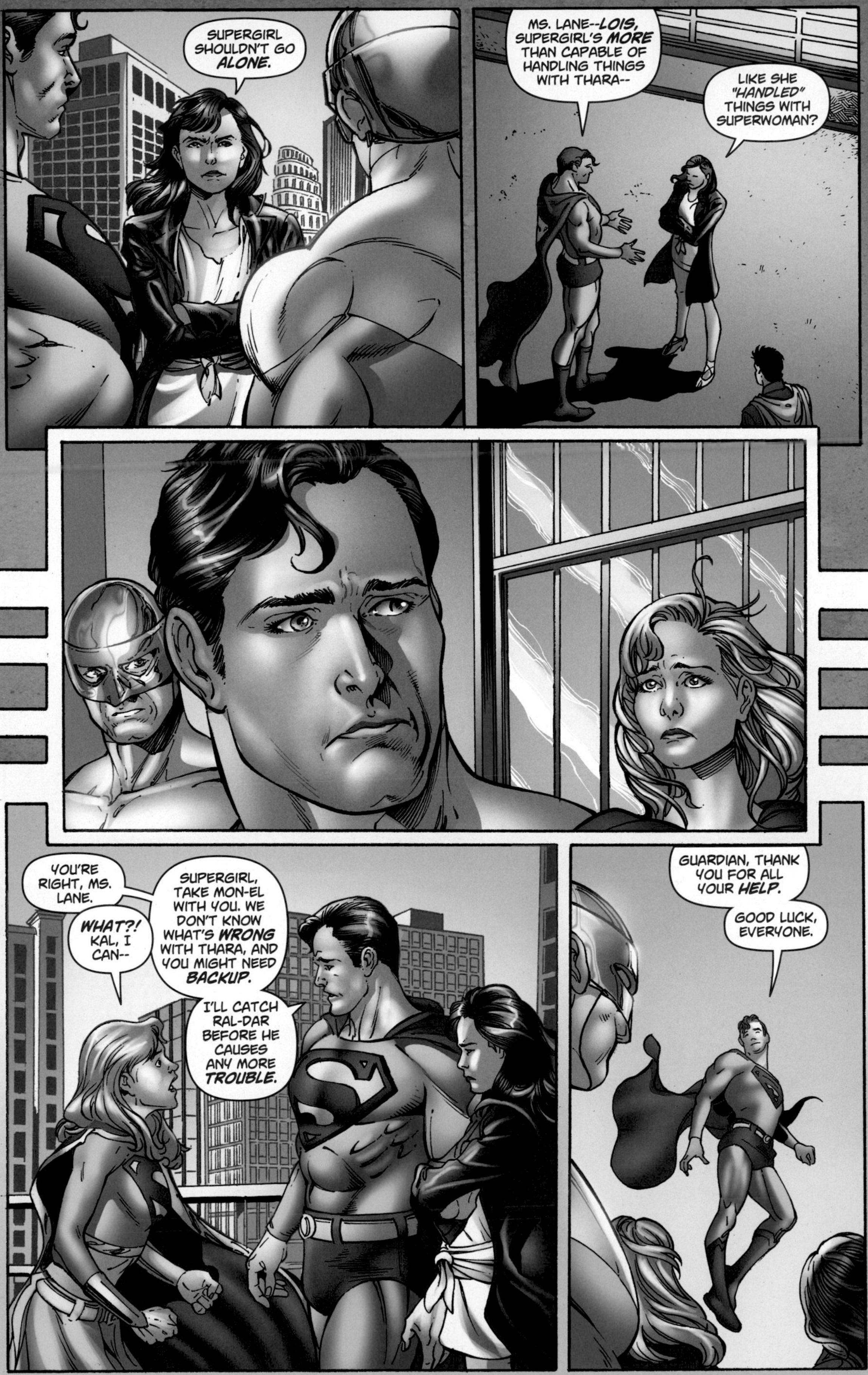
SUPERGIRL SHOULDN'T GO ALONE.
MS. LANE--LOIS, SUPERGIRL'S MORE THAN CAPABLE OF HANDLING THINGS WITH THARA--
LIKE SHE "HANDLED" THINGS WITH SUPERWOMAN?
YOU'RE RIGHT, MS. LANE.
WHAT?! KAL, I CAN--
SUPERGIRL, TAKE MON-EL WITH YOU. WE DON'T KNOW WHAT'S WRONG WITH THARA, AND YOU MIGHT NEED BACKUP.
I'LL CATCH RAL-DAR BEFORE HE CAUSES ANY MORE TROUBLE.
GUARDIAN, THANK YOU FOR ALL YOUR HELP.
GOOD LUCK, EVERYONE.

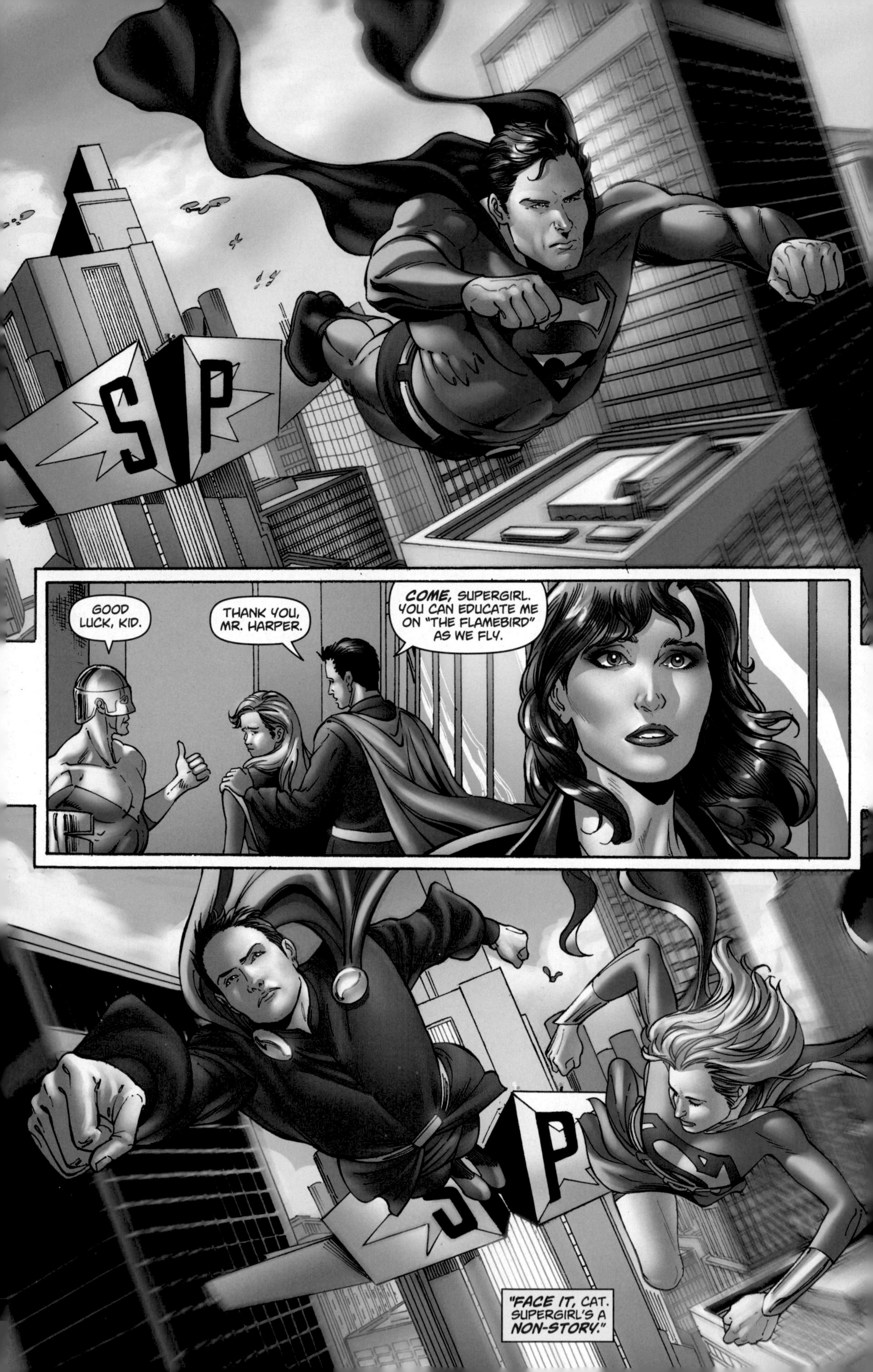
GOOD LUCK, KID.
THANK YOU, MR. HARPER.
COME, SUPERGIRL. YOU CAN EDUCATE ME ON "THE FLAMEBIRD" AS WE FLY.
"FACE IT, CAT. SUPERGIRL'S A NON-STORY."

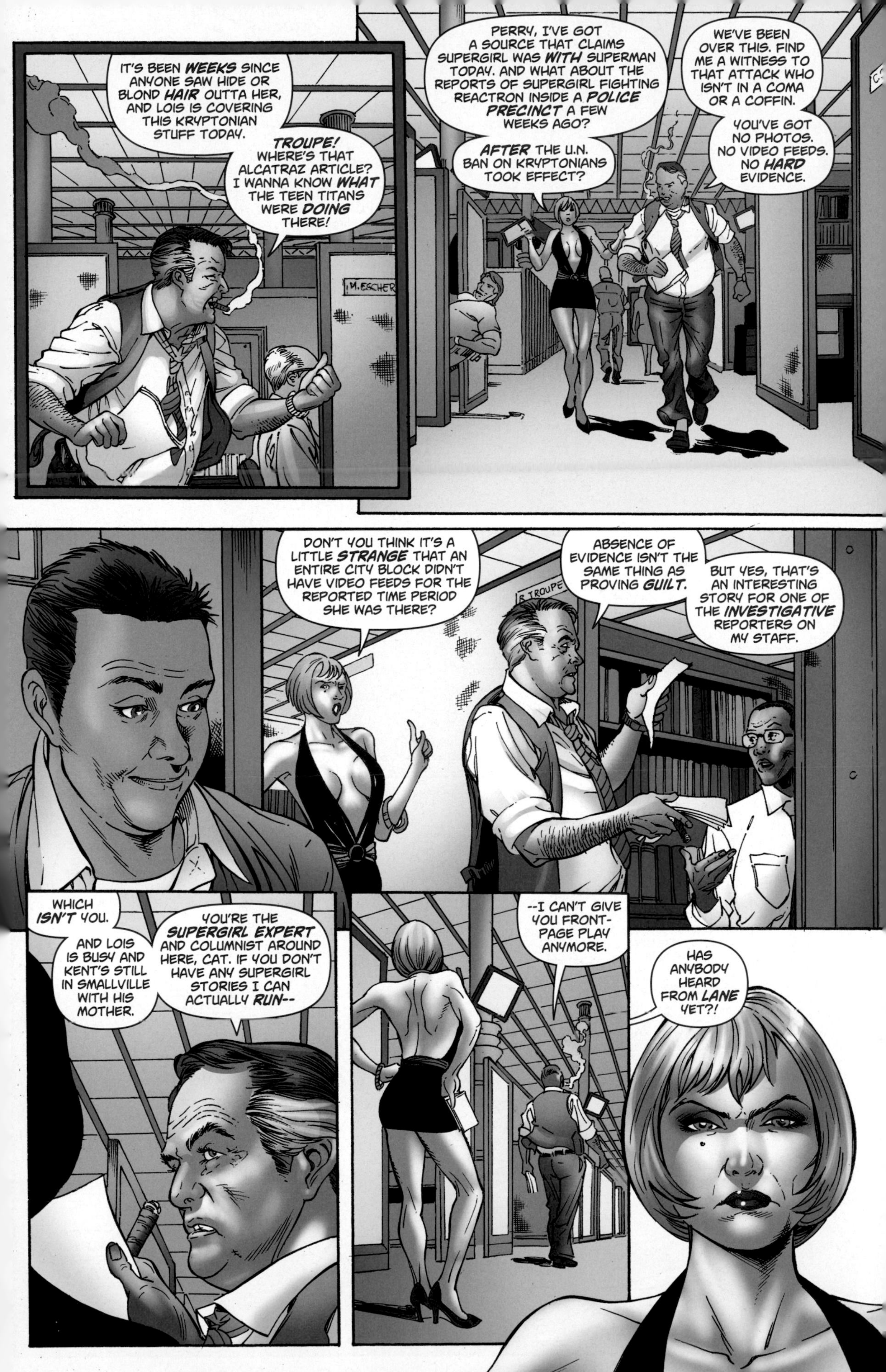
IT'S BEEN WEEKS SINCE ANYONE SAW HIDE OR BLOND HAIR OUTTA HER, AND LOIS IS COVERING THIS KRYPTONIAN STUFF TODAY.
TROUPE! WHERE'S THAT ALCATRAZ ARTICLE? I WANNA KNOW WHAT THE TEEN TITANS WERE DOING THERE!
M. ESCHER
PERRY, I'VE GOT A SOURCE THAT CLAIMS SUPERGIRL WAS WITH SUPERMAN TODAY. AND WHAT ABOUT THE REPORTS OF SUPERGIRL FIGHTING REACTRON INSIDE A POLICE PRECINCT A FEW WEEKS AGO?
AFTER THE U.N. BAN ON KRYPTONIANS TOOK EFFECT?
WE'VE BEEN OVER THIS. FIND ME A WITNESS TO THAT ATTACK WHO ISN'T IN A COMA OR A COFFIN.
YOU'VE GOT NO PHOTOS. NO VIDEO FEEDS. NO HARD EVIDENCE.
DON'T YOU THINK IT'S A LITTLE STRANGE THAT AN ENTIRE CITY BLOCK DIDN'T HAVE VIDEO FEEDS FOR THE REPORTED TIME PERIOD SHE WAS THERE?
ABSENCE OF EVIDENCE ISN'T THE SAME THING AS PROVING GUILT.
BUT YES, THAT'S AN INTERESTING STORY FOR ONE OF THE INVESTIGATIVE REPORTERS ON MY STAFF.
WHICH ISN'T YOU.
AND LOIS IS BUSY AND KENT'S STILL IN SMALLVILLE WITH HIS MOTHER.
YOU'RE THE SUPERGIRL EXPERT AND COLUMNIST AROUND HERE, CAT. IF YOU DON'T HAVE ANY SUPERGIRL STORIES I CAN ACTUALLY RUN--
--I CAN'T GIVE YOU FRONT-PAGE PLAY ANYMORE.
HAS ANYBODY HEARD FROM LANE YET?!

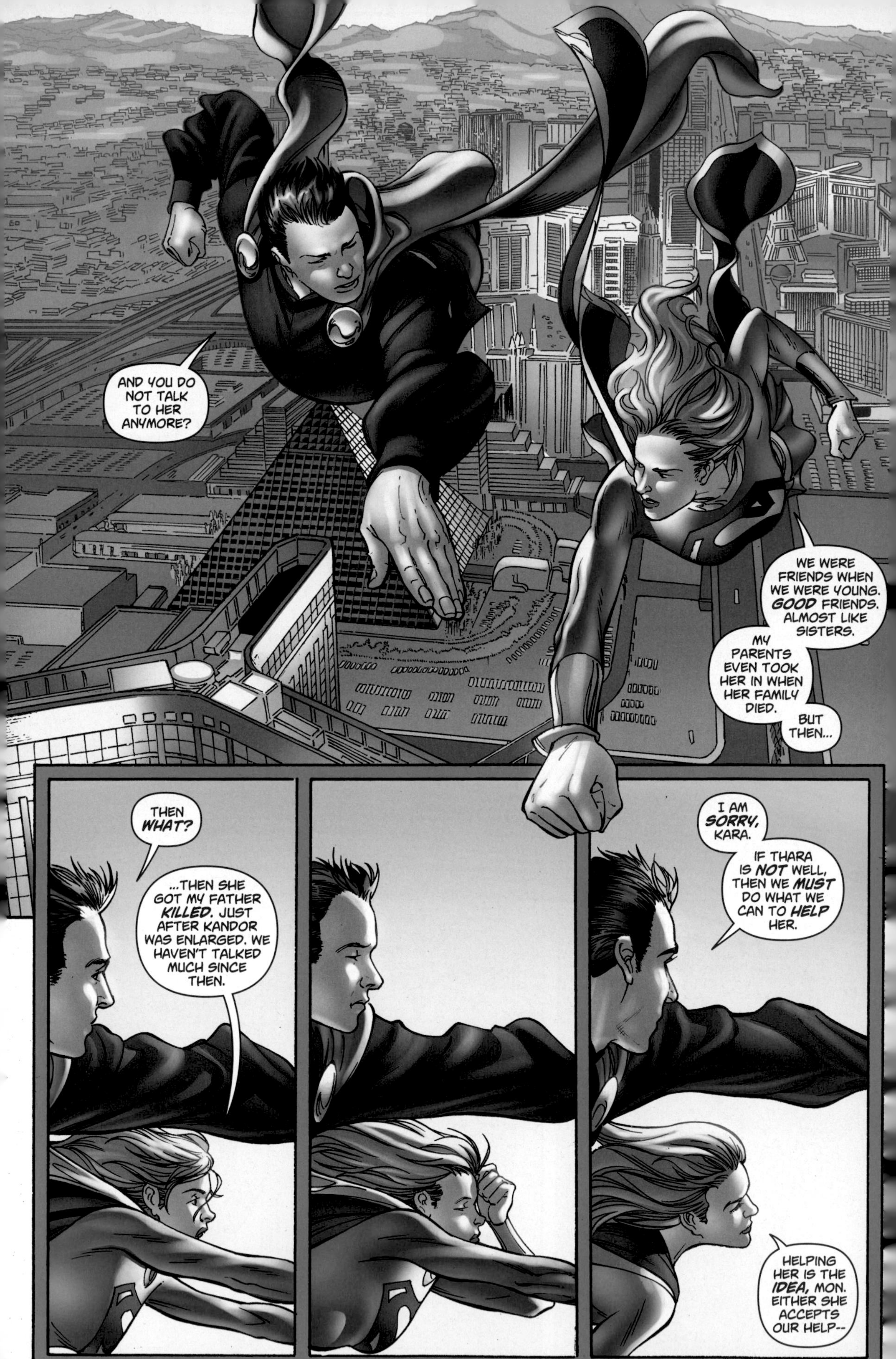
AND YOU DO NOT TALK TO HER ANYMORE?
WE WERE FRIENDS WHEN WE WERE YOUNG. GOOD FRIENDS. ALMOST LIKE SISTERS.
MY PARENTS EVEN TOOK HER IN WHEN HER FAMILY DIED.
BUT THEN...
THEN WHAT?
...THEN SHE GOT MY FATHER KILLED. JUST AFTER KANDOR WAS ENLARGED. WE HAVEN'T TALKED MUCH SINCE THEN.
I AM SORRY, KARA.
IF THARA IS NOT WELL, THEN WE MUST DO WHAT WE CAN TO HELP HER.
HELPING HER IS THE IDEA, MON. EITHER SHE ACCEPTS OUR HELP--

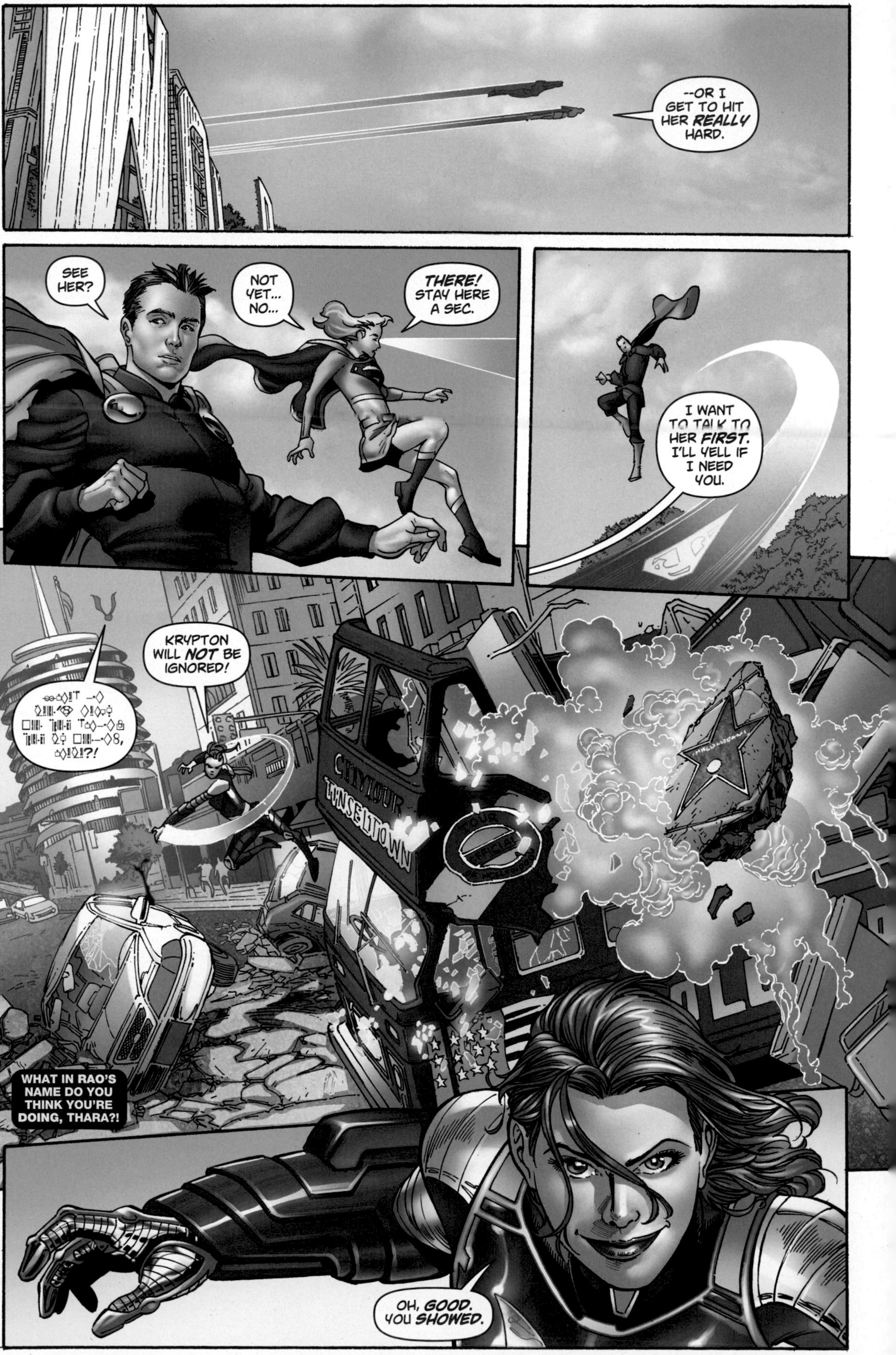
--OR I GET TO HIT HER **REALLY** HARD.
SEE HER?
NOT YET... NO...
THERE! STAY HERE A SEC.
I WANT TO TALK TO HER **FIRST**. I'LL YELL IF I NEED YOU.
KRYPTON WILL **NOT** BE IGNORED!
WHAT IN RAO'S NAME DO YOU THINK YOU'RE DOING, THARA?!
OH, **GOOD**. YOU **SHOWED**.

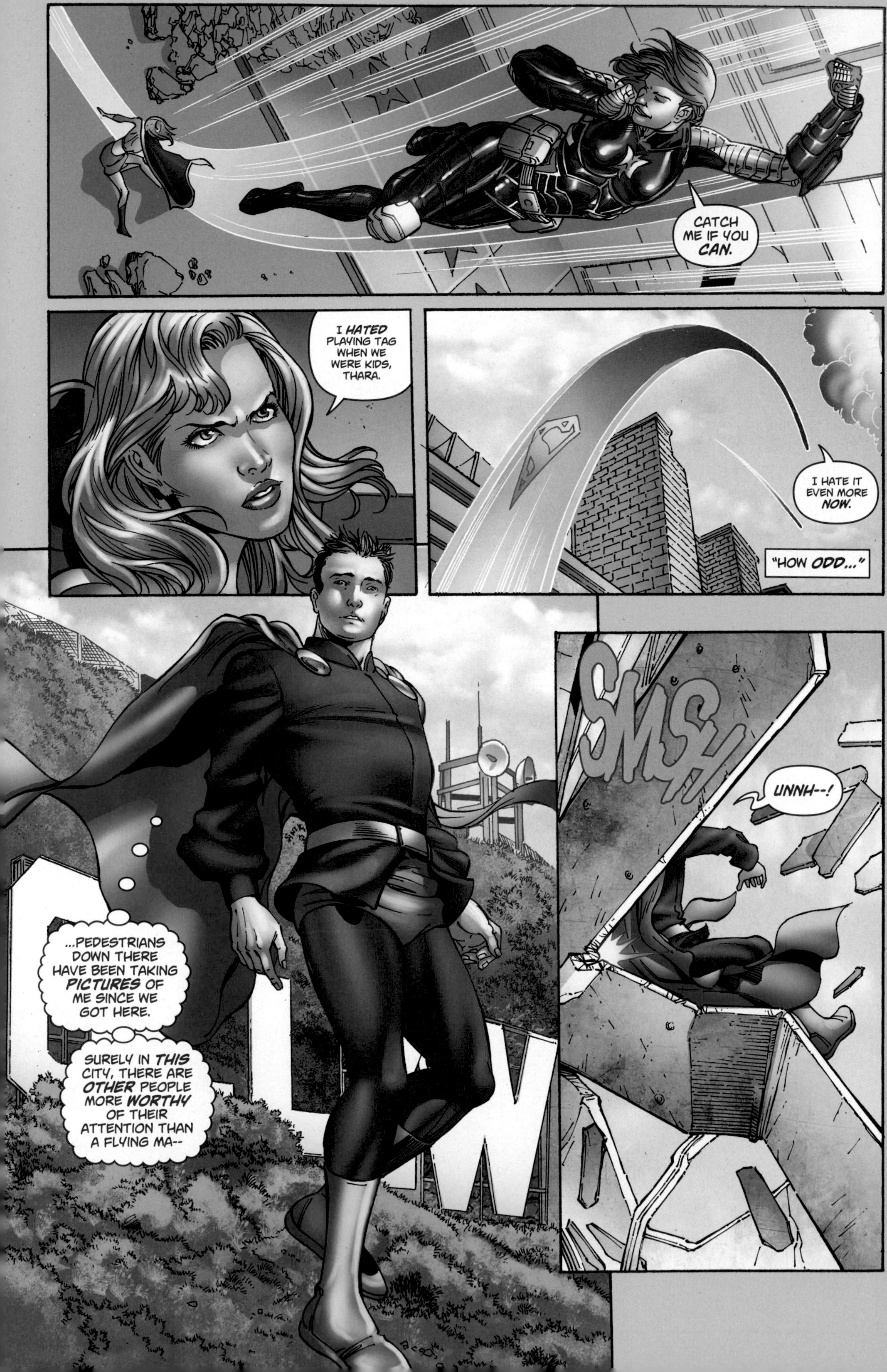

CATCH ME IF YOU CAN.
I HATED PLAYING TAG WHEN WE WERE KIDS, THARA.
I HATE IT EVEN MORE NOW.
"HOW ODD..."
...PEDESTRIANS DOWN THERE HAVE BEEN TAKING PICTURES OF ME SINCE WE GOT HERE.
SURELY IN THIS CITY, THERE ARE OTHER PEOPLE MORE WORTHY OF THEIR ATTENTION THAN A FLYING MA--
SMSH
UNNH--!

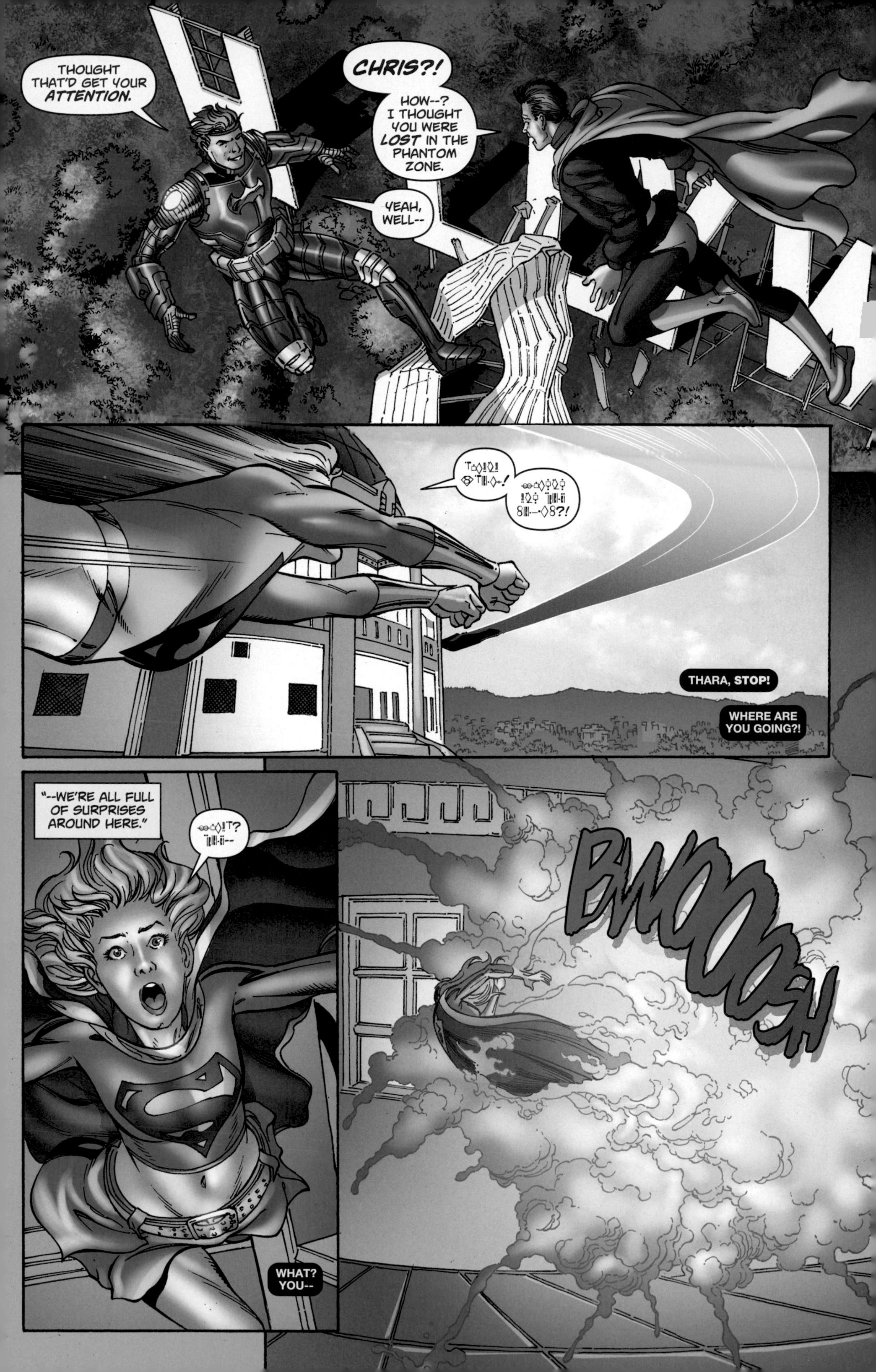
THOUGHT THAT'D GET YOUR ATTENTION.
CHRIS?!
HOW--? I THOUGHT YOU WERE LOST IN THE PHANTOM ZONE.
YEAH, WELL--
THARA, STOP!
WHERE ARE YOU GOING?!
"--WE'RE ALL FULL OF SURPRISES AROUND HERE."
BWOOOSH
WHAT? YOU--

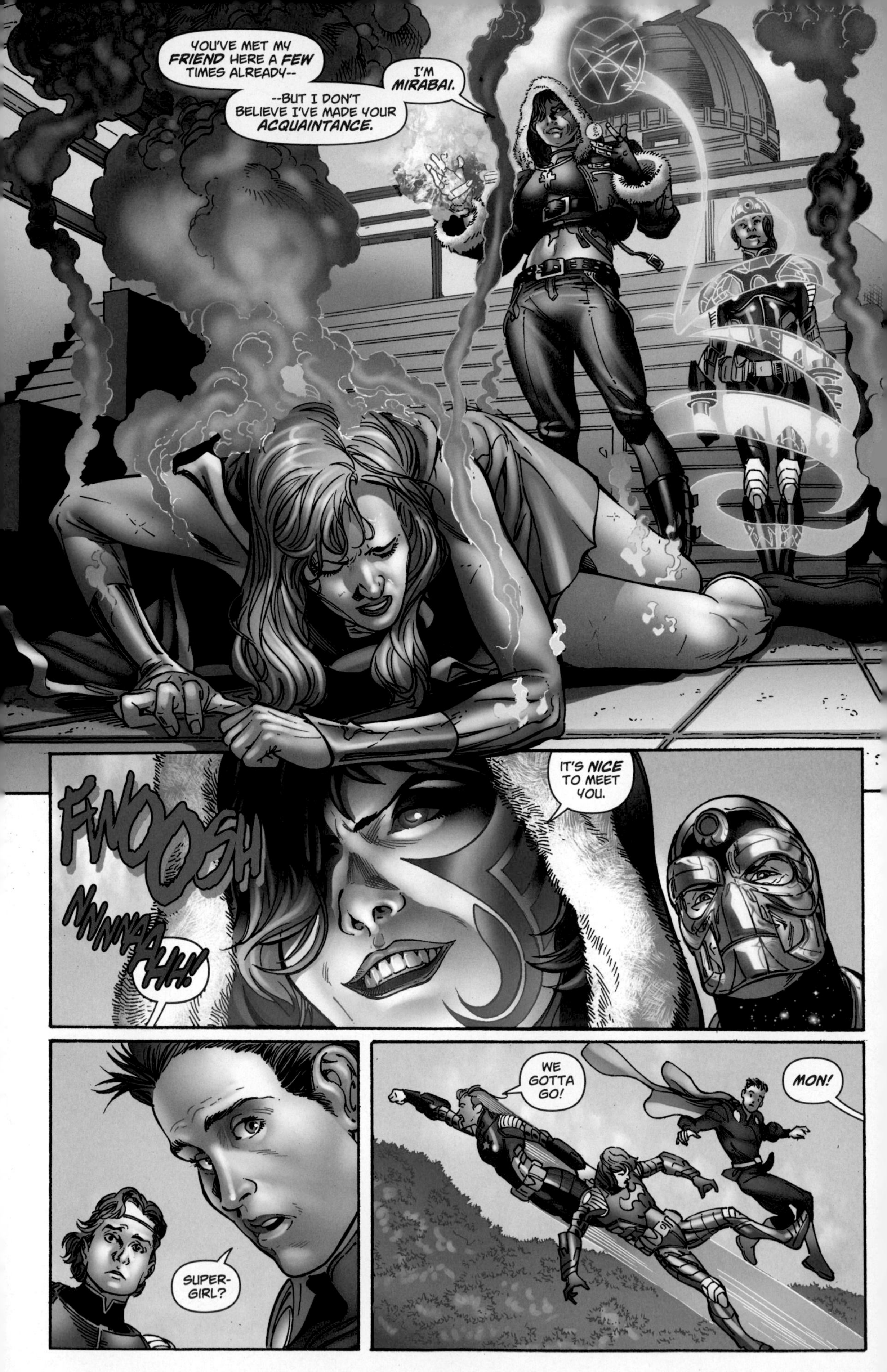
YOU'VE MET MY FRIEND HERE A FEW TIMES ALREADY--
--BUT I DON'T BELIEVE I'VE MADE YOUR ACQUAINTANCE.
I'M MIRABAI.
FWOOSH
IT'S NICE TO MEET YOU.
NNNAAHH!
SUPER-GIRL?
WE GOTTA GO!
MON!

WE HAVE TO **STOP** THEM!

SHE **TOLD** ME WHAT THEY WERE PLANNING!

WHERE ARE THEY--

METROPOLIS!

"SOMETHING **BIG** IS GOING TO HAPPEN IN **METROPOLIS**!"

HELLO?

BZZZT BZZZT

UNKNOWN CALLER

AT FOUR P.M. TOMORROW, THERE WILL BE A CAR OUTSIDE OF THE DAILY PLANET.

IT WILL TAKE YOU TO WGBS STUDIOS WHERE YOU WILL BE APPEARING ON MORGAN EDGE'S SHOW, "THE EDGE OF REASON."

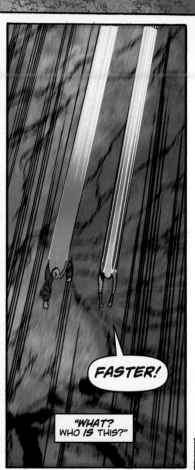

FASTER!

"WHAT? WHO **IS** THIS?"

AND **WHY** WOULD I GO ON EDGE'S SHOW?

YOU'LL **KNOW** WHY BY THE END OF THE DAY. FOUR P.M., MS. GRANT--

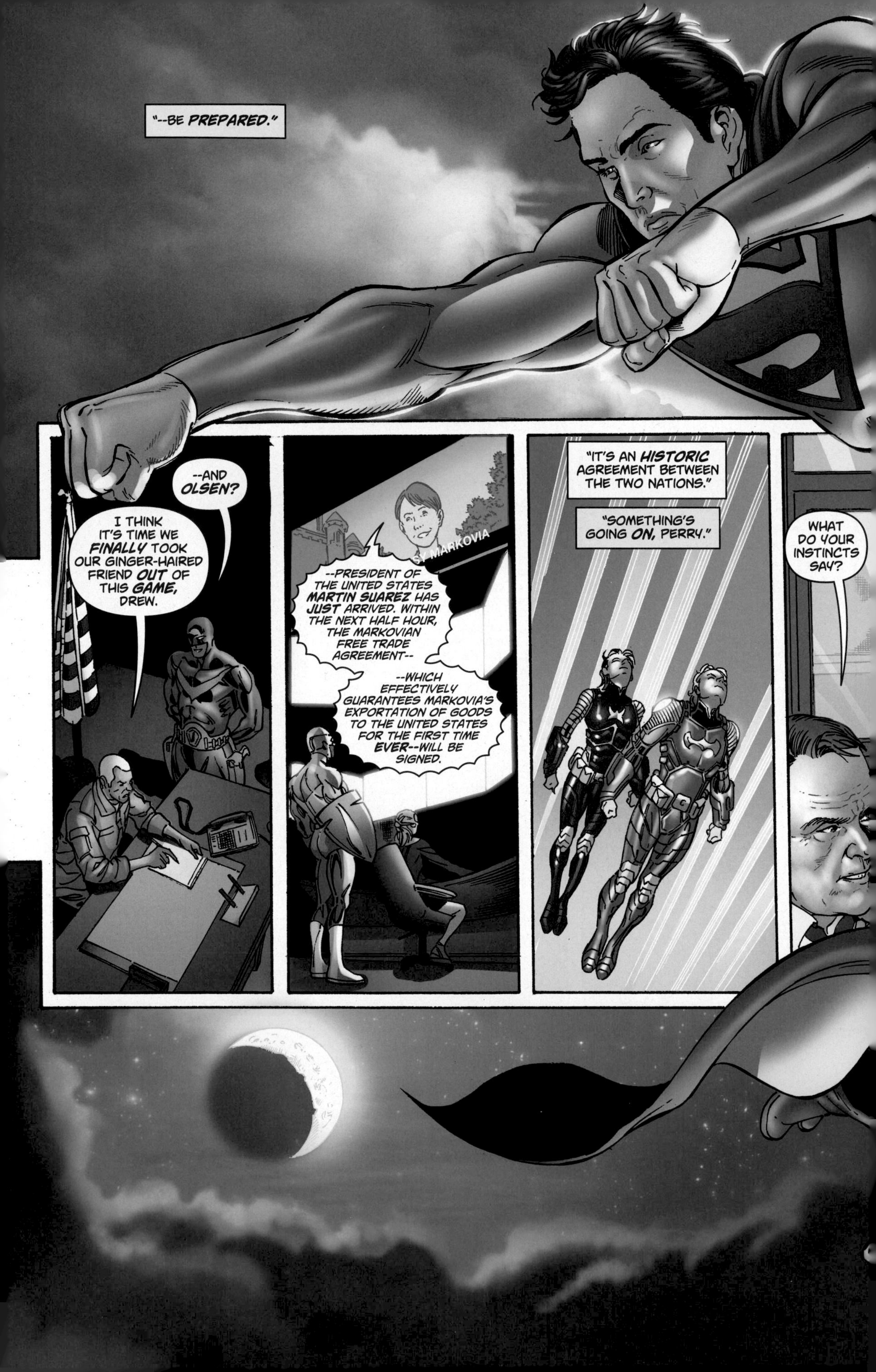
"--BE PREPARED."
--AND OLSEN?
I THINK IT'S TIME WE FINALLY TOOK OUR GINGER-HAIRED FRIEND OUT OF THIS GAME, DREW.
SY MARKOVIA
--PRESIDENT OF THE UNITED STATES MARTIN SUAREZ HAS JUST ARRIVED. WITHIN THE NEXT HALF HOUR, THE MARKOVIAN FREE TRADE AGREEMENT--
--WHICH EFFECTIVELY GUARANTEES MARKOVIA'S EXPORTATION OF GOODS TO THE UNITED STATES FOR THE FIRST TIME EVER--WILL BE SIGNED.
"IT'S AN HISTORIC AGREEMENT BETWEEN THE TWO NATIONS."
"SOMETHING'S GOING ON, PERRY."
WHAT DO YOUR INSTINCTS SAY?

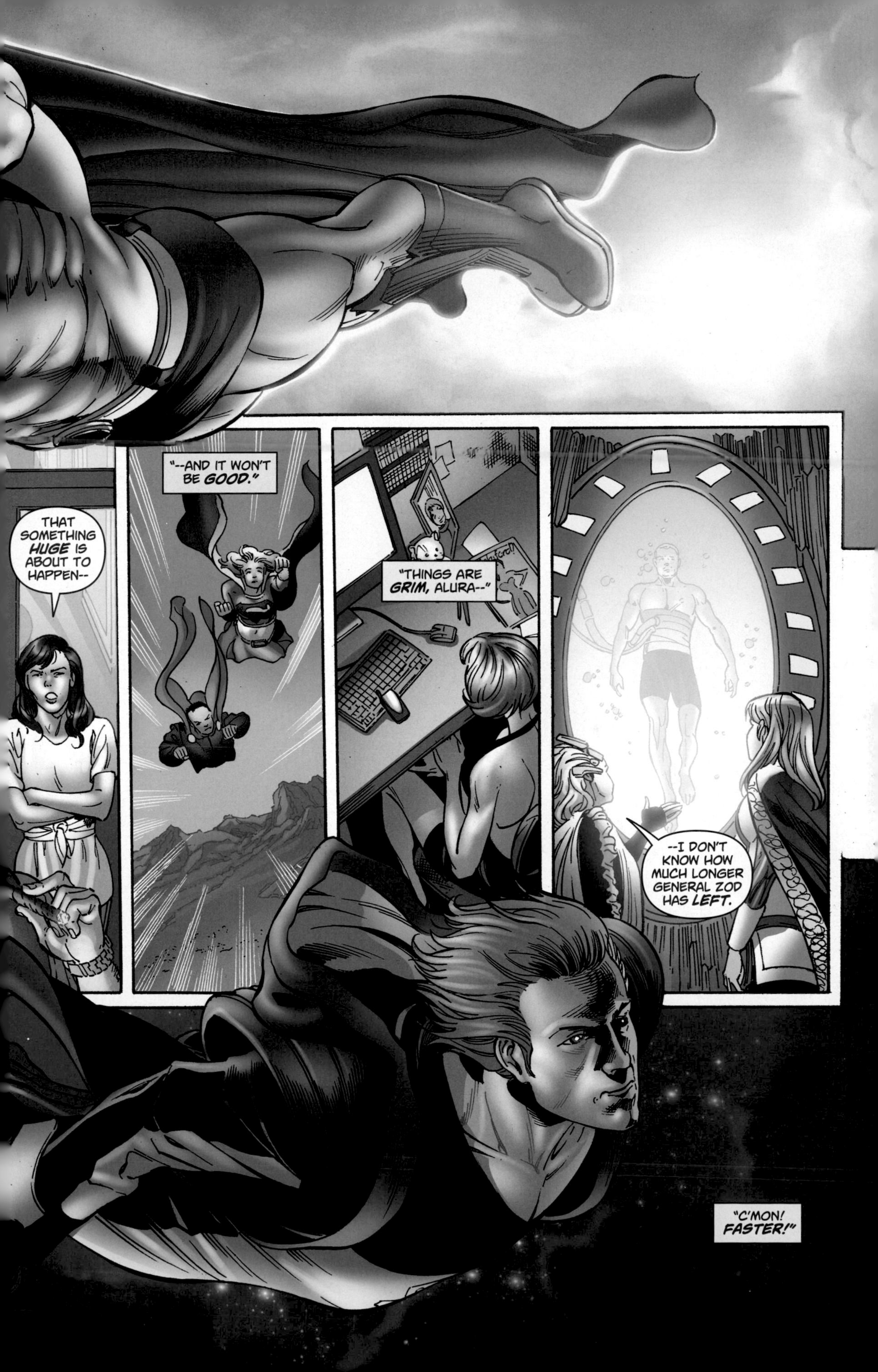
THAT SOMETHING HUGE IS ABOUT TO HAPPEN--
"--AND IT WON'T BE GOOD."
"THINGS ARE GRIM, ALURA--"
--I DON'T KNOW HOW MUCH LONGER GENERAL ZOD HAS LEFT.
"C'MON! FASTER!"

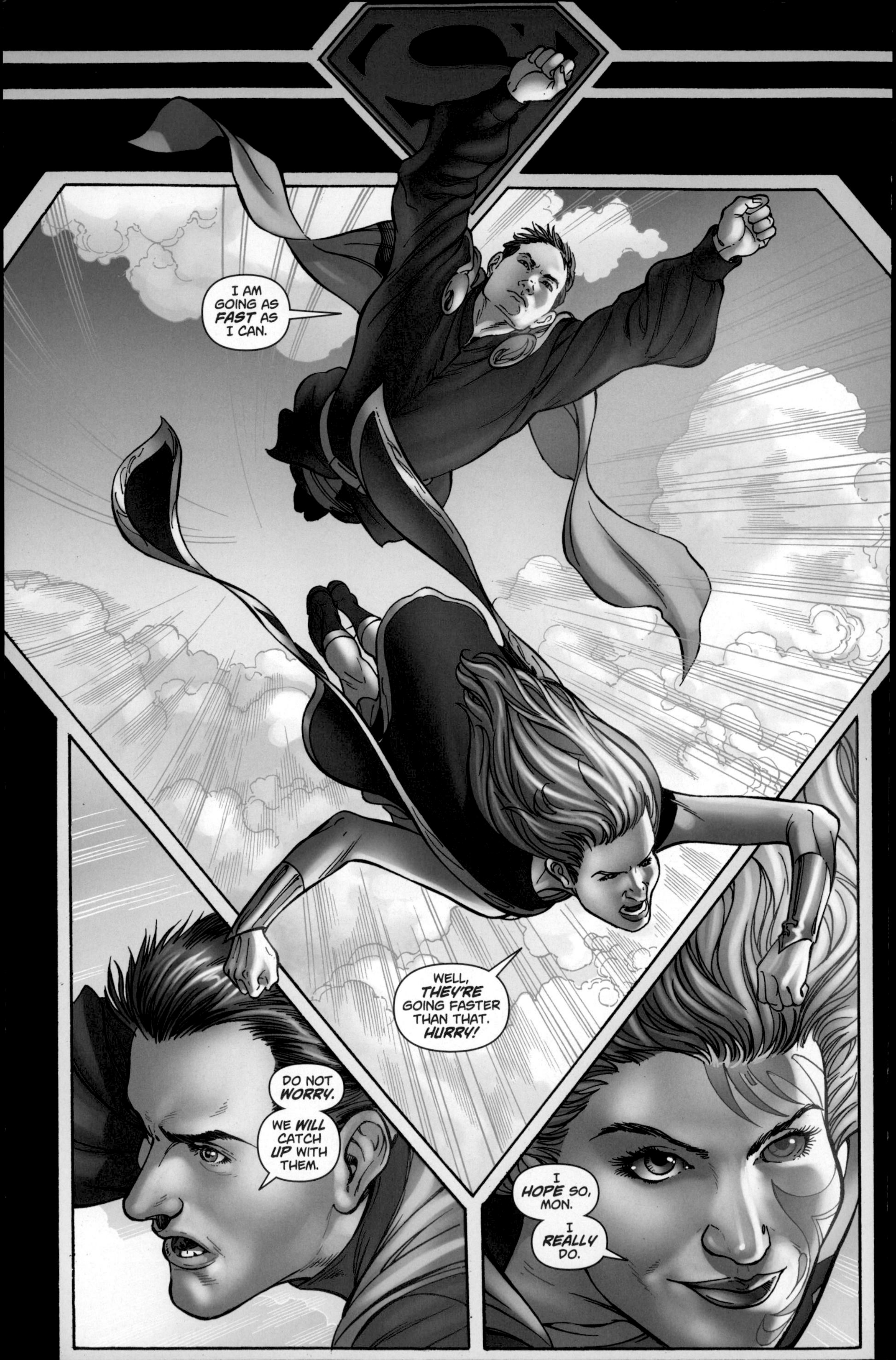
I AM GOING AS FAST AS I CAN.
WELL, THEY'RE GOING FASTER THAN THAT. HURRY!
DO NOT WORRY.
WE WILL CATCH UP WITH THEM.
I HOPE SO, MON.
I REALLY DO.

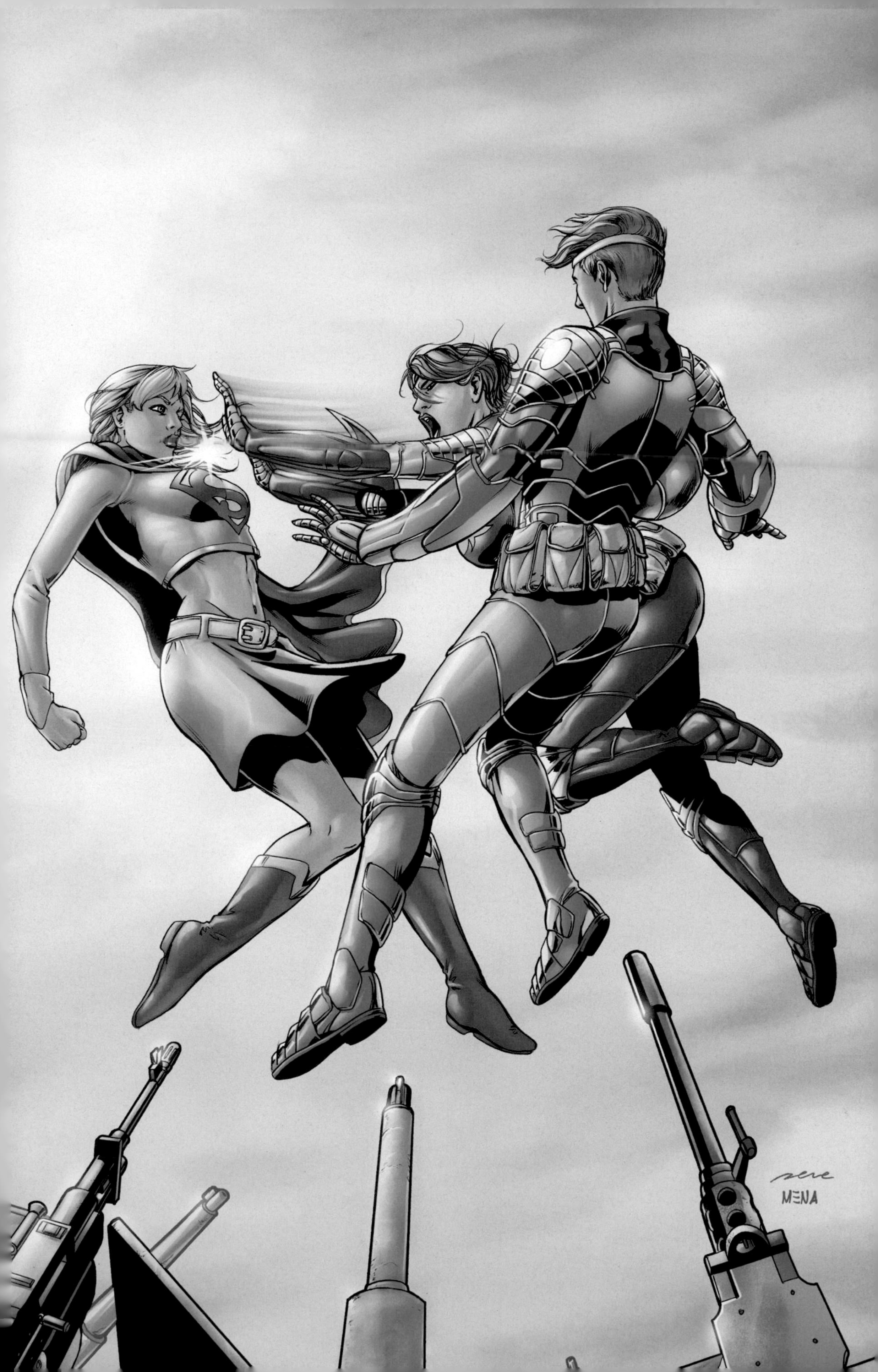

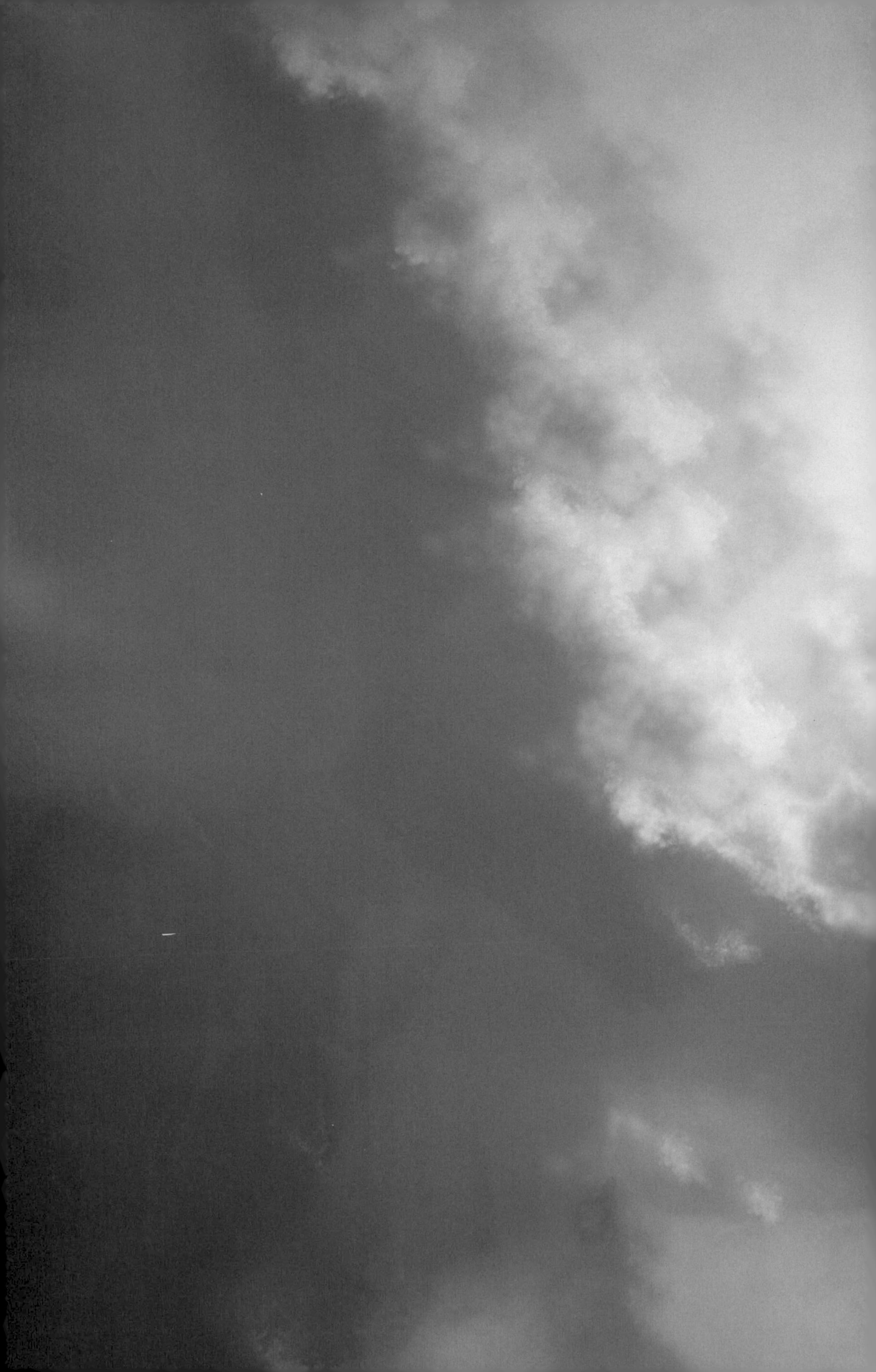

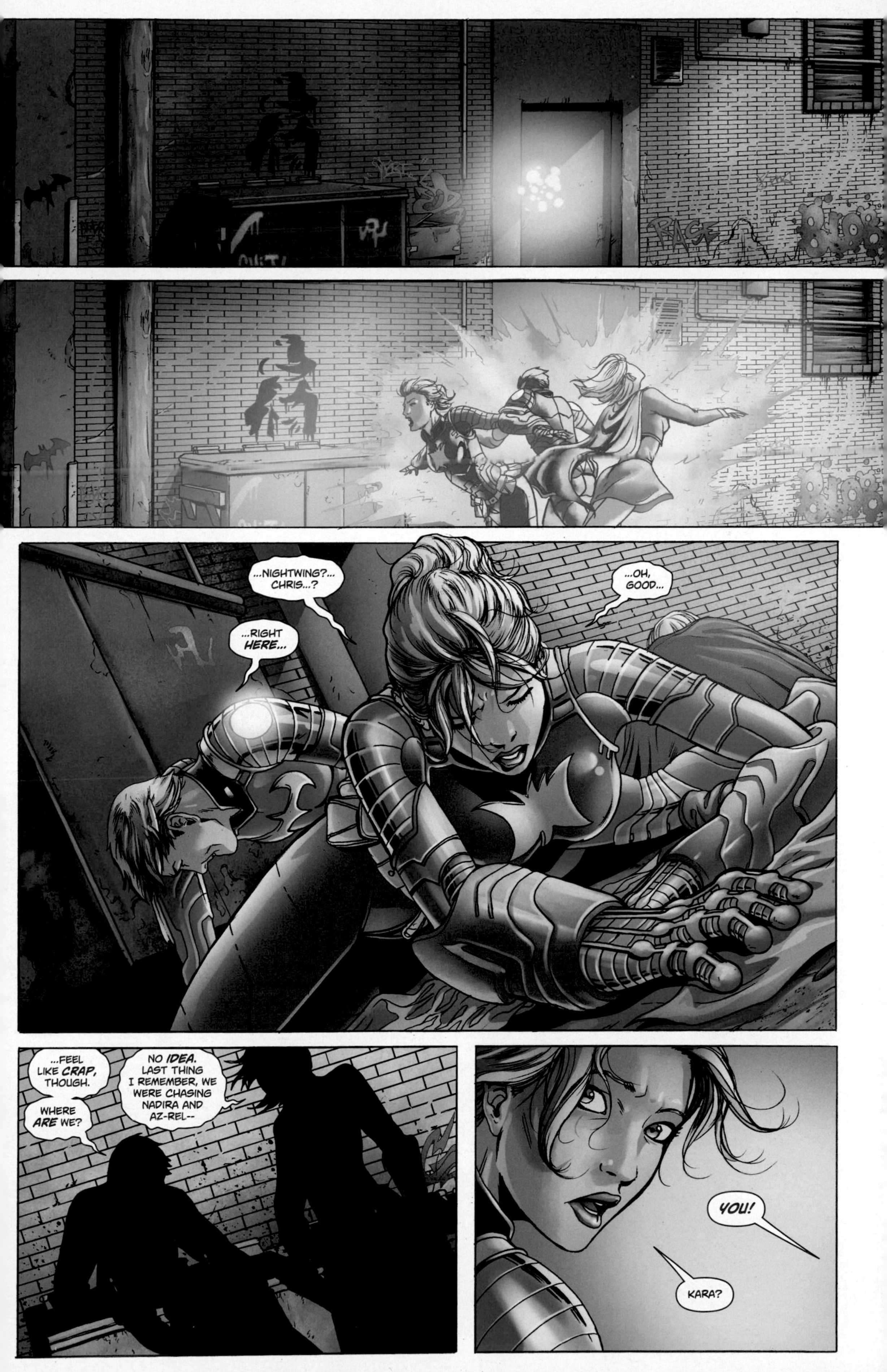
...NIGHTWING?... CHRIS...?
...RIGHT HERE...
...OH, GOOD...
...FEEL LIKE CRAP, THOUGH.
WHERE ARE WE?
NO IDEA. LAST THING I REMEMBER, WE WERE CHASING NADIRA AND AZ-REL--
YOU!
KARA?

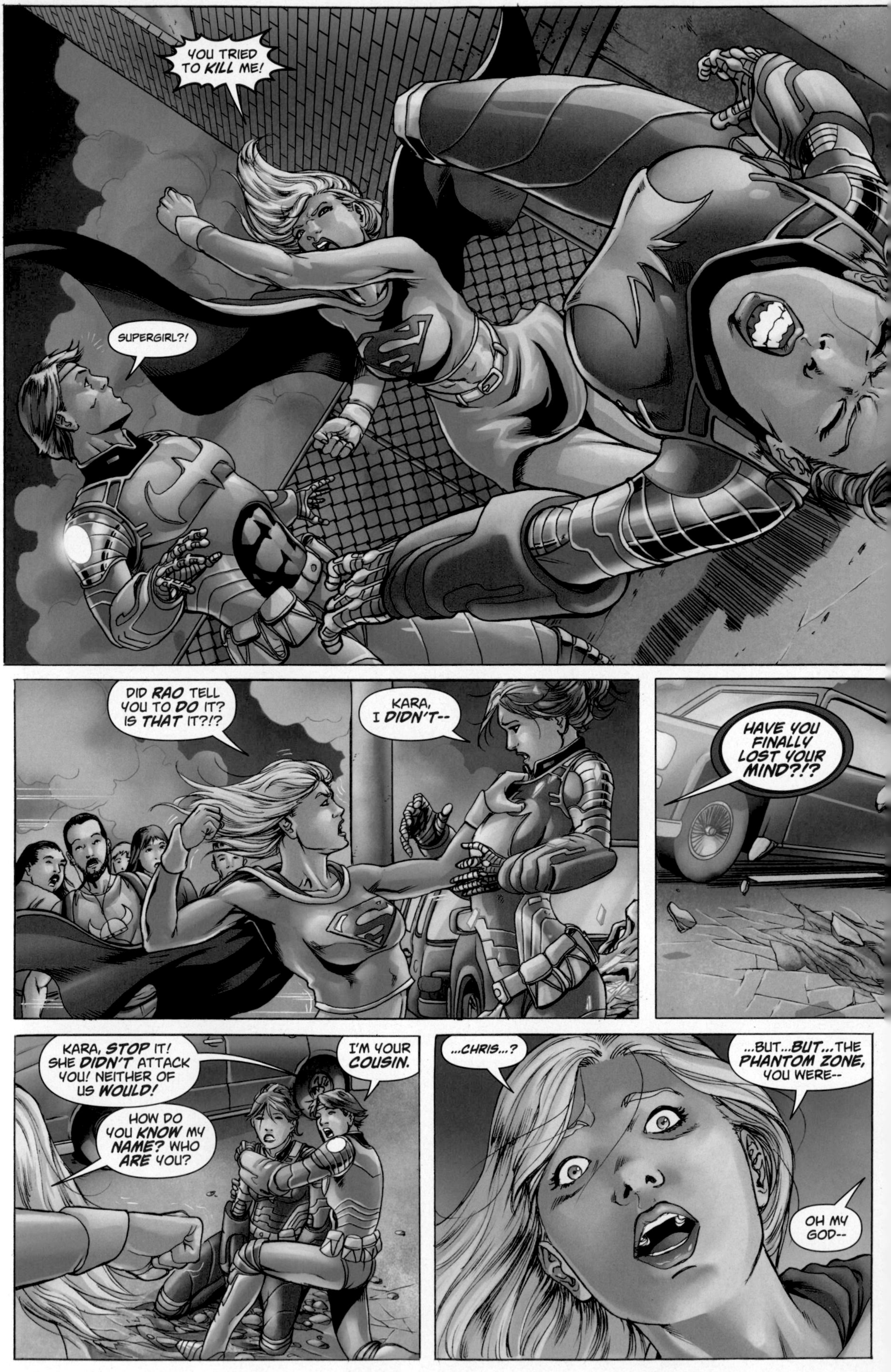
YOU TRIED TO KILL ME!
SUPERGIRL?!
DID RAO TELL YOU TO DO IT? IS THAT IT?!?
KARA, I DIDN'T--
HAVE YOU FINALLY LOST YOUR MIND?!?
KARA, STOP IT! SHE DIDN'T ATTACK YOU! NEITHER OF US WOULD!
I'M YOUR COUSIN.
HOW DO YOU KNOW MY NAME? WHO ARE YOU?
...CHRIS...?
...BUT...BUT...THE PHANTOM ZONE, YOU WERE--
OH MY GOD--

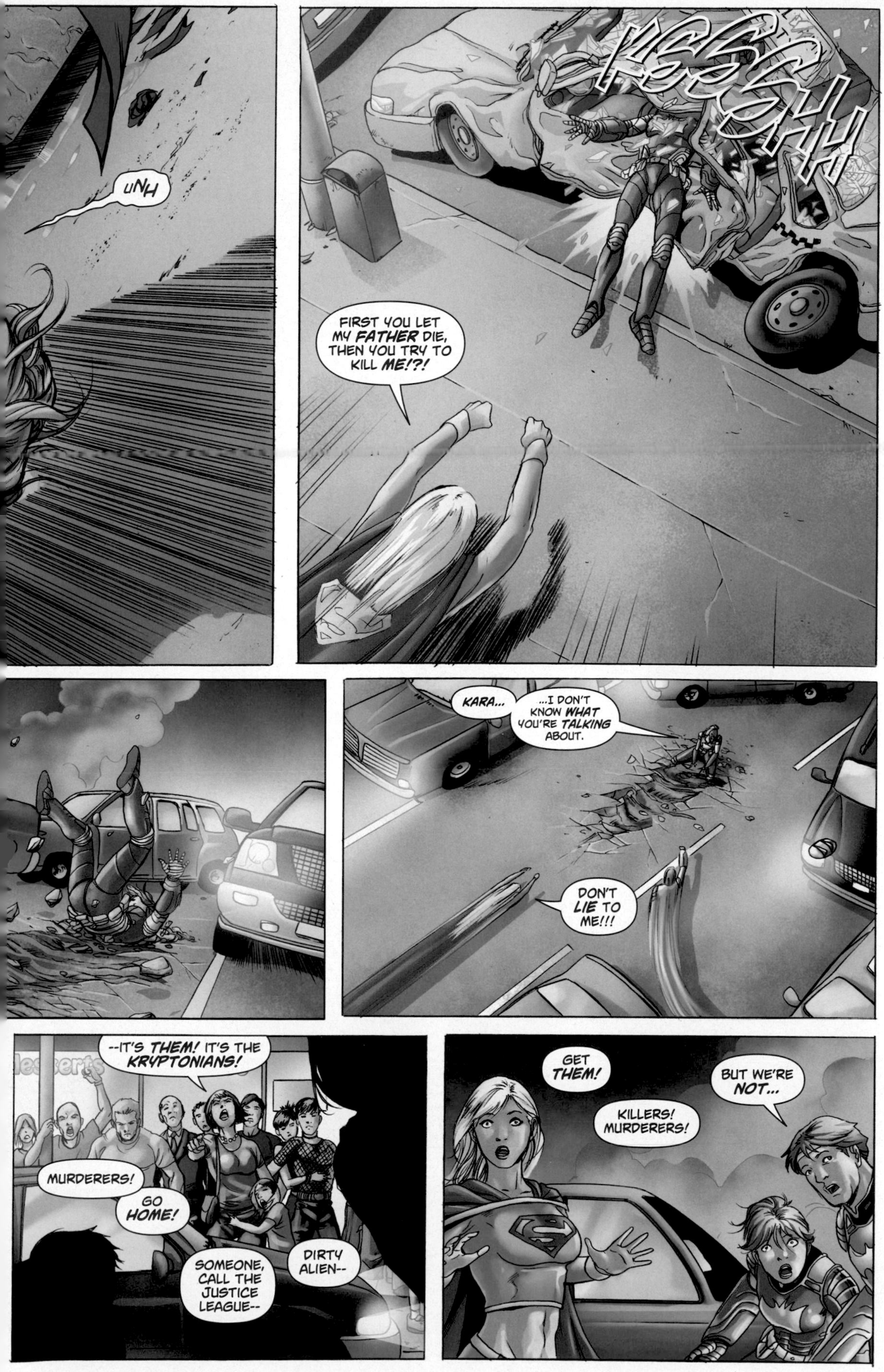
UNH
KSSSHH
FIRST YOU LET MY FATHER DIE, THEN YOU TRY TO KILL ME!?!
KARA...
...I DON'T KNOW WHAT YOU'RE TALKING ABOUT.
DON'T LIE TO ME!!!
--IT'S THEM! IT'S THE KRYPTONIANS!
MURDERERS!
GO HOME!
SOMEONE, CALL THE JUSTICE LEAGUE--
DIRTY ALIEN--
GET THEM!
KILLERS! MURDERERS!
BUT WE'RE NOT...

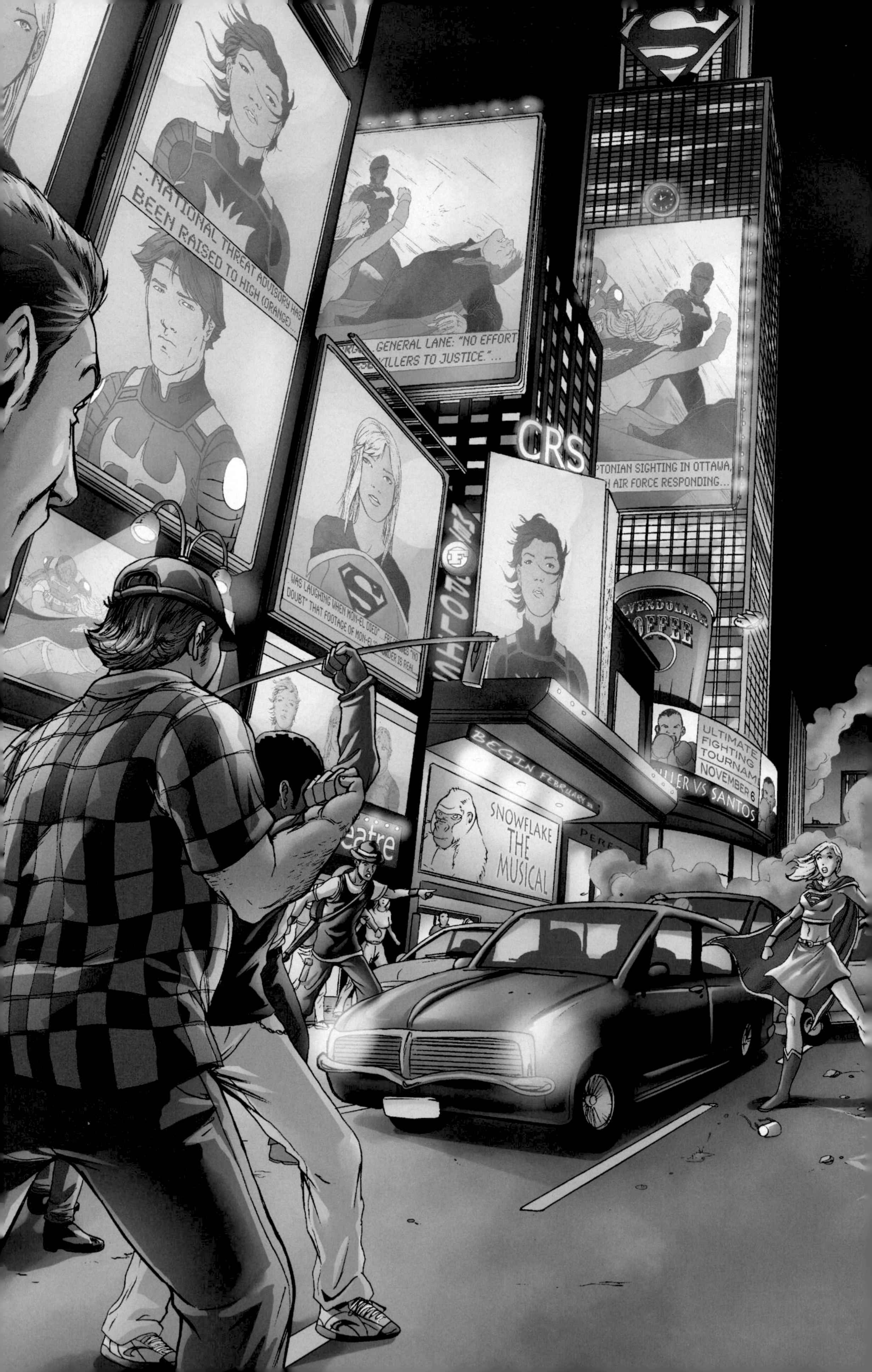

...NATIONAL THREAT ADVISORY HAS BEEN RAISED TO HIGH (ORANGE)...
GENERAL LANE: "NO EFFORT
KILLERS TO JUSTICE."...
CRS
PTONIAN SIGHTING IN OTTAWA,
AIR FORCE RESPONDING...
WAS LAUGHING WHEN MON-EL DIED"
DOUBT" THAT FOOTAGE OF MON-EL
BEGIN FEBRUARY
SNOWFLAKE THE MUSICAL
COFFEE
ULTIMATE FIGHTING TOURNAM
NOVEMBER 6
LLER VS SANTOS
eatre

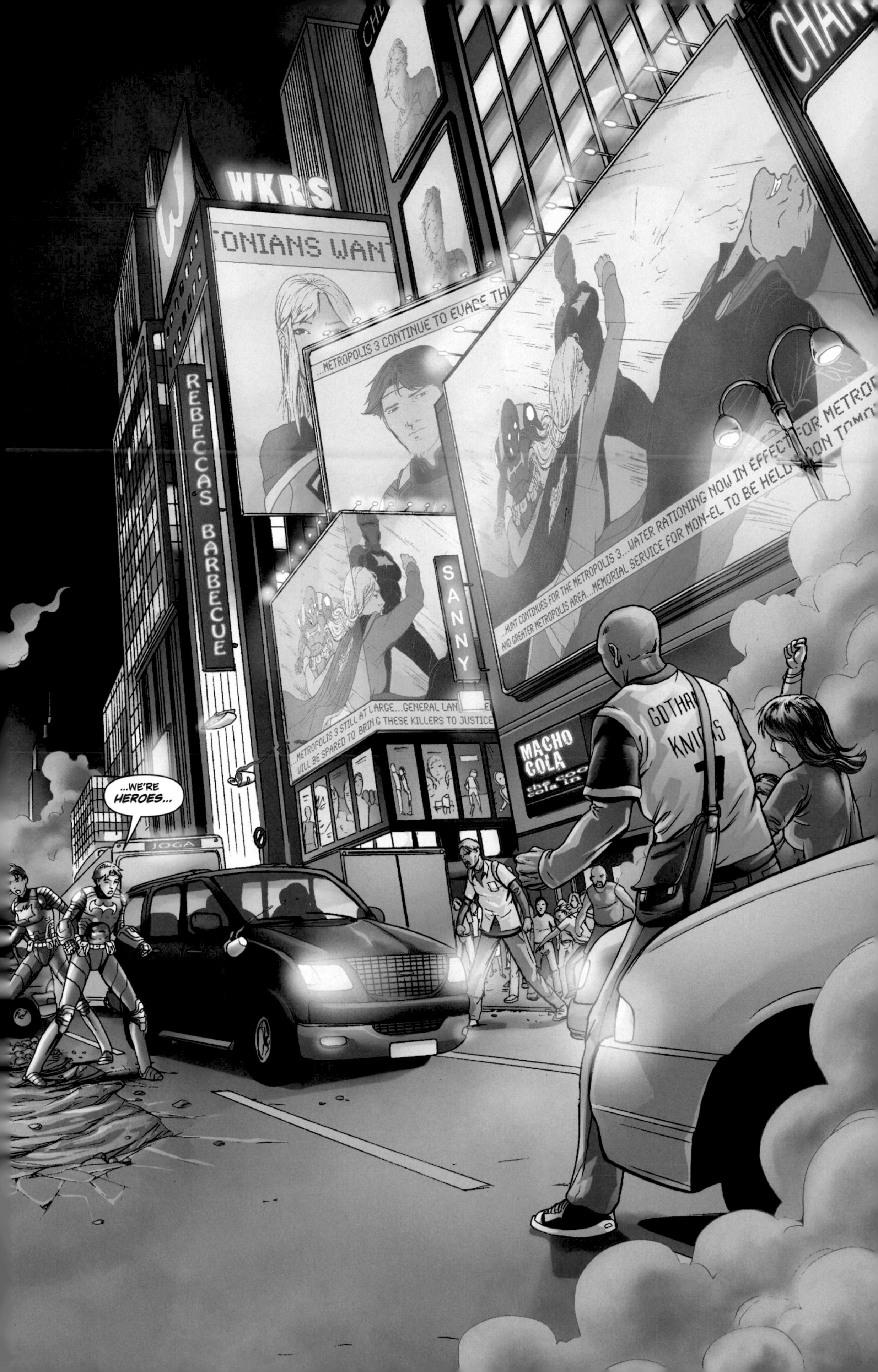

WKRS
TONIANS WANT
...METROPOLIS 3 CONTINUE TO EVADE TH
REBECCAS BARBECUE
...HUNT CONTINUES FOR THE METROPOLIS 3...WATER RATIONING NOW IN EFFECT FOR METRO
AND GREATER METROPOLIS AREA...MEMORIAL SERVICE FOR MON-EL TO BE HELD SOON TOMO
SANNY
...METROPOLIS 3 STILL AT LARGE...GENERAL LAN
WILL BE SPARED TO BRING THESE KILLERS TO JUSTICE
MACHO COLA
GOTHAM KNIGHTS
JOGA
...WE'RE HEROES...

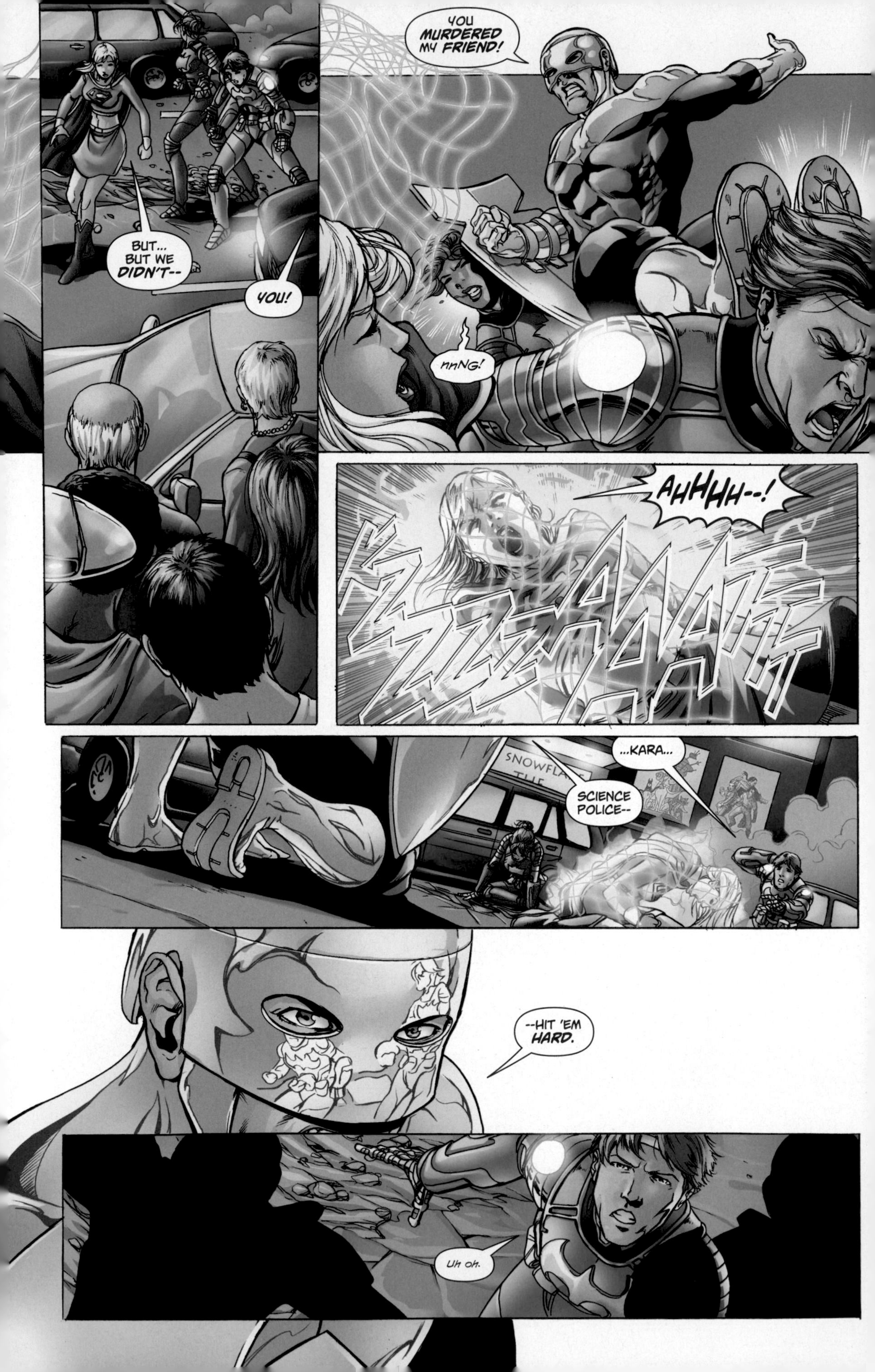

BUT... BUT WE DIDN'T--
YOU!
YOU MURDERED MY FRIEND!
nnNG!
AHHHH--!
KZZZZAAAATT
...KARA...
SCIENCE POLICE--
SNOWFLA
THE
--HIT 'EM HARD.
Uh oh.

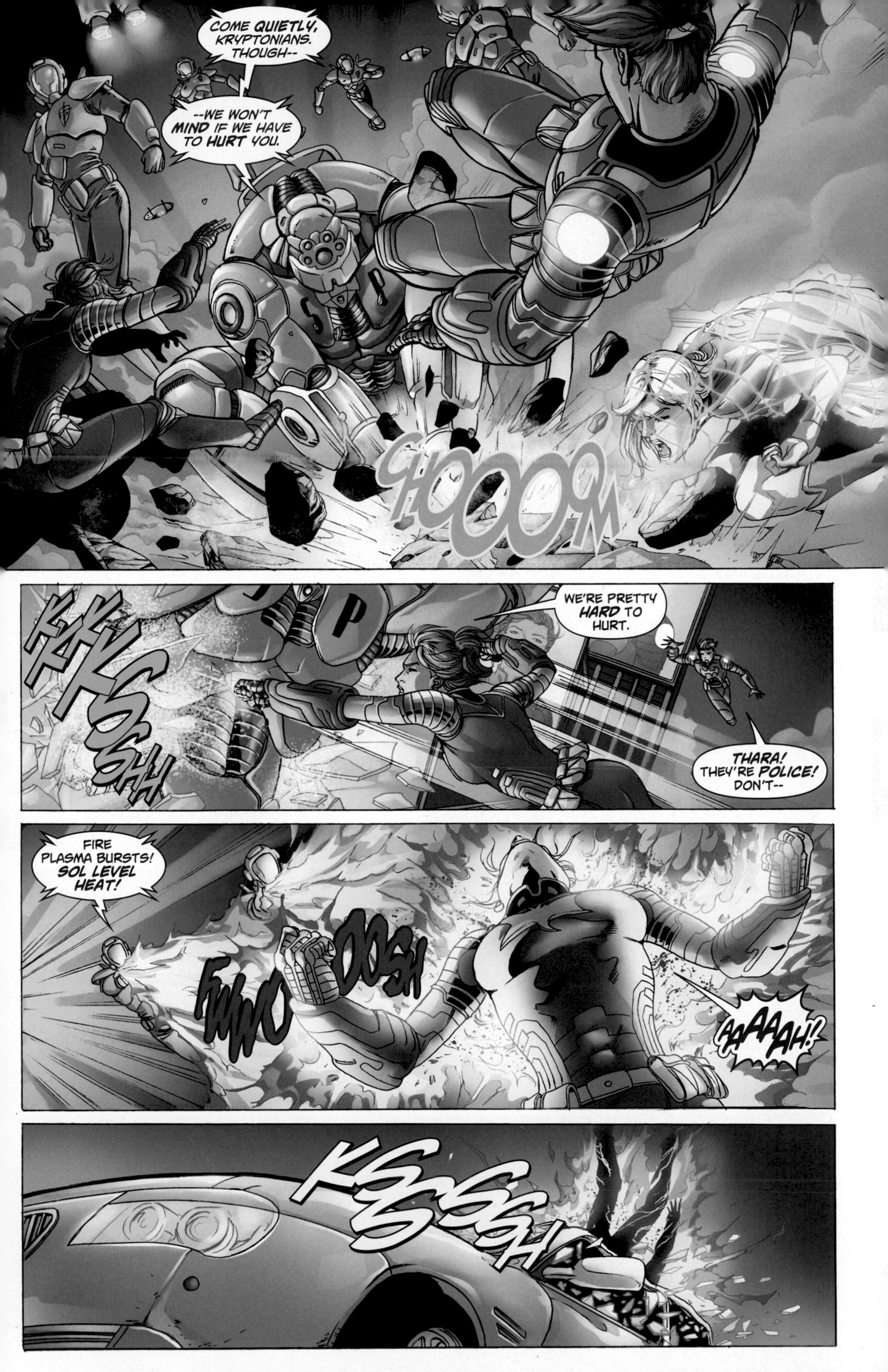
COME QUIETLY, KRYPTONIANS. THOUGH--
--WE WON'T MIND IF WE HAVE TO HURT YOU.
CHOOOOM
KAKKSSHH
WE'RE PRETTY HARD TO HURT.
THARA! THEY'RE POLICE! DON'T--
FIRE PLASMA BURSTS! SOL LEVEL HEAT!
FWWOOOSH
AAAAAH!
KSSSSCH

THARA!

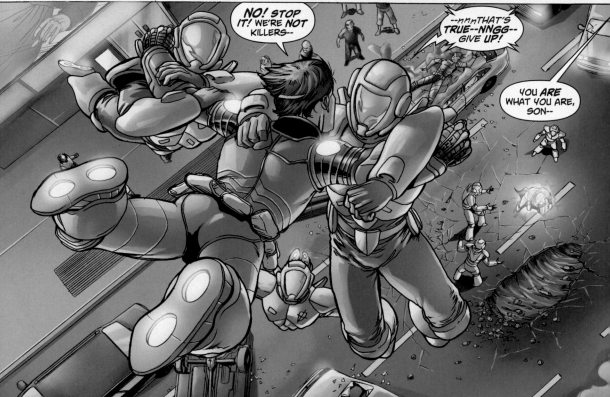

NO! STOP IT! WE'RE NOT KILLERS--

--nnnnTHAT'S TRUE--NNGG-- GIVE UP!

YOU ARE WHAT YOU ARE, SON--

--AND YOU'RE RESPONSIBLE FOR MON-EL'S DEATH.

I INTEND FOR YOU TO ANSWER FOR IT.

NNNNAA!

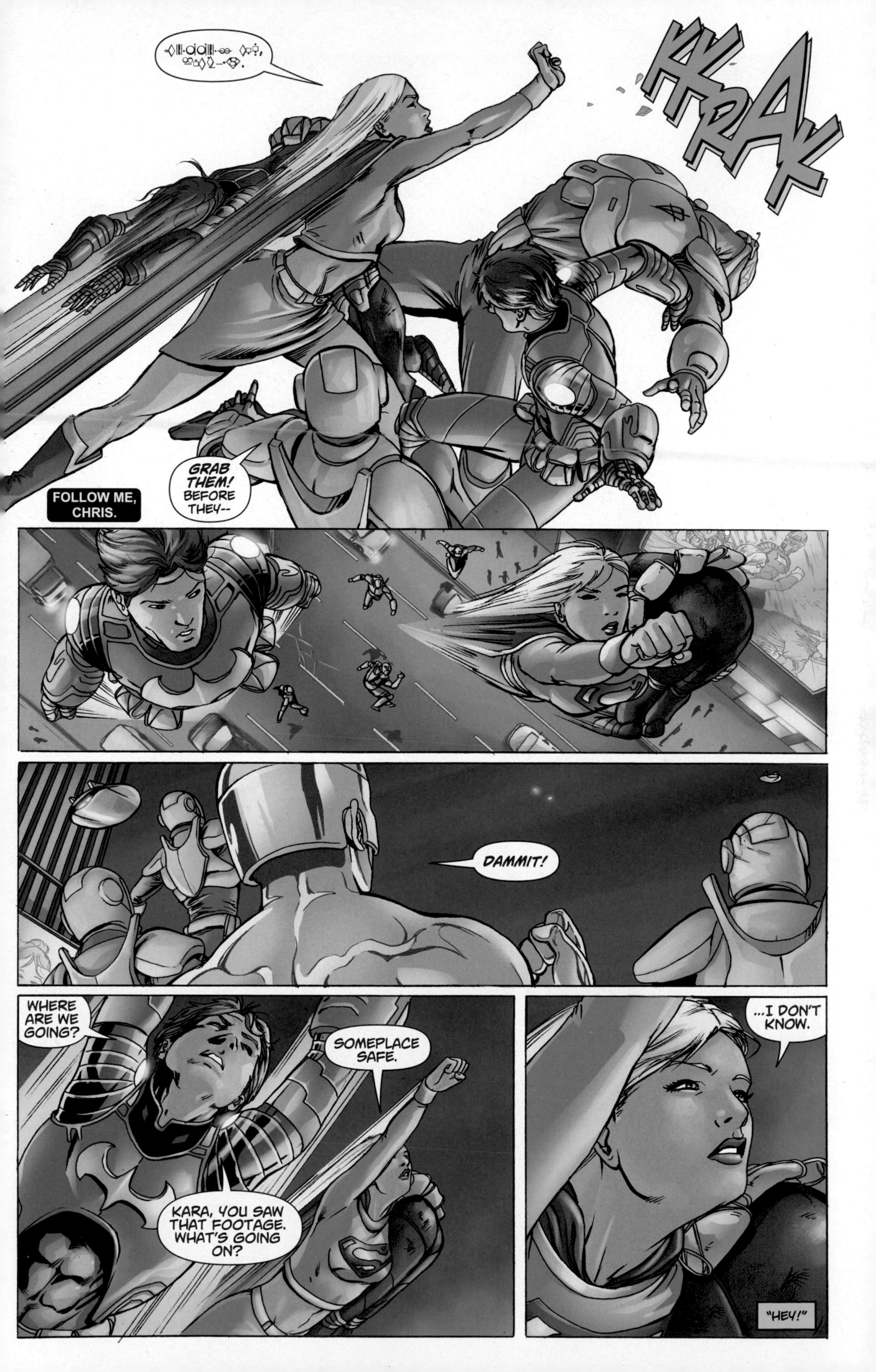

KKRAK
FOLLOW ME, CHRIS.
GRAB THEM! BEFORE THEY--
DAMMIT!
WHERE ARE WE GOING?
SOMEPLACE SAFE.
KARA, YOU SAW THAT FOOTAGE. WHAT'S GOING ON?
...I DON'T KNOW.
"HEY!"

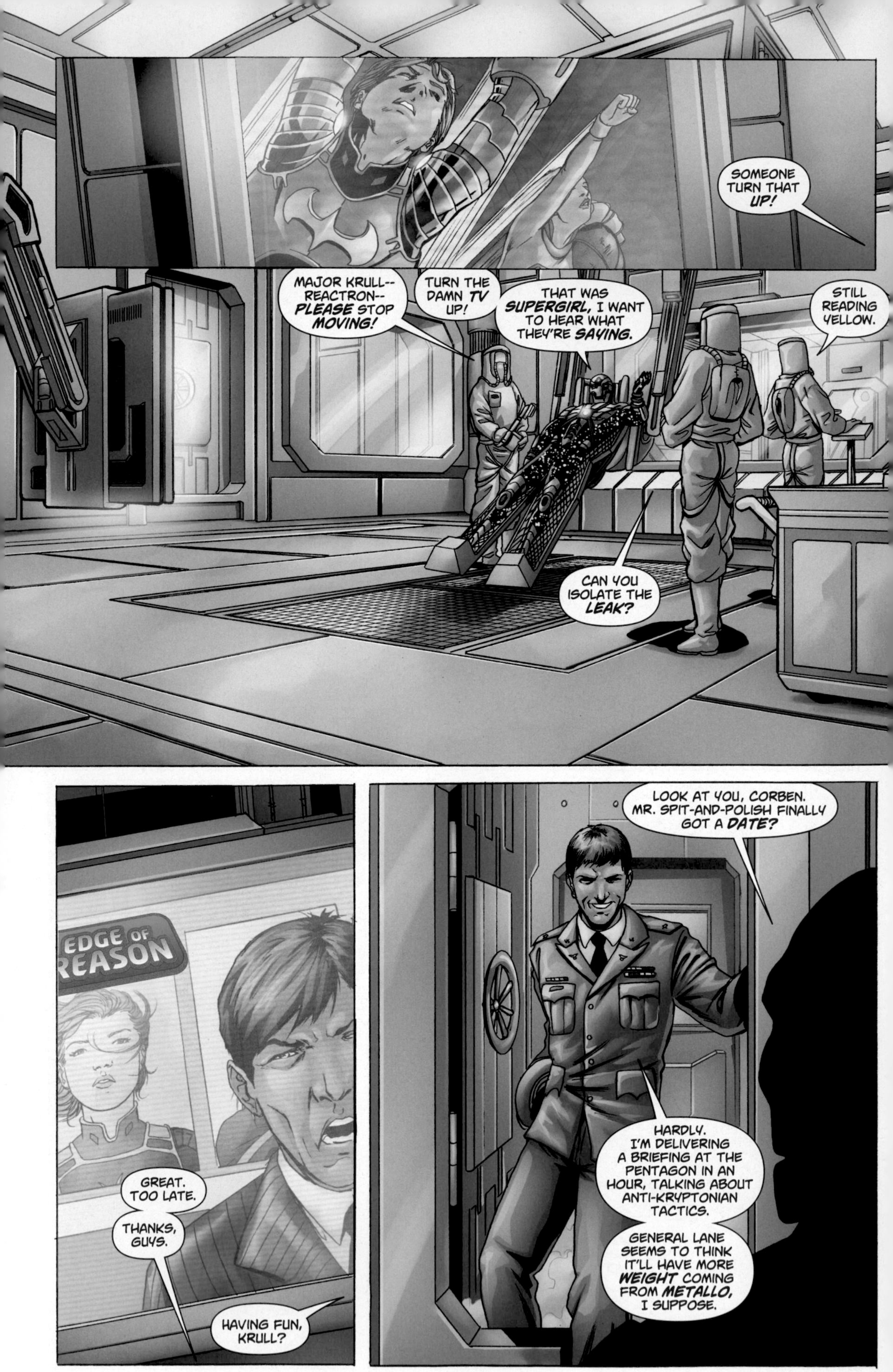
SOMEONE TURN THAT UP!
MAJOR KRULL-- REACTRON-- PLEASE STOP MOVING!
TURN THE DAMN TV UP!
THAT WAS SUPERGIRL, I WANT TO HEAR WHAT THEY'RE SAYING.
STILL READING YELLOW.
CAN YOU ISOLATE THE LEAK?
EDGE OF REASON
GREAT. TOO LATE.
THANKS, GUYS.
HAVING FUN, KRULL?
LOOK AT YOU, CORBEN. MR. SPIT-AND-POLISH FINALLY GOT A DATE?
HARDLY. I'M DELIVERING A BRIEFING AT THE PENTAGON IN AN HOUR, TALKING ABOUT ANTI-KRYPTONIAN TACTICS.
GENERAL LANE SEEMS TO THINK IT'LL HAVE MORE WEIGHT COMING FROM METALLO, I SUPPOSE.

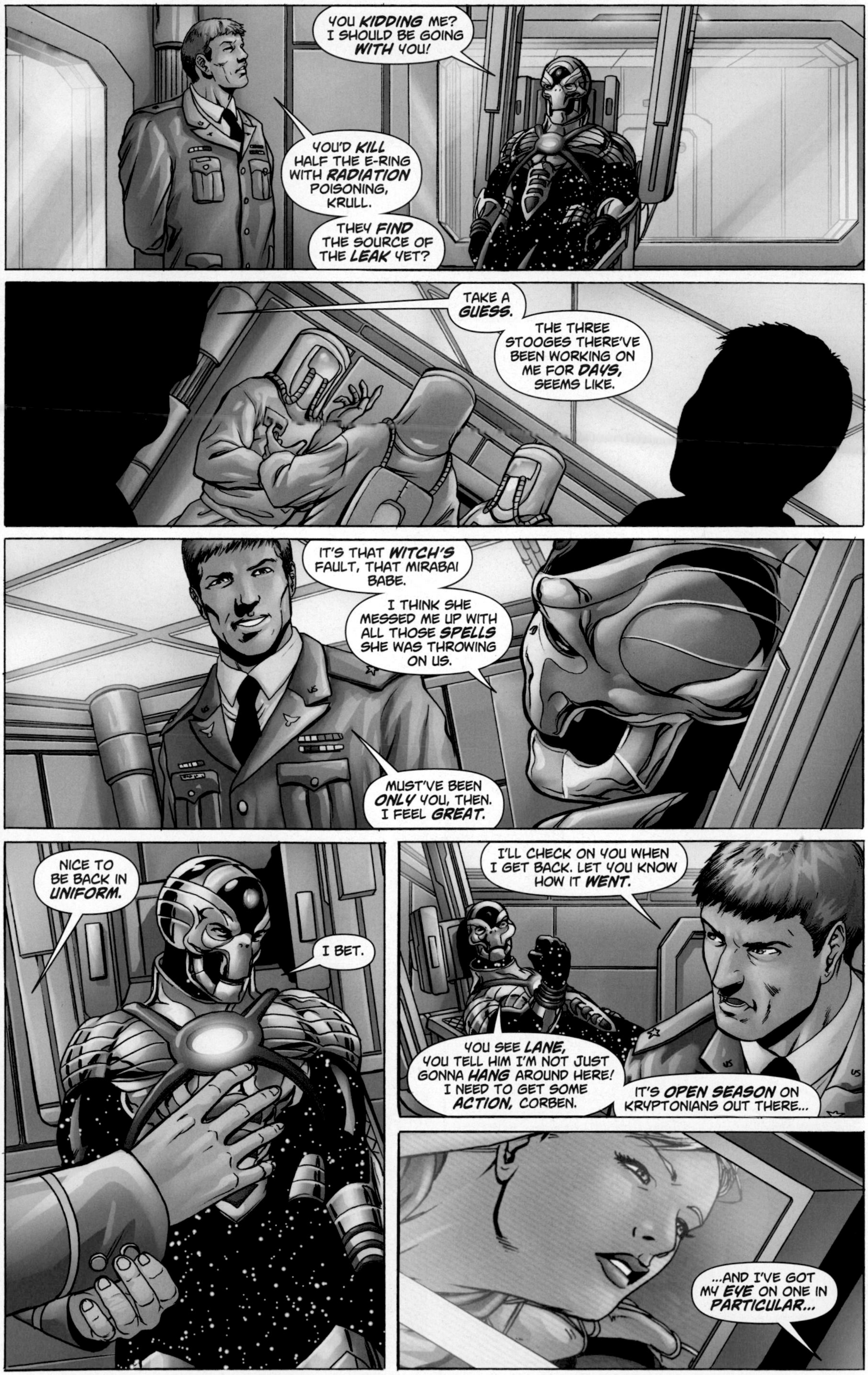
YOU KIDDING ME? I SHOULD BE GOING WITH YOU!
YOU'D KILL HALF THE E-RING WITH RADIATION POISONING, KRULL.
THEY FIND THE SOURCE OF THE LEAK YET?
TAKE A GUESS.
THE THREE STOOGES THERE'VE BEEN WORKING ON ME FOR DAYS, SEEMS LIKE.
IT'S THAT WITCH'S FAULT, THAT MIRABAI BABE.
I THINK SHE MESSED ME UP WITH ALL THOSE SPELLS SHE WAS THROWING ON US.
MUST'VE BEEN ONLY YOU, THEN. I FEEL GREAT.
NICE TO BE BACK IN UNIFORM.
I BET.
I'LL CHECK ON YOU WHEN I GET BACK. LET YOU KNOW HOW IT WENT.
YOU SEE LANE, YOU TELL HIM I'M NOT JUST GONNA HANG AROUND HERE! I NEED TO GET SOME ACTION, CORBEN.
IT'S OPEN SEASON ON KRYPTONIANS OUT THERE...
...AND I'VE GOT MY EYE ON ONE IN PARTICULAR...

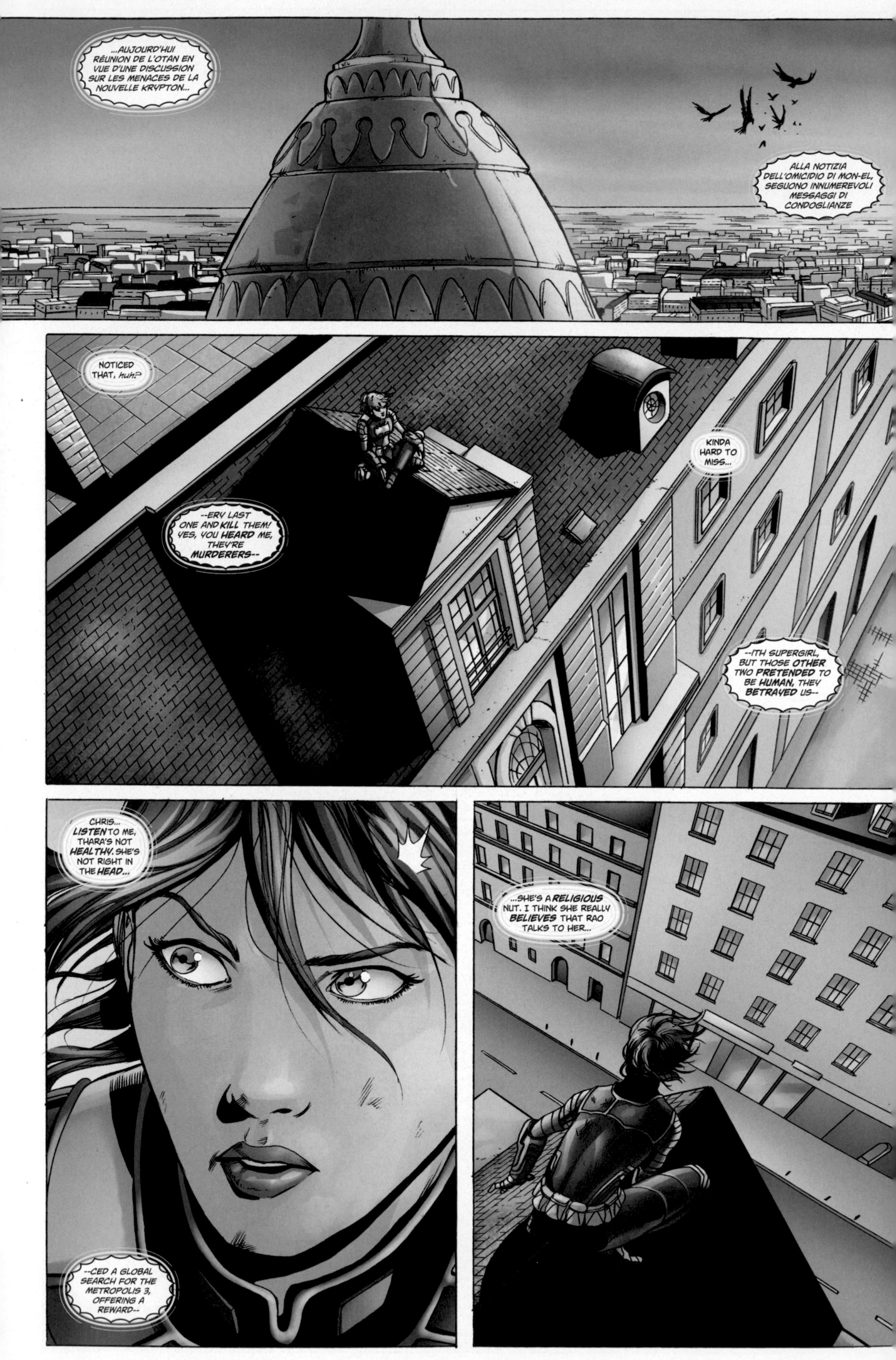
...AUJOURD'HUI RÉUNION DE L'OTAN EN VUE D'UNE DISCUSSION SUR LES MENACES DE LA NOUVELLE KRYPTON...
ALLA NOTIZIA DELL'OMICIDIO DI MON-EL, SEGUONO INNUMEREVOLI MESSAGGI DI CONDOGLIANZE
NOTICED THAT, *huh?*
KINDA HARD TO MISS...
--ERY LAST ONE AND **KILL** THEM! YES, YOU **HEARD** ME, THEY'RE **MURDERERS**--
--ITH SUPERGIRL, BUT THOSE **OTHER** TWO **PRETENDED** TO BE **HUMAN**, THEY **BETRAYED** US--
CHRIS... **LISTEN** TO ME, THARA'S NOT **HEALTHY**. SHE'S NOT RIGHT IN THE **HEAD**...
...SHE'S A **RELIGIOUS** NUT. I THINK SHE REALLY **BELIEVES** THAT RAO TALKS TO HER...
--CED A GLOBAL SEARCH FOR THE METROPOLIS 3, OFFERING A REWARD--

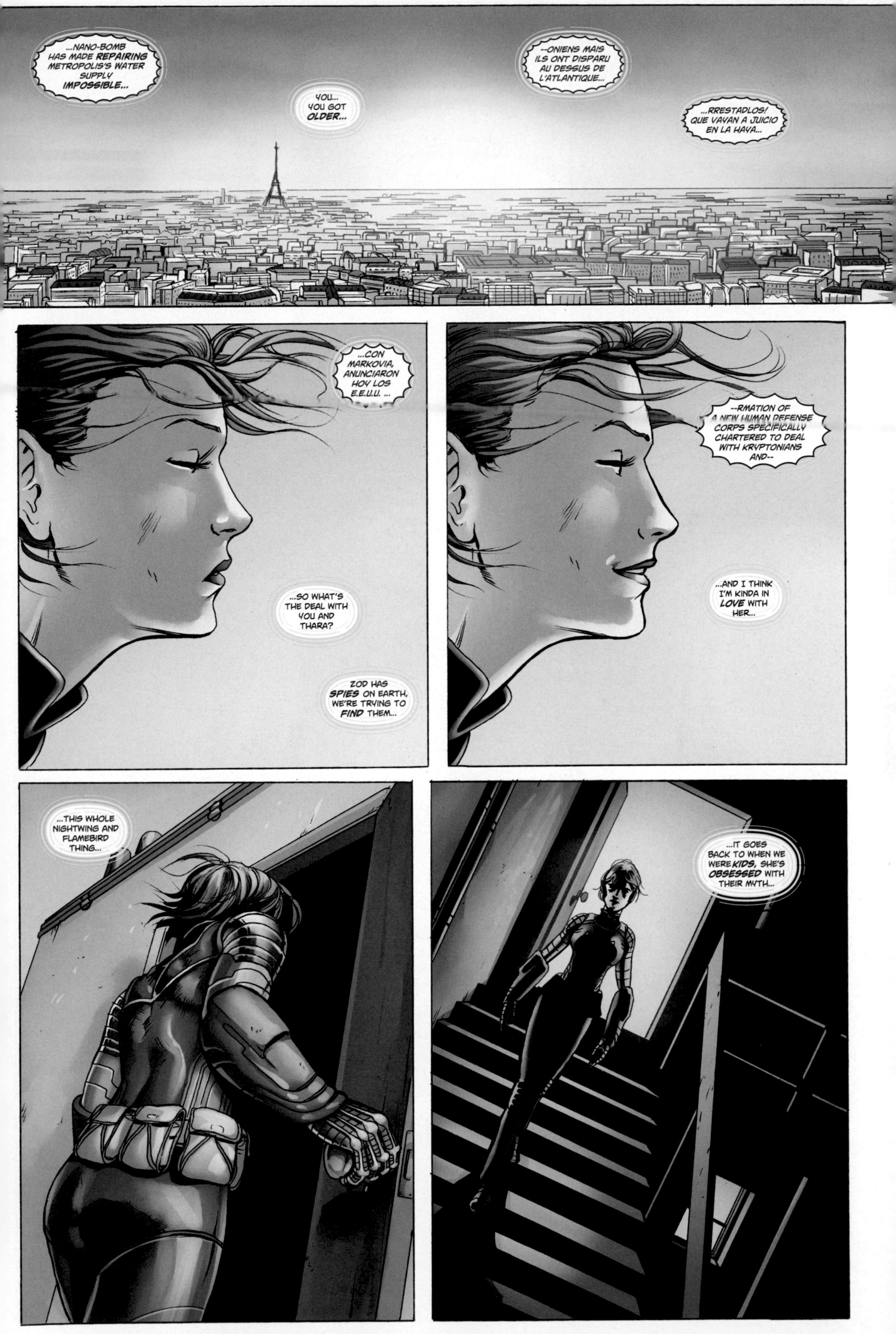
...NANO-BOMB HAS MADE REPAIRING METROPOLIS'S WATER SUPPLY IMPOSSIBLE...
YOU... YOU GOT OLDER...
--ONIENS MAIS ILS ONT DISPARU AU DESSUS DE L'ATLANTIQUE...
...RRESTADLOS! QUE VAYAN A JUICIO EN LA HAYA...
...CON MARKOVIA, ANUNCIARON HOY LOS E.E.U.U. ...
...SO WHAT'S THE DEAL WITH YOU AND THARA?
ZOD HAS SPIES ON EARTH, WE'RE TRYING TO FIND THEM...
--RMATION OF A NEW HUMAN DEFENSE CORPS SPECIFICALLY CHARTERED TO DEAL WITH KRYPTONIANS AND--
...AND I THINK I'M KINDA IN LOVE WITH HER...
...THIS WHOLE NIGHTWING AND FLAMEBIRD THING...
...IT GOES BACK TO WHEN WE WERE KIDS, SHE'S OBSESSED WITH THEIR MYTH...

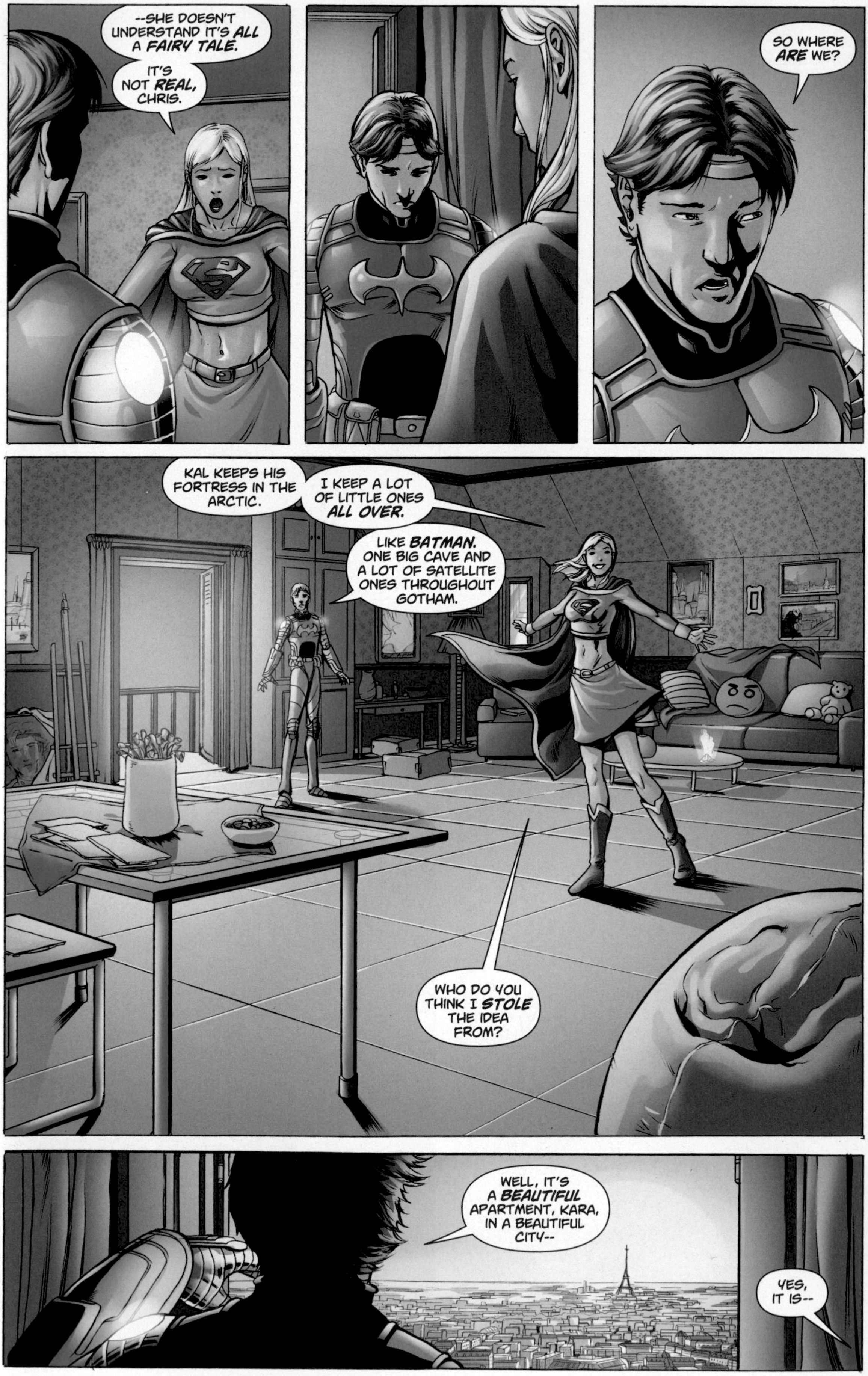
--SHE DOESN'T UNDERSTAND IT'S ALL A FAIRY TALE.
IT'S NOT REAL, CHRIS.
SO WHERE ARE WE?
KAL KEEPS HIS FORTRESS IN THE ARCTIC.
I KEEP A LOT OF LITTLE ONES ALL OVER.
LIKE BATMAN. ONE BIG CAVE AND A LOT OF SATELLITE ONES THROUGHOUT GOTHAM.
WHO DO YOU THINK I STOLE THE IDEA FROM?
WELL, IT'S A BEAUTIFUL APARTMENT, KARA, IN A BEAUTIFUL CITY--
YES, IT IS--

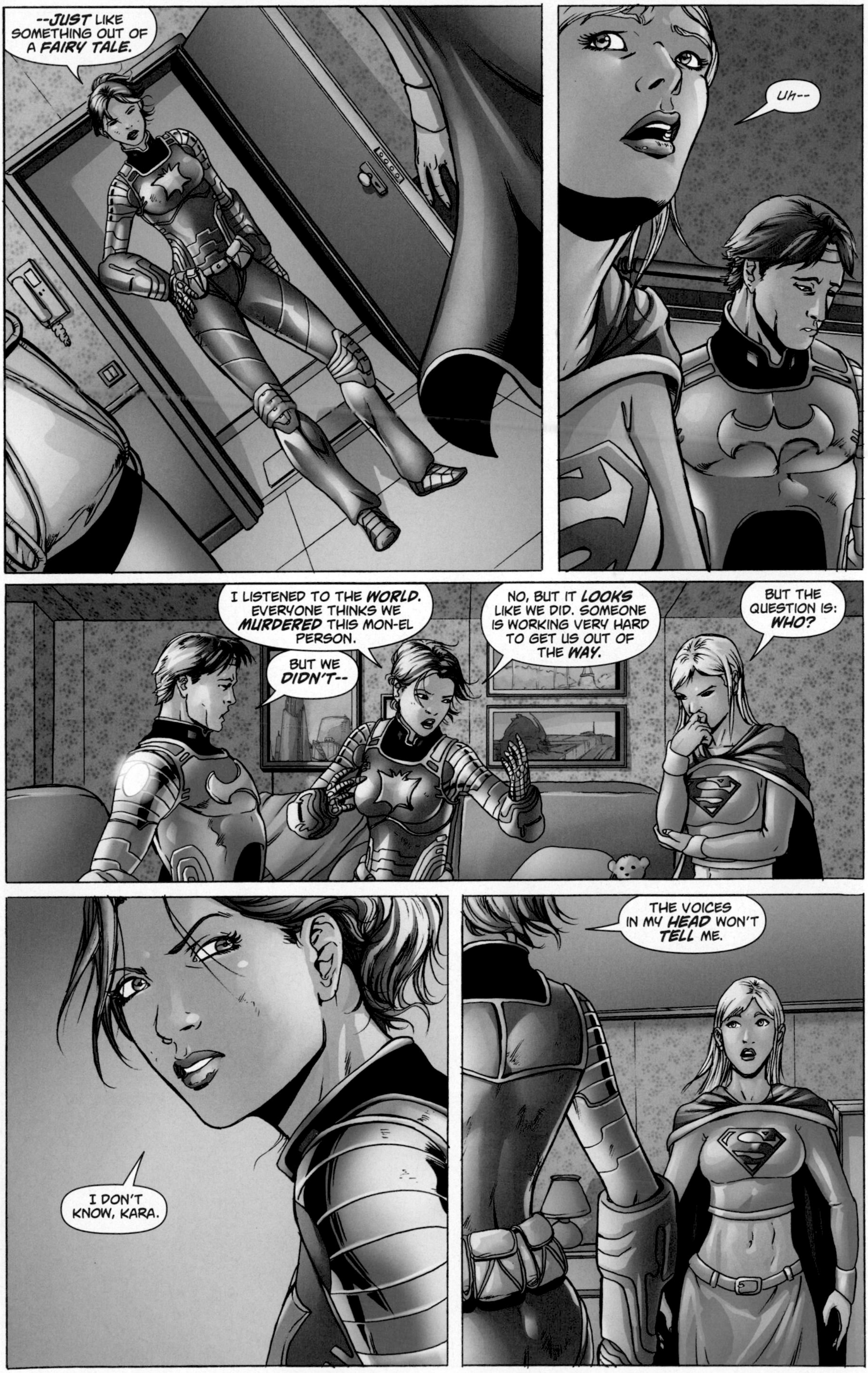

--JUST LIKE SOMETHING OUT OF A FAIRY TALE.
Uh--
I LISTENED TO THE WORLD. EVERYONE THINKS WE MURDERED THIS MON-EL PERSON.
BUT WE DIDN'T--
NO, BUT IT LOOKS LIKE WE DID. SOMEONE IS WORKING VERY HARD TO GET US OUT OF THE WAY.
BUT THE QUESTION IS: WHO?
I DON'T KNOW, KARA.
THE VOICES IN MY HEAD WON'T TELL ME.

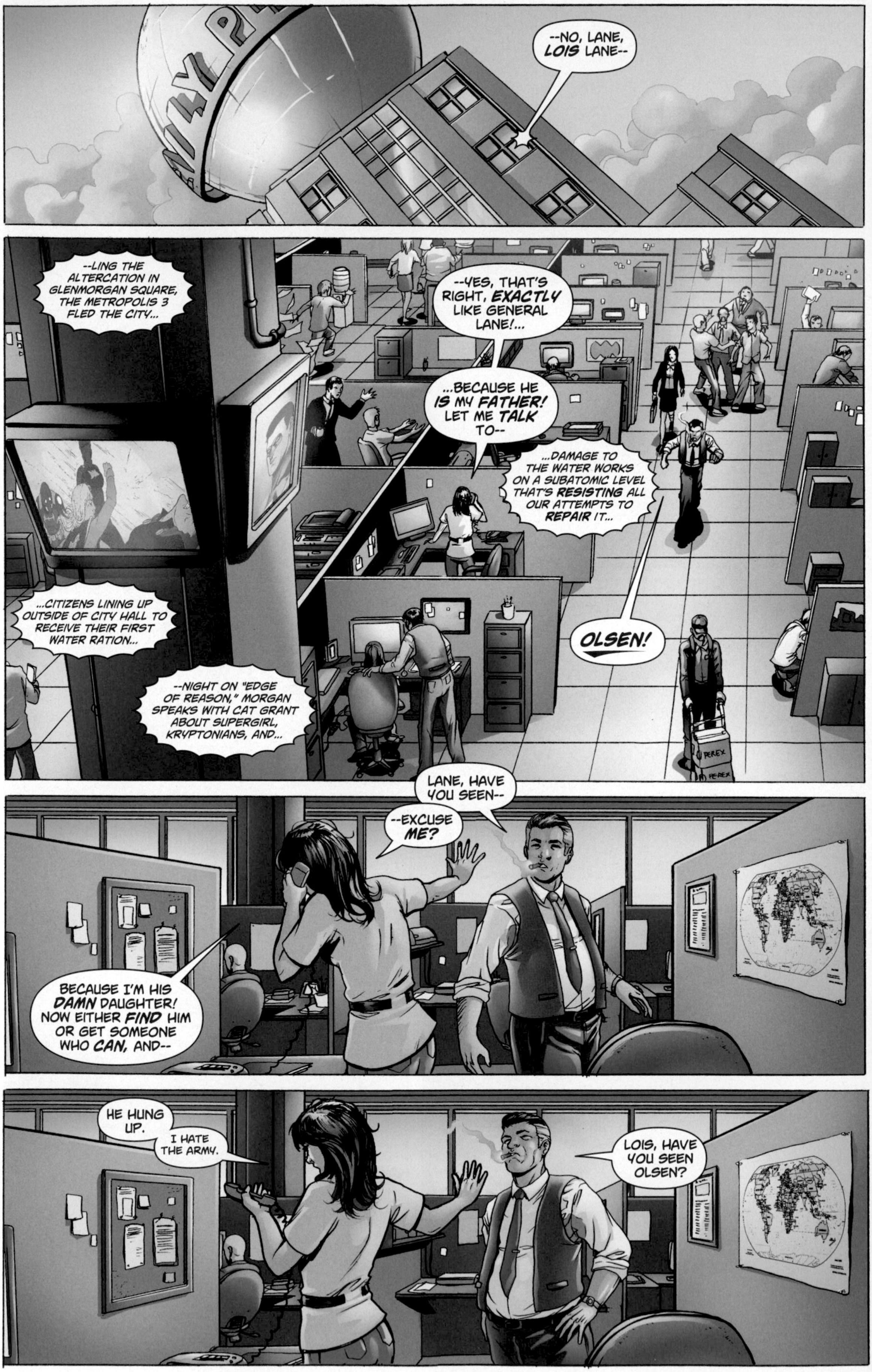
--NO, LANE, LOIS LANE--
--LING THE ALTERCATION IN GLENMORGAN SQUARE, THE METROPOLIS 3 FLED THE CITY...
--YES, THAT'S RIGHT, EXACTLY LIKE GENERAL LANE!...
...BECAUSE HE IS MY FATHER! LET ME TALK TO--
...DAMAGE TO THE WATER WORKS ON A SUBATOMIC LEVEL THAT'S RESISTING ALL OUR ATTEMPTS TO REPAIR IT...
...CITIZENS LINING UP OUTSIDE OF CITY HALL TO RECEIVE THEIR FIRST WATER RATION...
--NIGHT ON "EDGE OF REASON," MORGAN SPEAKS WITH CAT GRANT ABOUT SUPERGIRL, KRYPTONIANS, AND...
OLSEN!
LANE, HAVE YOU SEEN--
--EXCUSE ME?
BECAUSE I'M HIS DAMN DAUGHTER! NOW EITHER FIND HIM OR GET SOMEONE WHO CAN, AND--
HE HUNG UP.
I HATE THE ARMY.
LOIS, HAVE YOU SEEN OLSEN?

NO, SORRY, CHIEF.

GIMME A SEC?

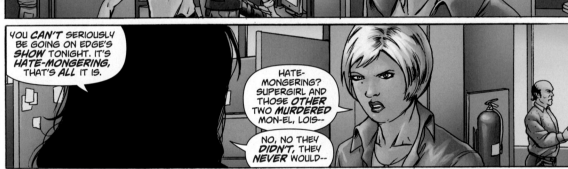

CAT! CAT, *WAIT!*

I'M LATE, LOIS. CAN YOU SHOUT AT ME *LATER?*

YOU *CAN'T* SERIOUSLY BE GOING ON EDGE'S *SHOW* TONIGHT. IT'S *HATE-MONGERING,* THAT'S *ALL* IT IS.

HATE-MONGERING? SUPERGIRL AND THOSE *OTHER* TWO *MURDERED* MON-EL, LOIS--

NO, NO THEY *DIDN'T,* THEY *NEVER* WOULD--

LOOK AT THE *TELEVISION!* THE WHOLE *WORLD* SAW IT!

VIDEO CAN BE *FAKED!*

THEY'VE *CONFIRMED* THAT THE *FOOTAGE* IS *UNALTERED!*

FACE IT, LOIS! THESE *ALIENS* THAT YOU'VE *CHAMPIONED* ALL THESE YEARS ARE *NOT* OUR FRIENDS...

...THEY'RE THE *ENEMY,* AND THE PEOPLE WHO *STAND* WITH THEM, WHO *DEFEND* THEM...

...THEY MIGHT WANT TO START *WATCHING* WHAT THEY SAY AND WHAT THEY *WRITE...*

...OR *SOMEONE* MIGHT THINK *THEY'RE* THE ENEMY, TOO....

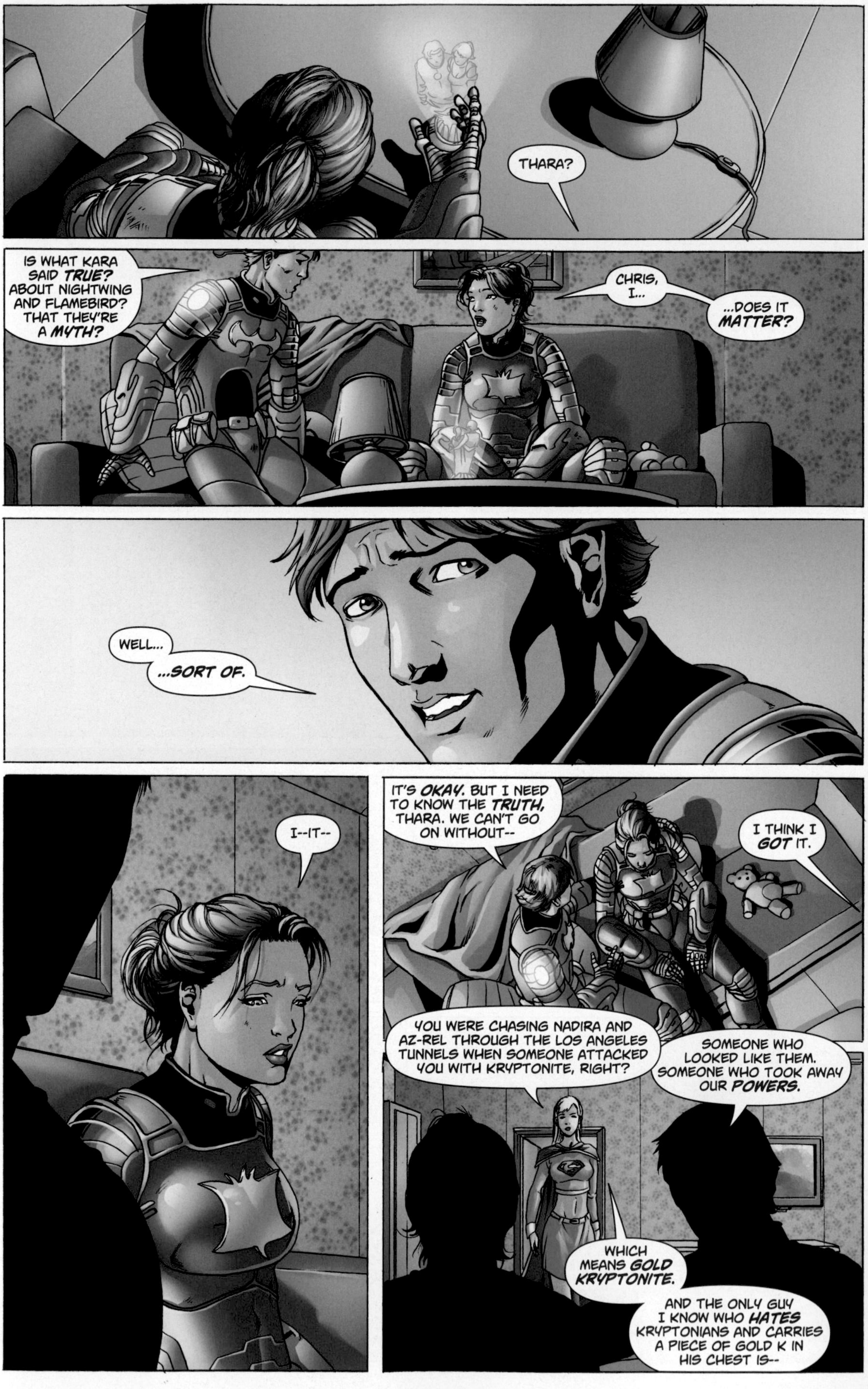
THARA?
IS WHAT KARA SAID TRUE? ABOUT NIGHTWING AND FLAMEBIRD? THAT THEY'RE A MYTH?
CHRIS, I...
...DOES IT MATTER?
WELL...
...SORT OF.
I--IT--
IT'S OKAY. BUT I NEED TO KNOW THE TRUTH, THARA. WE CAN'T GO ON WITHOUT--
I THINK I GOT IT.
YOU WERE CHASING NADIRA AND AZ-REL THROUGH THE LOS ANGELES TUNNELS WHEN SOMEONE ATTACKED YOU WITH KRYPTONITE, RIGHT?
SOMEONE WHO LOOKED LIKE THEM. SOMEONE WHO TOOK AWAY OUR POWERS.
WHICH MEANS GOLD KRYPTONITE.
AND THE ONLY GUY I KNOW WHO HATES KRYPTONIANS AND CARRIES A PIECE OF GOLD K IN HIS CHEST IS--

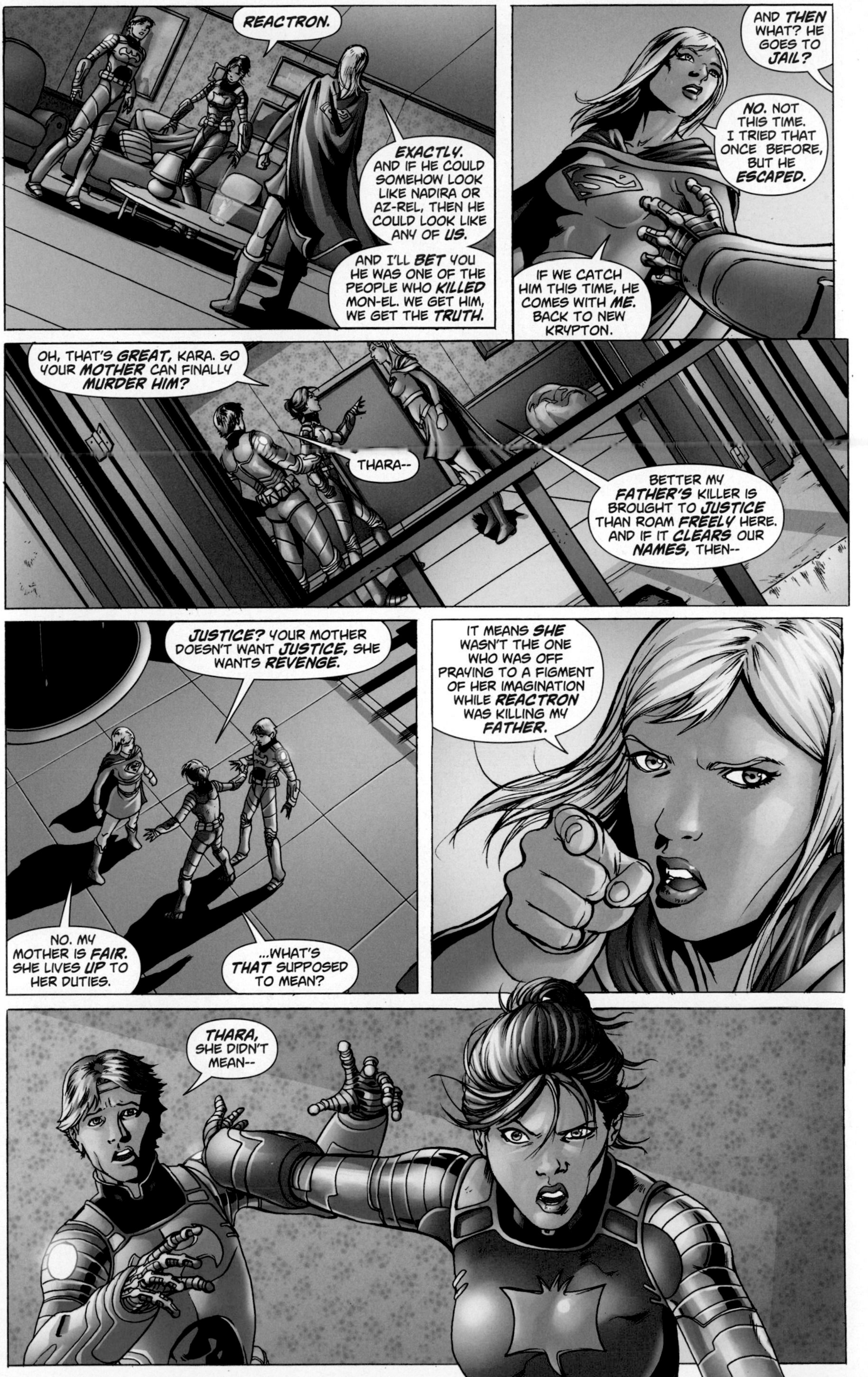
REACTRON.
EXACTLY. AND IF HE COULD SOMEHOW LOOK LIKE NADIRA OR AZ-REL, THEN HE COULD LOOK LIKE ANY OF US.
AND I'LL BET YOU HE WAS ONE OF THE PEOPLE WHO KILLED MON-EL. WE GET HIM, WE GET THE TRUTH.
AND THEN WHAT? HE GOES TO JAIL?
NO. NOT THIS TIME. I TRIED THAT ONCE BEFORE, BUT HE ESCAPED.
IF WE CATCH HIM THIS TIME, HE COMES WITH ME. BACK TO NEW KRYPTON.
OH, THAT'S GREAT, KARA. SO YOUR MOTHER CAN FINALLY MURDER HIM?
THARA--
BETTER MY FATHER'S KILLER IS BROUGHT TO JUSTICE THAN ROAM FREELY HERE. AND IF IT CLEARS OUR NAMES, THEN--
JUSTICE? YOUR MOTHER DOESN'T WANT JUSTICE, SHE WANTS REVENGE.
NO. MY MOTHER IS FAIR. SHE LIVES UP TO HER DUTIES.
...WHAT'S THAT SUPPOSED TO MEAN?
IT MEANS SHE WASN'T THE ONE WHO WAS OFF PRAYING TO A FIGMENT OF HER IMAGINATION WHILE REACTRON WAS KILLING MY FATHER.
THARA, SHE DIDN'T MEAN--

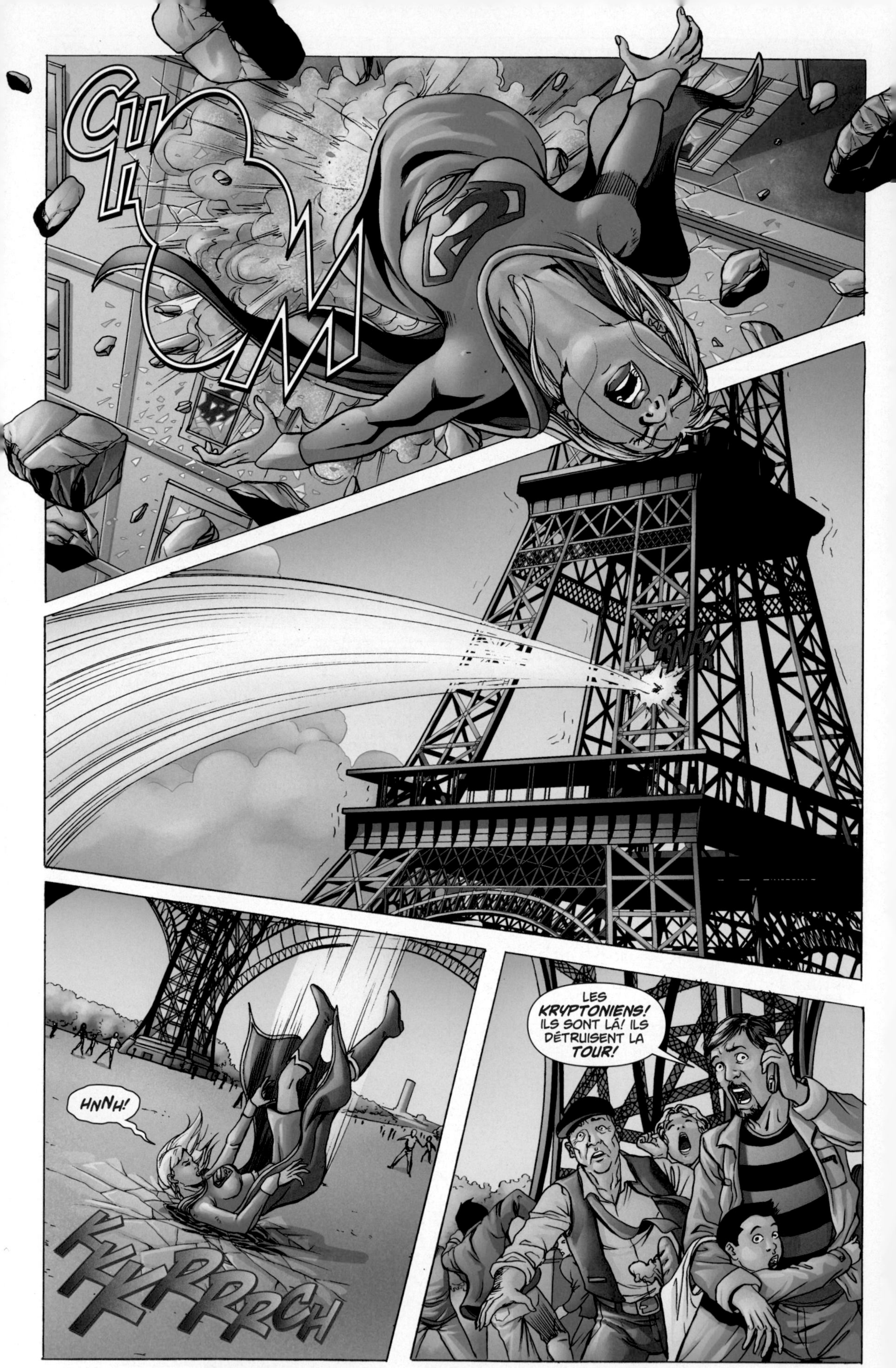
CRUNCH
CRNKK
HNNH!
KKKRRRRCH
LES KRYPTONIENS! ILS SONT LÀ! ILS DÉTRUISENT LA TOUR!

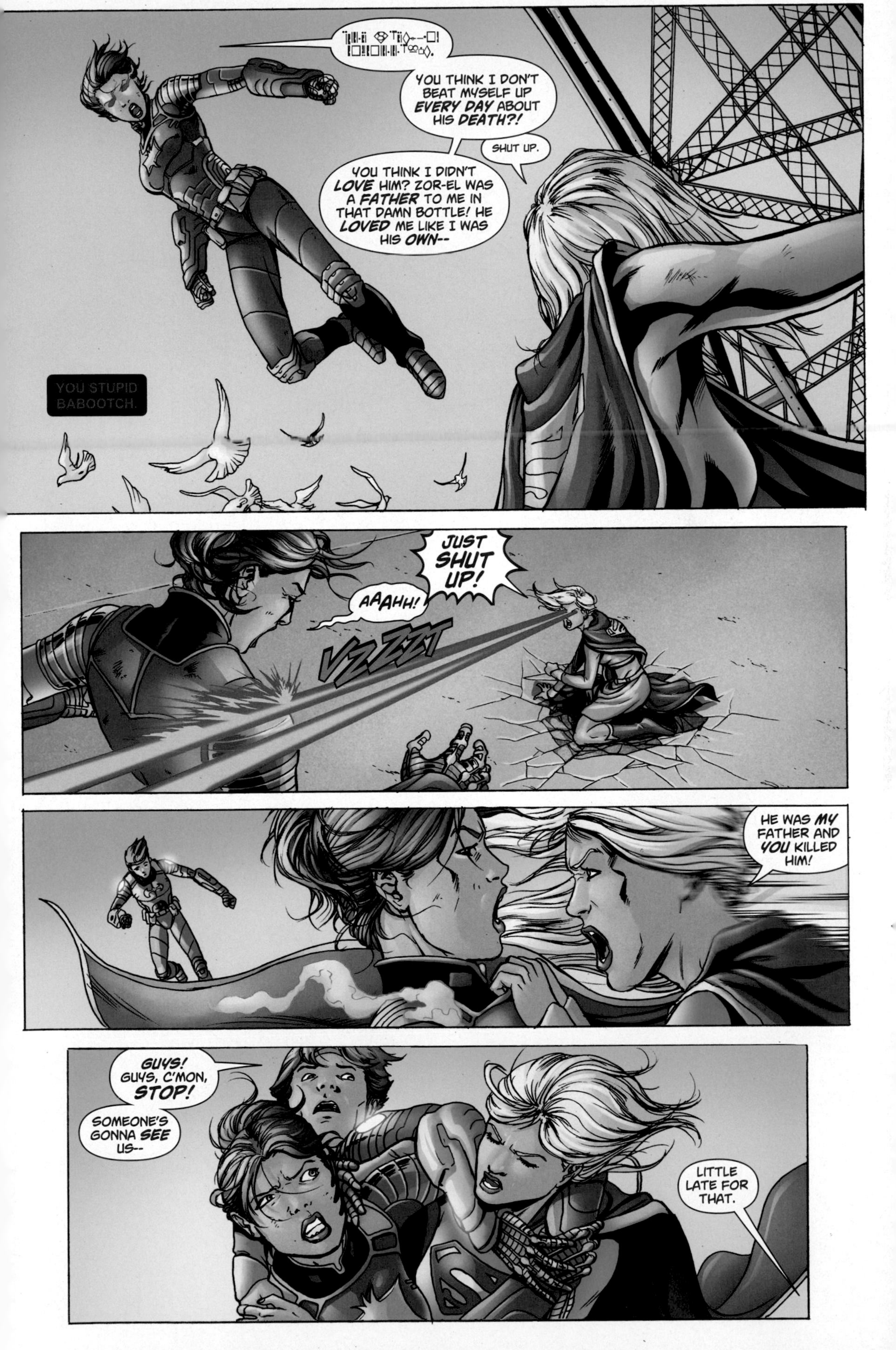
YOU THINK I DON'T BEAT MYSELF UP EVERY DAY ABOUT HIS DEATH?!
SHUT UP.
YOU THINK I DIDN'T LOVE HIM? ZOR-EL WAS A FATHER TO ME IN THAT DAMN BOTTLE! HE LOVED ME LIKE I WAS HIS OWN--
YOU STUPID BABOOTCH.
JUST SHUT UP!
AAAHH!
VZZZT
HE WAS MY FATHER AND YOU KILLED HIM!
GUYS! GUYS, C'MON, STOP!
SOMEONE'S GONNA SEE US--
LITTLE LATE FOR THAT.

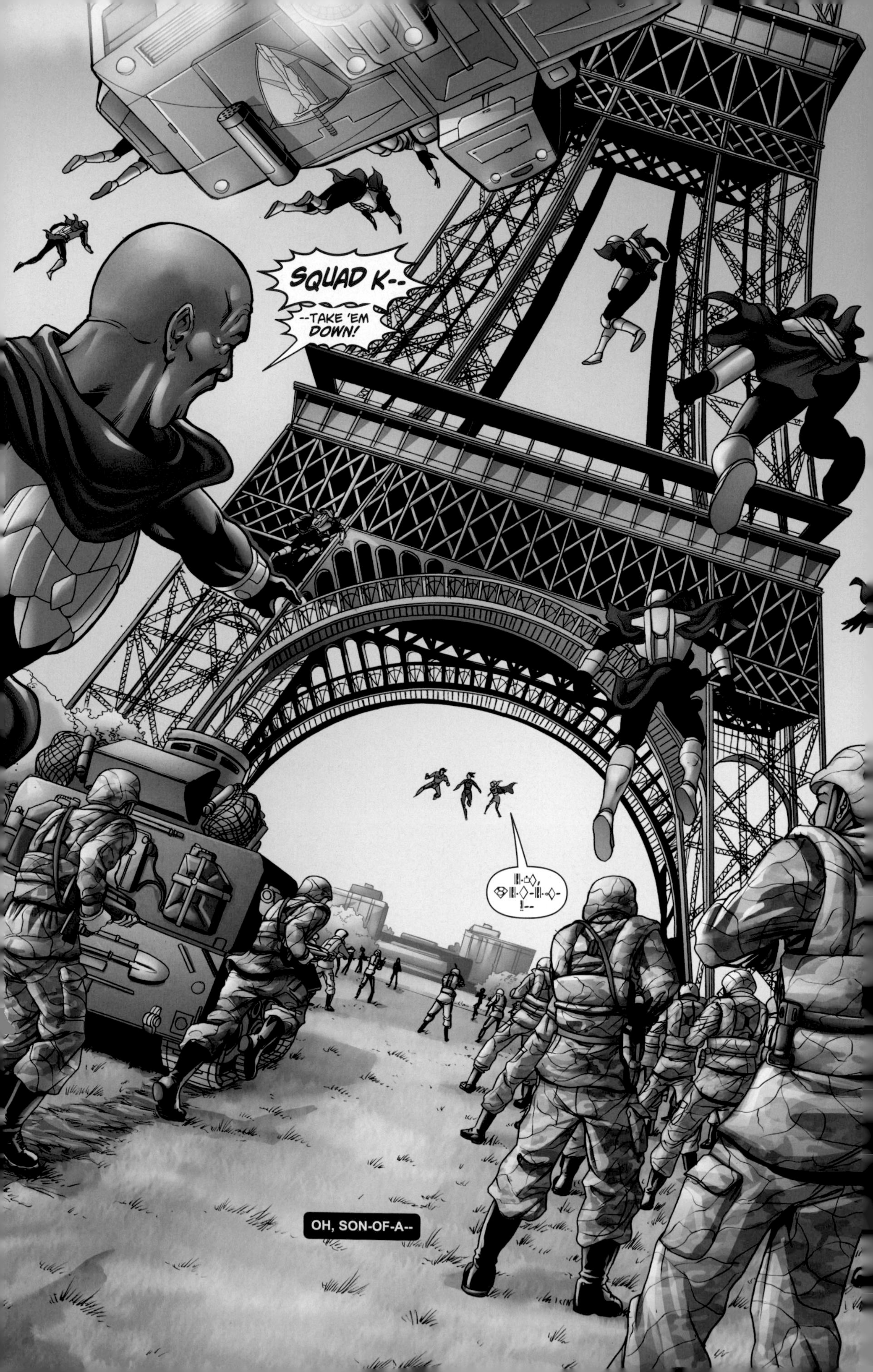
SQUAD K--
--TAKE 'EM DOWN!
OH, SON-OF-A--

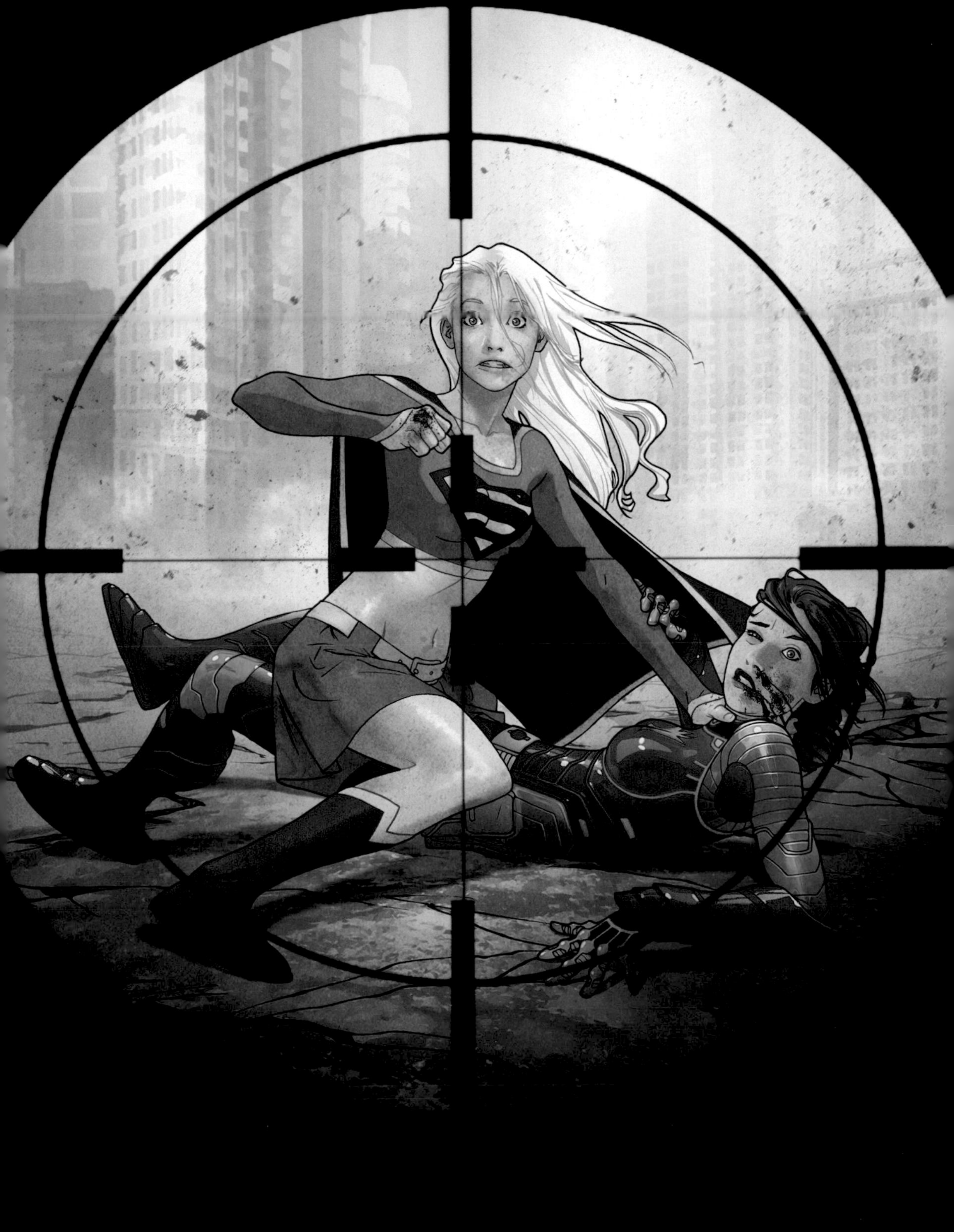

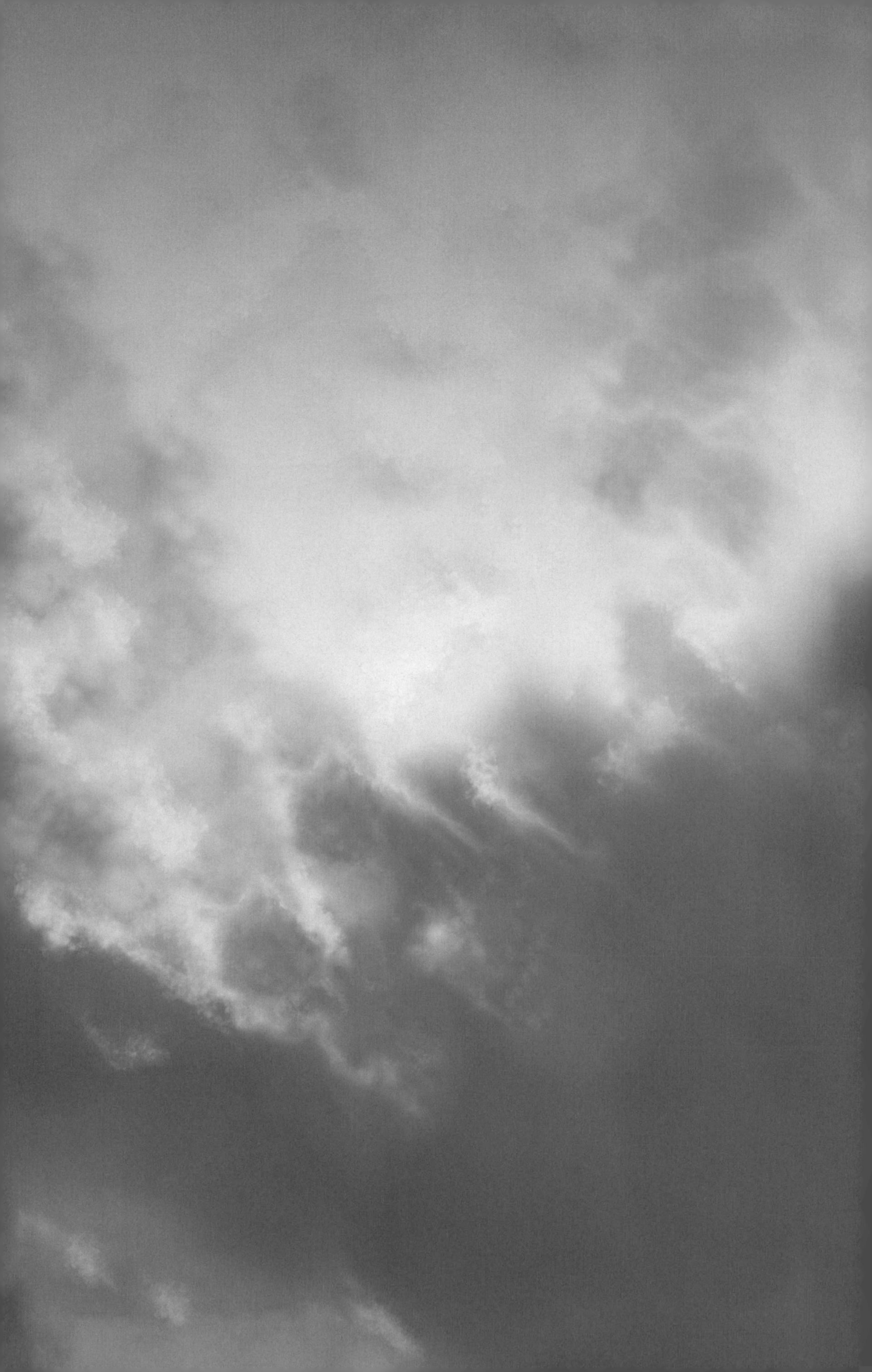

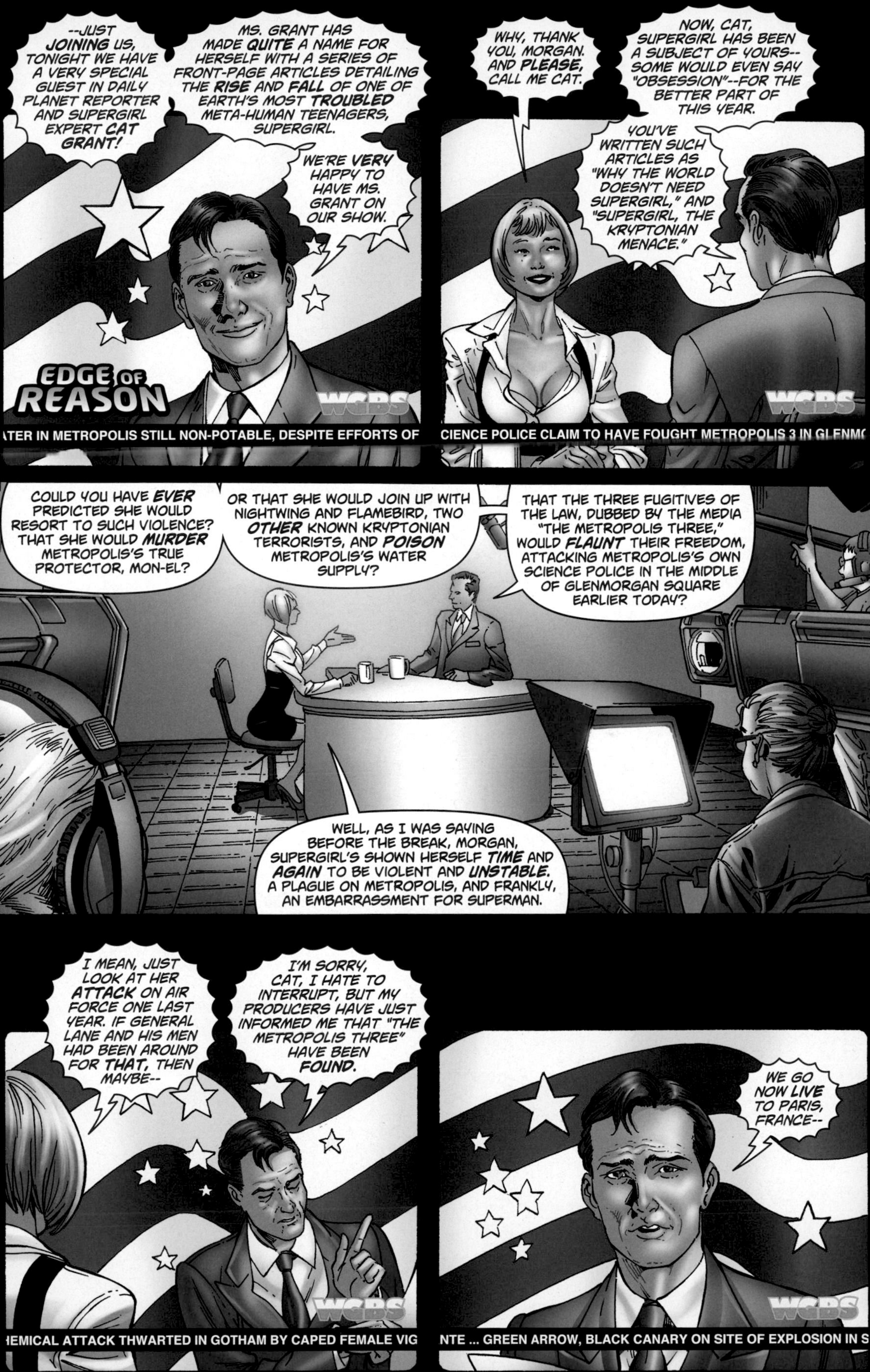
--JUST JOINING US, TONIGHT WE HAVE A VERY SPECIAL GUEST IN DAILY PLANET REPORTER AND SUPERGIRL EXPERT CAT GRANT!
MS. GRANT HAS MADE QUITE A NAME FOR HERSELF WITH A SERIES OF FRONT-PAGE ARTICLES DETAILING THE RISE AND FALL OF ONE OF EARTH'S MOST TROUBLED META-HUMAN TEENAGERS, SUPERGIRL.
WE'RE VERY HAPPY TO HAVE MS. GRANT ON OUR SHOW.
EDGE OF REASON
WGBS
ATER IN METROPOLIS STILL NON-POTABLE, DESPITE EFFORTS OF
WHY, THANK YOU, MORGAN. AND PLEASE, CALL ME CAT.
NOW, CAT, SUPERGIRL HAS BEEN A SUBJECT OF YOURS--SOME WOULD EVEN SAY "OBSESSION"--FOR THE BETTER PART OF THIS YEAR.
YOU'VE WRITTEN SUCH ARTICLES AS "WHY THE WORLD DOESN'T NEED SUPERGIRL," AND "SUPERGIRL, THE KRYPTONIAN MENACE."
WGBS
CIENCE POLICE CLAIM TO HAVE FOUGHT METROPOLIS 3 IN GLENM
COULD YOU HAVE EVER PREDICTED SHE WOULD RESORT TO SUCH VIOLENCE? THAT SHE WOULD MURDER METROPOLIS'S TRUE PROTECTOR, MON-EL?
OR THAT SHE WOULD JOIN UP WITH NIGHTWING AND FLAMEBIRD, TWO OTHER KNOWN KRYPTONIAN TERRORISTS, AND POISON METROPOLIS'S WATER SUPPLY?
THAT THE THREE FUGITIVES OF THE LAW, DUBBED BY THE MEDIA "THE METROPOLIS THREE," WOULD FLAUNT THEIR FREEDOM, ATTACKING METROPOLIS'S OWN SCIENCE POLICE IN THE MIDDLE OF GLENMORGAN SQUARE EARLIER TODAY?
WELL, AS I WAS SAYING BEFORE THE BREAK, MORGAN, SUPERGIRL'S SHOWN HERSELF TIME AND AGAIN TO BE VIOLENT AND UNSTABLE. A PLAGUE ON METROPOLIS, AND FRANKLY, AN EMBARRASSMENT FOR SUPERMAN.
I MEAN, JUST LOOK AT HER ATTACK ON AIR FORCE ONE LAST YEAR. IF GENERAL LANE AND HIS MEN HAD BEEN AROUND FOR THAT, THEN MAYBE--
I'M SORRY, CAT, I HATE TO INTERRUPT, BUT MY PRODUCERS HAVE JUST INFORMED ME THAT "THE METROPOLIS THREE" HAVE BEEN FOUND.
WGBS
HEMICAL ATTACK THWARTED IN GOTHAM BY CAPED FEMALE VIG
WE GO NOW LIVE TO PARIS, FRANCE--
WGBS
NTE ... GREEN ARROW, BLACK CANARY ON SITE OF EXPLOSION IN S

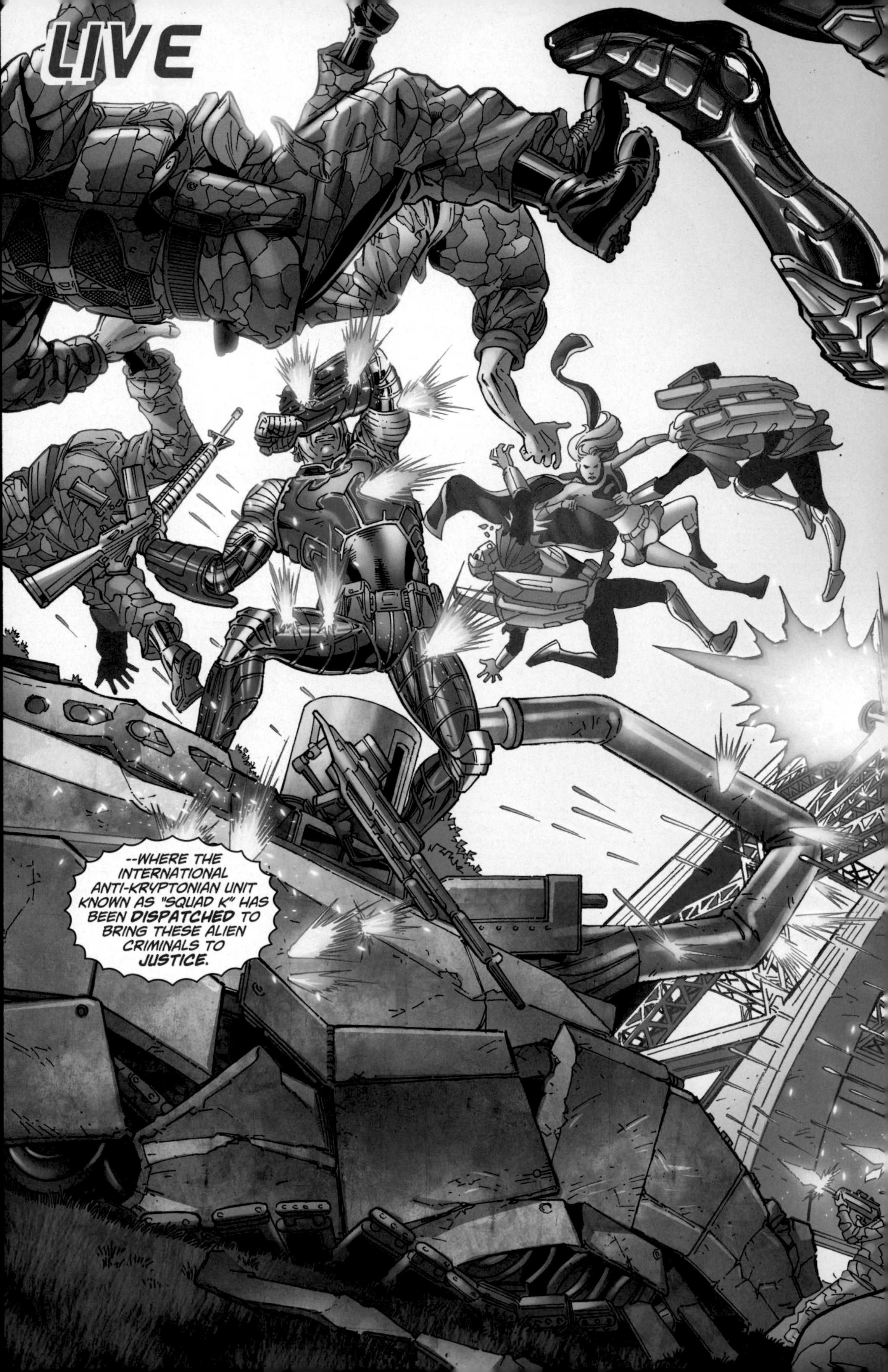
LIVE
--WHERE THE INTERNATIONAL ANTI-KRYPTONIAN UNIT KNOWN AS "SQUAD K" HAS BEEN DISPATCHED TO BRING THESE ALIEN CRIMINALS TO JUSTICE.

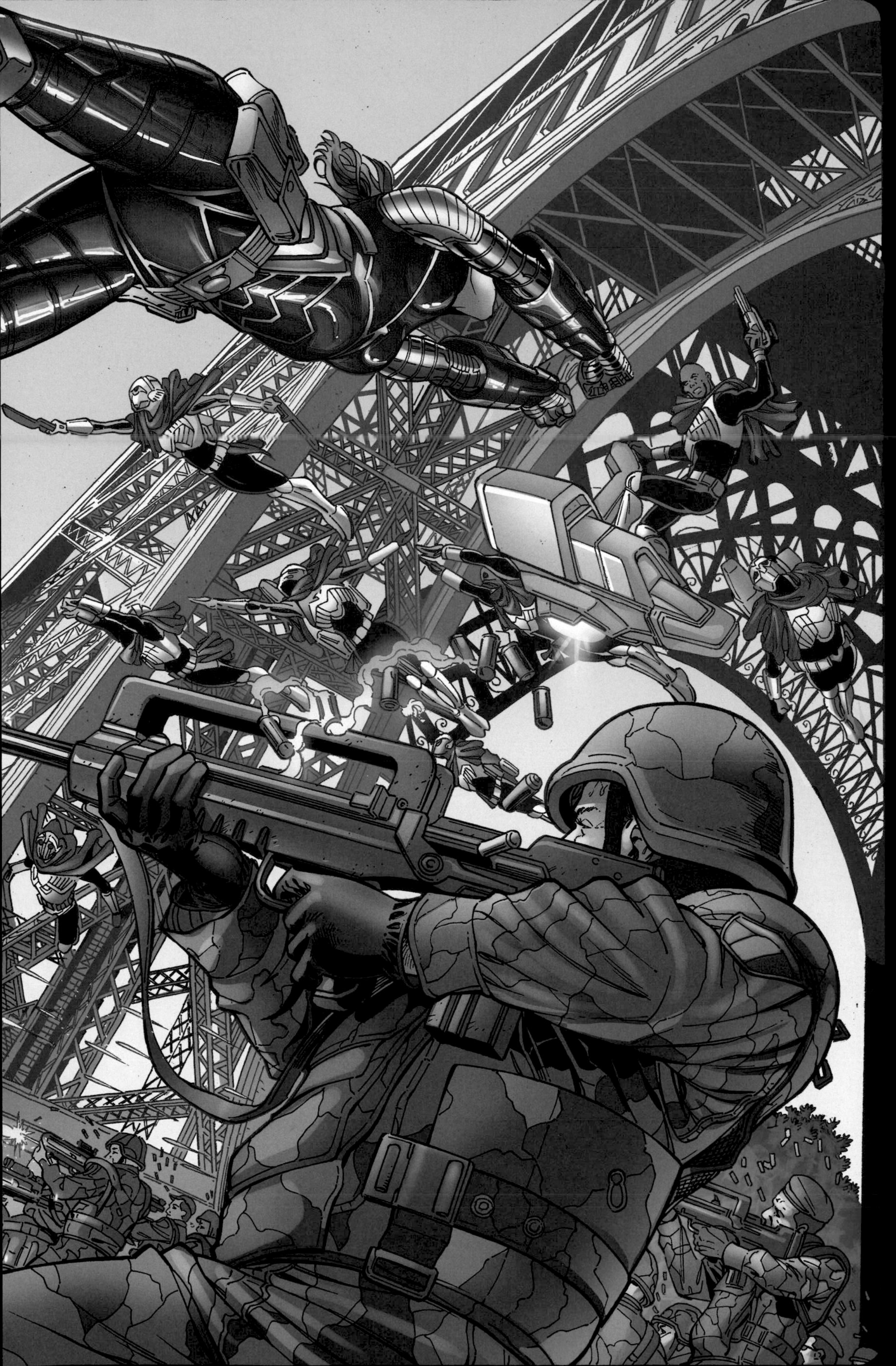

LIVE

CLEARLY A **DESPERATE** STRUGGLE, CAT...

ARIS. THREAT LEVEL IS: ORANGE. MET 3 BATTLING SQUAD K AT

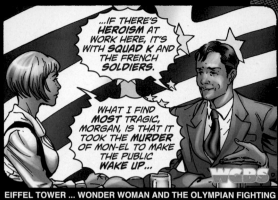

...IF THERE'S **HEROISM** AT WORK HERE, IT'S WITH **SQUAD K** AND THE **FRENCH SOLDIERS.**

WHAT I FIND **MOST TRAGIC,** MORGAN, IS THAT IT TOOK THE **MURDER** OF MON-EL TO MAKE THE PUBLIC **WAKE UP...**

EIFFEL TOWER ... WONDER WOMAN AND THE OLYMPIAN FIGHTING

LIVE

...IT'S KNOWN THAT SUPERGIRL IS THE **DAUGHTER** OF ALURA ZOR-EL, THE **RULER**-- OR SHOULD WE SAY **QUEEN?**--OF NEW KRYPTON.

THAT'S **CORRECT,** MORGAN. WHICH GOES TO WHAT I'VE BEEN SAYING...

...THAT SUPERGIRL, PERHAPS MORE THAN ANY **OTHER** KRYPTONIAN, IS AN **ENEMY** OF EARTH...

CEPTED OFFER OF NATO SUPPORT. BBC REPORTS THREE FIGHTER SQUADRONS

LIVE

SQUAD K SEEMS TO BE HOLDING THEIR **OWN** FOR THE MOMENT...

...AND I'M FRANKLY **TERRIFIED** BY WHAT THEY'LL DO TO US **NEXT** IF THEY CAN'T BE STOPPED.

MOBILIZING AT THE BORDER. GEN. LANE, "UNBRIDLED FAITH IN SQUAD K." PRESI

LIVE

...THOUGH THE **MILITARY** FORCES SEEM **LESS**--

DENT CONFIRMS FBI TO PURSUE

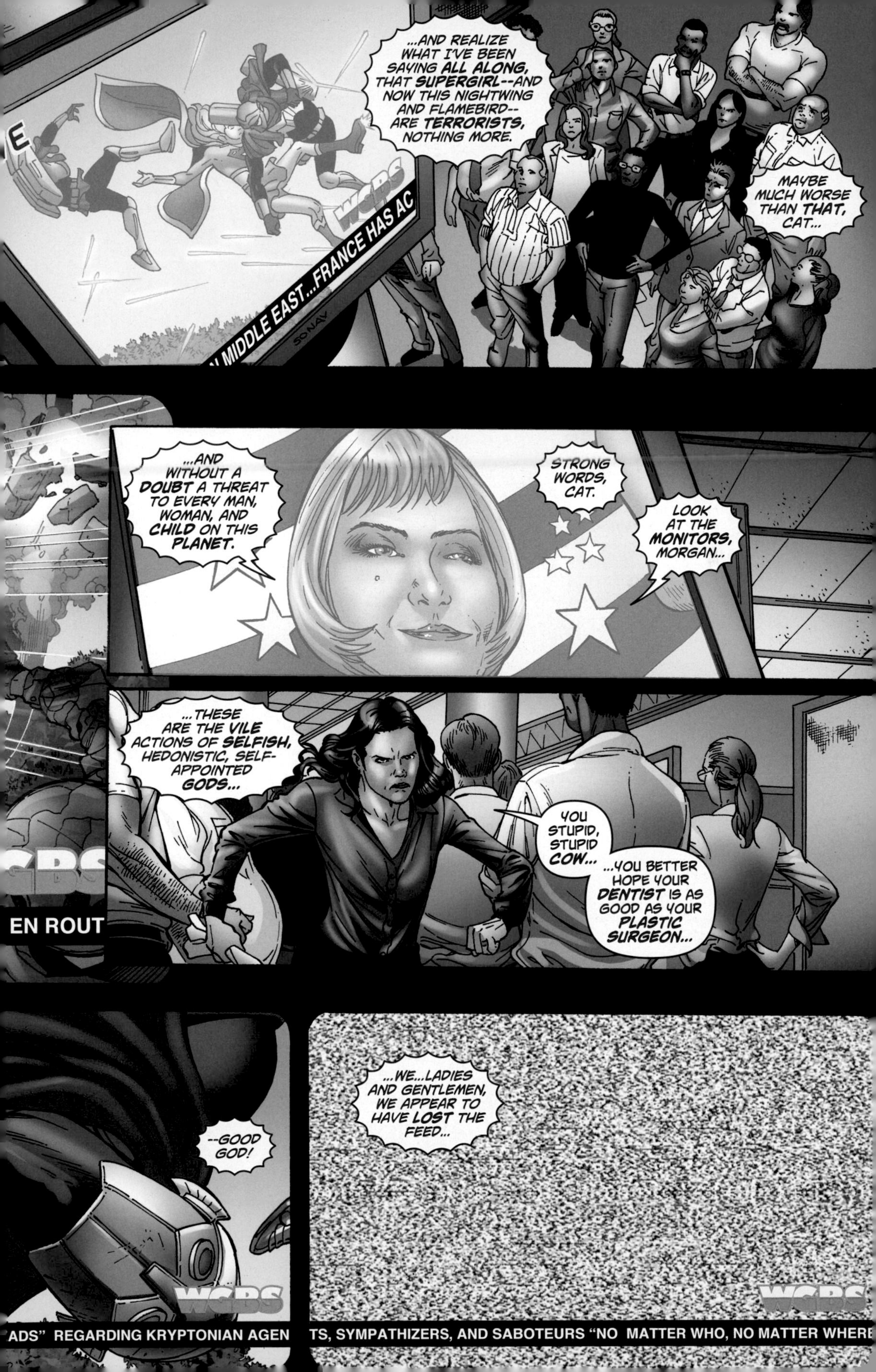
...AND REALIZE WHAT I'VE BEEN SAYING ALL ALONG, THAT SUPERGIRL--AND NOW THIS NIGHTWING AND FLAMEBIRD--ARE TERRORISTS, NOTHING MORE.
MAYBE MUCH WORSE THAN THAT, CAT...
WGBS
...MIDDLE EAST...FRANCE HAS AC
...AND WITHOUT A DOUBT A THREAT TO EVERY MAN, WOMAN, AND CHILD ON THIS PLANET.
STRONG WORDS, CAT.
LOOK AT THE MONITORS, MORGAN...
...THESE ARE THE VILE ACTIONS OF SELFISH, HEDONISTIC, SELF-APPOINTED GODS...
YOU STUPID, STUPID COW...
...YOU BETTER HOPE YOUR DENTIST IS AS GOOD AS YOUR PLASTIC SURGEON...
EN ROUT
--GOOD GOD!
...WE...LADIES AND GENTLEMEN, WE APPEAR TO HAVE LOST THE FEED...
WGBS
"ADS" REGARDING KRYPTONIAN AGEN TS, SYMPATHIZERS, AND SABOTEURS "NO MATTER WHO, NO MATTER WHERE

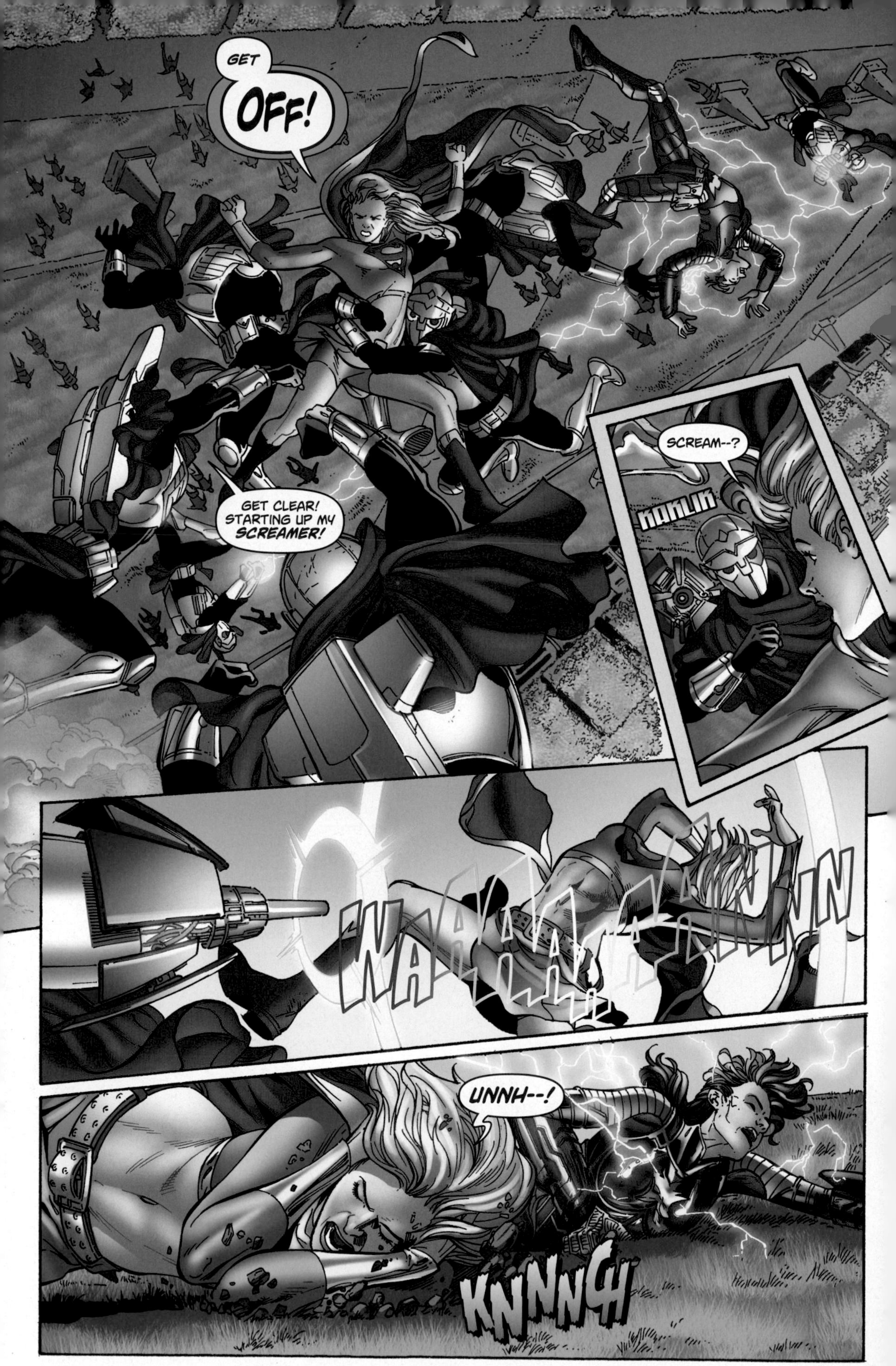
GET OFF!
GET CLEAR! STARTING UP MY SCREAMER!
SCREAM--?
KaKLIK
WAAAAAAAANNN
UNNH--!
KNNNGH

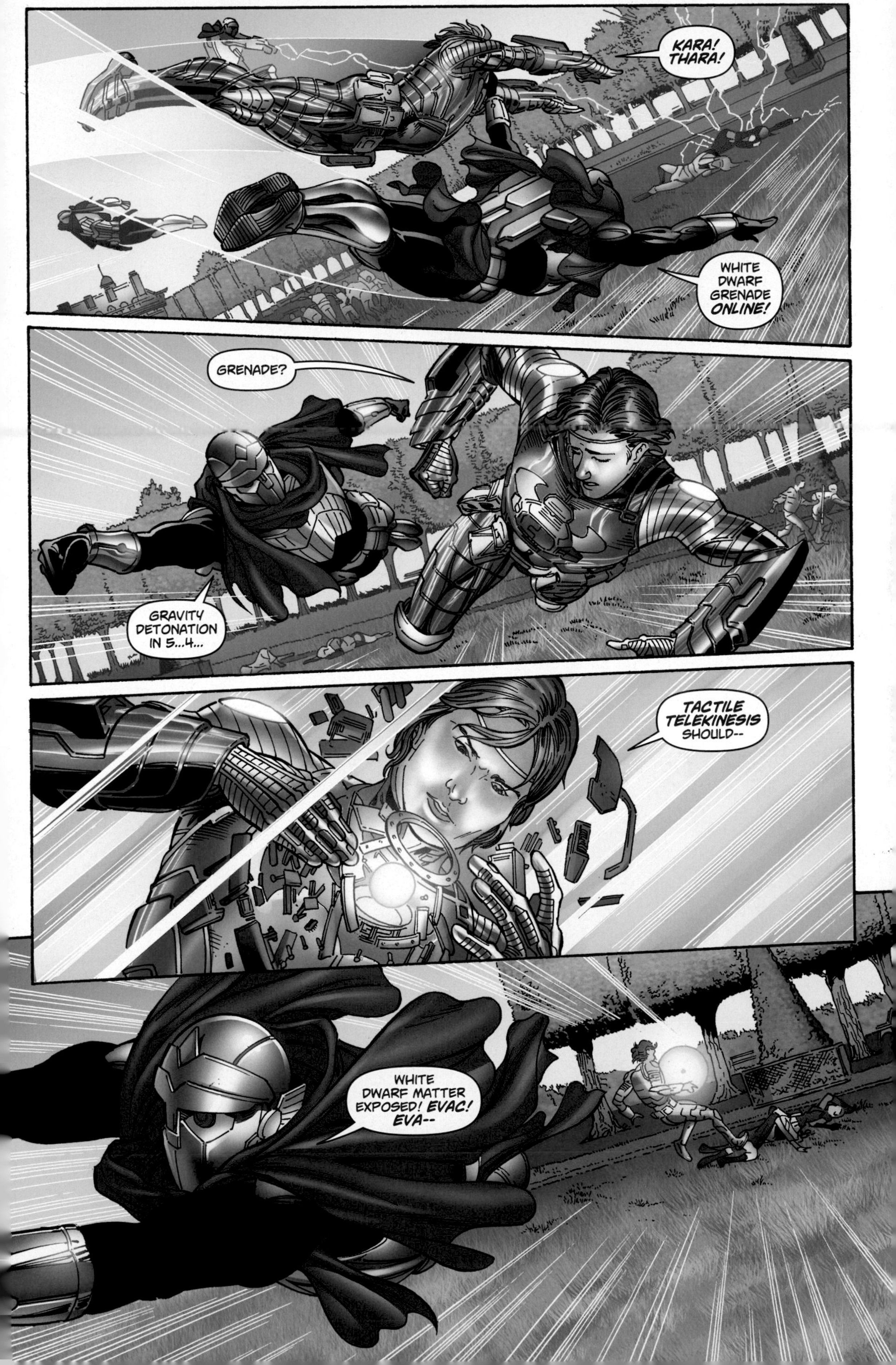
KARA! THARA!
WHITE DWARF GRENADE ONLINE!
GRENADE?
GRAVITY DETONATION IN 5...4...
TACTILE TELEKINESIS SHOULD--
WHITE DWARF MATTER EXPOSED! EVAC! EVA--

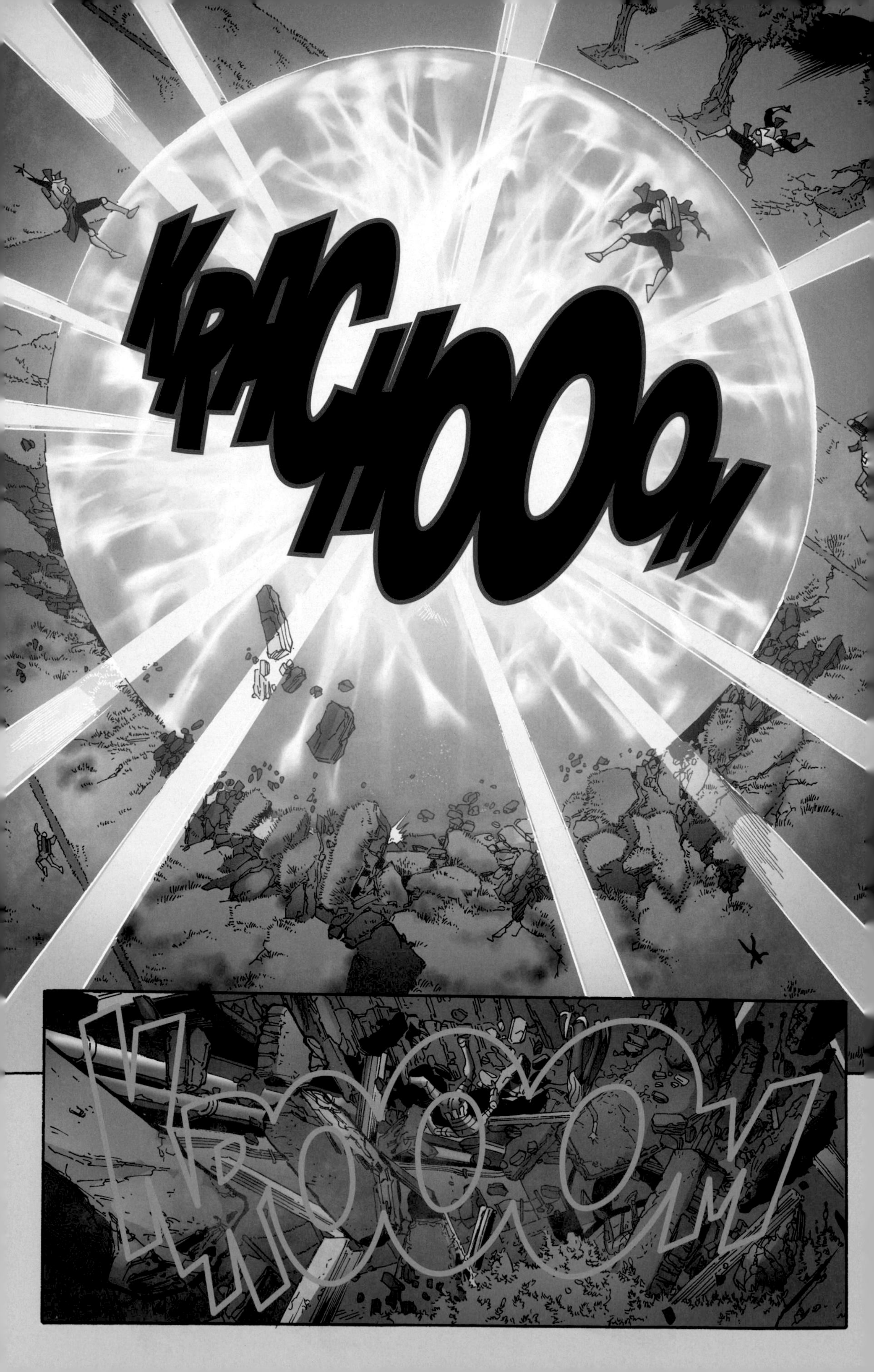
KRACHOOOM
KROOOM

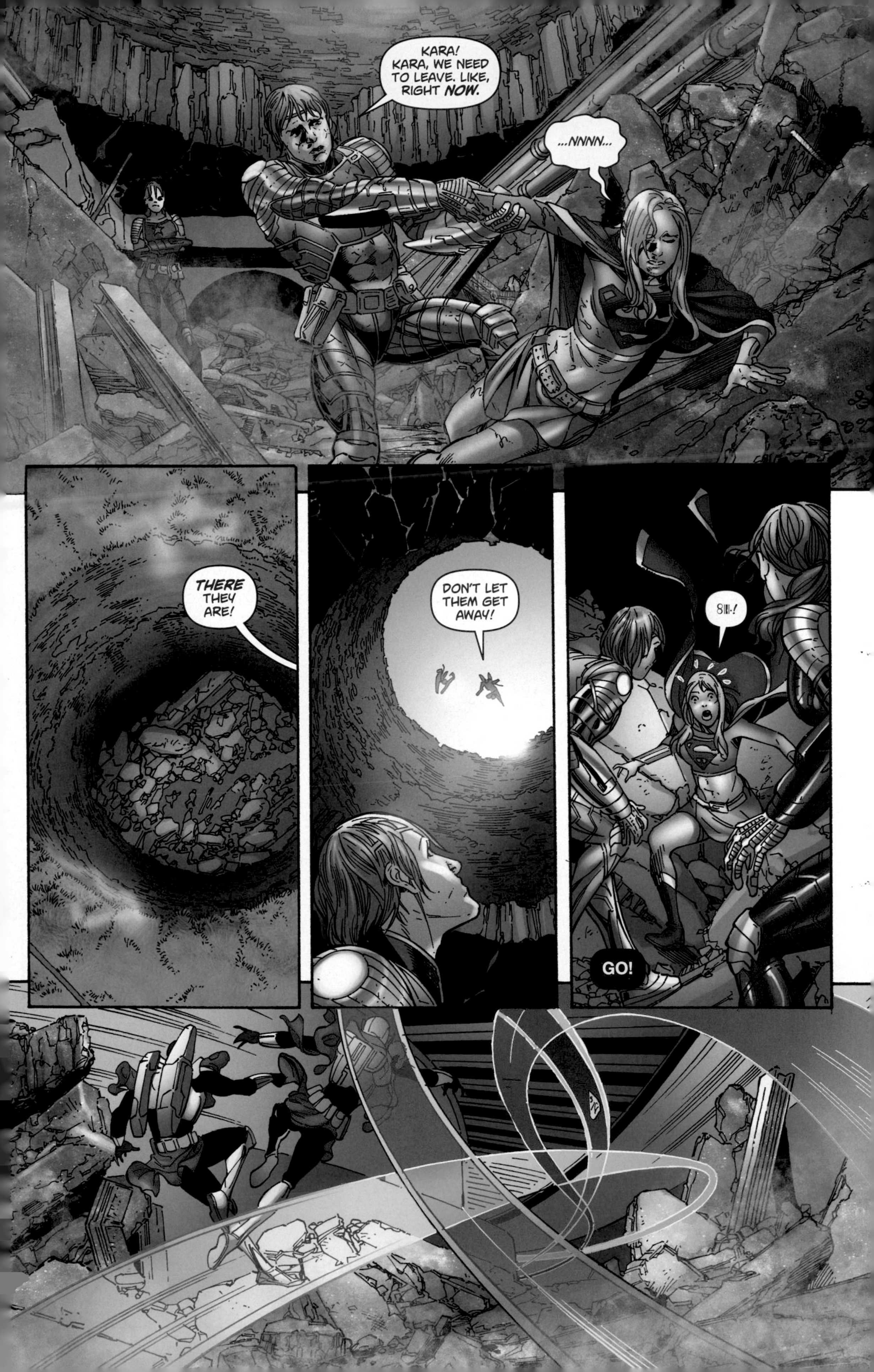
KARA! KARA, WE NEED TO LEAVE. LIKE, RIGHT NOW.
...NNNN...
THERE THEY ARE!
DON'T LET THEM GET AWAY!
GO!

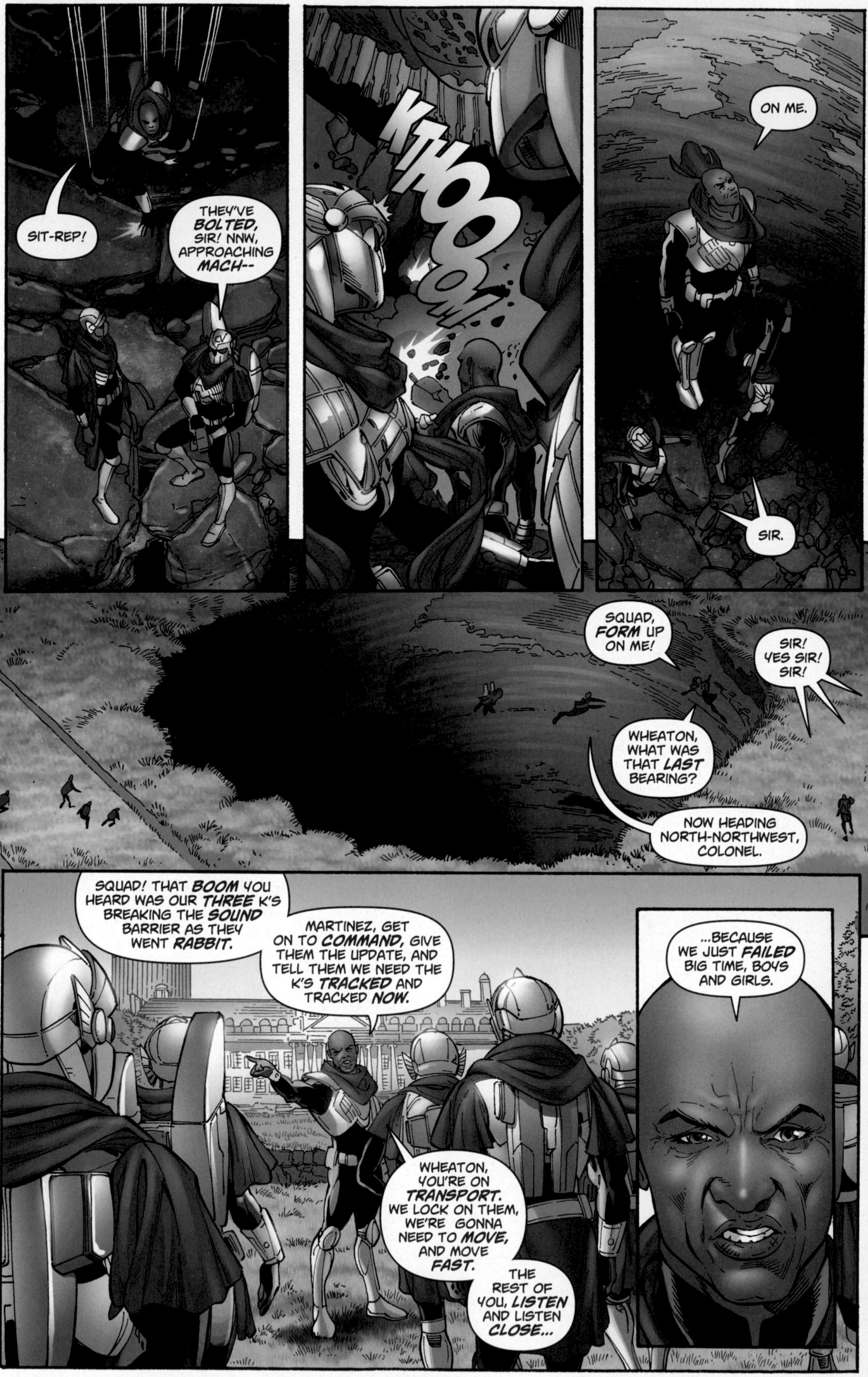
SIT-REP!
THEY'VE BOLTED, SIR! NNW, APPROACHING MACH--
KTHOOOM!
ON ME.
SIR.
SQUAD, FORM UP ON ME!
SIR! YES SIR! SIR!
WHEATON, WHAT WAS THAT LAST BEARING?
NOW HEADING NORTH-NORTHWEST, COLONEL.
SQUAD! THAT BOOM YOU HEARD WAS OUR THREE K'S BREAKING THE SOUND BARRIER AS THEY WENT RABBIT.
MARTINEZ, GET ON TO COMMAND, GIVE THEM THE UPDATE, AND TELL THEM WE NEED THE K'S TRACKED AND TRACKED NOW.
WHEATON, YOU'RE ON TRANSPORT. WE LOCK ON THEM, WE'RE GONNA NEED TO MOVE, AND MOVE FAST.
THE REST OF YOU, LISTEN AND LISTEN CLOSE...
...BECAUSE WE JUST FAILED BIG TIME, BOYS AND GIRLS.

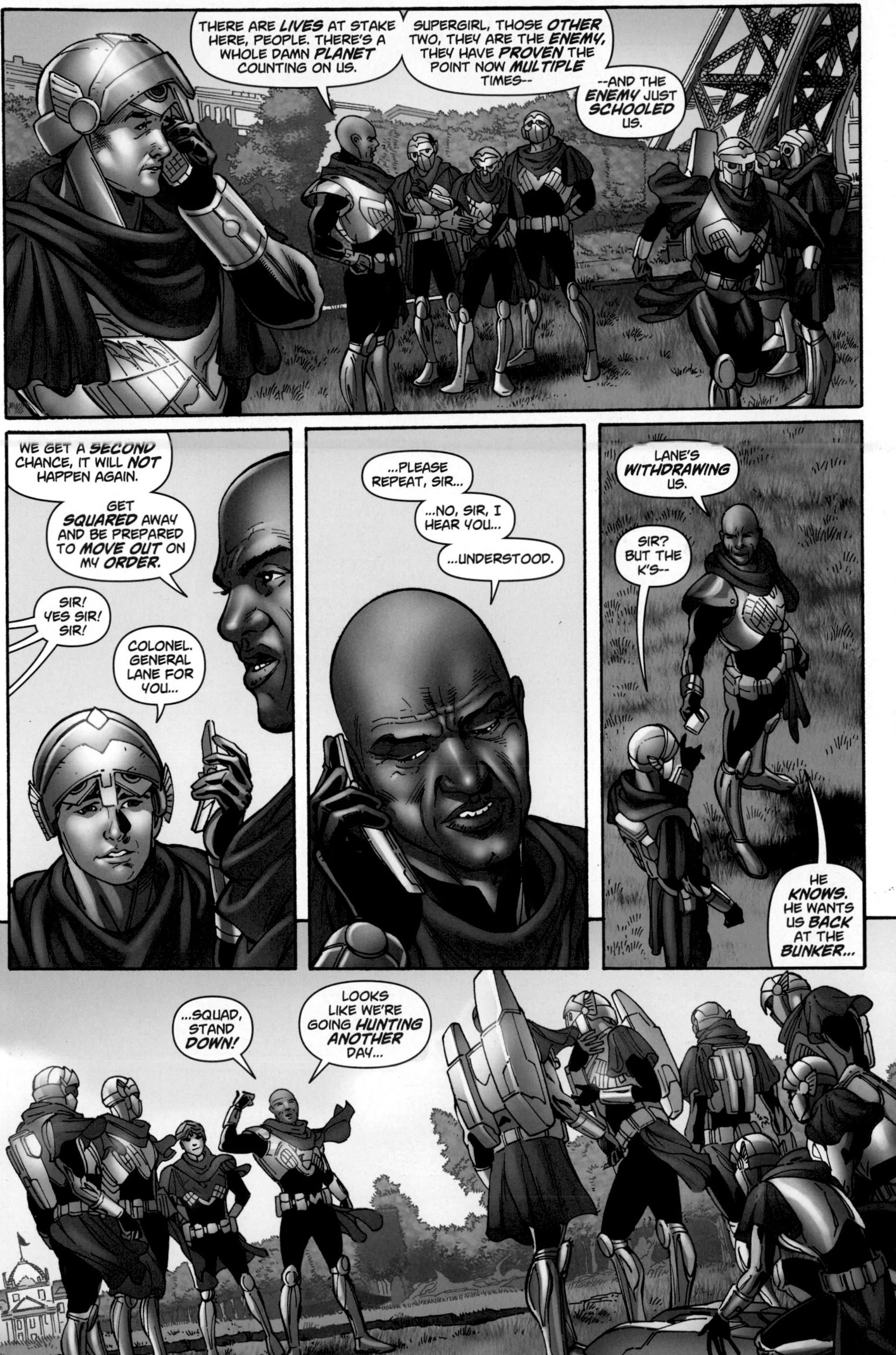
THERE ARE LIVES AT STAKE HERE, PEOPLE. THERE'S A WHOLE DAMN PLANET COUNTING ON US.
SUPERGIRL, THOSE OTHER TWO, THEY ARE THE ENEMY, THEY HAVE PROVEN THE POINT NOW MULTIPLE TIMES--
--AND THE ENEMY JUST SCHOOLED US.
WE GET A SECOND CHANCE, IT WILL NOT HAPPEN AGAIN.
GET SQUARED AWAY AND BE PREPARED TO MOVE OUT ON MY ORDER.
SIR! YES SIR! SIR!
COLONEL. GENERAL LANE FOR YOU...
...PLEASE REPEAT, SIR...
...NO, SIR, I HEAR YOU...
...UNDERSTOOD.
LANE'S WITHDRAWING US.
SIR? BUT THE K'S--
HE KNOWS. HE WANTS US BACK AT THE BUNKER...
...SQUAD, STAND DOWN!
LOOKS LIKE WE'RE GOING HUNTING ANOTHER DAY...

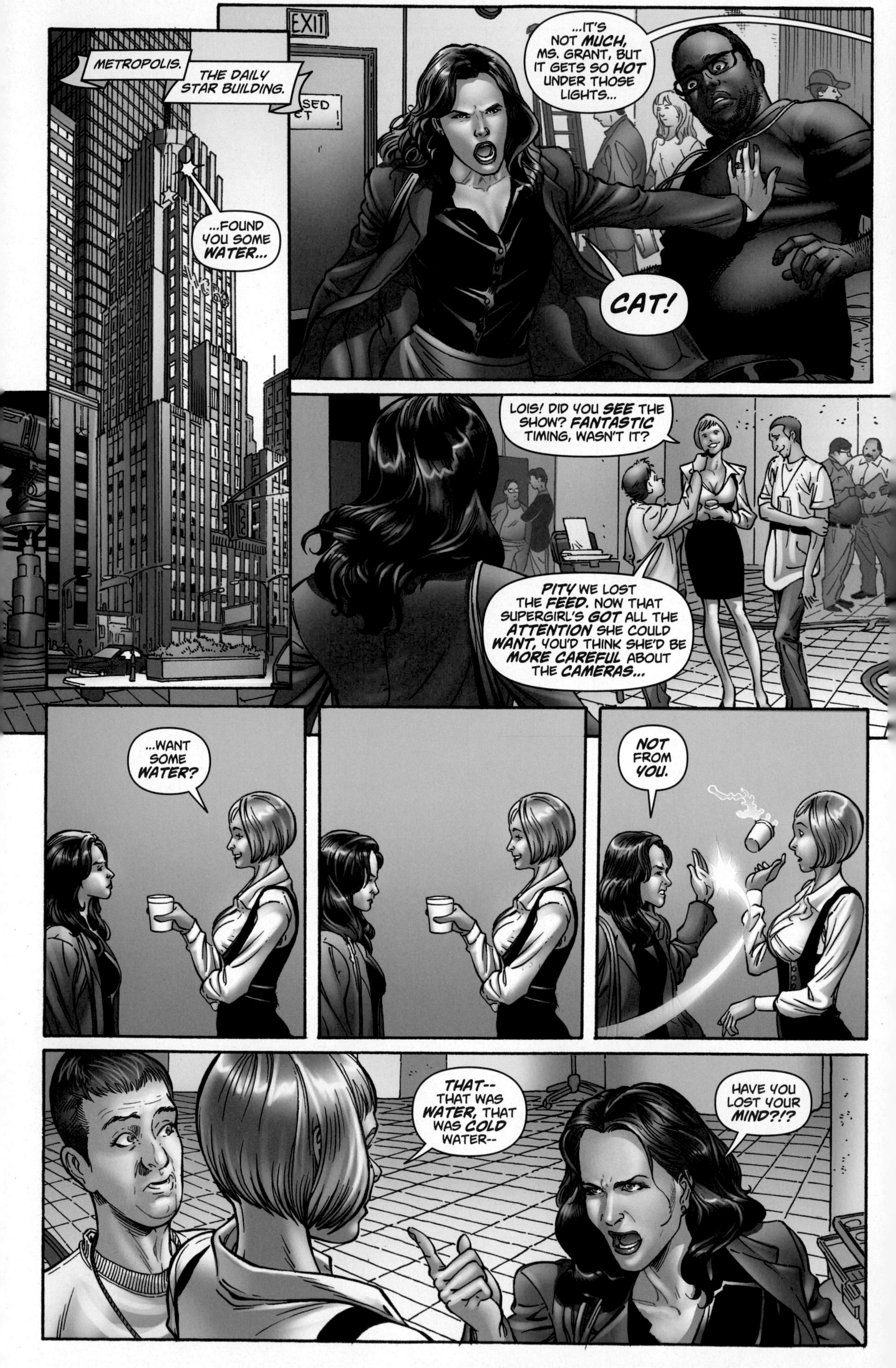
METROPOLIS.
THE DAILY STAR BUILDING.
...FOUND YOU SOME WATER...
...IT'S NOT MUCH, MS. GRANT, BUT IT GETS SO HOT UNDER THOSE LIGHTS...
CAT!
LOIS! DID YOU SEE THE SHOW? FANTASTIC TIMING, WASN'T IT?
PITY WE LOST THE FEED. NOW THAT SUPERGIRL'S GOT ALL THE ATTENTION SHE COULD WANT, YOU'D THINK SHE'D BE MORE CAREFUL ABOUT THE CAMERAS...
...WANT SOME WATER?
NOT FROM YOU.
THAT-- THAT WAS WATER, THAT WAS COLD WATER--
HAVE YOU LOST YOUR MIND?!?

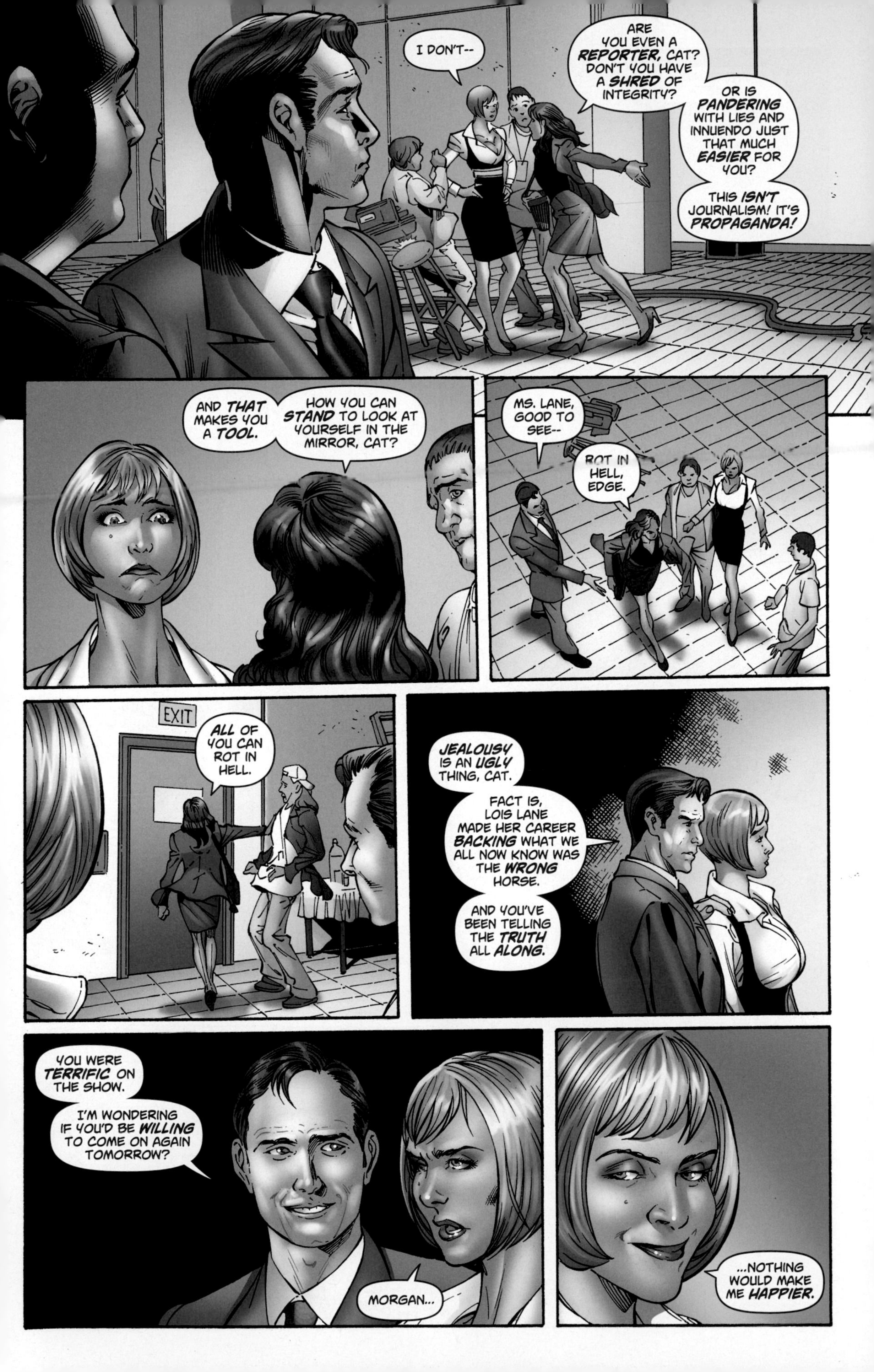
I DON'T--
ARE YOU EVEN A REPORTER, CAT? DON'T YOU HAVE A SHRED OF INTEGRITY?
OR IS PANDERING WITH LIES AND INNUENDO JUST THAT MUCH EASIER FOR YOU?
THIS ISN'T JOURNALISM! IT'S PROPAGANDA!
AND THAT MAKES YOU A TOOL.
HOW YOU CAN STAND TO LOOK AT YOURSELF IN THE MIRROR, CAT?
MS. LANE, GOOD TO SEE--
ROT IN HELL, EDGE.
EXIT
ALL OF YOU CAN ROT IN HELL.
JEALOUSY IS AN UGLY THING, CAT.
FACT IS, LOIS LANE MADE HER CAREER BACKING WHAT WE ALL NOW KNOW WAS THE WRONG HORSE.
AND YOU'VE BEEN TELLING THE TRUTH ALL ALONG.
YOU WERE TERRIFIC ON THE SHOW.
I'M WONDERING IF YOU'D BE WILLING TO COME ON AGAIN TOMORROW?
MORGAN...
...NOTHING WOULD MAKE ME HAPPIER.

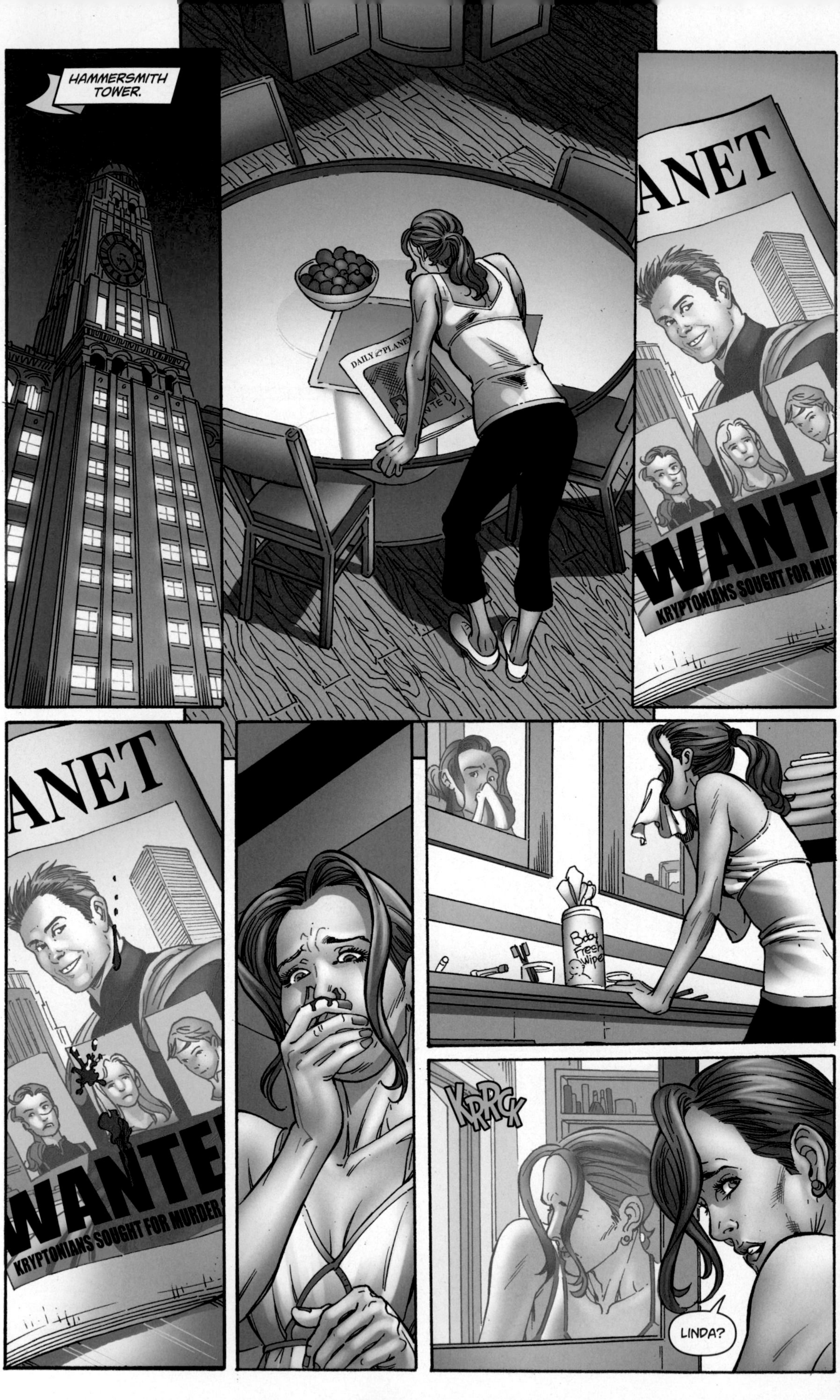
HAMMERSMITH TOWER.
DAILY PLANET
ANET
WANTE
KRYPTONIANS SOUGHT FOR MU
ANET
WANTE
KRYPTONIANS SOUGHT FOR MURDER
Baby Fresh Wipes
KRRCK
LINDA?

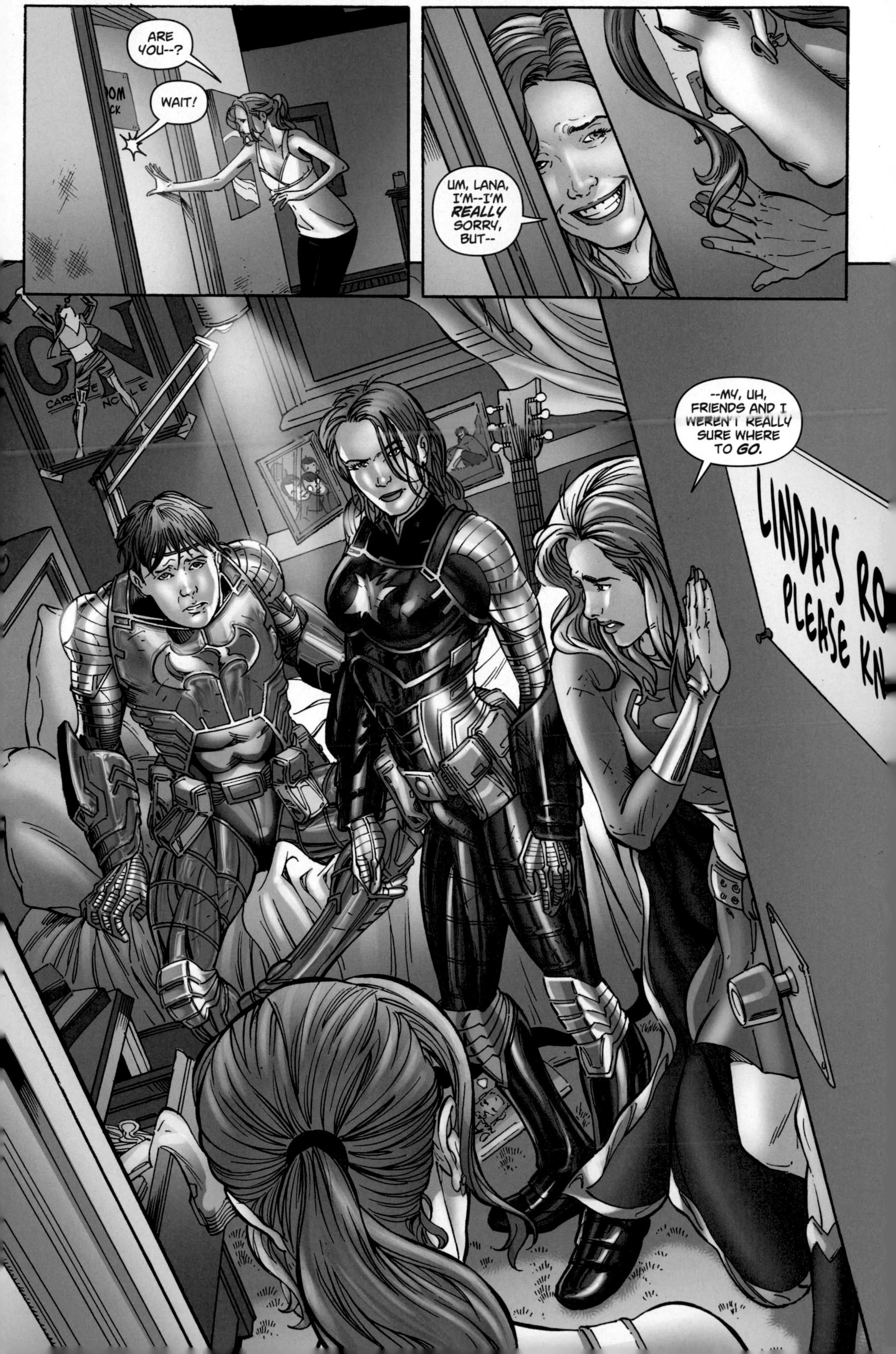

ARE YOU--?
WAIT!
UM, LANA, I'M--I'M *REALLY* SORRY, BUT--
--MY, UH, FRIENDS AND I WEREN'T REALLY SURE WHERE TO *GO*.
LINDA'S RO
PLEASE KN

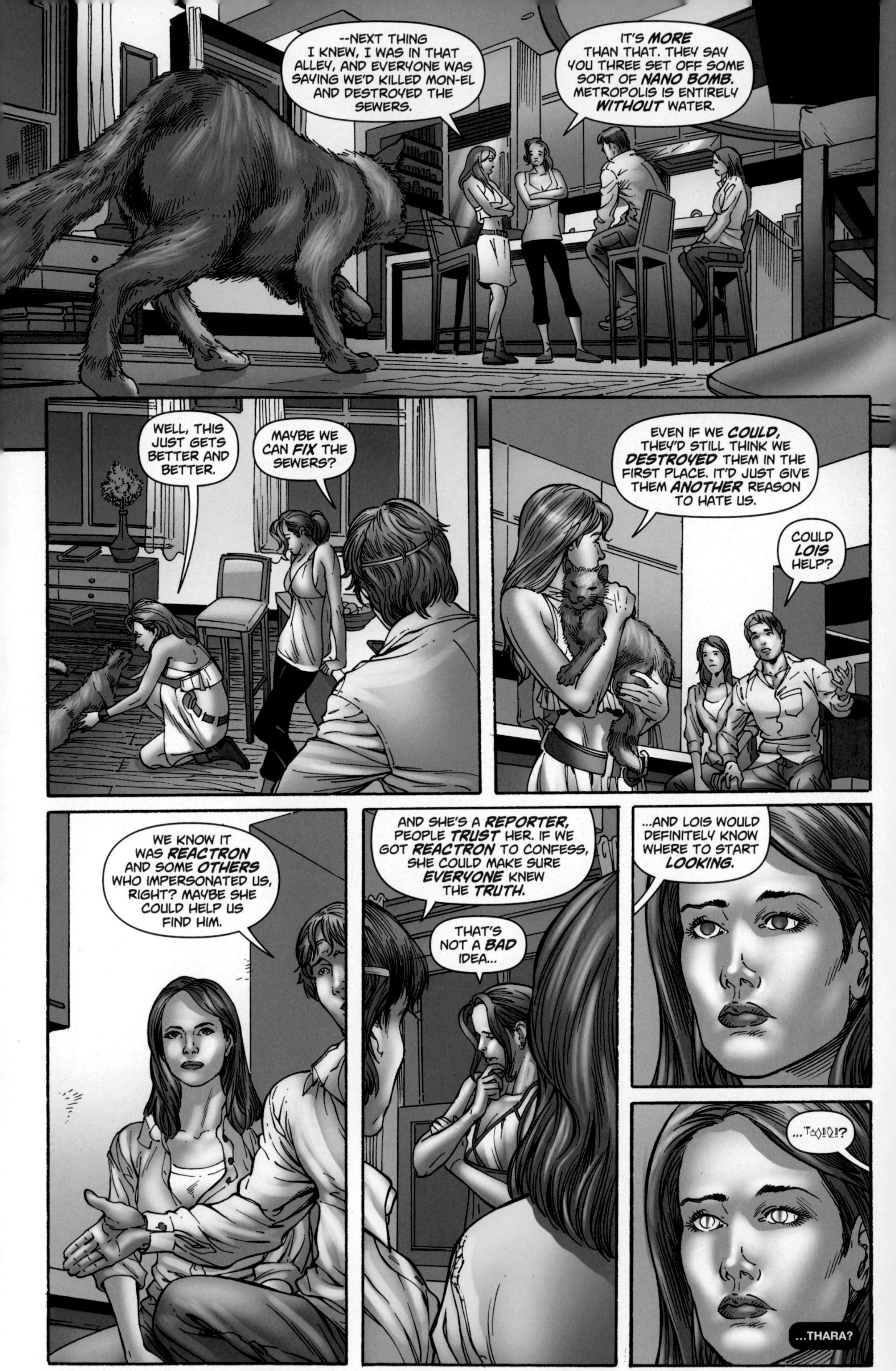
--NEXT THING I KNEW, I WAS IN THAT ALLEY, AND EVERYONE WAS SAYING WE'D KILLED MON-EL AND DESTROYED THE SEWERS.
IT'S MORE THAN THAT. THEY SAY YOU THREE SET OFF SOME SORT OF NANO BOMB. METROPOLIS IS ENTIRELY WITHOUT WATER.
WELL, THIS JUST GETS BETTER AND BETTER.
MAYBE WE CAN FIX THE SEWERS?
EVEN IF WE COULD, THEY'D STILL THINK WE DESTROYED THEM IN THE FIRST PLACE. IT'D JUST GIVE THEM ANOTHER REASON TO HATE US.
COULD LOIS HELP?
WE KNOW IT WAS REACTRON AND SOME OTHERS WHO IMPERSONATED US, RIGHT? MAYBE SHE COULD HELP US FIND HIM.
AND SHE'S A REPORTER, PEOPLE TRUST HER. IF WE GOT REACTRON TO CONFESS, SHE COULD MAKE SURE EVERYONE KNEW THE TRUTH.
THAT'S NOT A BAD IDEA...
...AND LOIS WOULD DEFINITELY KNOW WHERE TO START LOOKING.
...THARA?

◇○⟩!!'T?

⫶!!⫶-⫶ ⫶!-⫶!'T?

WHAT?

YOU OKAY?

◇!!⫶·
T⚬◇⫶2◇'⚬· ⚬⫶⫶-⚬8 ⚬⫶!⫶-⚬8 ⚬⚬-'T⚬ ⚬!⫶!'◇ ◇2-◇□⫶.

NO. THERE'S SOMETHING WRONG WITH KARA'S FRIEND.

YOU *PROBABLY* HAVEN'T HEARD--

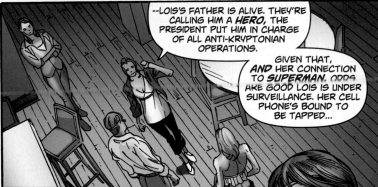

--LOIS'S FATHER IS ALIVE. THEY'RE CALLING HIM A *HERO*, THE PRESIDENT PUT HIM IN CHARGE OF ALL ANTI-KRYPTONIAN OPERATIONS.

GIVEN THAT, *AND* HER CONNECTION TO *SUPERMAN*, ODDS ARE GOOD LOIS IS UNDER SURVEILLANCE. HER CELL PHONE'S BOUND TO BE TAPPED...

...SO WE'RE GONNA HAVE TO BE SNEAKY ABOUT TALKING TO HER.

KARA, THARA, STAY HERE. TWO OF US APPROACHING HER WILL RAISE *LESS* SUSPICION THAN *FOUR*.

CHRIS, I'D LOSE THAT HEADBAND BEFORE WE GET DOWNSTAIRS.

AND HONEY, I LIKE THIS APARTMENT. *TRY* TO GET ALONG WITH HER.

WE'LL BE BACK SHORTLY.

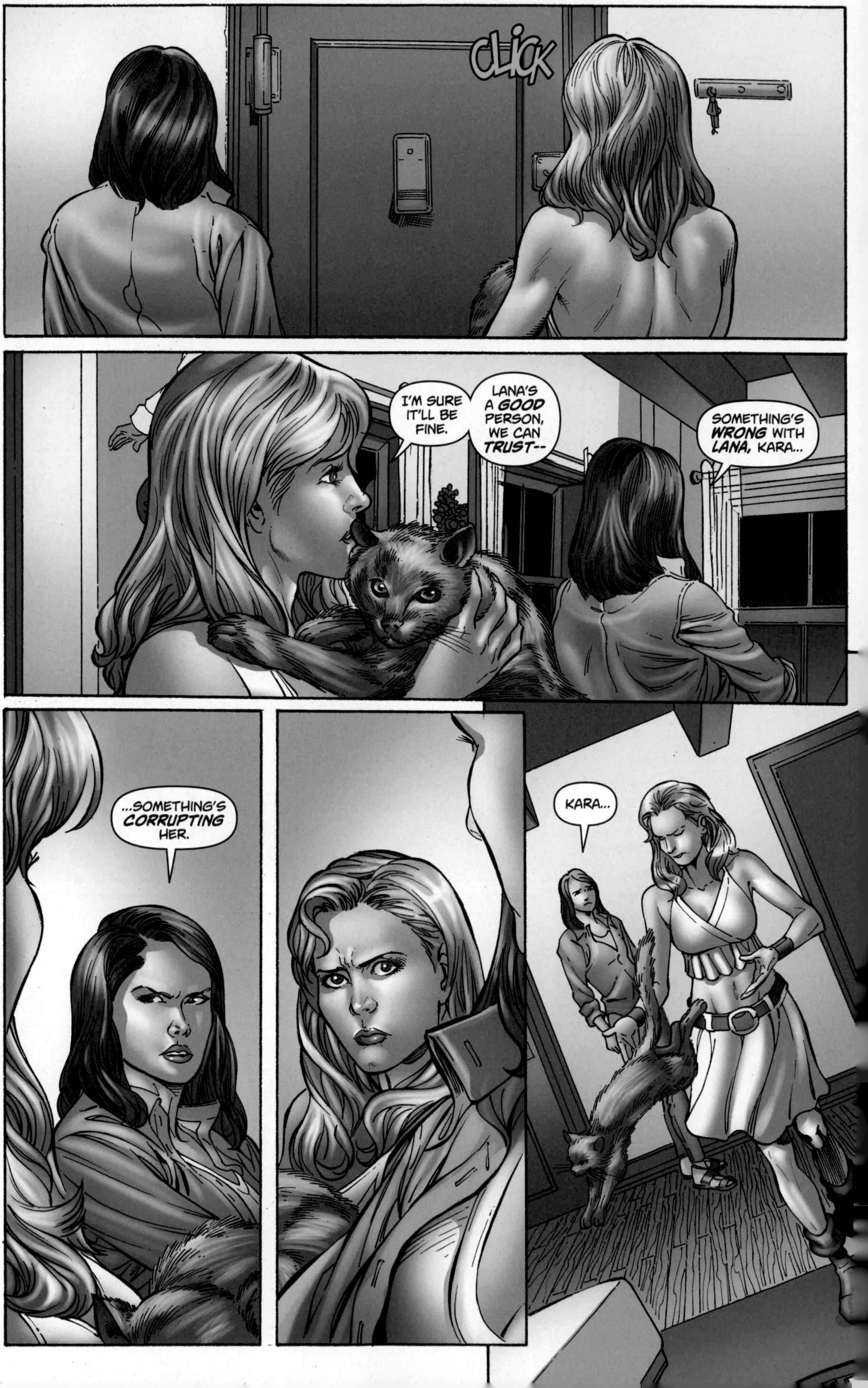
CLICK
I'M SURE IT'LL BE FINE.
LANA'S A GOOD PERSON, WE CAN TRUST--
SOMETHING'S WRONG WITH LANA, KARA...
...SOMETHING'S CORRUPTING HER.
KARA...

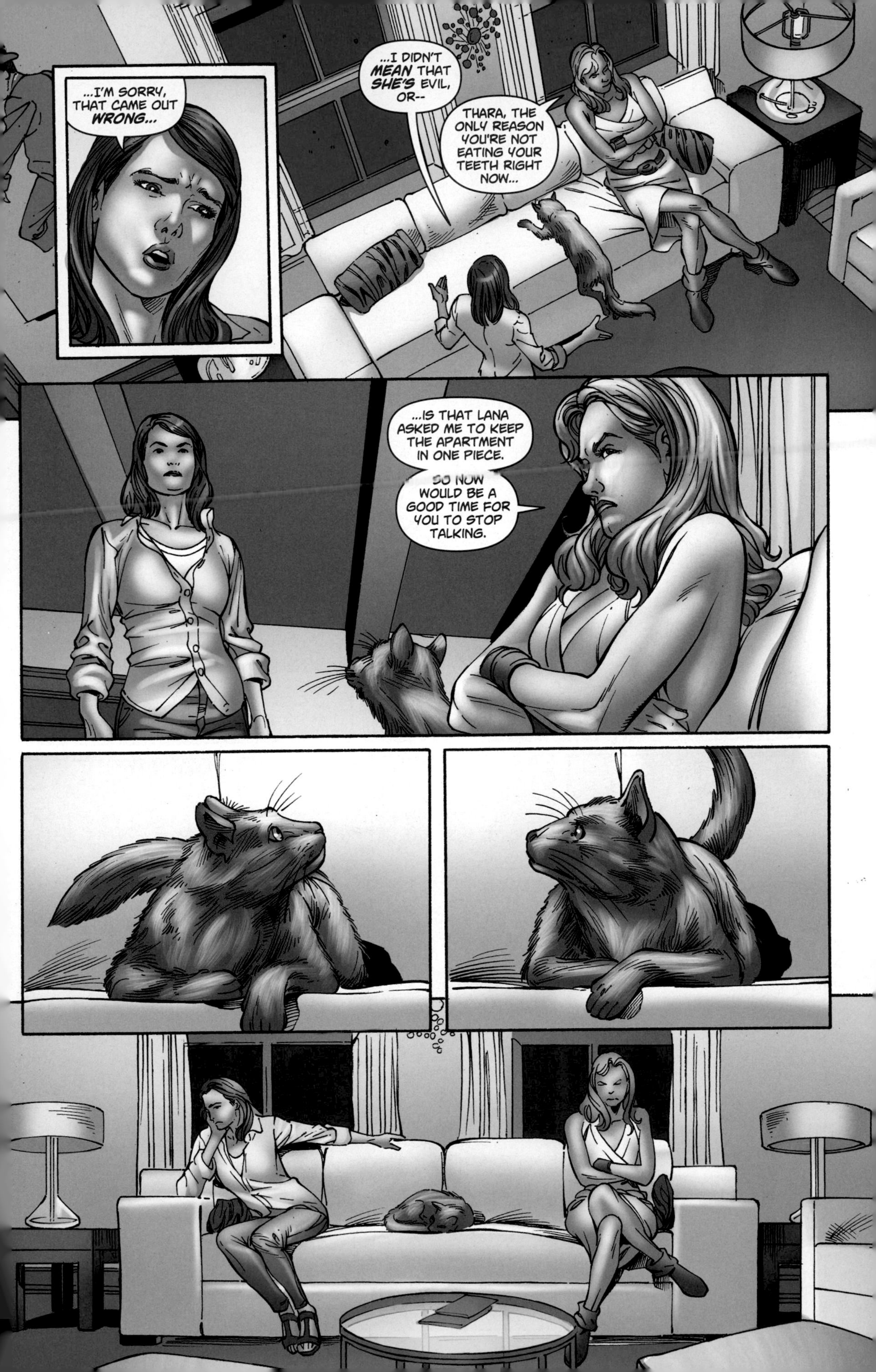
...I'M SORRY, THAT CAME OUT WRONG...
...I DIDN'T MEAN THAT SHE'S EVIL, OR--
THARA, THE ONLY REASON YOU'RE NOT EATING YOUR TEETH RIGHT NOW...
...IS THAT LANA ASKED ME TO KEEP THE APARTMENT IN ONE PIECE.
SO NOW WOULD BE A GOOD TIME FOR YOU TO STOP TALKING.

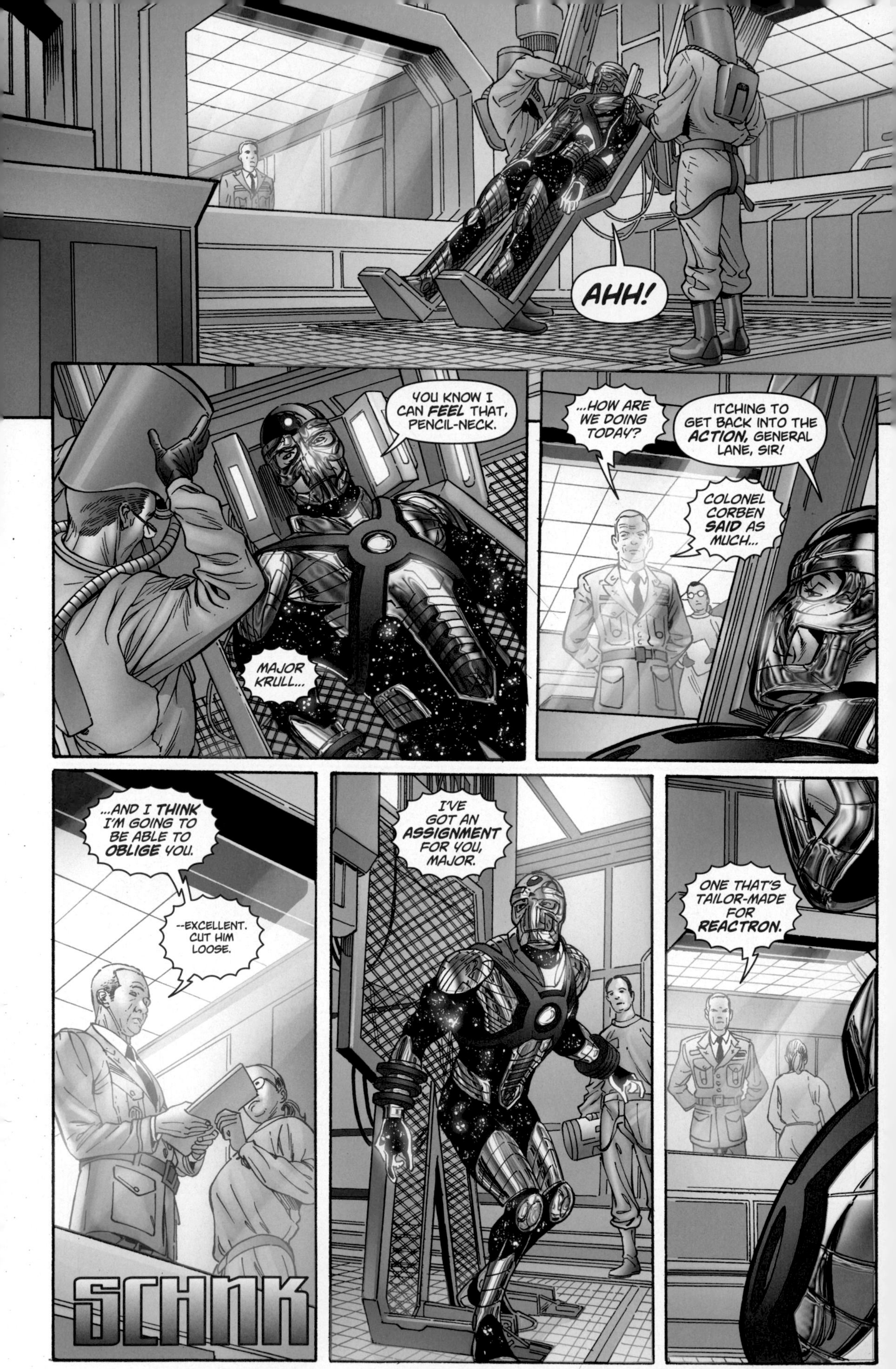
AHH!
YOU KNOW I CAN FEEL THAT, PENCIL-NECK.
MAJOR KRULL...
...HOW ARE WE DOING TODAY?
ITCHING TO GET BACK INTO THE ACTION, GENERAL LANE, SIR!
COLONEL CORBEN SAID AS MUCH...
...AND I THINK I'M GOING TO BE ABLE TO OBLIGE YOU.
--EXCELLENT. CUT HIM LOOSE.
SCHNK
I'VE GOT AN ASSIGNMENT FOR YOU, MAJOR.
ONE THAT'S TAILOR-MADE FOR REACTRON.

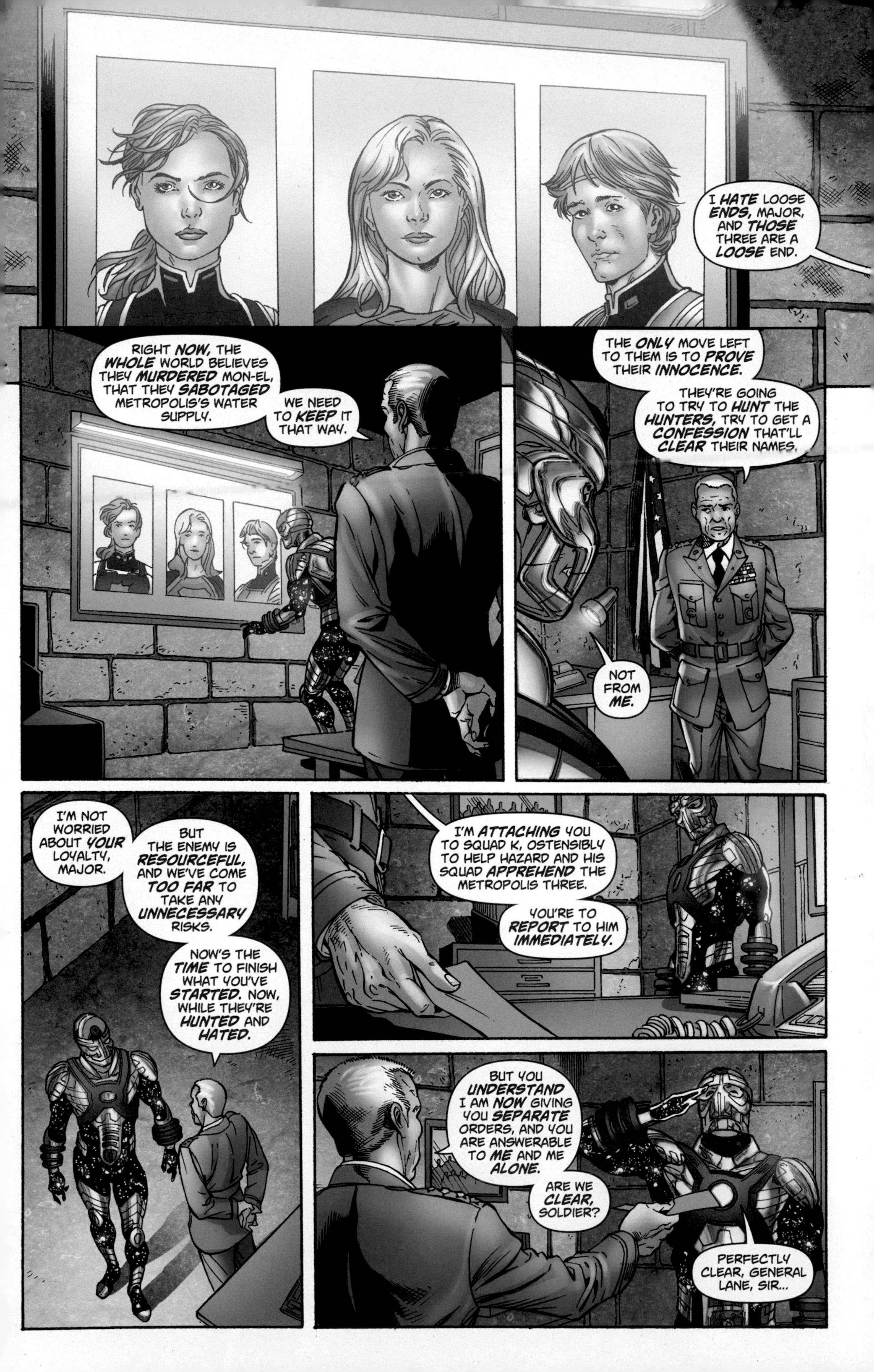
I HATE LOOSE ENDS, MAJOR, AND THOSE THREE ARE A LOOSE END.
RIGHT NOW, THE WHOLE WORLD BELIEVES THEY MURDERED MON-EL, THAT THEY SABOTAGED METROPOLIS'S WATER SUPPLY.
WE NEED TO KEEP IT THAT WAY.
THE ONLY MOVE LEFT TO THEM IS TO PROVE THEIR INNOCENCE.
THEY'RE GOING TO TRY TO HUNT THE HUNTERS, TRY TO GET A CONFESSION THAT'LL CLEAR THEIR NAMES.
NOT FROM ME.
I'M NOT WORRIED ABOUT YOUR LOYALTY, MAJOR.
BUT THE ENEMY IS RESOURCEFUL, AND WE'VE COME TOO FAR TO TAKE ANY UNNECESSARY RISKS.
NOW'S THE TIME TO FINISH WHAT YOU'VE STARTED. NOW, WHILE THEY'RE HUNTED AND HATED.
I'M ATTACHING YOU TO SQUAD K, OSTENSIBLY TO HELP HAZARD AND HIS SQUAD APPREHEND THE METROPOLIS THREE.
YOU'RE TO REPORT TO HIM IMMEDIATELY.
BUT YOU UNDERSTAND I AM NOW GIVING YOU SEPARATE ORDERS, AND YOU ARE ANSWERABLE TO ME AND ME ALONE.
ARE WE CLEAR, SOLDIER?
PERFECTLY CLEAR, GENERAL LANE, SIR...

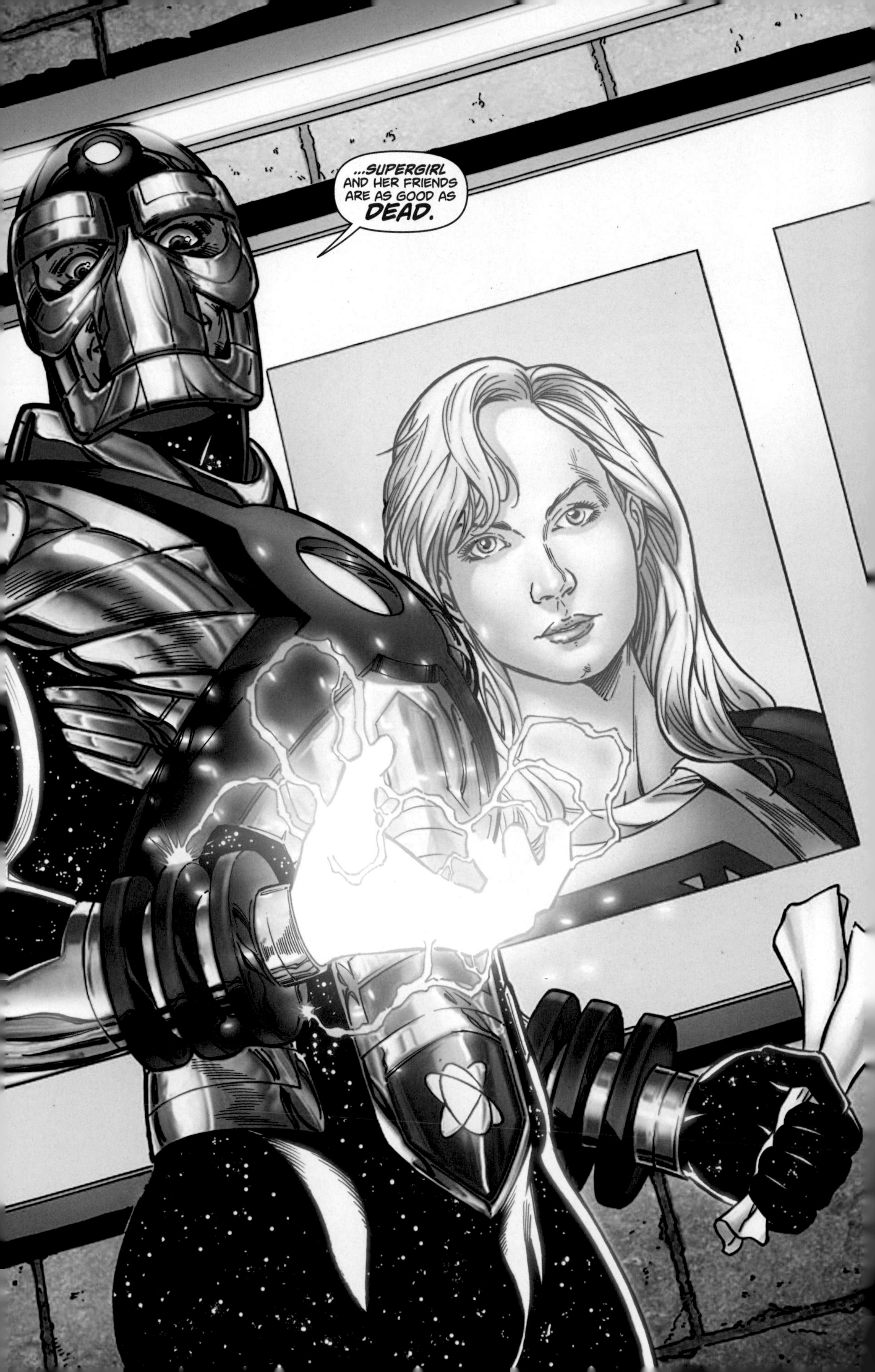
...SUPERGIRL AND HER FRIENDS ARE AS GOOD AS DEAD.

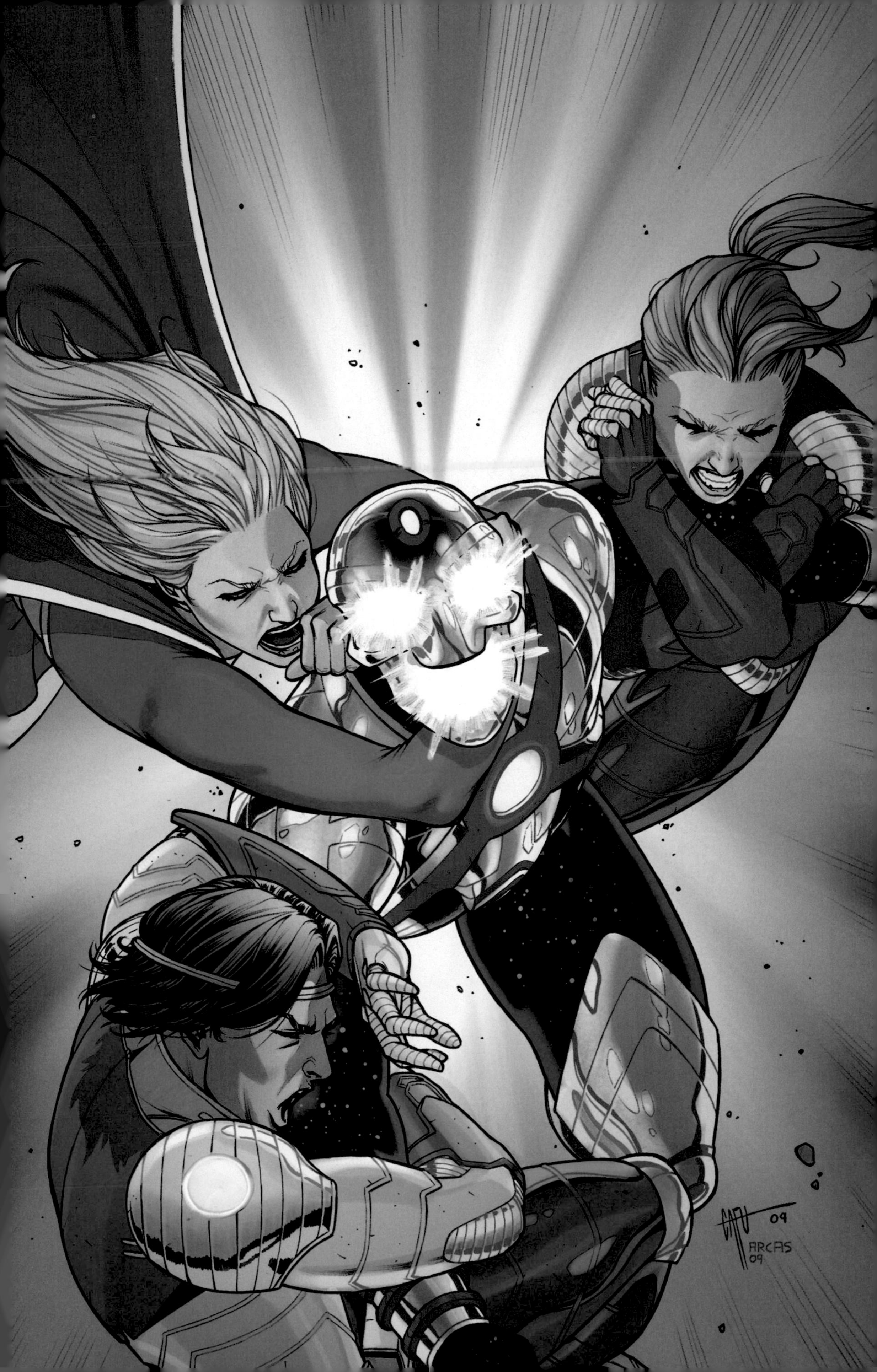

09
ARCAS
09

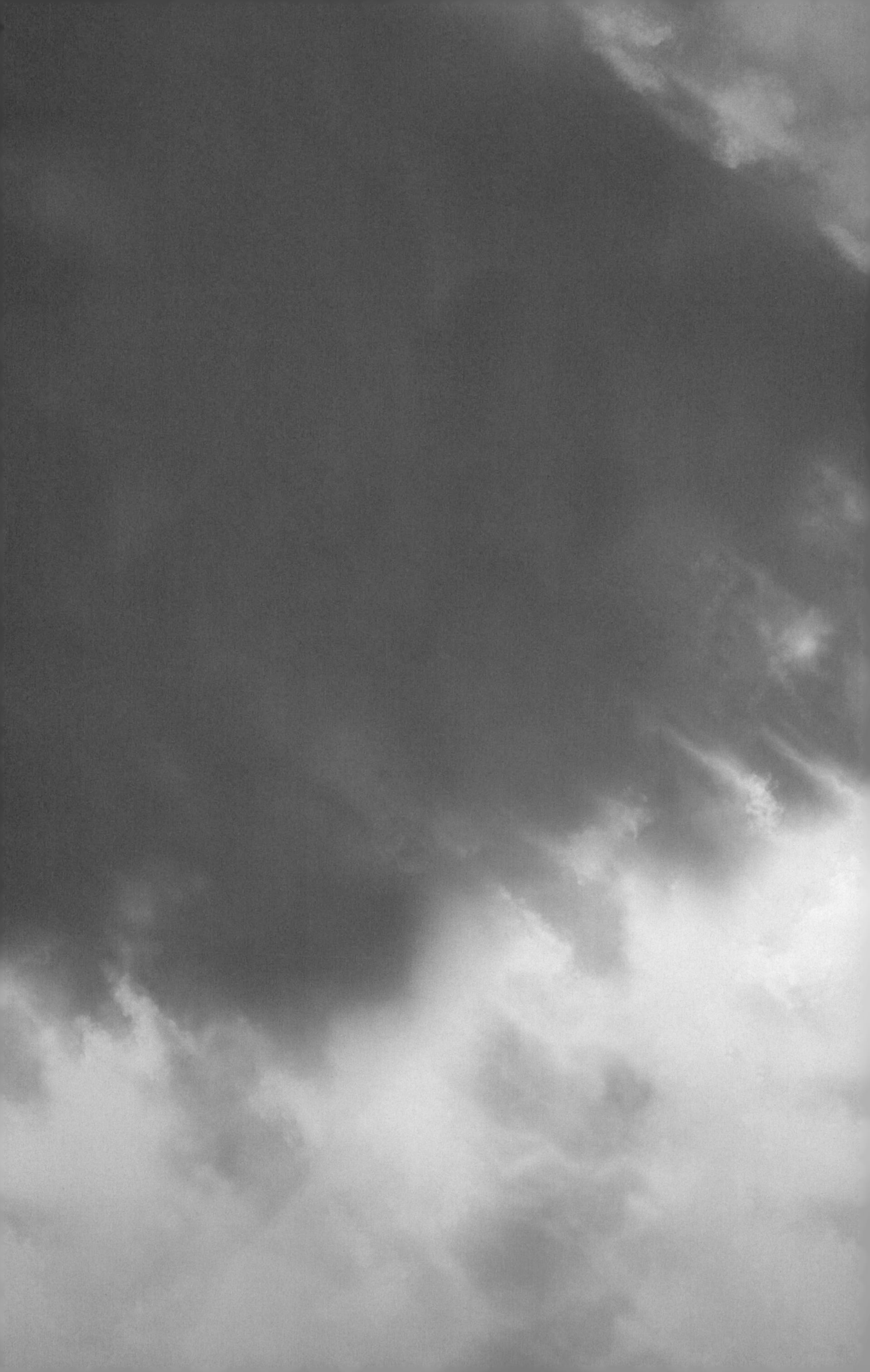

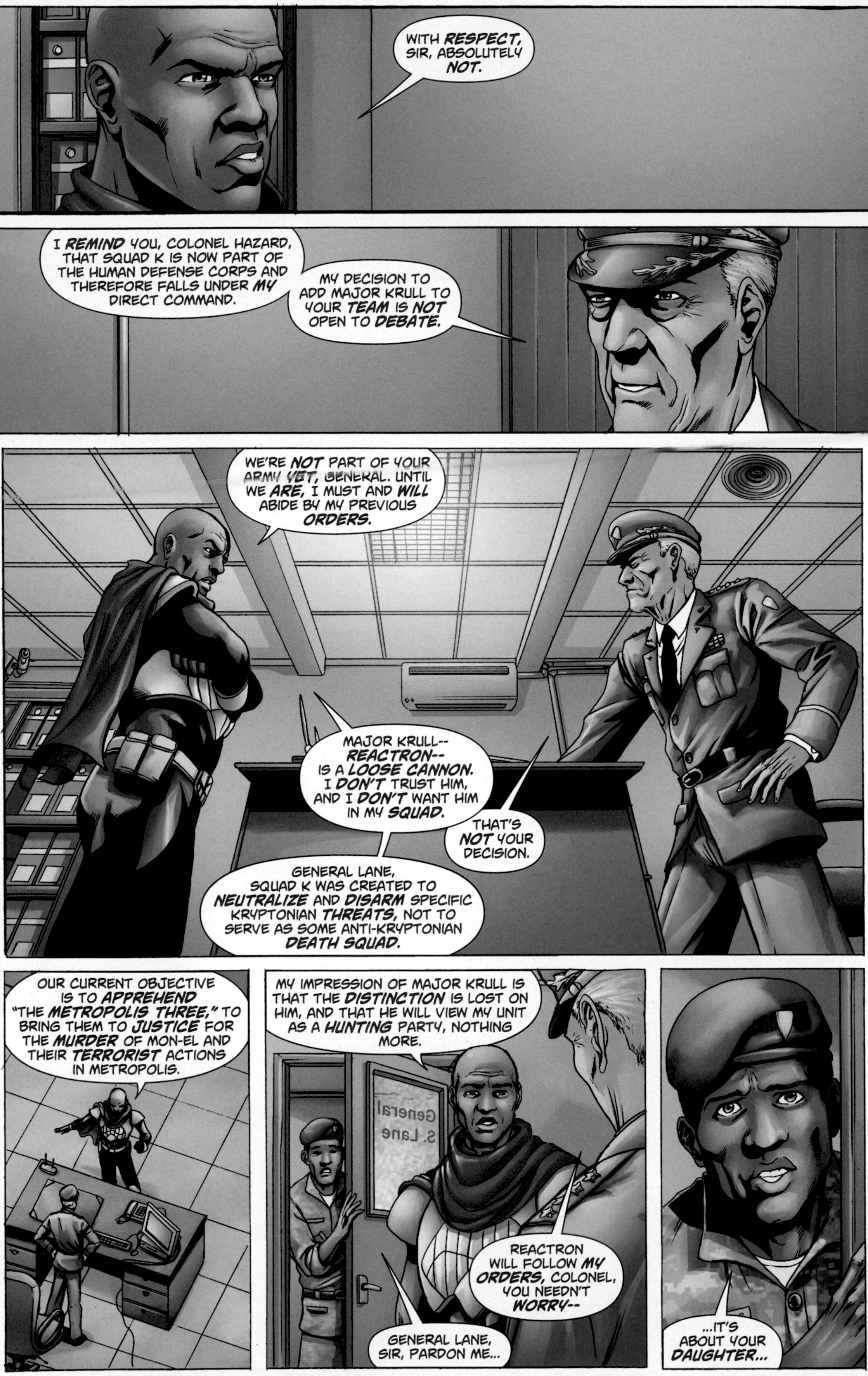
WITH RESPECT, SIR, ABSOLUTELY NOT.
I REMIND YOU, COLONEL HAZARD, THAT SQUAD K IS NOW PART OF THE HUMAN DEFENSE CORPS AND THEREFORE FALLS UNDER MY DIRECT COMMAND.
MY DECISION TO ADD MAJOR KRULL TO YOUR TEAM IS NOT OPEN TO DEBATE.
WE'RE NOT PART OF YOUR ARMY YET, GENERAL. UNTIL WE ARE, I MUST AND WILL ABIDE BY MY PREVIOUS ORDERS.
MAJOR KRULL-- REACTRON-- IS A LOOSE CANNON. I DON'T TRUST HIM, AND I DON'T WANT HIM IN MY SQUAD.
THAT'S NOT YOUR DECISION.
GENERAL LANE, SQUAD K WAS CREATED TO NEUTRALIZE AND DISARM SPECIFIC KRYPTONIAN THREATS, NOT TO SERVE AS SOME ANTI-KRYPTONIAN DEATH SQUAD.
OUR CURRENT OBJECTIVE IS TO APPREHEND "THE METROPOLIS THREE," TO BRING THEM TO JUSTICE FOR THE MURDER OF MON-EL AND THEIR TERRORIST ACTIONS IN METROPOLIS.
MY IMPRESSION OF MAJOR KRULL IS THAT THE DISTINCTION IS LOST ON HIM, AND THAT HE WILL VIEW MY UNIT AS A HUNTING PARTY, NOTHING MORE.
General S. Lane
REACTRON WILL FOLLOW MY ORDERS, COLONEL, YOU NEEDN'T WORRY--
GENERAL LANE, SIR, PARDON ME...
...IT'S ABOUT YOUR DAUGHTER...

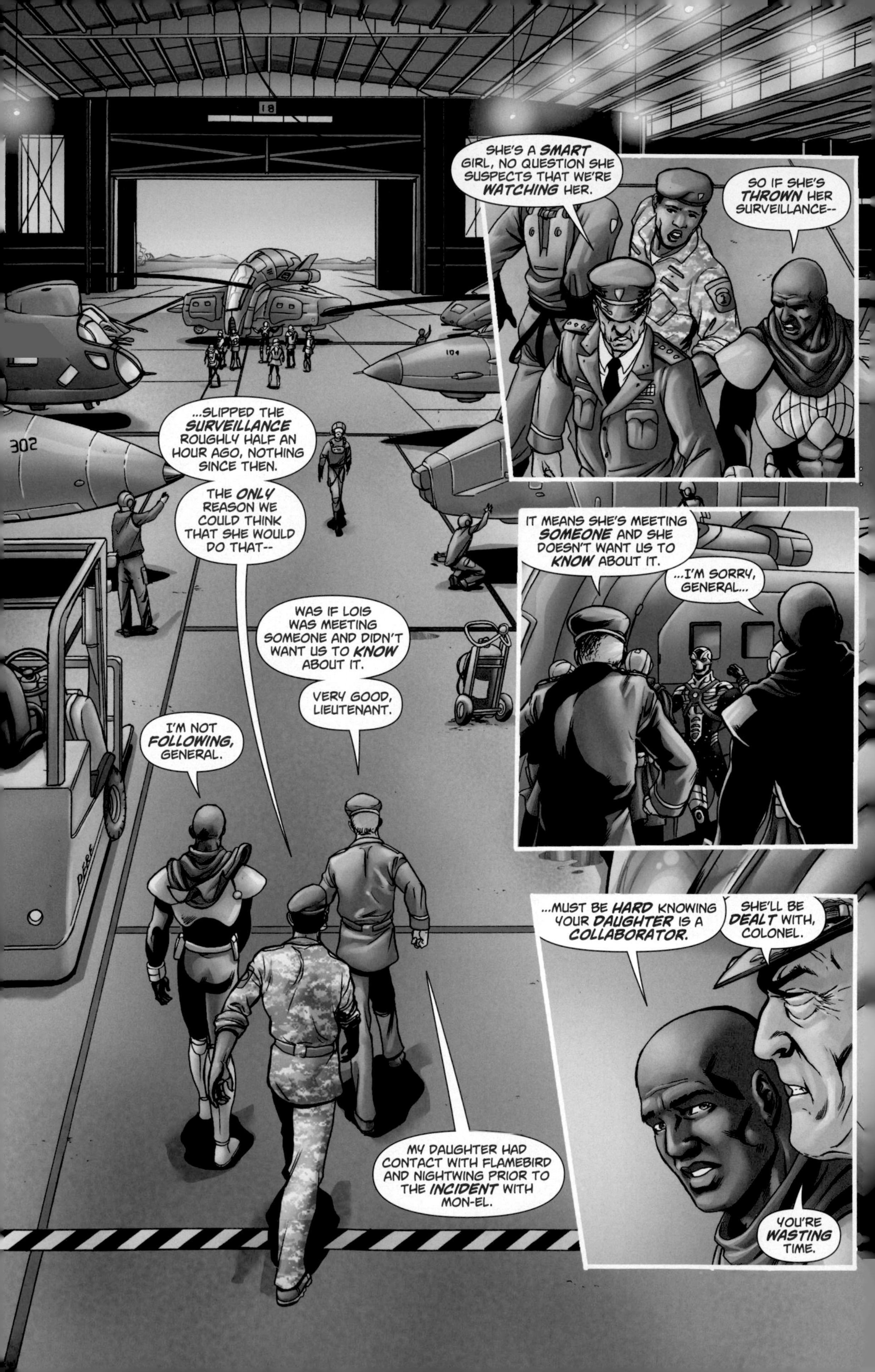
...SLIPPED THE SURVEILLANCE ROUGHLY HALF AN HOUR AGO, NOTHING SINCE THEN.
THE ONLY REASON WE COULD THINK THAT SHE WOULD DO THAT--
WAS IF LOIS WAS MEETING SOMEONE AND DIDN'T WANT US TO KNOW ABOUT IT.
VERY GOOD, LIEUTENANT.
I'M NOT FOLLOWING, GENERAL.
MY DAUGHTER HAD CONTACT WITH FLAMEBIRD AND NIGHTWING PRIOR TO THE INCIDENT WITH MON-EL.
SHE'S A SMART GIRL, NO QUESTION SHE SUSPECTS THAT WE'RE WATCHING HER.
SO IF SHE'S THROWN HER SURVEILLANCE--
IT MEANS SHE'S MEETING SOMEONE AND SHE DOESN'T WANT US TO KNOW ABOUT IT.
...I'M SORRY, GENERAL...
...MUST BE HARD KNOWING YOUR DAUGHTER IS A COLLABORATOR.
SHE'LL BE DEALT WITH, COLONEL.
YOU'RE WASTING TIME.

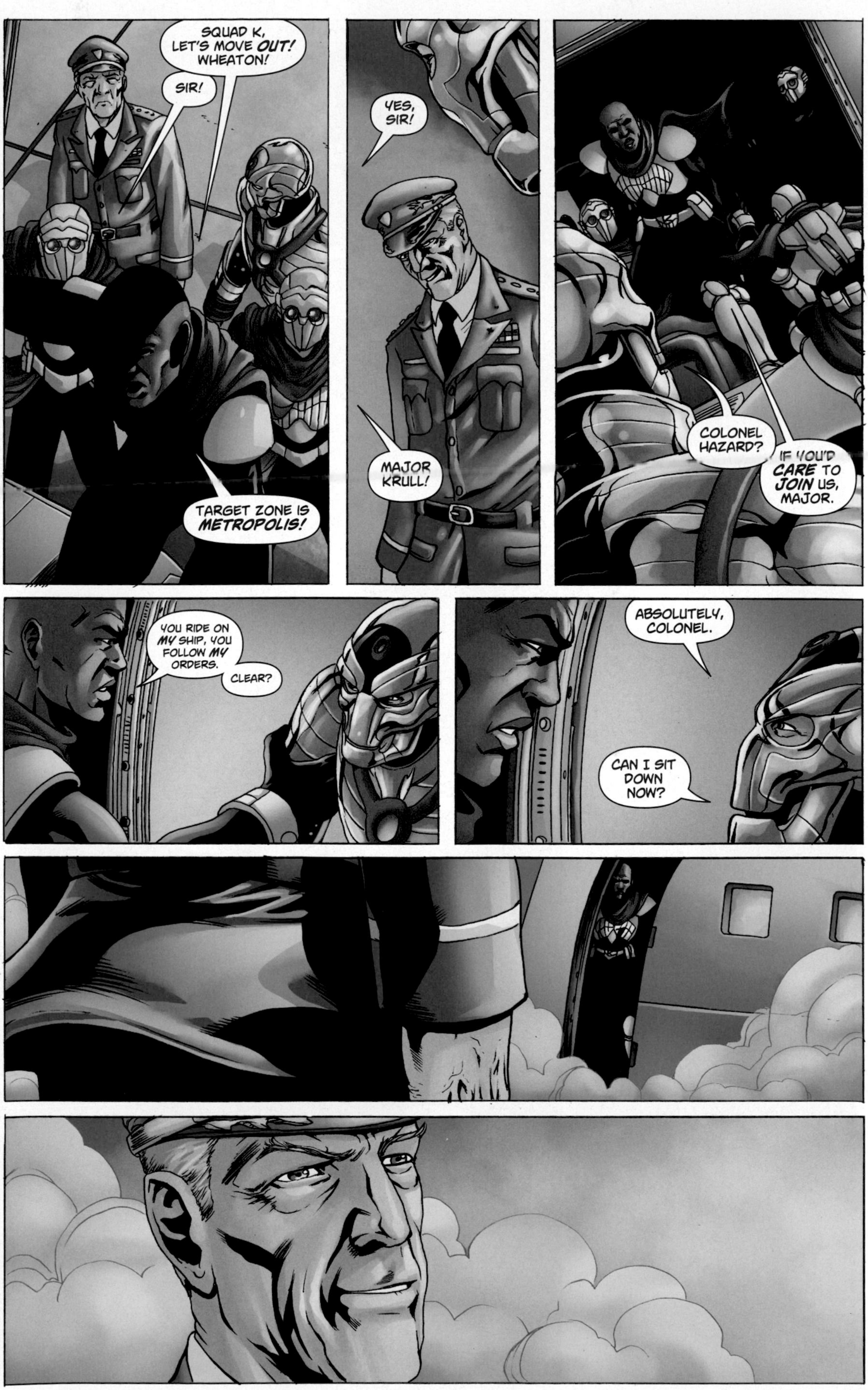
SQUAD K, LET'S MOVE OUT! WHEATON!
SIR!
TARGET ZONE IS METROPOLIS!
YES, SIR!
MAJOR KRULL!
COLONEL HAZARD?
IF YOU'D CARE TO JOIN US, MAJOR.
YOU RIDE ON MY SHIP, YOU FOLLOW MY ORDERS.
CLEAR?
ABSOLUTELY, COLONEL.
CAN I SIT DOWN NOW?

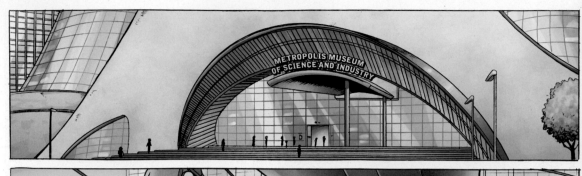

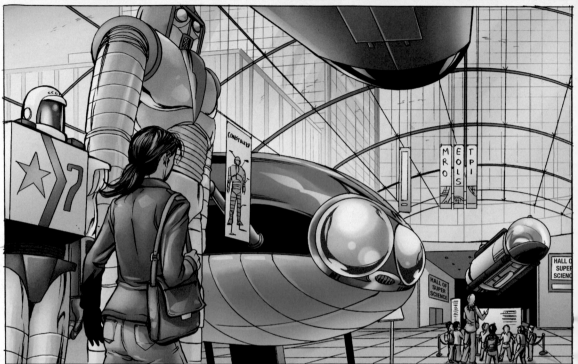

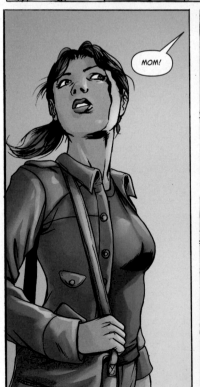

METROPOLIS MUSEUM OF SCIENCE AND INDUSTRY
HALL OF SUPER SCIENCE
MOM!
UP HERE!
REPLICA OF THE BLUE BEETLE'S BATTLE BUG! WATCH YOUR STEP!
"MOM"?
KARA CAN EXPLAIN IT.

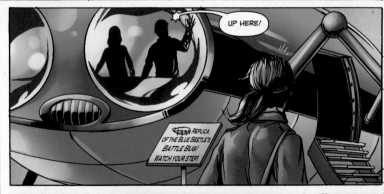

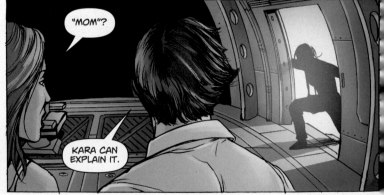

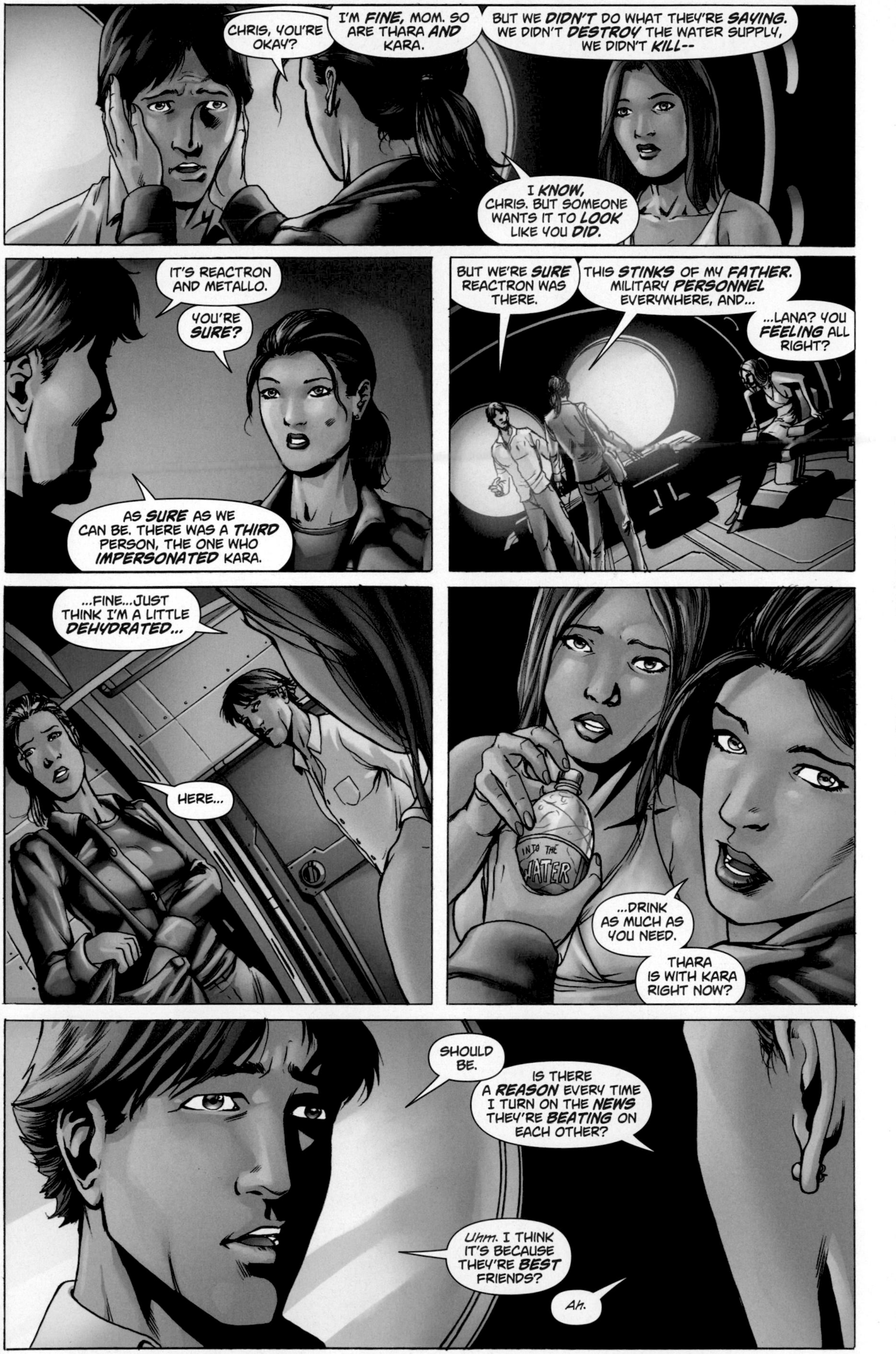
CHRIS, YOU'RE OKAY?
I'M FINE, MOM. SO ARE THARA AND KARA.
BUT WE DIDN'T DO WHAT THEY'RE SAYING. WE DIDN'T DESTROY THE WATER SUPPLY, WE DIDN'T KILL--
I KNOW, CHRIS. BUT SOMEONE WANTS IT TO LOOK LIKE YOU DID.
IT'S REACTRON AND METALLO.
YOU'RE SURE?
AS SURE AS WE CAN BE. THERE WAS A THIRD PERSON, THE ONE WHO IMPERSONATED KARA.
BUT WE'RE SURE REACTRON WAS THERE.
THIS STINKS OF MY FATHER. MILITARY PERSONNEL EVERYWHERE, AND...
...LANA? YOU FEELING ALL RIGHT?
...FINE...JUST THINK I'M A LITTLE DEHYDRATED...
HERE...
INTO THE WATER
...DRINK AS MUCH AS YOU NEED.
THARA IS WITH KARA RIGHT NOW?
SHOULD BE.
IS THERE A REASON EVERY TIME I TURN ON THE NEWS THEY'RE BEATING ON EACH OTHER?
Uhm. I THINK IT'S BECAUSE THEY'RE BEST FRIENDS?
Ah.

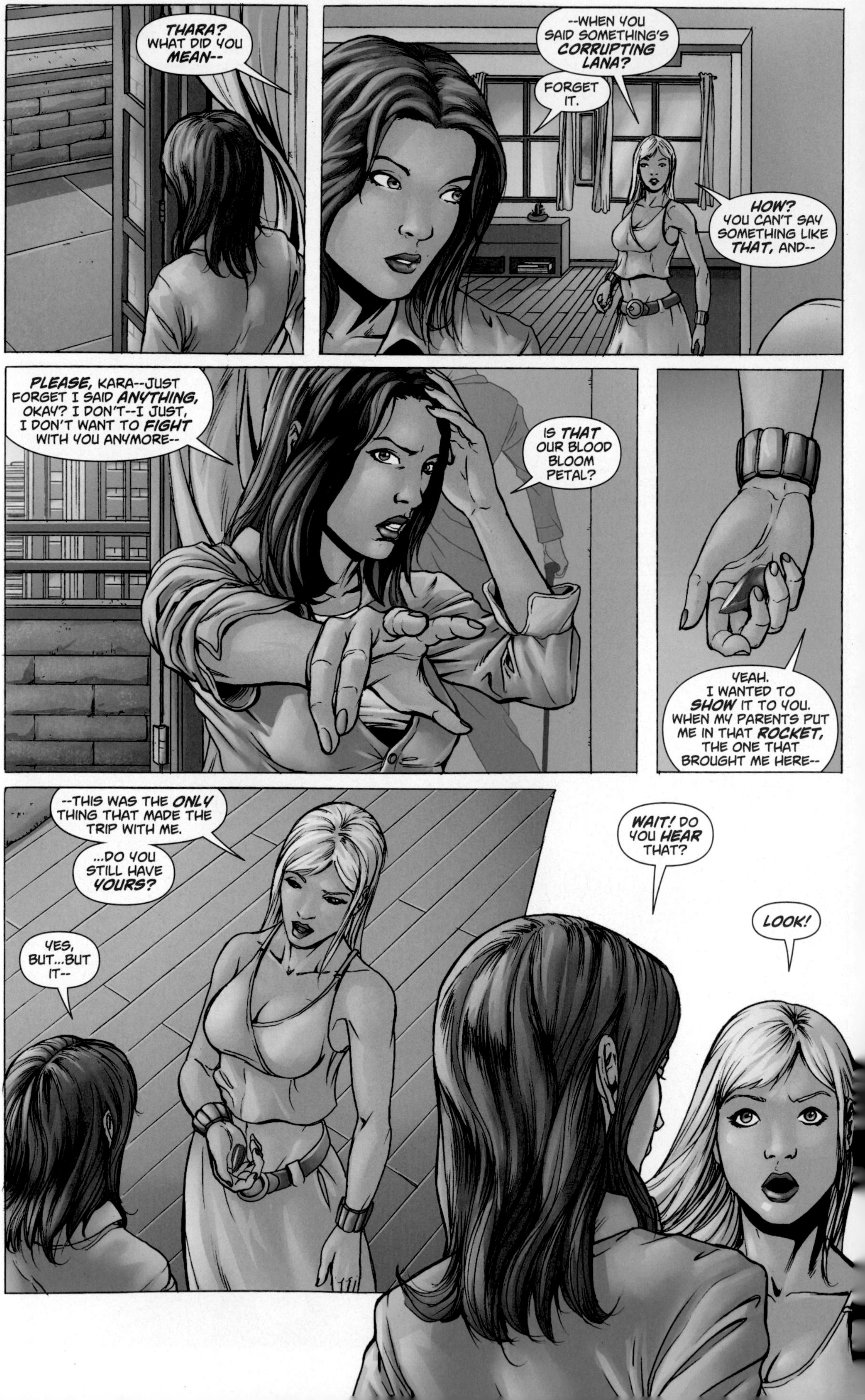

THARA? WHAT DID YOU MEAN--
--WHEN YOU SAID SOMETHING'S CORRUPTING LANA?
FORGET IT.
HOW? YOU CAN'T SAY SOMETHING LIKE THAT, AND--
PLEASE, KARA--JUST FORGET I SAID ANYTHING, OKAY? I DON'T--I JUST, I DON'T WANT TO FIGHT WITH YOU ANYMORE--
IS THAT OUR BLOOD BLOOM PETAL?
YEAH. I WANTED TO SHOW IT TO YOU. WHEN MY PARENTS PUT ME IN THAT ROCKET, THE ONE THAT BROUGHT ME HERE--
--THIS WAS THE ONLY THING THAT MADE THE TRIP WITH ME.
...DO YOU STILL HAVE YOURS?
YES, BUT...BUT IT--
WAIT! DO YOU HEAR THAT?
LOOK!

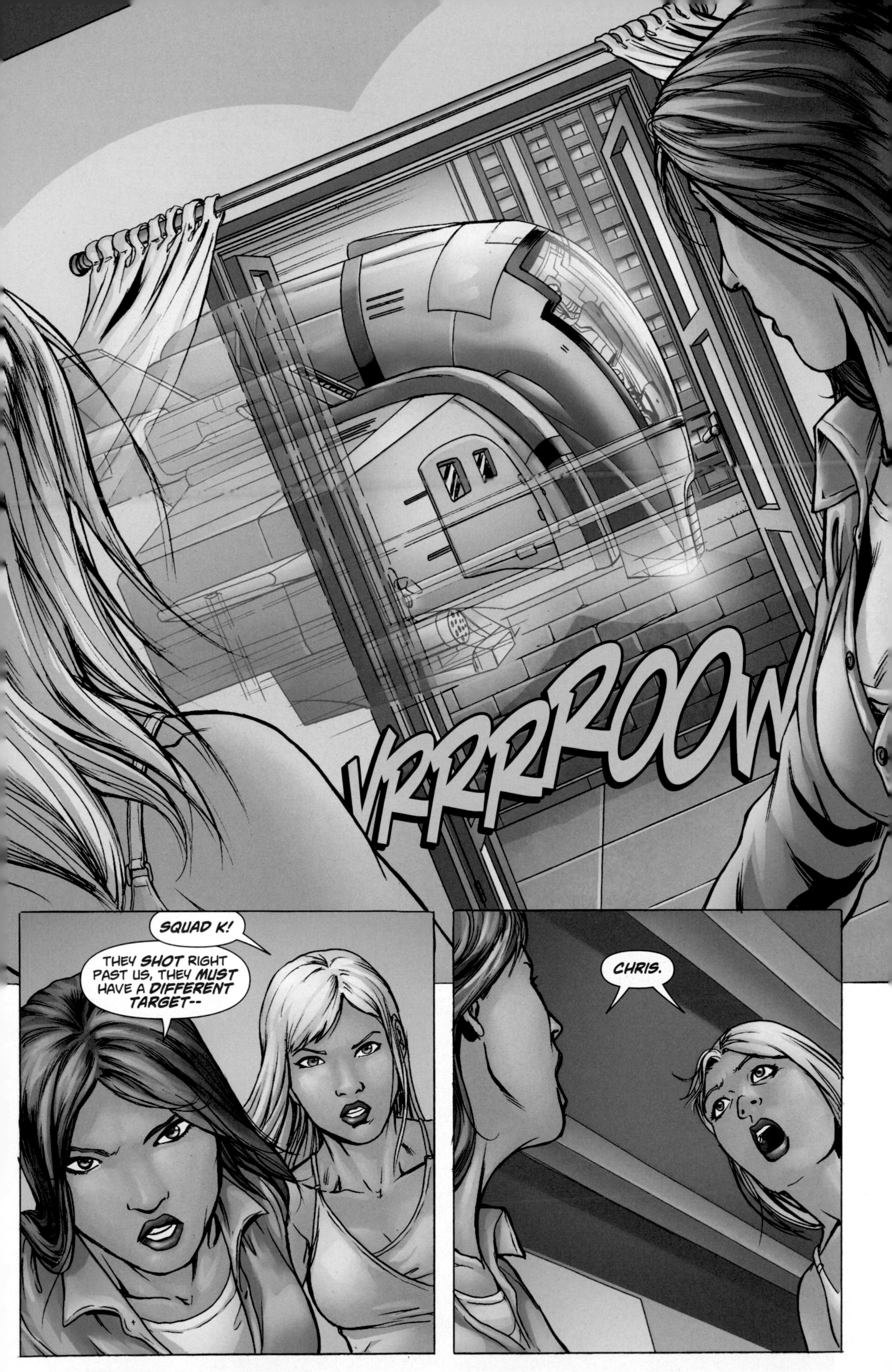
VRRRROOOW
SQUAD K!
THEY SHOT RIGHT PAST US, THEY MUST HAVE A DIFFERENT TARGET--
CHRIS.

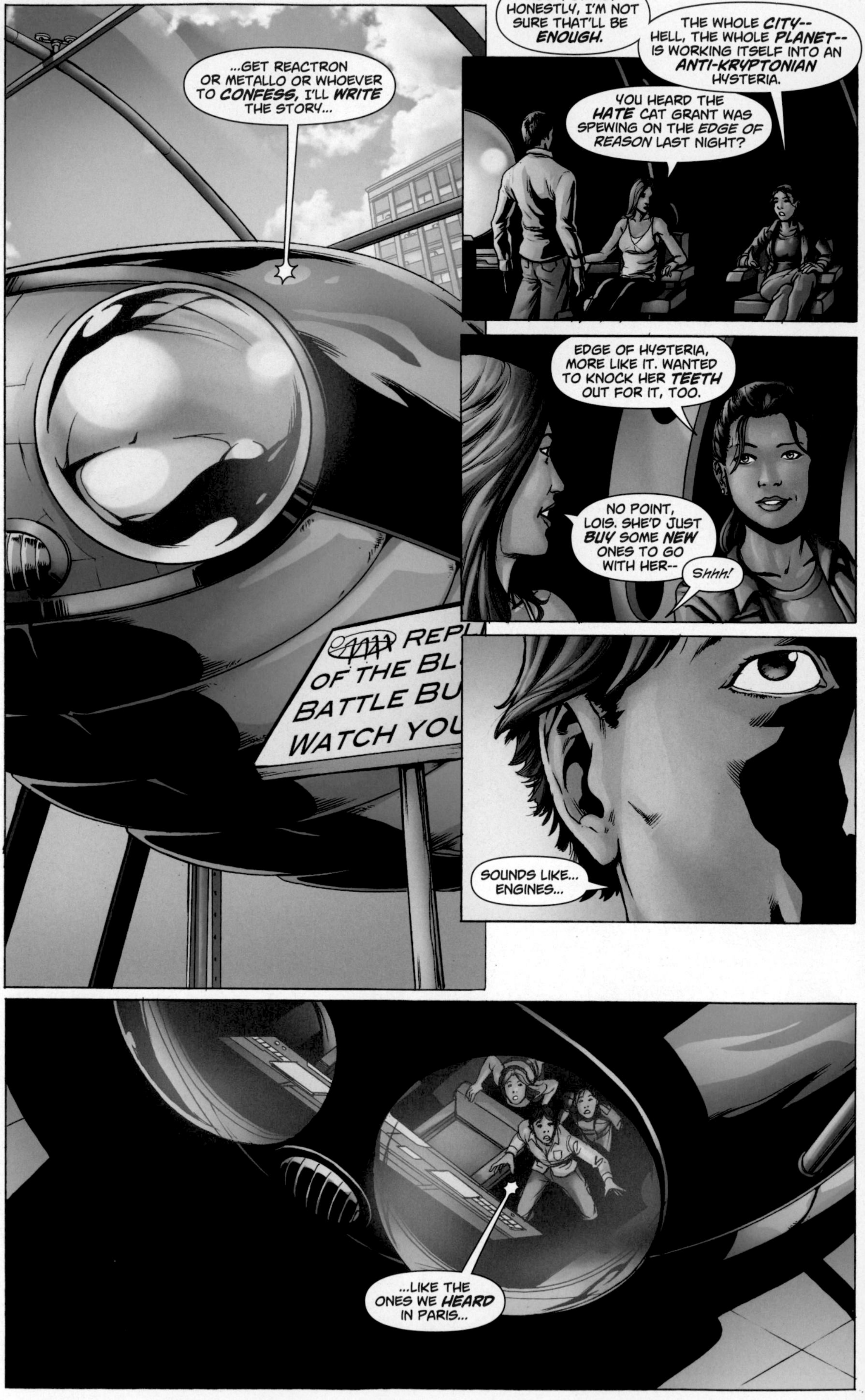
...GET REACTRON OR METALLO OR WHOEVER TO CONFESS, I'LL WRITE THE STORY...
...BUT, CHRIS, HONESTLY, I'M NOT SURE THAT'LL BE ENOUGH.
THE WHOLE CITY-- HELL, THE WHOLE PLANET-- IS WORKING ITSELF INTO AN ANTI-KRYPTONIAN HYSTERIA.
YOU HEARD THE HATE CAT GRANT WAS SPEWING ON THE EDGE OF REASON LAST NIGHT?
EDGE OF HYSTERIA, MORE LIKE IT. WANTED TO KNOCK HER TEETH OUT FOR IT, TOO.
NO POINT, LOIS. SHE'D JUST BUY SOME NEW ONES TO GO WITH HER--
Shhh!
REPL
OF THE BL
BATTLE BU
WATCH YOU
SOUNDS LIKE... ENGINES...
...LIKE THE ONES WE HEARD IN PARIS...

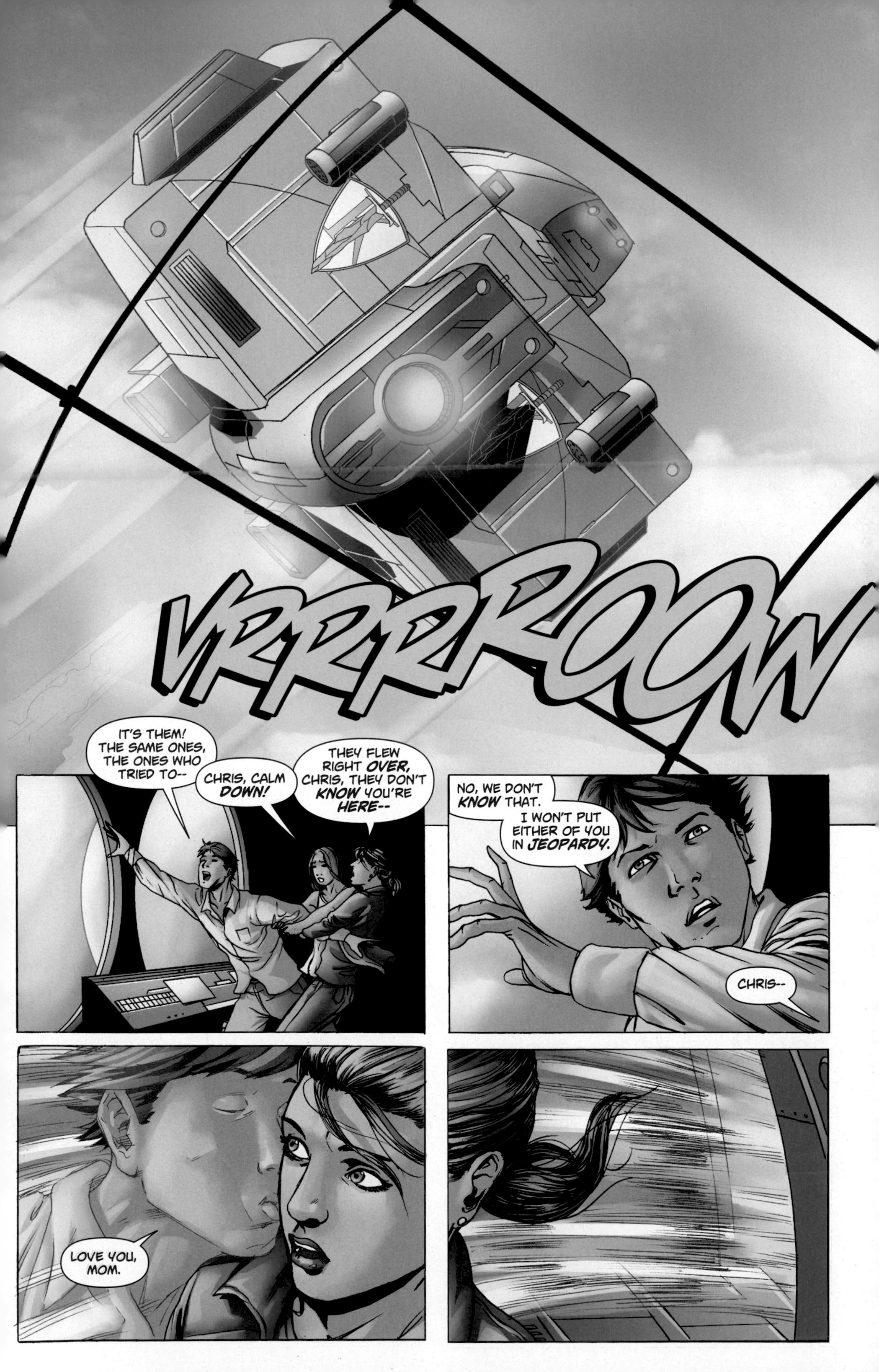
VRRROOOW
IT'S THEM! THE SAME ONES, THE ONES WHO TRIED TO--
CHRIS, CALM DOWN!
THEY FLEW RIGHT OVER, CHRIS, THEY DON'T KNOW YOU'RE HERE--
NO, WE DON'T KNOW THAT.
I WON'T PUT EITHER OF YOU IN JEOPARDY.
CHRIS--
LOVE YOU, MOM.

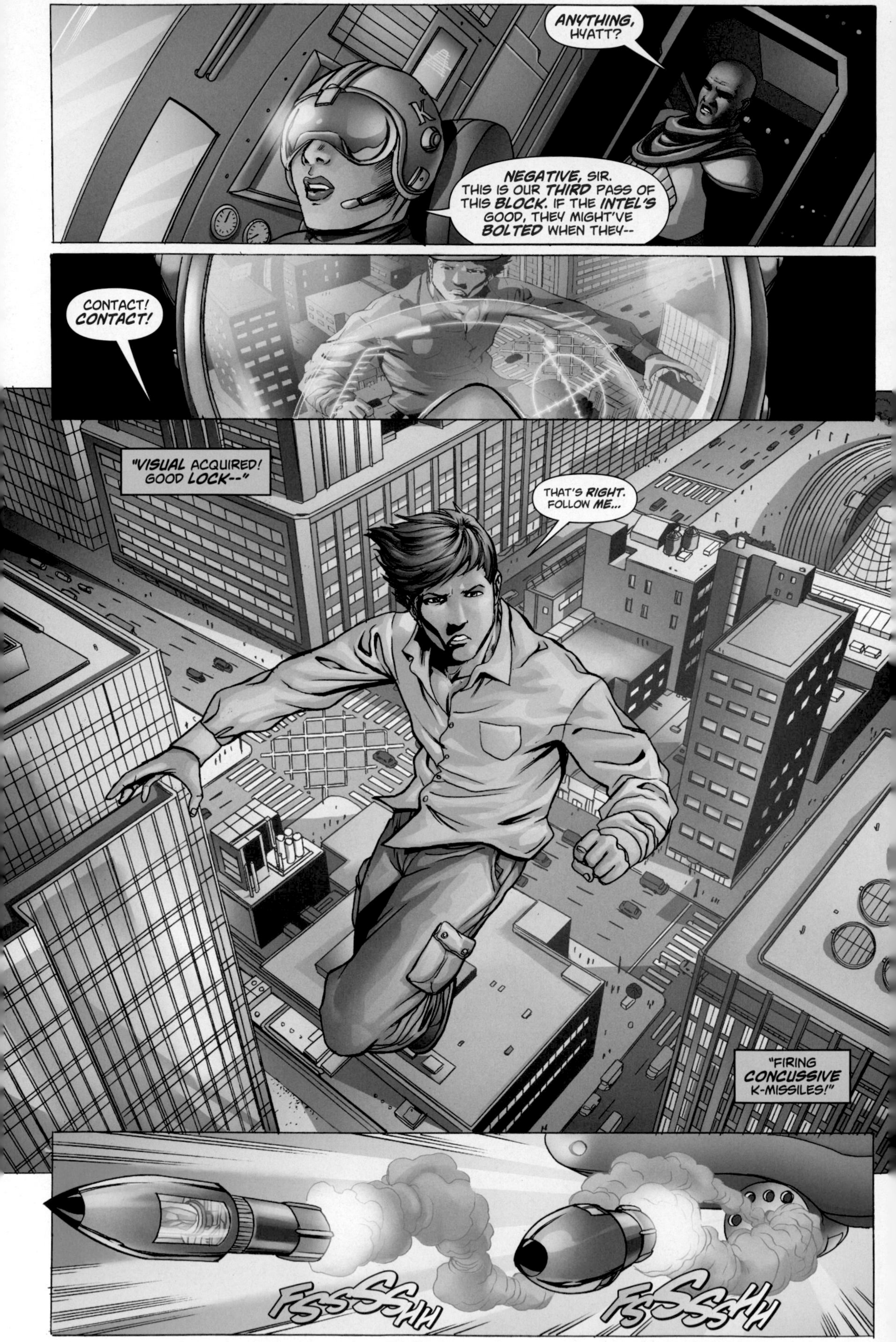
ANYTHING, HYATT?
NEGATIVE, SIR. THIS IS OUR THIRD PASS OF THIS BLOCK. IF THE INTEL'S GOOD, THEY MIGHT'VE BOLTED WHEN THEY--
CONTACT! CONTACT!
"VISUAL ACQUIRED! GOOD LOCK--"
THAT'S RIGHT. FOLLOW ME...
"FIRING CONCUSSIVE K-MISSILES!"
FSSSSSHH
FSSSSHH

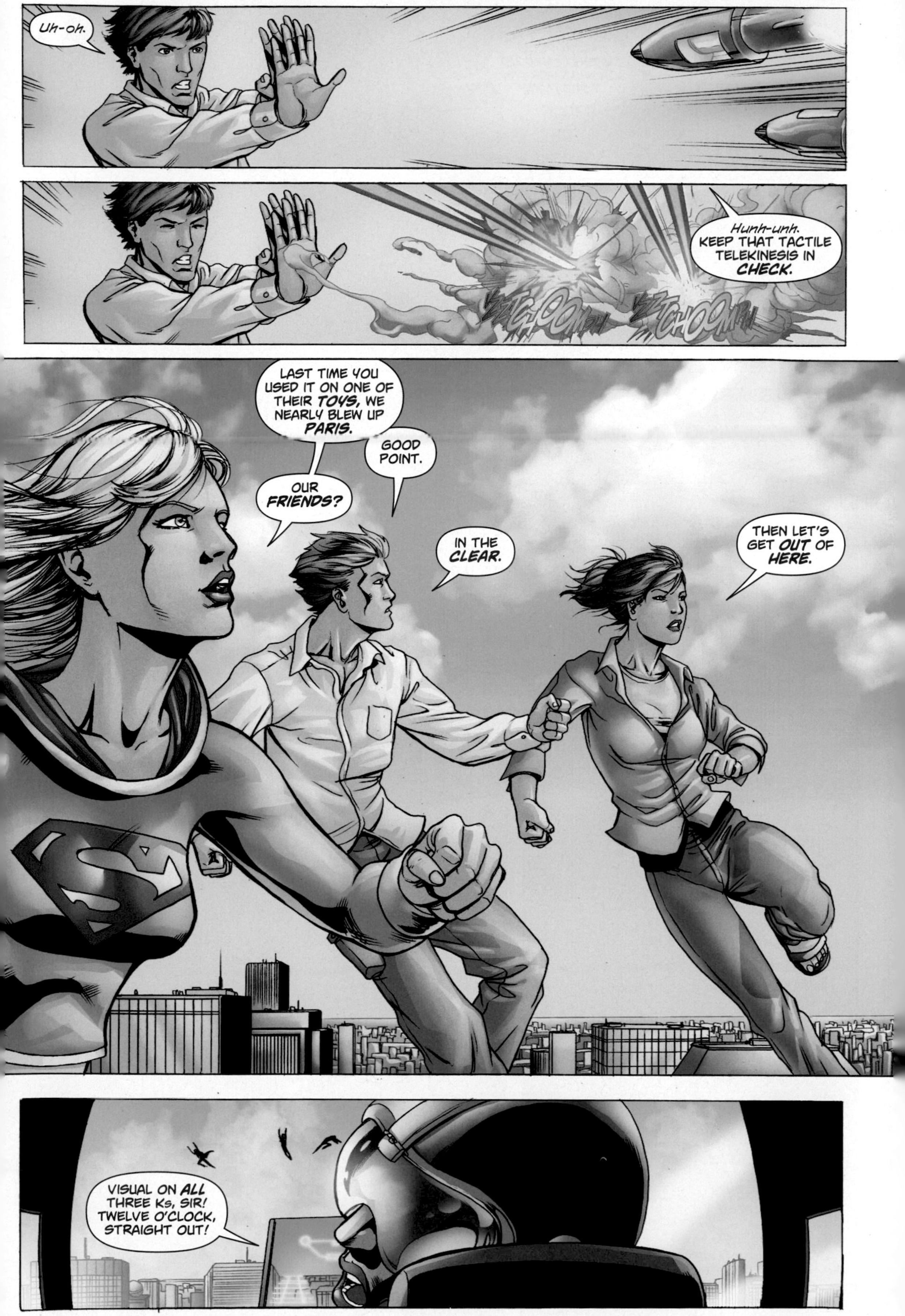
Uh-oh.
Hunh-unh. KEEP THAT TACTILE TELEKINESIS IN CHECK.
VZZTCHOOMMM
VZZTCHOOMMM
LAST TIME YOU USED IT ON ONE OF THEIR TOYS, WE NEARLY BLEW UP PARIS.
GOOD POINT.
OUR FRIENDS?
IN THE CLEAR.
THEN LET'S GET OUT OF HERE.
VISUAL ON ALL THREE Ks, SIR! TWELVE O'CLOCK, STRAIGHT OUT!

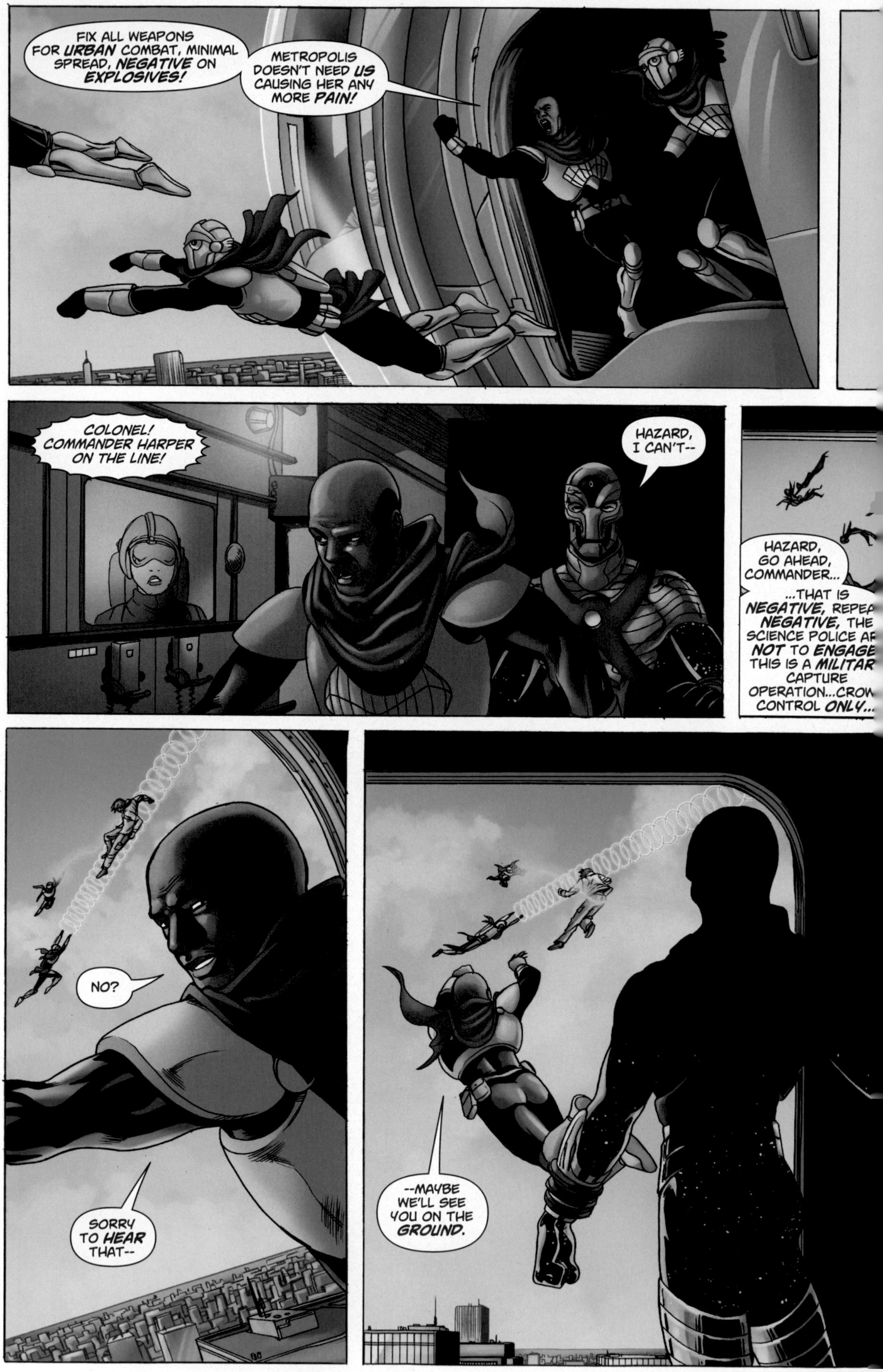
FIX ALL WEAPONS FOR URBAN COMBAT, MINIMAL SPREAD, NEGATIVE ON EXPLOSIVES!
METROPOLIS DOESN'T NEED US CAUSING HER ANY MORE PAIN!
COLONEL! COMMANDER HARPER ON THE LINE!
HAZARD, I CAN'T--
HAZARD, GO AHEAD, COMMANDER...
...THAT IS NEGATIVE, REPEA NEGATIVE, THE SCIENCE POLICE AR NOT TO ENGAGE THIS IS A MILITAR CAPTURE OPERATION...CROW CONTROL ONLY...
NO?
SORRY TO HEAR THAT--
--MAYBE WE'LL SEE YOU ON THE GROUND.

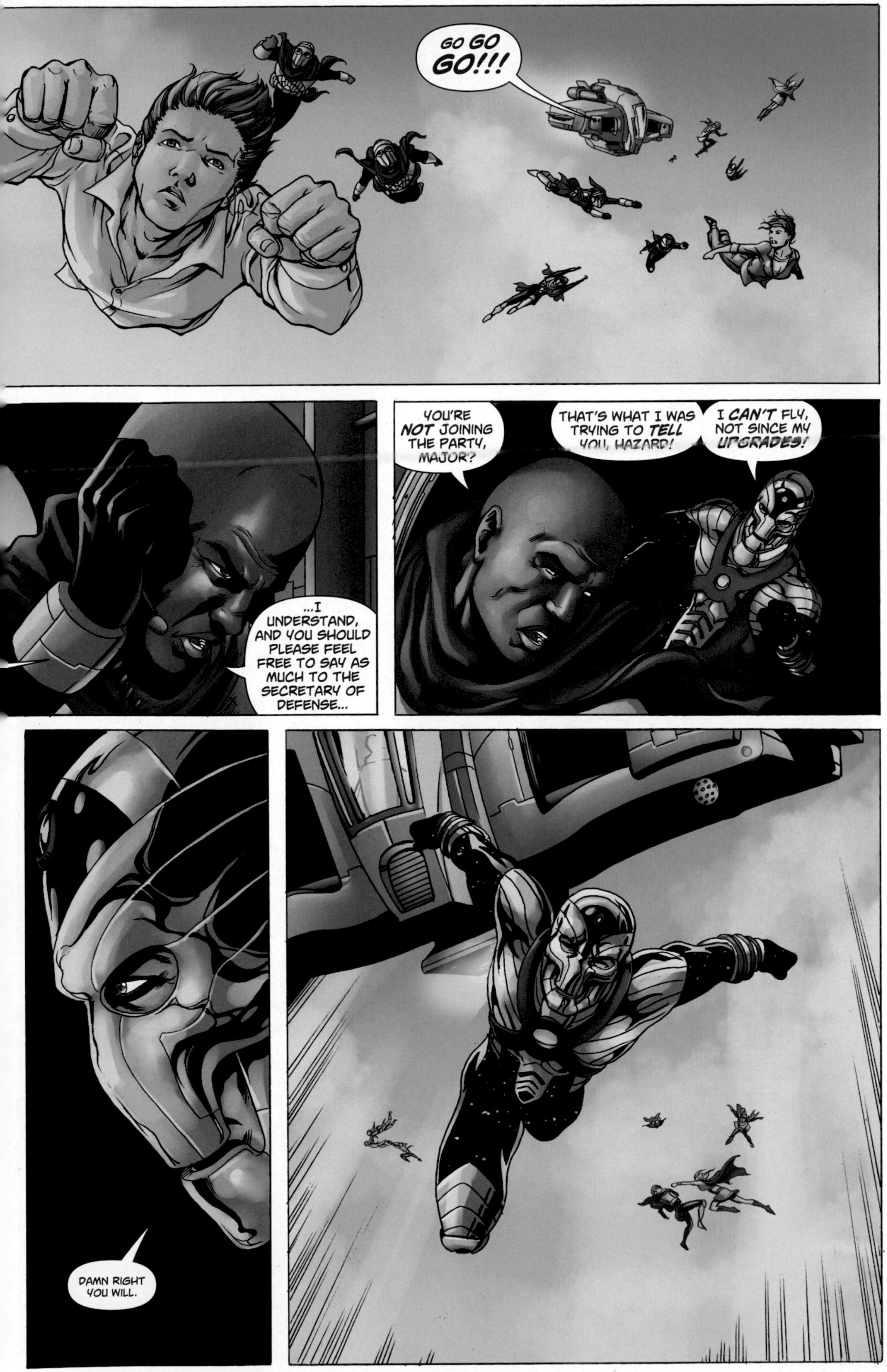
GO GO GO!!!
...I UNDERSTAND, AND YOU SHOULD PLEASE FEEL FREE TO SAY AS MUCH TO THE SECRETARY OF DEFENSE...
YOU'RE NOT JOINING THE PARTY, MAJOR?
THAT'S WHAT I WAS TRYING TO TELL YOU, HAZARD!
I CAN'T FLY, NOT SINCE MY UPGRADES!
DAMN RIGHT YOU WILL.

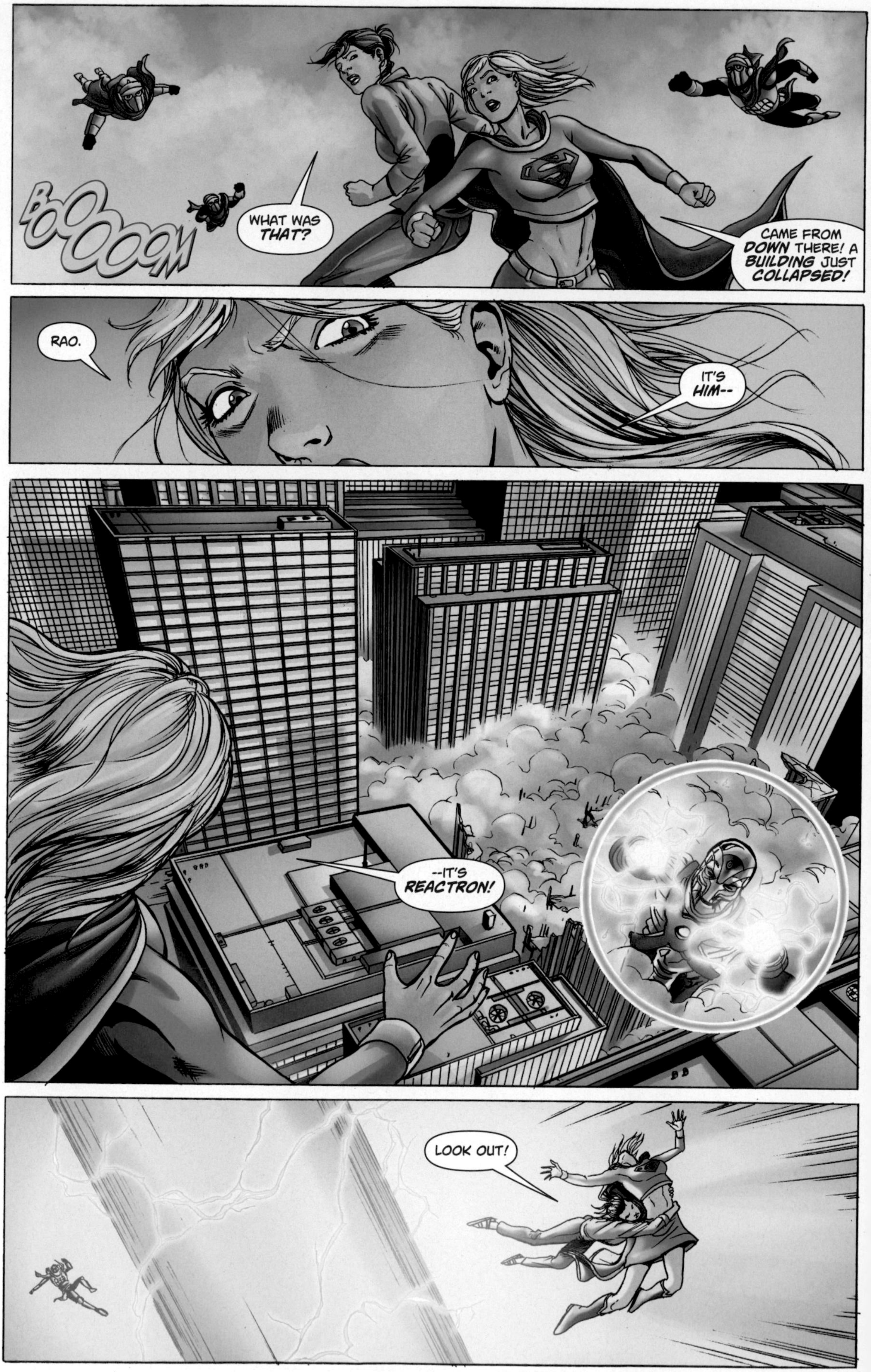
BOOOOOM
WHAT WAS THAT?
CAME FROM DOWN THERE! A BUILDING JUST COLLAPSED!
RAO.
IT'S HIM--
--IT'S REACTRON!
LOOK OUT!

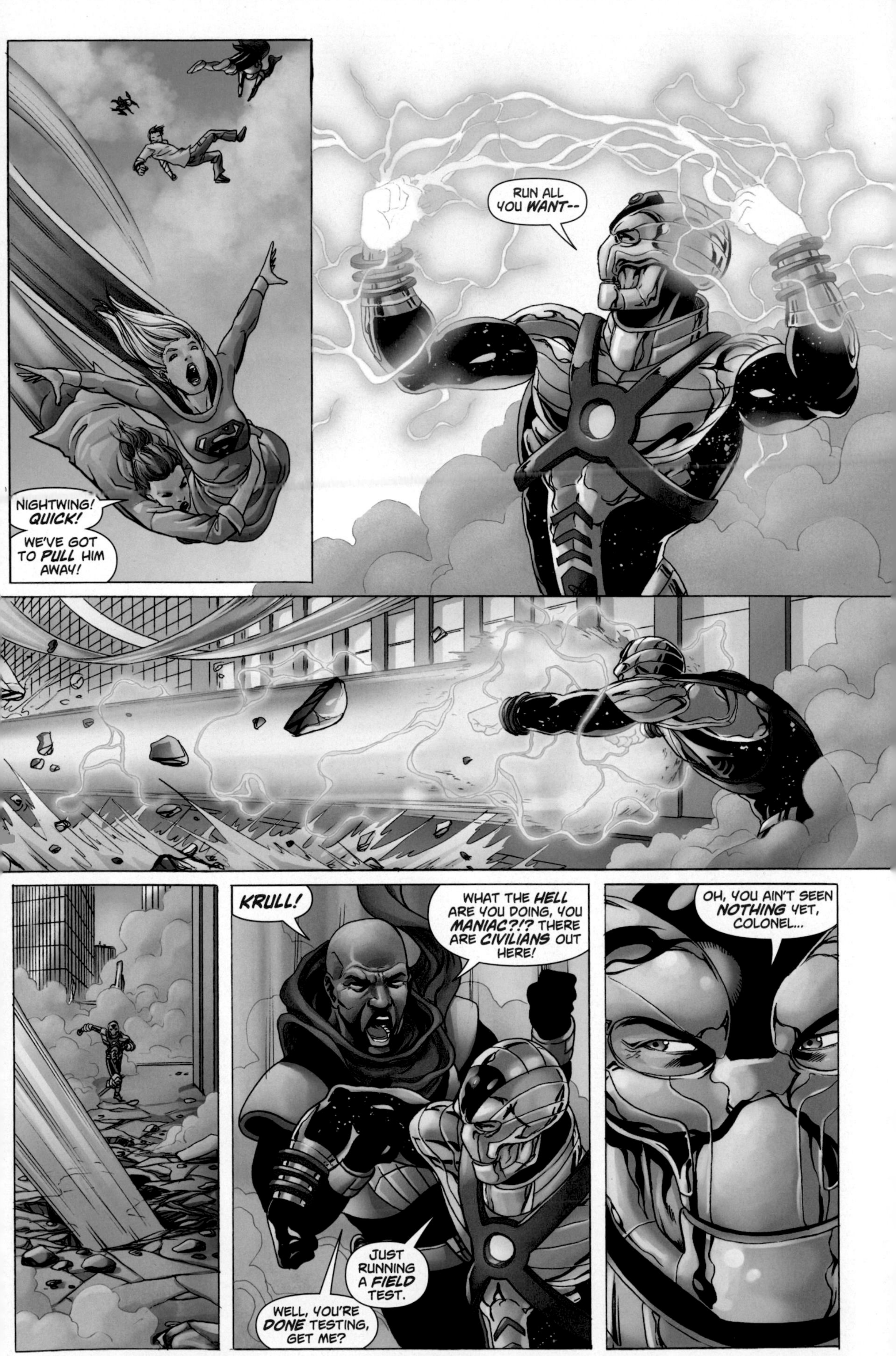
RUN ALL YOU WANT--
NIGHTWING! QUICK!
WE'VE GOT TO PULL HIM AWAY!
KRULL!
WHAT THE HELL ARE YOU DOING, YOU MANIAC?!? THERE ARE CIVILIANS OUT HERE!
JUST RUNNING A FIELD TEST.
WELL, YOU'RE DONE TESTING, GET ME?
OH, YOU AIN'T SEEN NOTHING YET, COLONEL...

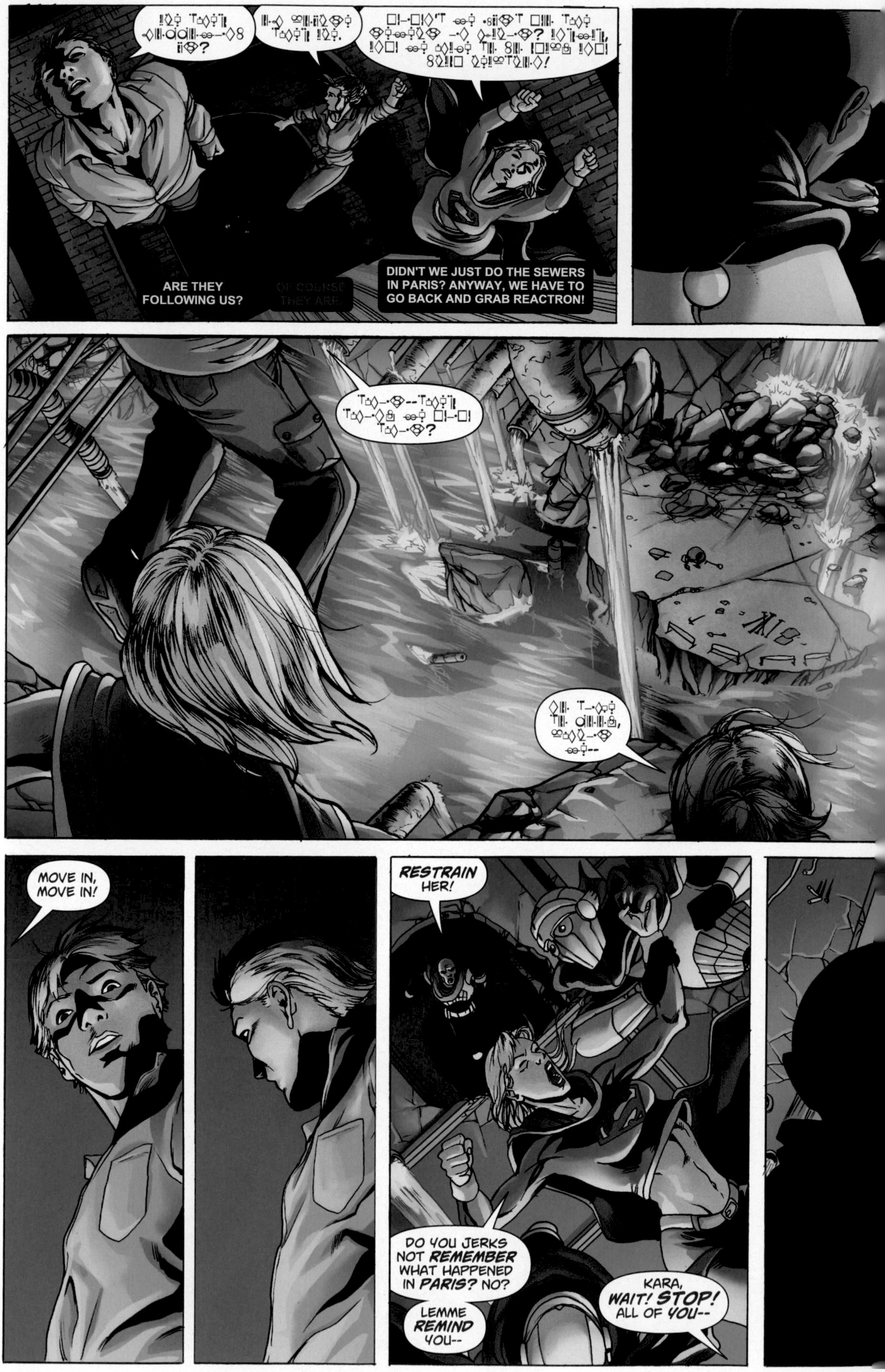
ARE THEY FOLLOWING US?
OF COURSE THEY ARE.
DIDN'T WE JUST DO THE SEWERS IN PARIS? ANYWAY, WE HAVE TO GO BACK AND GRAB REACTRON!
MOVE IN, MOVE IN!
RESTRAIN HER!
DO YOU JERKS NOT REMEMBER WHAT HAPPENED IN PARIS? NO?
LEMME REMIND YOU--
KARA, WAIT! STOP! ALL OF YOU--

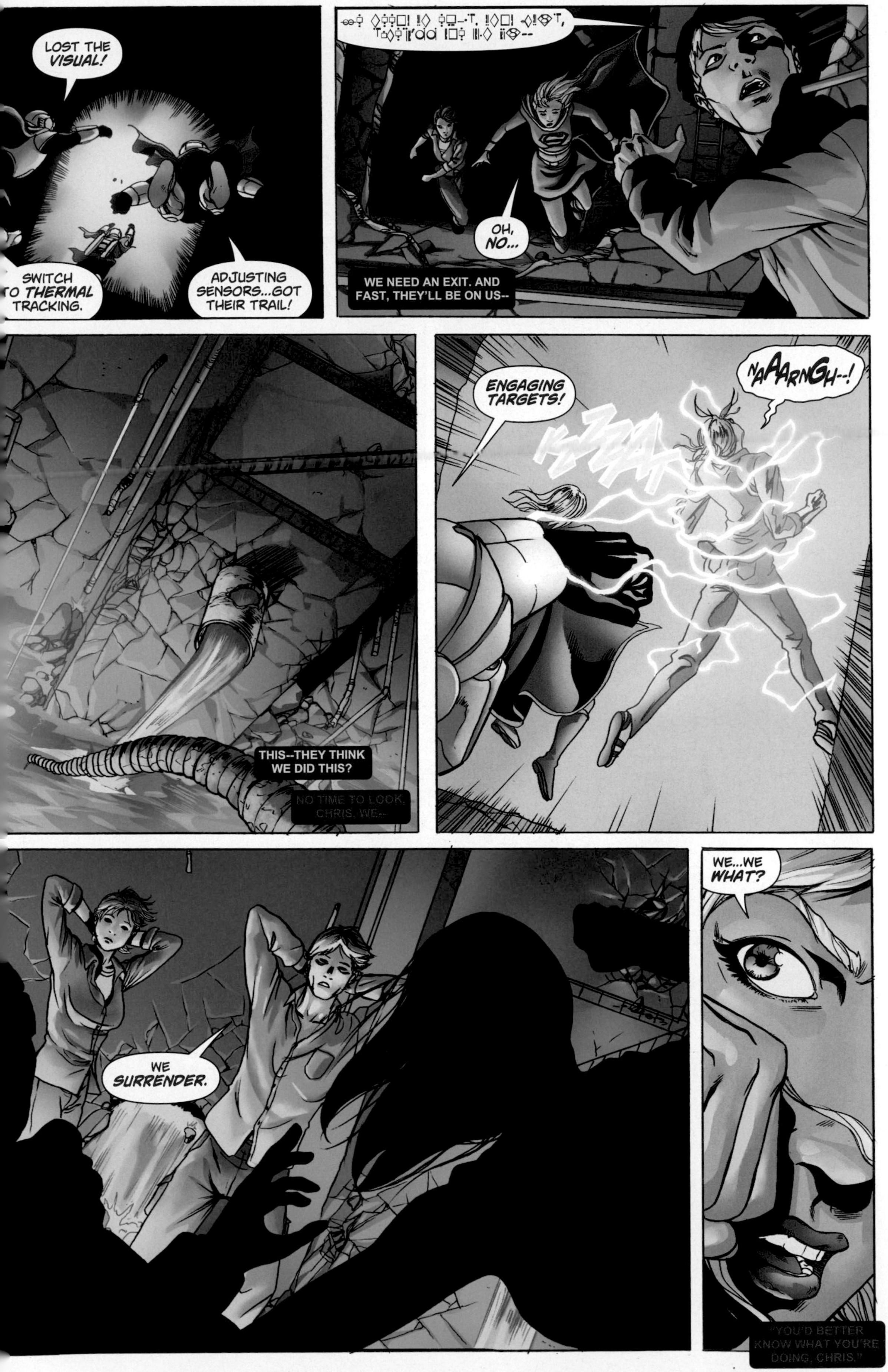
LOST THE VISUAL!
SWITCH TO THERMAL TRACKING.
ADJUSTING SENSORS...GOT THEIR TRAIL!
OH, NO...
WE NEED AN EXIT. AND FAST, THEY'LL BE ON US--
THIS--THEY THINK WE DID THIS?
NO TIME TO LOOK, CHRIS. WE--
ENGAGING TARGETS!
KRZZAK
NAAARNGH--!
WE SURRENDER.
WE...WE WHAT?
"YOU'D BETTER KNOW WHAT YOU'RE DOING, CHRIS."

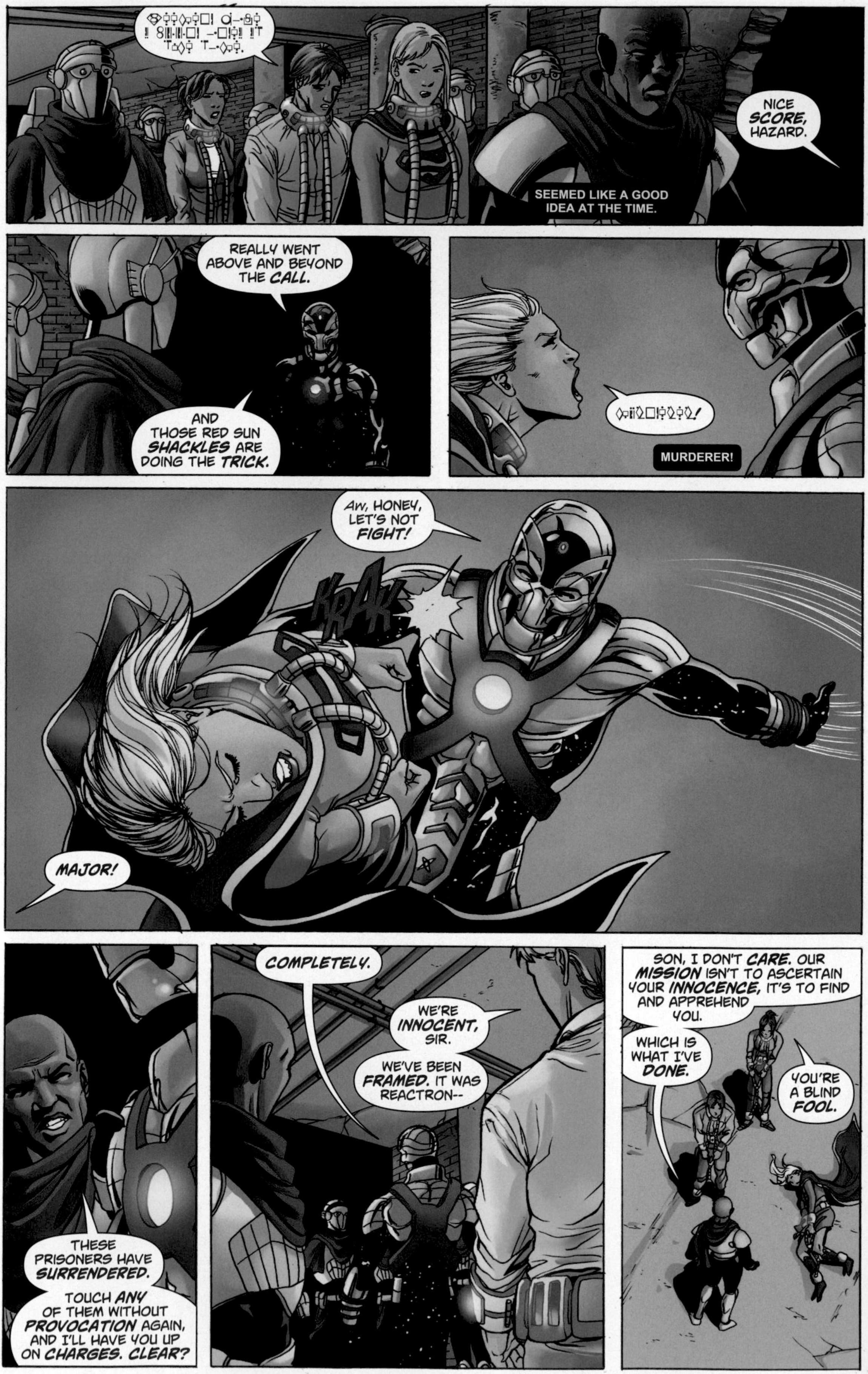
SEEMED LIKE A GOOD IDEA AT THE TIME.
NICE SCORE, HAZARD.
REALLY WENT ABOVE AND BEYOND THE CALL.
AND THOSE RED SUN SHACKLES ARE DOING THE TRICK.
MURDERER!
AW, HONEY, LET'S NOT FIGHT!
KRAK
MAJOR!
THESE PRISONERS HAVE SURRENDERED.
TOUCH ANY OF THEM WITHOUT PROVOCATION AGAIN, AND I'LL HAVE YOU UP ON CHARGES. CLEAR?
COMPLETELY.
WE'RE INNOCENT, SIR.
WE'VE BEEN FRAMED. IT WAS REACTRON--
SON, I DON'T CARE. OUR MISSION ISN'T TO ASCERTAIN YOUR INNOCENCE, IT'S TO FIND AND APPREHEND YOU.
WHICH IS WHAT I'VE DONE.
YOU'RE A BLIND FOOL.

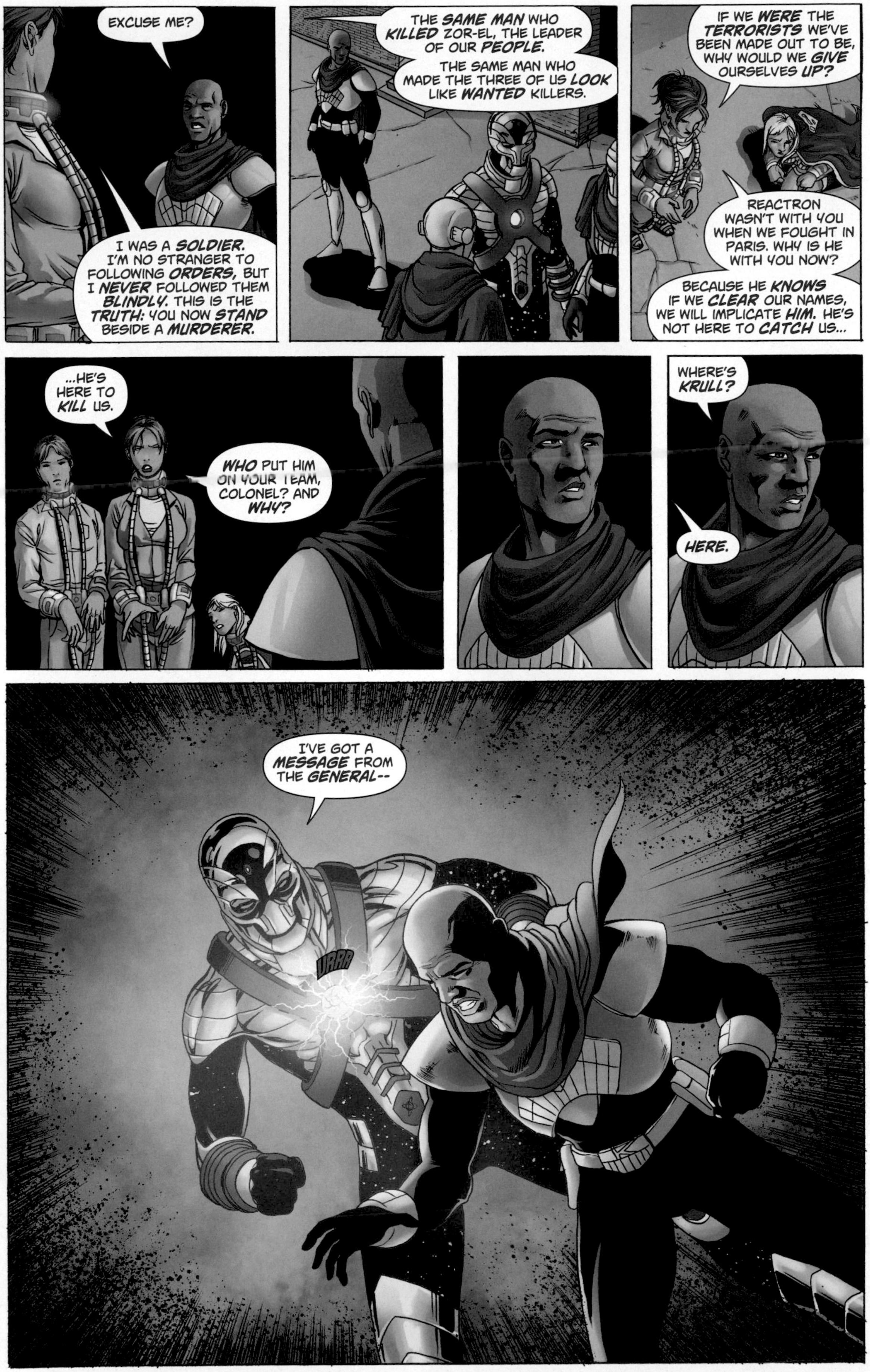
EXCUSE ME?
I WAS A SOLDIER. I'M NO STRANGER TO FOLLOWING ORDERS, BUT I NEVER FOLLOWED THEM BLINDLY. THIS IS THE TRUTH: YOU NOW STAND BESIDE A MURDERER.
THE SAME MAN WHO KILLED ZOR-EL, THE LEADER OF OUR PEOPLE.
THE SAME MAN WHO MADE THE THREE OF US LOOK LIKE WANTED KILLERS.
IF WE WERE THE TERRORISTS WE'VE BEEN MADE OUT TO BE, WHY WOULD WE GIVE OURSELVES UP?
REACTRON WASN'T WITH YOU WHEN WE FOUGHT IN PARIS. WHY IS HE WITH YOU NOW?
BECAUSE HE KNOWS IF WE CLEAR OUR NAMES, WE WILL IMPLICATE HIM. HE'S NOT HERE TO CATCH US...
...HE'S HERE TO KILL US.
WHO PUT HIM ON YOUR TEAM, COLONEL? AND WHY?
WHERE'S KRULL?
HERE.
I'VE GOT A MESSAGE FROM THE GENERAL--
URRR

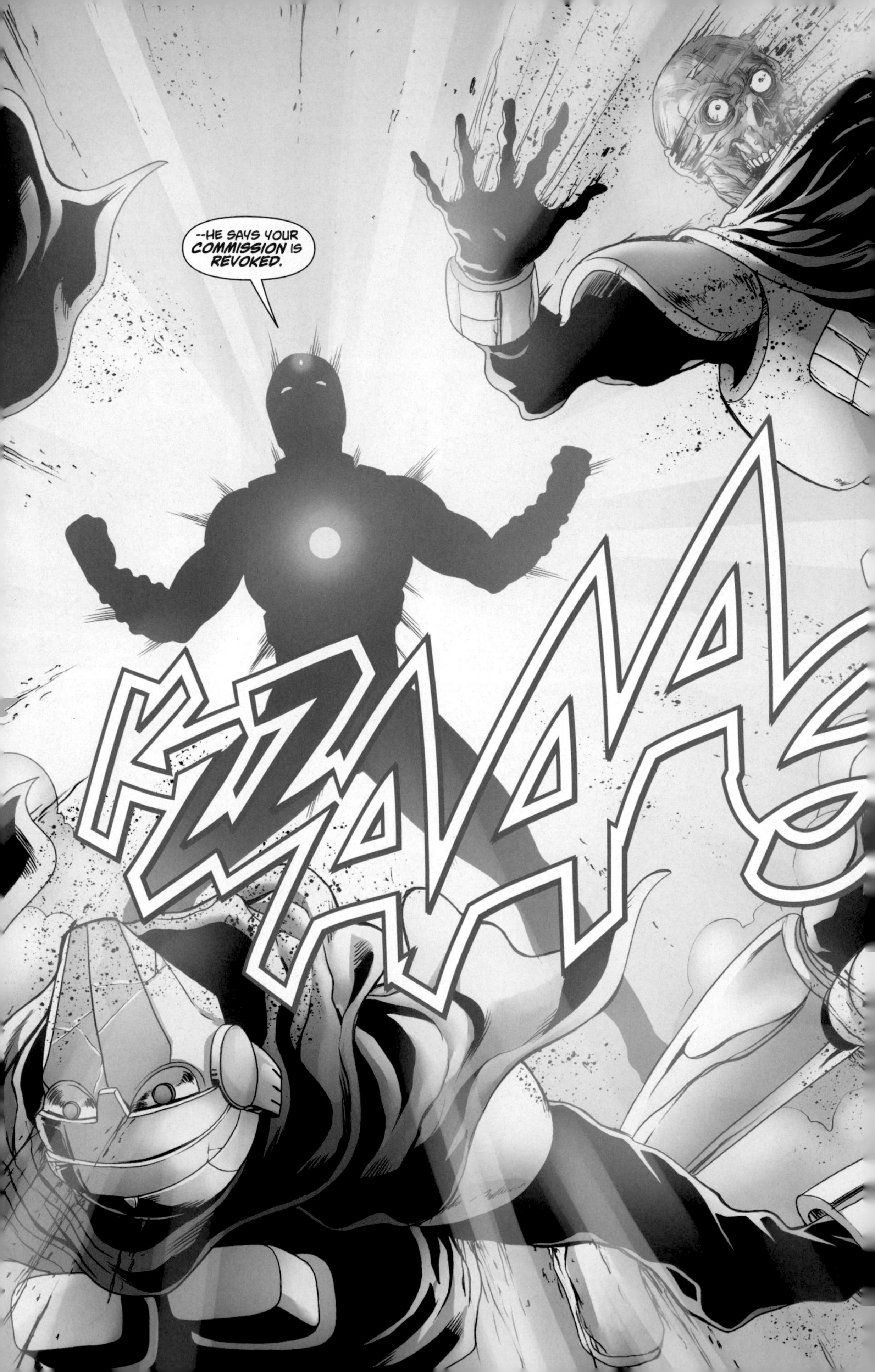
--HE SAYS YOUR COMMISSION IS REVOKED.
KZAAAK

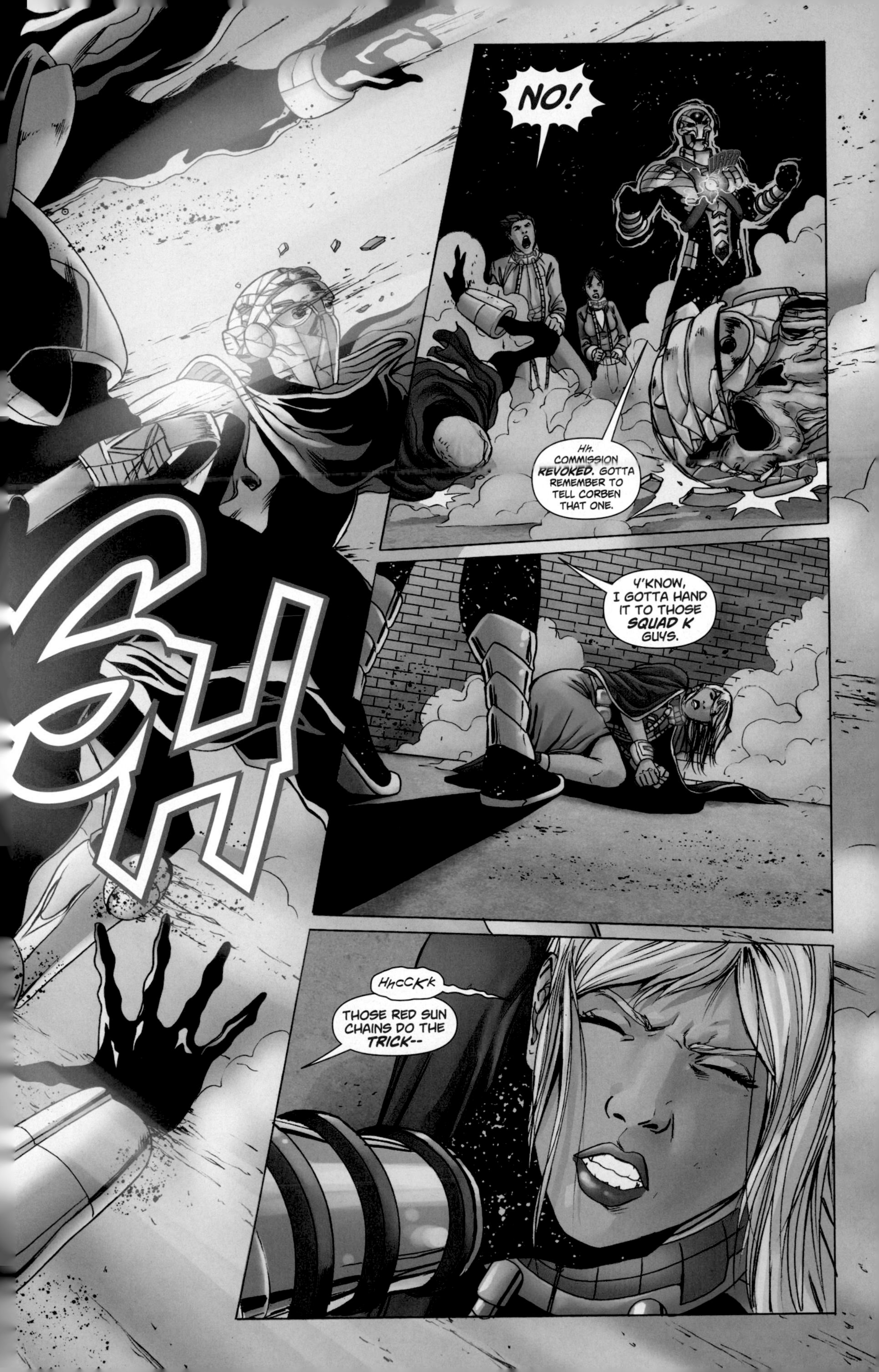
SHH
NO!
Hh. COMMISSION REVOKED. GOTTA REMEMBER TO TELL CORBEN THAT ONE.
Y'KNOW, I GOTTA HAND IT TO THOSE SQUAD K GUYS.
HnCCKk
THOSE RED SUN CHAINS DO THE TRICK--

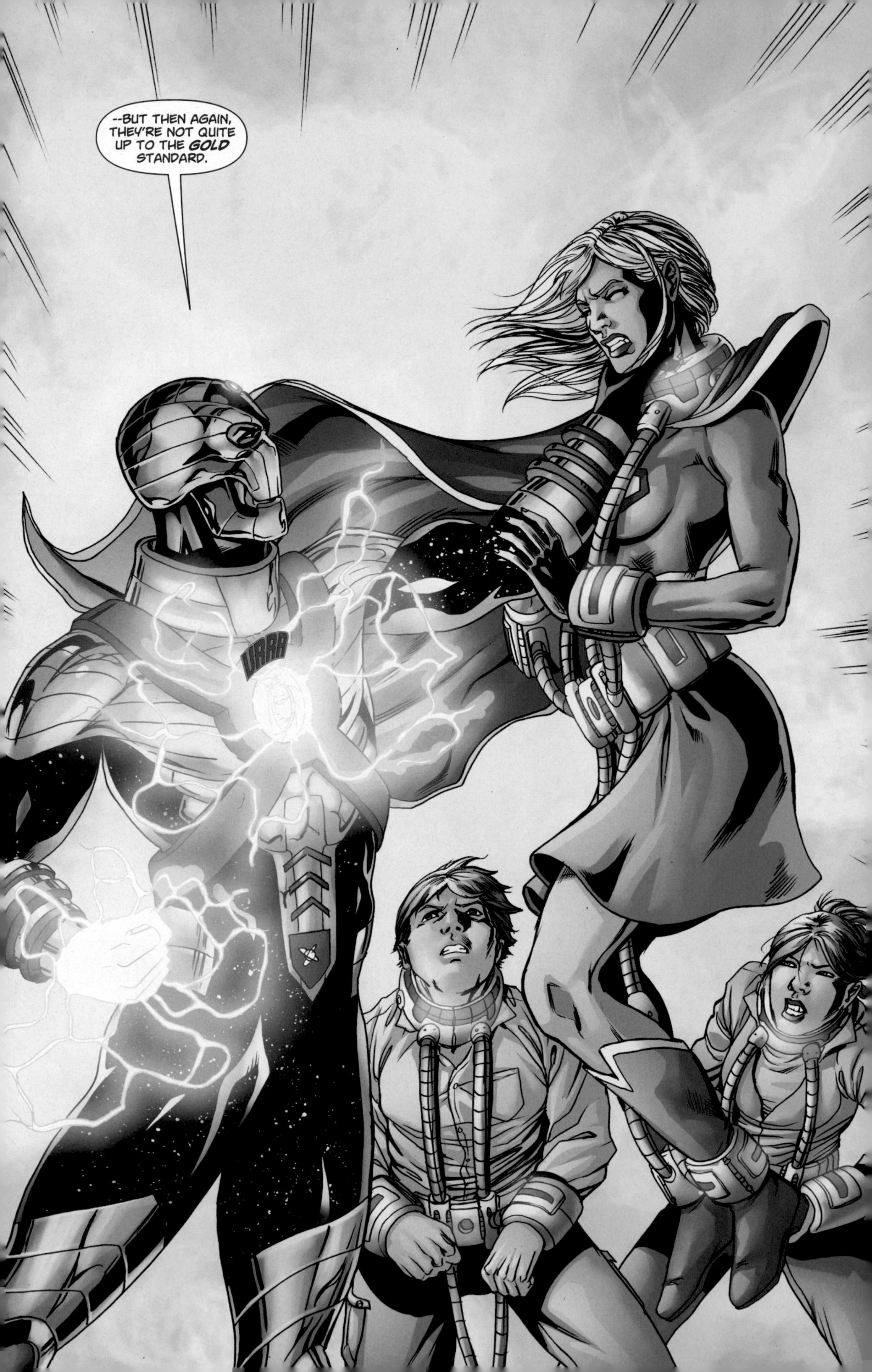
--BUT THEN AGAIN, THEY'RE NOT QUITE UP TO THE GOLD STANDARD.
URRR

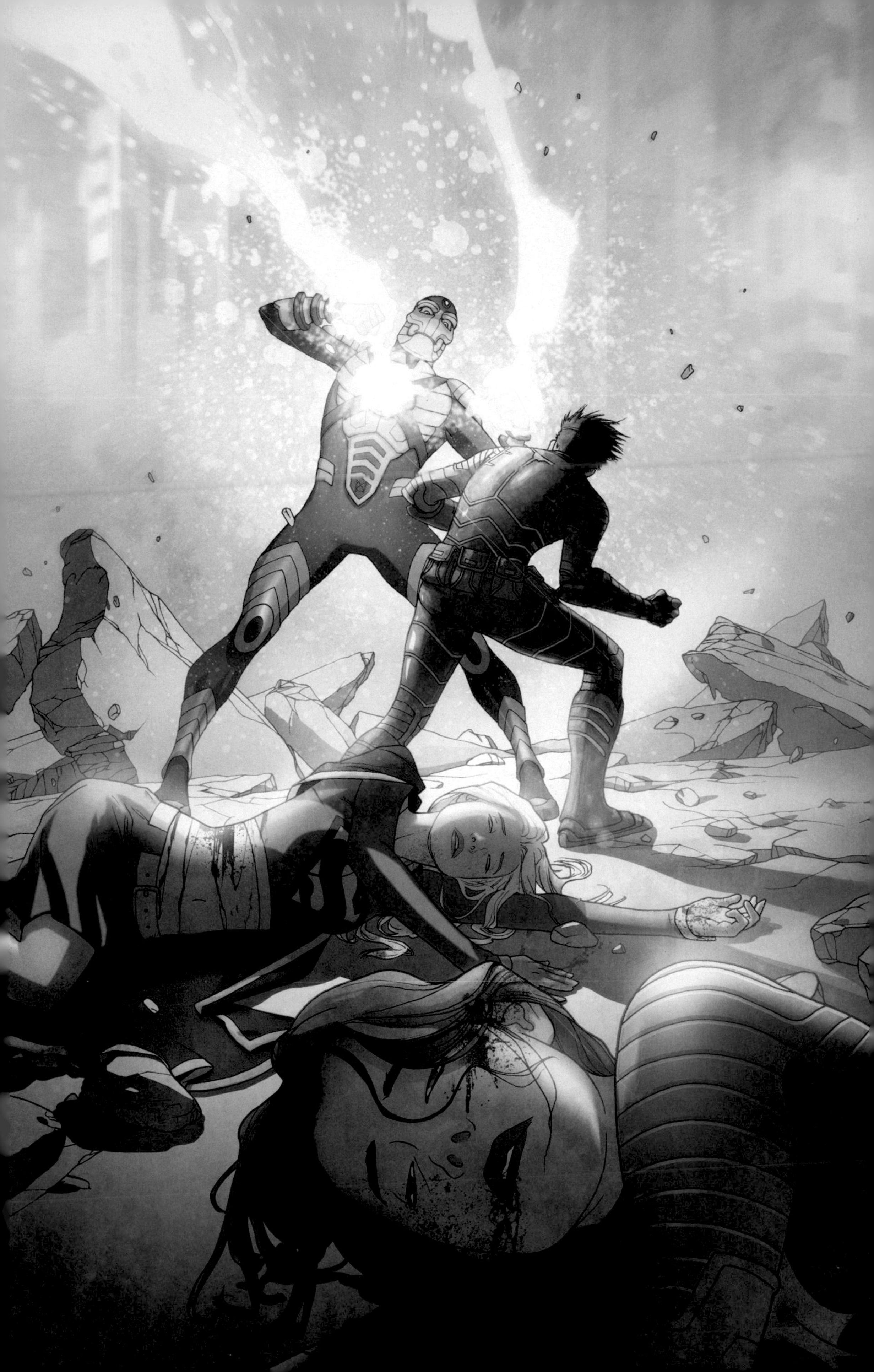

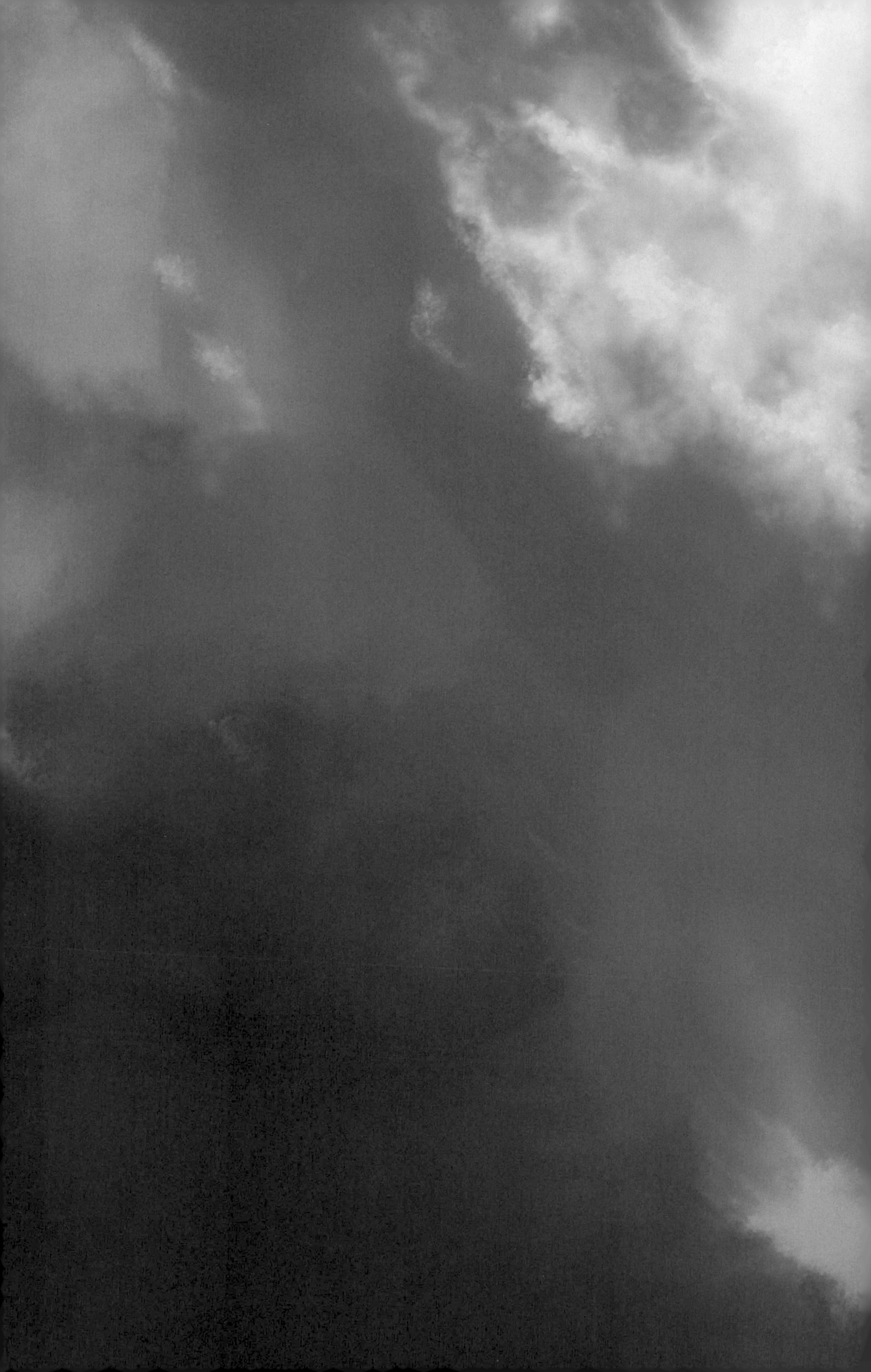

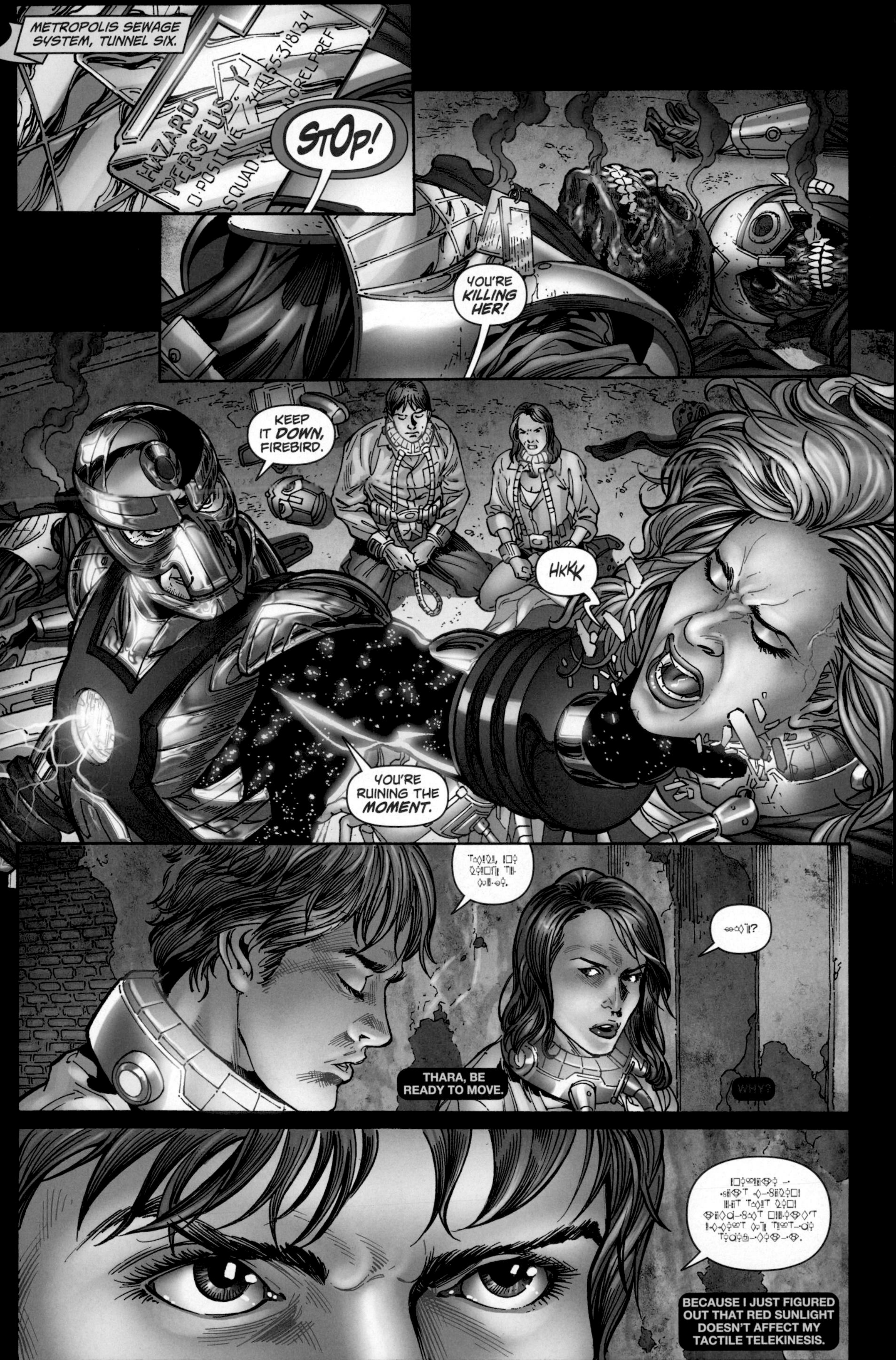
METROPOLIS SEWAGE SYSTEM, TUNNEL SIX.
HAZARD
PERSEUS
STOP!
YOU'RE KILLING HER!
KEEP IT DOWN, FIREBIRD.
HKKK
YOU'RE RUINING THE MOMENT.
THARA, BE READY TO MOVE.
WHY?
BECAUSE I JUST FIGURED OUT THAT RED SUNLIGHT DOESN'T AFFECT MY TACTILE TELEKINESIS.

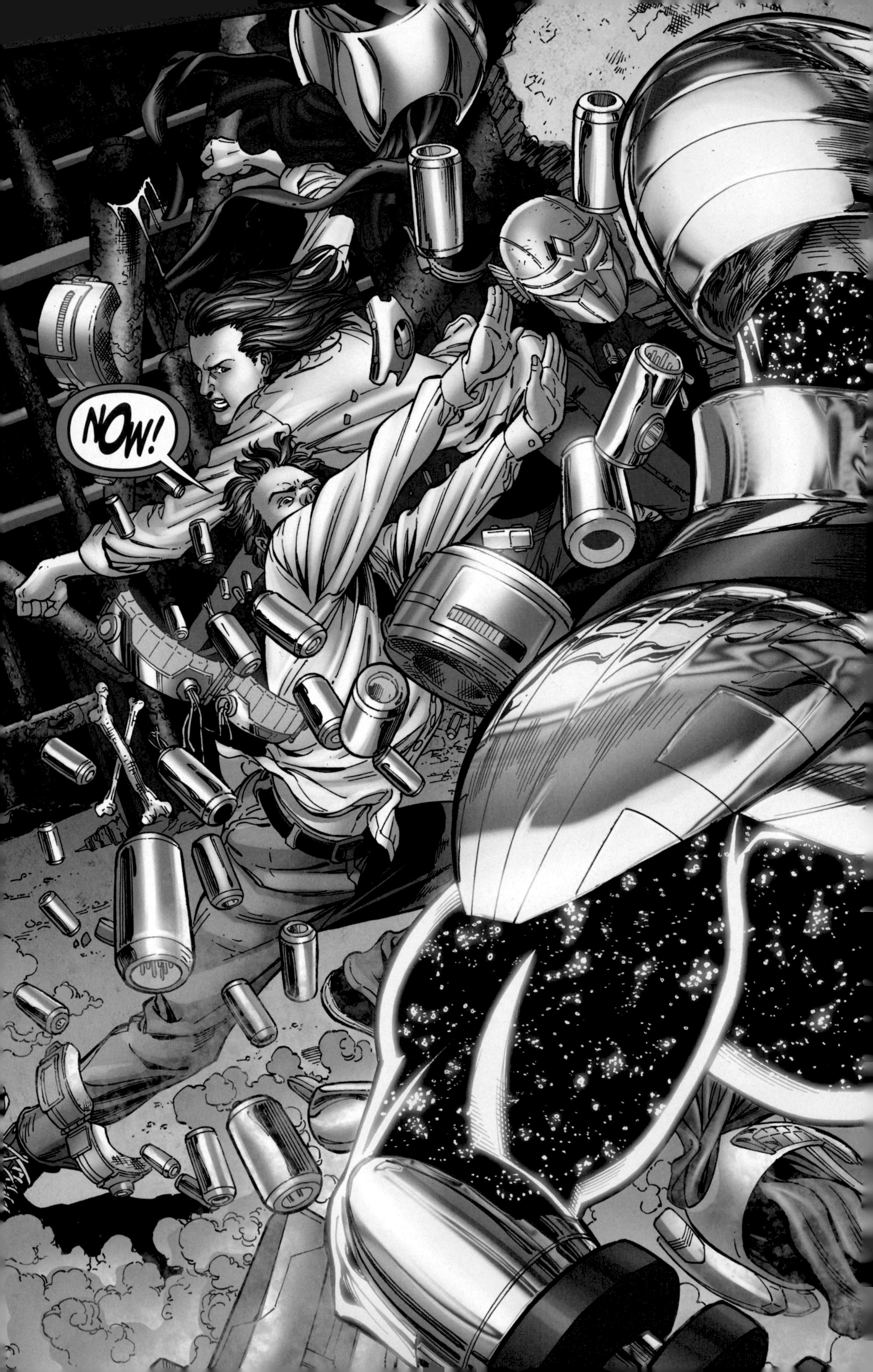
NOW!

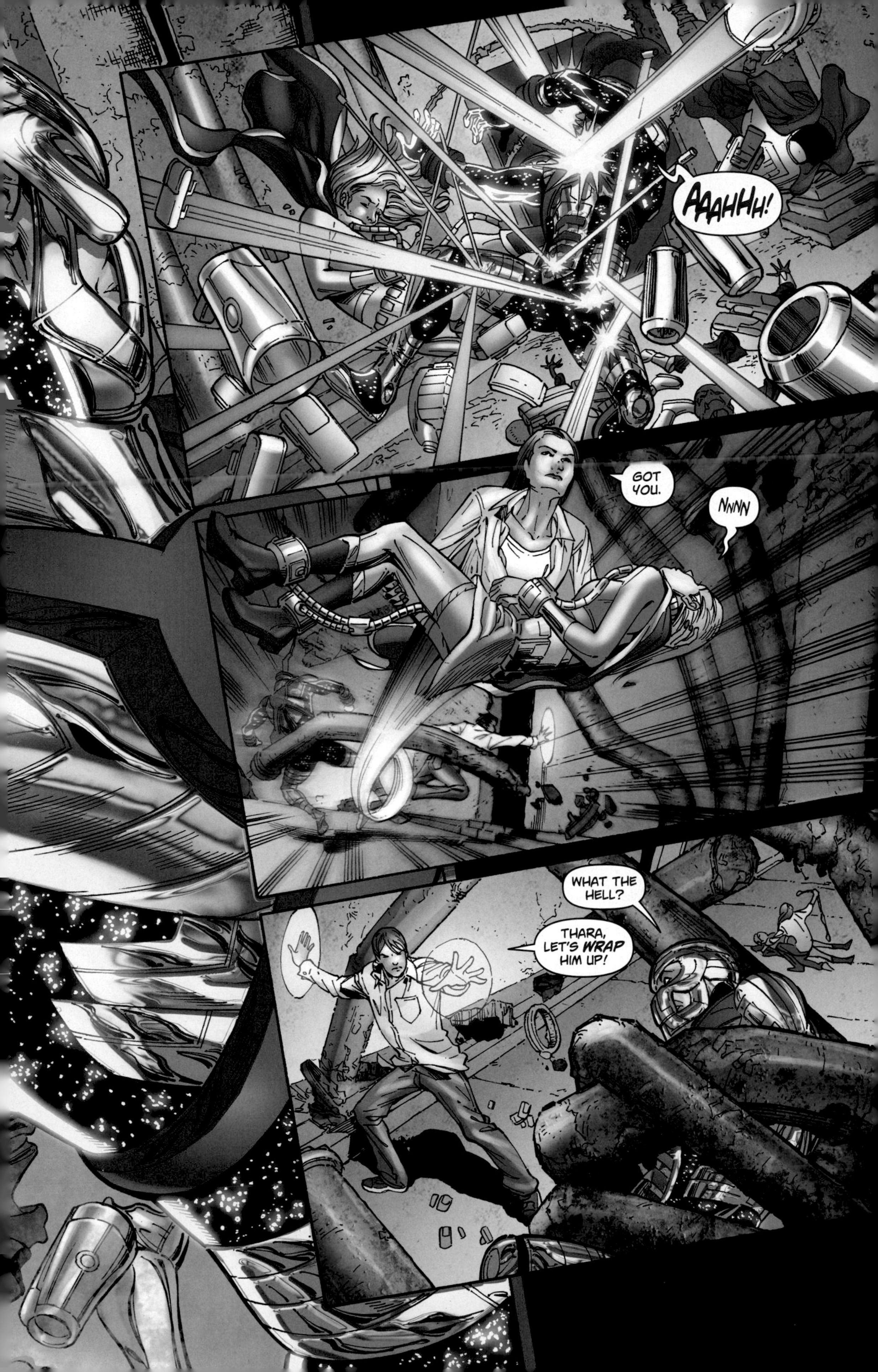
AAAHHH!
GOT YOU.
NNNN
WHAT THE HELL?
THARA, LET'S WRAP HIM UP!

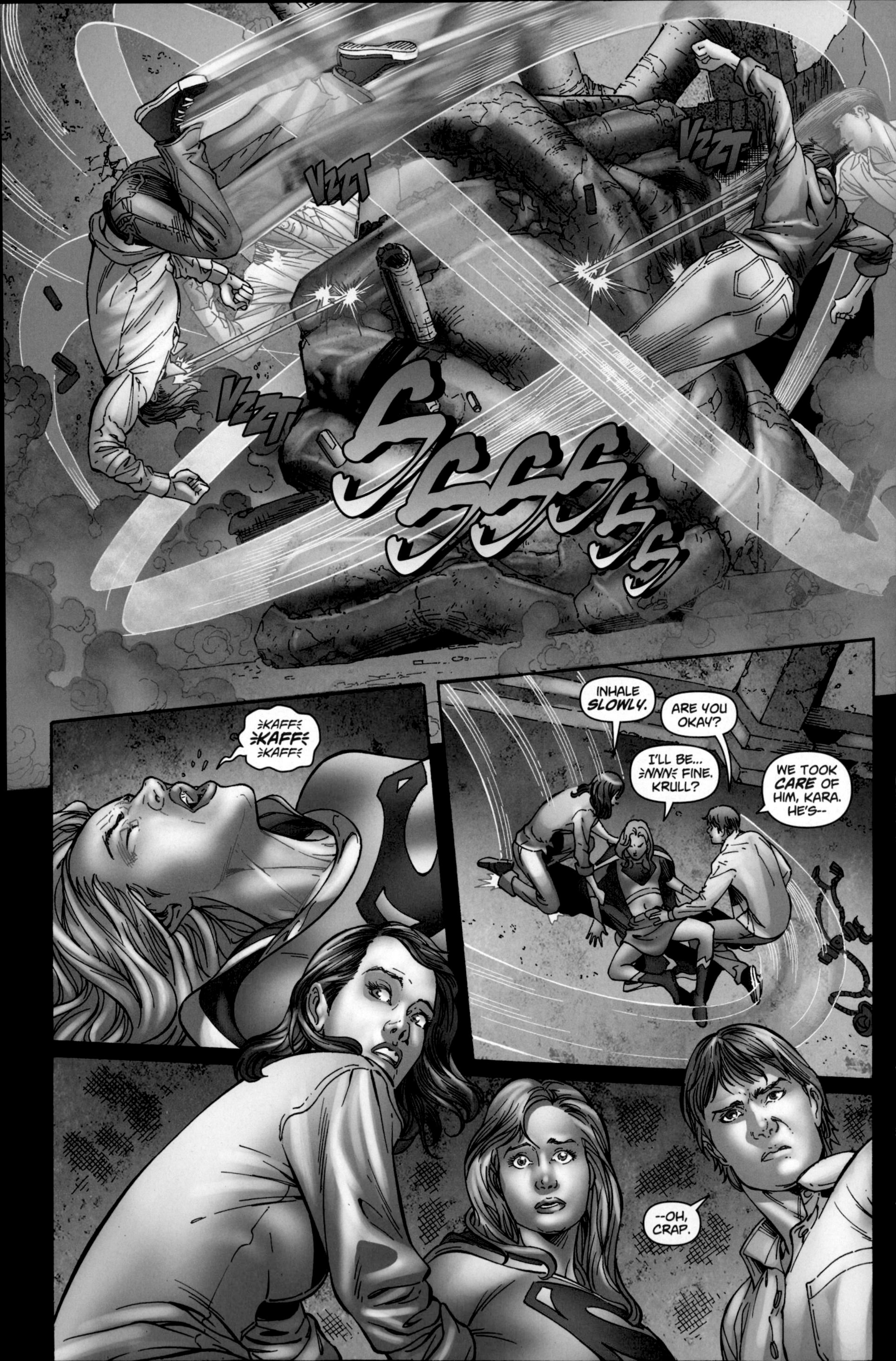
VZZT
VZZT
VZZT
SSSSSS
KAFF KAFF KAFF
INHALE SLOWLY.
ARE YOU OKAY?
I'LL BE... NNN FINE. KRULL?
WE TOOK CARE OF HIM, KARA. HE'S--
--OH, CRAP.

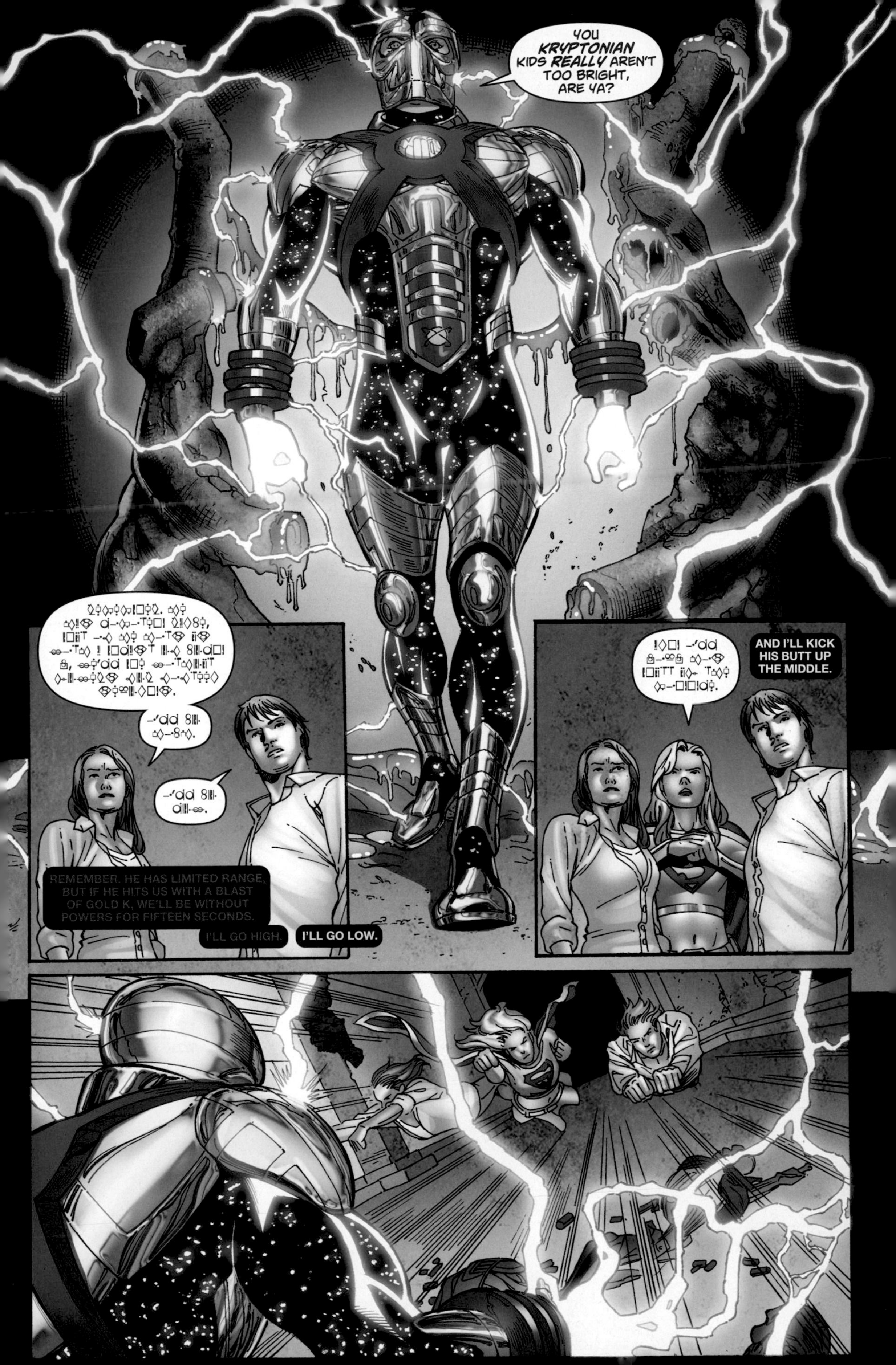
YOU KRYPTONIAN KIDS REALLY AREN'T TOO BRIGHT, ARE YA?
REMEMBER. HE HAS LIMITED RANGE, BUT IF HE HITS US WITH A BLAST OF GOLD K, WE'LL BE WITHOUT POWERS FOR FIFTEEN SECONDS.
I'LL GO HIGH.
I'LL GO LOW.
AND I'LL KICK HIS BUTT UP THE MIDDLE.

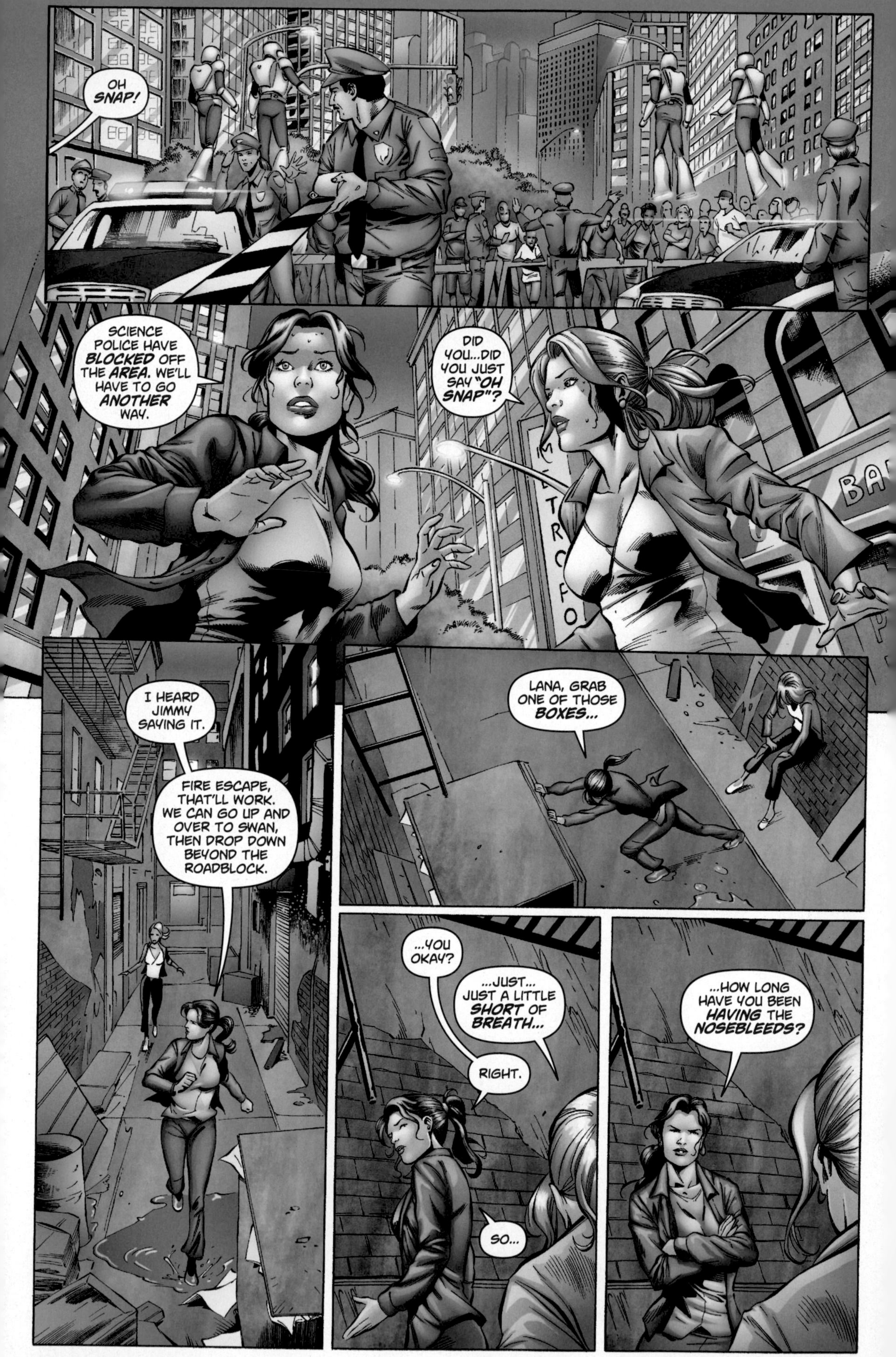
OH SNAP!
SCIENCE POLICE HAVE BLOCKED OFF THE AREA. WE'LL HAVE TO GO ANOTHER WAY.
DID YOU...DID YOU JUST SAY "OH SNAP"?
I HEARD JIMMY SAYING IT.
FIRE ESCAPE, THAT'LL WORK. WE CAN GO UP AND OVER TO SWAN, THEN DROP DOWN BEYOND THE ROADBLOCK.
LANA, GRAB ONE OF THOSE BOXES...
...YOU OKAY?
...JUST... JUST A LITTLE SHORT OF BREATH...
RIGHT.
SO...
...HOW LONG HAVE YOU BEEN HAVING THE NOSEBLEEDS?

OH, GOD--

YEAH, I *THOUGHT* I SAW *DRIED BLOOD* BACK AT THE *MUSEUM.*

PROBLEM WITH *NO* RUNNING WATER, YOU'VE GOT NO WAY TO *CLEAN UP.*

I'VE BEEN USING THOSE WET TOWLETTES, YOU KNOW.

BEEN USING THEM A *LOT?*

MORE THAN I'D *LIKE.*

I'VE BEEN GETTING *HEADACHES,* TOO.

HAVING A *HARD* TIME KEEPING *FOOD* DOWN.

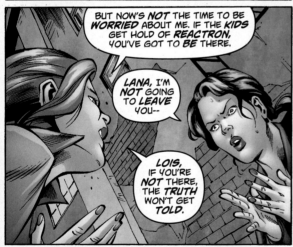

BUT NOW'S *NOT* THE TIME TO BE *WORRIED* ABOUT ME. IF THE *KIDS* GET HOLD OF *REACTRON,* YOU'VE GOT TO *BE* THERE.

LANA, I'M *NOT* GOING TO *LEAVE* YOU--

LOIS, IF YOU'RE *NOT* THERE, THE *TRUTH* WON'T GET *TOLD.*

I'LL GO BACK TO MY PLACE, I'LL BE *FINE.*

YOU'RE *SURE?*

POSITIVE. *GO.*

I'LL BE FINE.

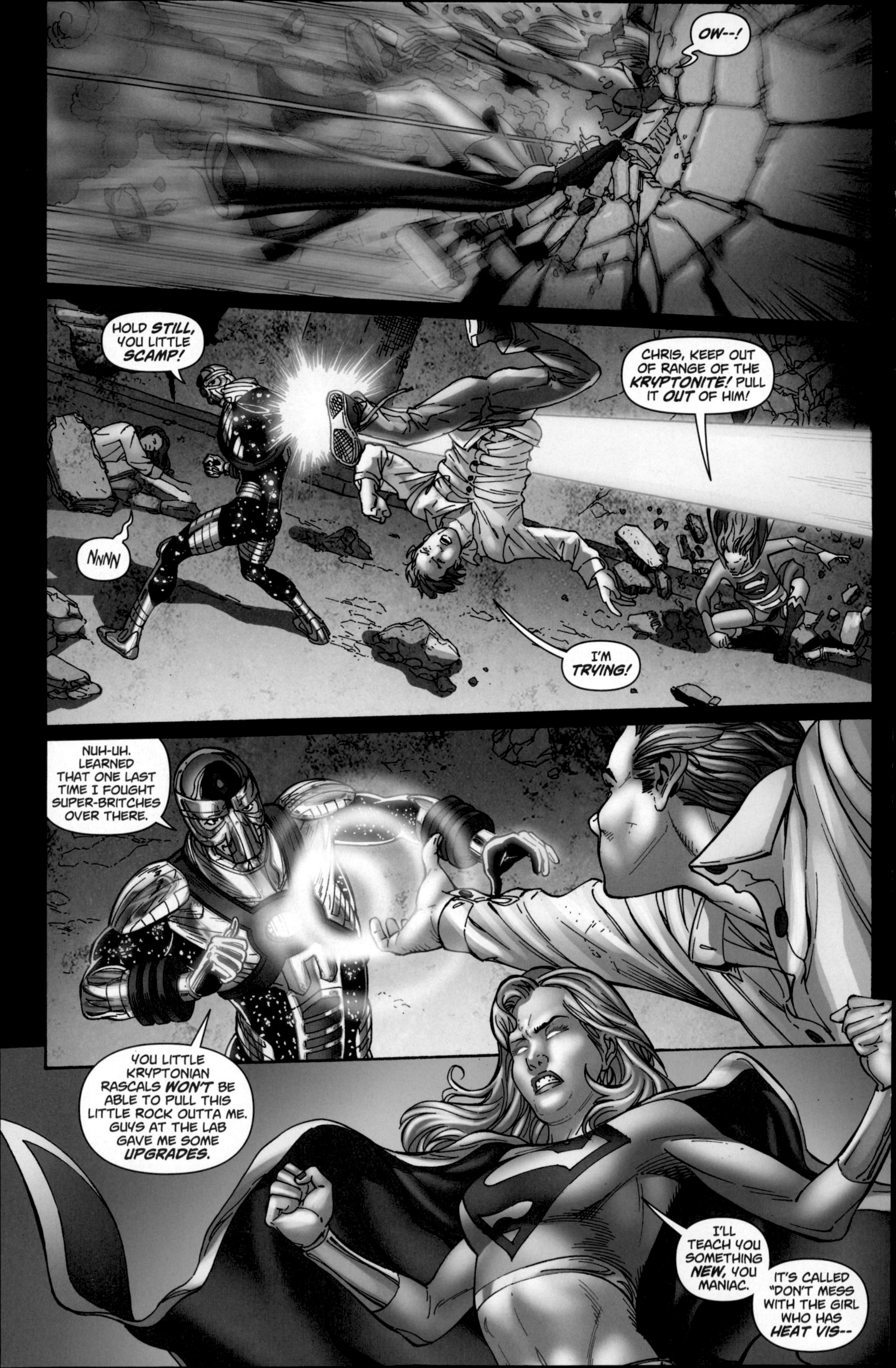
OW--!
HOLD STILL, YOU LITTLE SCAMP!
CHRIS, KEEP OUT OF RANGE OF THE KRYPTONITE! PULL IT OUT OF HIM!
NNNN
I'M TRYING!
NUH-UH. LEARNED THAT ONE LAST TIME I FOUGHT SUPER-BRITCHES OVER THERE.
YOU LITTLE KRYPTONIAN RASCALS WON'T BE ABLE TO PULL THIS LITTLE ROCK OUTTA ME. GUYS AT THE LAB GAVE ME SOME UPGRADES.
I'LL TEACH YOU SOMETHING NEW, YOU MANIAC.
IT'S CALLED "DON'T MESS WITH THE GIRL WHO HAS HEAT VIS--

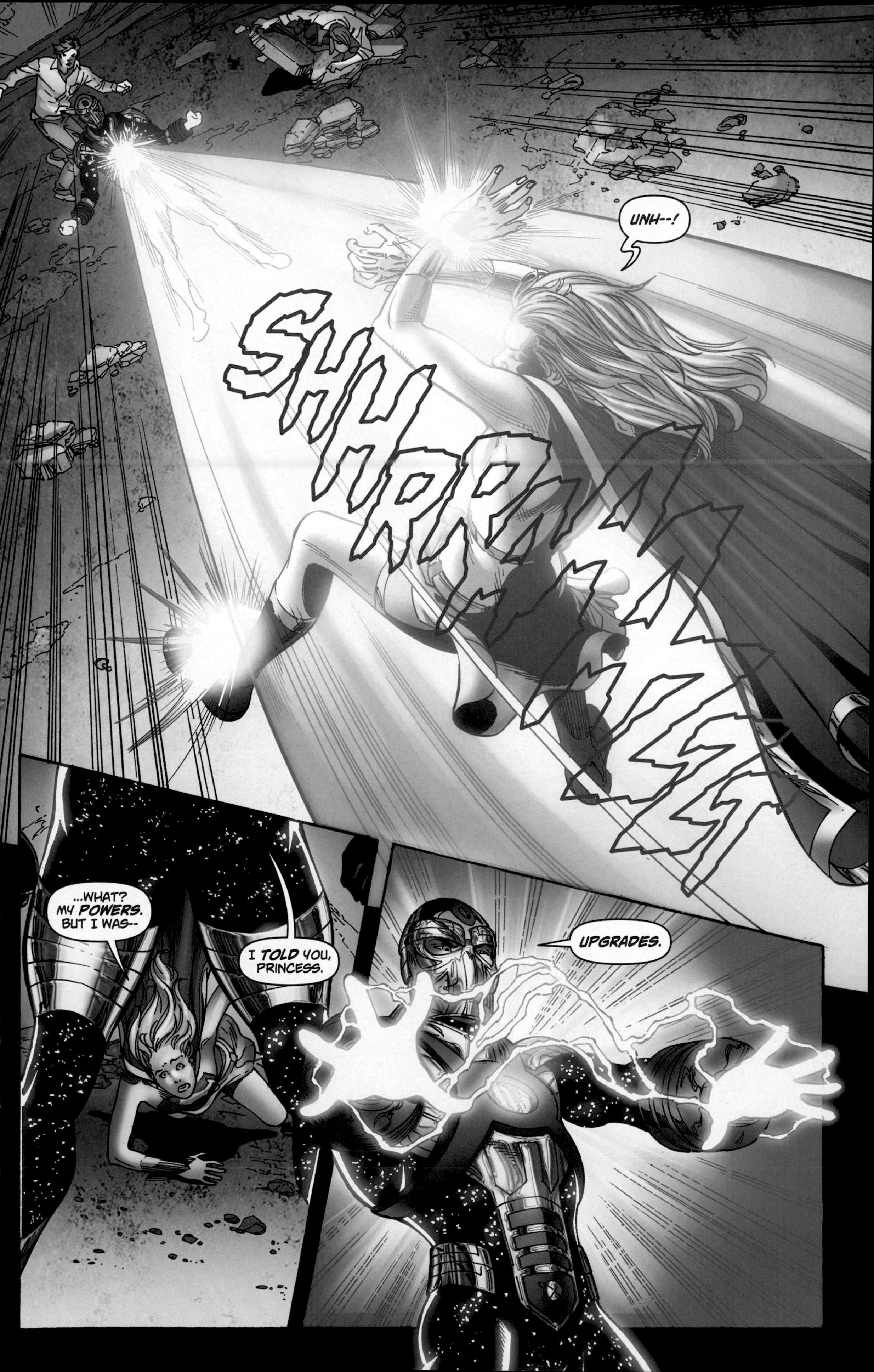
UNH--!
SHHRRAAAKKT
...WHAT? MY POWERS. BUT I WAS--
I TOLD YOU, PRINCESS.
UPGRADES.

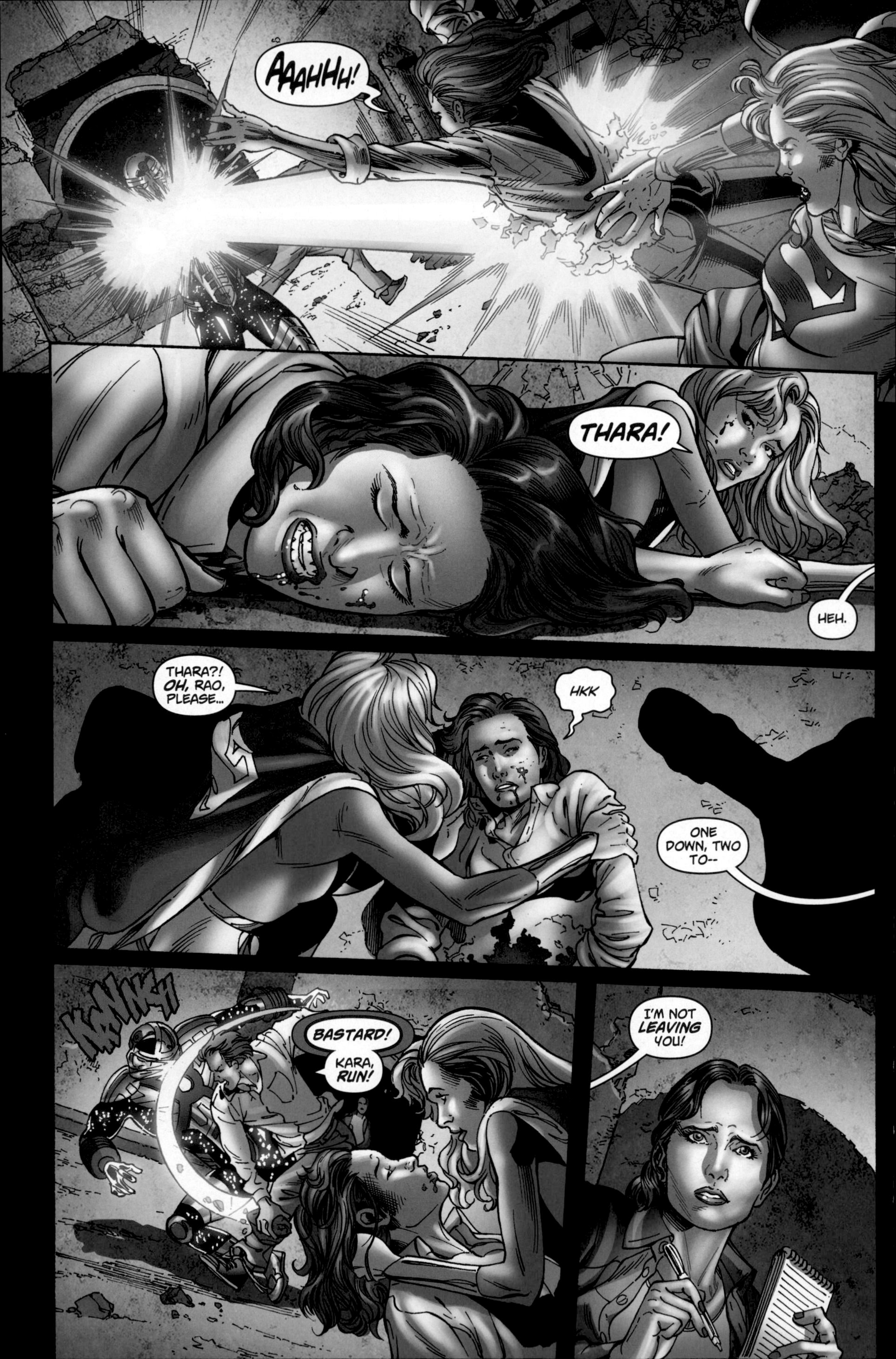
AAAHHH!
THARA!
HEH.
THARA?! OH, RAO, PLEASE...
HKK
ONE DOWN, TWO TO--
KNNNKH
BASTARD!
KARA, RUN!
I'M NOT LEAVING YOU!

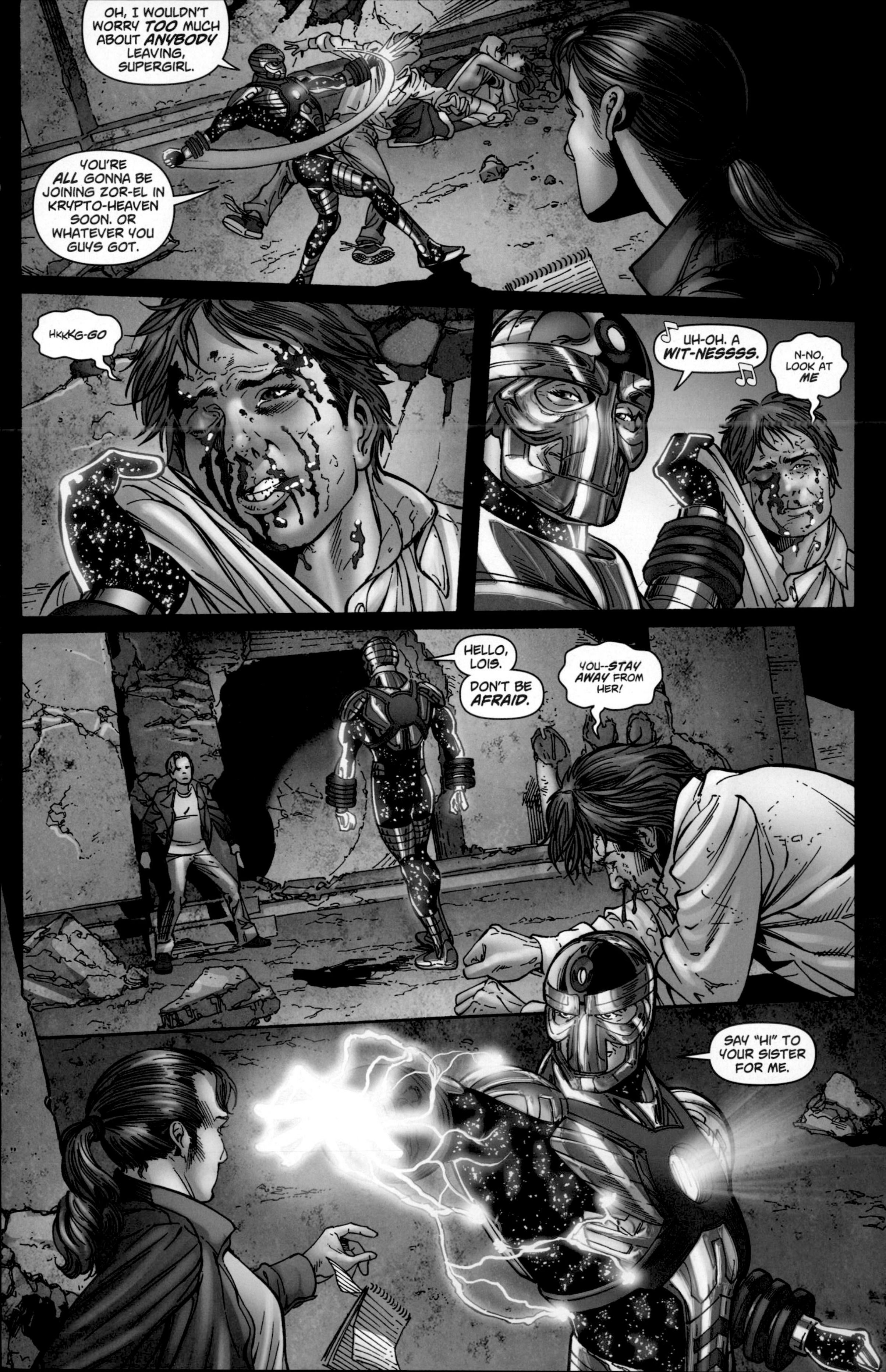
OH, I WOULDN'T WORRY TOO MUCH ABOUT ANYBODY LEAVING, SUPERGIRL.
YOU'RE ALL GONNA BE JOINING ZOR-EL IN KRYPTO-HEAVEN SOON. OR WHATEVER YOU GUYS GOT.
HKKKG-GO
UH-OH. A WIT-NESSSS.
N-NO, LOOK AT ME
HELLO, LOIS.
DON'T BE AFRAID.
YOU--STAY AWAY FROM HER!
SAY "HI" TO YOUR SISTER FOR ME.

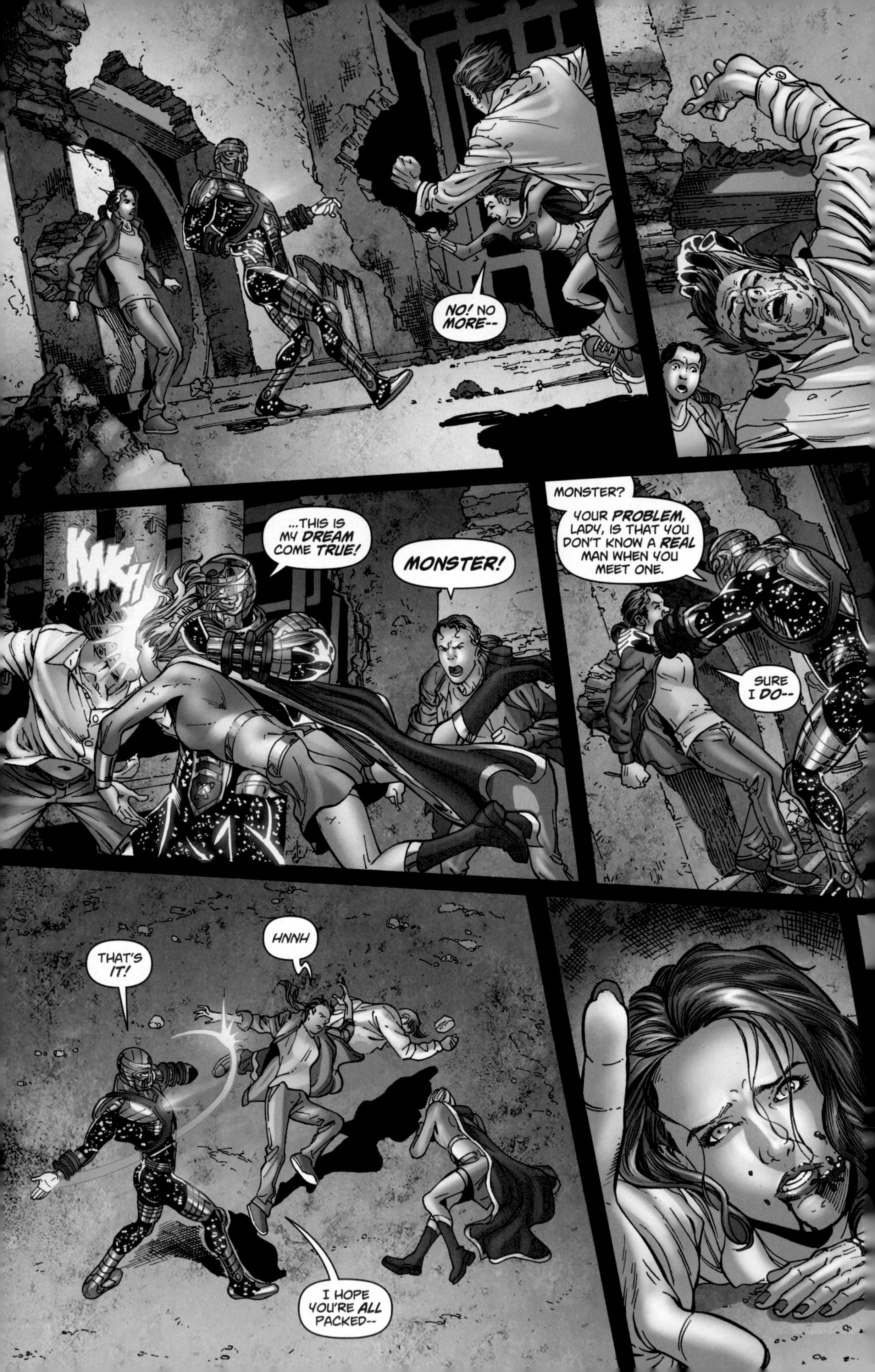
NO! NO MORE--
KNKH!!
...THIS IS MY DREAM COME TRUE!
MONSTER!
MONSTER?
YOUR PROBLEM, LADY, IS THAT YOU DON'T KNOW A REAL MAN WHEN YOU MEET ONE.
SURE I DO--
THAT'S IT!
HNNH
I HOPE YOU'RE ALL PACKED--

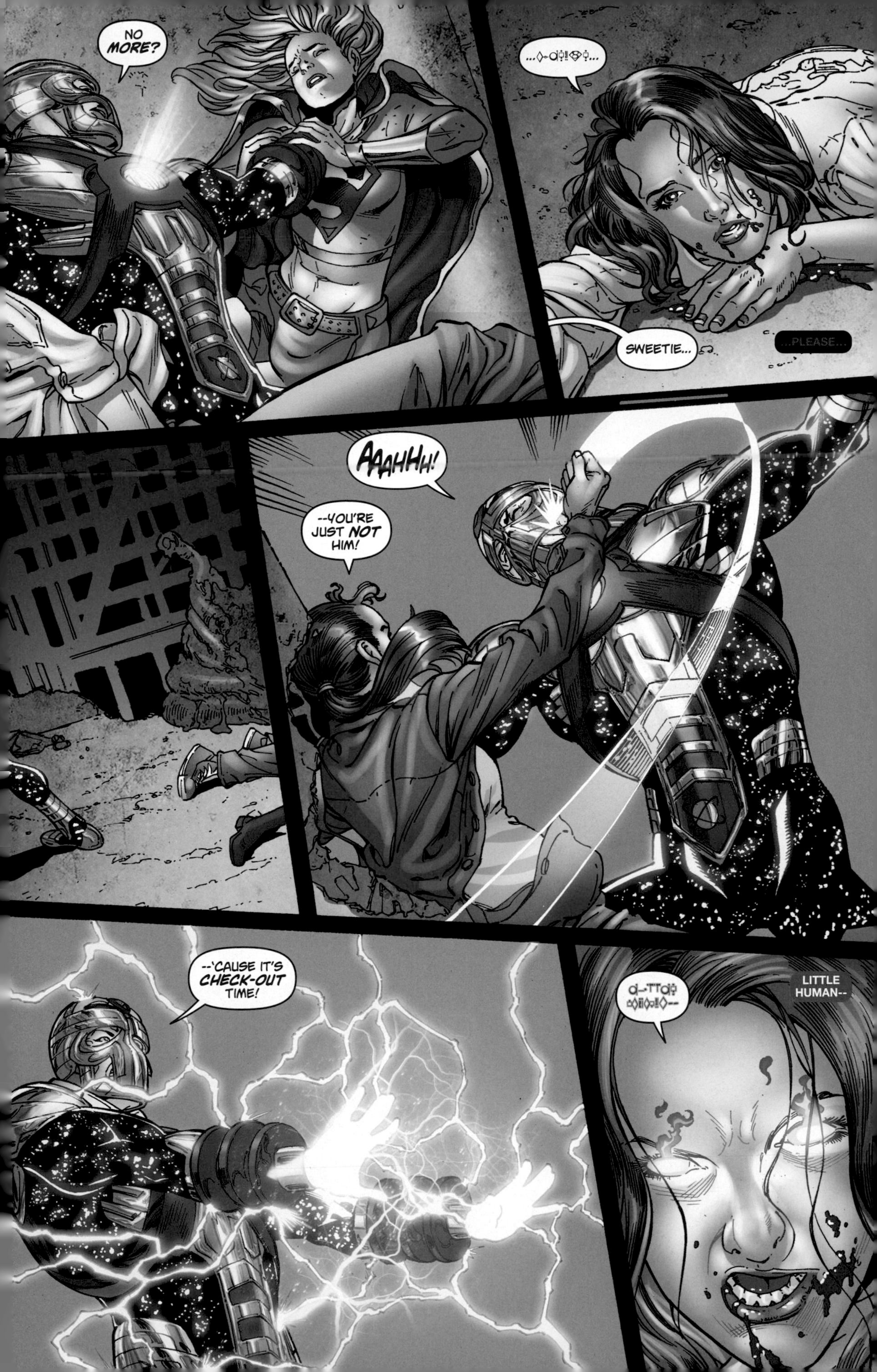
NO MORE?
SWEETIE...
...PLEASE...
AAAHHH!
--YOU'RE JUST NOT HIM!
--'CAUSE IT'S CHECK-OUT TIME!
LITTLE HUMAN--

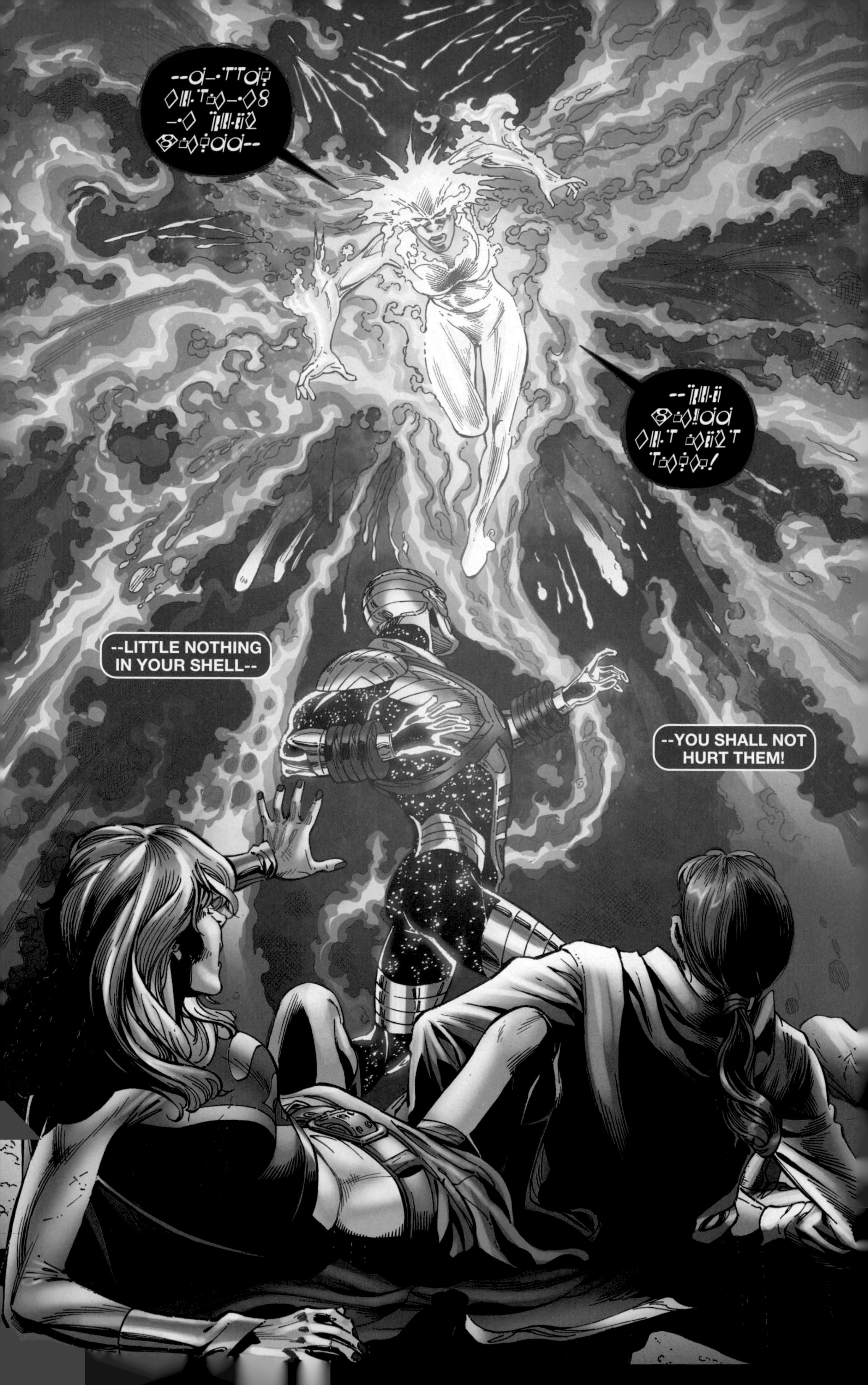
--LITTLE NOTHING IN YOUR SHELL--
--YOU SHALL NOT HURT THEM!

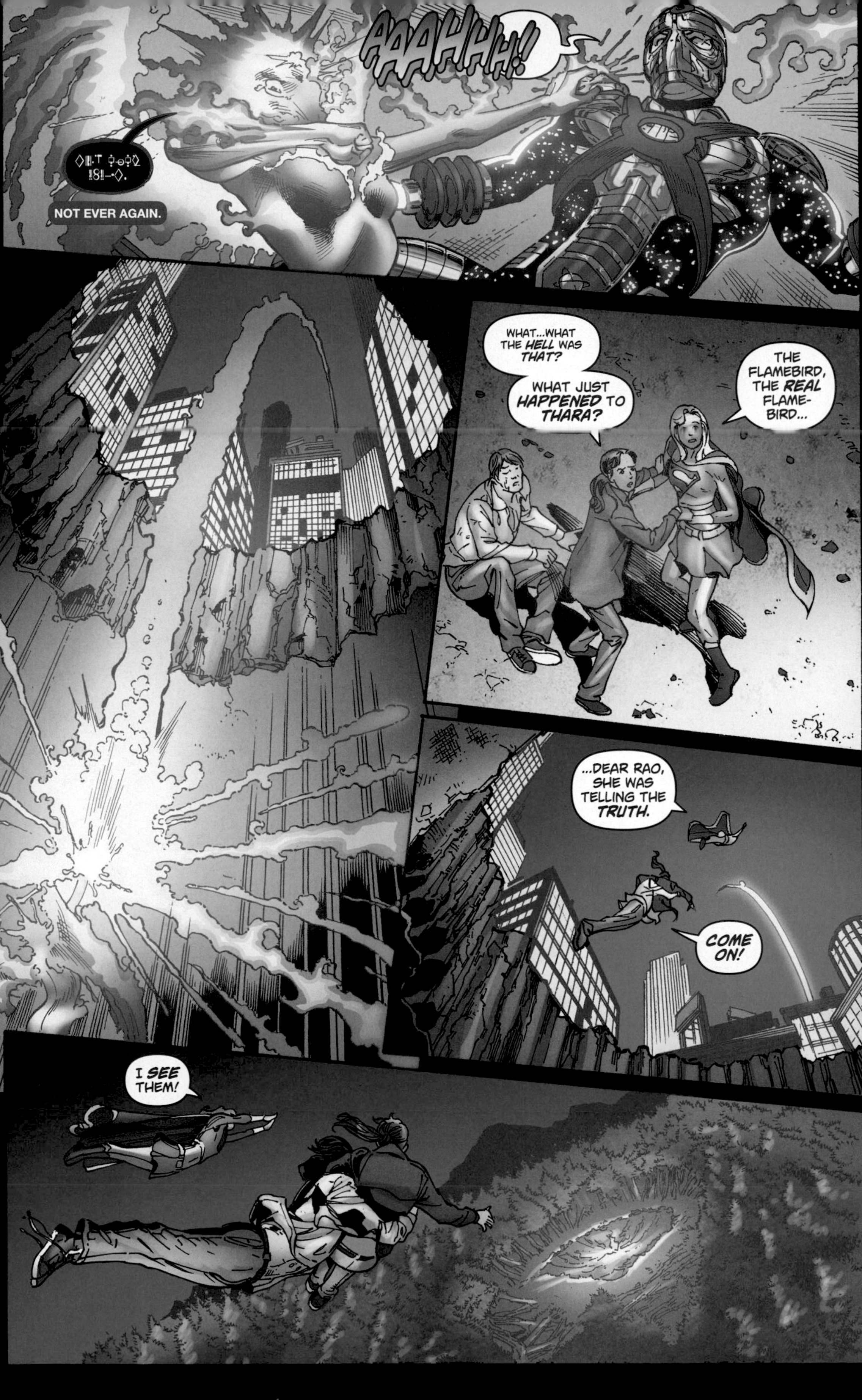
AAAHHH!
◊|||·T ♀-⊖-♀Ω !|8|!-·◊.
NOT EVER AGAIN.
WHAT...WHAT THE HELL WAS THAT?
WHAT JUST HAPPENED TO THARA?
THE FLAMEBIRD, THE REAL FLAME-BIRD...
...DEAR RAO, SHE WAS TELLING THE TRUTH.
COME ON!
I SEE THEM!

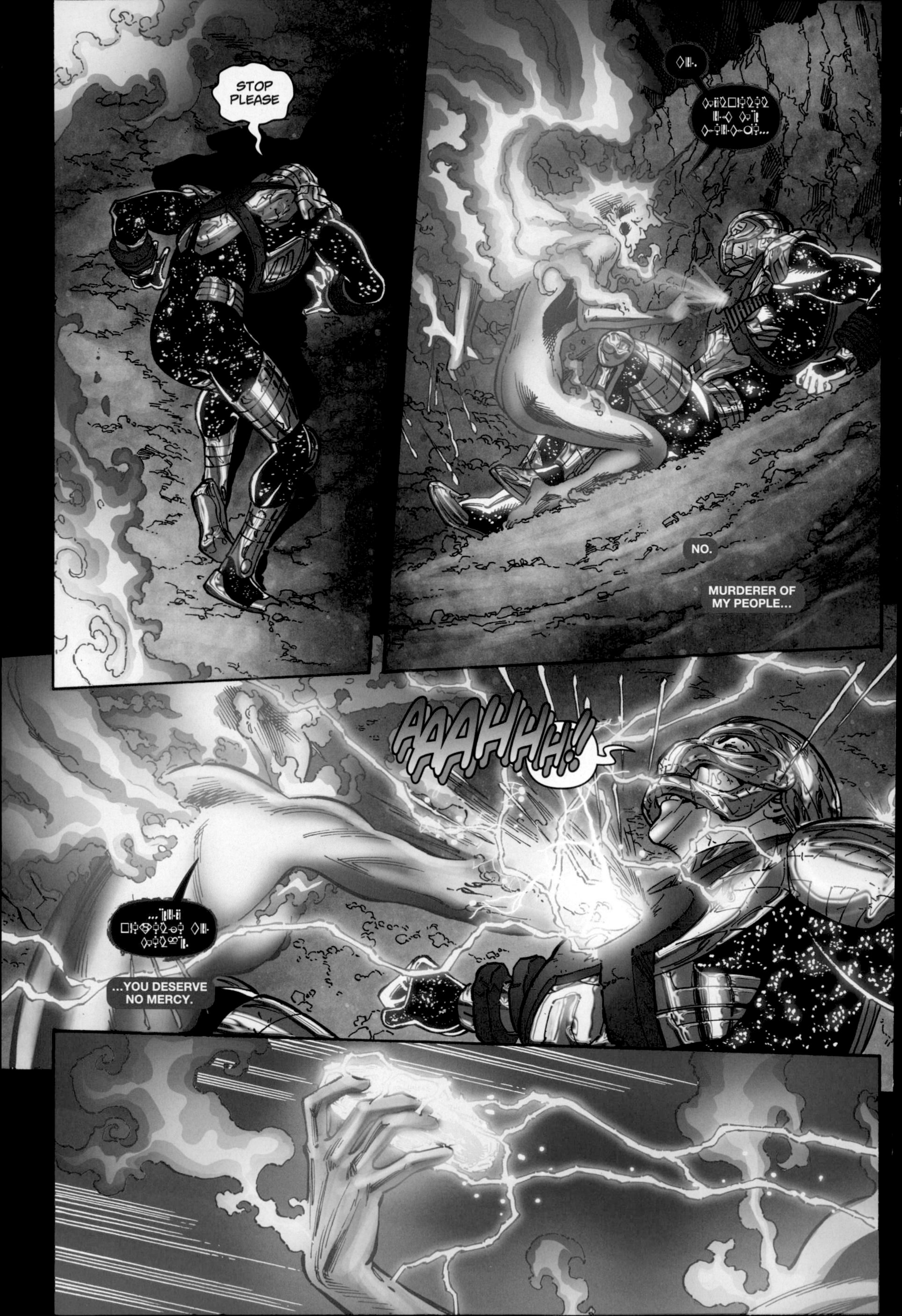
STOP PLEASE
NO.
MURDERER OF MY PEOPLE...
AAAHHHH!
...YOU DESERVE NO MERCY.

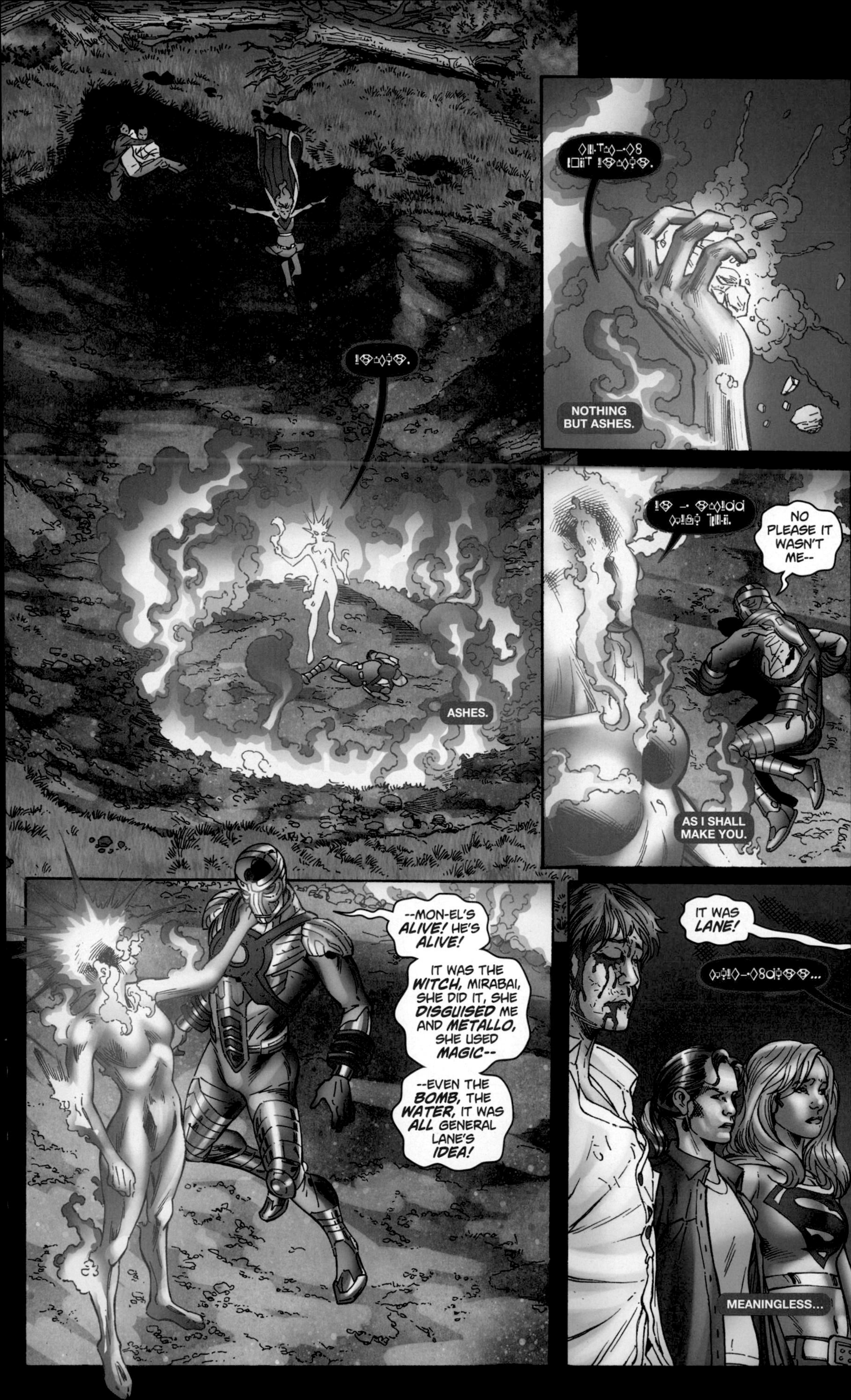
ASHES.
NOTHING BUT ASHES.
NO PLEASE IT WASN'T ME--
AS I SHALL MAKE YOU.
--MON-EL'S ALIVE! HE'S ALIVE!
IT WAS THE WITCH, MIRABAI, SHE DID IT, SHE DISGUISED ME AND METALLO, SHE USED MAGIC--
--EVEN THE BOMB, THE WATER, IT WAS ALL GENERAL LANE'S IDEA!
IT WAS LANE!
MEANINGLESS...

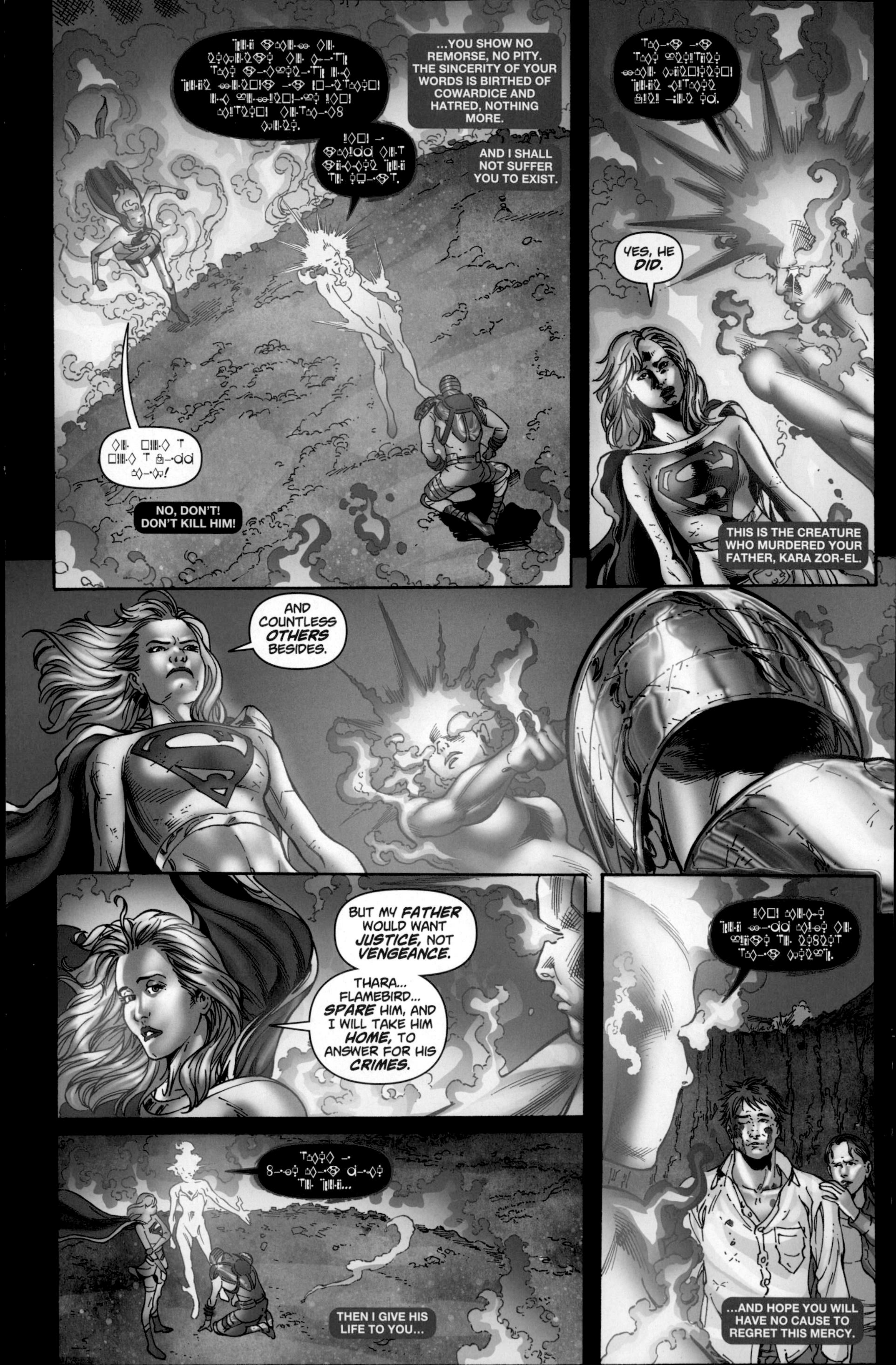
...YOU SHOW NO REMORSE, NO PITY. THE SINCERITY OF YOUR WORDS IS BIRTHED OF COWARDICE AND HATRED, NOTHING MORE.
AND I SHALL NOT SUFFER YOU TO EXIST.
NO, DON'T! DON'T KILL HIM!
THIS IS THE CREATURE WHO MURDERED YOUR FATHER, KARA ZOR-EL.
YES, HE DID.
AND COUNTLESS OTHERS BESIDES.
BUT MY FATHER WOULD WANT JUSTICE, NOT VENGEANCE.
THARA... FLAMEBIRD... SPARE HIM, AND I WILL TAKE HIM HOME, TO ANSWER FOR HIS CRIMES.
THEN I GIVE HIS LIFE TO YOU...
...AND HOPE YOU WILL HAVE NO CAUSE TO REGRET THIS MERCY.

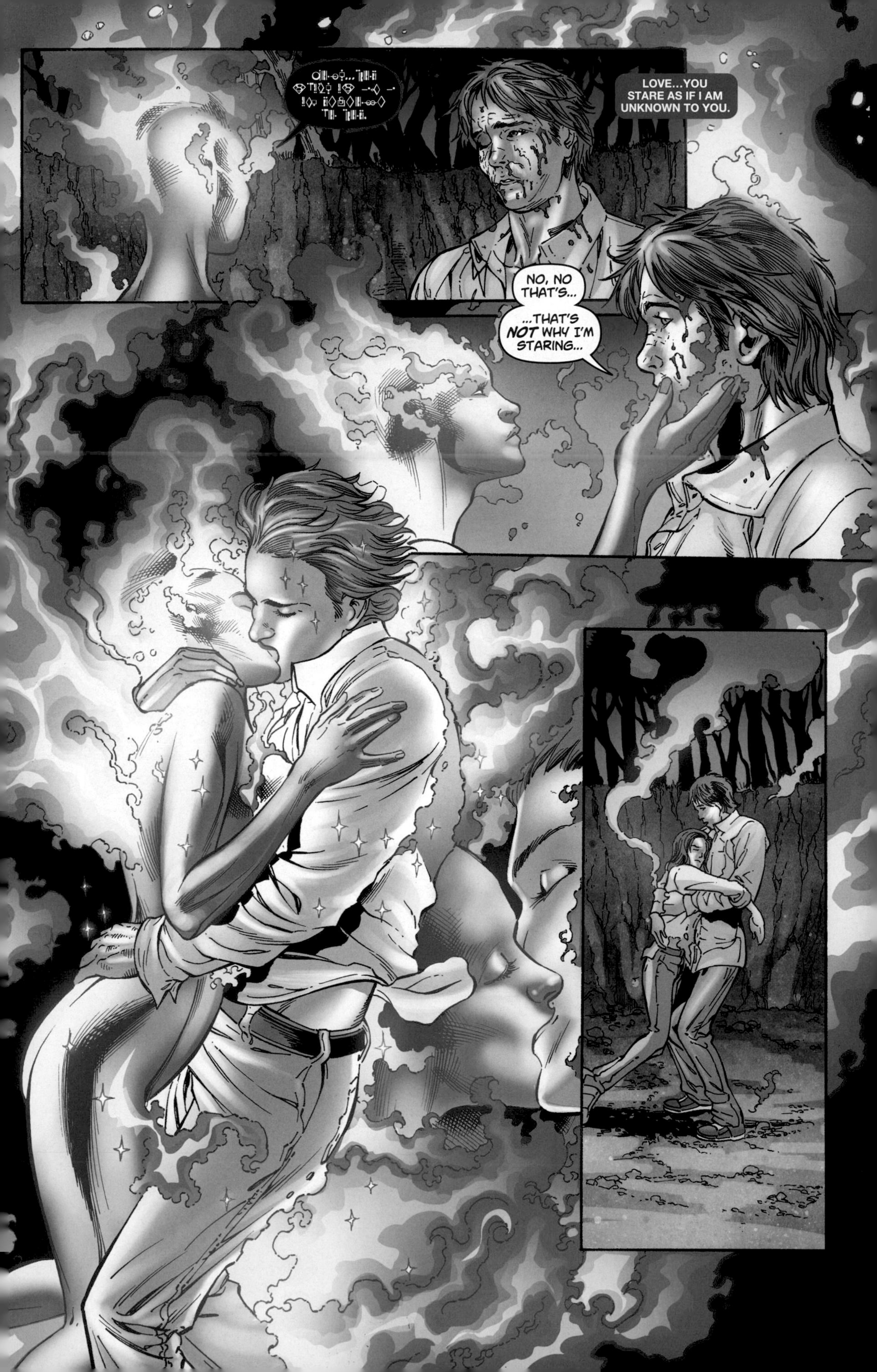
LOVE…YOU STARE AS IF I AM UNKNOWN TO YOU.
NO, NO THAT'S…
…THAT'S **NOT** WHY I'M STARING…

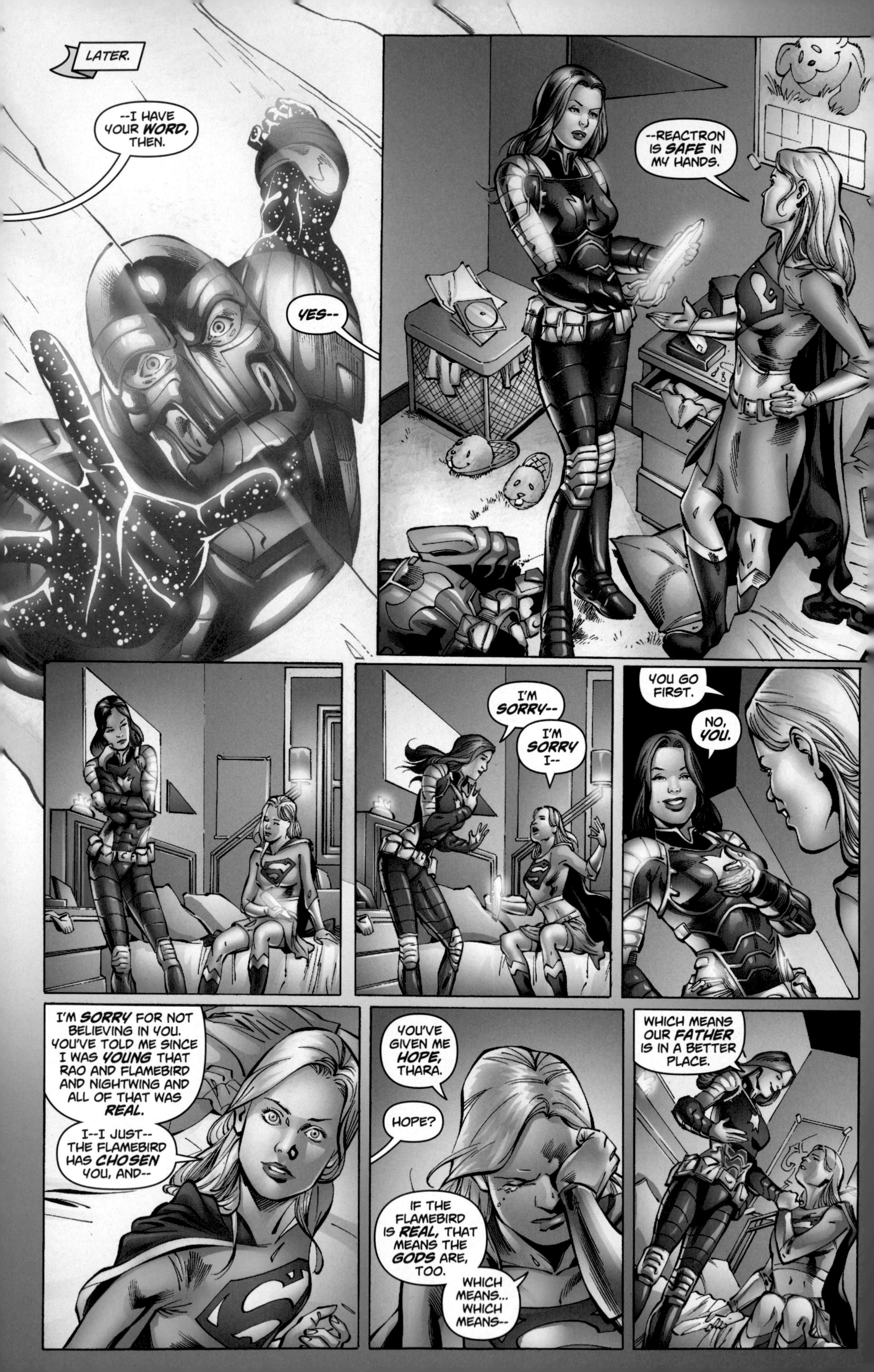
LATER.
--I HAVE YOUR WORD, THEN.
YES--
--REACTRON IS SAFE IN MY HANDS.
I'M SORRY--
I'M SORRY I--
YOU GO FIRST.
NO, YOU.
I'M SORRY FOR NOT BELIEVING IN YOU. YOU'VE TOLD ME SINCE I WAS YOUNG THAT RAO AND FLAMEBIRD AND NIGHTWING AND ALL OF THAT WAS REAL.
I--I JUST-- THE FLAMEBIRD HAS CHOSEN YOU, AND--
YOU'VE GIVEN ME HOPE, THARA.
HOPE?
IF THE FLAMEBIRD IS REAL, THAT MEANS THE GODS ARE, TOO.
WHICH MEANS... WHICH MEANS--
WHICH MEANS OUR FATHER IS IN A BETTER PLACE.

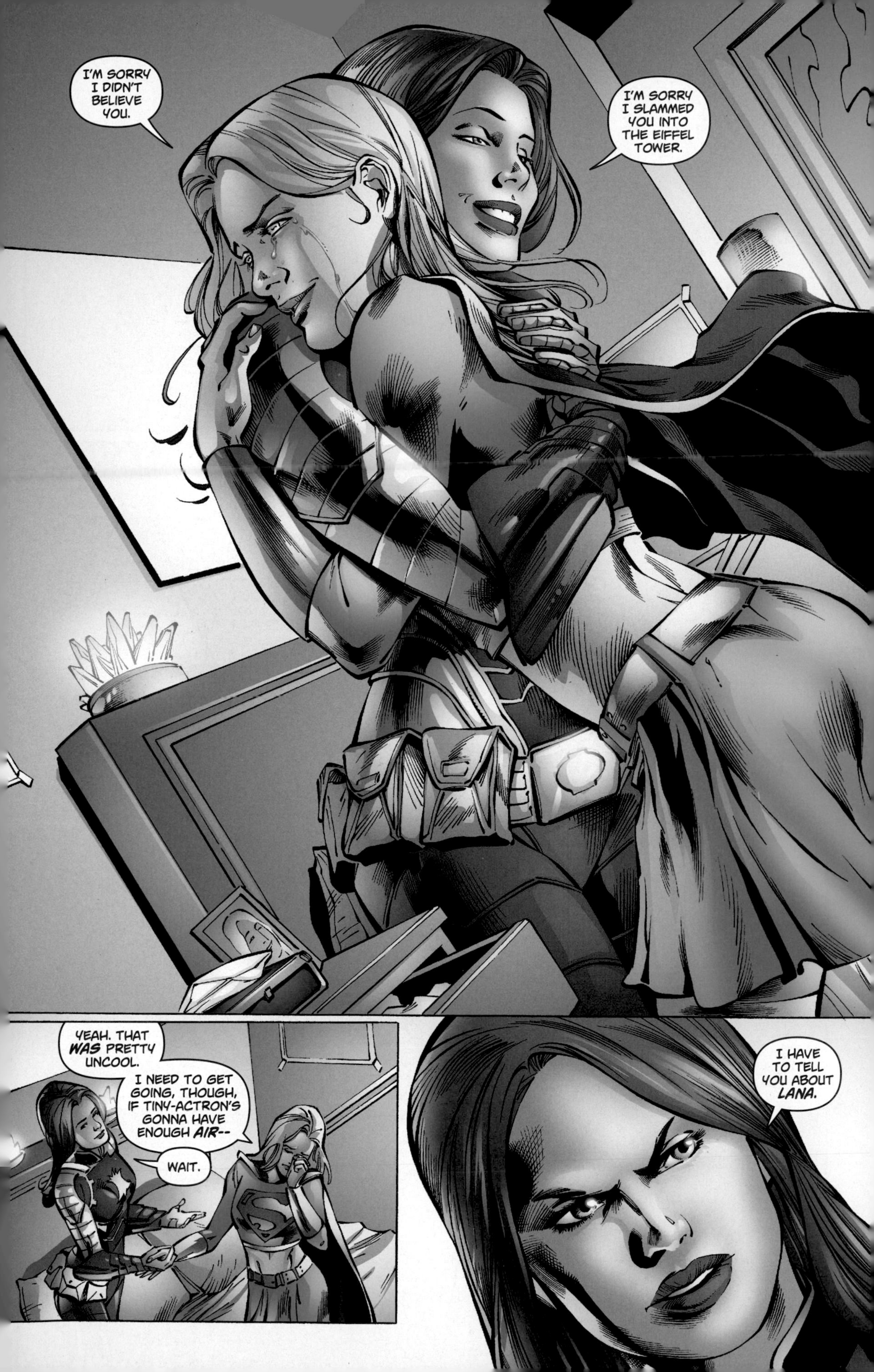
I'M SORRY I DIDN'T BELIEVE YOU.
I'M SORRY I SLAMMED YOU INTO THE EIFFEL TOWER.
YEAH. THAT **WAS** PRETTY UNCOOL.
I NEED TO GET GOING, THOUGH, IF TINY-ACTRON'S GONNA HAVE ENOUGH **AIR**--
WAIT.
I HAVE TO TELL YOU ABOUT **LANA**.

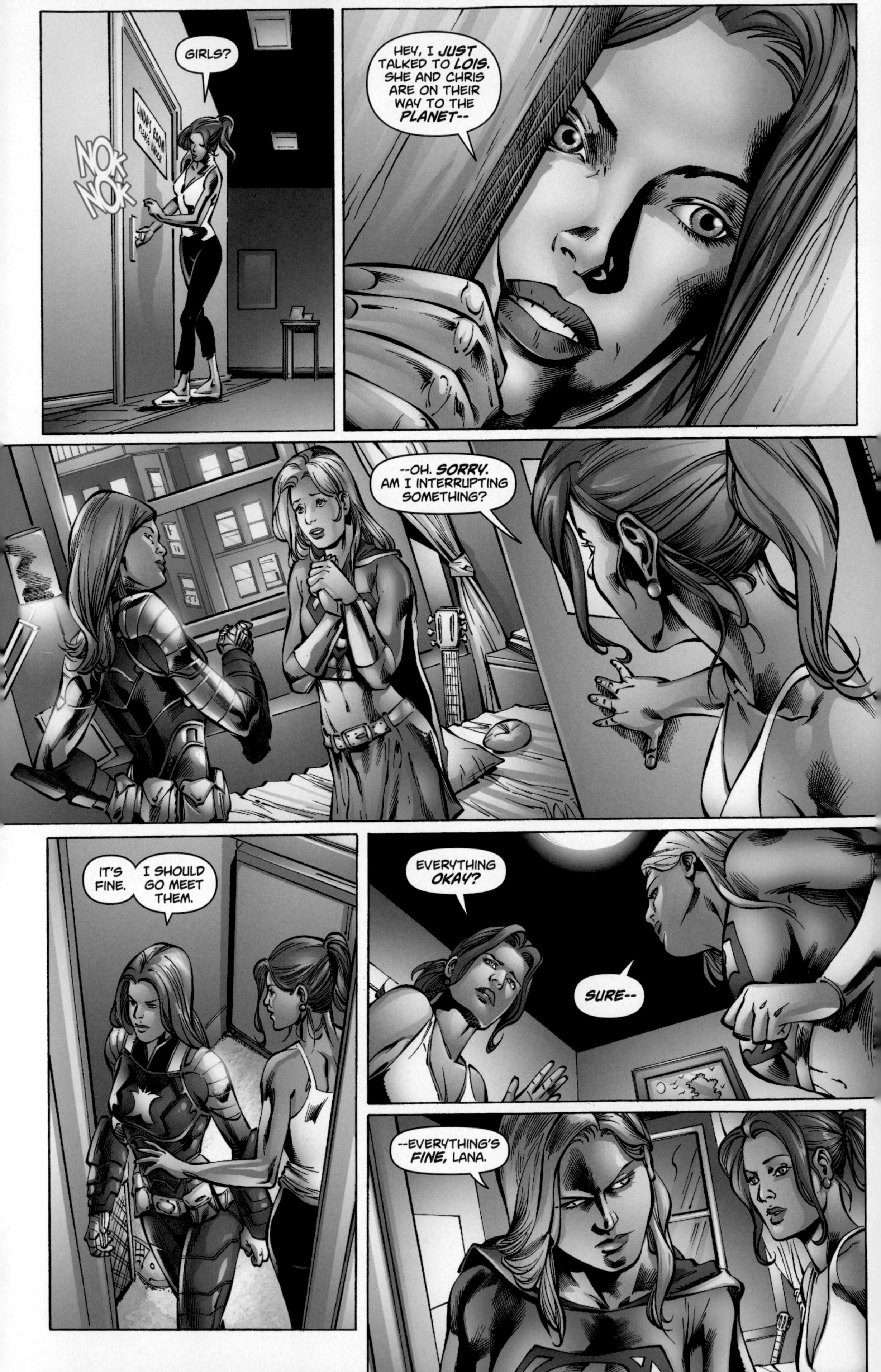
GIRLS?
LINDA'S ROOM PLEASE KNOCK
NOK NOK
HEY, I JUST TALKED TO LOIS. SHE AND CHRIS ARE ON THEIR WAY TO THE PLANET--
--OH. SORRY. AM I INTERRUPTING SOMETHING?
IT'S FINE.
I SHOULD GO MEET THEM.
EVERYTHING OKAY?
SURE--
--EVERYTHING'S FINE, LANA.

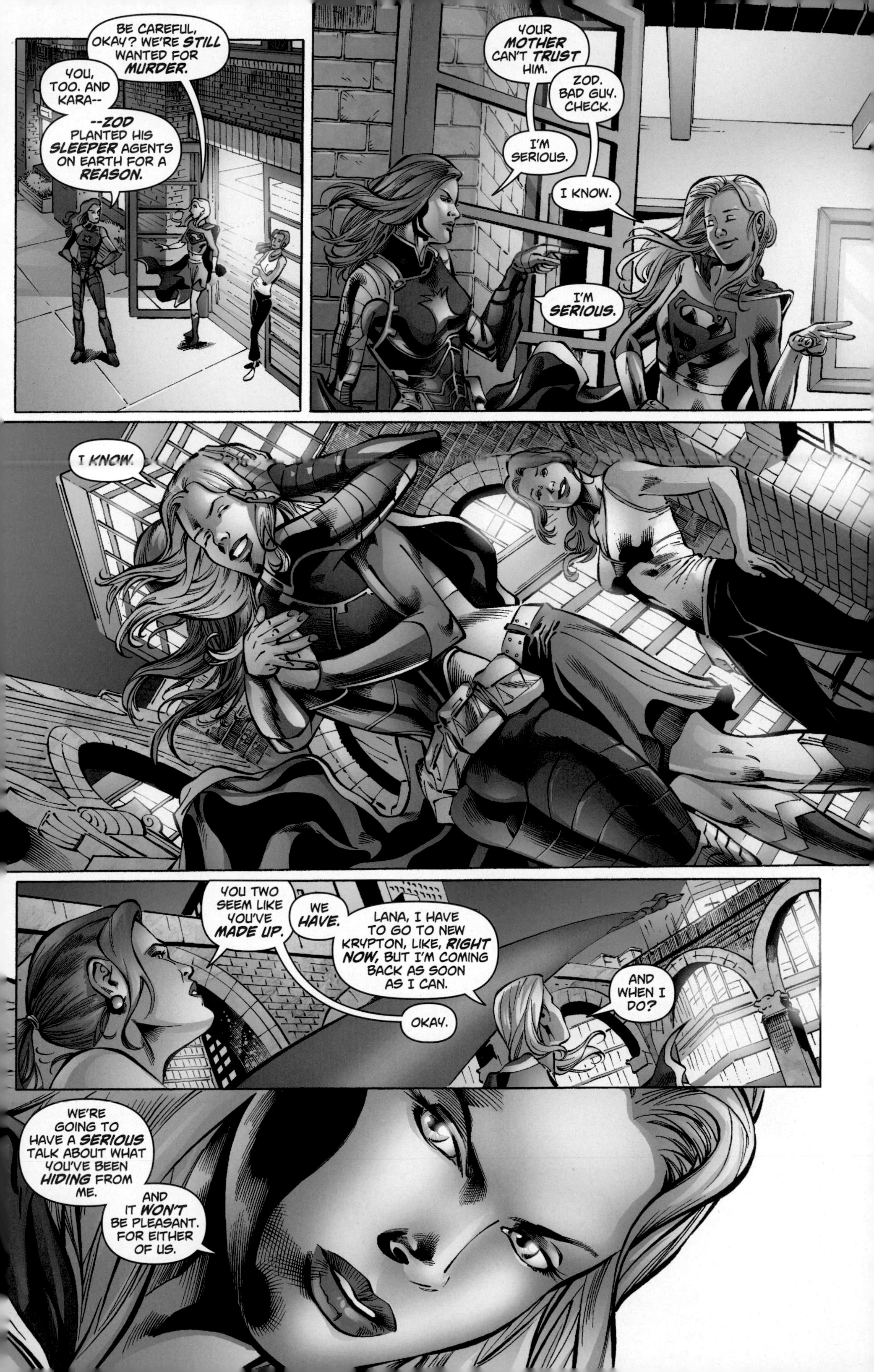
BE CAREFUL, OKAY? WE'RE STILL WANTED FOR MURDER.
YOU, TOO. AND KARA--
--ZOD PLANTED HIS SLEEPER AGENTS ON EARTH FOR A REASON.
YOUR MOTHER CAN'T TRUST HIM.
ZOD. BAD GUY. CHECK.
I'M SERIOUS.
I KNOW.
I'M SERIOUS.
I KNOW.
YOU TWO SEEM LIKE YOU'VE MADE UP.
WE HAVE.
LANA, I HAVE TO GO TO NEW KRYPTON, LIKE, RIGHT NOW, BUT I'M COMING BACK AS SOON AS I CAN.
OKAY.
AND WHEN I DO?
WE'RE GOING TO HAVE A SERIOUS TALK ABOUT WHAT YOU'VE BEEN HIDING FROM ME.
AND IT WON'T BE PLEASANT. FOR EITHER OF US.

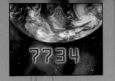

METALLO

ALTER EGO: John Corben

BASE OF OPERATIONS: Project 7734 Bunker (location unknown); Metropolis

POWERS/ABILITIES: Metallo possesses a super hard skeleton laced with metallo, the alloy from which he draws his codename. Within his chest is a piece of Green Kryptonite, giving him the ability to harm, and eventually kill, Kryptonians.

HISTORY: JOHN CORBEN was [REDACTED BY THE U.S. ARMY – REDACTED BY THE U.S. ARMY – REDACTED BY THE U.S. ARMY – REDACTED BY THE U.S. ARMY – REDACTED BY THE U.S. ARMY] a test subject for [REDACTED BY THE U.S. ARMY – REDACTED BY THE U.S. ARMY] Kryptonite heart and a metallic alloy lacing his chest cavity. Naming himself Metallo after the type of metal in his body, Corben [REDACTED BY THE U.S. ARMY – REDACTED BY THE U.S. ARMY] and a long history with Lois Lane.

Corben was stunned when the Green Kryptonite in his chest was able to take down the Man of Steel, but was eventually stopped by Superman. The once [REDACTED BY THE U.S. ARMY] was now a full-fledged super-villain.

Recently Metallo has been recruited into Project: 7734 by **GENERAL LANE**. He and Reactron were part of an elite team that infiltrated Kandor after its enlargement. They murdered several Kryptonians, including the Kryptonian leader **ZOR-EL**, before being evacuated from the city by Superwoman. Now a man wanted by the Kryptonian government, Metallo is smart enough to lie low before showing his face again.

REACTRON

ALTER EGO: Major Benjamin Krull

BASE OF OPERATIONS: Project 7734 Bunker (location unknown); Metropolis

POWERS/ABILITIES: Reactron has a piece of Gold Kryptonite embedded in his chest, giving him the ability to neutralize a Kryptonian's powers for approximately fifteen seconds. He's also able to fire blasts of energy from his hands.

HISTORY: BENJAMIN KRULL was a loser who didn't know what to do with his life until he joined the U.S. Army. One night, while guarding an experimental [REDACTED BY THE U.S. ARMY], Krull was injured. Knowing he was going to die, Dr. [REDACTED BY THE U.S. ARMY], the man in charge of Project [REDACTED BY THE U.S. ARMY], decided Krull needed a new uniform, one that they hoped would prolong his life: the Star-Suit.

Soon after his initial defeat at the hands of Supergirl, Krull was approached by General Lane with an offer to join Project 7734. Krull accepted, and he was fitted for a new suit — one with a piece of Gold Kryptonite in the middle.

Reactron was part of an elite team that infiltrated Kandor when it appeared on Earth, and was directly responsible for the death of the Kryptonian leader Zor-El. It is unknown what the ramifications will be once a Kryptonian finally gets hold of him. Fortunately for him, the piece of Gold Kryptonite in his chest will make it a fair fight.

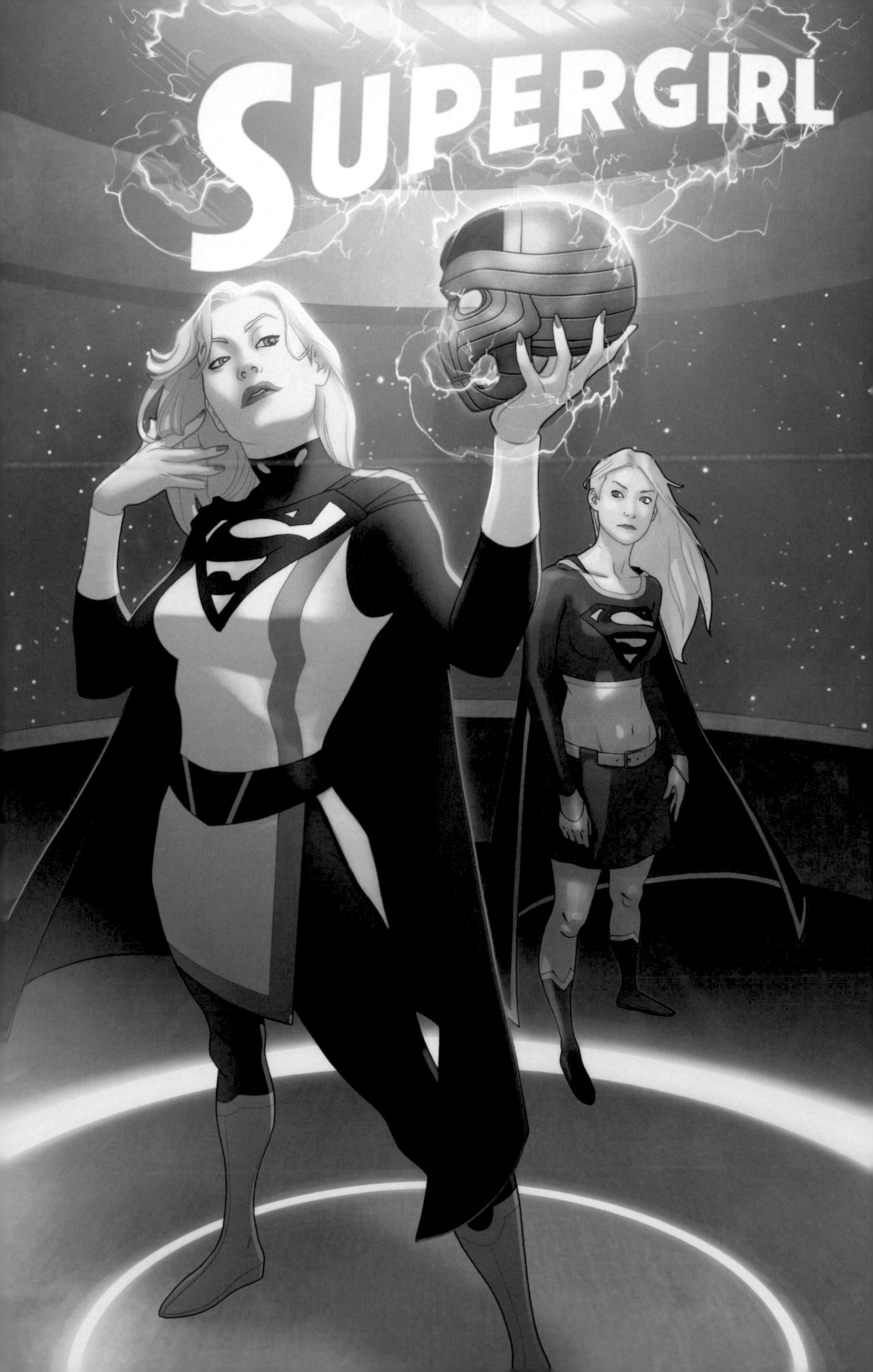
SUPERGIRL

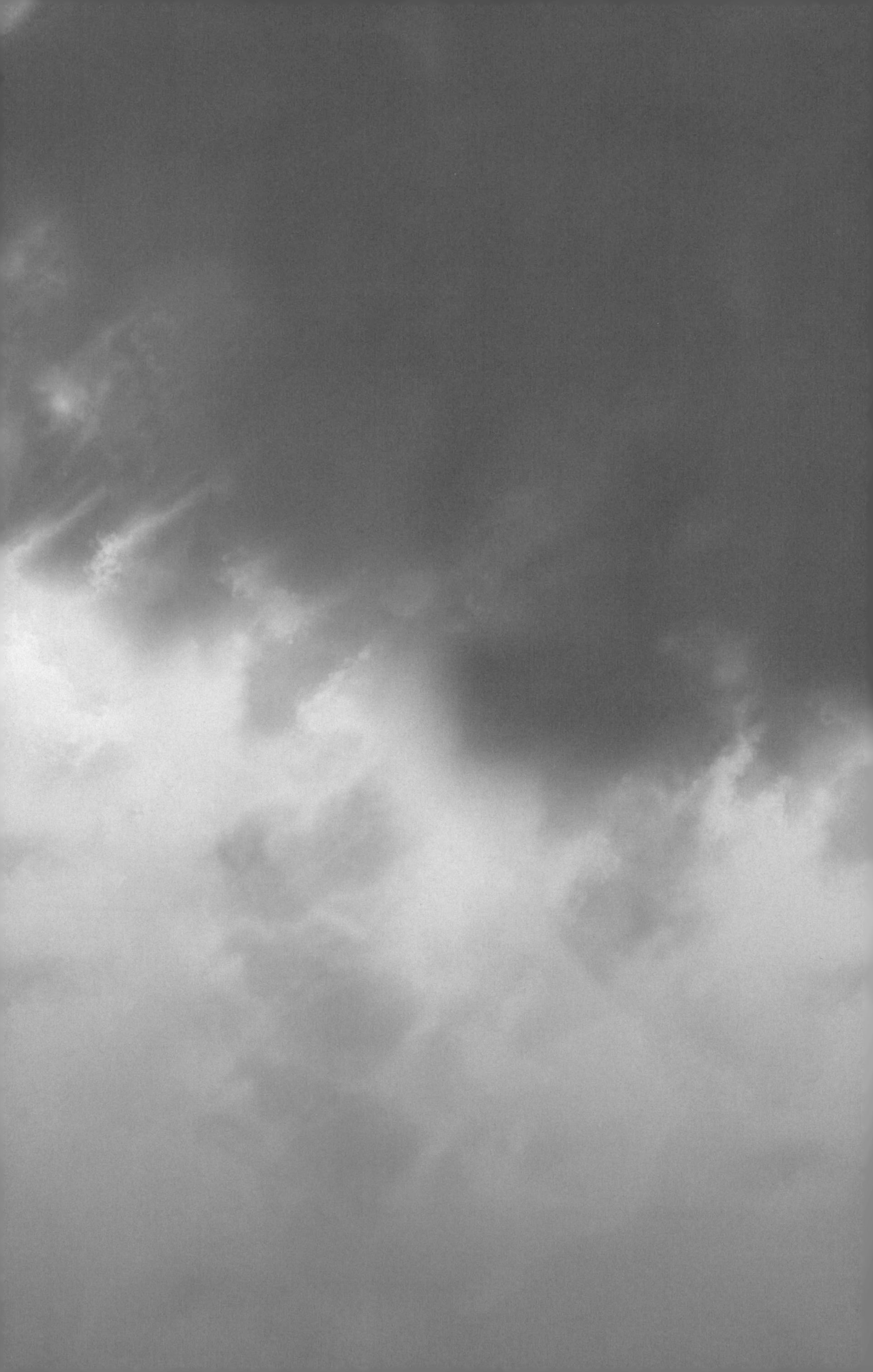

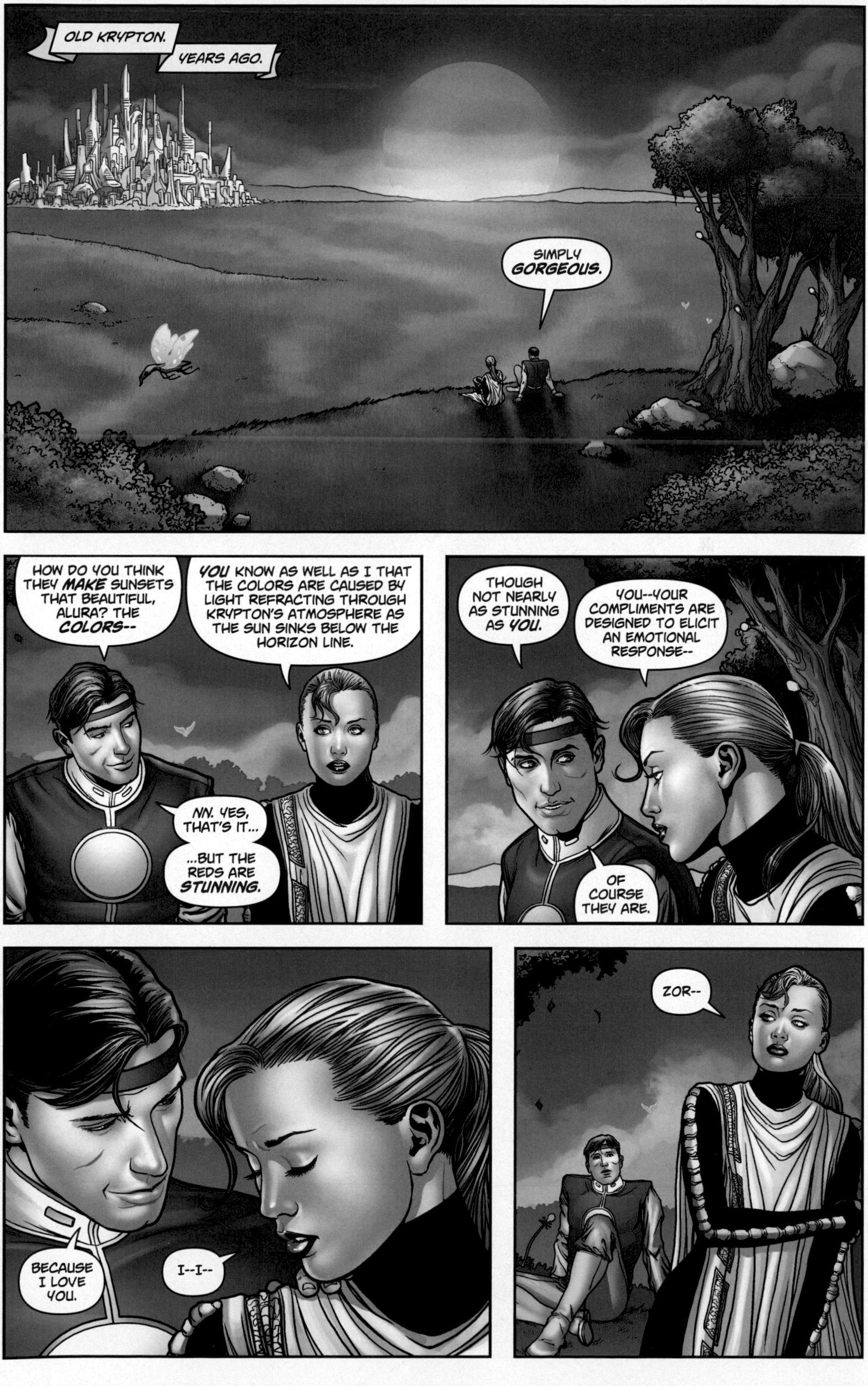
OLD KRYPTON.
YEARS AGO.
SIMPLY GORGEOUS.
HOW DO YOU THINK THEY MAKE SUNSETS THAT BEAUTIFUL, ALURA? THE COLORS--
YOU KNOW AS WELL AS I THAT THE COLORS ARE CAUSED BY LIGHT REFRACTING THROUGH KRYPTON'S ATMOSPHERE AS THE SUN SINKS BELOW THE HORIZON LINE.
NN. YES, THAT'S IT...
...BUT THE REDS ARE STUNNING.
THOUGH NOT NEARLY AS STUNNING AS YOU.
YOU--YOUR COMPLIMENTS ARE DESIGNED TO ELICIT AN EMOTIONAL RESPONSE--
OF COURSE THEY ARE.
BECAUSE I LOVE YOU.
I--I--
ZOR--

...STILL? WE'VE BEEN SEEING EACH OTHER FOR MONTHS, ALURA, AND STILL YOU WON'T SAY WHAT IT IS YOU *FEEL* FOR ME.

DO YOU THINK *SO* LITTLE OF ME YOU CAN'T BEAR TO OPEN UP? WHY EVEN BOTHER TO KEEP *SEEING* ME?

WHAT'S THE *POINT?*

NO, IT'S...

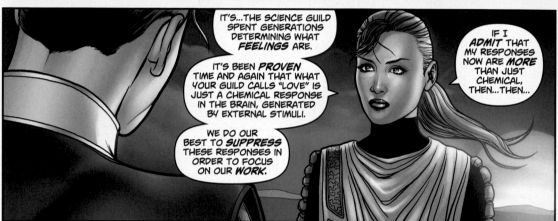

IT'S...THE SCIENCE GUILD SPENT GENERATIONS DETERMINING WHAT *FEELINGS* ARE.

IT'S BEEN *PROVEN* TIME AND AGAIN THAT WHAT YOUR GUILD CALLS "LOVE" IS JUST A CHEMICAL RESPONSE IN THE BRAIN, GENERATED BY EXTERNAL STIMULI.

WE DO OUR BEST TO *SUPPRESS* THESE RESPONSES IN ORDER TO FOCUS ON OUR *WORK.*

IF I *ADMIT* THAT MY RESPONSES NOW ARE *MORE* THAN JUST CHEMICAL, THEN...THEN...

THEN *WHAT?*

THEN I WILL HAVE BECOME SOMEONE *DIFFERENT. CHANGED* MY LIFE, MY THOUGHTS, MY WHOLE *EXISTENCE* COMPLETELY. FOR YOU.

NO. FOR *US.*

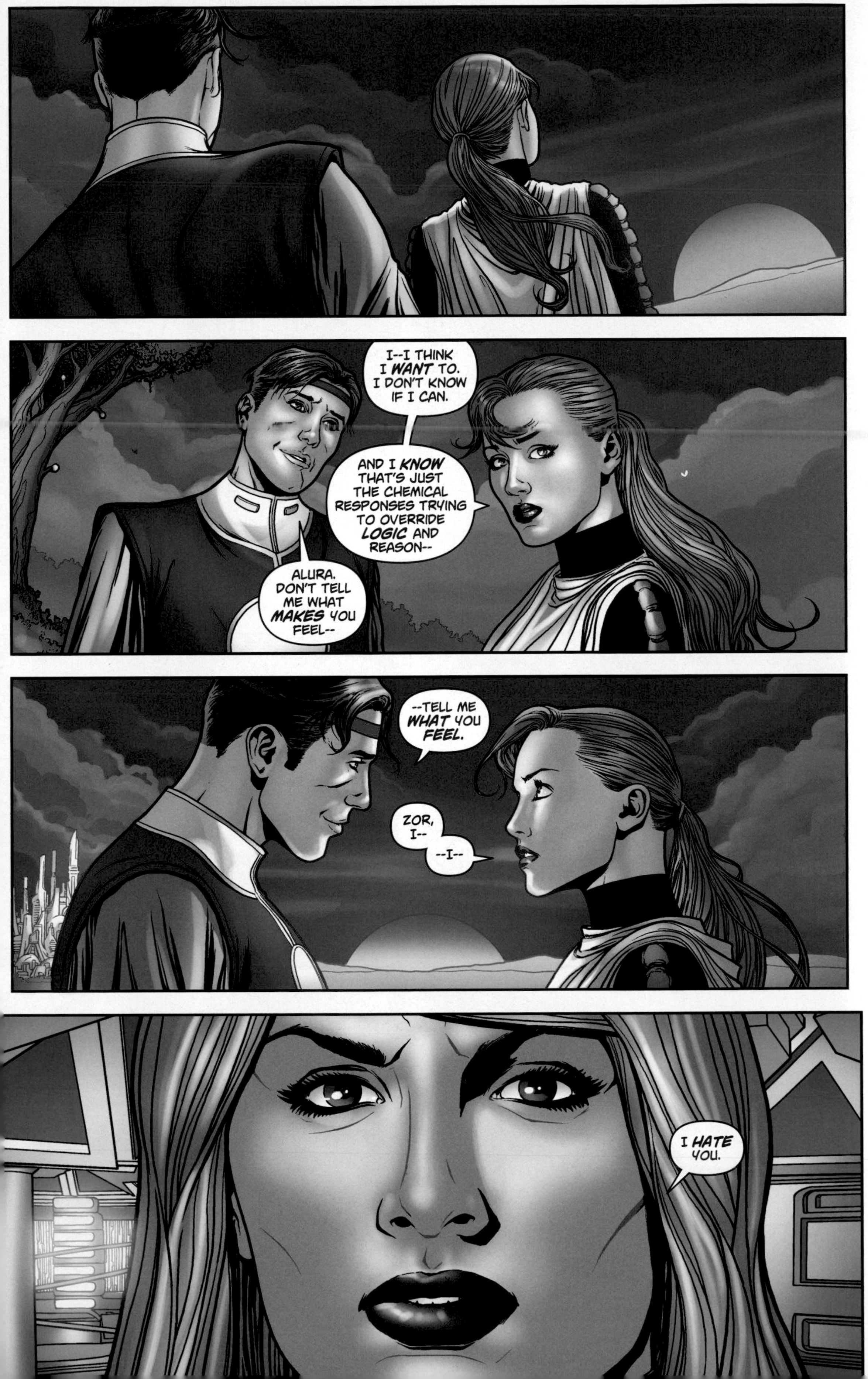
I--I THINK I WANT TO. I DON'T KNOW IF I CAN.
AND I KNOW THAT'S JUST THE CHEMICAL RESPONSES TRYING TO OVERRIDE LOGIC AND REASON--
ALURA. DON'T TELL ME WHAT MAKES YOU FEEL--
--TELL ME WHAT YOU FEEL.
ZOR, I--
--I--
I HATE YOU.

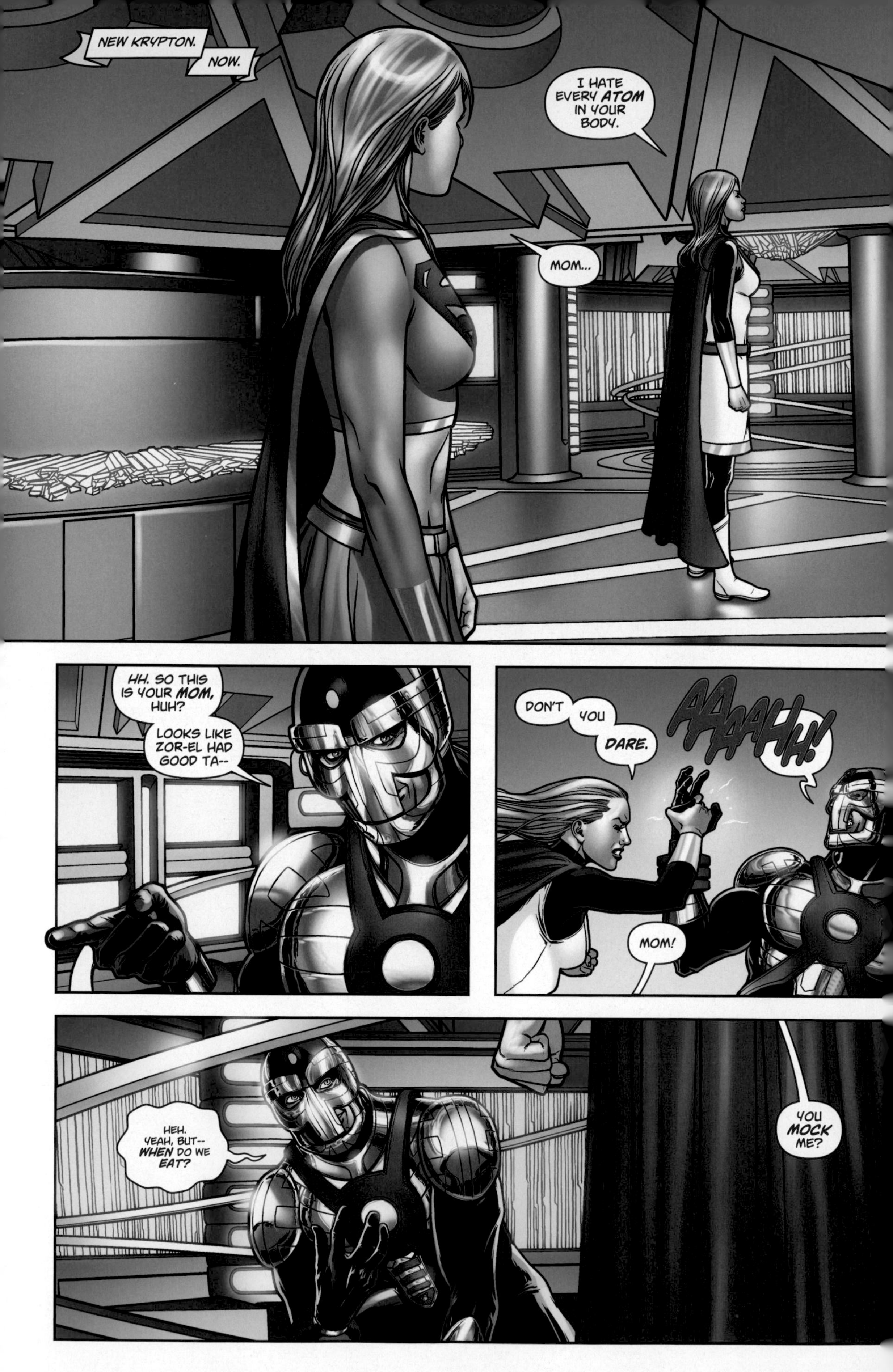
NEW KRYPTON.
NOW.
I HATE EVERY ATOM IN YOUR BODY.
MOM...
HH. SO THIS IS YOUR MOM, HUH?
LOOKS LIKE ZOR-EL HAD GOOD TA--
DON'T YOU DARE.
AAAAAHH!
MOM!
HEH. YEAH, BUT-- WHEN DO WE EAT?
YOU MOCK ME?

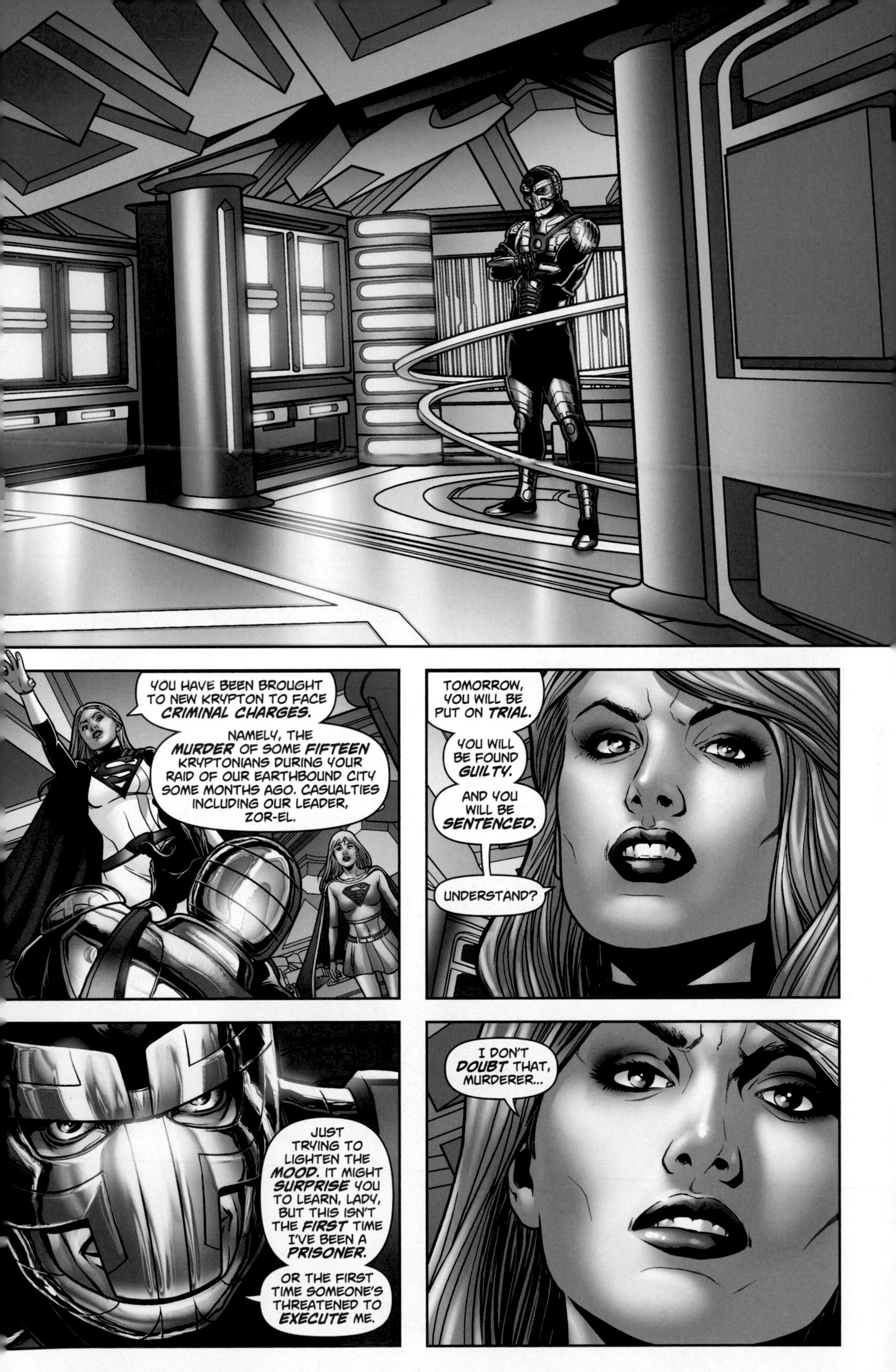

YOU HAVE BEEN BROUGHT TO NEW KRYPTON TO FACE CRIMINAL CHARGES.
NAMELY, THE MURDER OF SOME FIFTEEN KRYPTONIANS DURING YOUR RAID OF OUR EARTHBOUND CITY SOME MONTHS AGO. CASUALTIES INCLUDING OUR LEADER, ZOR-EL.
TOMORROW, YOU WILL BE PUT ON TRIAL.
YOU WILL BE FOUND GUILTY.
AND YOU WILL BE SENTENCED.
UNDERSTAND?
JUST TRYING TO LIGHTEN THE MOOD. IT MIGHT SURPRISE YOU TO LEARN, LADY, BUT THIS ISN'T THE FIRST TIME I'VE BEEN A PRISONER.
OR THE FIRST TIME SOMEONE'S THREATENED TO EXECUTE ME.
I DON'T DOUBT THAT, MURDERER...

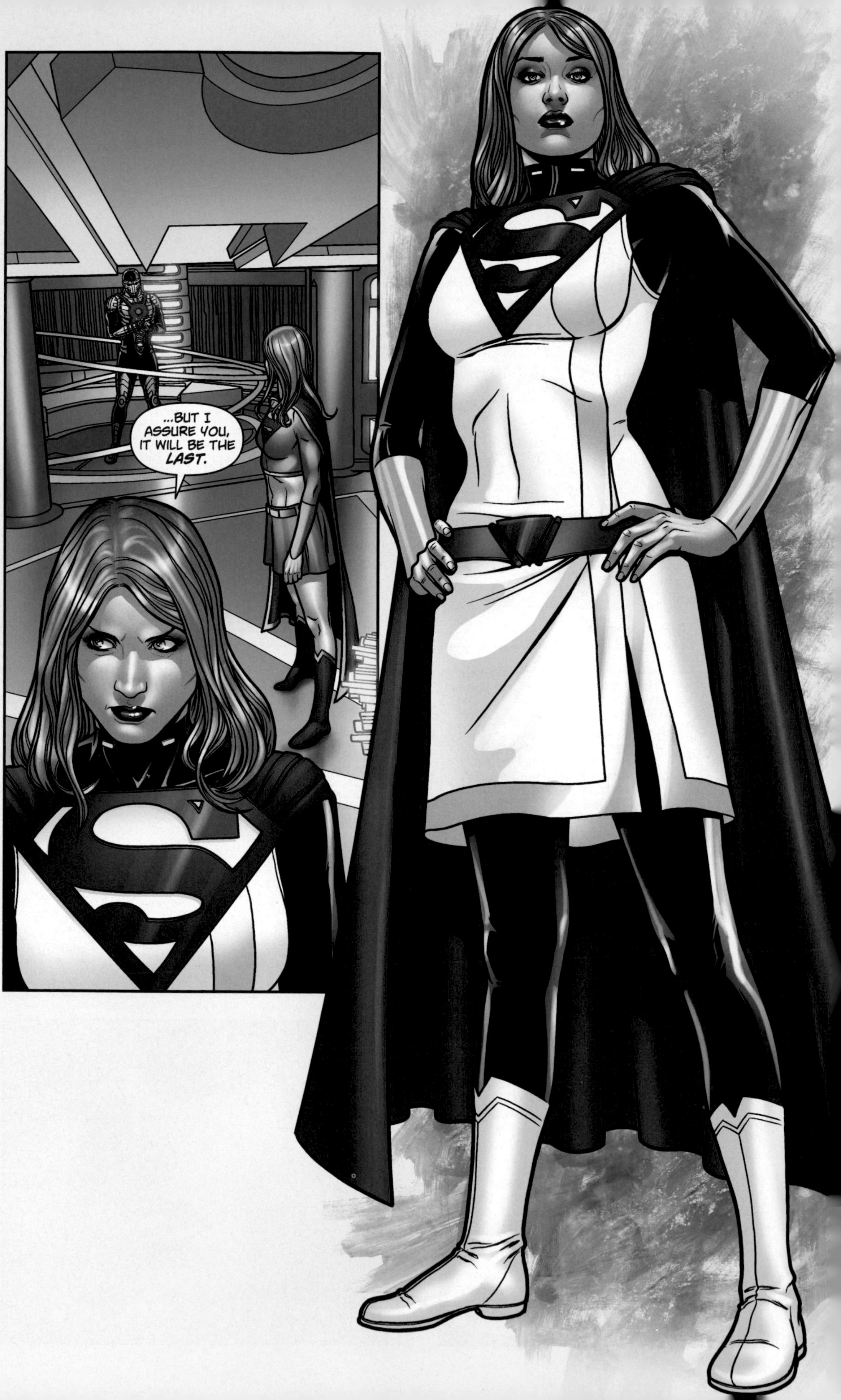
...BUT I ASSURE YOU, IT WILL BE THE LAST.

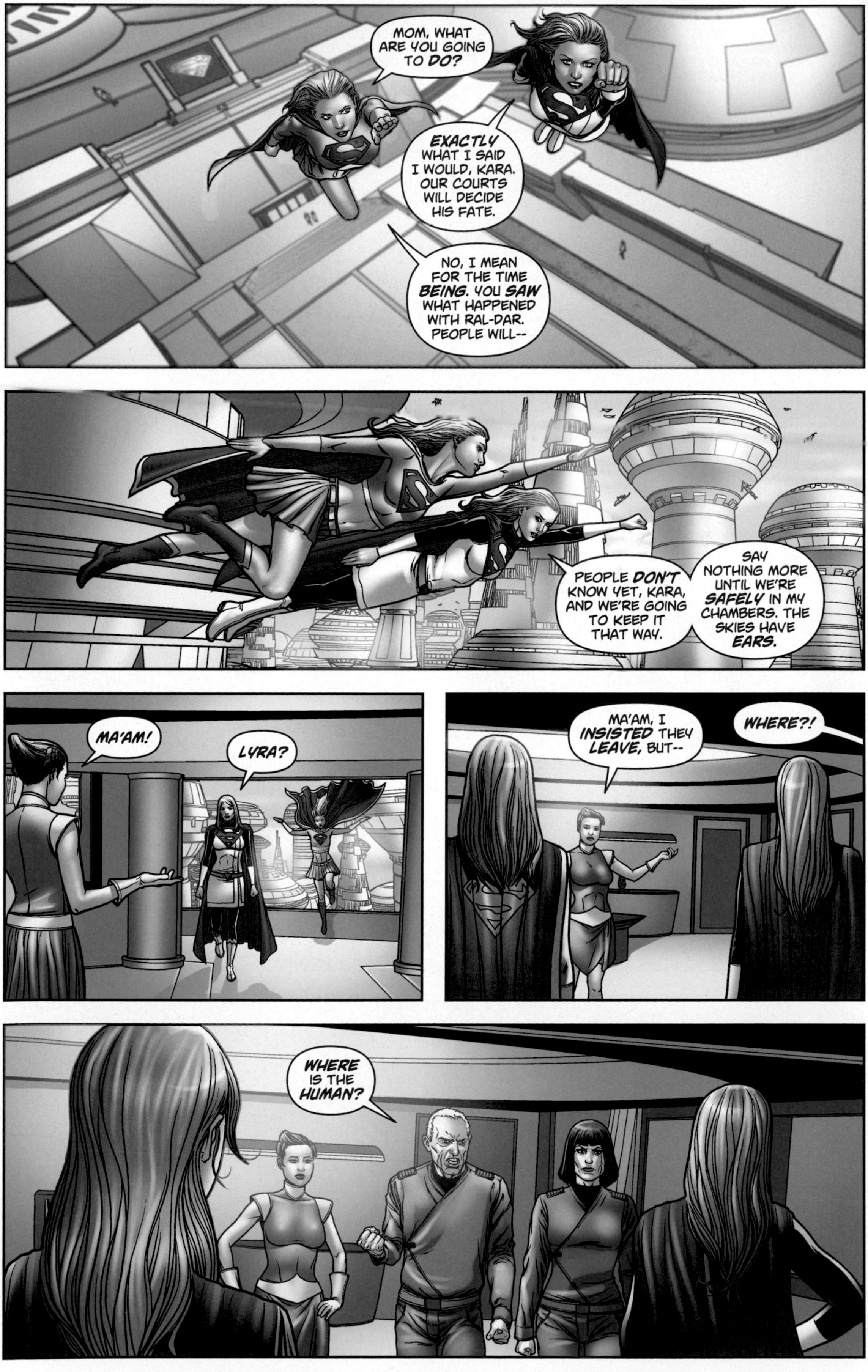
MOM, WHAT ARE YOU GOING TO DO?
EXACTLY WHAT I SAID I WOULD, KARA. OUR COURTS WILL DECIDE HIS FATE.
NO, I MEAN FOR THE TIME BEING. YOU SAW WHAT HAPPENED WITH RAL-DAR. PEOPLE WILL--
PEOPLE DON'T KNOW YET, KARA, AND WE'RE GOING TO KEEP IT THAT WAY.
SAY NOTHING MORE UNTIL WE'RE SAFELY IN MY CHAMBERS. THE SKIES HAVE EARS.
MA'AM!
LYRA?
MA'AM, I INSISTED THEY LEAVE, BUT--
WHERE?!
WHERE IS THE HUMAN?

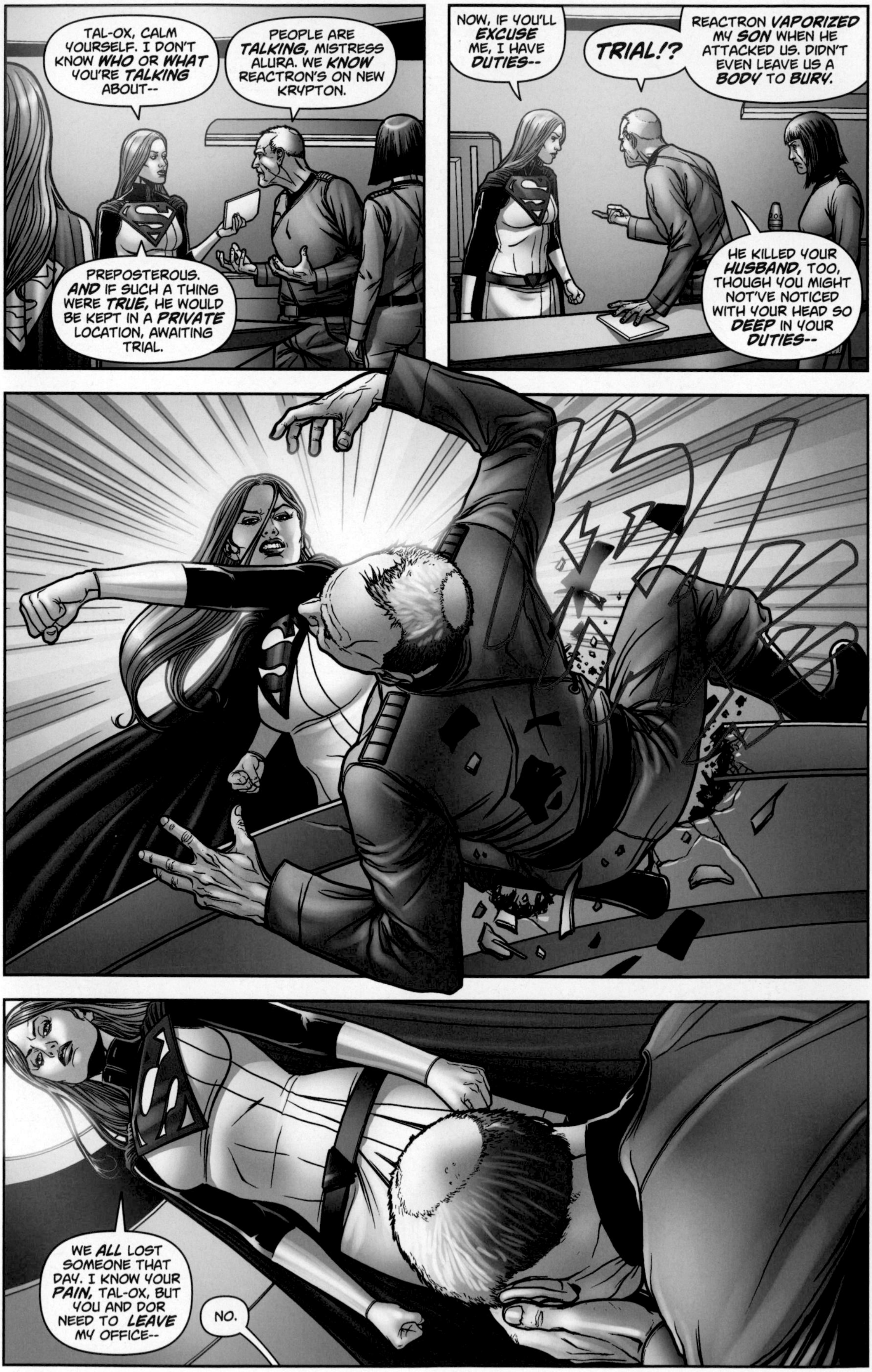
TAL-OX, CALM YOURSELF. I DON'T KNOW WHO OR WHAT YOU'RE TALKING ABOUT--
PEOPLE ARE TALKING, MISTRESS ALURA. WE KNOW REACTRON'S ON NEW KRYPTON.
PREPOSTEROUS. AND IF SUCH A THING WERE TRUE, HE WOULD BE KEPT IN A PRIVATE LOCATION, AWAITING TRIAL.
NOW, IF YOU'LL EXCUSE ME, I HAVE DUTIES--
TRIAL!?
REACTRON VAPORIZED MY SON WHEN HE ATTACKED US. DIDN'T EVEN LEAVE US A BODY TO BURY.
HE KILLED YOUR HUSBAND, TOO, THOUGH YOU MIGHT NOT'VE NOTICED WITH YOUR HEAD SO DEEP IN YOUR DUTIES--
WE ALL LOST SOMEONE THAT DAY. I KNOW YOUR PAIN, TAL-OX, BUT YOU AND DOR NEED TO LEAVE MY OFFICE--
NO.

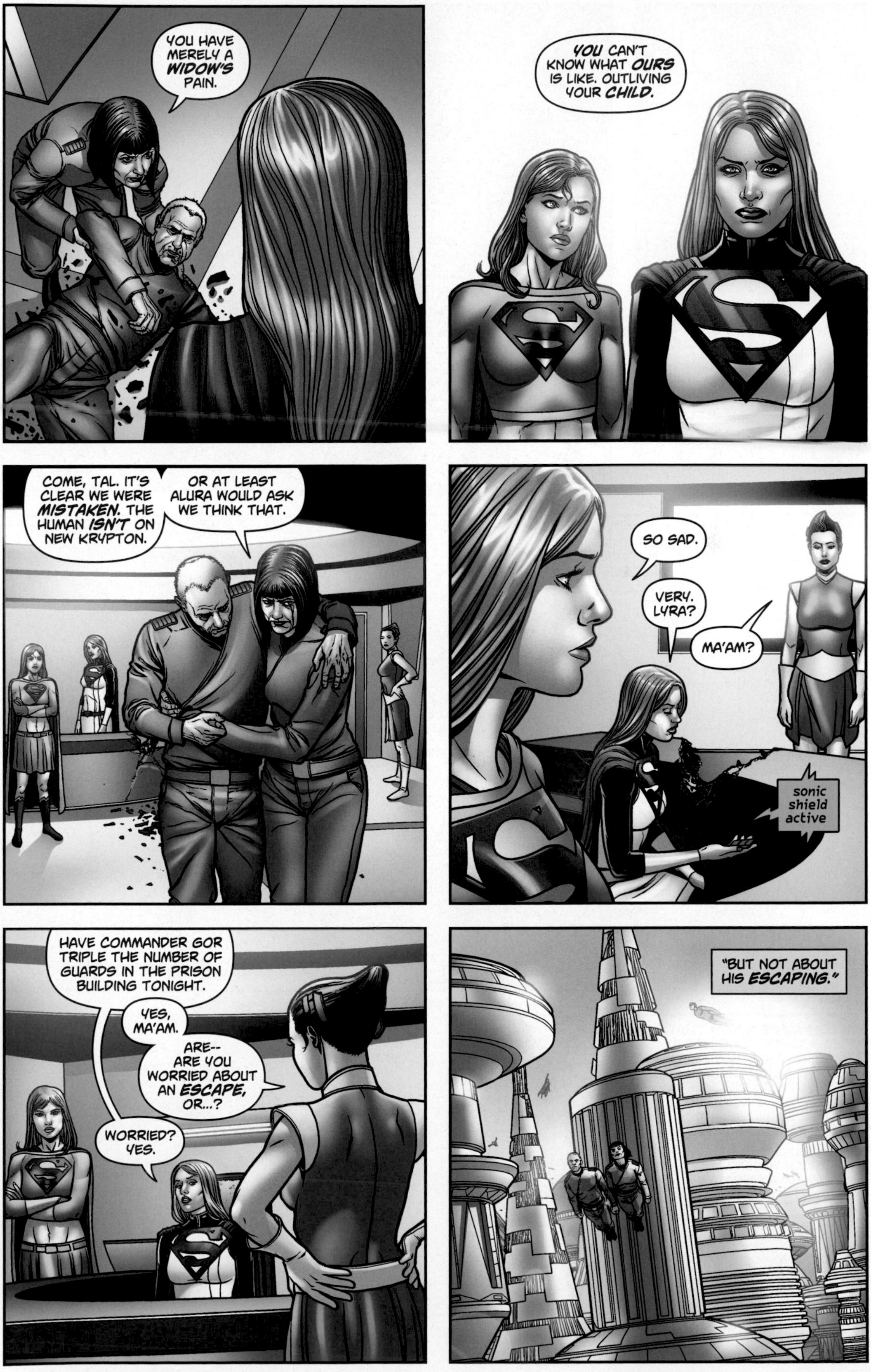
YOU HAVE MERELY A WIDOW'S PAIN.
YOU CAN'T KNOW WHAT OURS IS LIKE. OUTLIVING YOUR CHILD.
COME, TAL. IT'S CLEAR WE WERE MISTAKEN. THE HUMAN ISN'T ON NEW KRYPTON.
OR AT LEAST ALURA WOULD ASK WE THINK THAT.
SO SAD.
VERY. LYRA?
MA'AM?
sonic shield active
HAVE COMMANDER GOR TRIPLE THE NUMBER OF GUARDS IN THE PRISON BUILDING TONIGHT.
YES, MA'AM.
ARE-- ARE YOU WORRIED ABOUT AN ESCAPE, OR...?
WORRIED? YES.
"BUT NOT ABOUT HIS ESCAPING."

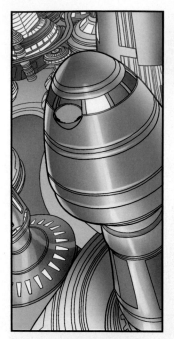

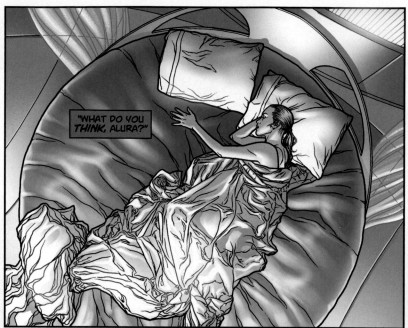

"WHAT DO YOU *THINK*, ALURA?"

ABOUT OUR GETTING *MARRIED*?

I THINK YOU'VE *LOST* YOUR *MIND*.

LOST IT? HM.

WELL, I *HAVE* HEARD THAT THE SCIENCE GUILD HAS A MACHINE THAT CAN *SAP* MEN'S WILLS, TURNING THEM INTO MINDLESS, MARRIED *SLAVES*.

YOU ARTISTS HAVE SUCH WONDERFULLY *VIVID* IMAGINATIONS.

WE *LIVE* TO IMAGINE. AND I'M IMAGINING A LIFE SPENT WITH *YOU*. WHAT DO YOU THINK?

I THINK, ZOR, THAT ONCE WE TAKE A MARRIAGE OATH BEFORE OUR *GODS*, WE'RE *PERMANENT*.

FOREVER.

ARE YOU... ARE YOU *POSITIVE* THAT'S WHAT YOU *WANT*?

HERE. FEEL.

WHAT? WHY--

YOUR HEARTBEAT *SKIPS* WHEN YOU LIE. KEEP YOUR HAND THERE.

WE ARE WHAT I WANT, ALURA. I WANT US TO BE *TOGETHER* AS HUSBAND AND WIFE.

FOREVER.

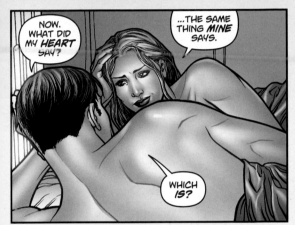

NOW. WHAT DID MY *HEART* SAY?

...THE SAME THING *MINE* SAYS.

WHICH *IS?*

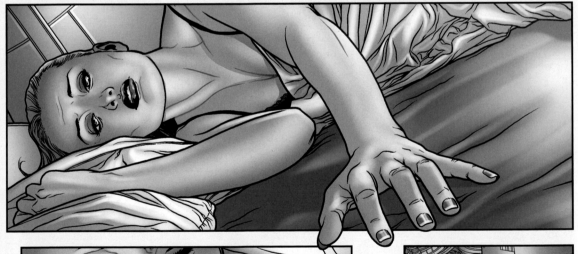

"ARBITRATORS OF THE *COURT*--"

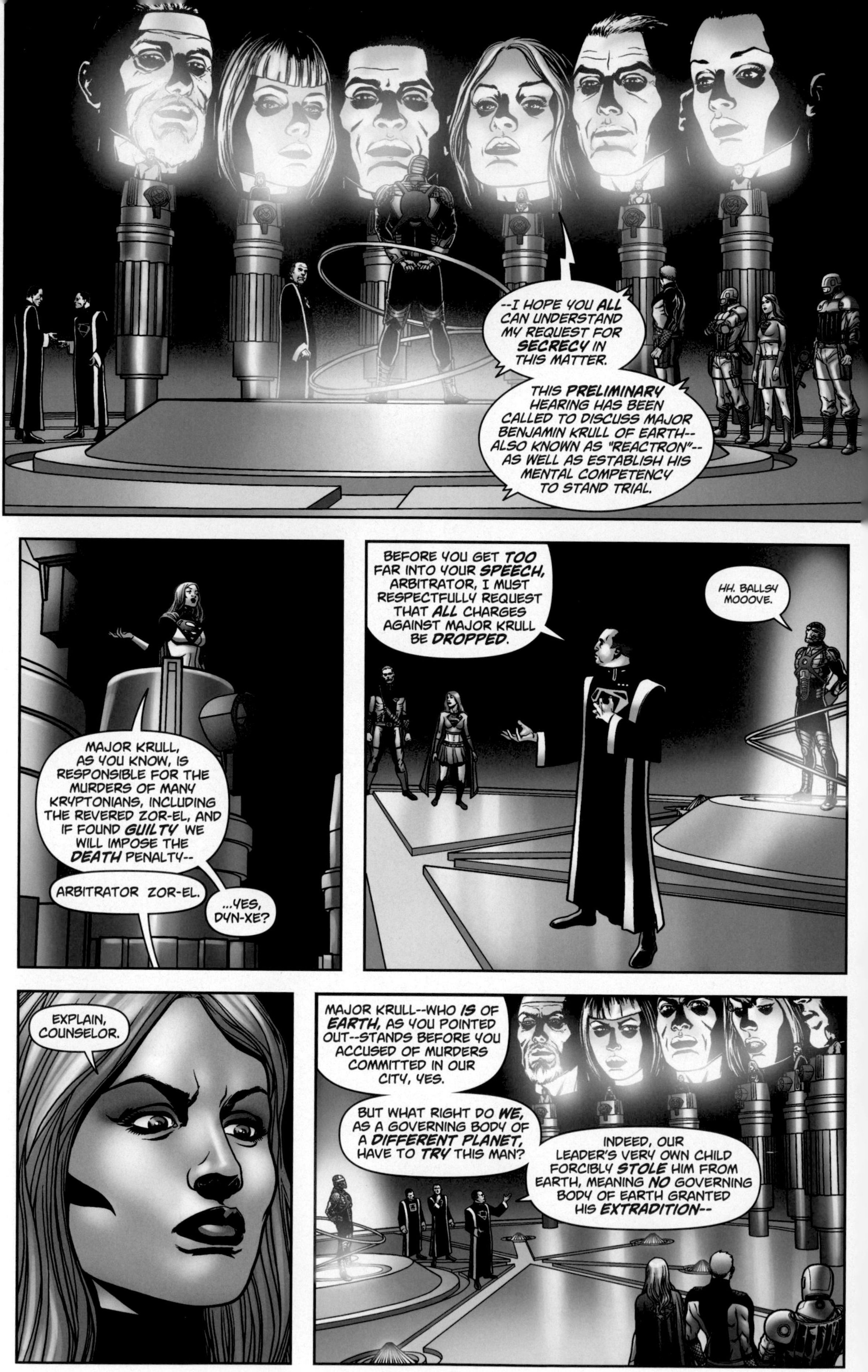
--I HOPE YOU ALL CAN UNDERSTAND MY REQUEST FOR SECRECY IN THIS MATTER.
THIS PRELIMINARY HEARING HAS BEEN CALLED TO DISCUSS MAJOR BENJAMIN KRULL OF EARTH--ALSO KNOWN AS "REACTRON"--AS WELL AS ESTABLISH HIS MENTAL COMPETENCY TO STAND TRIAL.
MAJOR KRULL, AS YOU KNOW, IS RESPONSIBLE FOR THE MURDERS OF MANY KRYPTONIANS, INCLUDING THE REVERED ZOR-EL, AND IF FOUND GUILTY WE WILL IMPOSE THE DEATH PENALTY--
ARBITRATOR ZOR-EL.
...YES, DYN-XE?
BEFORE YOU GET TOO FAR INTO YOUR SPEECH, ARBITRATOR, I MUST RESPECTFULLY REQUEST THAT ALL CHARGES AGAINST MAJOR KRULL BE DROPPED.
HH. BALLSY MOOOVE.
EXPLAIN, COUNSELOR.
MAJOR KRULL--WHO IS OF EARTH, AS YOU POINTED OUT--STANDS BEFORE YOU ACCUSED OF MURDERS COMMITTED IN OUR CITY, YES.
BUT WHAT RIGHT DO WE, AS A GOVERNING BODY OF A DIFFERENT PLANET, HAVE TO TRY THIS MAN?
INDEED, OUR LEADER'S VERY OWN CHILD FORCIBLY STOLE HIM FROM EARTH, MEANING NO GOVERNING BODY OF EARTH GRANTED HIS EXTRADITION--

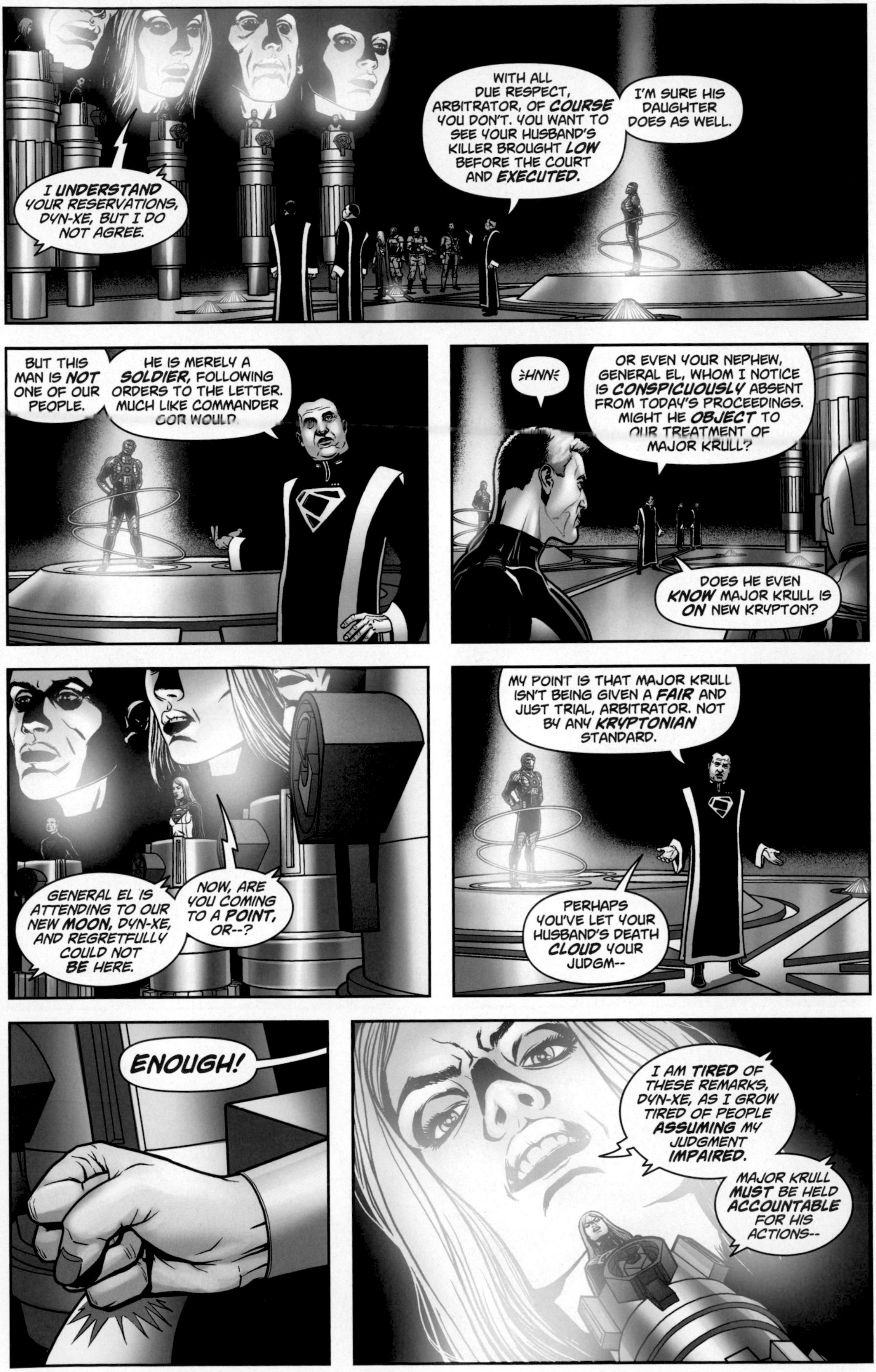
I UNDERSTAND YOUR RESERVATIONS, DYN-XE, BUT I DO NOT AGREE.
WITH ALL DUE RESPECT, ARBITRATOR, OF COURSE YOU DON'T. YOU WANT TO SEE YOUR HUSBAND'S KILLER BROUGHT LOW BEFORE THE COURT AND EXECUTED.
I'M SURE HIS DAUGHTER DOES AS WELL.
BUT THIS MAN IS NOT ONE OF OUR PEOPLE.
HE IS MERELY A SOLDIER, FOLLOWING ORDERS TO THE LETTER. MUCH LIKE COMMANDER GOR WOULD.
HNN
OR EVEN YOUR NEPHEW, GENERAL EL, WHOM I NOTICE IS CONSPICUOUSLY ABSENT FROM TODAY'S PROCEEDINGS. MIGHT HE OBJECT TO OUR TREATMENT OF MAJOR KRULL?
DOES HE EVEN KNOW MAJOR KRULL IS ON NEW KRYPTON?
GENERAL EL IS ATTENDING TO OUR NEW MOON, DYN-XE, AND REGRETFULLY COULD NOT BE HERE.
NOW, ARE YOU COMING TO A POINT, OR--?
MY POINT IS THAT MAJOR KRULL ISN'T BEING GIVEN A FAIR AND JUST TRIAL, ARBITRATOR. NOT BY ANY KRYPTONIAN STANDARD.
PERHAPS YOU'VE LET YOUR HUSBAND'S DEATH CLOUD YOUR JUDGM--
ENOUGH!
I AM TIRED OF THESE REMARKS, DYN-XE, AS I GROW TIRED OF PEOPLE ASSUMING MY JUDGMENT IMPAIRED.
MAJOR KRULL MUST BE HELD ACCOUNTABLE FOR HIS ACTIONS--

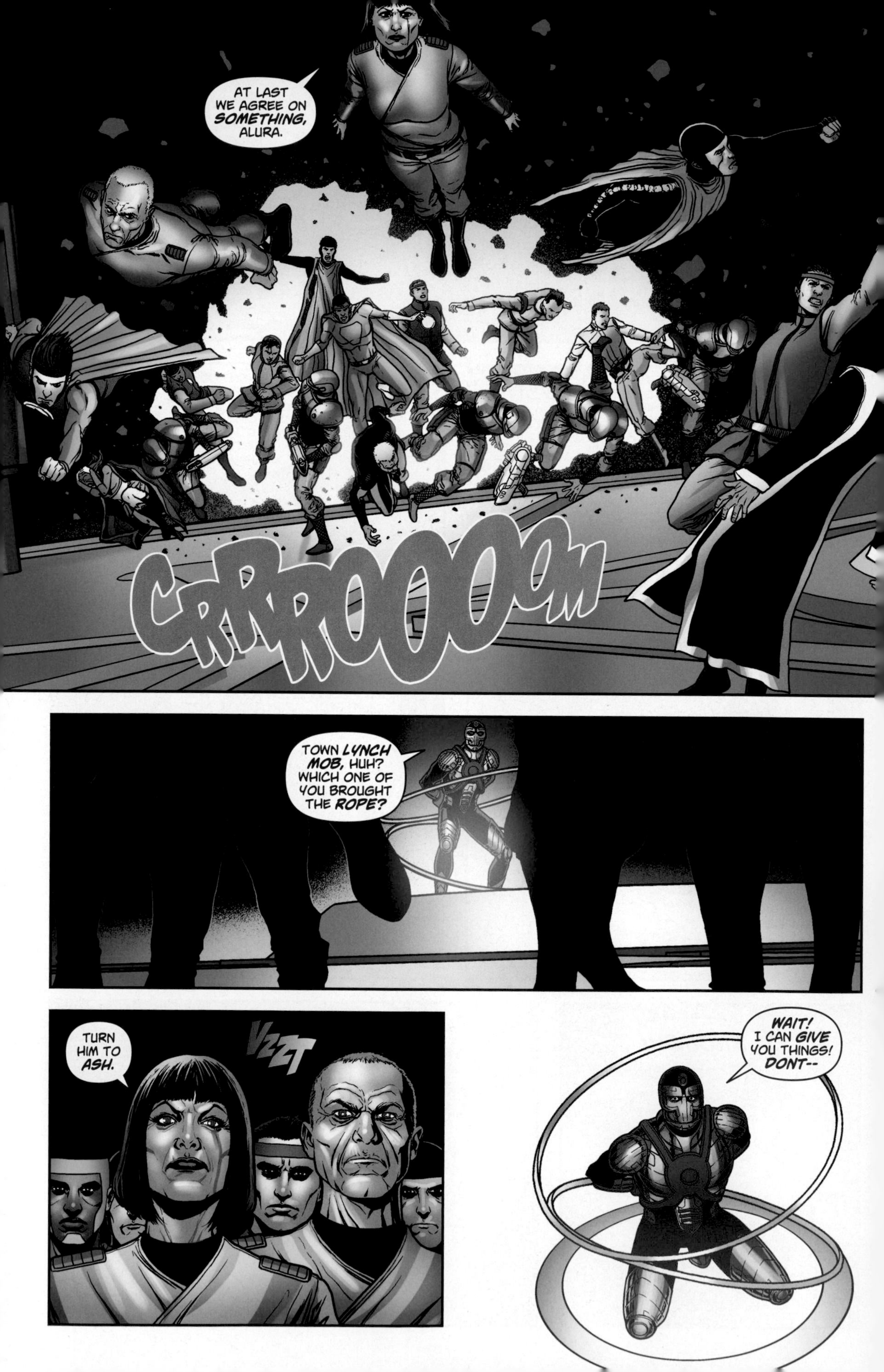
AT LAST WE AGREE ON SOMETHING, ALURA.
CRRROOOOOM
TOWN LYNCH MOB, HUH? WHICH ONE OF YOU BROUGHT THE ROPE?
TURN HIM TO ASH.
VZZT
WAIT! I CAN GIVE YOU THINGS! DONT--

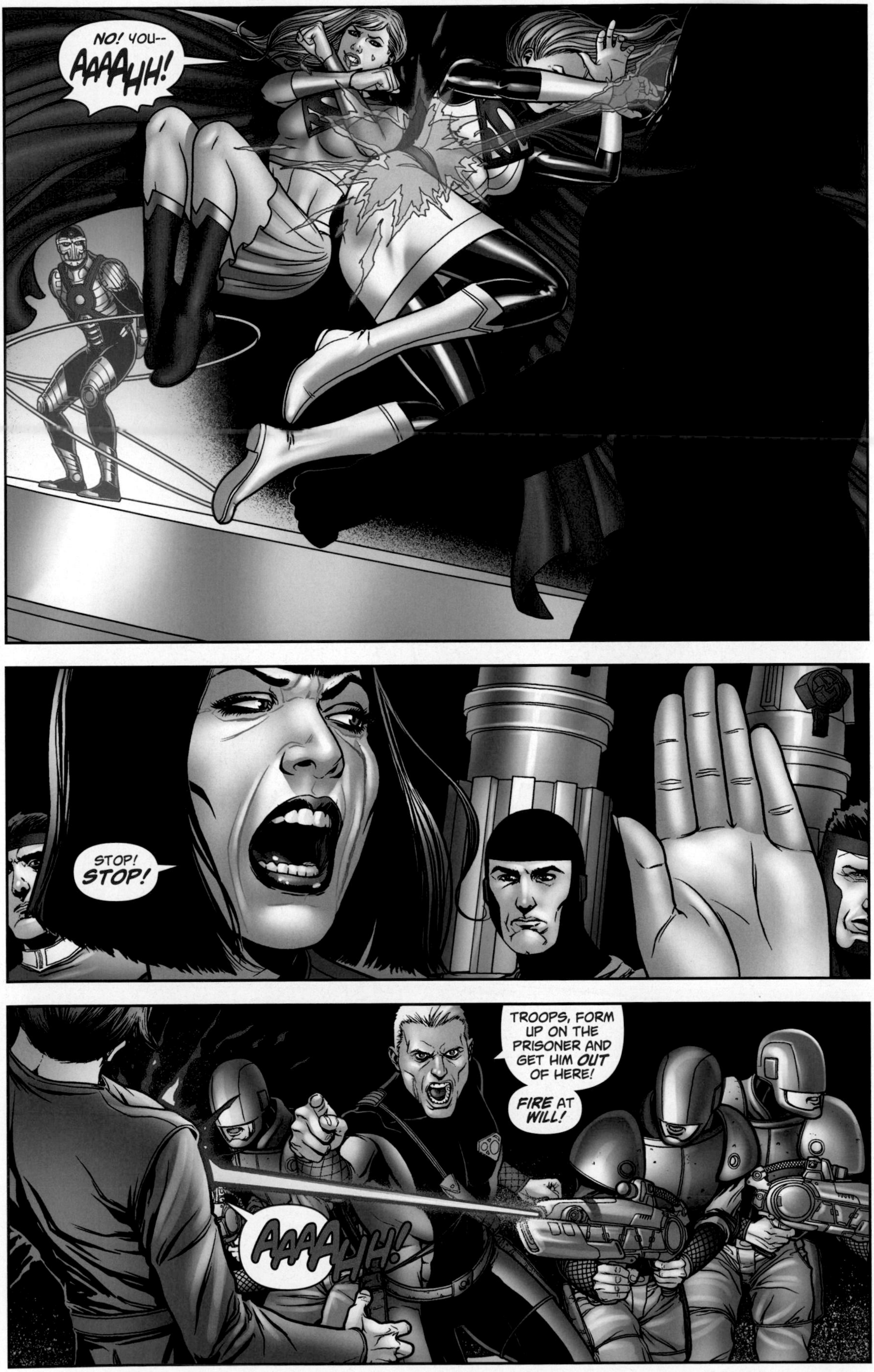
NO! YOU--
AAAAHH!
STOP!
STOP!
TROOPS, FORM UP ON THE PRISONER AND GET HIM OUT OF HERE!
FIRE AT WILL!
AAAAHH!

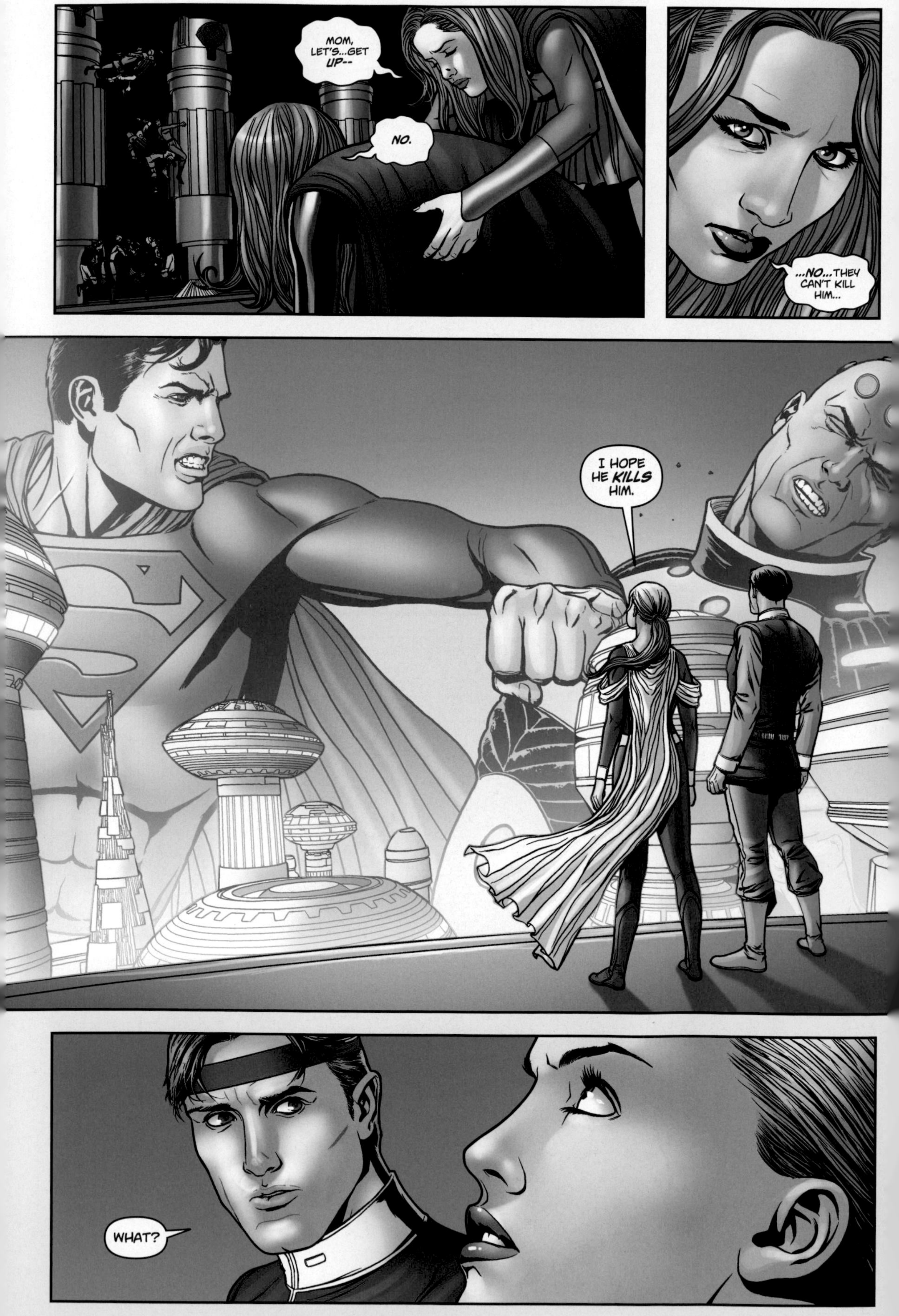
MOM, LET'S...GET UP--
NO.
...NO...THEY CAN'T KILL HIM...
I HOPE HE KILLS HIM.
WHAT?

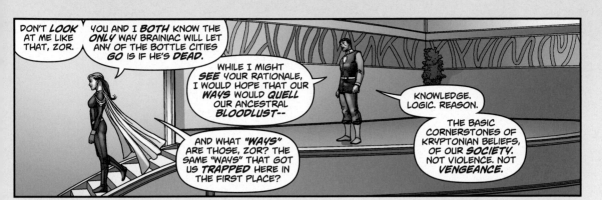

DON'T *LOOK* AT ME LIKE THAT, ZOR.

YOU AND I *BOTH* KNOW THE *ONLY* WAY BRAINIAC WILL LET ANY OF THE BOTTLE CITIES *GO* IS IF HE'S *DEAD.*

WHILE I MIGHT *SEE* YOUR RATIONALE, I WOULD HOPE THAT OUR *WAYS* WOULD *QUELL* OUR ANCESTRAL *BLOODLUST*--

AND WHAT *"WAYS"* ARE THOSE, ZOR? THE SAME *"WAYS"* THAT GOT US *TRAPPED* HERE IN THE FIRST PLACE?

KNOWLEDGE. LOGIC. REASON.

THE BASIC CORNERSTONES OF KRYPTONIAN BELIEFS, OF OUR *SOCIETY.* NOT VIOLENCE. NOT *VENGEANCE.*

THIS, COMING FROM *YOU,* THE *"ARTIST"?*

YOU'RE ASKING ME TO BE *LESS* EMOTIONAL? *FEEL* LESS *HATE?* HE *KILLED* MOST OF ARGO CITY WHEN HE CLAIMED US HIS OWN.

I KNOW YOU *HATE* BRAINIAC FOR ALL HE'S DONE TO US. TO OUR *FRIENDS.* WE ALL DO.

BUT WHO WE *ARE* SHOULD *OUTWEIGH* THAT HATRED. OUTWEIGH THAT *NEED* FOR VENGEANCE.

WE SHOULD BE *ABOVE* IT, AS LEADERS.

WE ARE *KRYPTONIANS.*

"REMEMBER THAT, ALURA."

DOR TAL-OX!

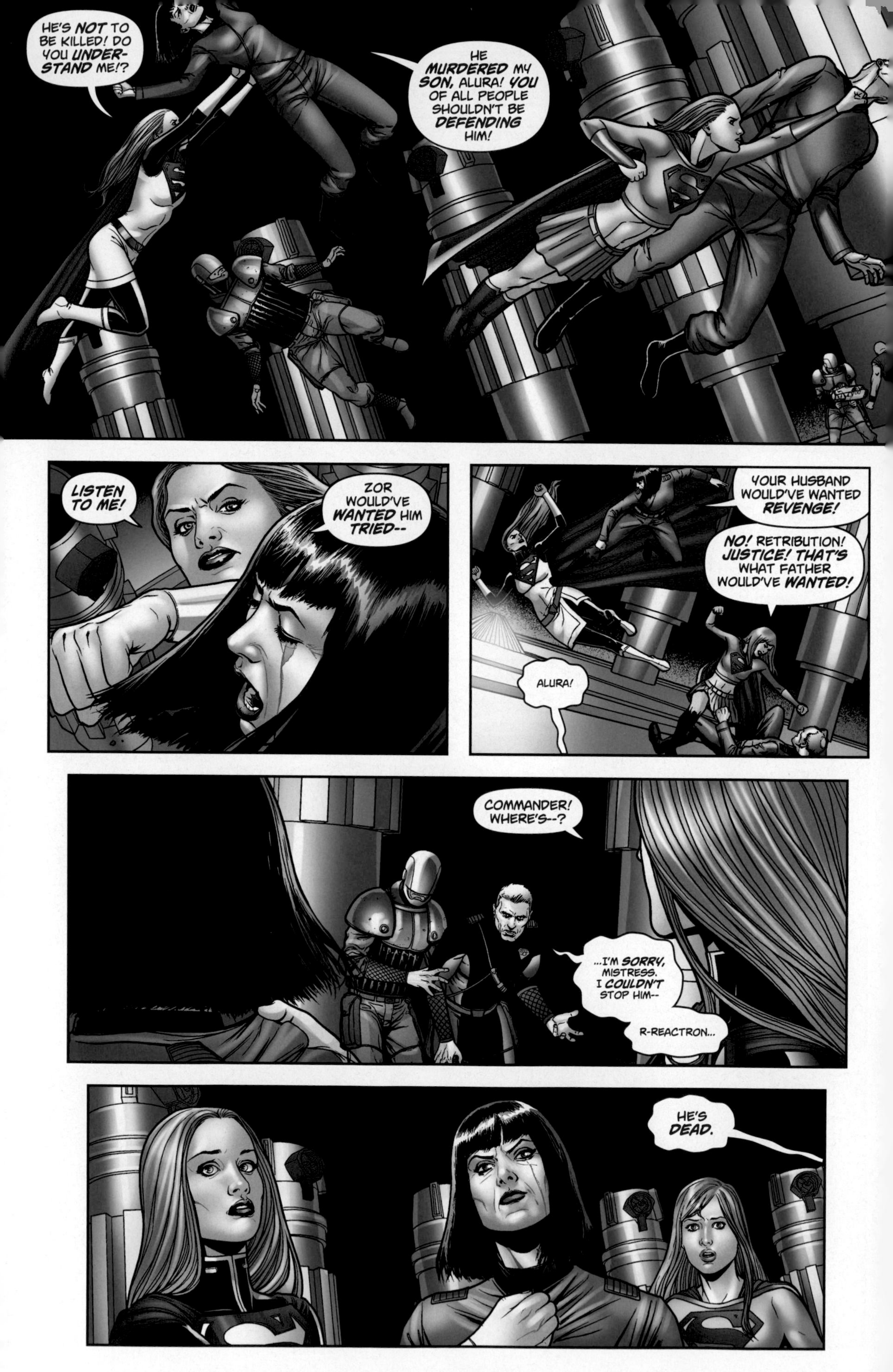
HE'S NOT TO BE KILLED! DO YOU UNDER-STAND ME!?
HE MURDERED MY SON, ALURA! YOU OF ALL PEOPLE SHOULDN'T BE DEFENDING HIM!
LISTEN TO ME!
ZOR WOULD'VE WANTED HIM TRIED--
YOUR HUSBAND WOULD'VE WANTED REVENGE!
NO! RETRIBUTION! JUSTICE! THAT'S WHAT FATHER WOULD'VE WANTED!
ALURA!
COMMANDER! WHERE'S--?
...I'M SORRY, MISTRESS. I COULDN'T STOP HIM--
R-REACTRON...
HE'S DEAD.

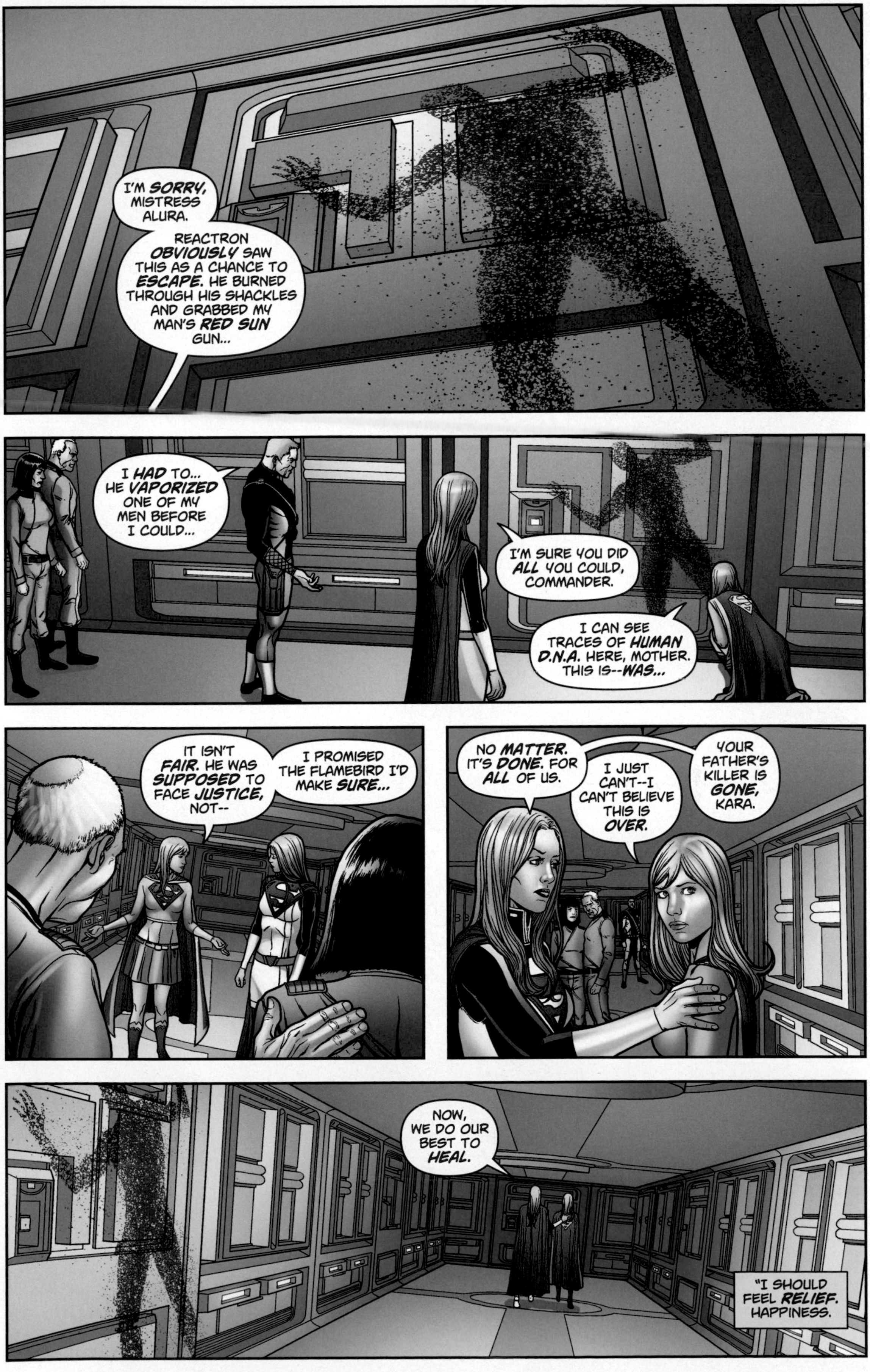
I'M SORRY, MISTRESS ALURA.
REACTRON OBVIOUSLY SAW THIS AS A CHANCE TO ESCAPE. HE BURNED THROUGH HIS SHACKLES AND GRABBED MY MAN'S RED SUN GUN...
I HAD TO... HE VAPORIZED ONE OF MY MEN BEFORE I COULD...
I'M SURE YOU DID ALL YOU COULD, COMMANDER.
I CAN SEE TRACES OF HUMAN D.N.A. HERE, MOTHER. THIS IS--WAS...
IT ISN'T FAIR. HE WAS SUPPOSED TO FACE JUSTICE, NOT--
I PROMISED THE FLAMEBIRD I'D MAKE SURE...
NO MATTER. IT'S DONE. FOR ALL OF US.
YOUR FATHER'S KILLER IS GONE, KARA.
I JUST CAN'T--I CAN'T BELIEVE THIS IS OVER.
NOW, WE DO OUR BEST TO HEAL.
"I SHOULD FEEL RELIEF. HAPPINESS.

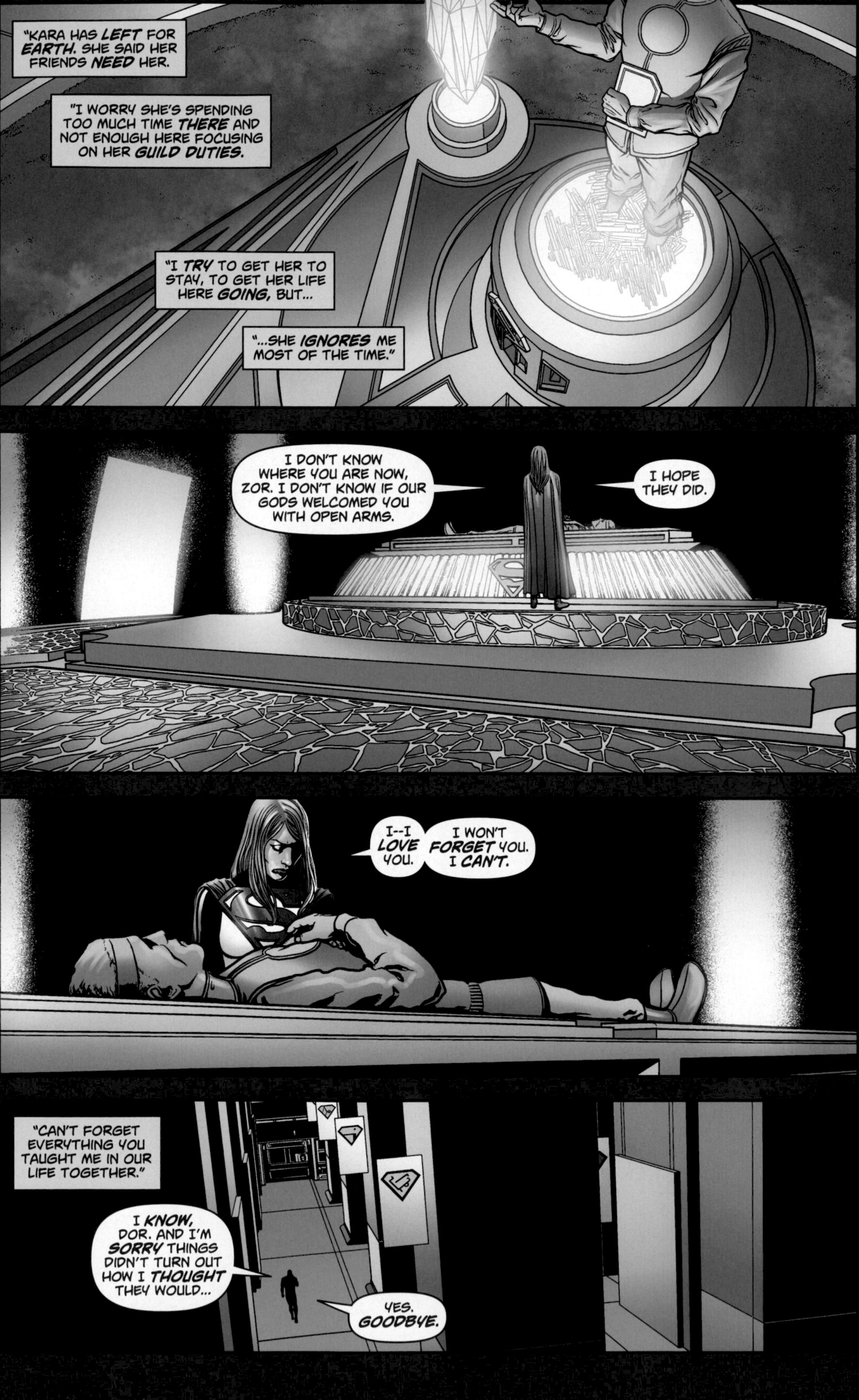
"KARA HAS LEFT FOR EARTH. SHE SAID HER FRIENDS NEED HER.
"I WORRY SHE'S SPENDING TOO MUCH TIME THERE AND NOT ENOUGH HERE FOCUSING ON HER GUILD DUTIES.
"I TRY TO GET HER TO STAY, TO GET HER LIFE HERE GOING, BUT...
"...SHE IGNORES ME MOST OF THE TIME."
I DON'T KNOW WHERE YOU ARE NOW, ZOR. I DON'T KNOW IF OUR GODS WELCOMED YOU WITH OPEN ARMS.
I HOPE THEY DID.
I--I LOVE YOU.
I WON'T FORGET YOU. I CAN'T.
"CAN'T FORGET EVERYTHING YOU TAUGHT ME IN OUR LIFE TOGETHER."
I KNOW, DOR. AND I'M SORRY THINGS DIDN'T TURN OUT HOW I THOUGHT THEY WOULD...
YES. GOODBYE.

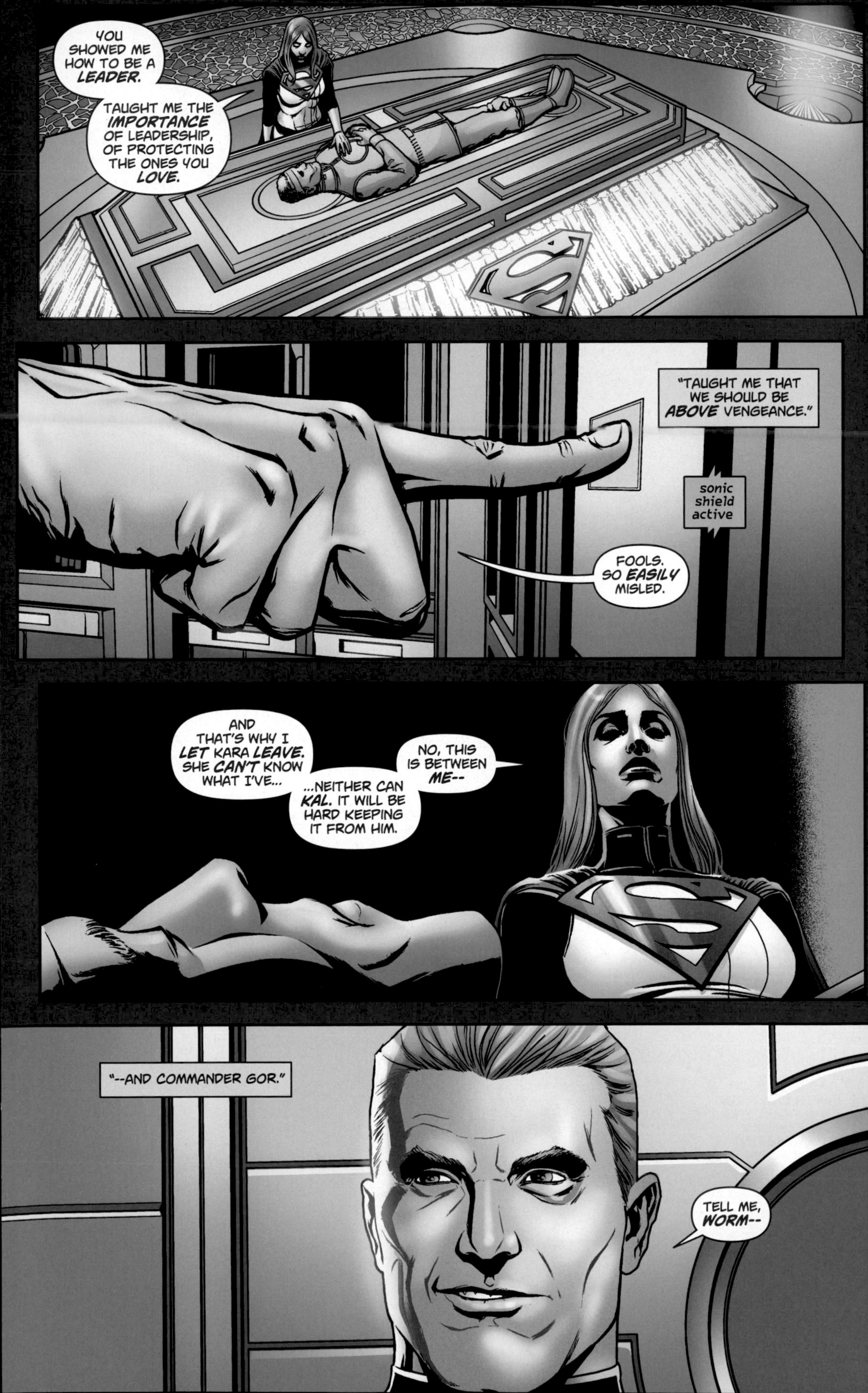
YOU SHOWED ME HOW TO BE A LEADER.
TAUGHT ME THE IMPORTANCE OF LEADERSHIP, OF PROTECTING THE ONES YOU LOVE.
"TAUGHT ME THAT WE SHOULD BE ABOVE VENGEANCE."
sonic shield active
FOOLS. SO EASILY MISLED.
AND THAT'S WHY I LET KARA LEAVE. SHE CAN'T KNOW WHAT I'VE...
...NEITHER CAN KAL. IT WILL BE HARD KEEPING IT FROM HIM.
NO, THIS IS BETWEEN ME--
"--AND COMMANDER GOR."
TELL ME, WORM--

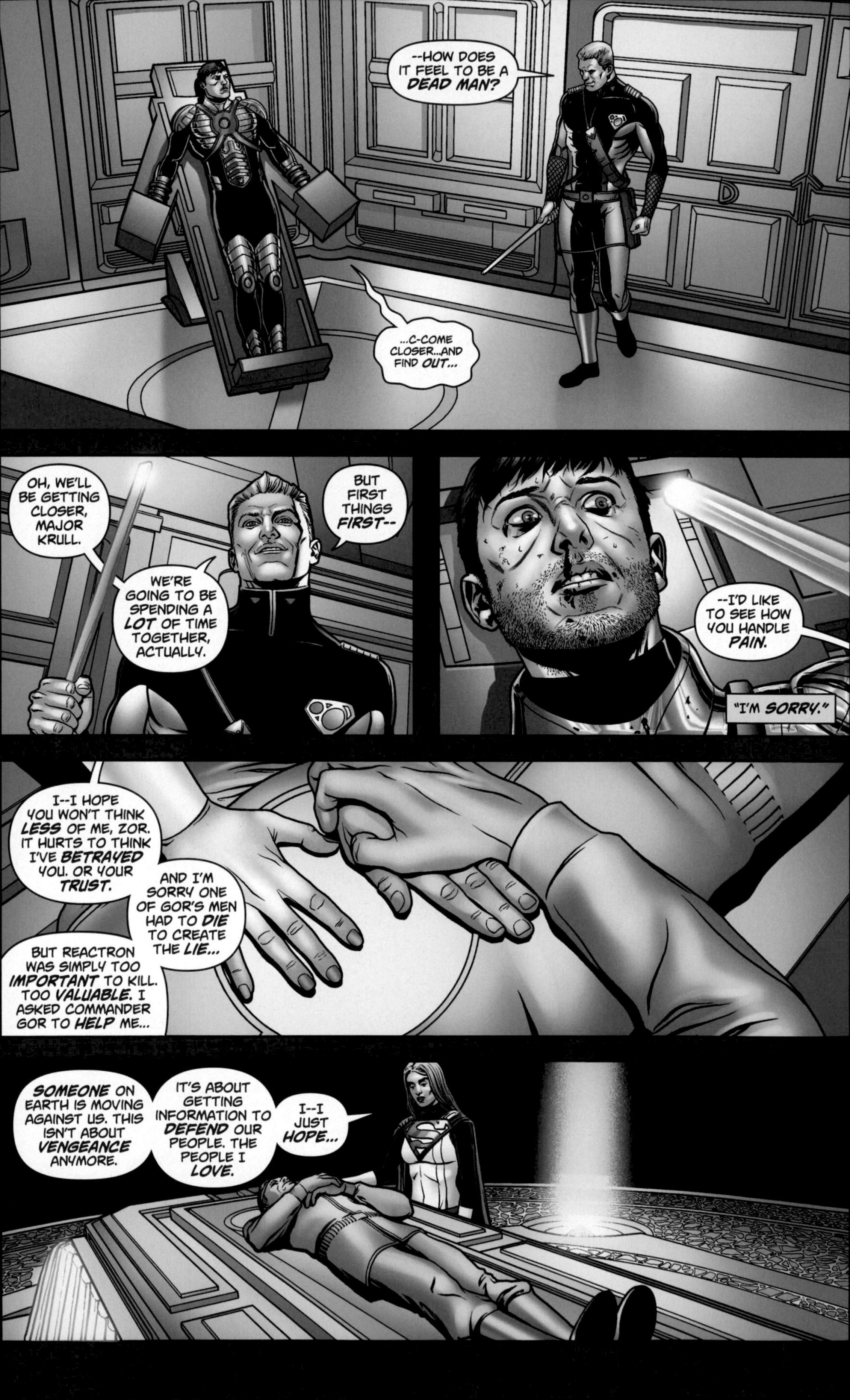
--HOW DOES IT FEEL TO BE A DEAD MAN?
...C-COME CLOSER...AND FIND OUT...
OH, WE'LL BE GETTING CLOSER, MAJOR KRULL.
WE'RE GOING TO BE SPENDING A LOT OF TIME TOGETHER, ACTUALLY.
BUT FIRST THINGS FIRST--
--I'D LIKE TO SEE HOW YOU HANDLE PAIN.
"I'M SORRY."
I--I HOPE YOU WON'T THINK LESS OF ME, ZOR. IT HURTS TO THINK I'VE BETRAYED YOU. OR YOUR TRUST.
AND I'M SORRY ONE OF GOR'S MEN HAD TO DIE TO CREATE THE LIE...
BUT REACTRON WAS SIMPLY TOO IMPORTANT TO KILL. TOO VALUABLE. I ASKED COMMANDER GOR TO HELP ME...
SOMEONE ON EARTH IS MOVING AGAINST US. THIS ISN'T ABOUT VENGEANCE ANYMORE.
IT'S ABOUT GETTING INFORMATION TO DEFEND OUR PEOPLE. THE PEOPLE I LOVE.
I--I JUST HOPE...

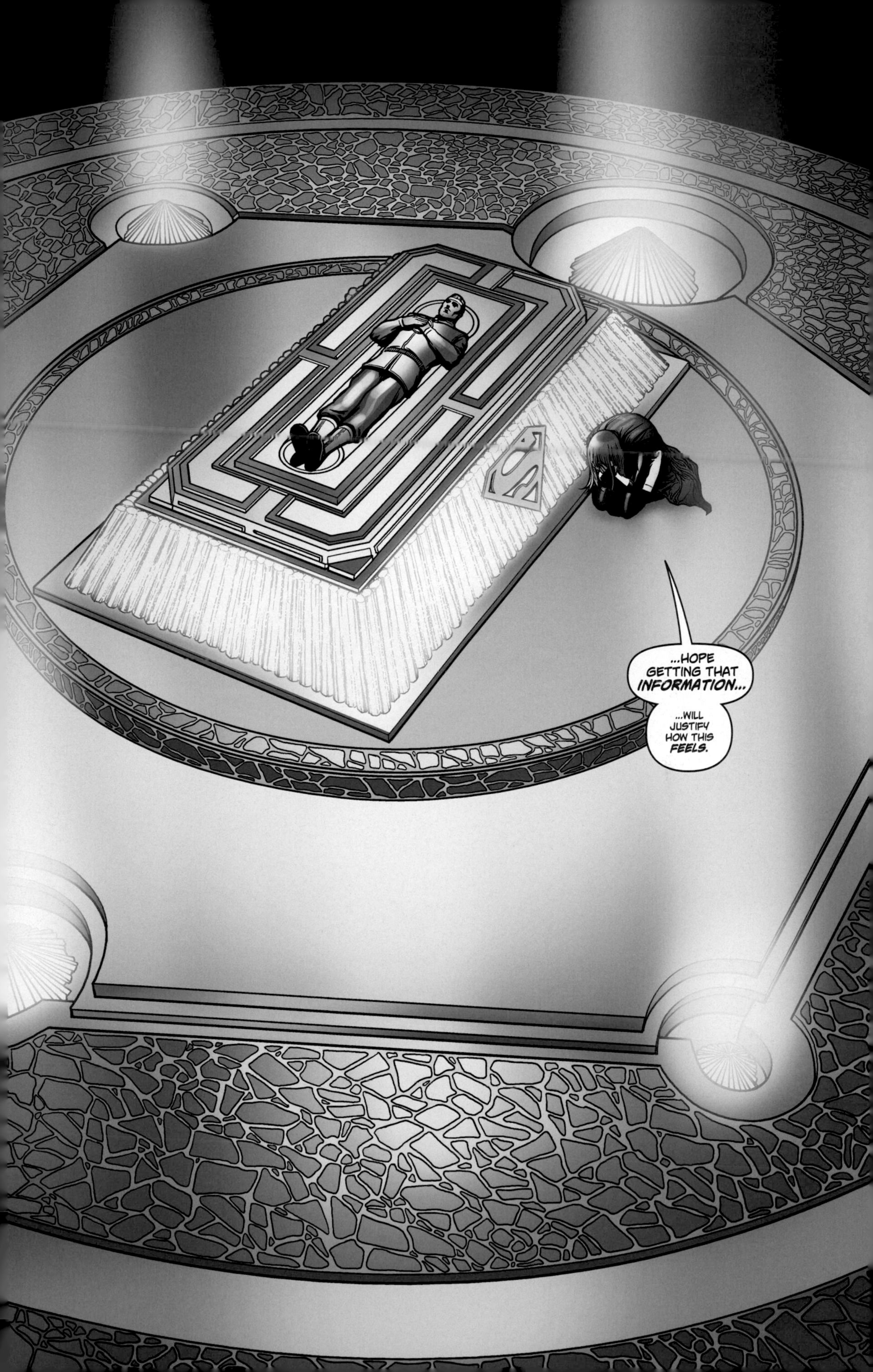
...HOPE GETTING THAT INFORMATION...
...WILL JUSTIFY HOW THIS FEELS.

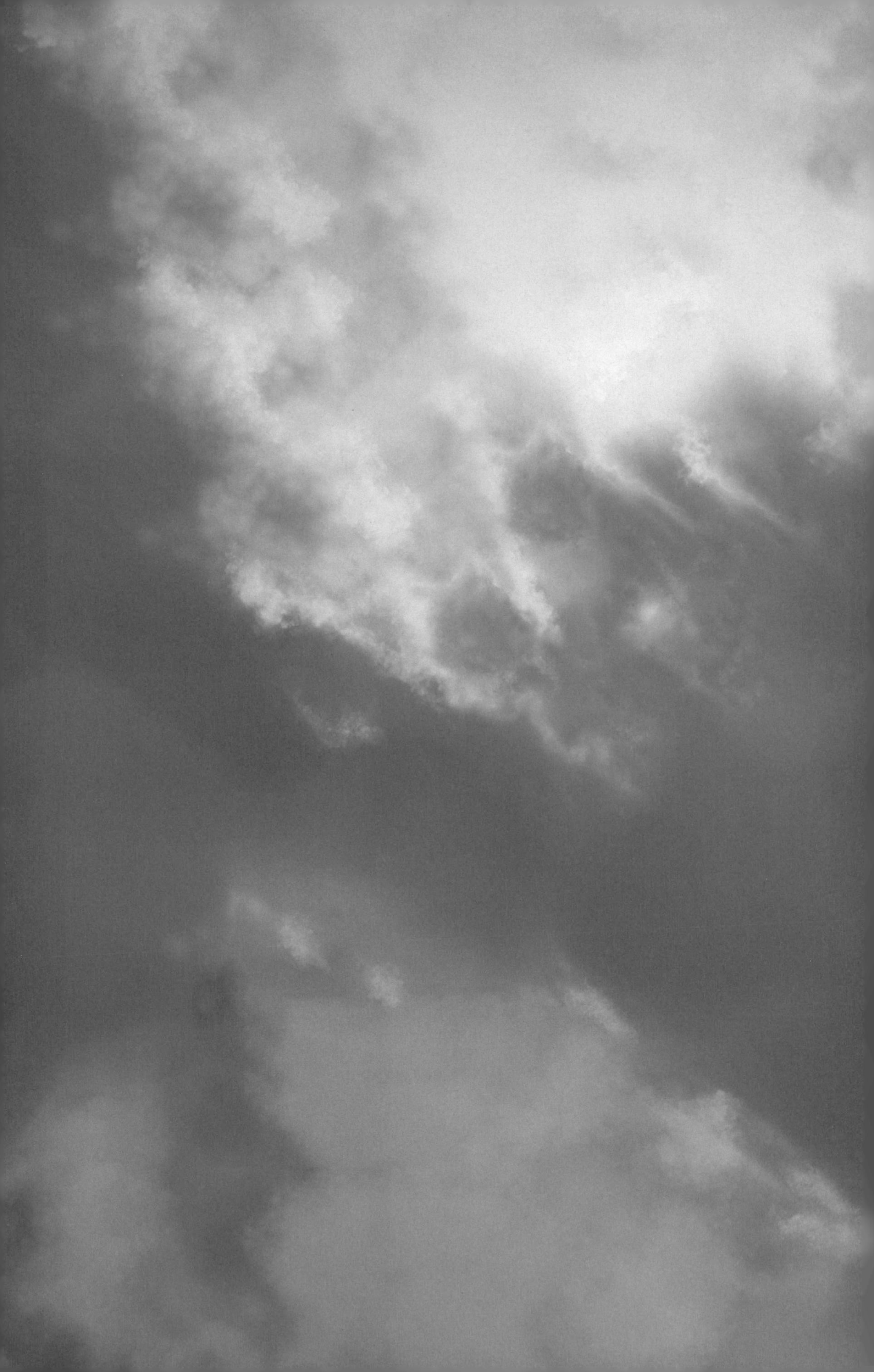

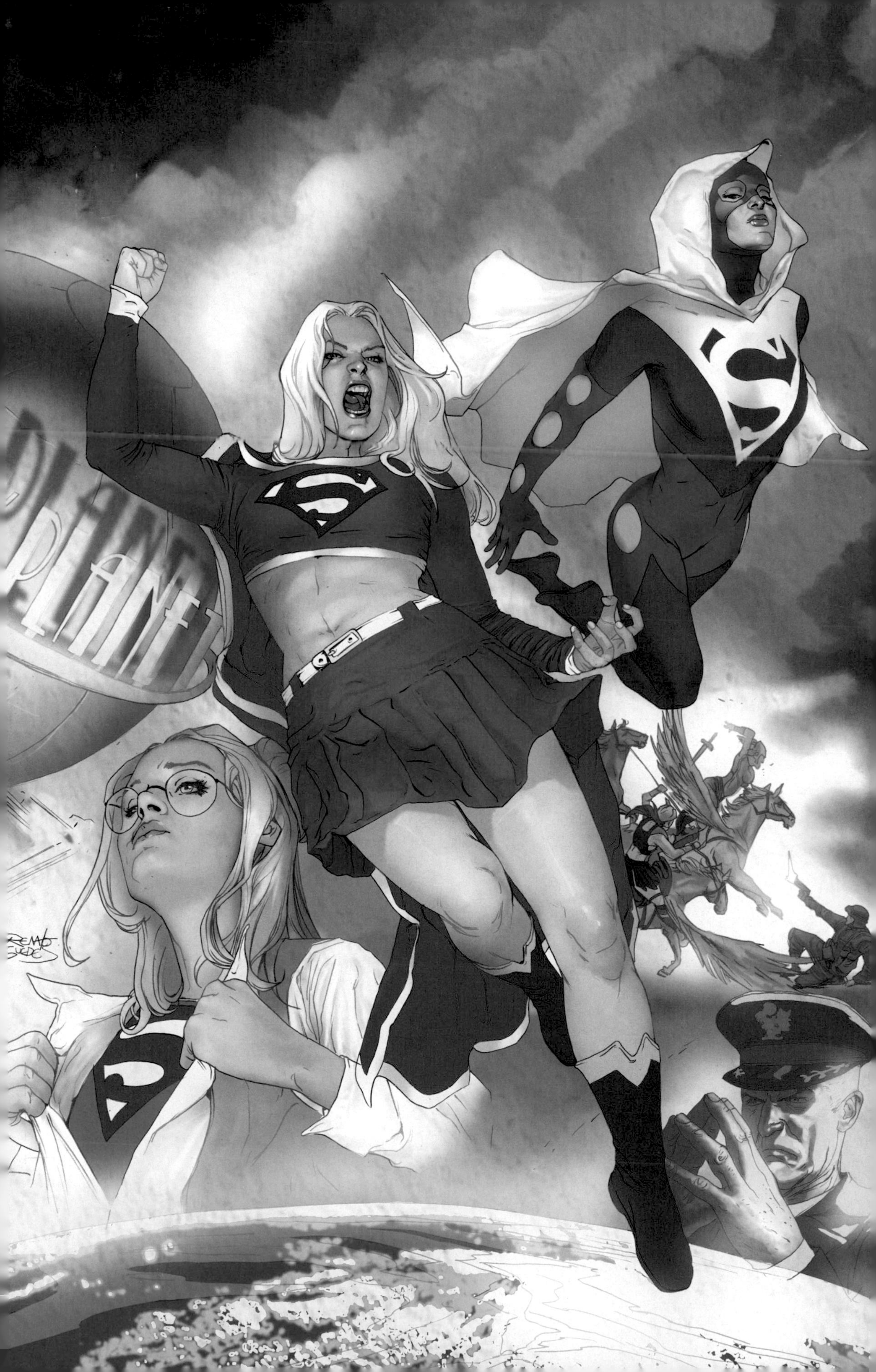

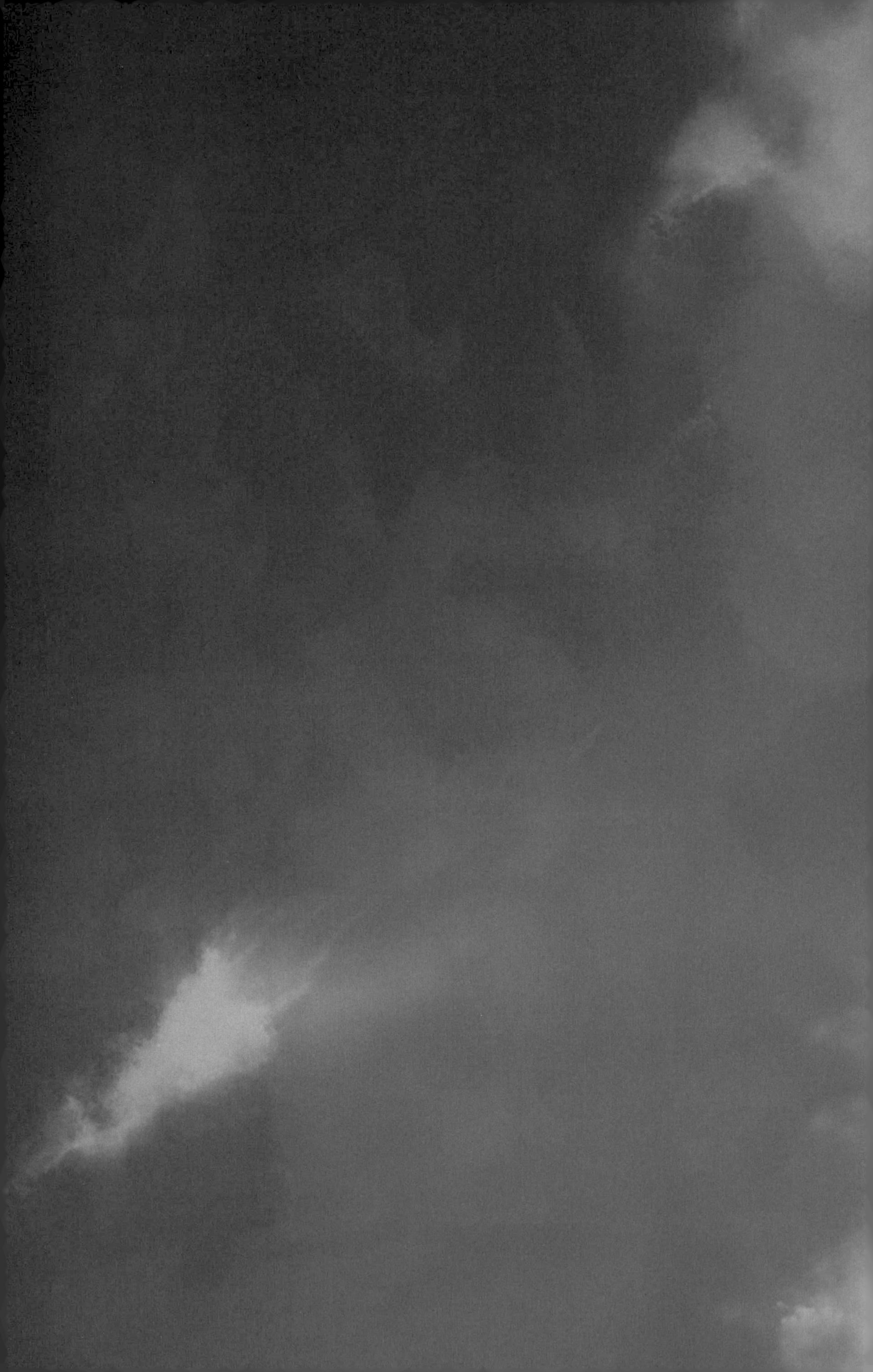

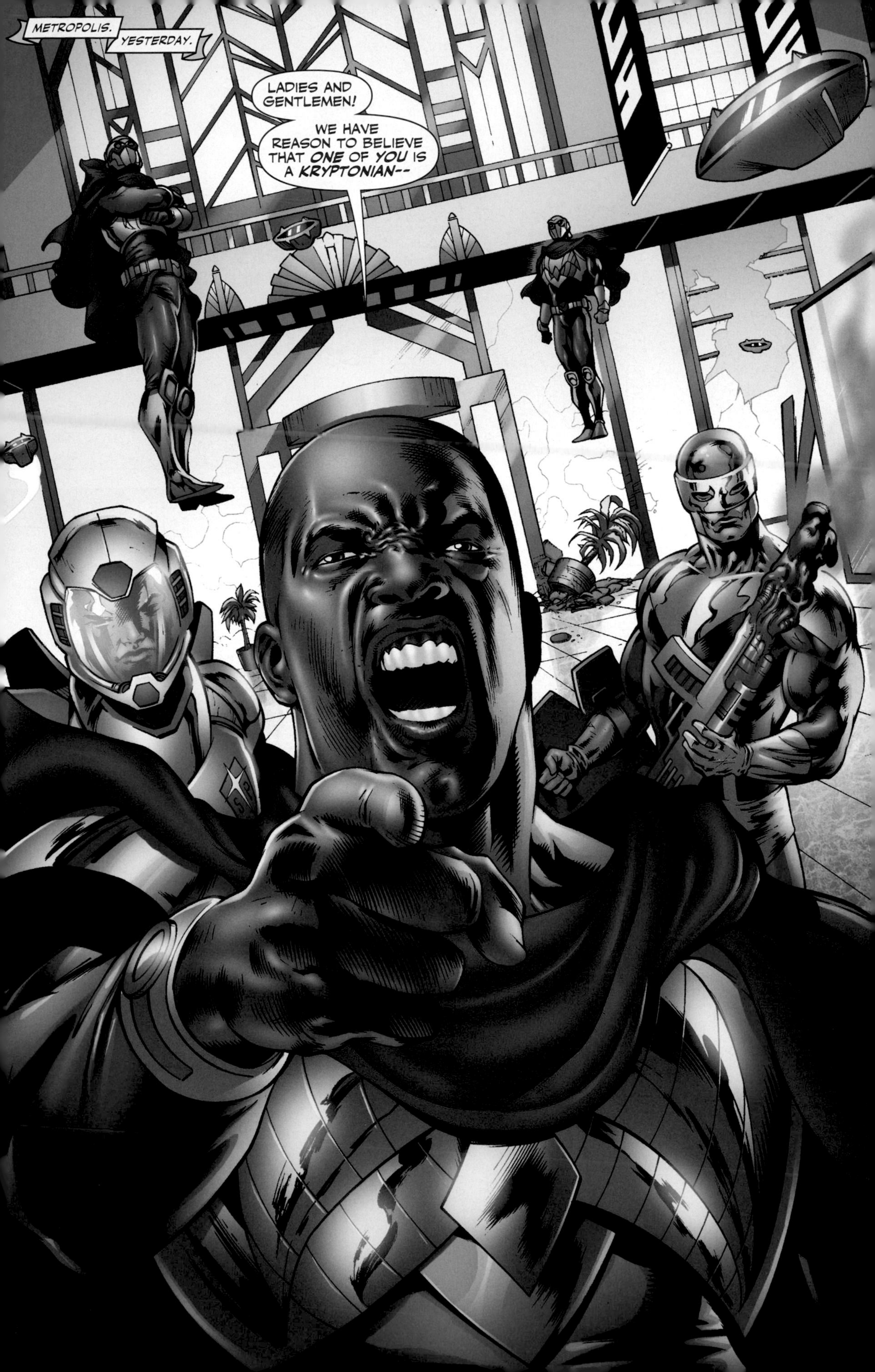
METROPOLIS.
YESTERDAY.
LADIES AND GENTLEMEN!
WE HAVE REASON TO BELIEVE THAT *ONE* OF *YOU* IS A *KRYPTONIAN*--

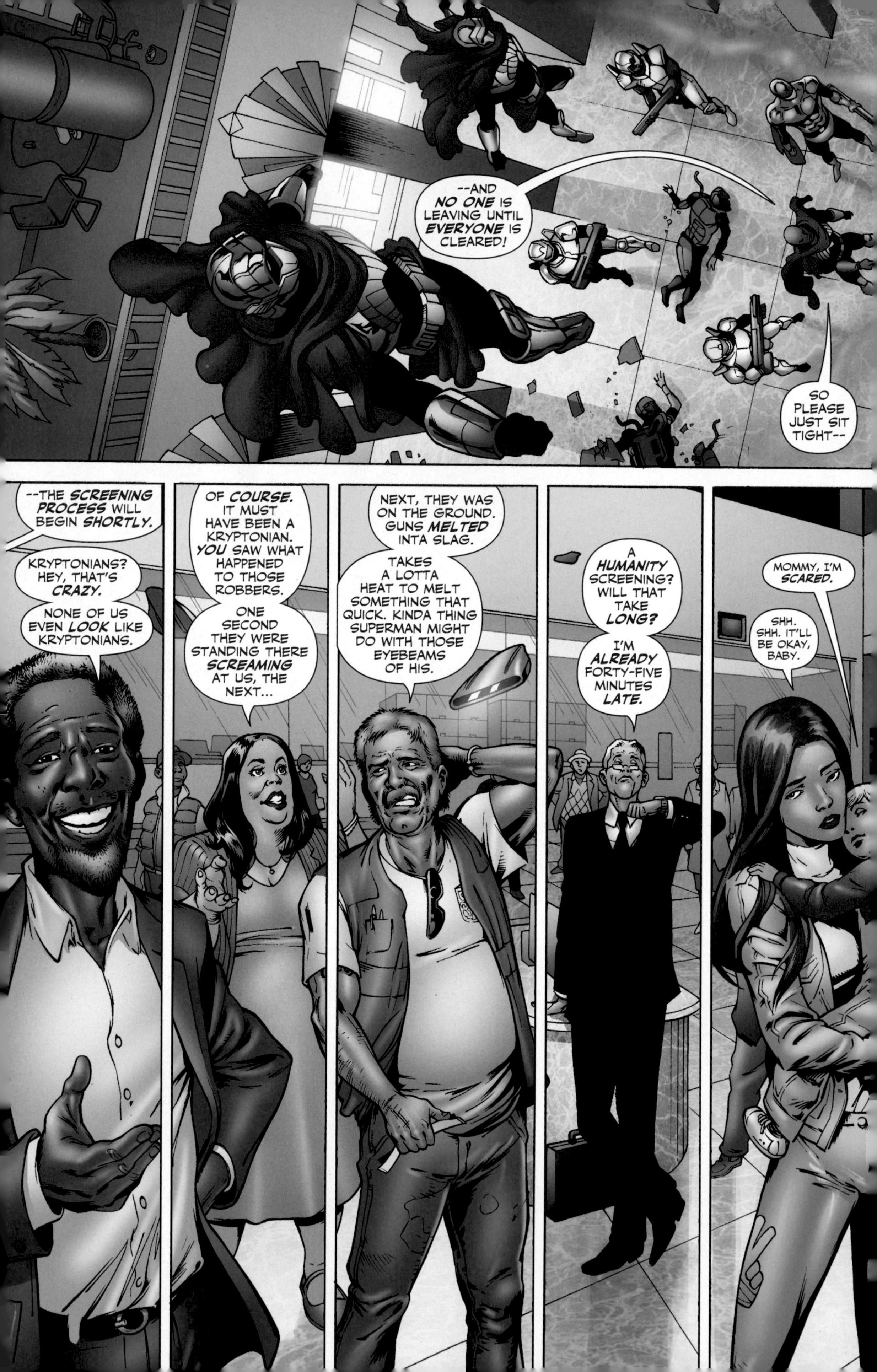
--AND *NO ONE* IS LEAVING UNTIL *EVERYONE* IS CLEARED!
SO PLEASE JUST SIT TIGHT--
--THE *SCREENING PROCESS* WILL BEGIN *SHORTLY.*
KRYPTONIANS? HEY, THAT'S *CRAZY.*
NONE OF US EVEN *LOOK* LIKE KRYPTONIANS.
OF *COURSE.* IT MUST HAVE BEEN A KRYPTONIAN. *YOU* SAW WHAT HAPPENED TO THOSE ROBBERS.
ONE SECOND THEY WERE STANDING THERE *SCREAMING* AT US, THE NEXT...
NEXT, THEY WAS ON THE GROUND. GUNS *MELTED* INTA SLAG.
TAKES A LOTTA HEAT TO MELT SOMETHING THAT QUICK. KINDA THING SUPERMAN MIGHT DO WITH THOSE EYEBEAMS OF HIS.
A *HUMANITY* SCREENING? WILL THAT TAKE *LONG?*
I'M *ALREADY* FORTY-FIVE MINUTES *LATE.*
MOMMY, I'M *SCARED.*
SHH. SHH. IT'LL BE OKAY, BABY.

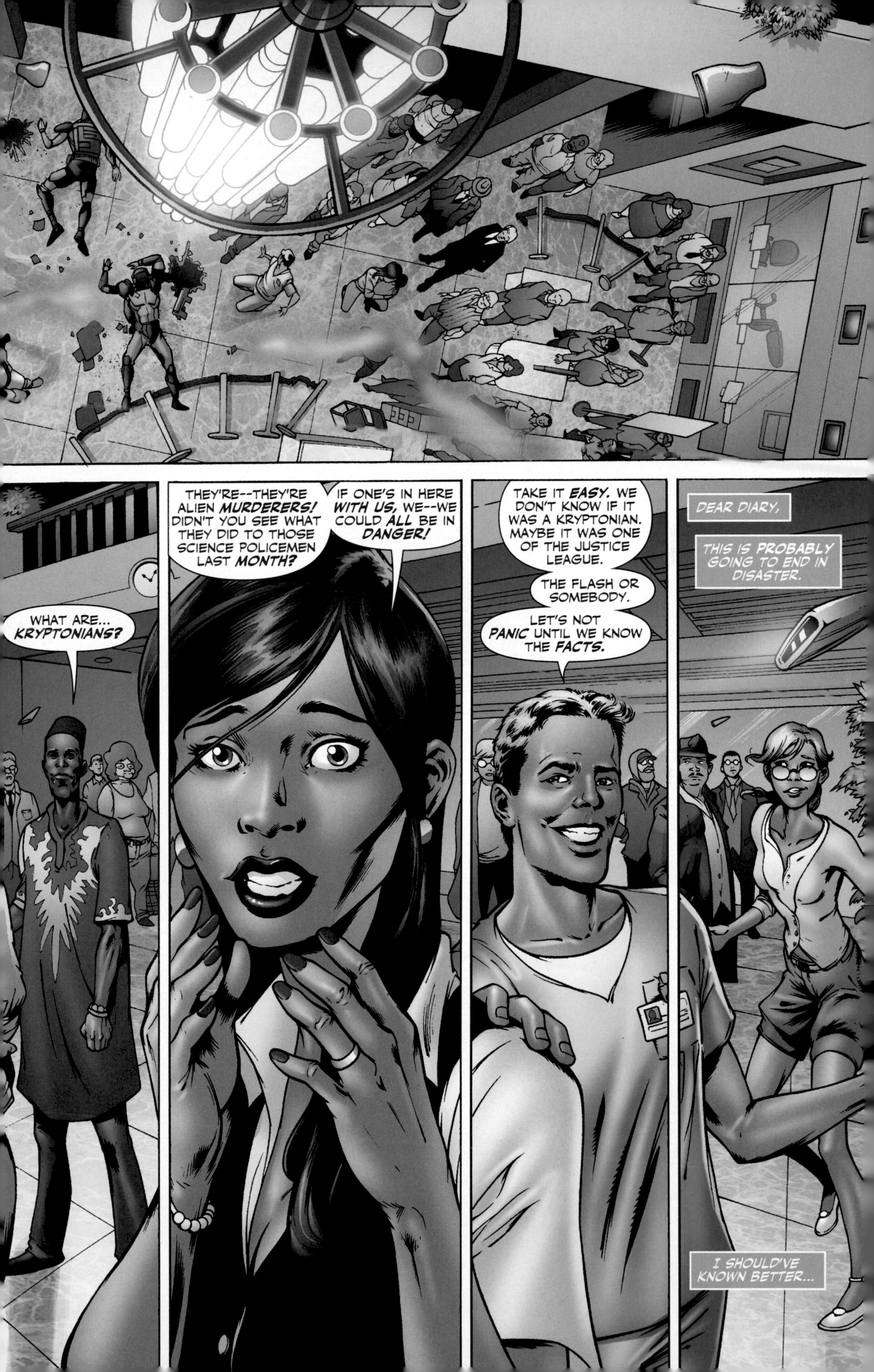
WHAT ARE... KRYPTONIANS?
THEY'RE--THEY'RE ALIEN MURDERERS! DIDN'T YOU SEE WHAT THEY DID TO THOSE SCIENCE POLICEMEN LAST MONTH?
IF ONE'S IN HERE WITH US, WE--WE COULD ALL BE IN DANGER!
TAKE IT EASY. WE DON'T KNOW IF IT WAS A KRYPTONIAN. MAYBE IT WAS ONE OF THE JUSTICE LEAGUE.
THE FLASH OR SOMEBODY.
LET'S NOT PANIC UNTIL WE KNOW THE FACTS.
DEAR DIARY,
THIS IS PROBABLY GOING TO END IN DISASTER.
I SHOULD'VE KNOWN BETTER...

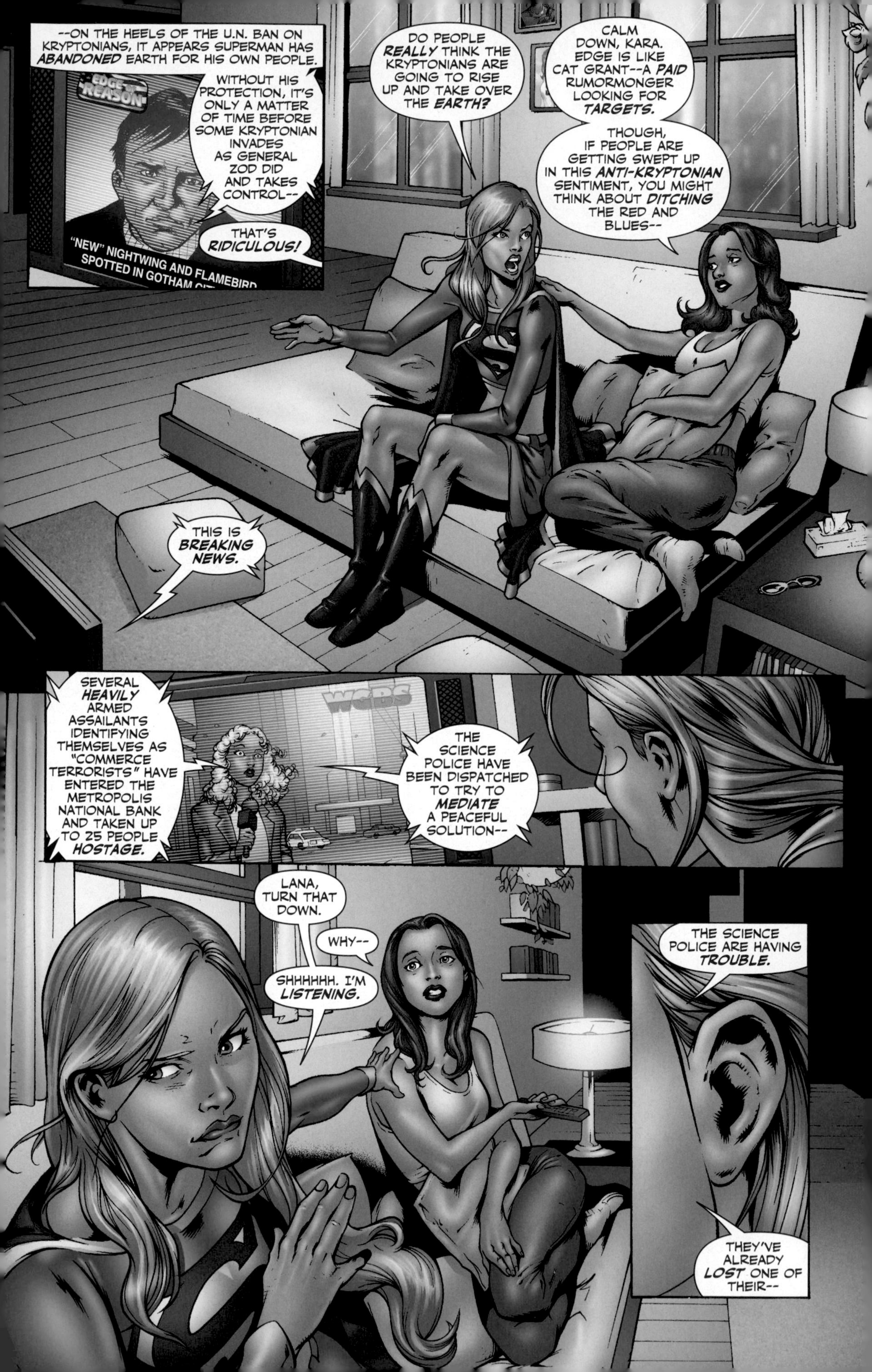
--ON THE HEELS OF THE U.N. BAN ON KRYPTONIANS, IT APPEARS SUPERMAN HAS ABANDONED EARTH FOR HIS OWN PEOPLE.
EDGE OF REASON
WITHOUT HIS PROTECTION, IT'S ONLY A MATTER OF TIME BEFORE SOME KRYPTONIAN INVADES AS GENERAL ZOD DID AND TAKES CONTROL--
THAT'S RIDICULOUS!
"NEW" NIGHTWING AND FLAMEBIRD SPOTTED IN GOTHAM CITY
DO PEOPLE REALLY THINK THE KRYPTONIANS ARE GOING TO RISE UP AND TAKE OVER THE EARTH?
CALM DOWN, KARA. EDGE IS LIKE CAT GRANT--A PAID RUMORMONGER LOOKING FOR TARGETS.
THOUGH, IF PEOPLE ARE GETTING SWEPT UP IN THIS ANTI-KRYPTONIAN SENTIMENT, YOU MIGHT THINK ABOUT DITCHING THE RED AND BLUES--
THIS IS BREAKING NEWS.
SEVERAL HEAVILY ARMED ASSAILANTS IDENTIFYING THEMSELVES AS "COMMERCE TERRORISTS" HAVE ENTERED THE METROPOLIS NATIONAL BANK AND TAKEN UP TO 25 PEOPLE HOSTAGE.
WGBS
THE SCIENCE POLICE HAVE BEEN DISPATCHED TO TRY TO MEDIATE A PEACEFUL SOLUTION--
LANA, TURN THAT DOWN.
WHY--
SHHHHHH. I'M LISTENING.
THE SCIENCE POLICE ARE HAVING TROUBLE.
THEY'VE ALREADY LOST ONE OF THEIR--

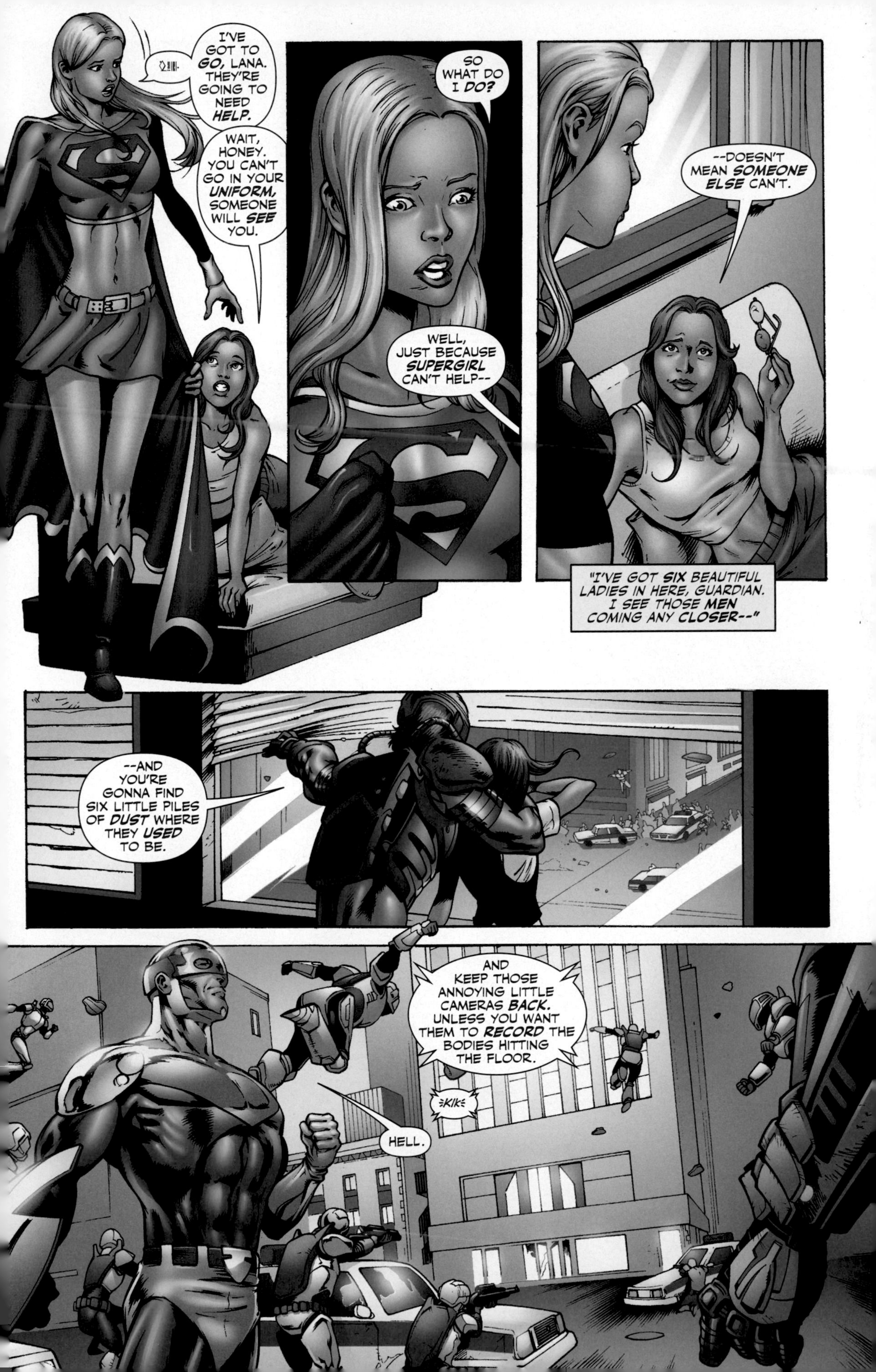

I'VE GOT TO *GO,* LANA. THEY'RE GOING TO NEED *HELP.*
WAIT, HONEY. YOU CAN'T GO IN YOUR *UNIFORM,* SOMEONE WILL *SEE* YOU.
SO WHAT DO I *DO?*
WELL, JUST BECAUSE *SUPERGIRL* CAN'T HELP--
--DOESN'T MEAN *SOMEONE ELSE* CAN'T.
"I'VE GOT *SIX* BEAUTIFUL LADIES IN HERE, GUARDIAN. I SEE THOSE *MEN* COMING ANY *CLOSER*--"
--AND YOU'RE GONNA FIND SIX LITTLE PILES OF *DUST* WHERE THEY *USED* TO BE.
AND KEEP THOSE ANNOYING LITTLE CAMERAS *BACK.* UNLESS YOU WANT THEM TO *RECORD* THE BODIES HITTING THE FLOOR.
KIK
HELL.

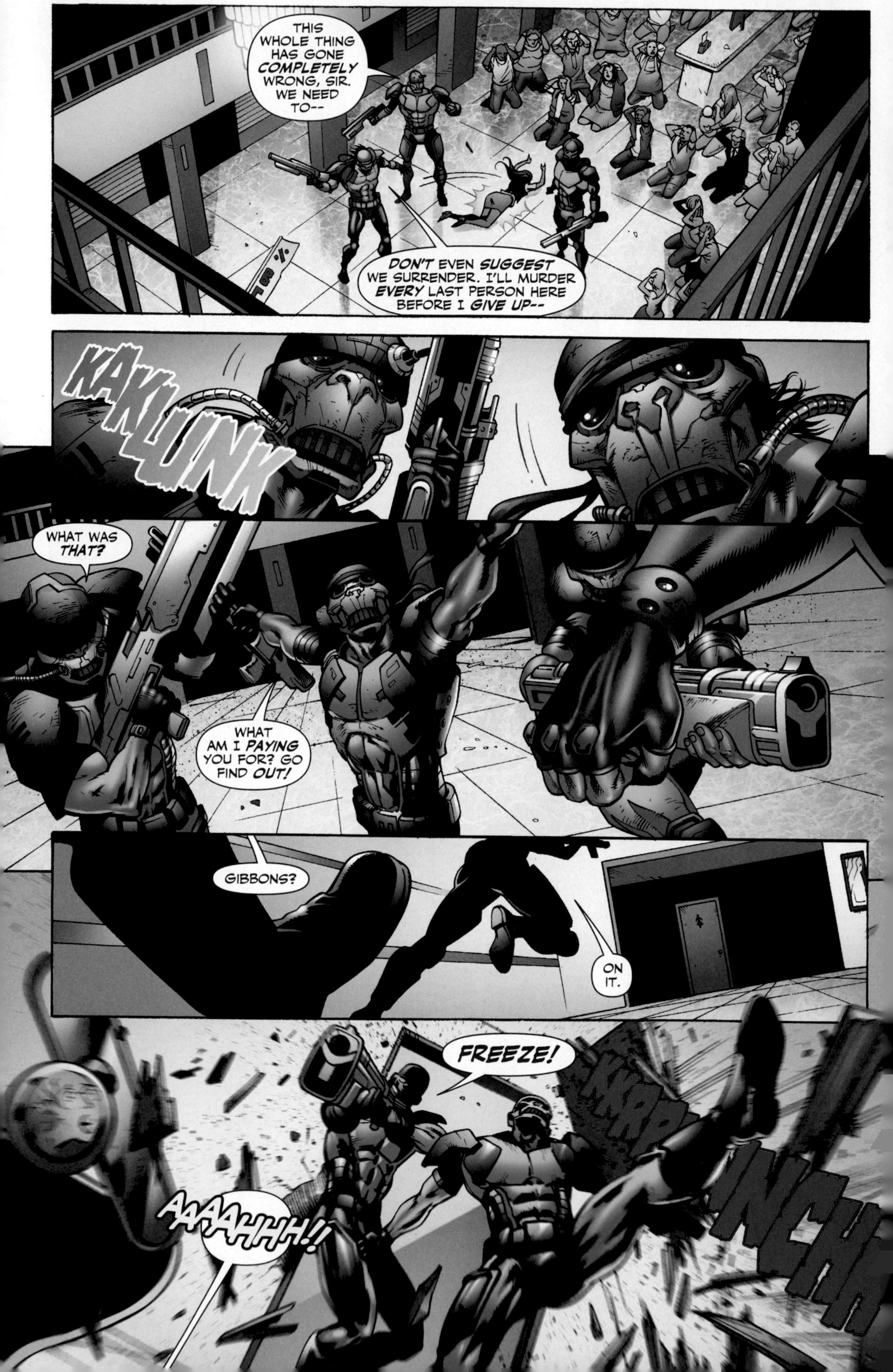
THIS WHOLE THING HAS GONE COMPLETELY WRONG, SIR. WE NEED TO--
DON'T EVEN SUGGEST WE SURRENDER. I'LL MURDER EVERY LAST PERSON HERE BEFORE I GIVE UP--
KAKLUNK
WHAT WAS THAT?
WHAT AM I PAYING YOU FOR? GO FIND OUT!
GIBBONS?
ON IT.
FREEZE!
AAAAHHH!!

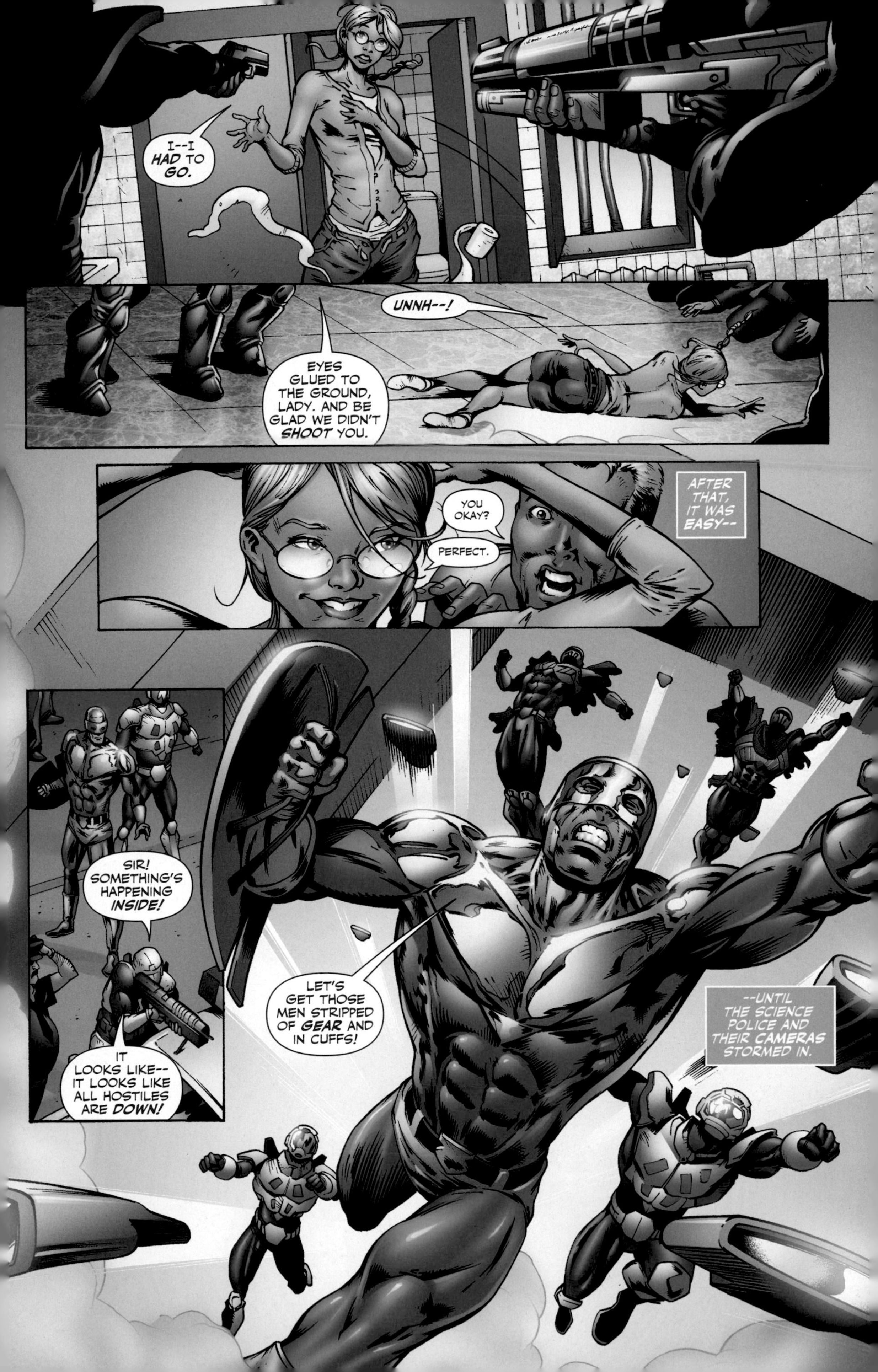
I--I HAD TO GO.
UNNH--!
EYES GLUED TO THE GROUND, LADY. AND BE GLAD WE DIDN'T SHOOT YOU.
YOU OKAY?
PERFECT.
AFTER THAT, IT WAS EASY--
SIR! SOMETHING'S HAPPENING INSIDE!
IT LOOKS LIKE-- IT LOOKS LIKE ALL HOSTILES ARE DOWN!
LET'S GET THOSE MEN STRIPPED OF GEAR AND IN CUFFS!
--UNTIL THE SCIENCE POLICE AND THEIR CAMERAS STORMED IN.

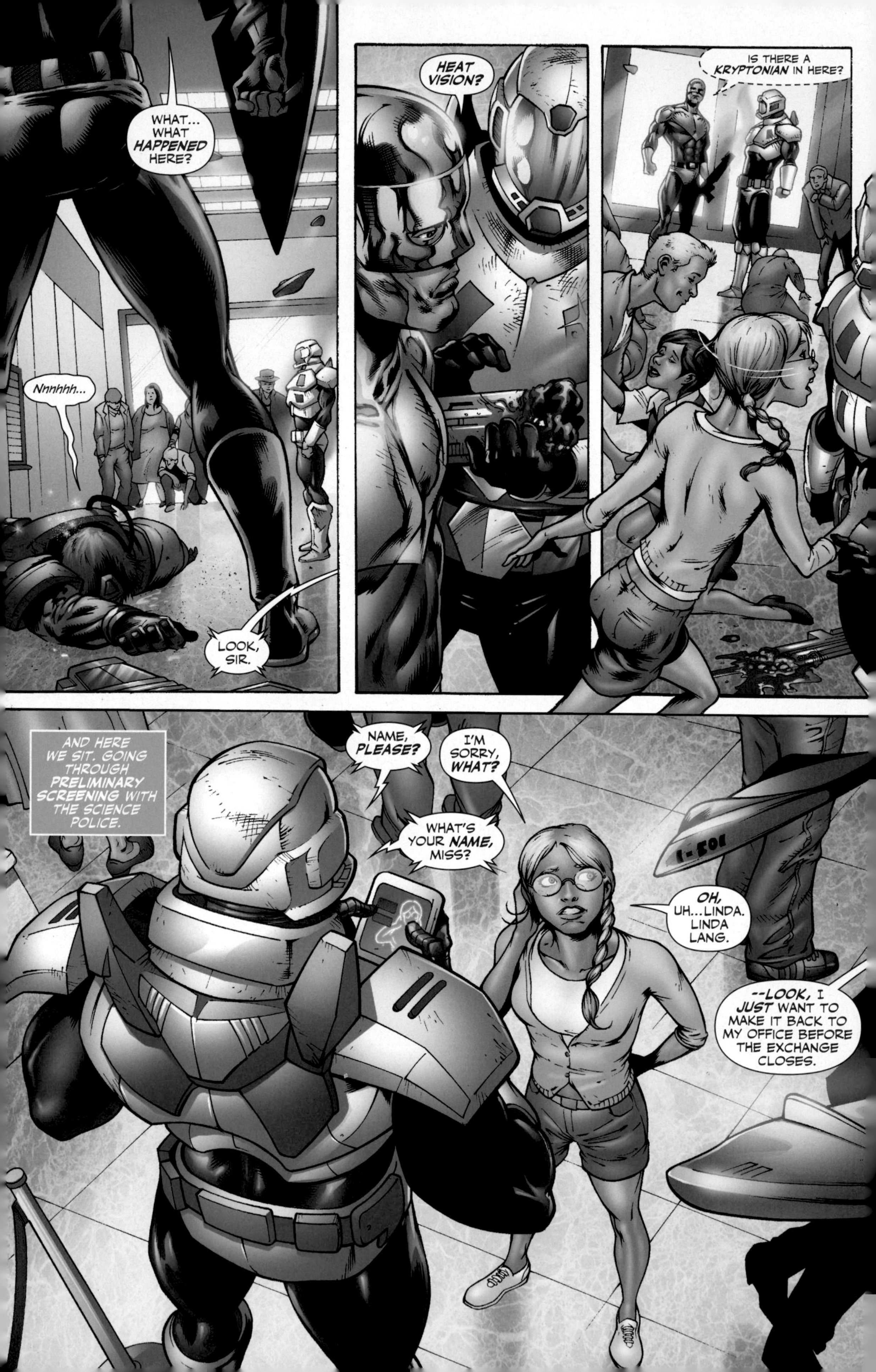
WHAT... WHAT HAPPENED HERE?
Nnnhhh...
LOOK, SIR.
HEAT VISION?
IS THERE A KRYPTONIAN IN HERE?
AND HERE WE SIT. GOING THROUGH PRELIMINARY SCREENING WITH THE SCIENCE POLICE.
NAME, PLEASE?
I'M SORRY, WHAT?
WHAT'S YOUR NAME, MISS?
OH, UH...LINDA. LINDA LANG.
--LOOK, I JUST WANT TO MAKE IT BACK TO MY OFFICE BEFORE THE EXCHANGE CLOSES.

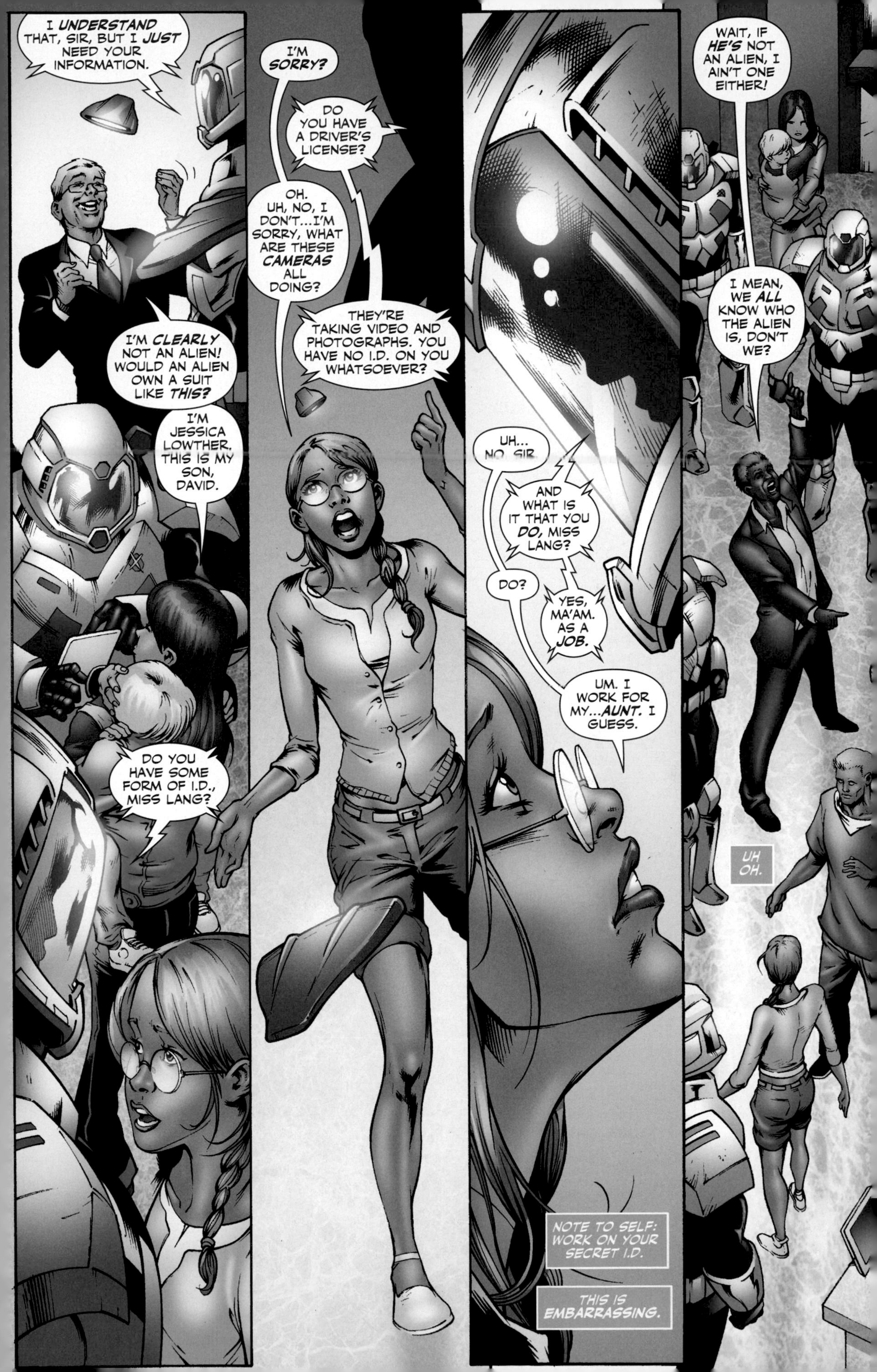
I UNDERSTAND THAT, SIR, BUT I JUST NEED YOUR INFORMATION.
I'M CLEARLY NOT AN ALIEN! WOULD AN ALIEN OWN A SUIT LIKE THIS?
I'M JESSICA LOWTHER. THIS IS MY SON, DAVID.
DO YOU HAVE SOME FORM OF I.D., MISS LANG?
I'M SORRY?
DO YOU HAVE A DRIVER'S LICENSE?
OH. UH, NO, I DON'T...I'M SORRY, WHAT ARE THESE CAMERAS ALL DOING?
THEY'RE TAKING VIDEO AND PHOTOGRAPHS. YOU HAVE NO I.D. ON YOU WHATSOEVER?
UH... NO, SIR.
AND WHAT IS IT THAT YOU DO, MISS LANG?
DO?
YES, MA'AM. AS A JOB.
UM. I WORK FOR MY...AUNT. I GUESS.
NOTE TO SELF: WORK ON YOUR SECRET I.D.
THIS IS EMBARRASSING.
WAIT, IF HE'S NOT AN ALIEN, I AIN'T ONE EITHER!
I MEAN, WE ALL KNOW WHO THE ALIEN IS, DON'T WE?
UH OH.

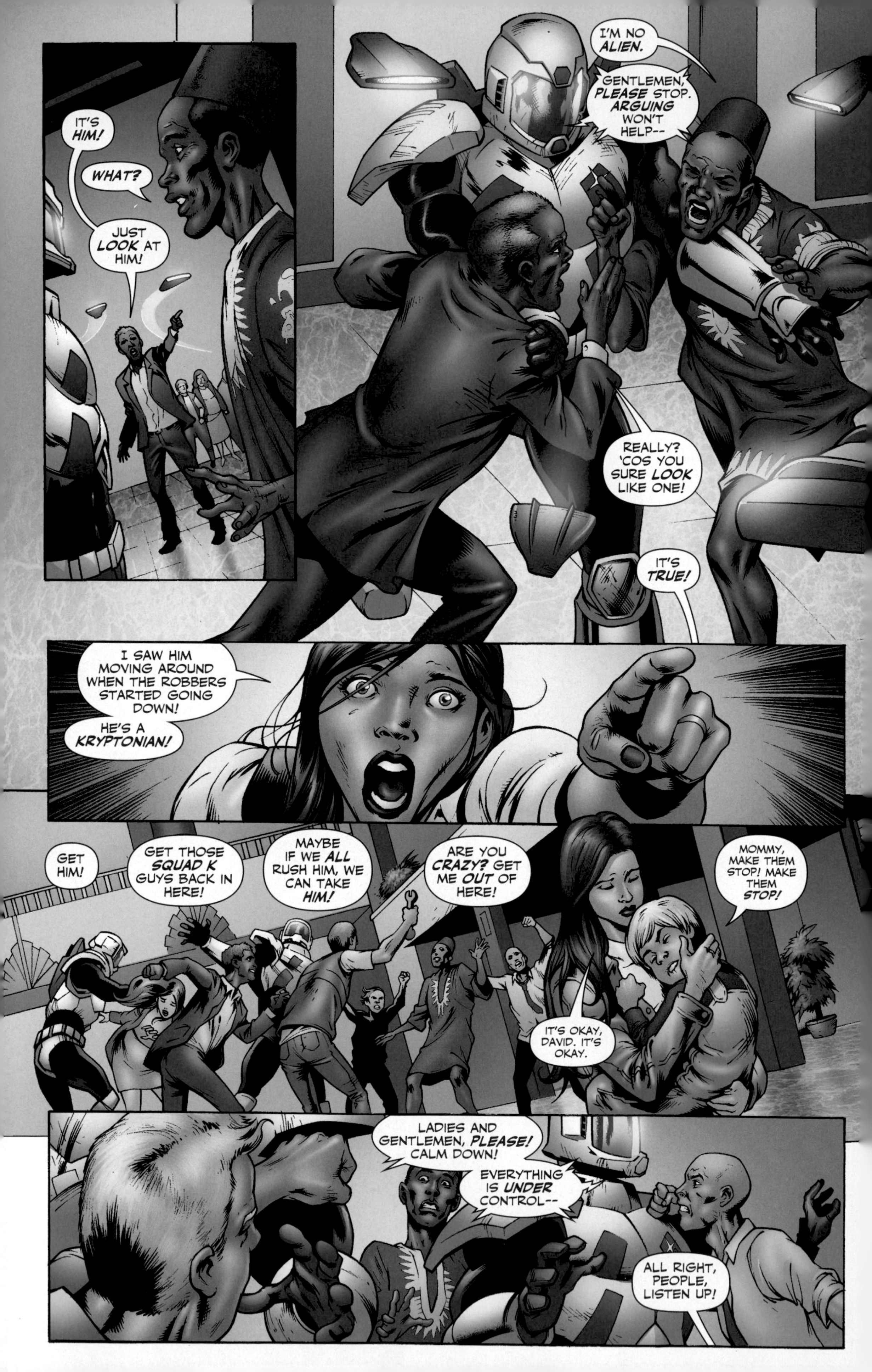
IT'S HIM!
WHAT?
JUST LOOK AT HIM!
I'M NO ALIEN.
GENTLEMEN, PLEASE STOP. ARGUING WON'T HELP--
REALLY? 'COS YOU SURE LOOK LIKE ONE!
IT'S TRUE!
I SAW HIM MOVING AROUND WHEN THE ROBBERS STARTED GOING DOWN!
HE'S A KRYPTONIAN!
GET HIM!
GET THOSE SQUAD K GUYS BACK IN HERE!
MAYBE IF WE ALL RUSH HIM, WE CAN TAKE HIM!
ARE YOU CRAZY? GET ME OUT OF HERE!
MOMMY, MAKE THEM STOP! MAKE THEM STOP!
IT'S OKAY, DAVID. IT'S OKAY.
LADIES AND GENTLEMEN, PLEASE! CALM DOWN!
EVERYTHING IS UNDER CONTROL--
ALL RIGHT, PEOPLE, LISTEN UP!

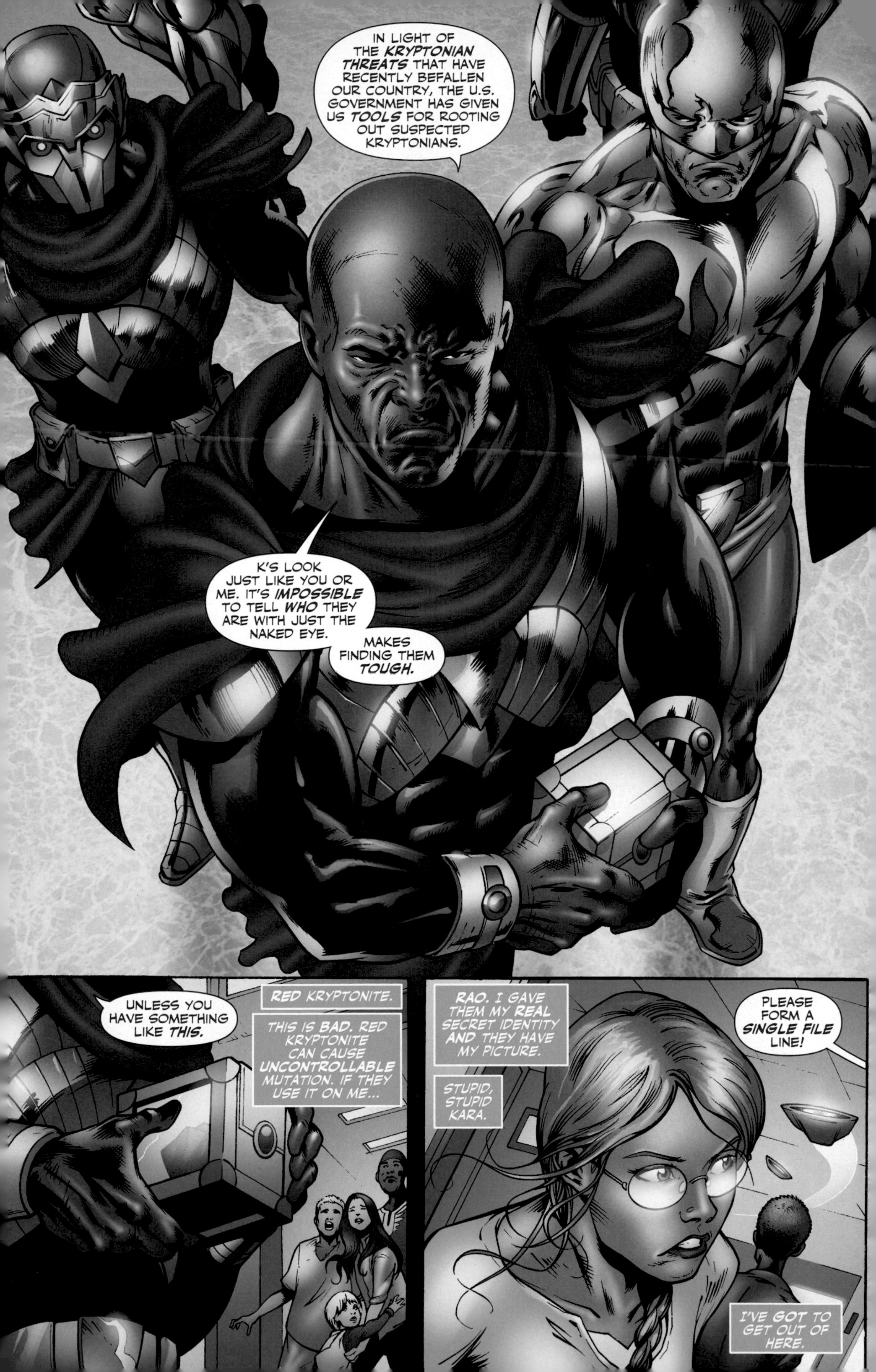
IN LIGHT OF THE KRYPTONIAN THREATS THAT HAVE RECENTLY BEFALLEN OUR COUNTRY, THE U.S. GOVERNMENT HAS GIVEN US TOOLS FOR ROOTING OUT SUSPECTED KRYPTONIANS.
K'S LOOK JUST LIKE YOU OR ME. IT'S IMPOSSIBLE TO TELL WHO THEY ARE WITH JUST THE NAKED EYE.
MAKES FINDING THEM TOUGH.
UNLESS YOU HAVE SOMETHING LIKE THIS.
RED KRYPTONITE.
THIS IS BAD. RED KRYPTONITE CAN CAUSE UNCONTROLLABLE MUTATION. IF THEY USE IT ON ME...
RAO. I GAVE THEM MY REAL SECRET IDENTITY AND THEY HAVE MY PICTURE.
STUPID, STUPID KARA.
PLEASE FORM A SINGLE FILE LINE!
I'VE GOT TO GET OUT OF HERE.

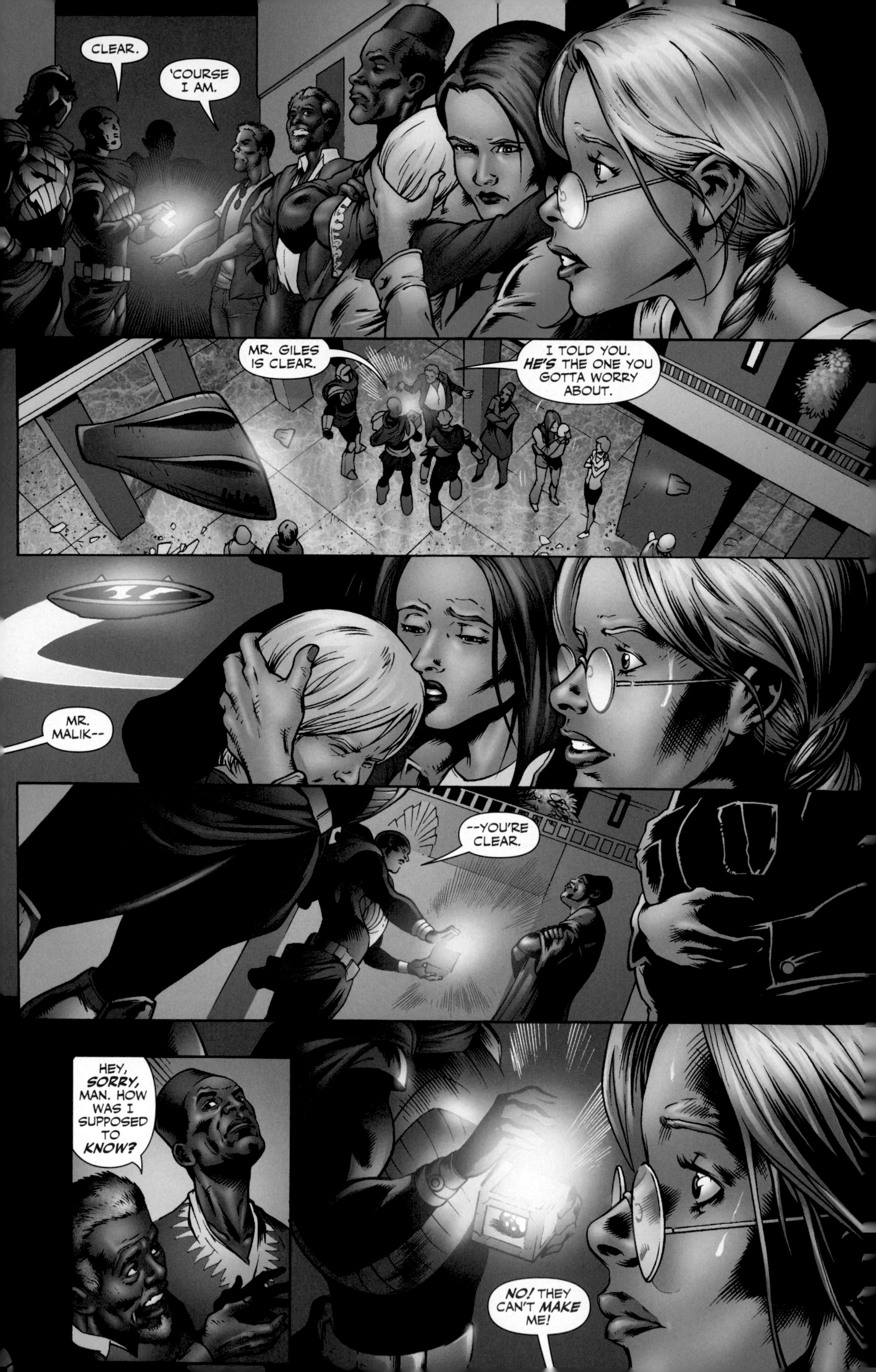
CLEAR.
'COURSE I AM.
MR. GILES IS CLEAR.
I TOLD YOU. HE'S THE ONE YOU GOTTA WORRY ABOUT.
MR. MALIK--
--YOU'RE CLEAR.
HEY, SORRY, MAN. HOW WAS I SUPPOSED TO KNOW?
NO! THEY CAN'T MAKE ME!

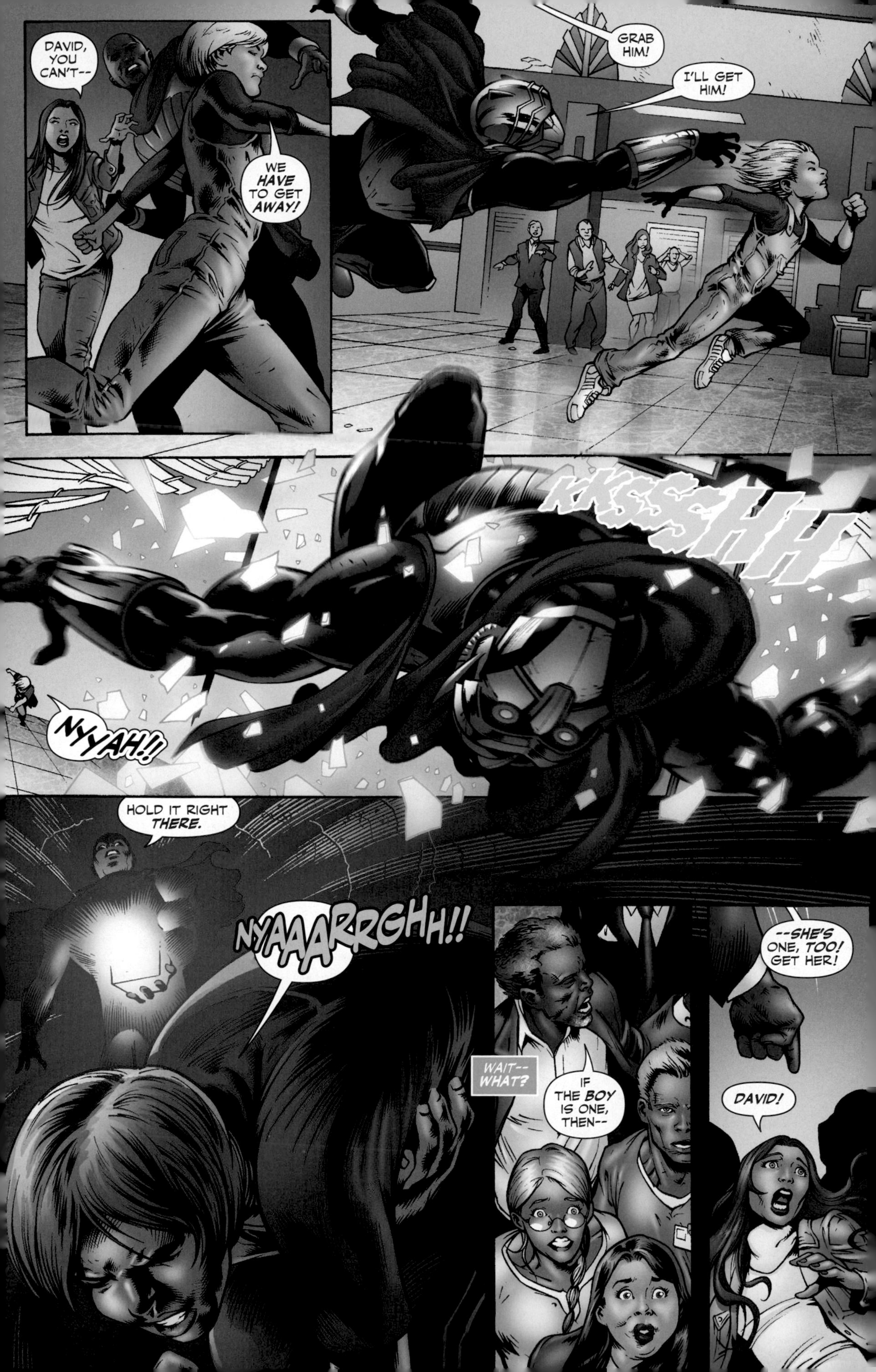
DAVID, YOU CAN'T--
WE HAVE TO GET AWAY!
GRAB HIM!
I'LL GET HIM!
KKSSSHH
NYYAH!!
HOLD IT RIGHT THERE.
NYAAARRGHH!!
WAIT-- WHAT?
IF THE BOY IS ONE, THEN--
--SHE'S ONE, TOO! GET HER!
DAVID!

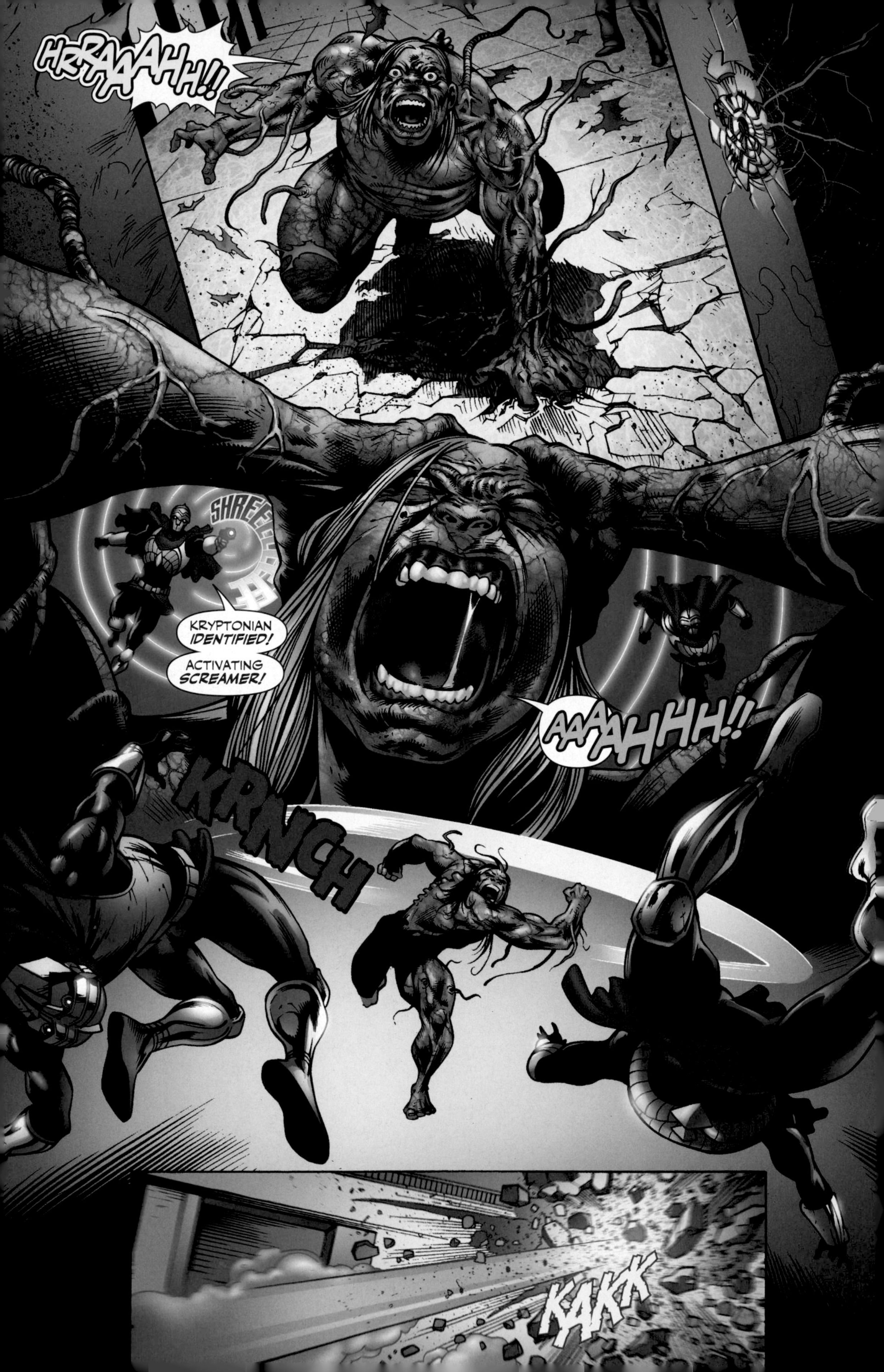
HRRAAAHHH!!
SHREEEEEEE
KRYPTONIAN IDENTIFIED!
ACTIVATING SCREAMER!
AAAAHHHH!!
KRNCH
KAKK

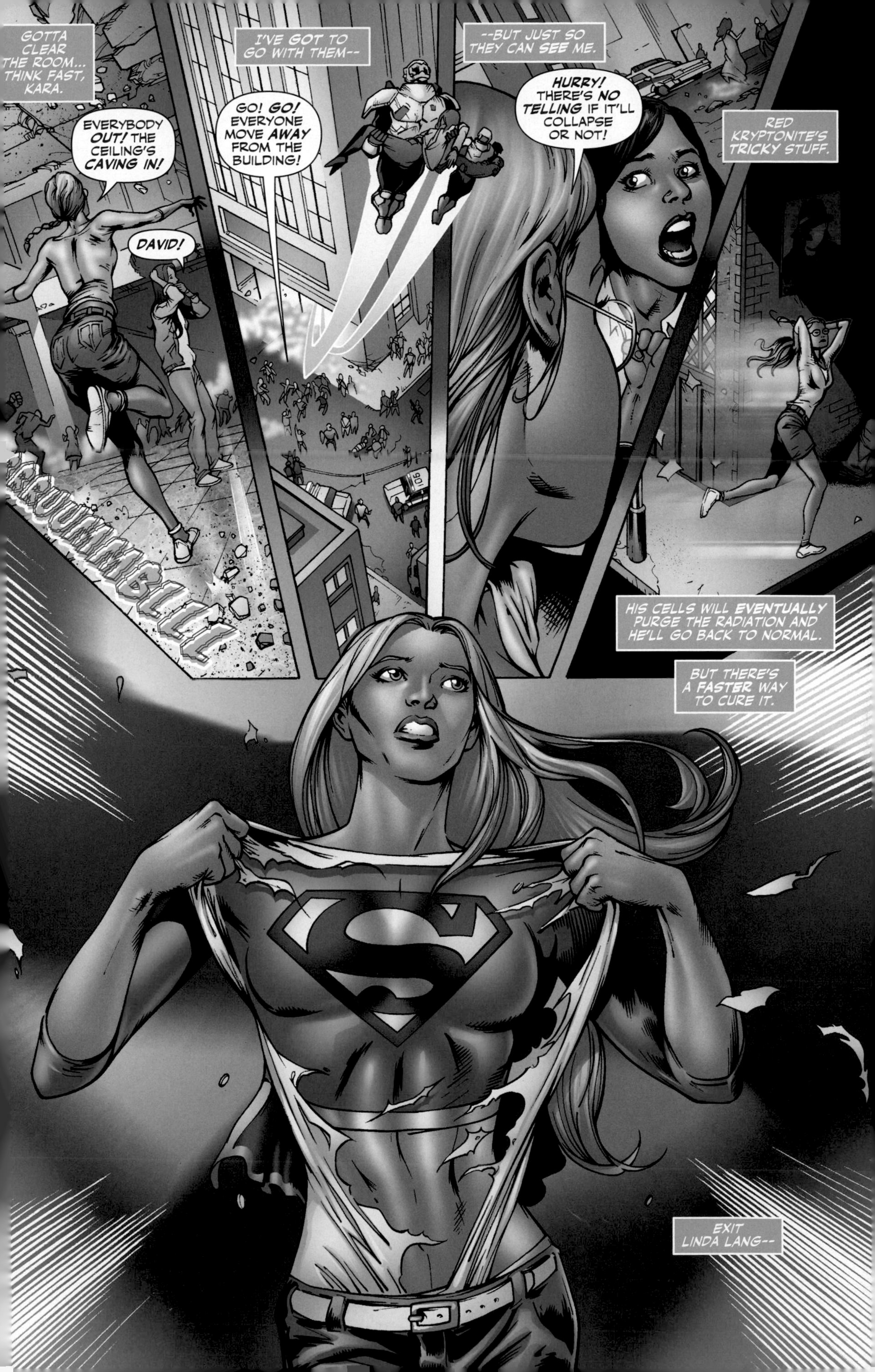

GOTTA CLEAR THE ROOM... THINK FAST, KARA.
EVERYBODY OUT! THE CEILING'S CAVING IN!
DAVID!
I'VE GOT TO GO WITH THEM--
GO! GO! EVERYONE MOVE AWAY FROM THE BUILDING!
--BUT JUST SO THEY CAN SEE ME.
HURRY! THERE'S NO TELLING IF IT'LL COLLAPSE OR NOT!
RED KRYPTONITE'S TRICKY STUFF.
KRRUUMBLLL
HIS CELLS WILL EVENTUALLY PURGE THE RADIATION AND HE'LL GO BACK TO NORMAL.
BUT THERE'S A FASTER WAY TO CURE IT.
EXIT LINDA LANG--

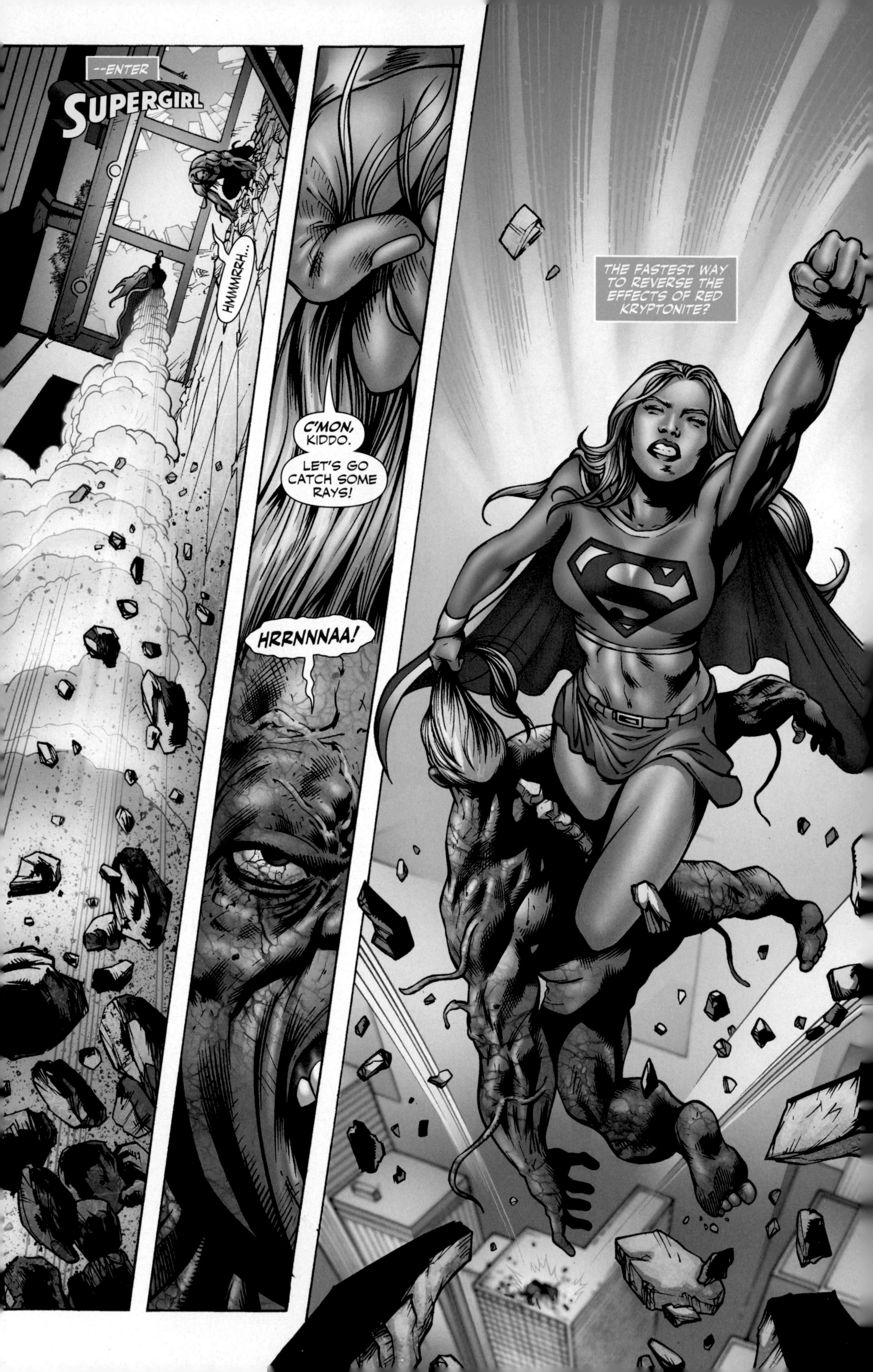
--ENTER
SUPERGIRL
HMMMRRH...
C'MON, KIDDO.
LET'S GO CATCH SOME RAYS!
HRRNNNAA!
THE FASTEST WAY TO REVERSE THE EFFECTS OF RED KRYPTONITE?

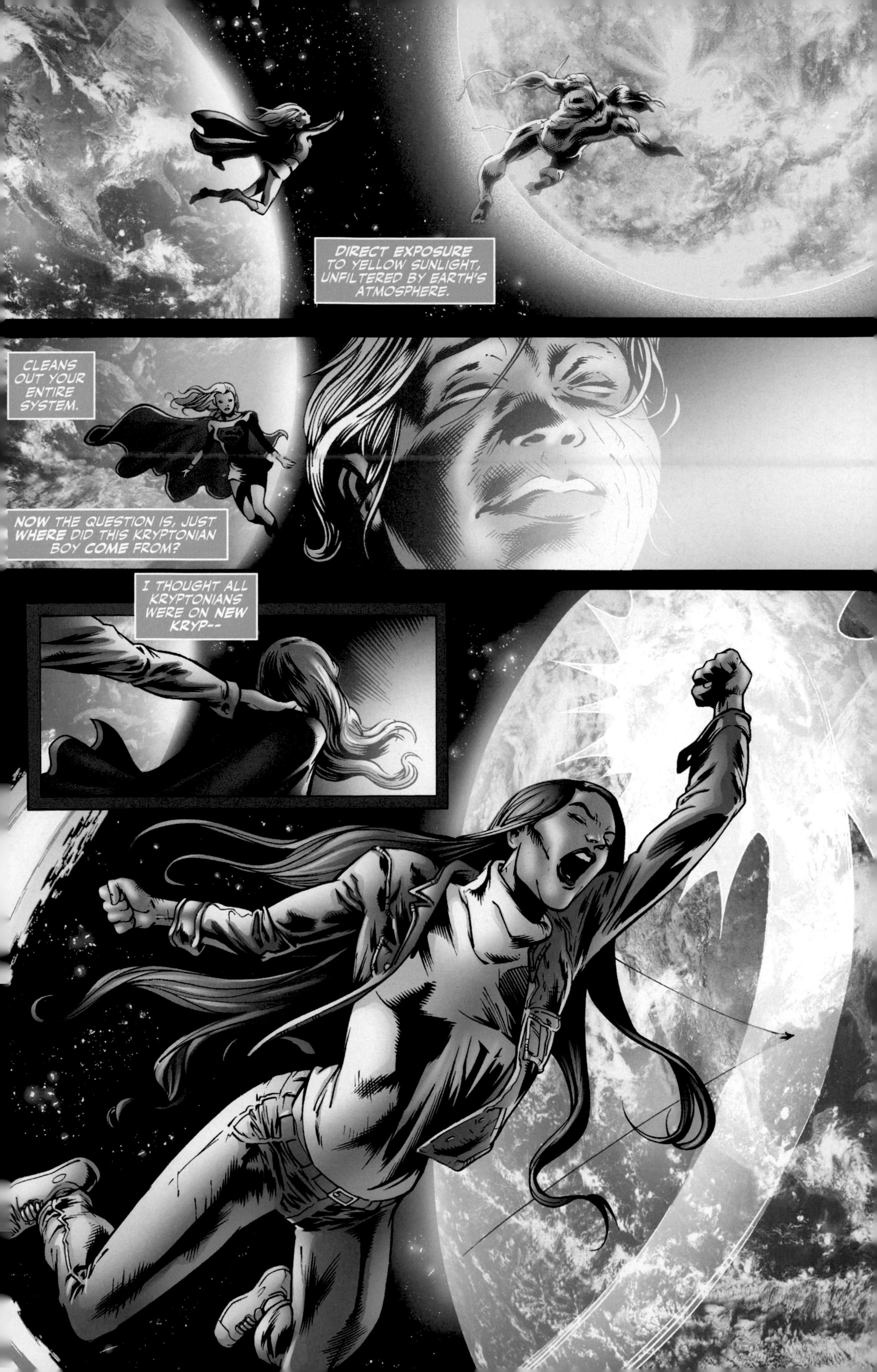
DIRECT EXPOSURE TO YELLOW SUNLIGHT, UNFILTERED BY EARTH'S ATMOSPHERE.
CLEANS OUT YOUR ENTIRE SYSTEM.
NOW THE QUESTION IS, JUST WHERE DID THIS KRYPTONIAN BOY COME FROM?
I THOUGHT ALL KRYPTONIANS WERE ON NEW KRYP--

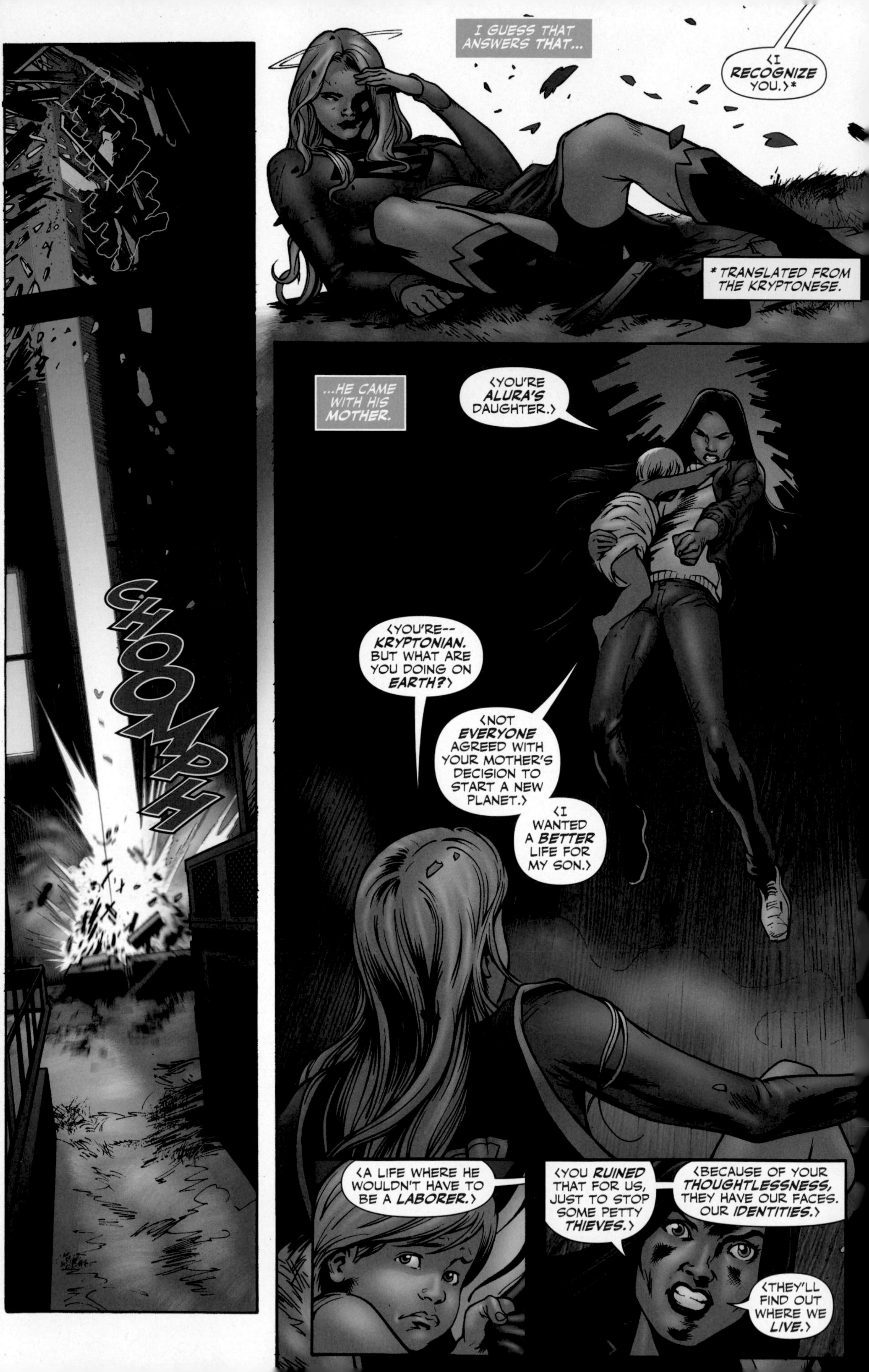
CHOOMPH
I GUESS THAT ANSWERS THAT...
‹I RECOGNIZE YOU.›*
*TRANSLATED FROM THE KRYPTONESE.
...HE CAME WITH HIS MOTHER.
‹YOU'RE ALURA'S DAUGHTER.›
‹YOU'RE-- KRYPTONIAN. BUT WHAT ARE YOU DOING ON EARTH?›
‹NOT EVERYONE AGREED WITH YOUR MOTHER'S DECISION TO START A NEW PLANET.›
‹I WANTED A BETTER LIFE FOR MY SON.›
‹A LIFE WHERE HE WOULDN'T HAVE TO BE A LABORER.›
‹YOU RUINED THAT FOR US, JUST TO STOP SOME PETTY THIEVES.›
‹BECAUSE OF YOUR THOUGHTLESSNESS, THEY HAVE OUR FACES. OUR IDENTITIES.›
‹THEY'LL FIND OUT WHERE WE LIVE.›

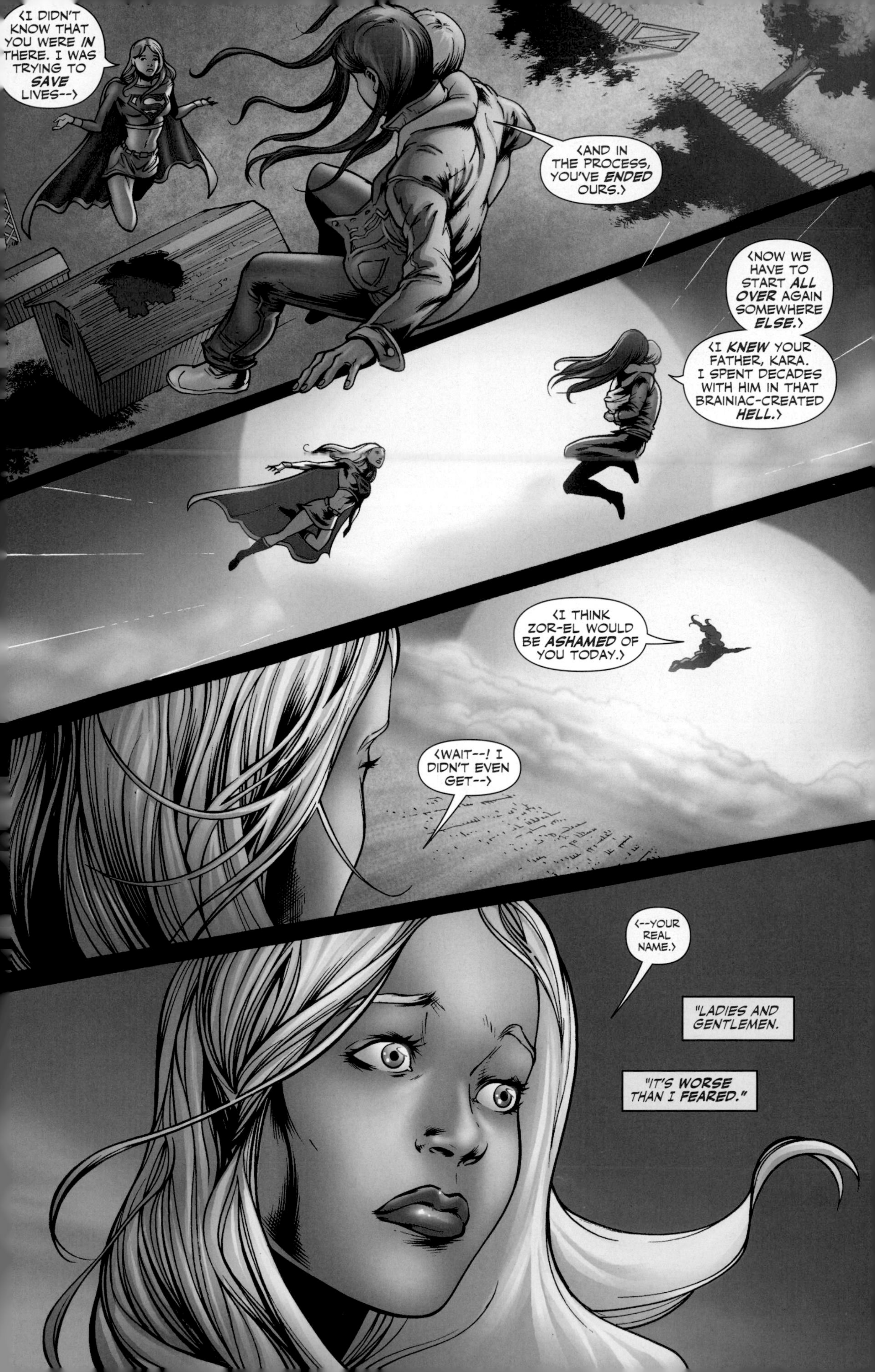

‹I DIDN'T KNOW THAT YOU WERE *IN* THERE. I WAS TRYING TO *SAVE* LIVES--›
‹AND IN THE PROCESS, YOU'VE *ENDED* OURS.›
‹NOW WE HAVE TO START *ALL OVER* AGAIN SOMEWHERE *ELSE*.›
‹I *KNEW* YOUR FATHER, KARA. I SPENT DECADES WITH HIM IN THAT BRAINIAC-CREATED *HELL*.›
‹I THINK ZOR-EL WOULD BE *ASHAMED* OF YOU TODAY.›
‹WAIT--! I DIDN'T EVEN GET--›
‹--YOUR REAL NAME.›
"LADIES AND GENTLEMEN.
"IT'S *WORSE* THAN I *FEARED*."

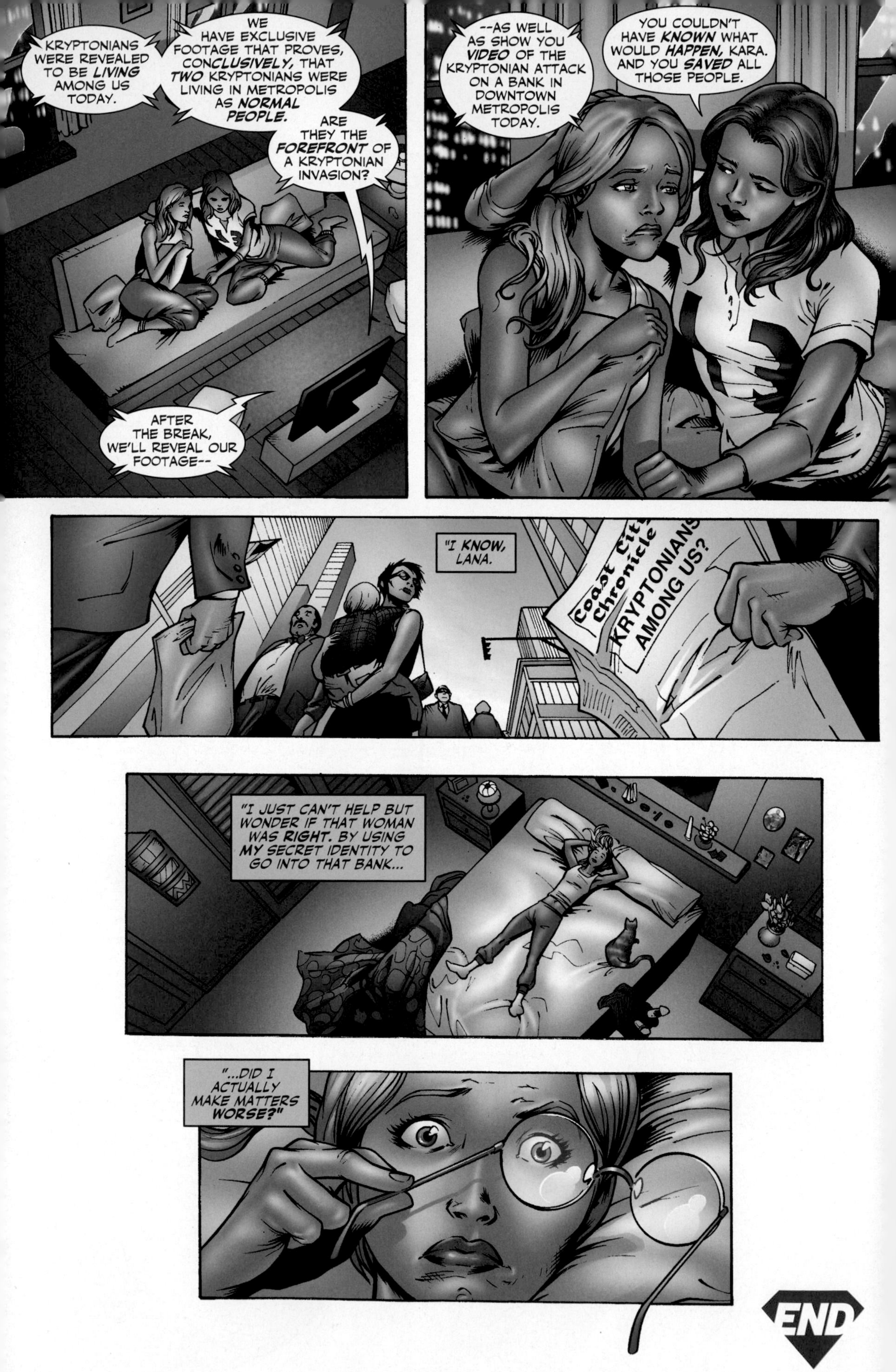
KRYPTONIANS WERE REVEALED TO BE LIVING AMONG US TODAY.
WE HAVE EXCLUSIVE FOOTAGE THAT PROVES, CONCLUSIVELY, THAT TWO KRYPTONIANS WERE LIVING IN METROPOLIS AS NORMAL PEOPLE.
ARE THEY THE FOREFRONT OF A KRYPTONIAN INVASION?
AFTER THE BREAK, WE'LL REVEAL OUR FOOTAGE--
--AS WELL AS SHOW YOU VIDEO OF THE KRYPTONIAN ATTACK ON A BANK IN DOWNTOWN METROPOLIS TODAY.
YOU COULDN'T HAVE KNOWN WHAT WOULD HAPPEN, KARA. AND YOU SAVED ALL THOSE PEOPLE.
"I KNOW, LANA.
Coast City Chronicle
KRYPTONIANS AMONG US?
"I JUST CAN'T HELP BUT WONDER IF THAT WOMAN WAS RIGHT. BY USING MY SECRET IDENTITY TO GO INTO THAT BANK...
"...DID I ACTUALLY MAKE MATTERS WORSE?"
END

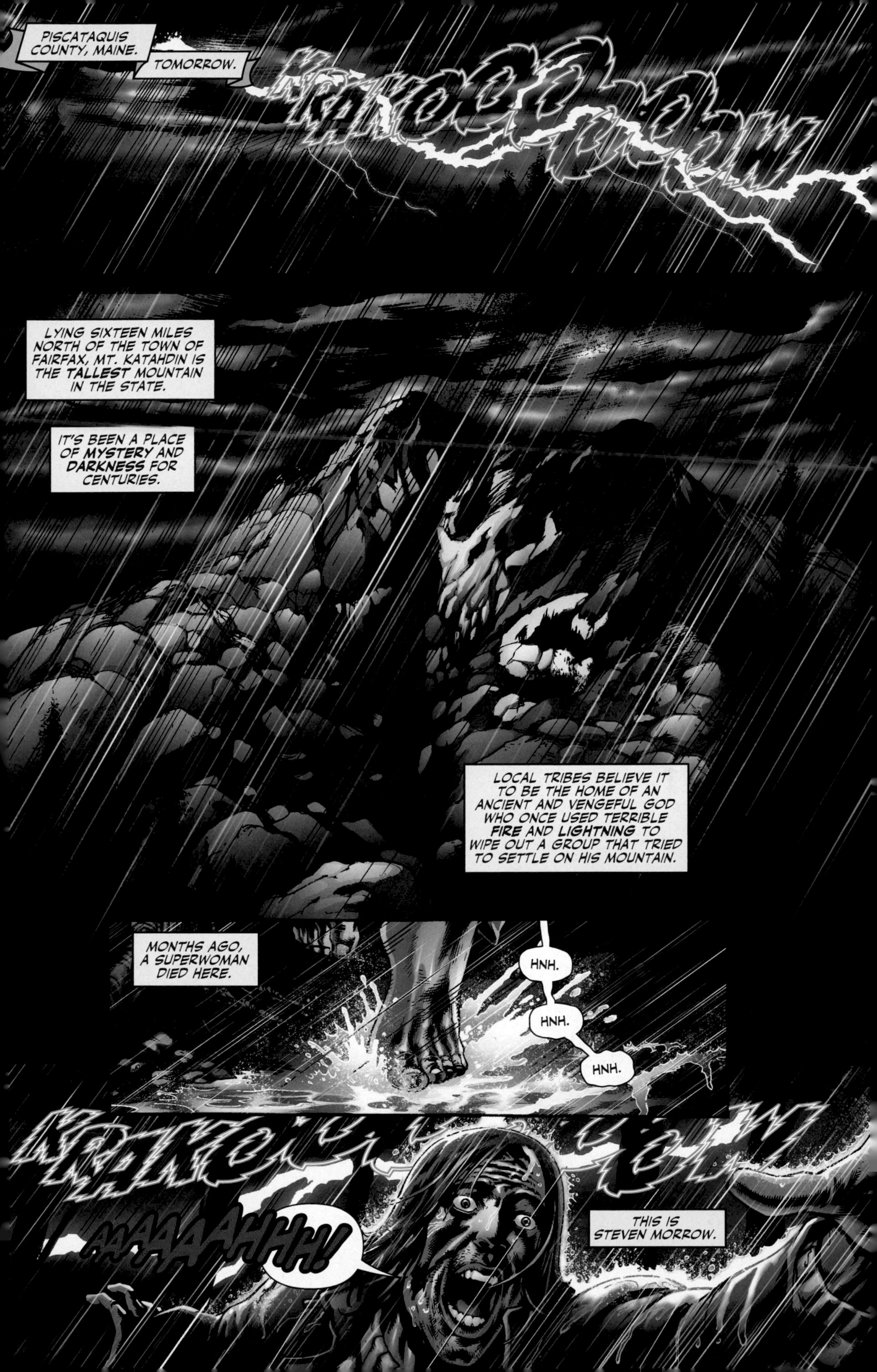
PISCATAQUIS COUNTY, MAINE.
TOMORROW.
LYING SIXTEEN MILES NORTH OF THE TOWN OF FAIRFAX, MT. KATAHDIN IS THE TALLEST MOUNTAIN IN THE STATE.
IT'S BEEN A PLACE OF MYSTERY AND DARKNESS FOR CENTURIES.
LOCAL TRIBES BELIEVE IT TO BE THE HOME OF AN ANCIENT AND VENGEFUL GOD WHO ONCE USED TERRIBLE FIRE AND LIGHTNING TO WIPE OUT A GROUP THAT TRIED TO SETTLE ON HIS MOUNTAIN.
MONTHS AGO, A SUPERWOMAN DIED HERE.
HNH.
HNH.
HNH.
AAAAAHHH!
THIS IS STEVEN MORROW.

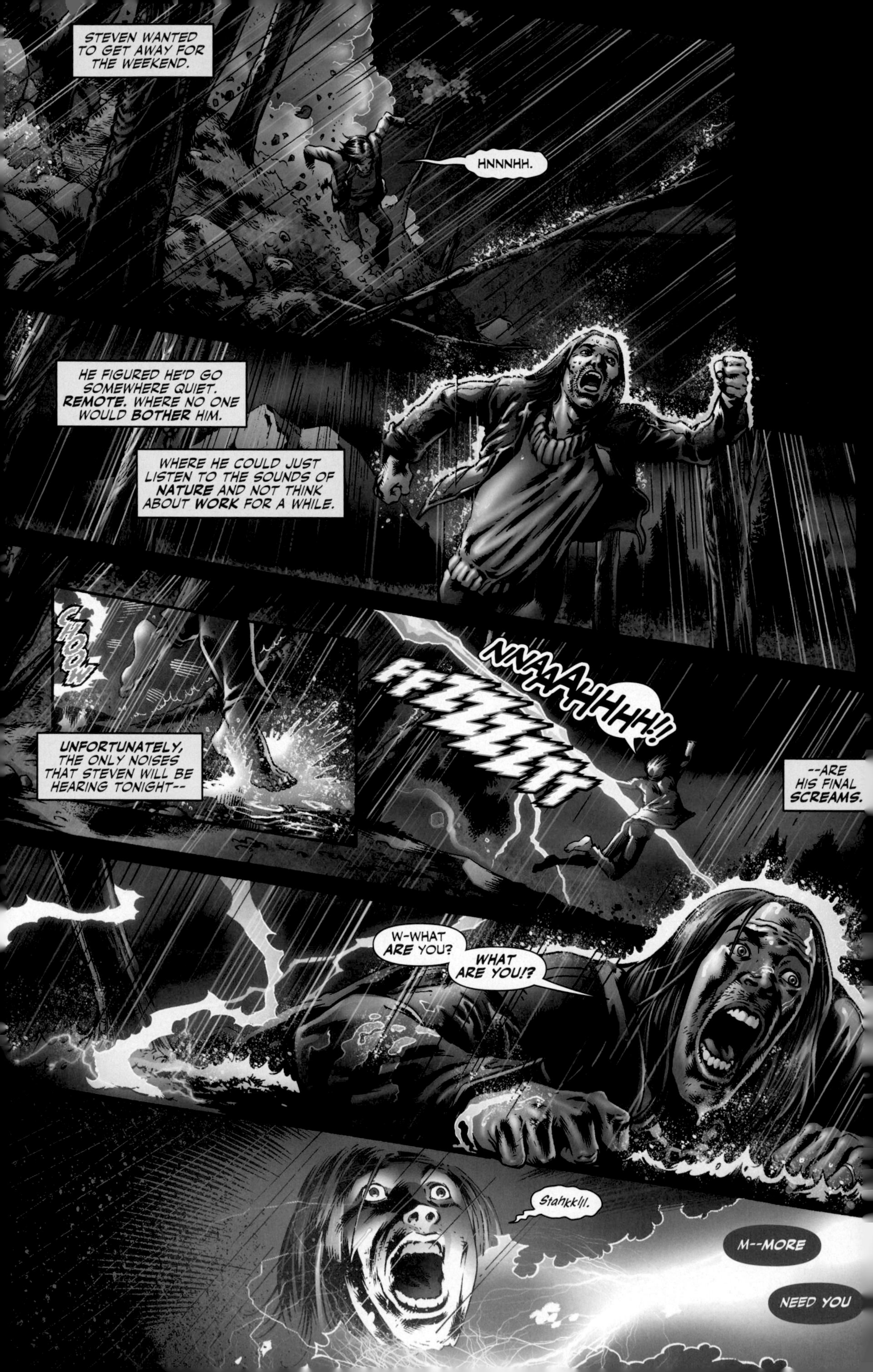

STEVEN WANTED TO GET AWAY FOR THE WEEKEND.
HNNNHH.
HE FIGURED HE'D GO SOMEWHERE QUIET. REMOTE. WHERE NO ONE WOULD BOTHER HIM.
WHERE HE COULD JUST LISTEN TO THE SOUNDS OF NATURE AND NOT THINK ABOUT WORK FOR A WHILE.
CHOOM
UNFORTUNATELY, THE ONLY NOISES THAT STEVEN WILL BE HEARING TONIGHT--
NNAAAHHH!!
FFZZZTT
--ARE HIS FINAL SCREAMS.
W-WHAT ARE YOU?
WHAT ARE YOU!?
Stahkklll.
M--MORE
NEED YOU

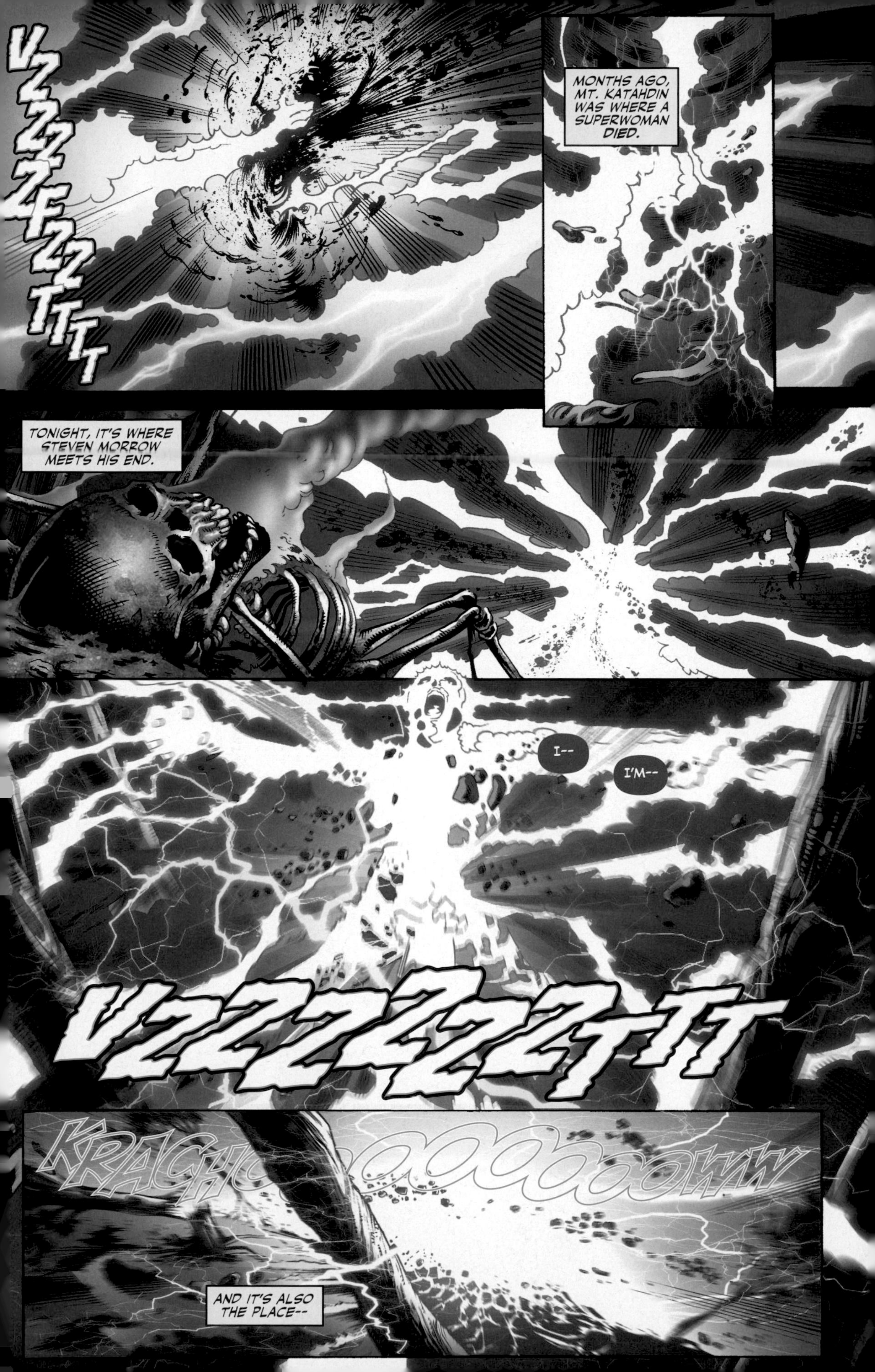
VZZZZFZZZTTTTT
MONTHS AGO, MT. KATAHDIN WAS WHERE A SUPERWOMAN DIED.
TONIGHT, IT'S WHERE STEVEN MORROW MEETS HIS END.
I--
I'M--
VZZZZZZZZTTT
KRACHOOOOOOOOOOOWW
AND IT'S ALSO THE PLACE--

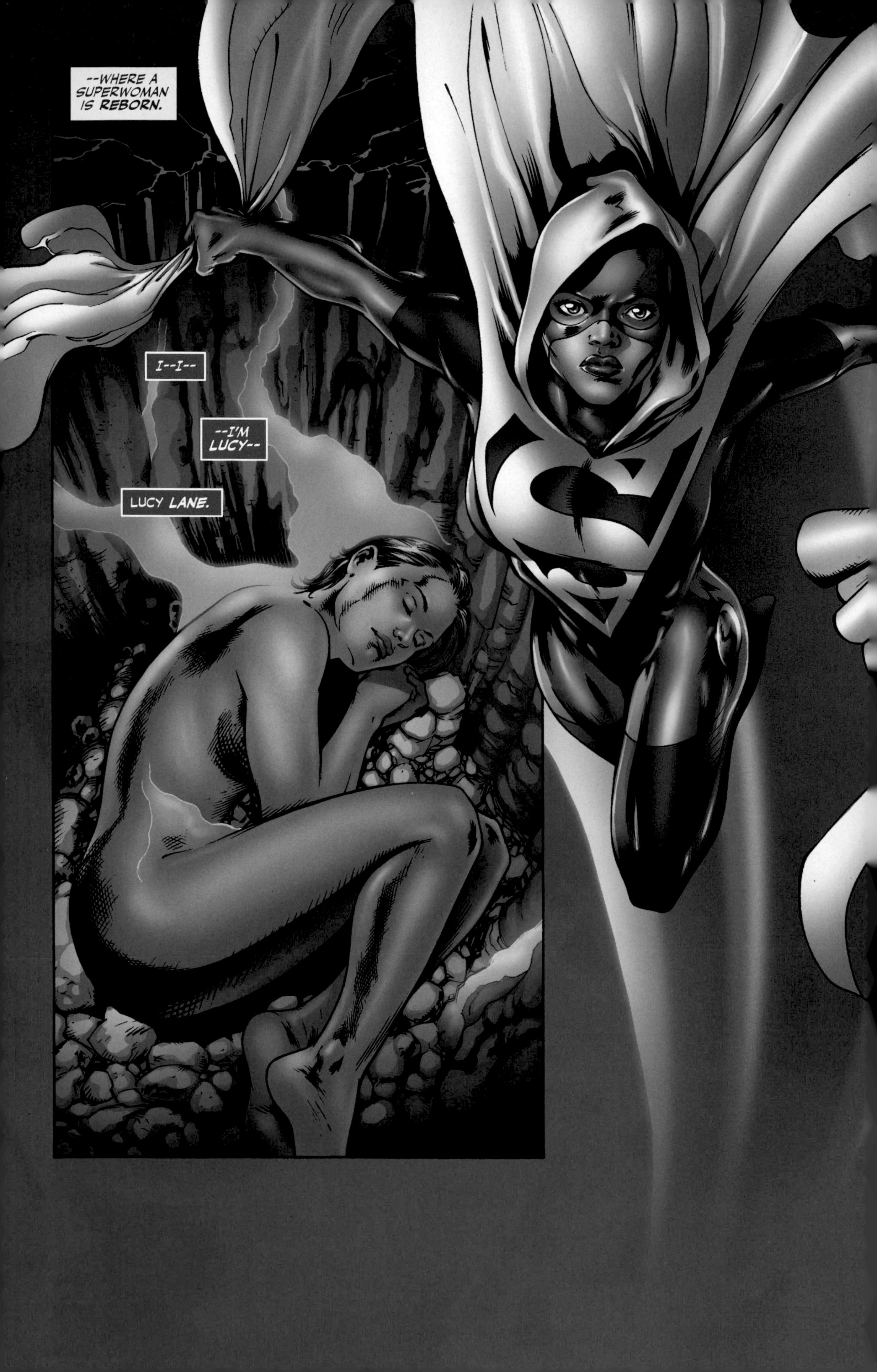
--WHERE A SUPERWOMAN IS REBORN.
I--I--
--I'M LUCY--
LUCY LANE.

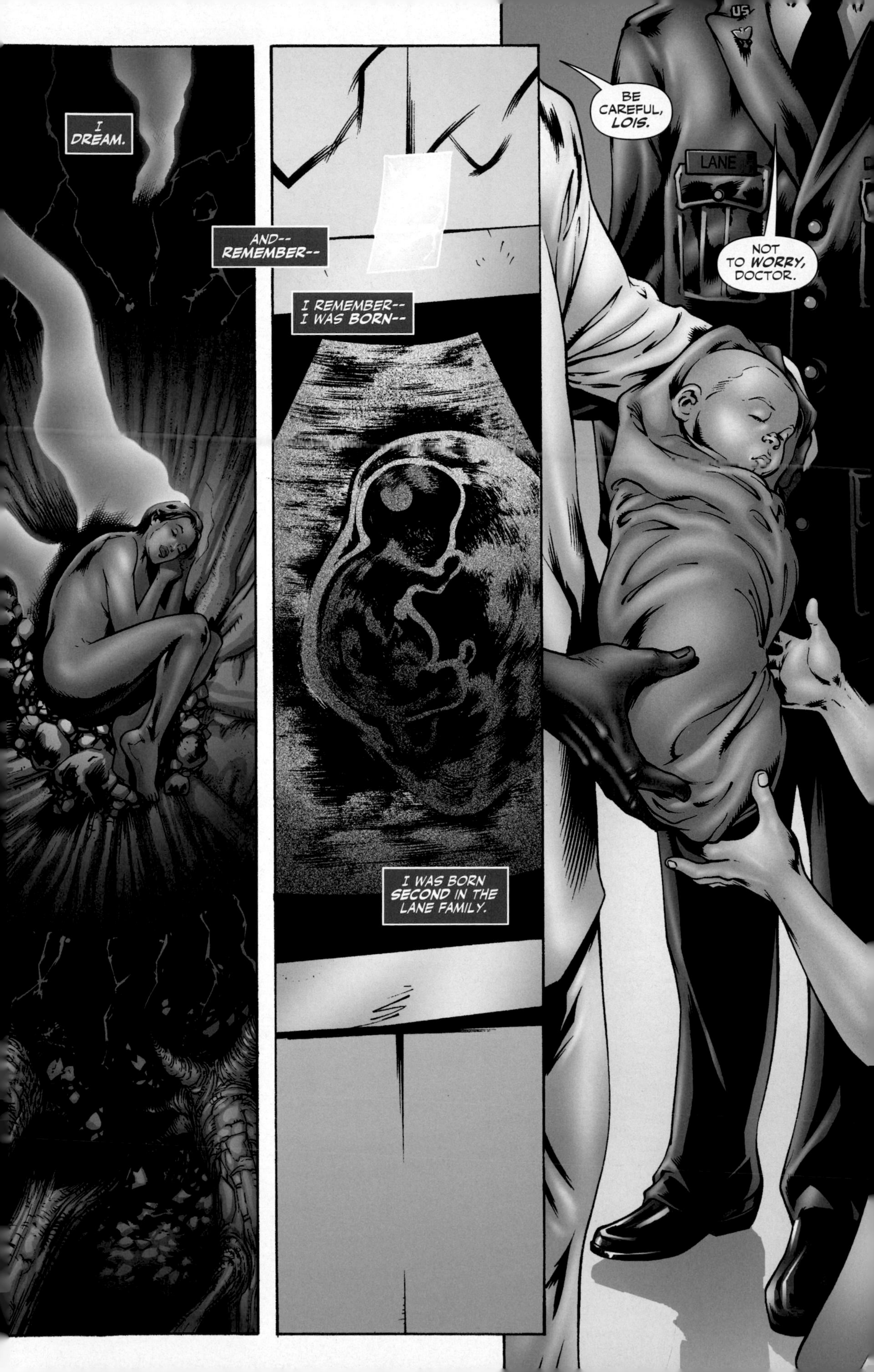
I DREAM.
AND-- REMEMBER--
I REMEMBER-- I WAS BORN--
I WAS BORN SECOND IN THE LANE FAMILY.
BE CAREFUL, LOIS.
NOT TO WORRY, DOCTOR.
LANE
US

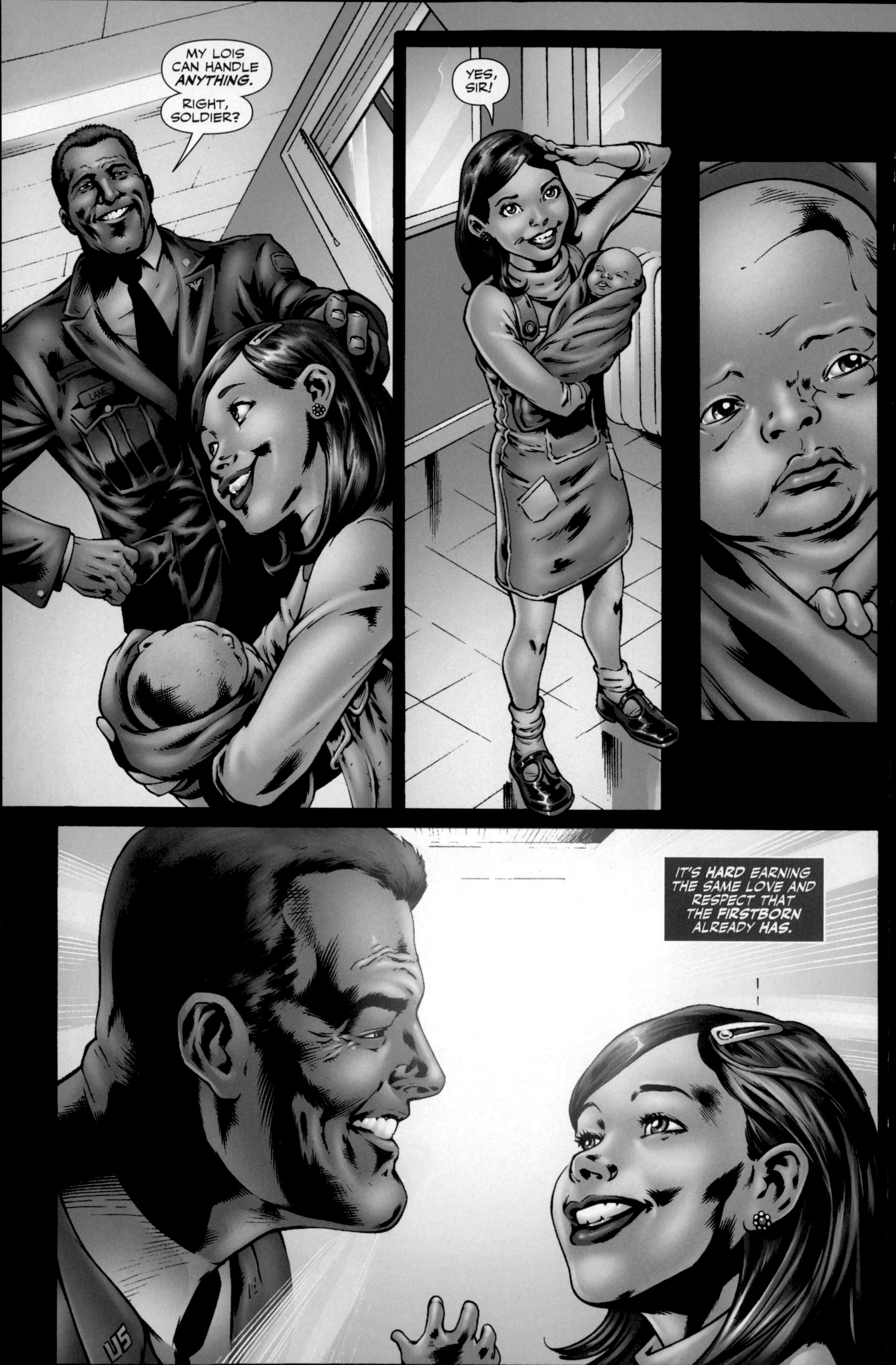
MY LOIS CAN HANDLE ANYTHING.
RIGHT, SOLDIER?
LANE
YES, SIR!
IT'S HARD EARNING THE SAME LOVE AND RESPECT THAT THE FIRSTBORN ALREADY HAS.
US

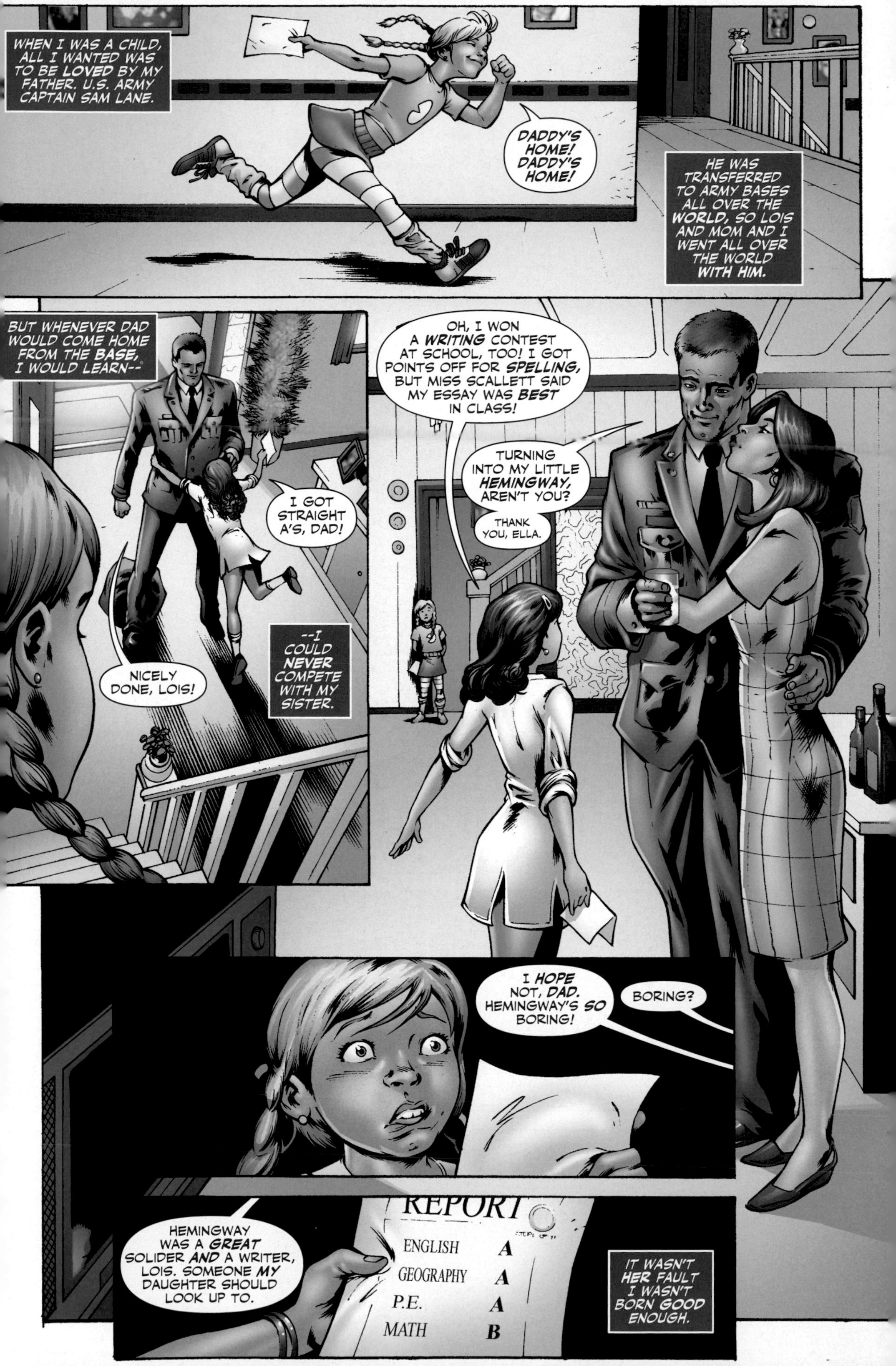
WHEN I WAS A CHILD, ALL I WANTED WAS TO BE LOVED BY MY FATHER. U.S. ARMY CAPTAIN SAM LANE.
DADDY'S HOME! DADDY'S HOME!
HE WAS TRANSFERRED TO ARMY BASES ALL OVER THE WORLD, SO LOIS AND MOM AND I WENT ALL OVER THE WORLD WITH HIM.
BUT WHENEVER DAD WOULD COME HOME FROM THE BASE, I WOULD LEARN--
I GOT STRAIGHT A'S, DAD!
NICELY DONE, LOIS!
--I COULD NEVER COMPETE WITH MY SISTER.
OH, I WON A WRITING CONTEST AT SCHOOL, TOO! I GOT POINTS OFF FOR SPELLING, BUT MISS SCALLETT SAID MY ESSAY WAS BEST IN CLASS!
TURNING INTO MY LITTLE HEMINGWAY, AREN'T YOU?
THANK YOU, ELLA.
I HOPE NOT, DAD. HEMINGWAY'S SO BORING!
BORING?
HEMINGWAY WAS A GREAT SOLIDER AND A WRITER, LOIS. SOMEONE MY DAUGHTER SHOULD LOOK UP TO.
REPORT
ENGLISH A
GEOGRAPHY A
P.E. A
MATH B
IT WASN'T HER FAULT I WASN'T BORN GOOD ENOUGH.

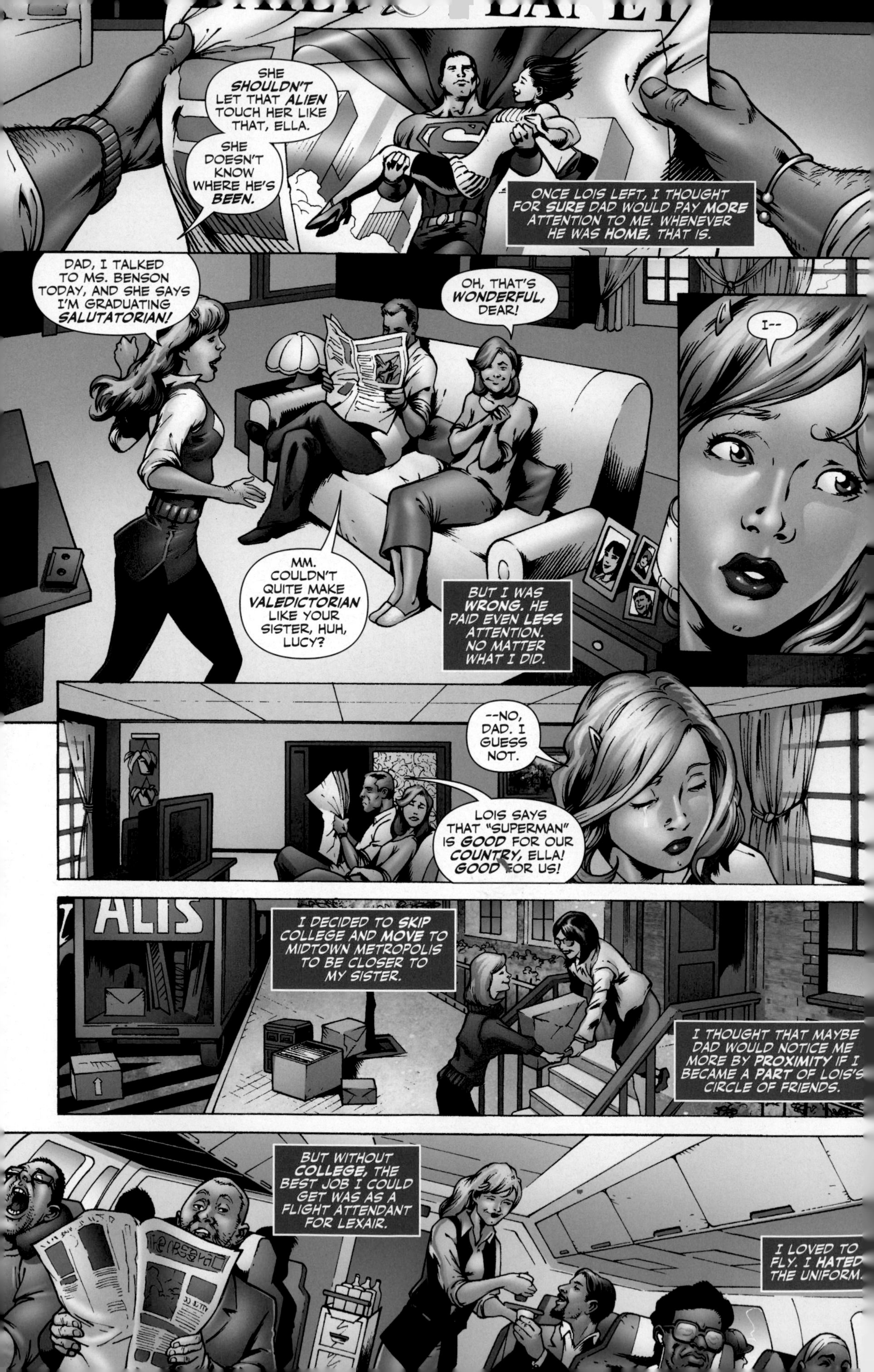

SHE SHOULDN'T LET THAT ALIEN TOUCH HER LIKE THAT, ELLA.
SHE DOESN'T KNOW WHERE HE'S BEEN.
ONCE LOIS LEFT, I THOUGHT FOR SURE DAD WOULD PAY MORE ATTENTION TO ME. WHENEVER HE WAS HOME, THAT IS.
DAD, I TALKED TO MS. BENSON TODAY, AND SHE SAYS I'M GRADUATING SALUTATORIAN!
OH, THAT'S WONDERFUL, DEAR!
MM. COULDN'T QUITE MAKE VALEDICTORIAN LIKE YOUR SISTER, HUH, LUCY?
BUT I WAS WRONG. HE PAID EVEN LESS ATTENTION. NO MATTER WHAT I DID.
I--
--NO, DAD. I GUESS NOT.
LOIS SAYS THAT "SUPERMAN" IS GOOD FOR OUR COUNTRY, ELLA! GOOD FOR US!
ALIS
I DECIDED TO SKIP COLLEGE AND MOVE TO MIDTOWN METROPOLIS TO BE CLOSER TO MY SISTER.
I THOUGHT THAT MAYBE DAD WOULD NOTICE ME MORE BY PROXIMITY IF I BECAME A PART OF LOIS'S CIRCLE OF FRIENDS.
BUT WITHOUT COLLEGE, THE BEST JOB I COULD GET WAS AS A FLIGHT ATTENDANT FOR LEXAIR.
I LOVED TO FLY. I HATED THE UNIFORM.

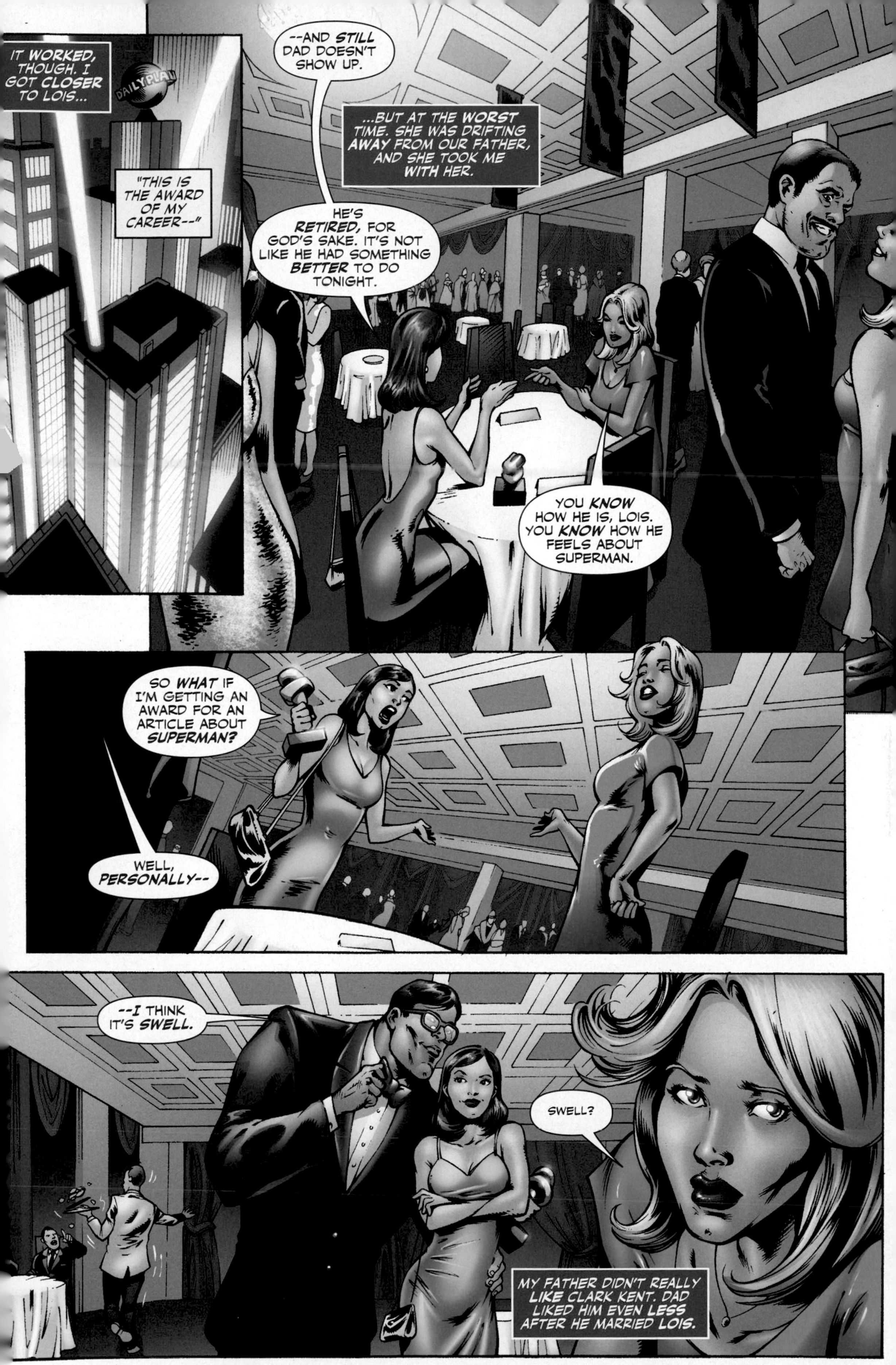

IT WORKED, THOUGH. I GOT CLOSER TO LOIS...
DAILY PLANET
"THIS IS THE AWARD OF MY CAREER--"
--AND STILL DAD DOESN'T SHOW UP.
...BUT AT THE WORST TIME. SHE WAS DRIFTING AWAY FROM OUR FATHER, AND SHE TOOK ME WITH HER.
HE'S RETIRED, FOR GOD'S SAKE. IT'S NOT LIKE HE HAD SOMETHING BETTER TO DO TONIGHT.
YOU KNOW HOW HE IS, LOIS. YOU KNOW HOW HE FEELS ABOUT SUPERMAN.
SO WHAT IF I'M GETTING AN AWARD FOR AN ARTICLE ABOUT SUPERMAN?
WELL, PERSONALLY--
--I THINK IT'S SWELL.
SWELL?
MY FATHER DIDN'T REALLY LIKE CLARK KENT. DAD LIKED HIM EVEN LESS AFTER HE MARRIED LOIS.

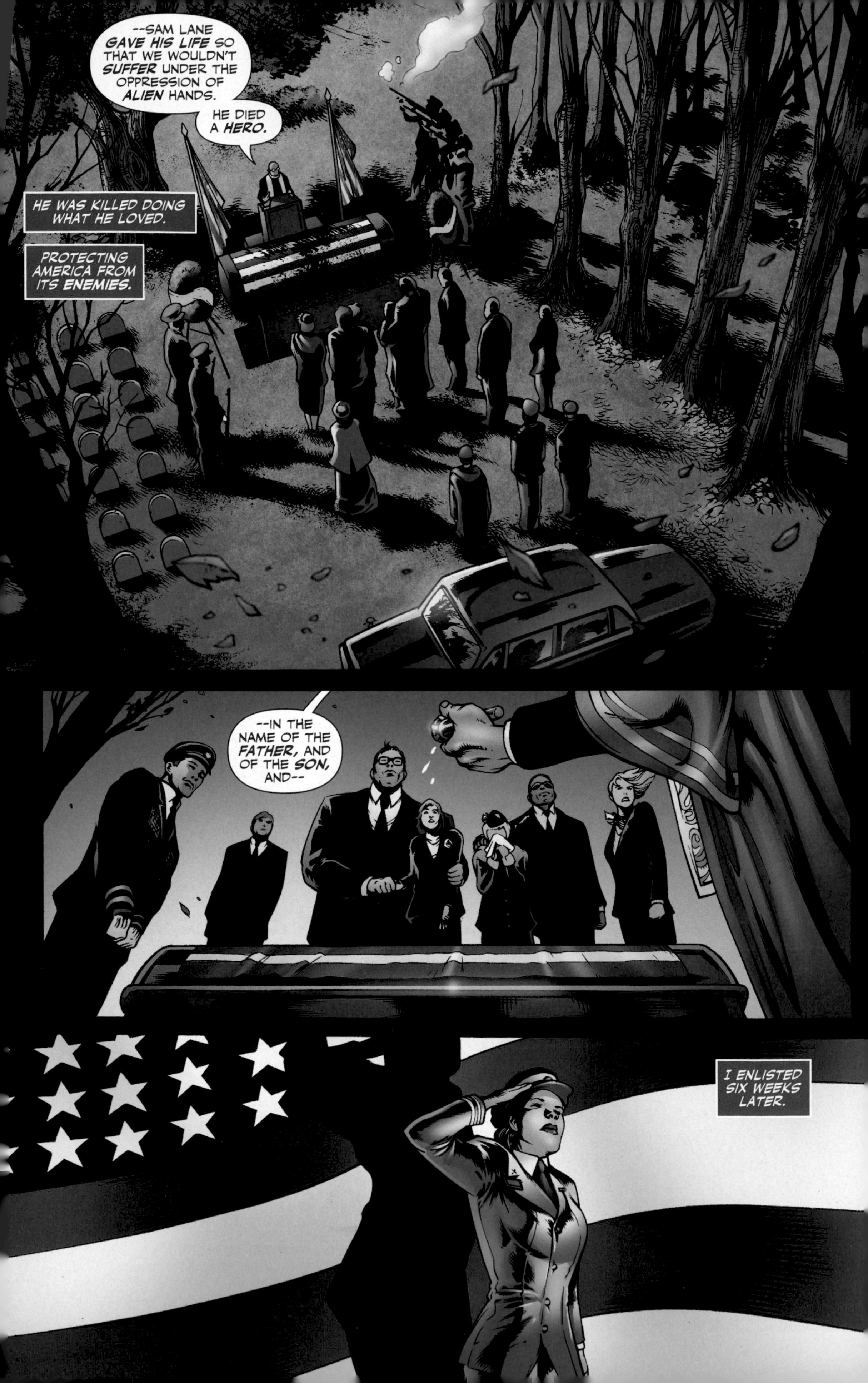
--SAM LANE GAVE HIS LIFE SO THAT WE WOULDN'T SUFFER UNDER THE OPPRESSION OF ALIEN HANDS.
HE DIED A HERO.
HE WAS KILLED DOING WHAT HE LOVED.
PROTECTING AMERICA FROM ITS ENEMIES.
--IN THE NAME OF THE FATHER, AND OF THE SON, AND--
I ENLISTED SIX WEEKS LATER.

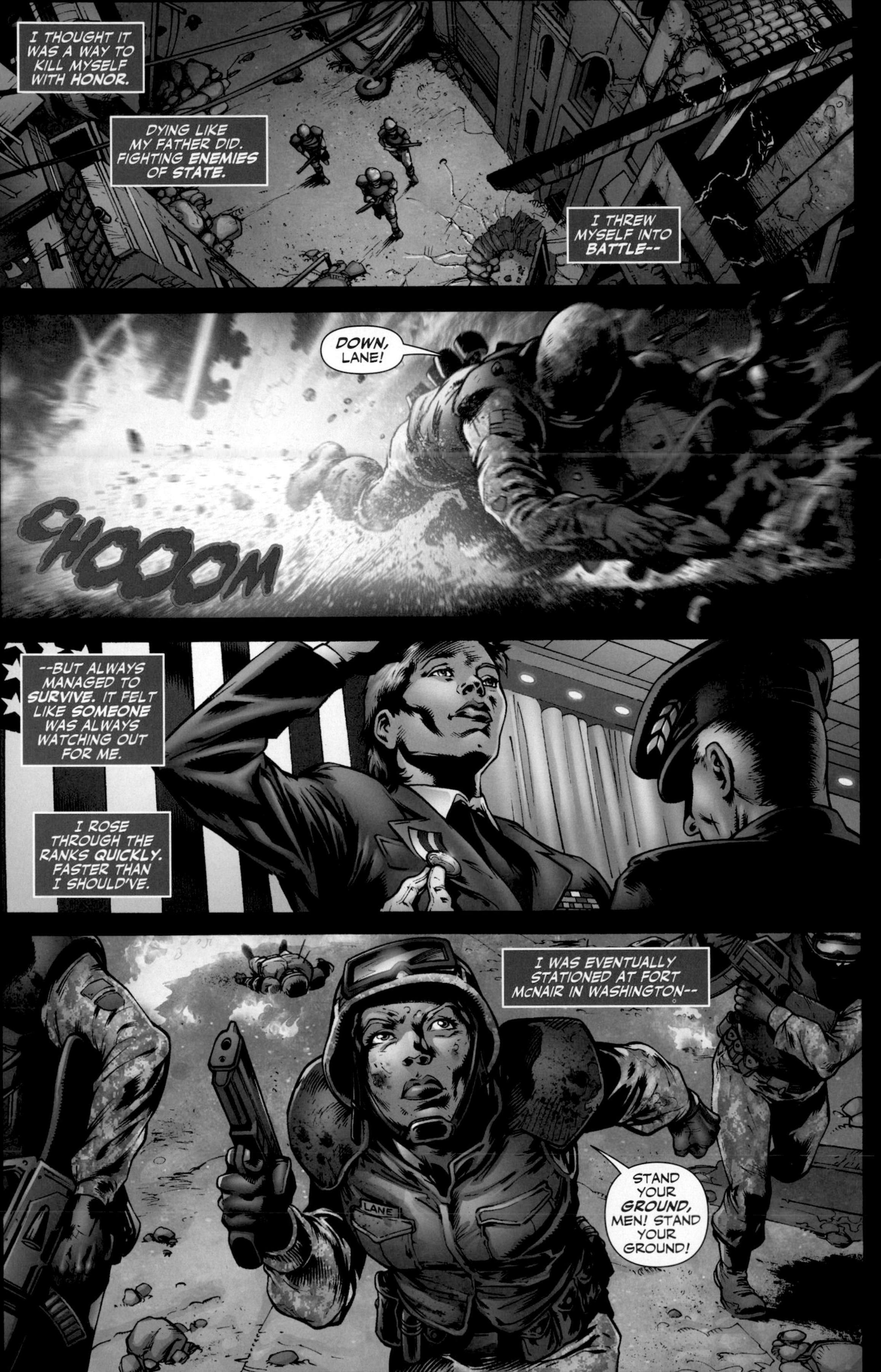

I THOUGHT IT WAS A WAY TO KILL MYSELF WITH HONOR.
DYING LIKE MY FATHER DID. FIGHTING ENEMIES OF STATE.
I THREW MYSELF INTO BATTLE--
DOWN, LANE!
CHOOOM
--BUT ALWAYS MANAGED TO SURVIVE. IT FELT LIKE SOMEONE WAS ALWAYS WATCHING OUT FOR ME.
I ROSE THROUGH THE RANKS QUICKLY. FASTER THAN I SHOULD'VE.
I WAS EVENTUALLY STATIONED AT FORT McNAIR IN WASHINGTON--
LANE
STAND YOUR GROUND, MEN! STAND YOUR GROUND!

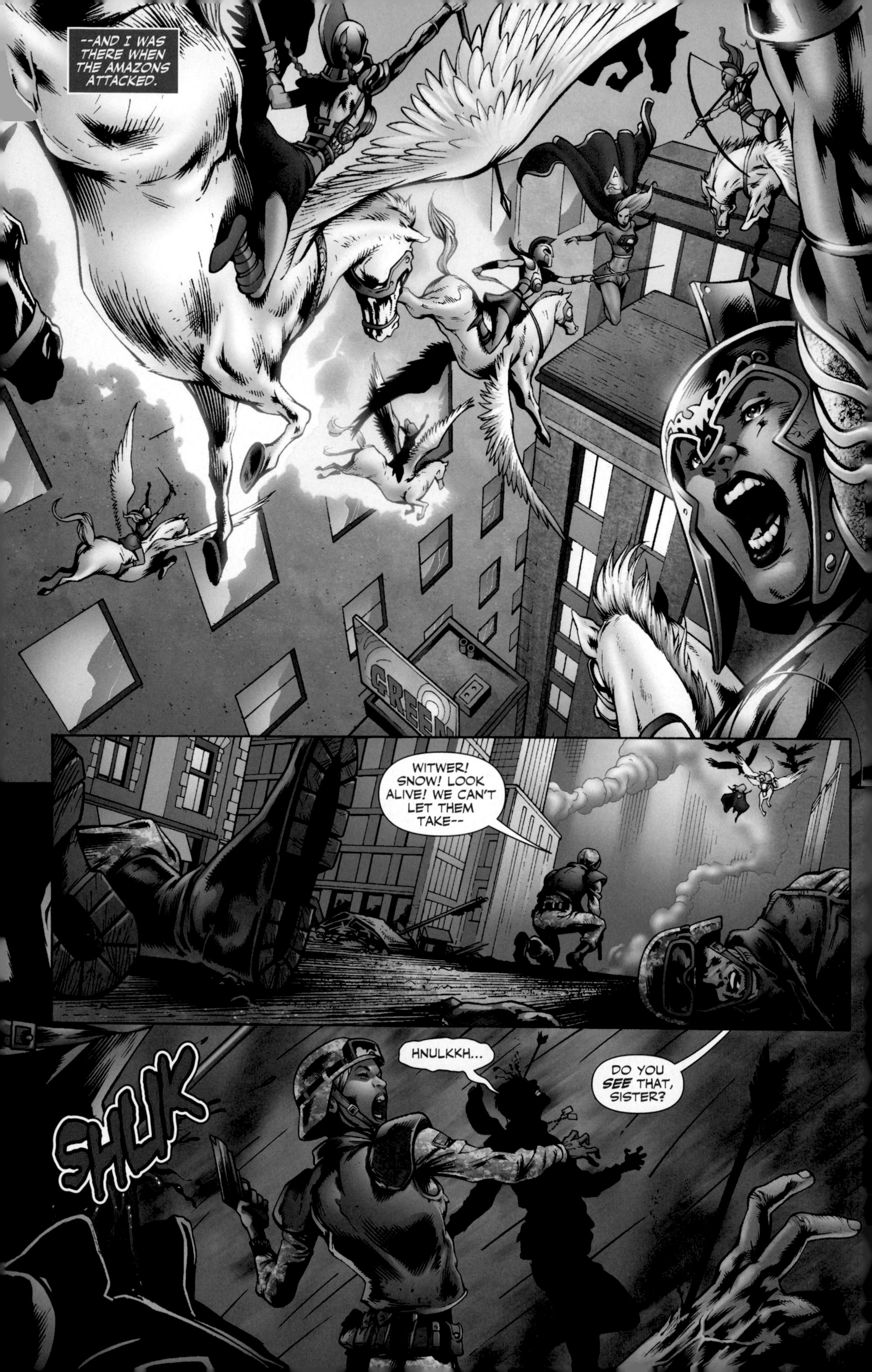
--AND I WAS THERE WHEN THE AMAZONS ATTACKED.
GREEN
WITWER! SNOW! LOOK ALIVE! WE CAN'T LET THEM TAKE--
SHUK
HNULKKH...
DO YOU SEE THAT, SISTER?

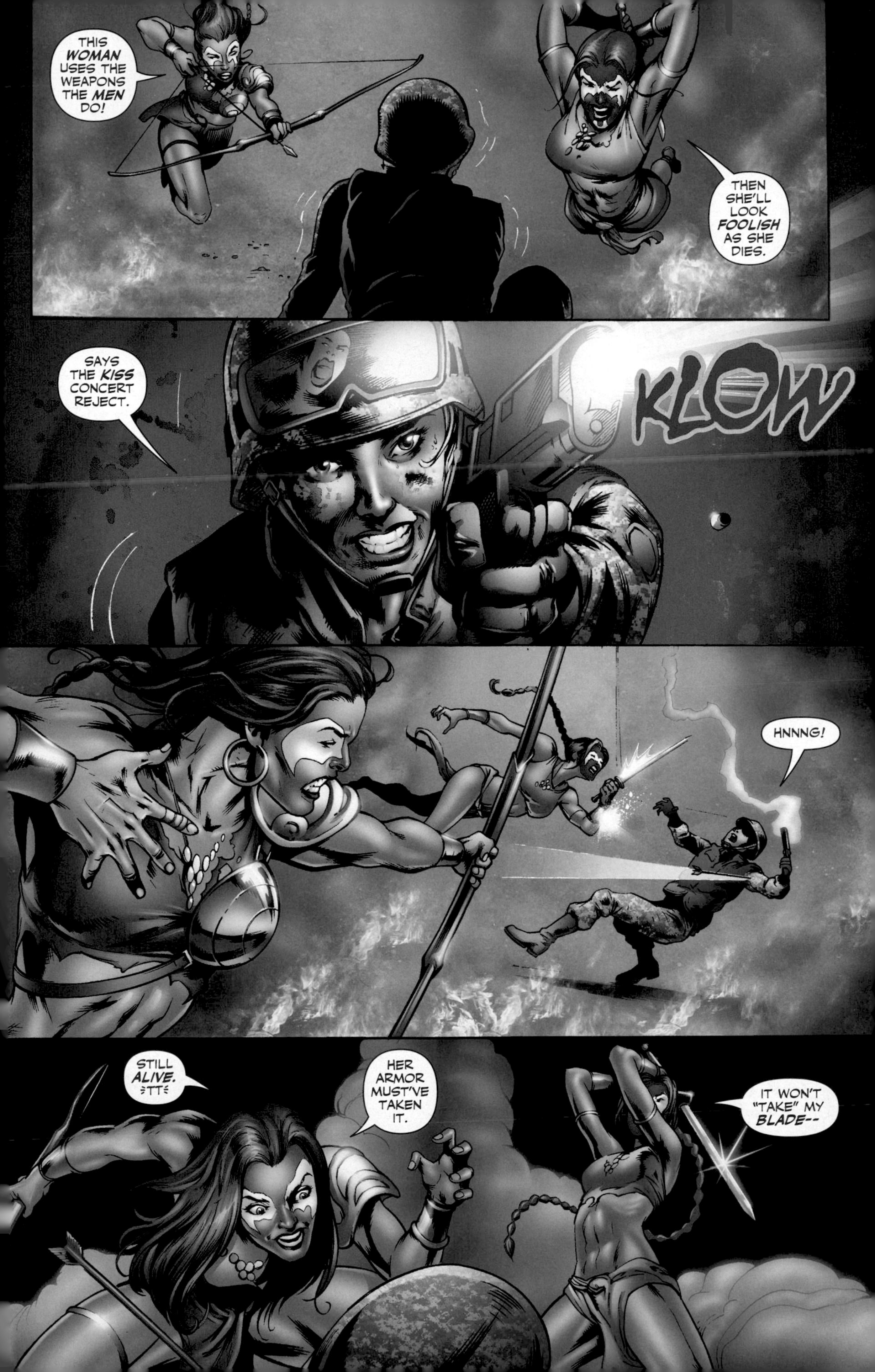
THIS WOMAN USES THE WEAPONS THE MEN DO!
THEN SHE'LL LOOK FOOLISH AS SHE DIES.
SAYS THE KISS CONCERT REJECT.
KLOW
HNNNG!
STILL ALIVE. TT
HER ARMOR MUST'VE TAKEN IT.
IT WON'T "TAKE" MY BLADE--

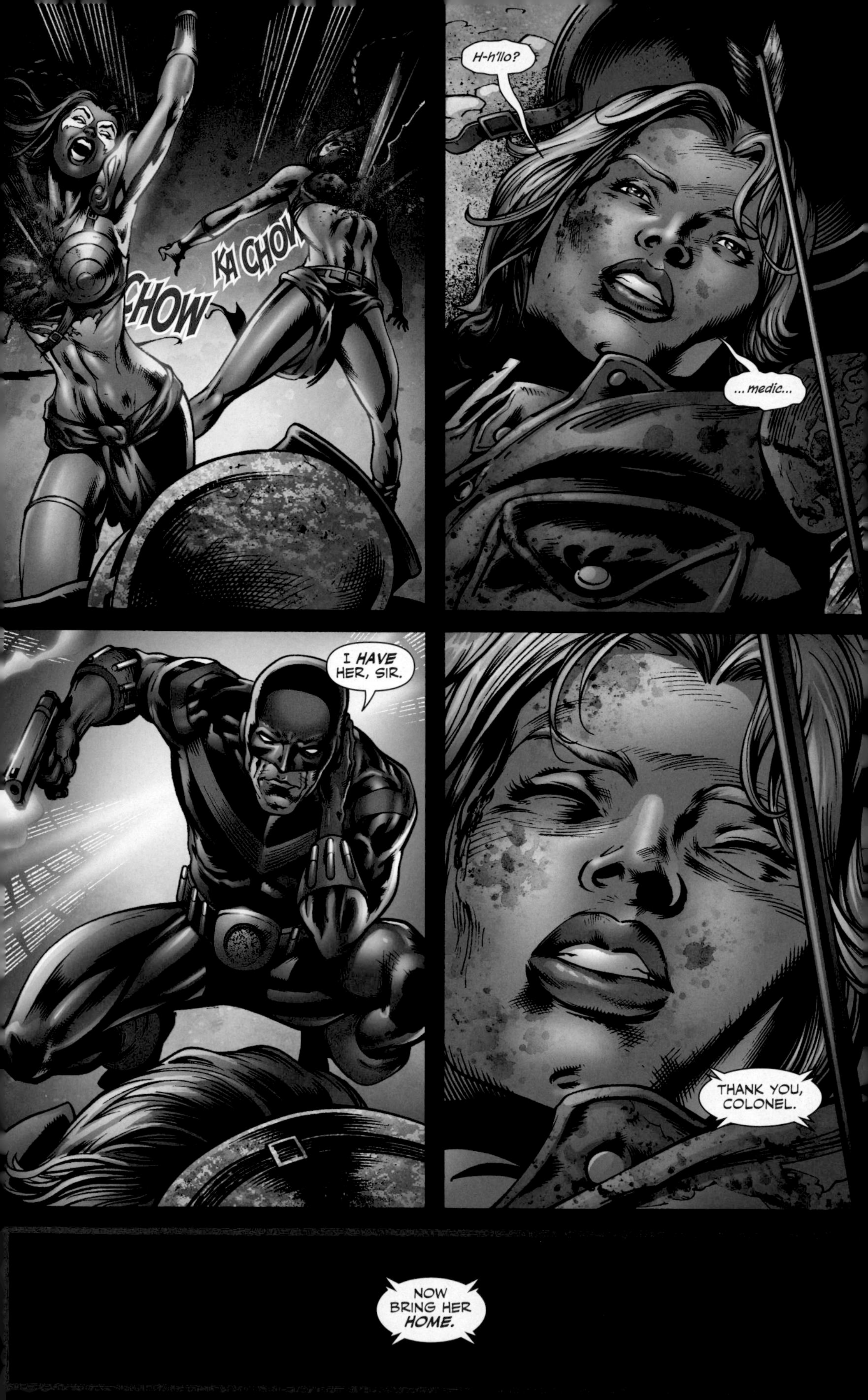
KA CHOW
CHOW
H-h'llo?
...medic...
I HAVE HER, SIR.
THANK YOU, COLONEL.
NOW BRING HER HOME.

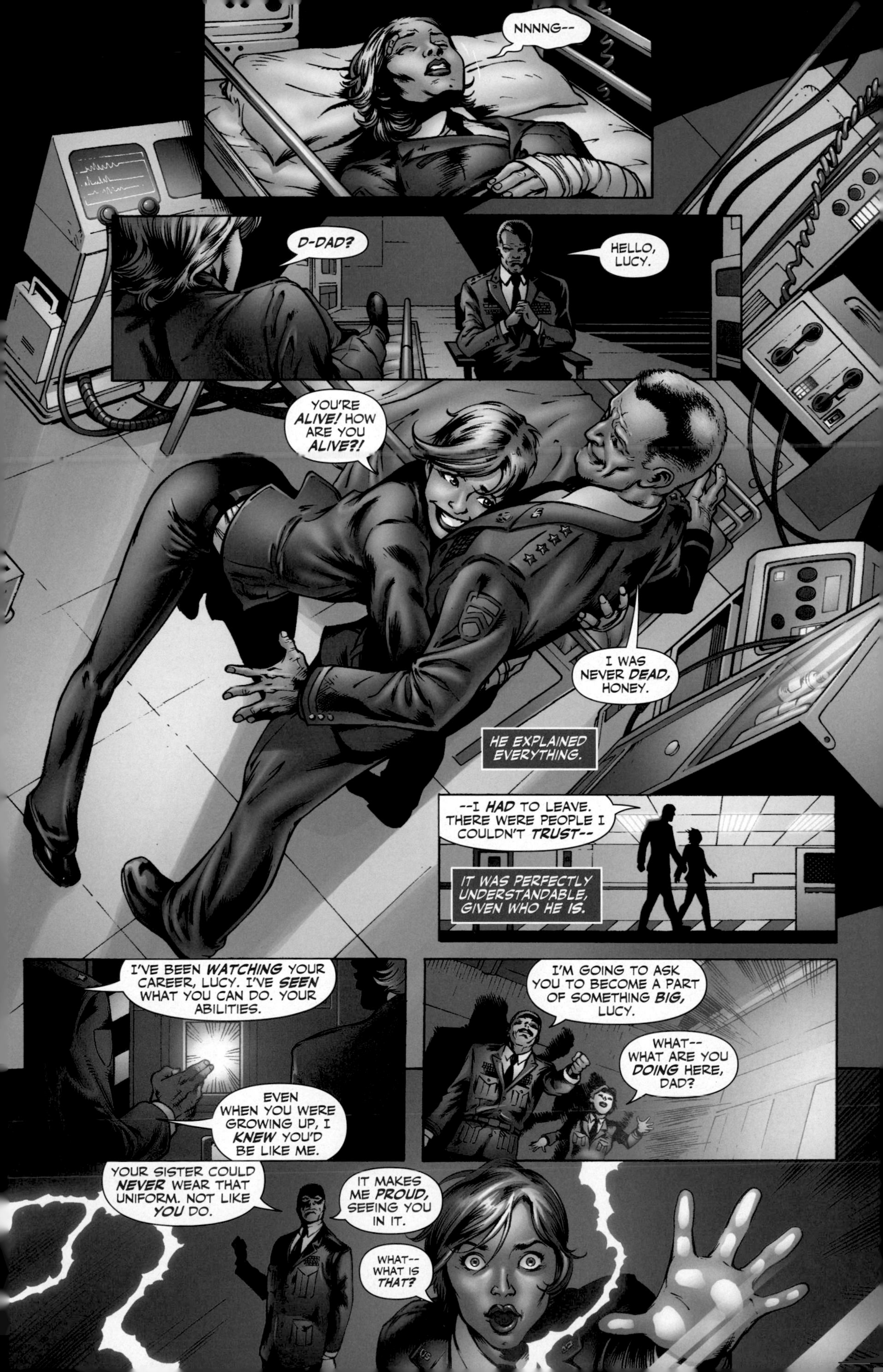
NNNNG--
D-DAD?
HELLO, LUCY.
YOU'RE ALIVE! HOW ARE YOU ALIVE?!
I WAS NEVER DEAD, HONEY.
HE EXPLAINED EVERYTHING.
--I HAD TO LEAVE. THERE WERE PEOPLE I COULDN'T TRUST--
IT WAS PERFECTLY UNDERSTANDABLE, GIVEN WHO HE IS.
I'VE BEEN WATCHING YOUR CAREER, LUCY. I'VE SEEN WHAT YOU CAN DO. YOUR ABILITIES.
EVEN WHEN YOU WERE GROWING UP, I KNEW YOU'D BE LIKE ME.
I'M GOING TO ASK YOU TO BECOME A PART OF SOMETHING BIG, LUCY.
WHAT-- WHAT ARE YOU DOING HERE, DAD?
YOUR SISTER COULD NEVER WEAR THAT UNIFORM. NOT LIKE YOU DO.
IT MAKES ME PROUD, SEEING YOU IN IT.
WHAT-- WHAT IS THAT?

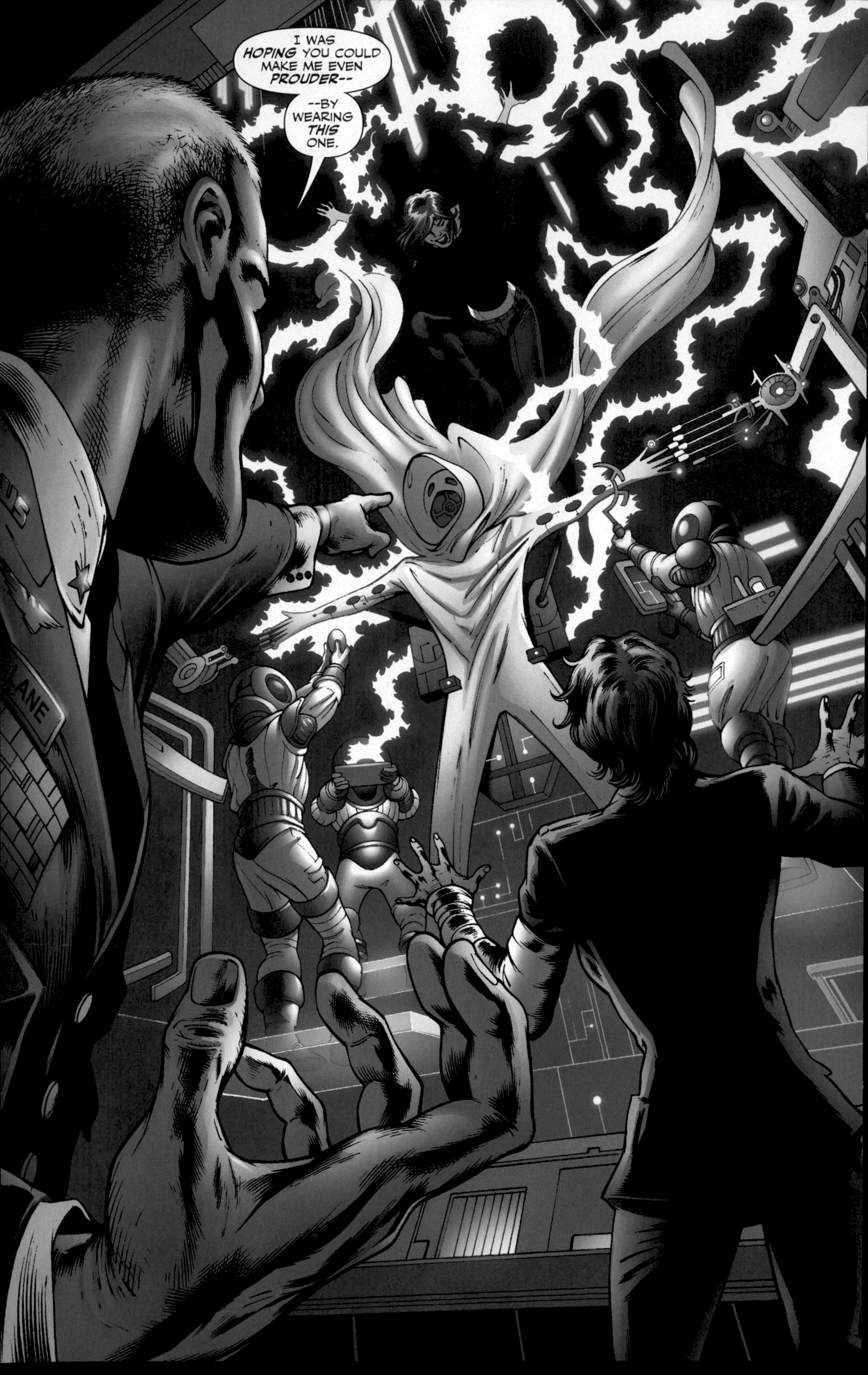
I WAS *HOPING* YOU COULD MAKE ME EVEN *PROUDER*--
--BY WEARING *THIS* ONE.
LANE

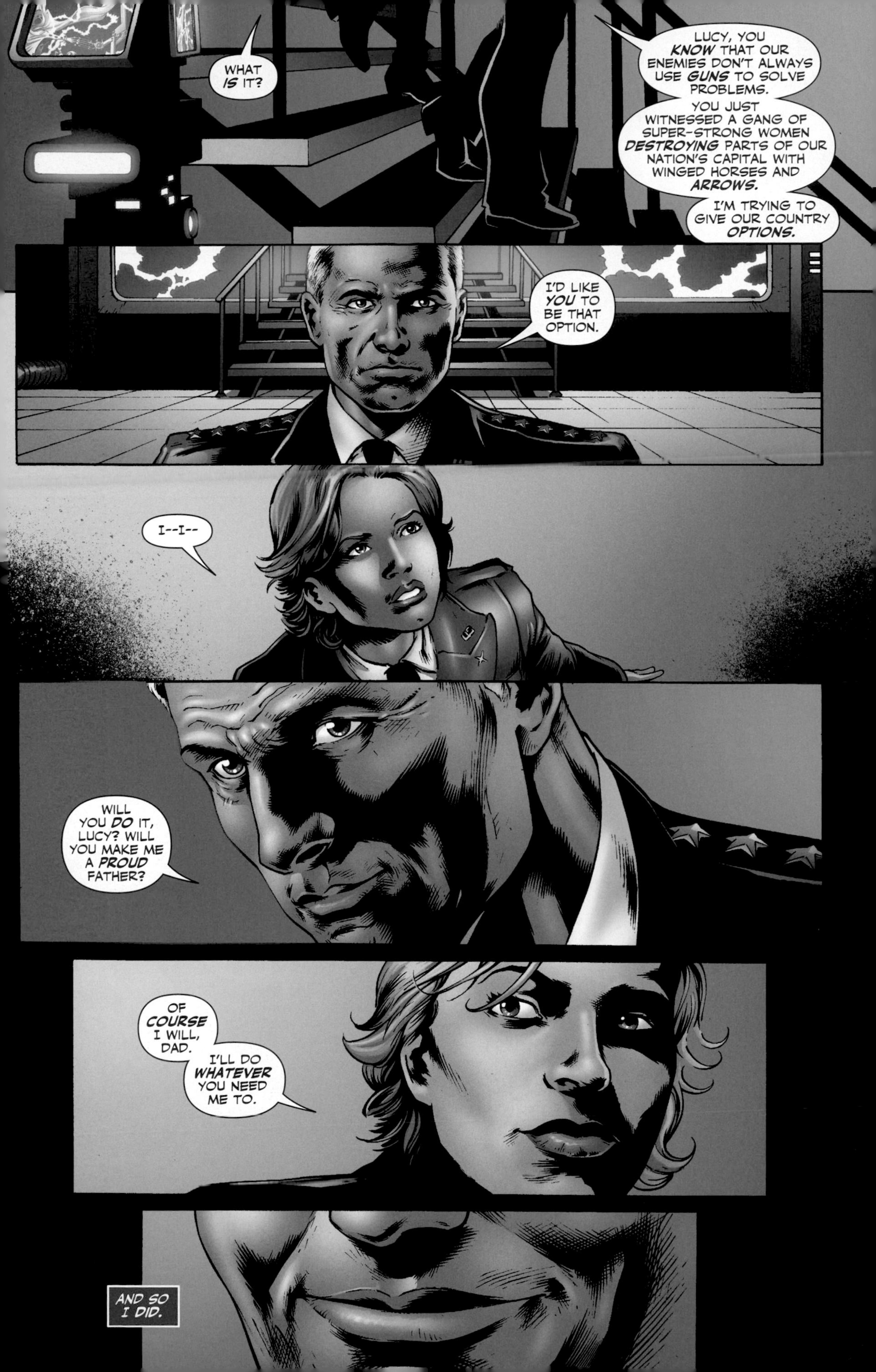
WHAT IS IT?
LUCY, YOU KNOW THAT OUR ENEMIES DON'T ALWAYS USE GUNS TO SOLVE PROBLEMS.
YOU JUST WITNESSED A GANG OF SUPER-STRONG WOMEN DESTROYING PARTS OF OUR NATION'S CAPITAL WITH WINGED HORSES AND ARROWS.
I'M TRYING TO GIVE OUR COUNTRY OPTIONS.
I'D LIKE YOU TO BE THAT OPTION.
I--I--
WILL YOU DO IT, LUCY? WILL YOU MAKE ME A PROUD FATHER?
OF COURSE I WILL, DAD.
I'LL DO WHATEVER YOU NEED ME TO.
AND SO I DID.

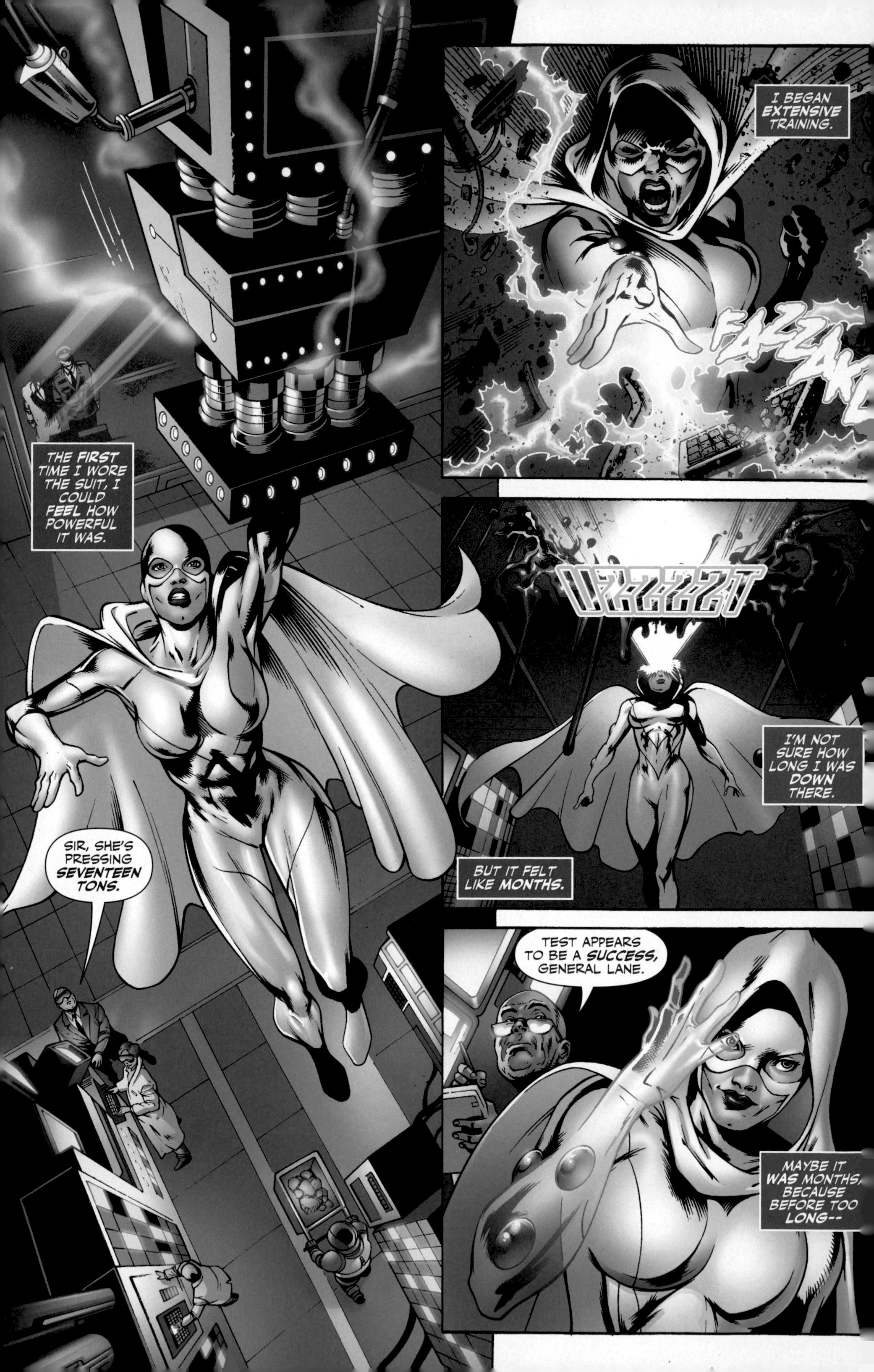
THE FIRST TIME I WORE THE SUIT, I COULD FEEL HOW POWERFUL IT WAS.
SIR, SHE'S PRESSING SEVENTEEN TONS.
I BEGAN EXTENSIVE TRAINING.
I'M NOT SURE HOW LONG I WAS DOWN THERE.
BUT IT FELT LIKE MONTHS.
TEST APPEARS TO BE A SUCCESS, GENERAL LANE.
MAYBE IT WAS MONTHS, BECAUSE BEFORE TOO LONG--

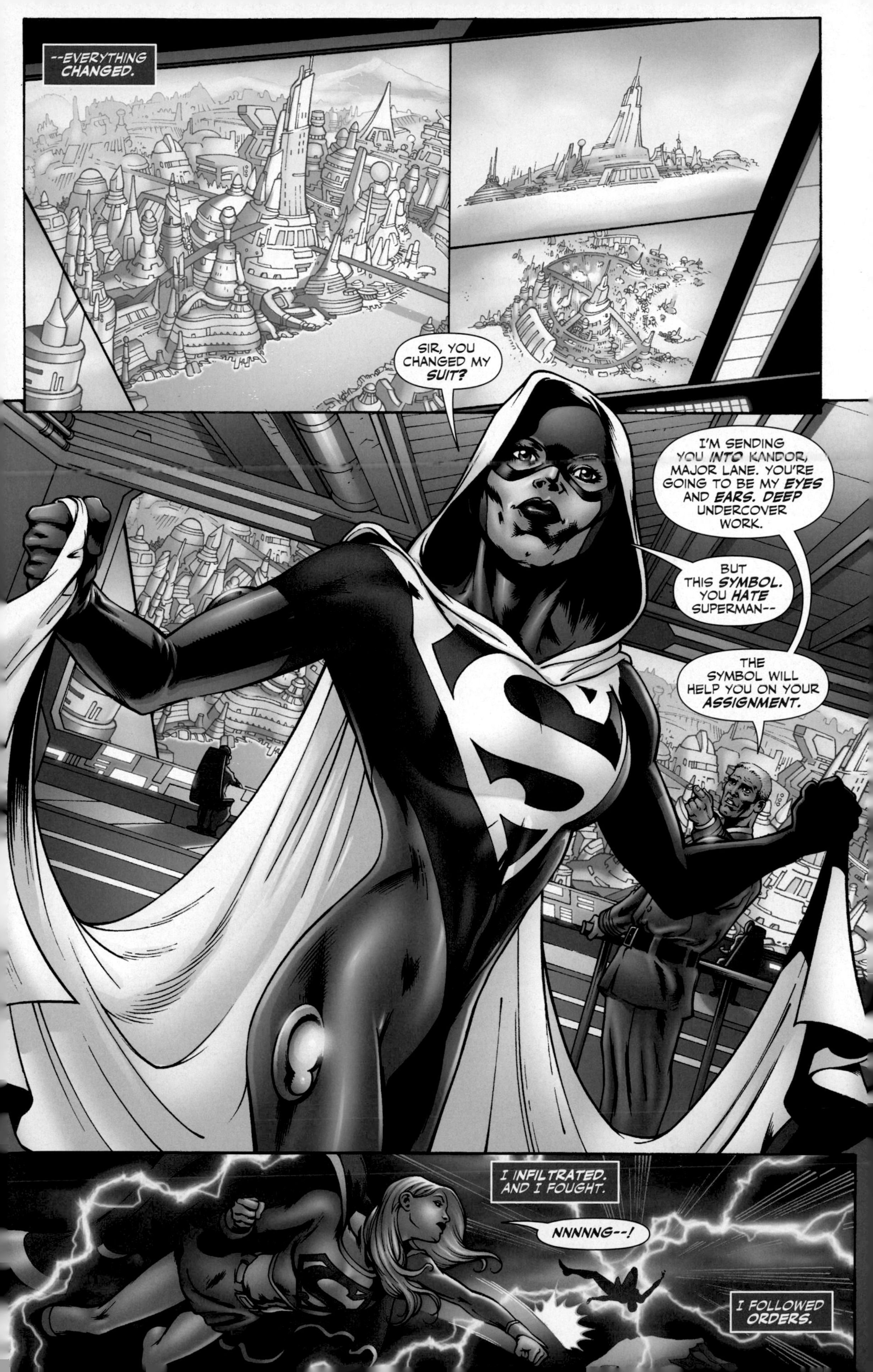
--EVERYTHING CHANGED.
SIR, YOU CHANGED MY SUIT?
I'M SENDING YOU INTO KANDOR, MAJOR LANE. YOU'RE GOING TO BE MY EYES AND EARS. DEEP UNDERCOVER WORK.
BUT THIS SYMBOL. YOU HATE SUPERMAN--
THE SYMBOL WILL HELP YOU ON YOUR ASSIGNMENT.
I INFILTRATED. AND I FOUGHT.
NNNNNG--!
I FOLLOWED ORDERS.

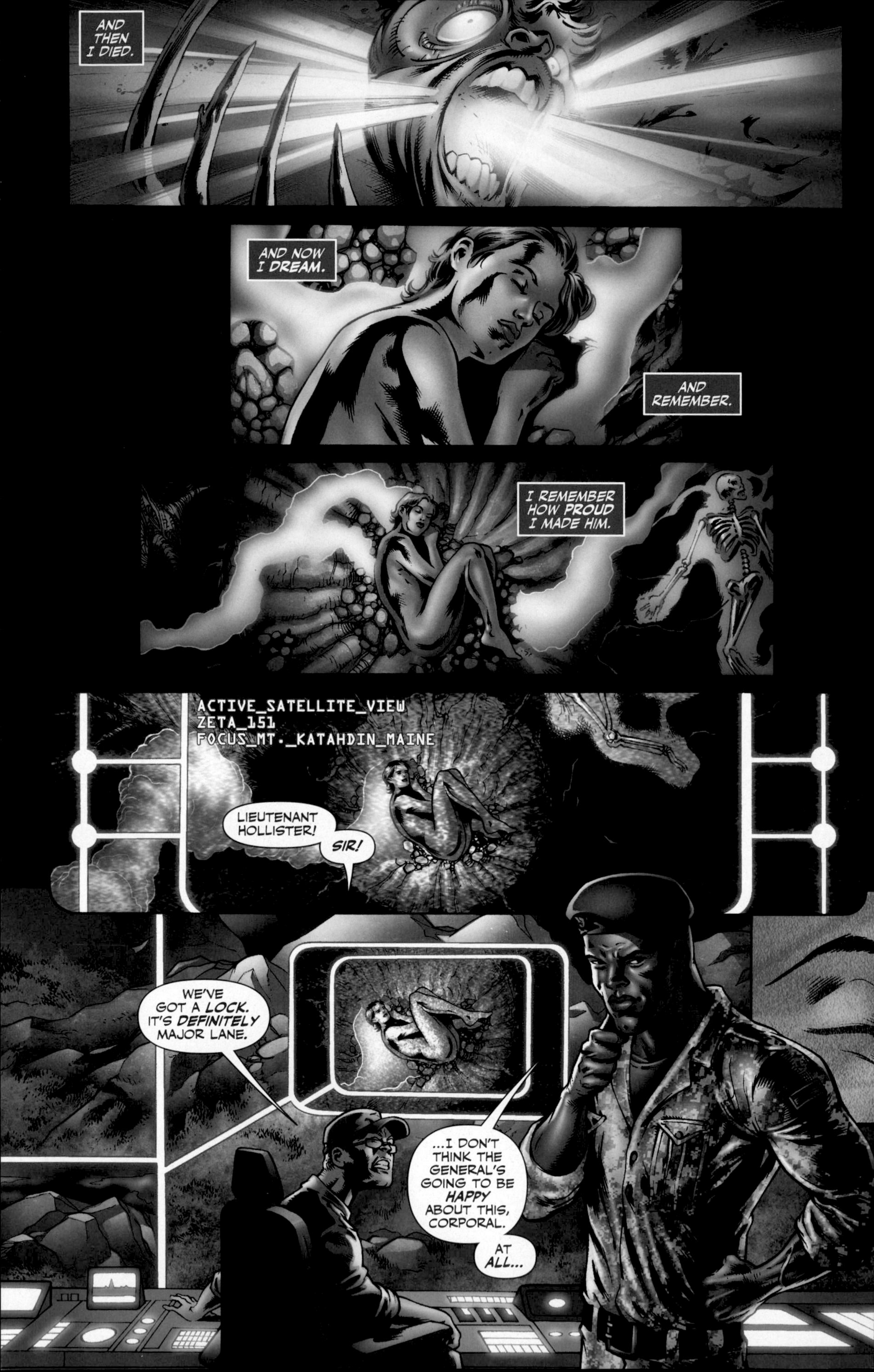

AND THEN I DIED.
AND NOW I DREAM.
AND REMEMBER.
I REMEMBER HOW PROUD I MADE HIM.
ACTIVE_SATELLITE_VIEW
ZETA_151
FOCUS_MT._KATAHDIN_MAINE
LIEUTENANT HOLLISTER!
SIR!
WE'VE GOT A LOCK. IT'S DEFINITELY MAJOR LANE.
...I DON'T THINK THE GENERAL'S GOING TO BE HAPPY ABOUT THIS, CORPORAL.
AT ALL...

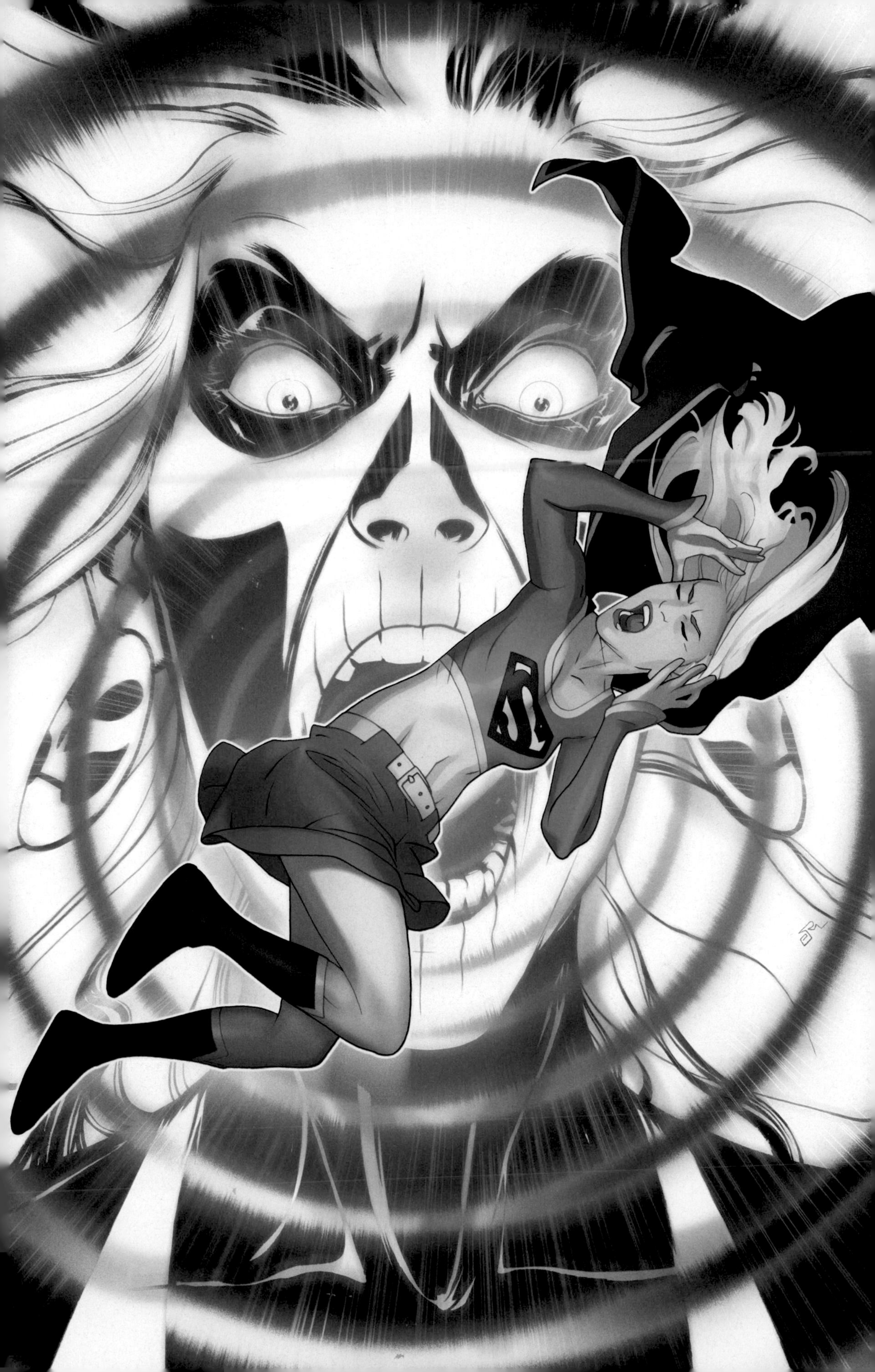

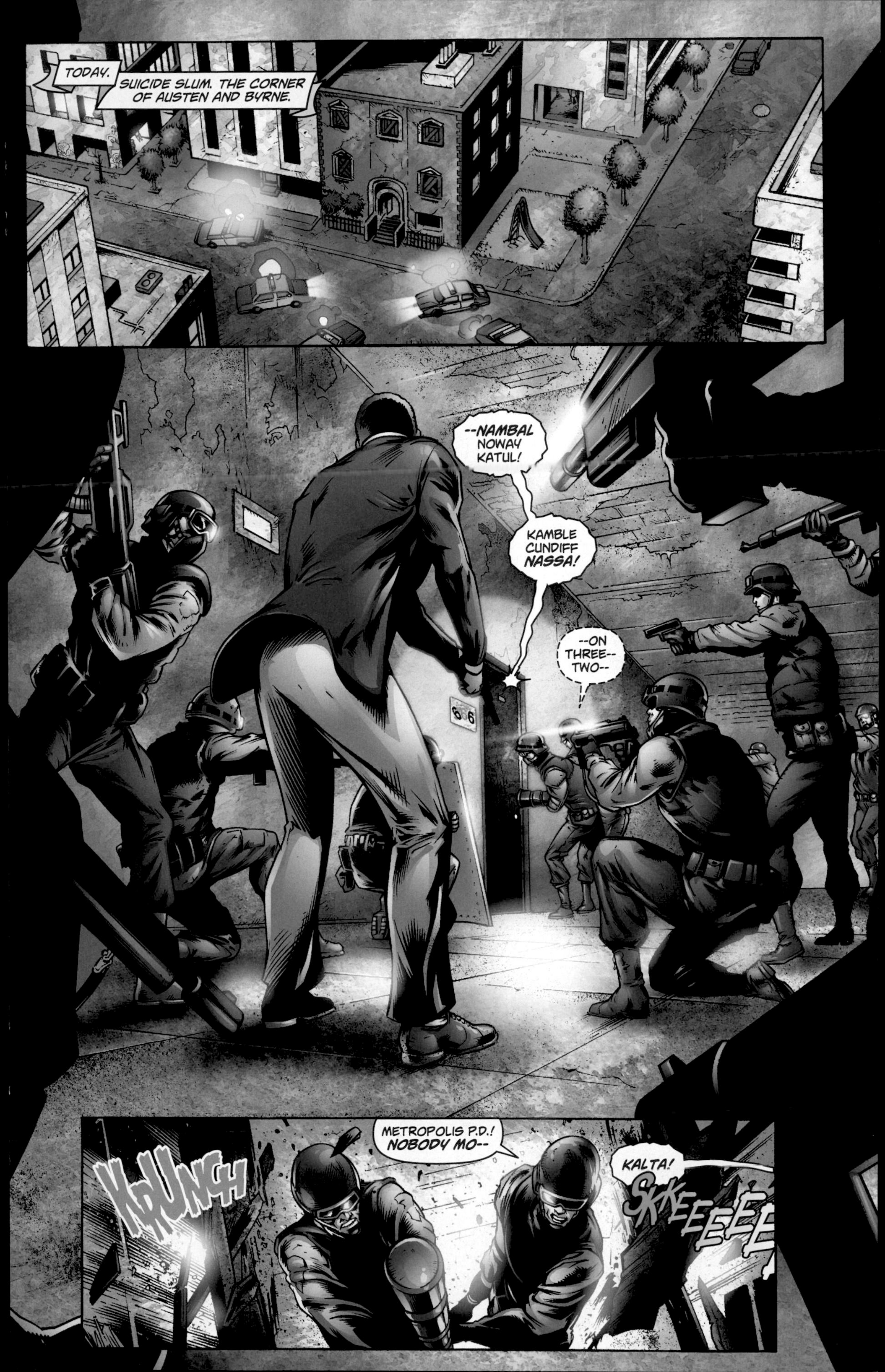
TODAY.
SUICIDE SLUM. THE CORNER OF AUSTEN AND BYRNE.
--NAMBAL NOWAY KATUL!
KAMBLE CUNDIFF NASSA!
--ON THREE-- TWO--
!
KRUNCH
METROPOLIS P.D.! NOBODY MO--
KALTA!
SKKEEEEE

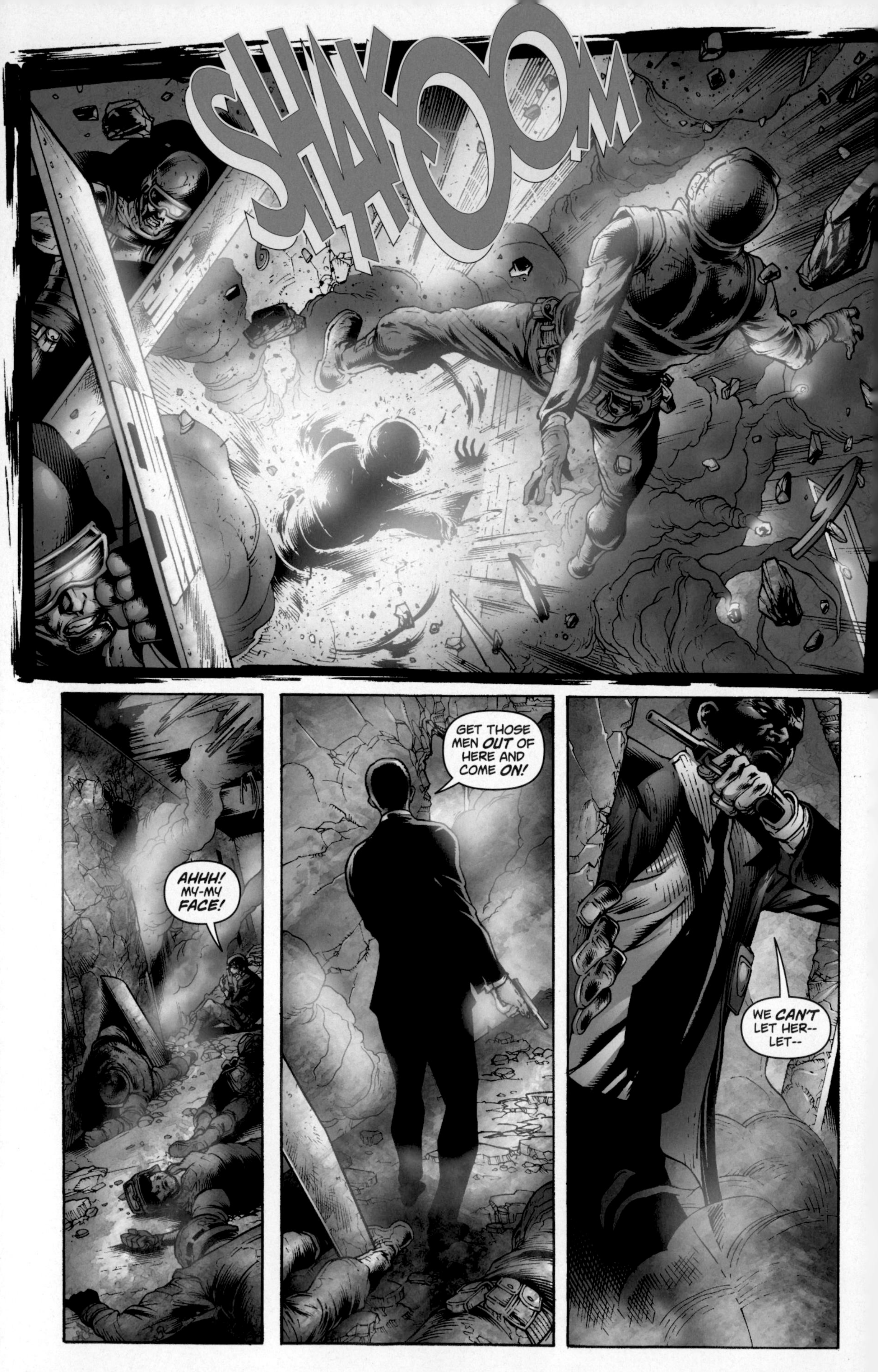
SHAKOOM
AHHH! MY-MY FACE!
GET THOSE MEN OUT OF HERE AND COME ON!
WE CAN'T LET HER-- LET--

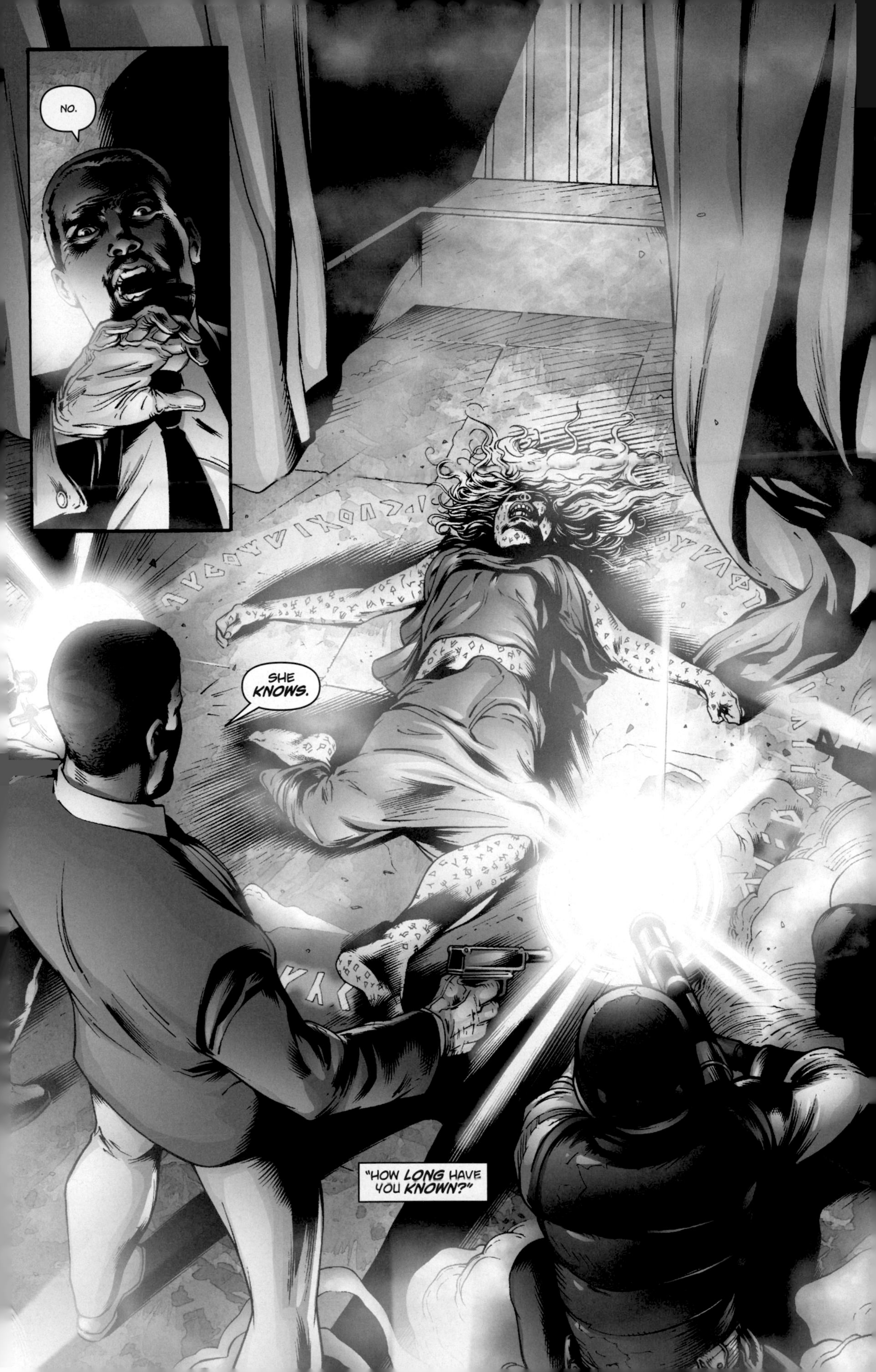
NO.
SHE KNOWS.
"HOW LONG HAVE YOU KNOWN?"

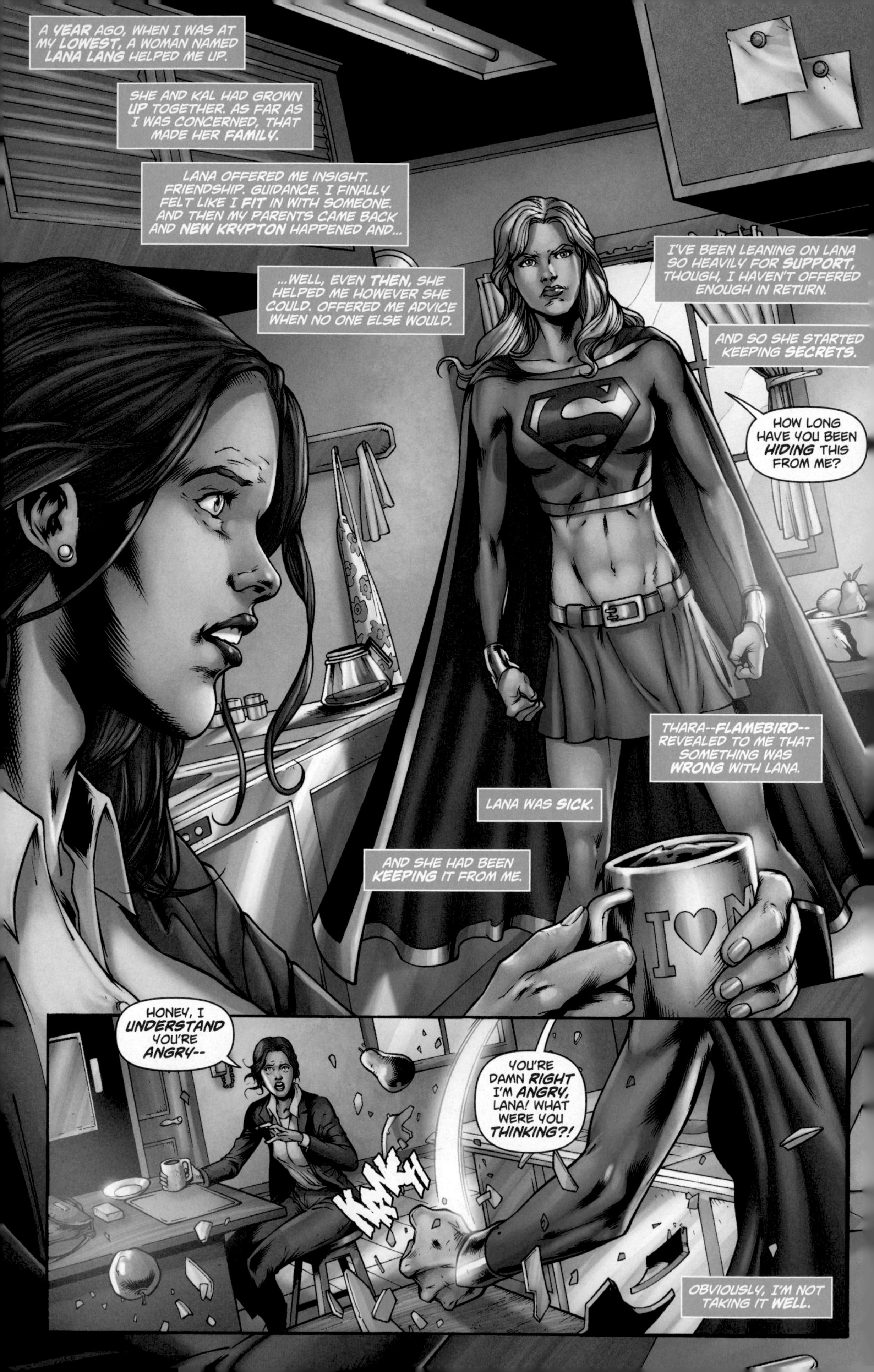
A YEAR AGO, WHEN I WAS AT MY LOWEST, A WOMAN NAMED LANA LANG HELPED ME UP.
SHE AND KAL HAD GROWN UP TOGETHER. AS FAR AS I WAS CONCERNED, THAT MADE HER FAMILY.
LANA OFFERED ME INSIGHT. FRIENDSHIP. GUIDANCE. I FINALLY FELT LIKE I FIT IN WITH SOMEONE. AND THEN MY PARENTS CAME BACK AND NEW KRYPTON HAPPENED AND...
...WELL, EVEN THEN, SHE HELPED ME HOWEVER SHE COULD. OFFERED ME ADVICE WHEN NO ONE ELSE WOULD.
I'VE BEEN LEANING ON LANA SO HEAVILY FOR SUPPORT, THOUGH, I HAVEN'T OFFERED ENOUGH IN RETURN.
AND SO SHE STARTED KEEPING SECRETS.
HOW LONG HAVE YOU BEEN HIDING THIS FROM ME?
THARA--FLAMEBIRD--REVEALED TO ME THAT SOMETHING WAS WRONG WITH LANA.
LANA WAS SICK.
AND SHE HAD BEEN KEEPING IT FROM ME.
I ♥ M
HONEY, I UNDERSTAND YOU'RE ANGRY--
YOU'RE DAMN RIGHT I'M ANGRY, LANA! WHAT WERE YOU THINKING?!
KRAKK!!
OBVIOUSLY, I'M NOT TAKING IT WELL.

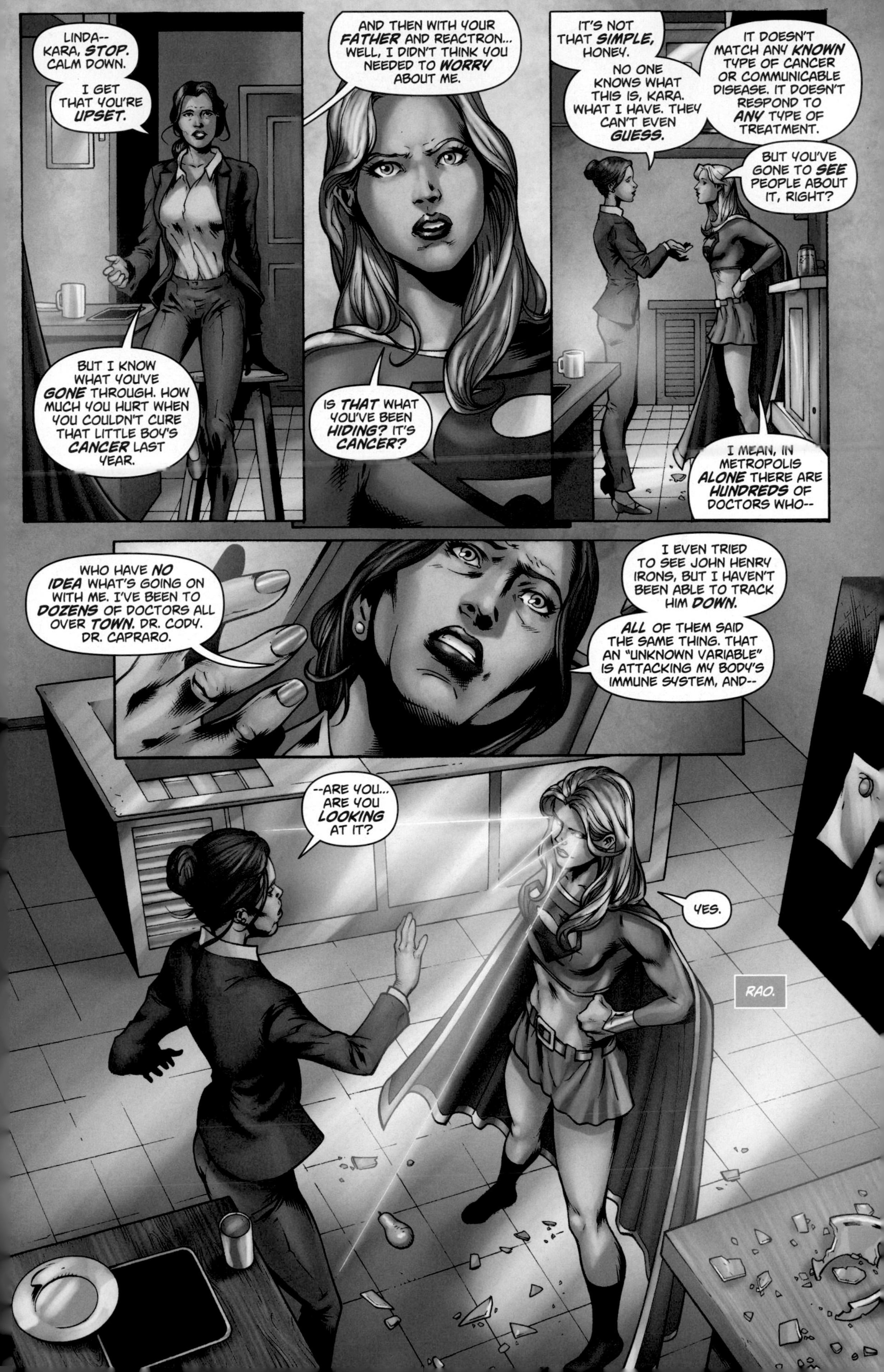
LINDA-- KARA, STOP. CALM DOWN.
I GET THAT YOU'RE UPSET.
BUT I KNOW WHAT YOU'VE GONE THROUGH. HOW MUCH YOU HURT WHEN YOU COULDN'T CURE THAT LITTLE BOY'S CANCER LAST YEAR.
AND THEN WITH YOUR FATHER AND REACTRON... WELL, I DIDN'T THINK YOU NEEDED TO WORRY ABOUT ME.
IS THAT WHAT YOU'VE BEEN HIDING? IT'S CANCER?
IT'S NOT THAT SIMPLE, HONEY.
NO ONE KNOWS WHAT THIS IS, KARA. WHAT I HAVE. THEY CAN'T EVEN GUESS.
IT DOESN'T MATCH ANY KNOWN TYPE OF CANCER OR COMMUNICABLE DISEASE. IT DOESN'T RESPOND TO ANY TYPE OF TREATMENT.
BUT YOU'VE GONE TO SEE PEOPLE ABOUT IT, RIGHT?
I MEAN, IN METROPOLIS ALONE THERE ARE HUNDREDS OF DOCTORS WHO--
WHO HAVE NO IDEA WHAT'S GOING ON WITH ME. I'VE BEEN TO DOZENS OF DOCTORS ALL OVER TOWN. DR. CODY. DR. CAPRARO.
I EVEN TRIED TO SEE JOHN HENRY IRONS, BUT I HAVEN'T BEEN ABLE TO TRACK HIM DOWN.
ALL OF THEM SAID THE SAME THING. THAT AN "UNKNOWN VARIABLE" IS ATTACKING MY BODY'S IMMUNE SYSTEM, AND--
--ARE YOU... ARE YOU LOOKING AT IT?
YES.
RAO.

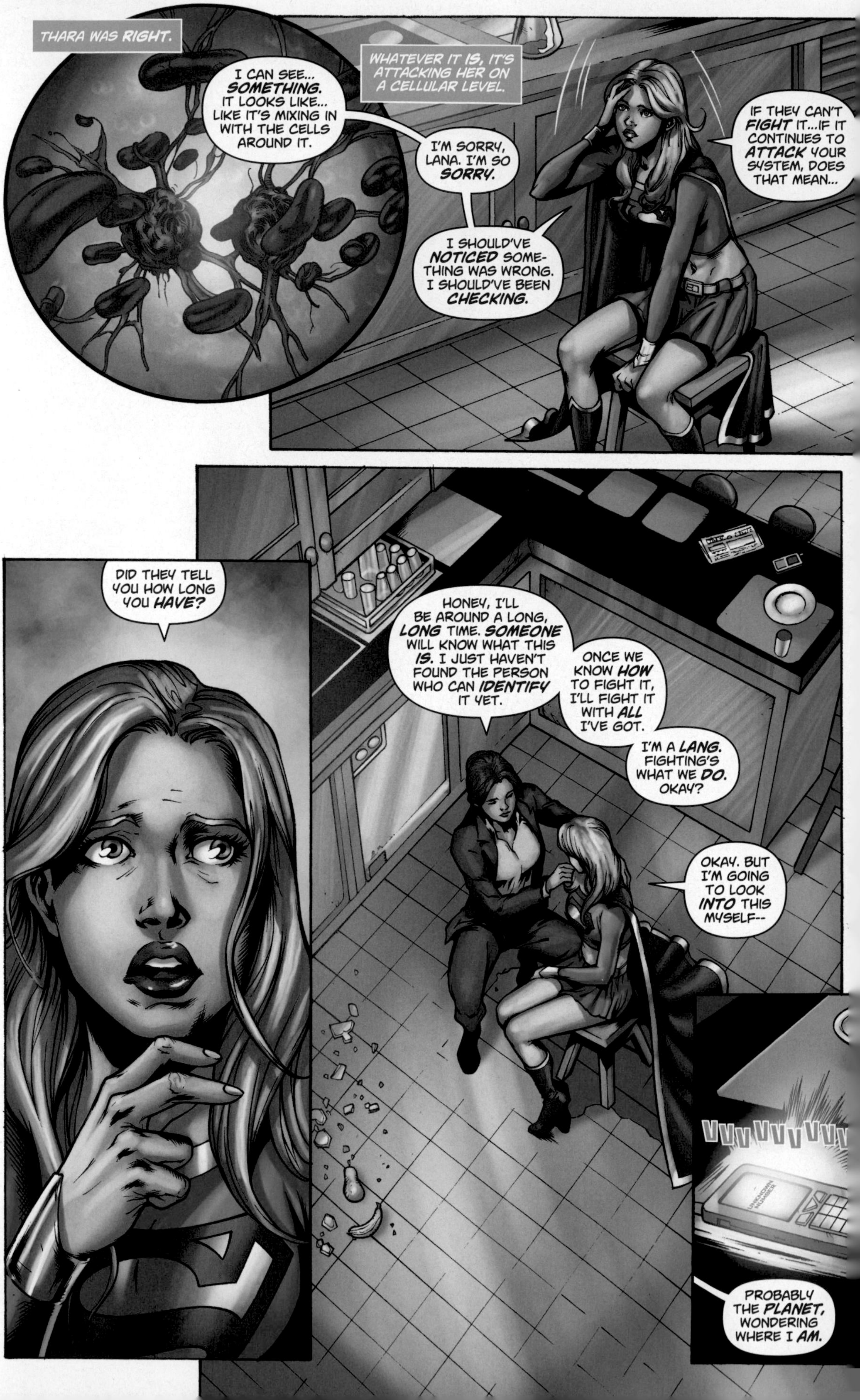

THARA WAS RIGHT.
I CAN SEE... SOMETHING. IT LOOKS LIKE... LIKE IT'S MIXING IN WITH THE CELLS AROUND IT.
WHATEVER IT IS, IT'S ATTACKING HER ON A CELLULAR LEVEL.
I'M SORRY, LANA. I'M SO SORRY.
I SHOULD'VE NOTICED SOMETHING WAS WRONG. I SHOULD'VE BEEN CHECKING.
IF THEY CAN'T FIGHT IT...IF IT CONTINUES TO ATTACK YOUR SYSTEM, DOES THAT MEAN...
DID THEY TELL YOU HOW LONG YOU HAVE?
HONEY, I'LL BE AROUND A LONG, LONG TIME. SOMEONE WILL KNOW WHAT THIS IS. I JUST HAVEN'T FOUND THE PERSON WHO CAN IDENTIFY IT YET.
ONCE WE KNOW HOW TO FIGHT IT, I'LL FIGHT IT WITH ALL I'VE GOT.
I'M A LANG. FIGHTING'S WHAT WE DO. OKAY?
OKAY. BUT I'M GOING TO LOOK INTO THIS MYSELF--
VVVVVVVVVV
UNKNOWN NUMBER
PROBABLY THE PLANET, WONDERING WHERE I AM.

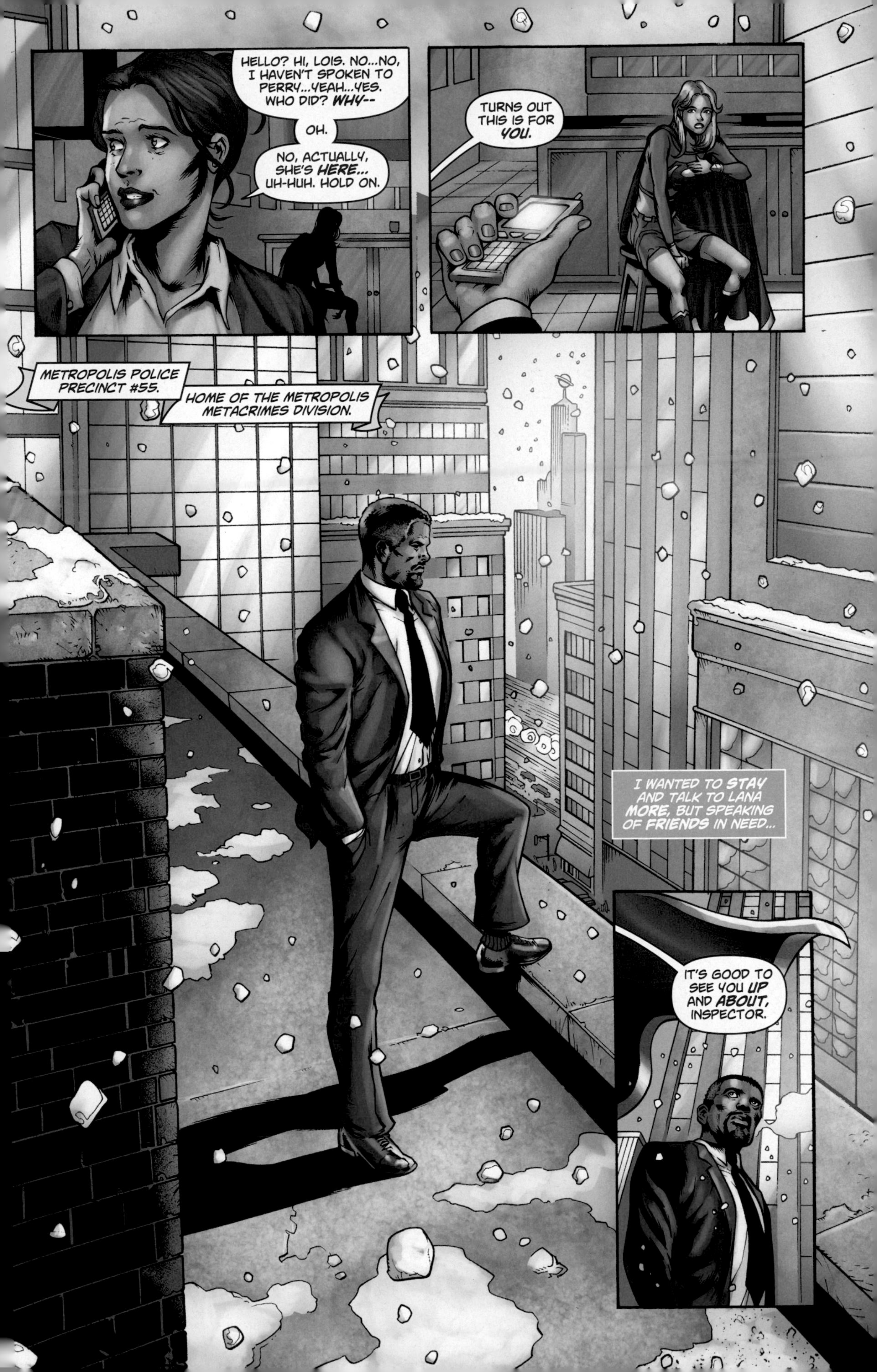
HELLO? HI, LOIS. NO...NO, I HAVEN'T SPOKEN TO PERRY...YEAH...YES. WHO DID? WHY--
OH.
NO, ACTUALLY, SHE'S HERE... UH-HUH. HOLD ON.
TURNS OUT THIS IS FOR YOU.
METROPOLIS POLICE PRECINCT #55.
HOME OF THE METROPOLIS METACRIMES DIVISION.
I WANTED TO STAY AND TALK TO LANA MORE, BUT SPEAKING OF FRIENDS IN NEED...
IT'S GOOD TO SEE YOU UP AND ABOUT, INSPECTOR.

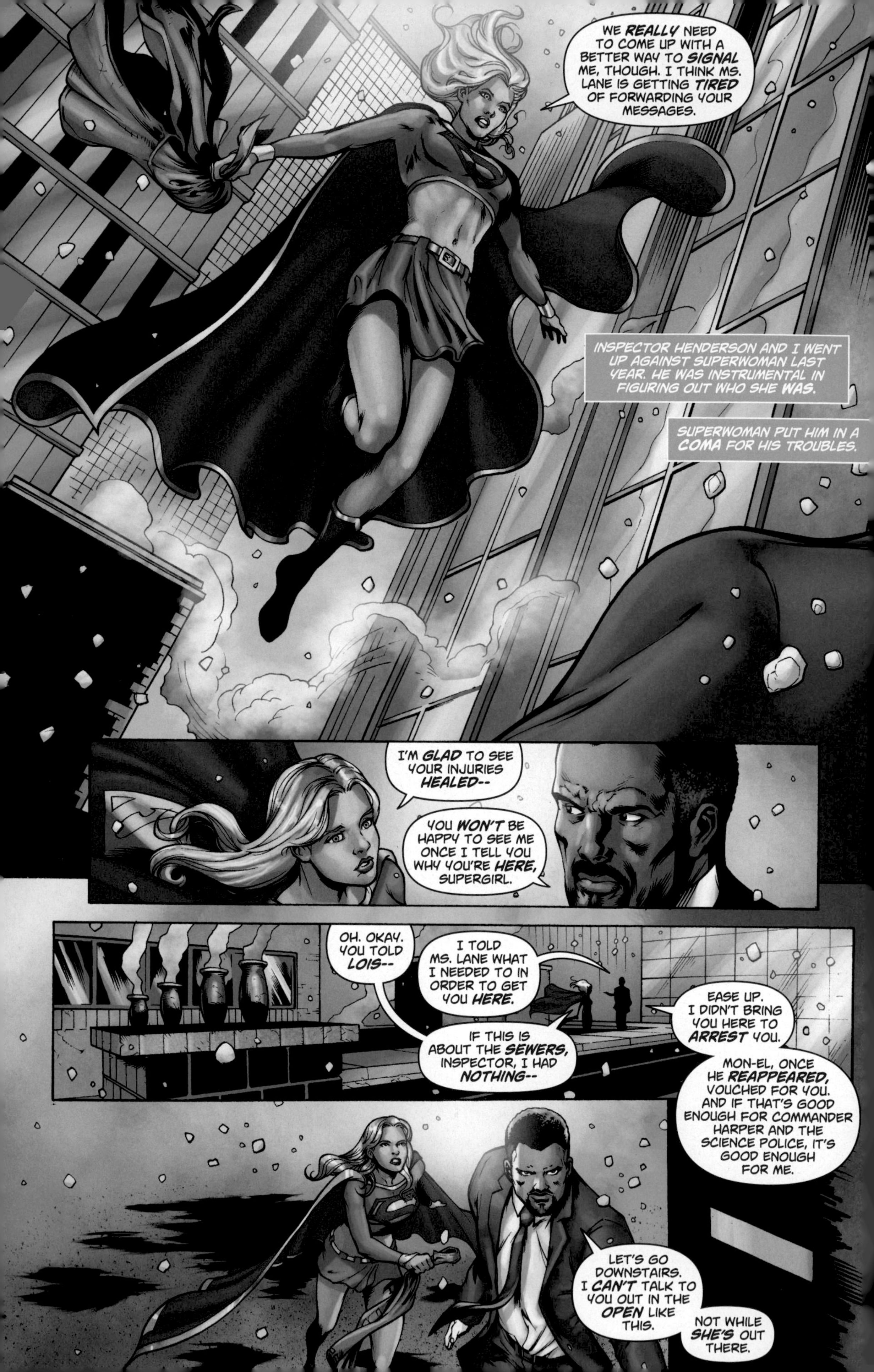
WE REALLY NEED TO COME UP WITH A BETTER WAY TO SIGNAL ME, THOUGH. I THINK MS. LANE IS GETTING TIRED OF FORWARDING YOUR MESSAGES.
INSPECTOR HENDERSON AND I WENT UP AGAINST SUPERWOMAN LAST YEAR. HE WAS INSTRUMENTAL IN FIGURING OUT WHO SHE WAS.
SUPERWOMAN PUT HIM IN A COMA FOR HIS TROUBLES.
I'M GLAD TO SEE YOUR INJURIES HEALED--
YOU WON'T BE HAPPY TO SEE ME ONCE I TELL YOU WHY YOU'RE HERE, SUPERGIRL.
OH. OKAY. YOU TOLD LOIS--
I TOLD MS. LANE WHAT I NEEDED TO IN ORDER TO GET YOU HERE.
IF THIS IS ABOUT THE SEWERS, INSPECTOR, I HAD NOTHING--
EASE UP. I DIDN'T BRING YOU HERE TO ARREST YOU.
MON-EL, ONCE HE REAPPEARED, VOUCHED FOR YOU. AND IF THAT'S GOOD ENOUGH FOR COMMANDER HARPER AND THE SCIENCE POLICE, IT'S GOOD ENOUGH FOR ME.
LET'S GO DOWNSTAIRS. I CAN'T TALK TO YOU OUT IN THE OPEN LIKE THIS.
NOT WHILE SHE'S OUT THERE.

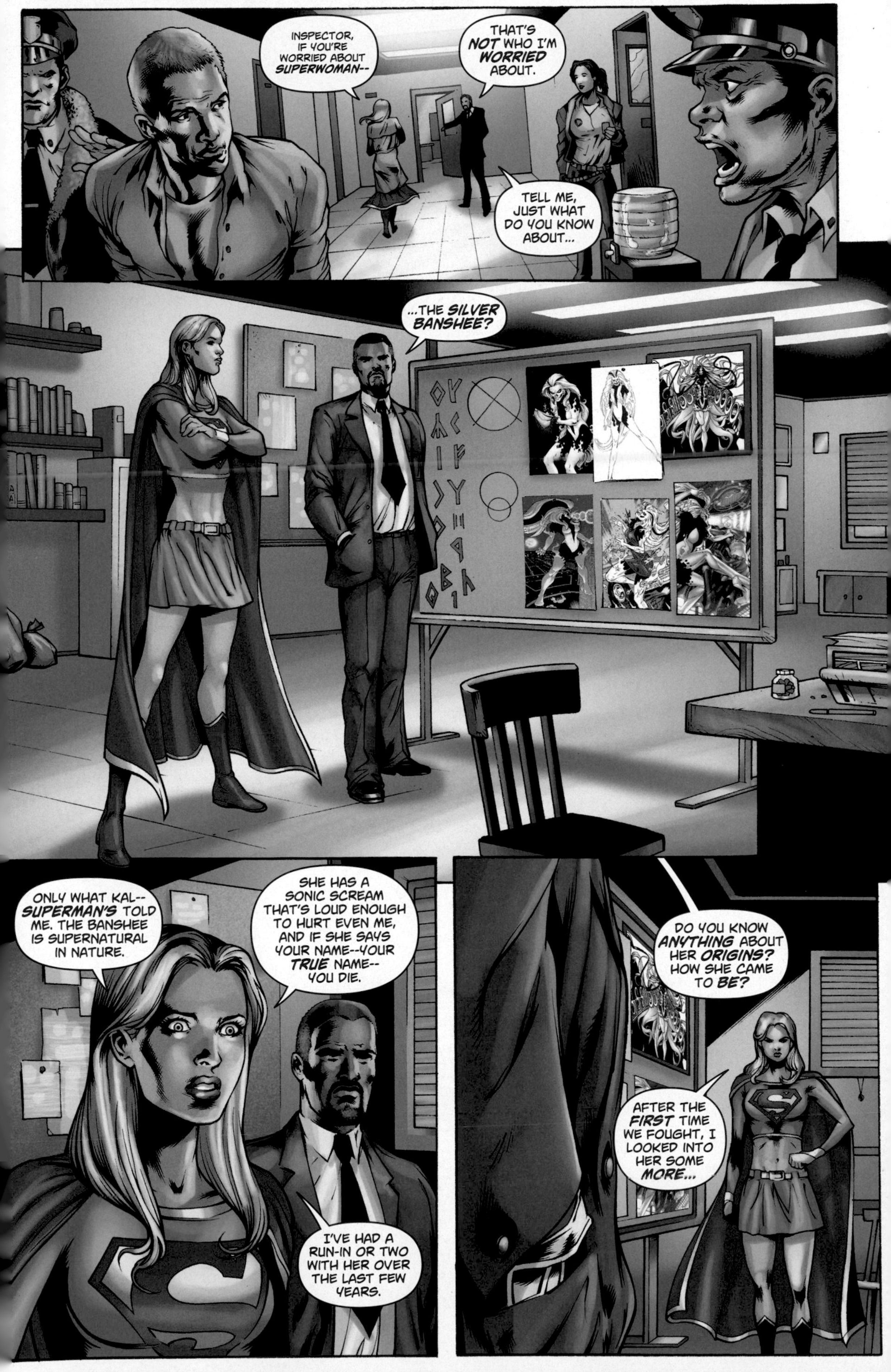
INSPECTOR, IF YOU'RE WORRIED ABOUT SUPERWOMAN--
THAT'S NOT WHO I'M WORRIED ABOUT.
TELL ME, JUST WHAT DO YOU KNOW ABOUT...
...THE SILVER BANSHEE?
ONLY WHAT KAL-- SUPERMAN'S TOLD ME. THE BANSHEE IS SUPERNATURAL IN NATURE.
SHE HAS A SONIC SCREAM THAT'S LOUD ENOUGH TO HURT EVEN ME, AND IF SHE SAYS YOUR NAME--YOUR TRUE NAME-- YOU DIE.
I'VE HAD A RUN-IN OR TWO WITH HER OVER THE LAST FEW YEARS.
DO YOU KNOW ANYTHING ABOUT HER ORIGINS? HOW SHE CAME TO BE?
AFTER THE FIRST TIME WE FOUGHT, I LOOKED INTO HER SOME MORE...

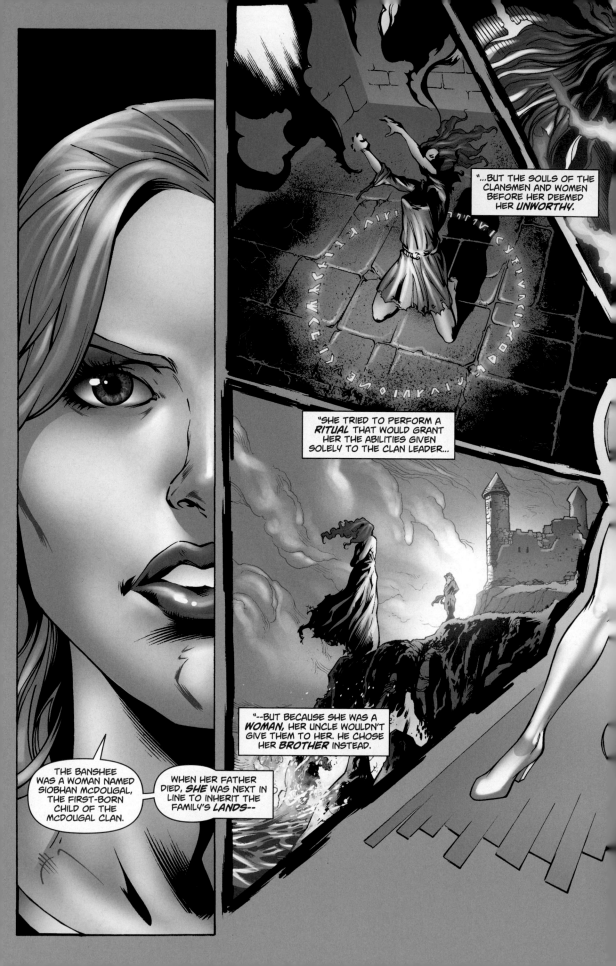

"...BUT THE SOULS OF THE CLANSMEN AND WOMEN BEFORE HER DEEMED HER *UNWORTHY*.

"SHE TRIED TO PERFORM A *RITUAL* THAT WOULD GRANT HER THE ABILITIES GIVEN SOLELY TO THE CLAN LEADER...

"--BUT BECAUSE SHE WAS A *WOMAN*, HER UNCLE WOULDN'T GIVE THEM TO HER. HE CHOSE HER *BROTHER* INSTEAD.

THE BANSHEE WAS A WOMAN NAMED SIOBHAN MCDOUGAL, THE FIRST-BORN CHILD OF THE MCDOUGAL CLAN.

WHEN HER FATHER DIED, *SHE* WAS NEXT IN LINE TO INHERIT THE FAMILY'S *LANDS*--

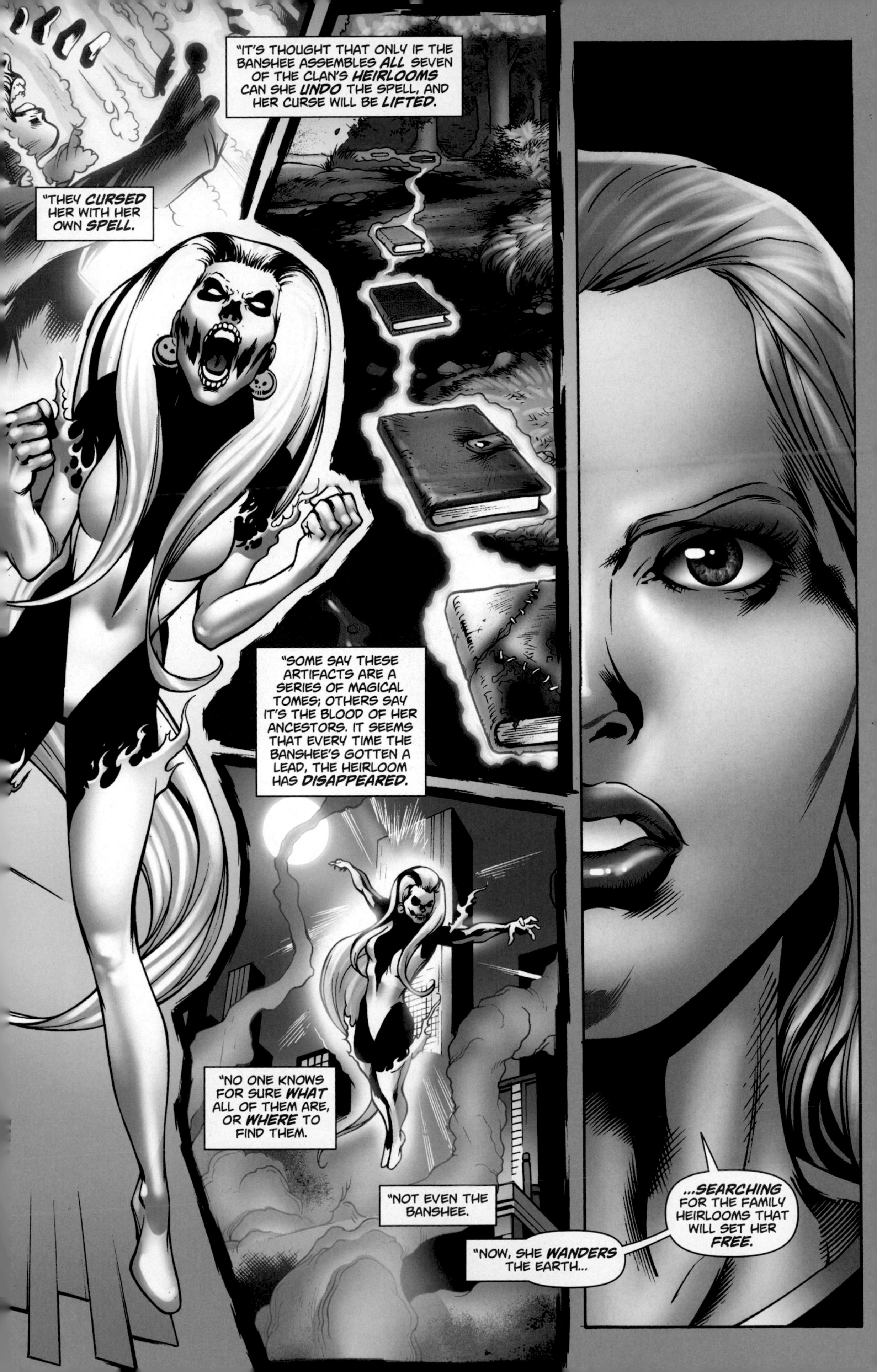
"THEY CURSED HER WITH HER OWN SPELL.
"IT'S THOUGHT THAT ONLY IF THE BANSHEE ASSEMBLES ALL SEVEN OF THE CLAN'S HEIRLOOMS CAN SHE UNDO THE SPELL, AND HER CURSE WILL BE LIFTED.
"SOME SAY THESE ARTIFACTS ARE A SERIES OF MAGICAL TOMES; OTHERS SAY IT'S THE BLOOD OF HER ANCESTORS. IT SEEMS THAT EVERY TIME THE BANSHEE'S GOTTEN A LEAD, THE HEIRLOOM HAS DISAPPEARED.
"NO ONE KNOWS FOR SURE WHAT ALL OF THEM ARE, OR WHERE TO FIND THEM.
"NOT EVEN THE BANSHEE.
"NOW, SHE WANDERS THE EARTH...
...SEARCHING FOR THE FAMILY HEIRLOOMS THAT WILL SET HER FREE.

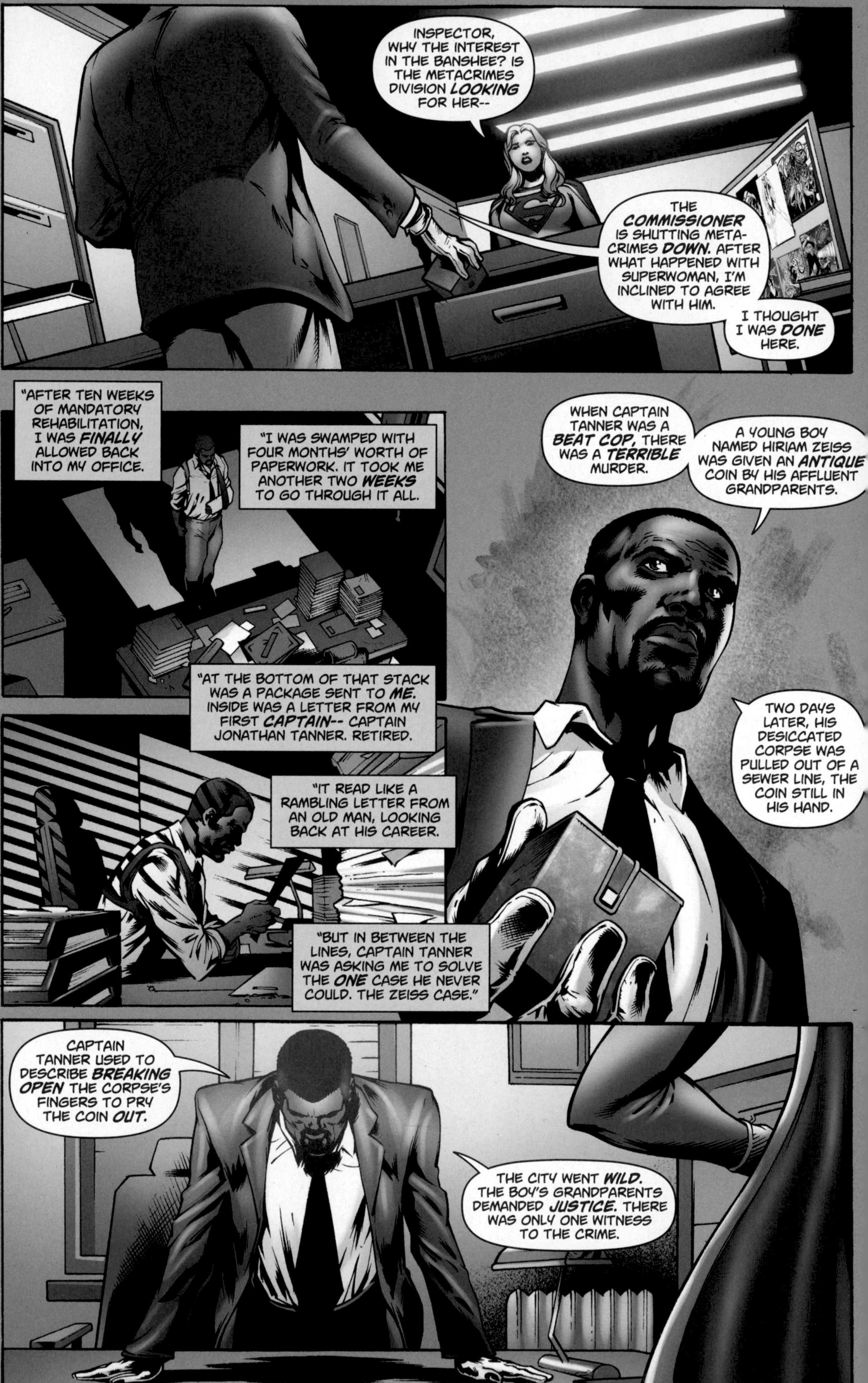
INSPECTOR, WHY THE INTEREST IN THE BANSHEE? IS THE METACRIMES DIVISION LOOKING FOR HER--
THE COMMISSIONER IS SHUTTING METACRIMES DOWN. AFTER WHAT HAPPENED WITH SUPERWOMAN, I'M INCLINED TO AGREE WITH HIM.
I THOUGHT I WAS DONE HERE.
"AFTER TEN WEEKS OF MANDATORY REHABILITATION, I WAS FINALLY ALLOWED BACK INTO MY OFFICE.
"I WAS SWAMPED WITH FOUR MONTHS' WORTH OF PAPERWORK. IT TOOK ME ANOTHER TWO WEEKS TO GO THROUGH IT ALL.
"AT THE BOTTOM OF THAT STACK WAS A PACKAGE SENT TO ME. INSIDE WAS A LETTER FROM MY FIRST CAPTAIN-- CAPTAIN JONATHAN TANNER. RETIRED.
"IT READ LIKE A RAMBLING LETTER FROM AN OLD MAN, LOOKING BACK AT HIS CAREER.
"BUT IN BETWEEN THE LINES, CAPTAIN TANNER WAS ASKING ME TO SOLVE THE ONE CASE HE NEVER COULD. THE ZEISS CASE."
WHEN CAPTAIN TANNER WAS A BEAT COP, THERE WAS A TERRIBLE MURDER.
A YOUNG BOY NAMED HIRIAM ZEISS WAS GIVEN AN ANTIQUE COIN BY HIS AFFLUENT GRANDPARENTS.
TWO DAYS LATER, HIS DESICCATED CORPSE WAS PULLED OUT OF A SEWER LINE, THE COIN STILL IN HIS HAND.
CAPTAIN TANNER USED TO DESCRIBE BREAKING OPEN THE CORPSE'S FINGERS TO PRY THE COIN OUT.
THE CITY WENT WILD. THE BOY'S GRANDPARENTS DEMANDED JUSTICE. THERE WAS ONLY ONE WITNESS TO THE CRIME.

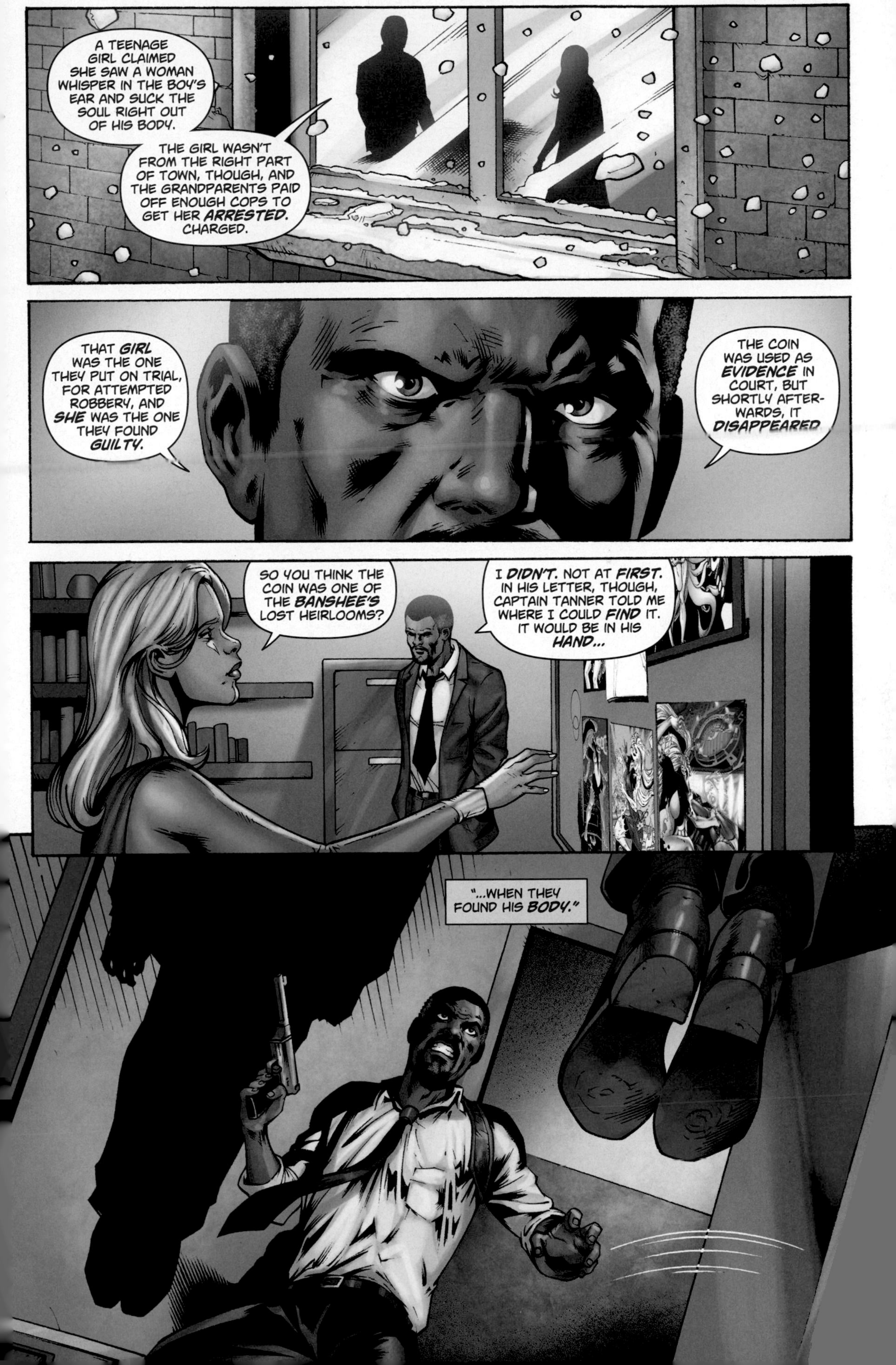
A TEENAGE GIRL CLAIMED SHE SAW A WOMAN WHISPER IN THE BOY'S EAR AND SUCK THE SOUL RIGHT OUT OF HIS BODY.
THE GIRL WASN'T FROM THE RIGHT PART OF TOWN, THOUGH, AND THE GRANDPARENTS PAID OFF ENOUGH COPS TO GET HER ARRESTED. CHARGED.
THAT GIRL WAS THE ONE THEY PUT ON TRIAL, FOR ATTEMPTED ROBBERY, AND SHE WAS THE ONE THEY FOUND GUILTY.
THE COIN WAS USED AS EVIDENCE IN COURT, BUT SHORTLY AFTER-WARDS, IT DISAPPEARED.
SO YOU THINK THE COIN WAS ONE OF THE BANSHEE'S LOST HEIRLOOMS?
I DIDN'T. NOT AT FIRST. IN HIS LETTER, THOUGH, CAPTAIN TANNER TOLD ME WHERE I COULD FIND IT. IT WOULD BE IN HIS HAND...
"...WHEN THEY FOUND HIS BODY."

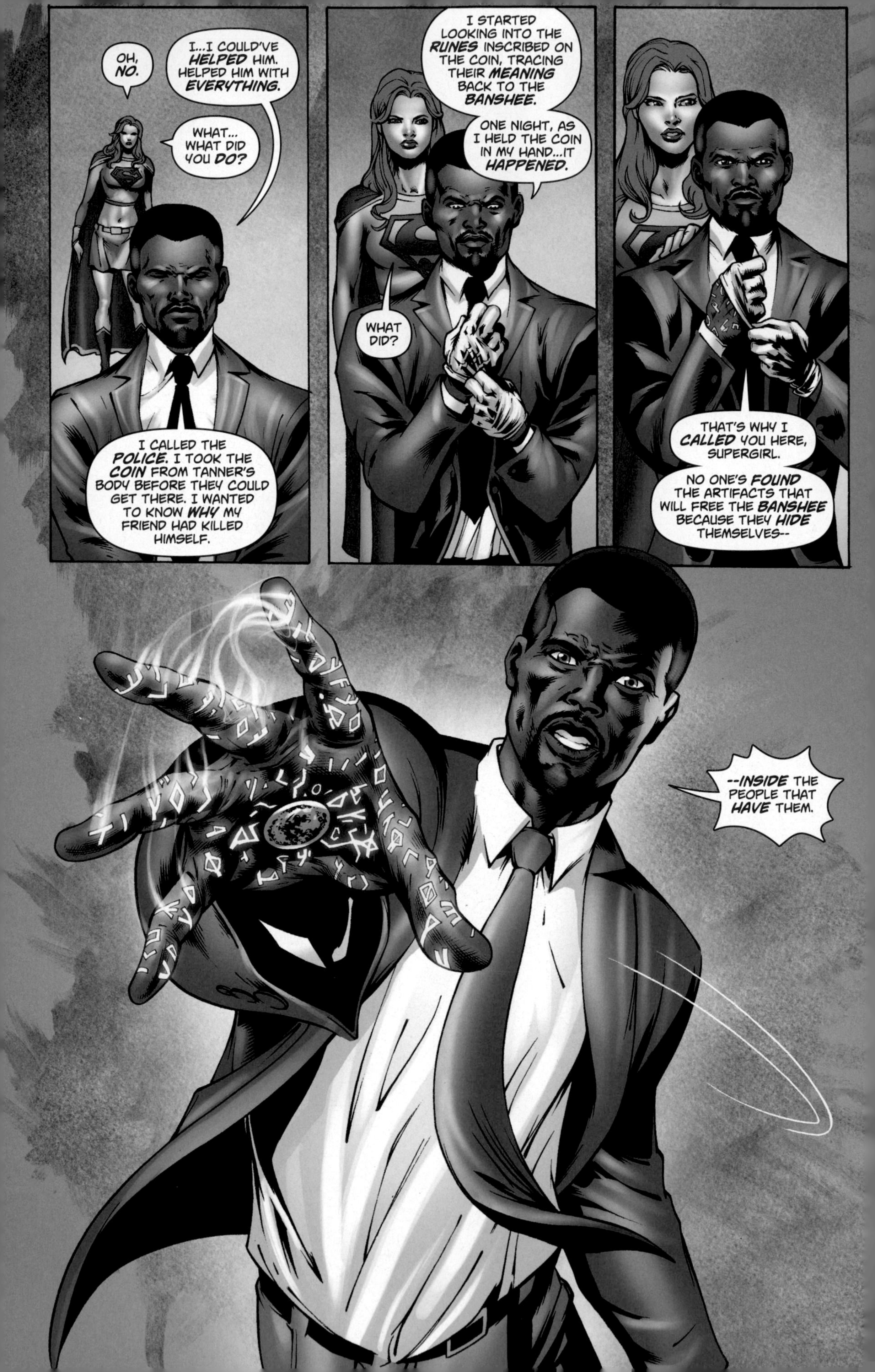
OH, NO.
I...I COULD'VE HELPED HIM. HELPED HIM WITH EVERYTHING.
WHAT... WHAT DID YOU DO?
I CALLED THE POLICE. I TOOK THE COIN FROM TANNER'S BODY BEFORE THEY COULD GET THERE. I WANTED TO KNOW WHY MY FRIEND HAD KILLED HIMSELF.
I STARTED LOOKING INTO THE RUNES INSCRIBED ON THE COIN, TRACING THEIR MEANING BACK TO THE BANSHEE.
ONE NIGHT, AS I HELD THE COIN IN MY HAND...IT HAPPENED.
WHAT DID?
THAT'S WHY I CALLED YOU HERE, SUPERGIRL.
NO ONE'S FOUND THE ARTIFACTS THAT WILL FREE THE BANSHEE BECAUSE THEY HIDE THEMSELVES--
--INSIDE THE PEOPLE THAT HAVE THEM.

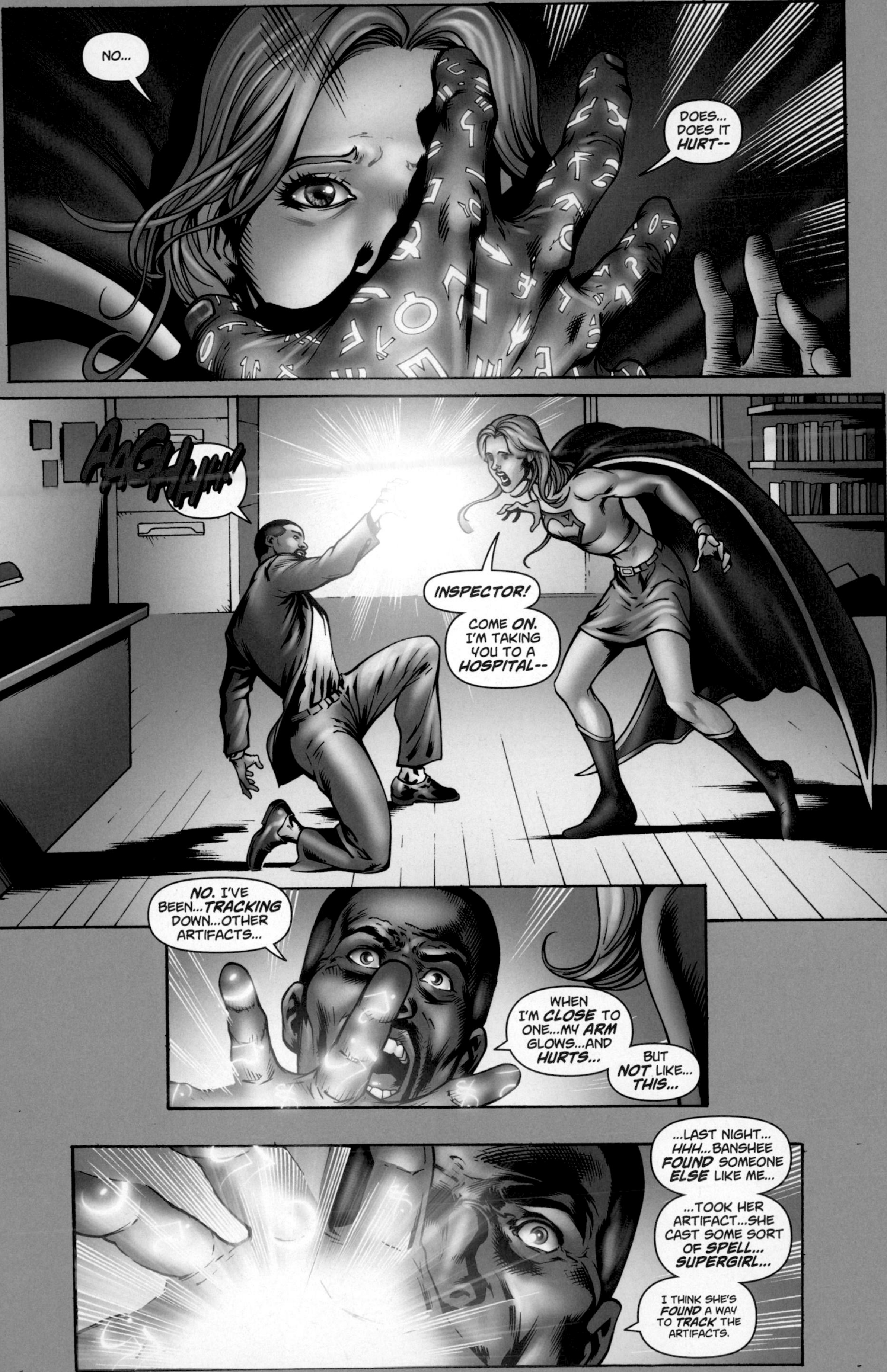
NO...
DOES... DOES IT HURT--
AAGHHHH!
INSPECTOR!
COME ON. I'M TAKING YOU TO A HOSPITAL--
NO. I'VE BEEN...TRACKING DOWN...OTHER ARTIFACTS...
WHEN I'M CLOSE TO ONE...MY ARM GLOWS...AND HURTS...
BUT NOT LIKE... THIS...
...LAST NIGHT... HHH...BANSHEE FOUND SOMEONE ELSE LIKE ME...
...TOOK HER ARTIFACT...SHE CAST SOME SORT OF SPELL... SUPERGIRL...
I THINK SHE'S FOUND A WAY TO TRACK THE ARTIFACTS.

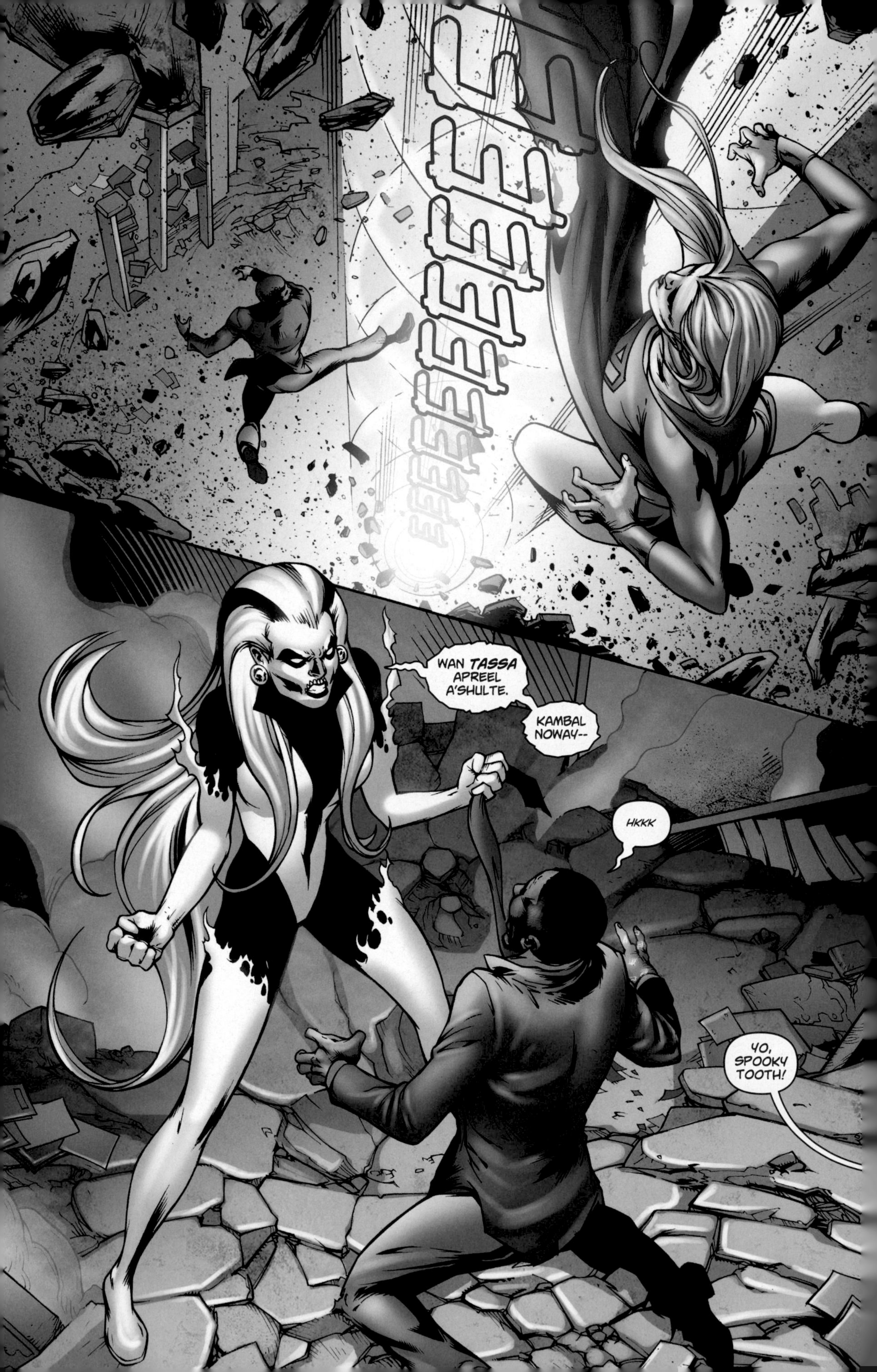
EEEEEEEEEE
WAN TASSA APREEL A'SHULTE.
KAMBAL NOWAY--
HKKK
YO, SPOOKY TOOTH!

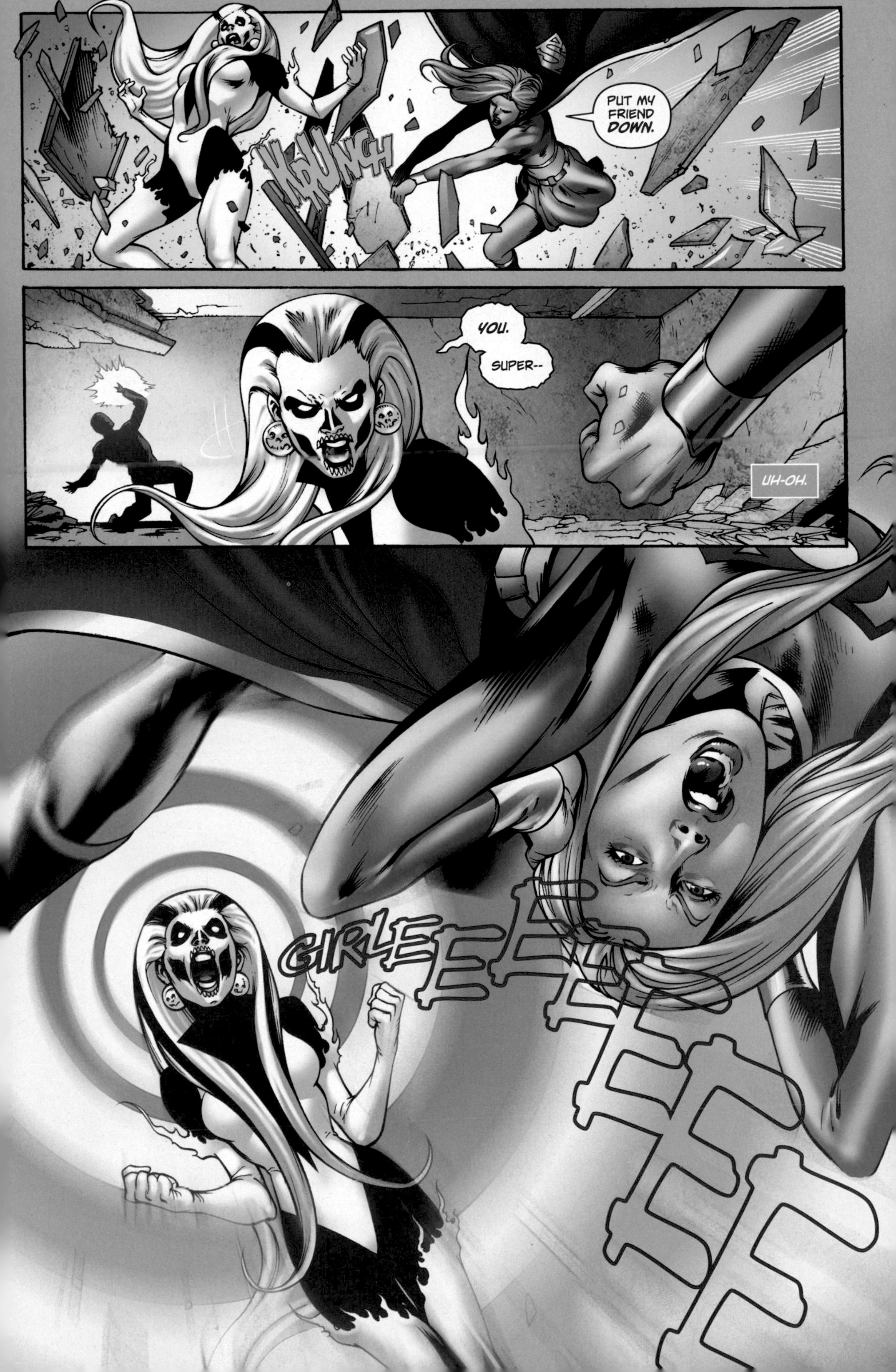
PUT MY FRIEND DOWN.
KRUNCH
YOU.
SUPER--
UH-OH.
GIRLEEEEEEEE

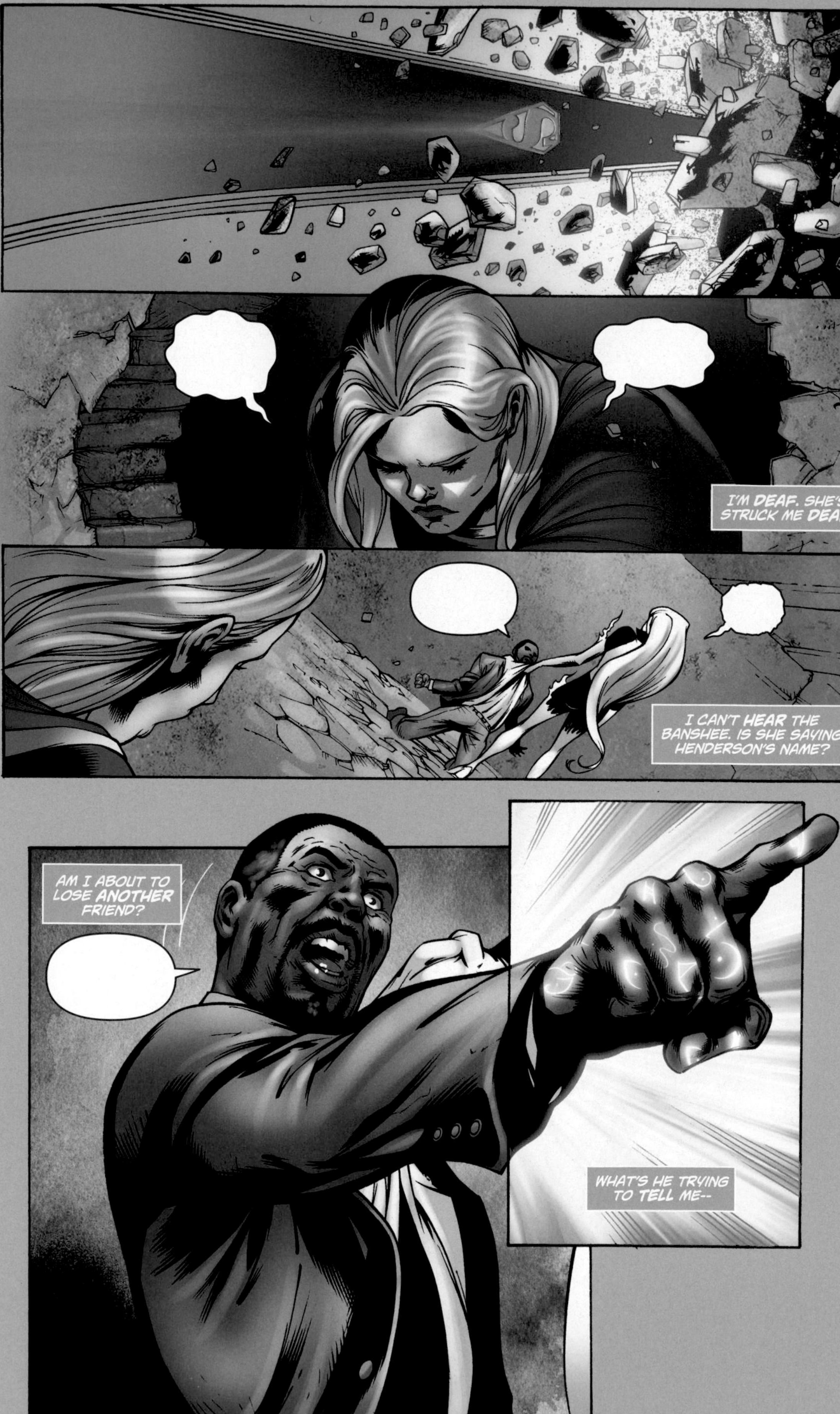
I'M DEAF. SHE'S STRUCK ME DEAF.
I CAN'T HEAR THE BANSHEE. IS SHE SAYING HENDERSON'S NAME?
AM I ABOUT TO LOSE ANOTHER FRIEND?
WHAT'S HE TRYING TO TELL ME--

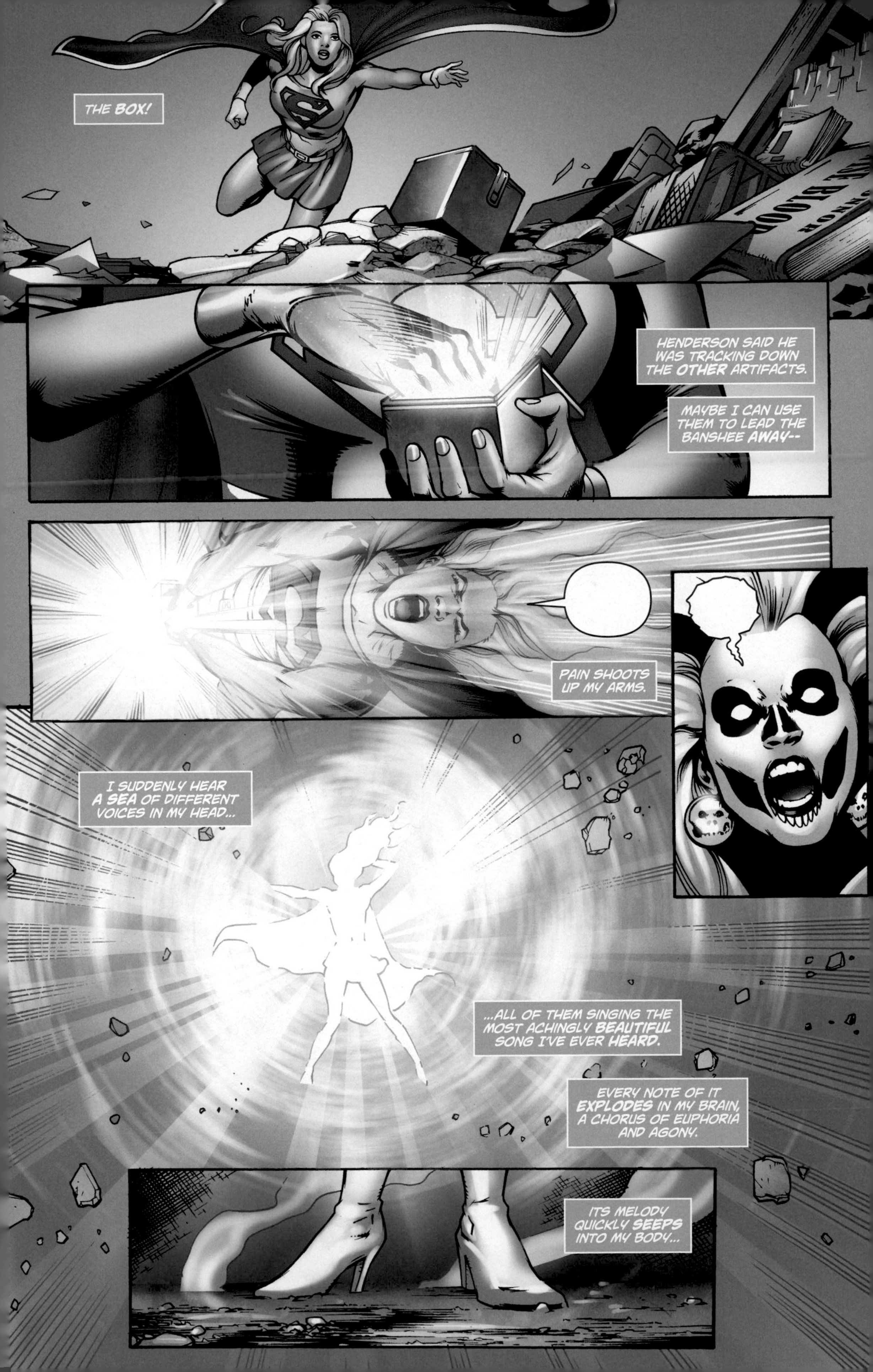
THE BOX!
HENDERSON SAID HE WAS TRACKING DOWN THE OTHER ARTIFACTS.
MAYBE I CAN USE THEM TO LEAD THE BANSHEE AWAY--
PAIN SHOOTS UP MY ARMS.
I SUDDENLY HEAR A SEA OF DIFFERENT VOICES IN MY HEAD...
...ALL OF THEM SINGING THE MOST ACHINGLY BEAUTIFUL SONG I'VE EVER HEARD.
EVERY NOTE OF IT EXPLODES IN MY BRAIN, A CHORUS OF EUPHORIA AND AGONY.
ITS MELODY QUICKLY SEEPS INTO MY BODY...

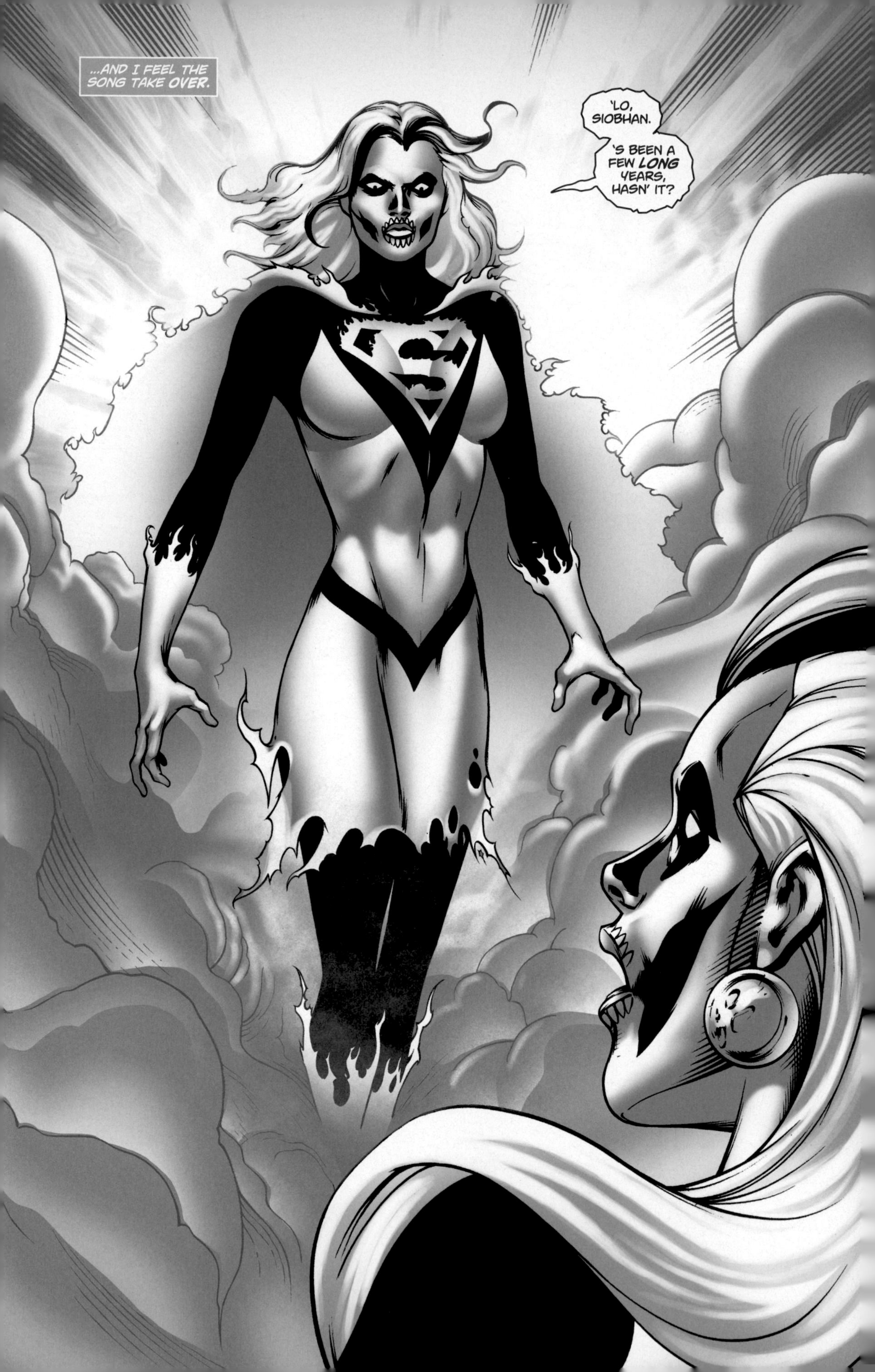
...AND I FEEL THE SONG TAKE OVER.
'LO, SIOBHAN.
'S BEEN A FEW LONG YEARS, HASN' IT?

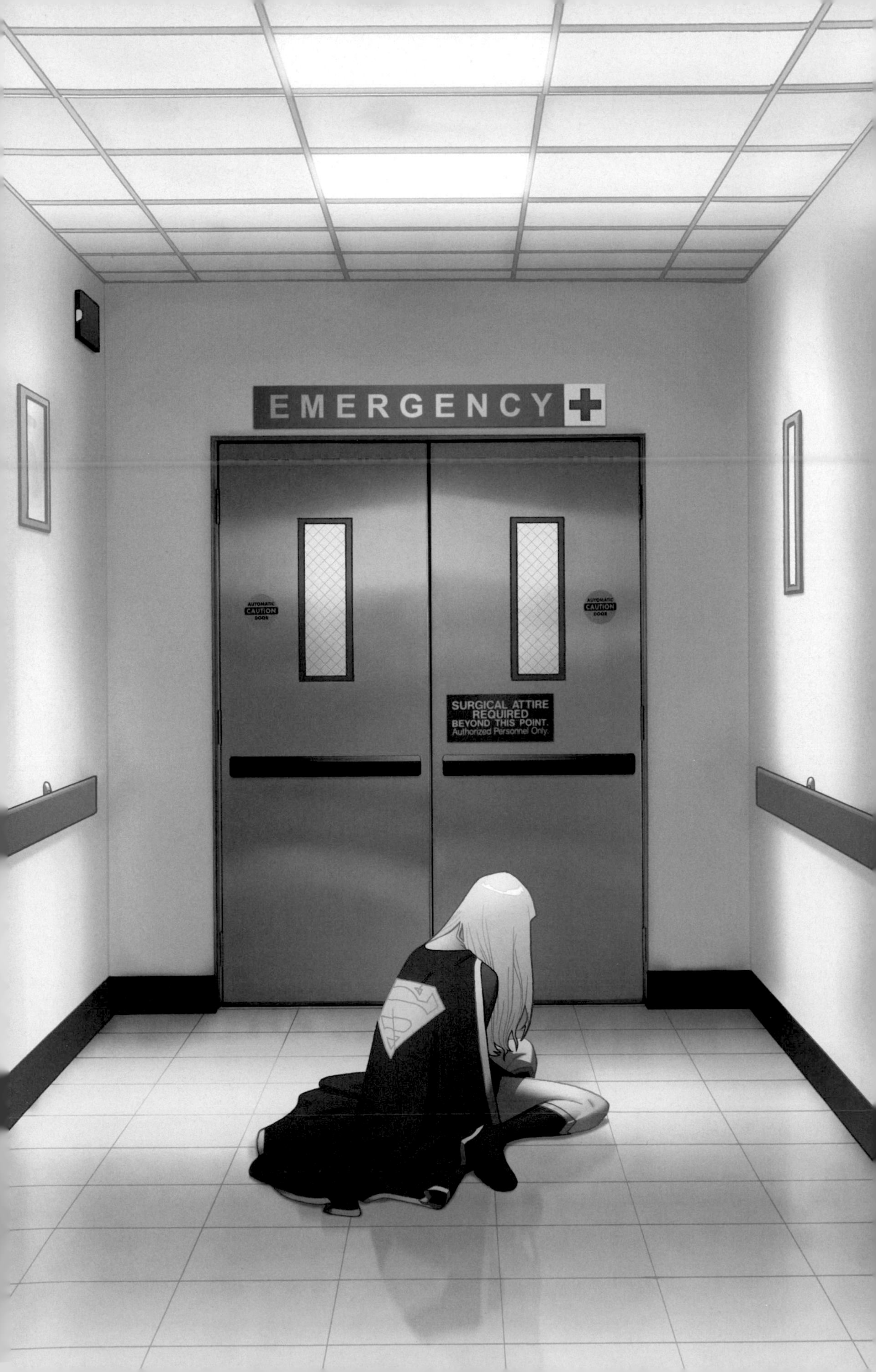
EMERGENCY
AUTOMATIC CAUTION DOOR
AUTOMATIC CAUTION DOOR
SURGICAL ATTIRE REQUIRED BEYOND THIS POINT.
Authorized Personnel Only.

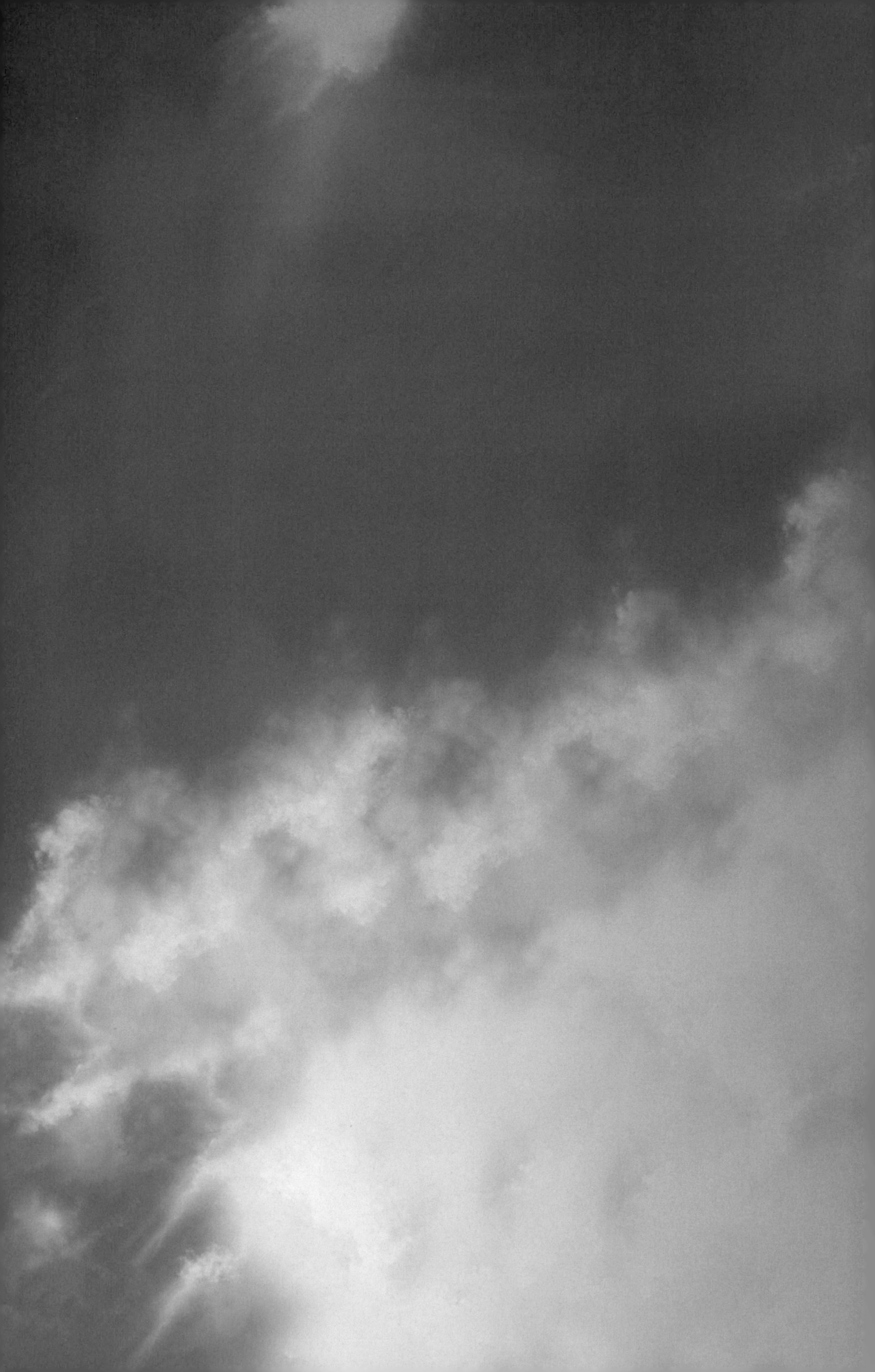

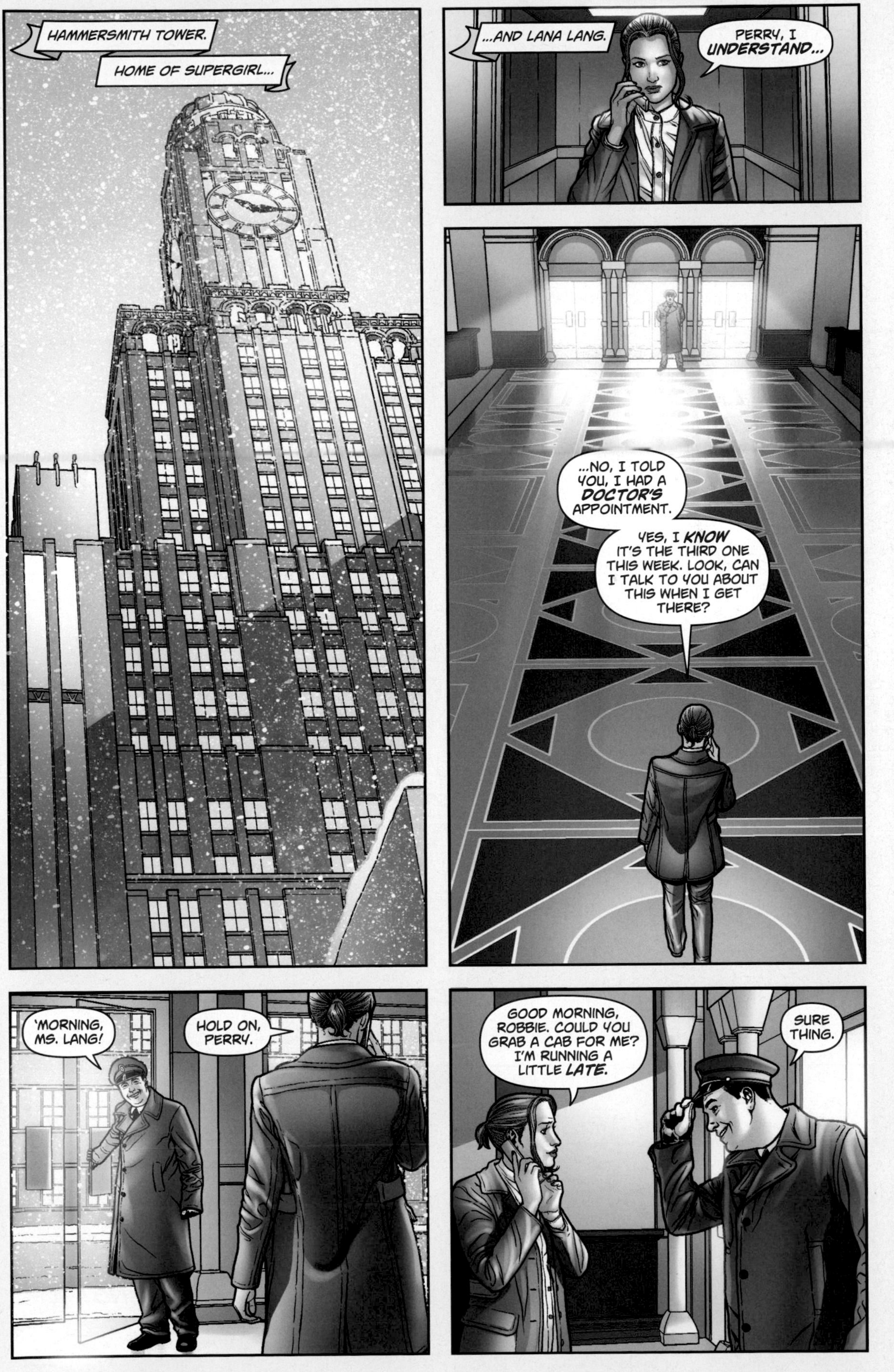
HAMMERSMITH TOWER.
HOME OF SUPERGIRL...
...AND LANA LANG.
PERRY, I UNDERSTAND...
...NO, I TOLD YOU, I HAD A DOCTOR'S APPOINTMENT.
YES, I KNOW IT'S THE THIRD ONE THIS WEEK. LOOK, CAN I TALK TO YOU ABOUT THIS WHEN I GET THERE?
'MORNING, MS. LANG!
HOLD ON, PERRY.
GOOD MORNING, ROBBIE. COULD YOU GRAB A CAB FOR ME? I'M RUNNING A LITTLE LATE.
SURE THING.

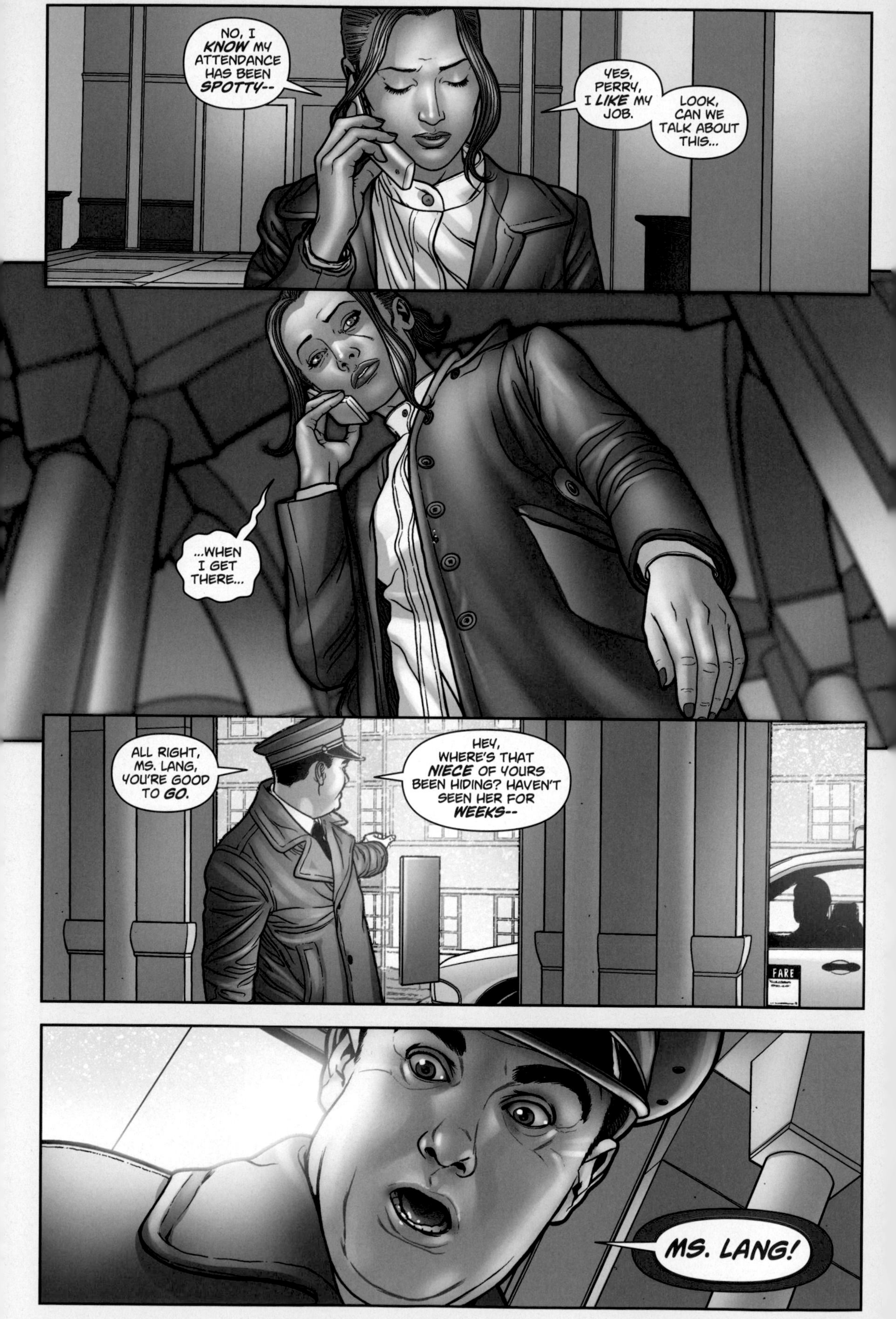
NO, I KNOW MY ATTENDANCE HAS BEEN SPOTTY--
YES, PERRY, I LIKE MY JOB.
LOOK, CAN WE TALK ABOUT THIS...
...WHEN I GET THERE...
ALL RIGHT, MS. LANG, YOU'RE GOOD TO GO.
HEY, WHERE'S THAT NIECE OF YOURS BEEN HIDING? HAVEN'T SEEN HER FOR WEEKS--
FARE
MS. LANG!

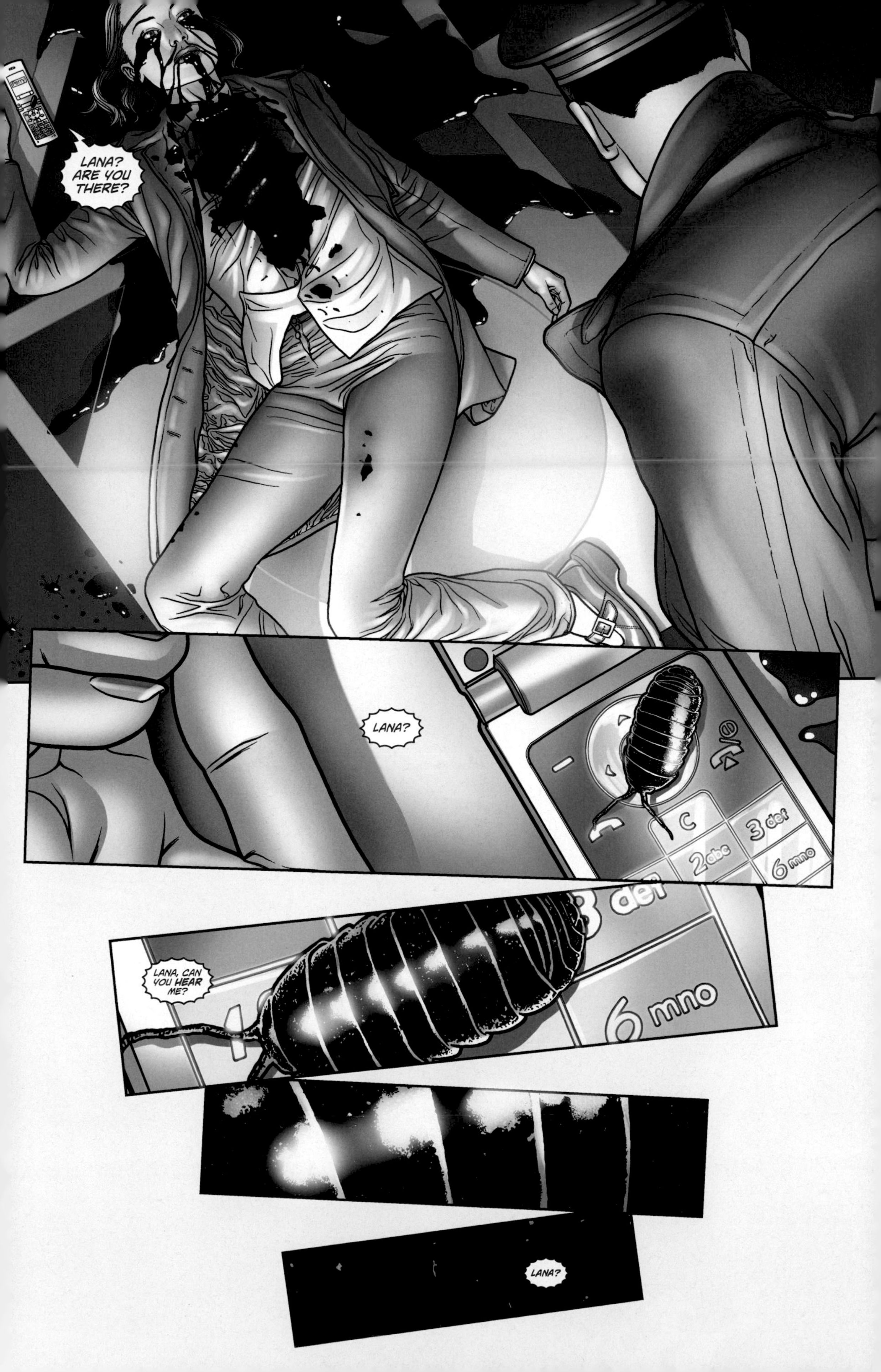

LANA? ARE YOU THERE?
LANA?
LANA, CAN YOU HEAR ME?
LANA?

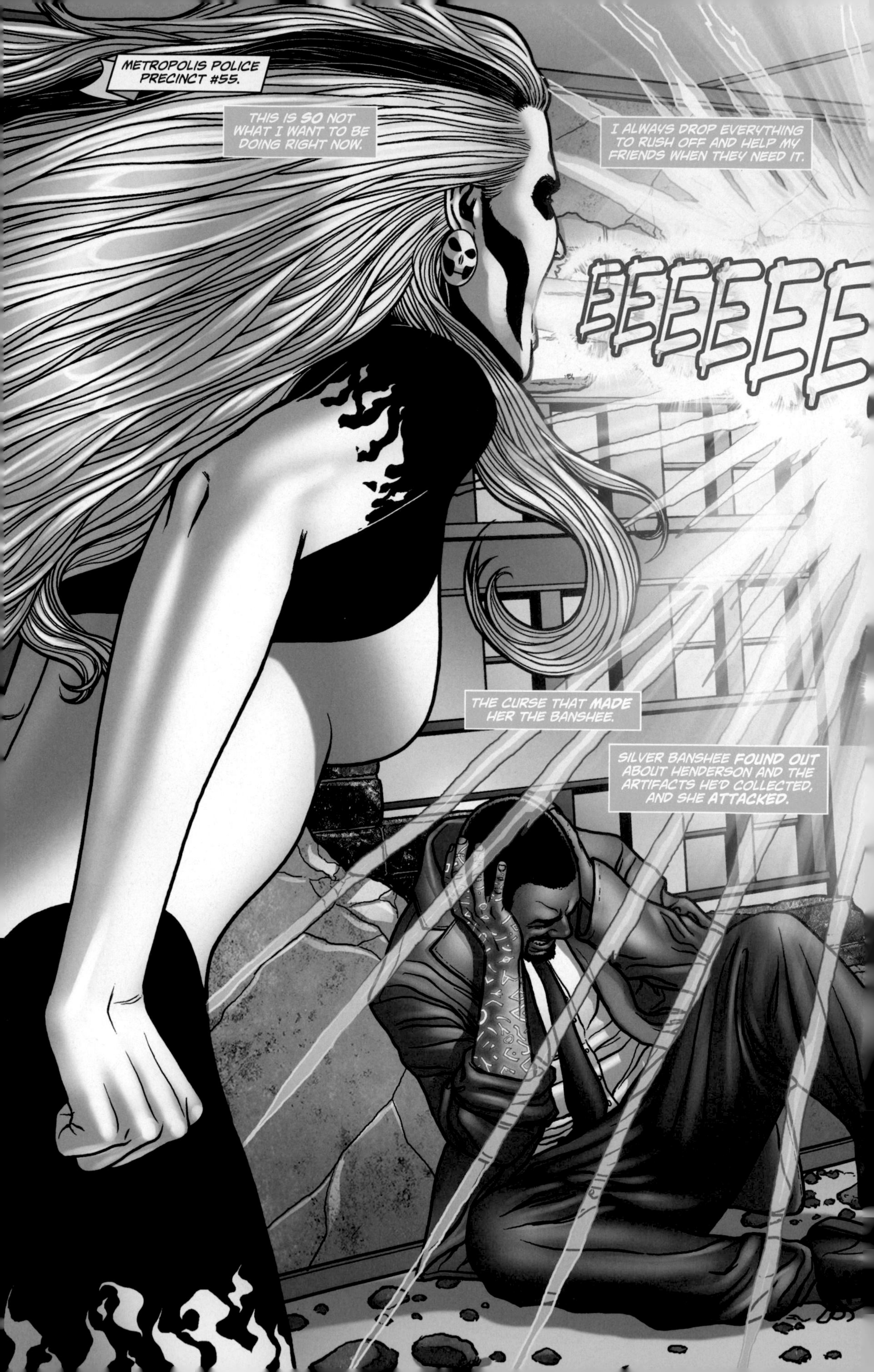
METROPOLIS POLICE PRECINCT #55.
THIS IS SO NOT WHAT I WANT TO BE DOING RIGHT NOW.
I ALWAYS DROP EVERYTHING TO RUSH OFF AND HELP MY FRIENDS WHEN THEY NEED IT.
EEEEEEE
THE CURSE THAT MADE HER THE BANSHEE.
SILVER BANSHEE FOUND OUT ABOUT HENDERSON AND THE ARTIFACTS HE'D COLLECTED, AND SHE ATTACKED.

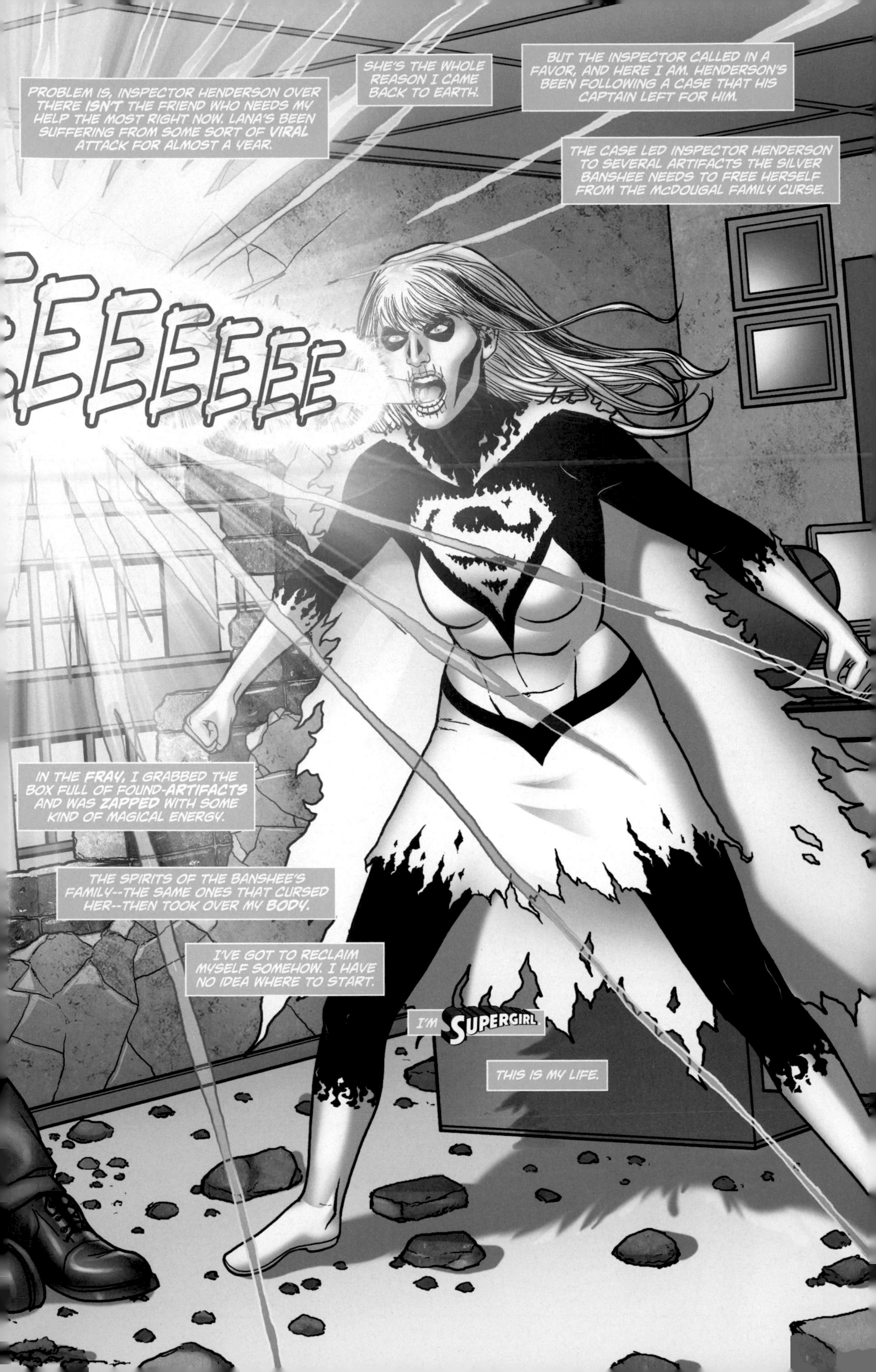

PROBLEM IS, INSPECTOR HENDERSON OVER THERE ISN'T THE FRIEND WHO NEEDS MY HELP THE MOST RIGHT NOW. LANA'S BEEN SUFFERING FROM SOME SORT OF VIRAL ATTACK FOR ALMOST A YEAR.
SHE'S THE WHOLE REASON I CAME BACK TO EARTH.
BUT THE INSPECTOR CALLED IN A FAVOR, AND HERE I AM. HENDERSON'S BEEN FOLLOWING A CASE THAT HIS CAPTAIN LEFT FOR HIM.
THE CASE LED INSPECTOR HENDERSON TO SEVERAL ARTIFACTS THE SILVER BANSHEE NEEDS TO FREE HERSELF FROM THE McDOUGAL FAMILY CURSE.
EEEEEEE
IN THE FRAY, I GRABBED THE BOX FULL OF FOUND-ARTIFACTS AND WAS ZAPPED WITH SOME KIND OF MAGICAL ENERGY.
THE SPIRITS OF THE BANSHEE'S FAMILY--THE SAME ONES THAT CURSED HER--THEN TOOK OVER MY BODY.
I'VE GOT TO RECLAIM MYSELF SOMEHOW. I HAVE NO IDEA WHERE TO START.
I'M SUPERGIRL.
THIS IS MY LIFE.

QUIET.

≥HK≥

≥HHHHHK≥

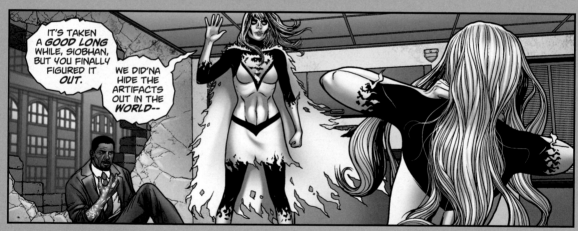

IT'S TAKEN A **GOOD LONG** WHILE, SIOBHAN, BUT YOU FINALLY FIGURED IT **OUT.**

WE DID'NA HIDE THE ARTIFACTS OUT IN THE **WORLD--**

--WE HID THEM IN **PEOPLE.**

OH, WE DID OUR **BEST** TO KEEP THOSE PEOPLE AWAY FROM YE, TOO. KILLIN WHO WE HAD TO, WHEN WE HAD TO.

COULDN'T MAKE IT **EASIER** FOR YOU THAN IT WAS FOR ANY OF THE **OTHER** McDOUGALS, COULD WE, SIOBHAN?

S-SUPERGIRL...?

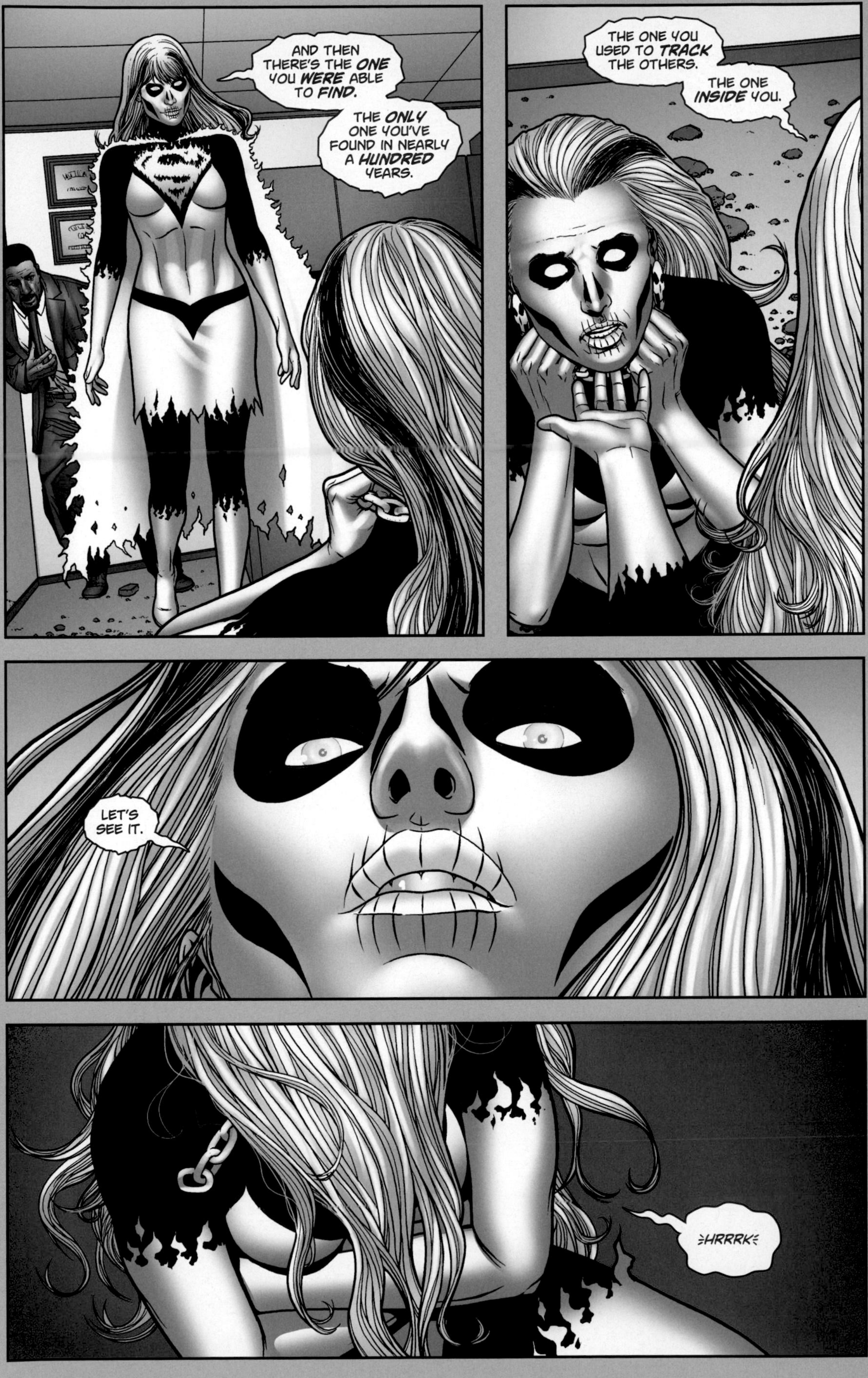
AND THEN THERE'S THE ONE YOU WERE ABLE TO FIND.
THE ONLY ONE YOU'VE FOUND IN NEARLY A HUNDRED YEARS.
THE ONE YOU USED TO TRACK THE OTHERS.
THE ONE INSIDE YOU.
LET'S SEE IT.
HRRRK

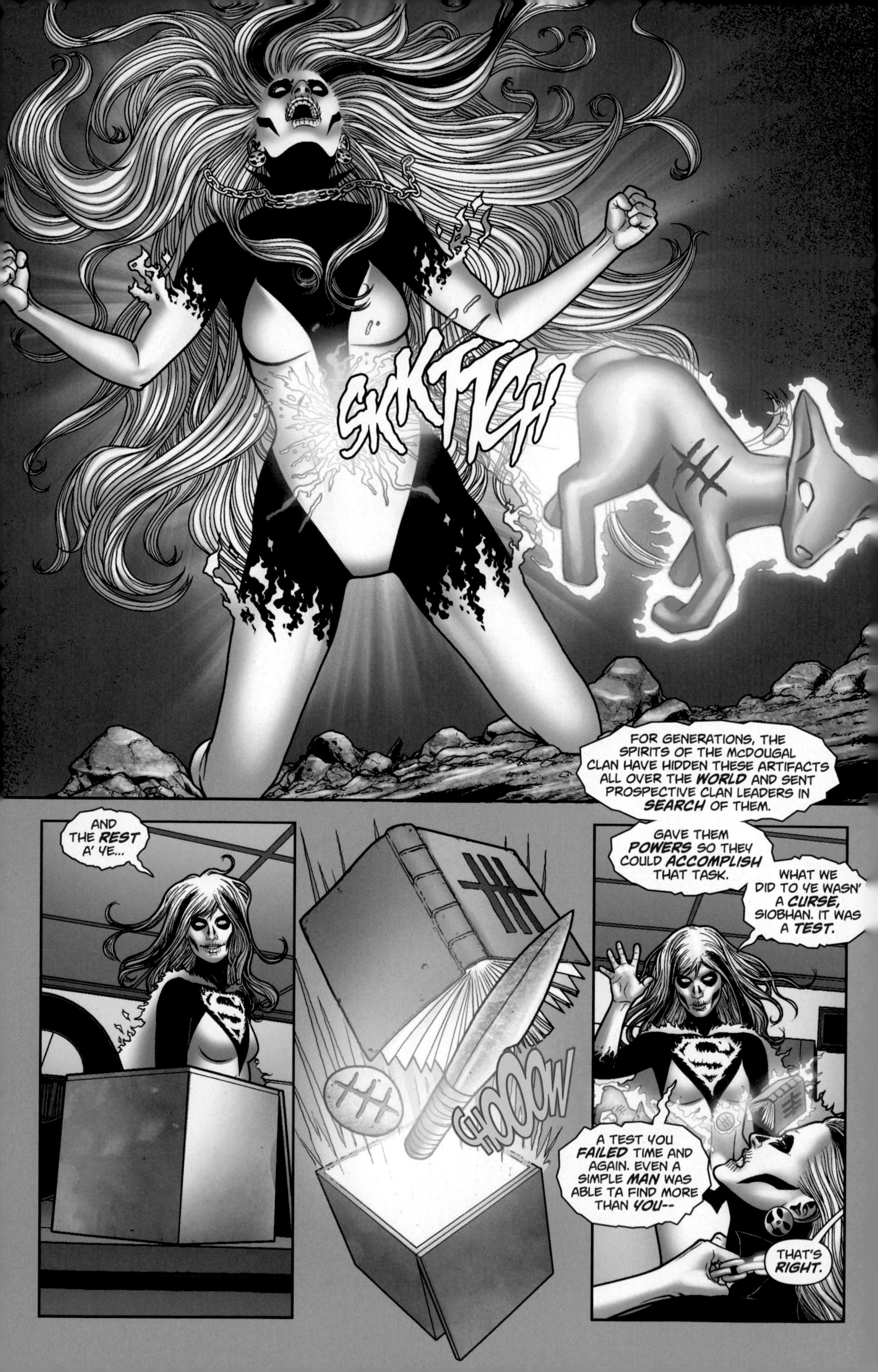
SKKTTCH
FOR GENERATIONS, THE SPIRITS OF THE McDOUGAL CLAN HAVE HIDDEN THESE ARTIFACTS ALL OVER THE WORLD AND SENT PROSPECTIVE CLAN LEADERS IN SEARCH OF THEM.
AND THE REST A' YE...
CHOOOW
GAVE THEM POWERS SO THEY COULD ACCOMPLISH THAT TASK.
WHAT WE DID TO YE WASN' A CURSE, SIOBHAN. IT WAS A TEST.
A TEST YOU FAILED TIME AND AGAIN. EVEN A SIMPLE MAN WAS ABLE TA FIND MORE THAN YOU--
THAT'S RIGHT.

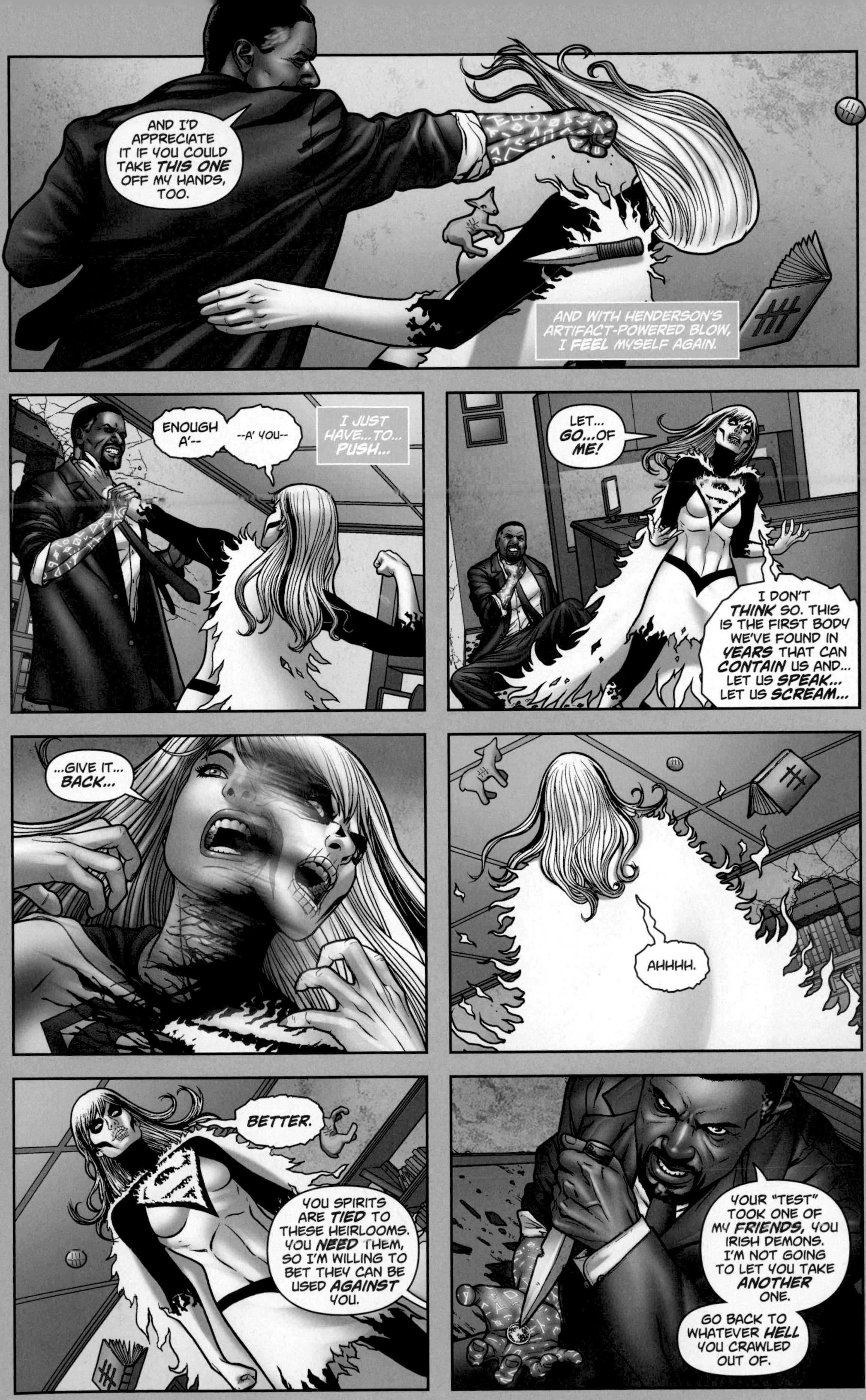
AND I'D APPRECIATE IT IF YOU COULD TAKE THIS ONE OFF MY HANDS, TOO.
AND WITH HENDERSON'S ARTIFACT-POWERED BLOW, I FEEL MYSELF AGAIN.
ENOUGH A'--
--A' YOU--
I JUST HAVE...TO... PUSH...
LET... GO...OF ME!
I DON'T THINK SO. THIS IS THE FIRST BODY WE'VE FOUND IN YEARS THAT CAN CONTAIN US AND... LET US SPEAK... LET US SCREAM...
...GIVE IT... BACK...
AHHHH.
BETTER.
YOU SPIRITS ARE TIED TO THESE HEIRLOOMS. YOU NEED THEM, SO I'M WILLING TO BET THEY CAN BE USED AGAINST YOU.
YOUR "TEST" TOOK ONE OF MY FRIENDS, YOU IRISH DEMONS. I'M NOT GOING TO LET YOU TAKE ANOTHER ONE.
GO BACK TO WHATEVER HELL YOU CRAWLED OUT OF.

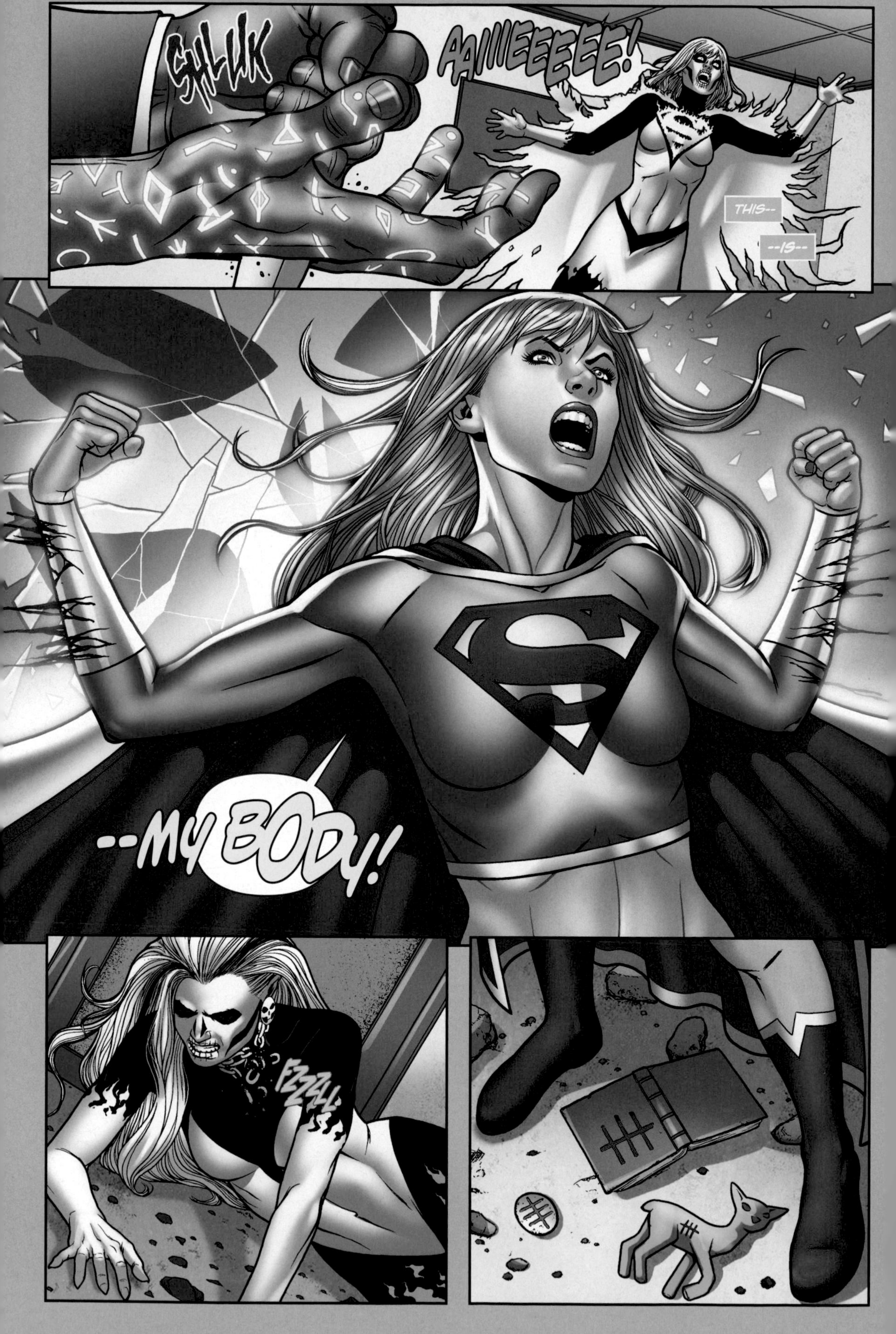
SHLUK
AAIIIEEEEEE!
THIS--
--IS--
--MY BODY!
FZZZLL

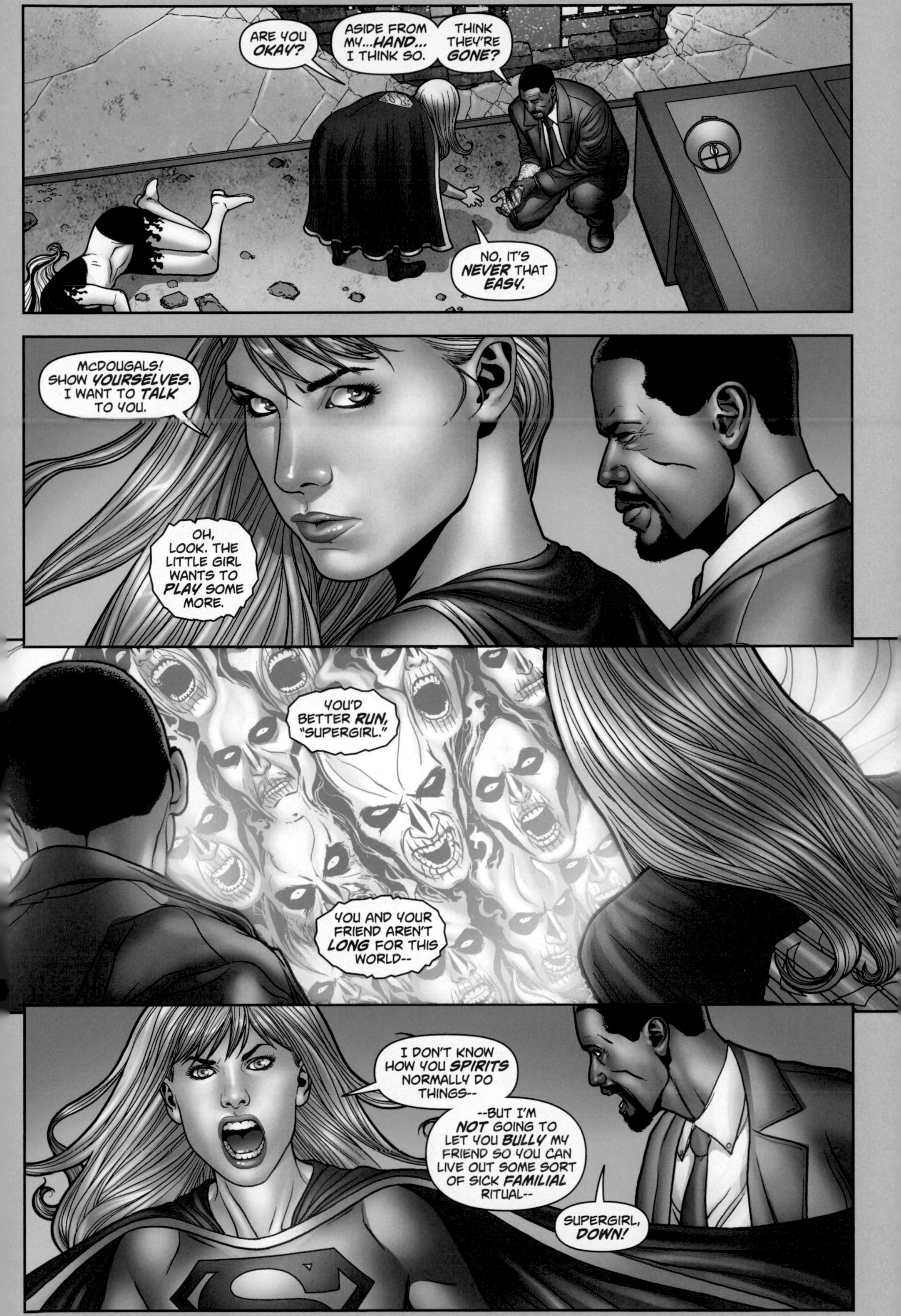
ARE YOU OKAY?
ASIDE FROM MY...HAND... I THINK SO.
THINK THEY'RE GONE?
NO, IT'S NEVER THAT EASY.
McDOUGALS! SHOW YOURSELVES. I WANT TO TALK TO YOU.
OH, LOOK. THE LITTLE GIRL WANTS TO PLAY SOME MORE.
YOU'D BETTER RUN, "SUPERGIRL."
YOU AND YOUR FRIEND AREN'T LONG FOR THIS WORLD--
I DON'T KNOW HOW YOU SPIRITS NORMALLY DO THINGS--
--BUT I'M NOT GOING TO LET YOU BULLY MY FRIEND SO YOU CAN LIVE OUT SOME SORT OF SICK FAMILIAL RITUAL--
SUPERGIRL, DOWN!

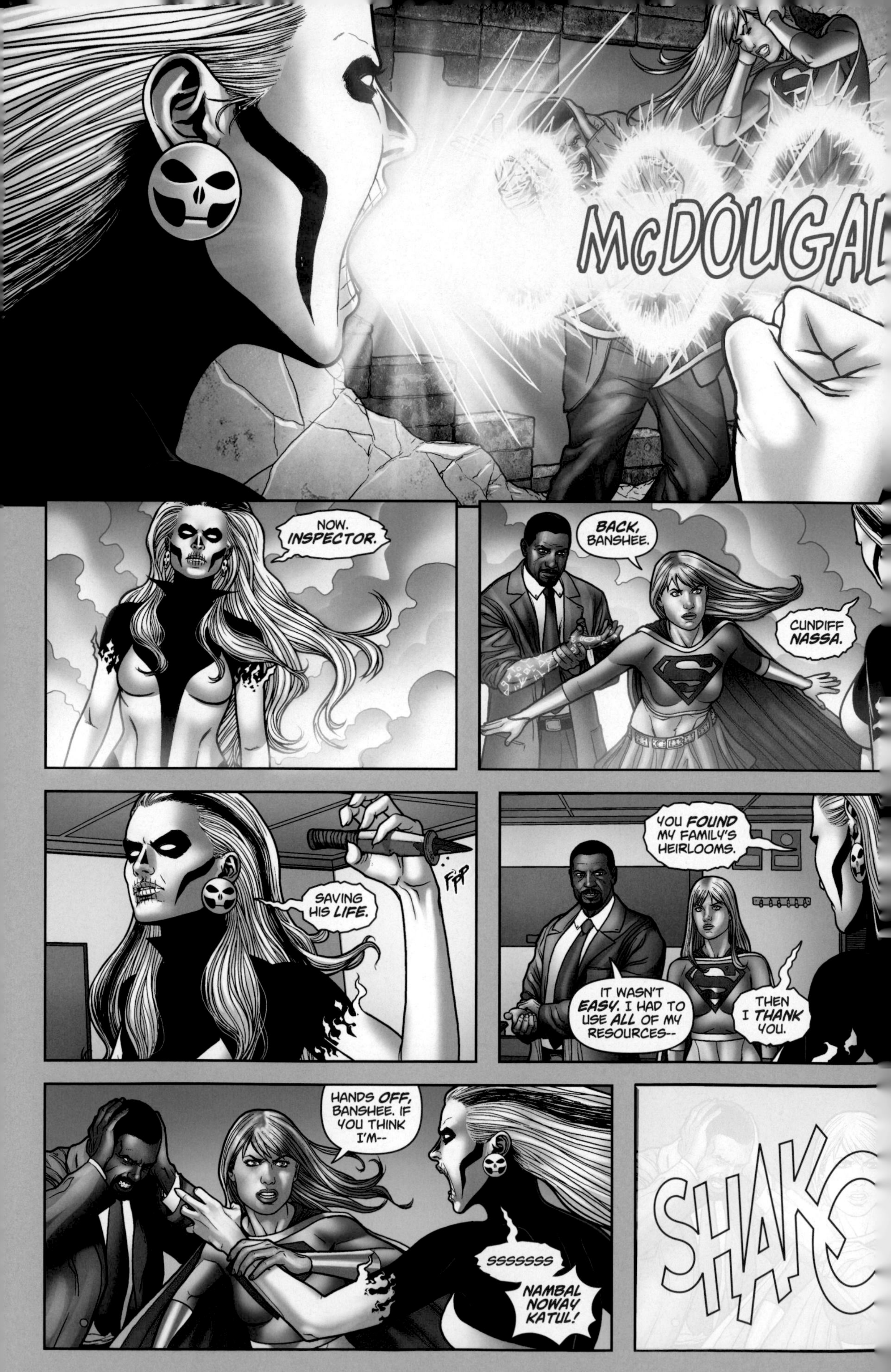
McDOUGAL
NOW. INSPECTOR.
BACK, BANSHEE.
CUNDIFF NASSA.
SAVING HIS LIFE.
FPP
YOU FOUND MY FAMILY'S HEIRLOOMS.
IT WASN'T EASY. I HAD TO USE ALL OF MY RESOURCES--
THEN I THANK YOU.
HANDS OFF, BANSHEE. IF YOU THINK I'M--
SSSSSSS
NAMBAL NOWAY KATUL!
SHAKO

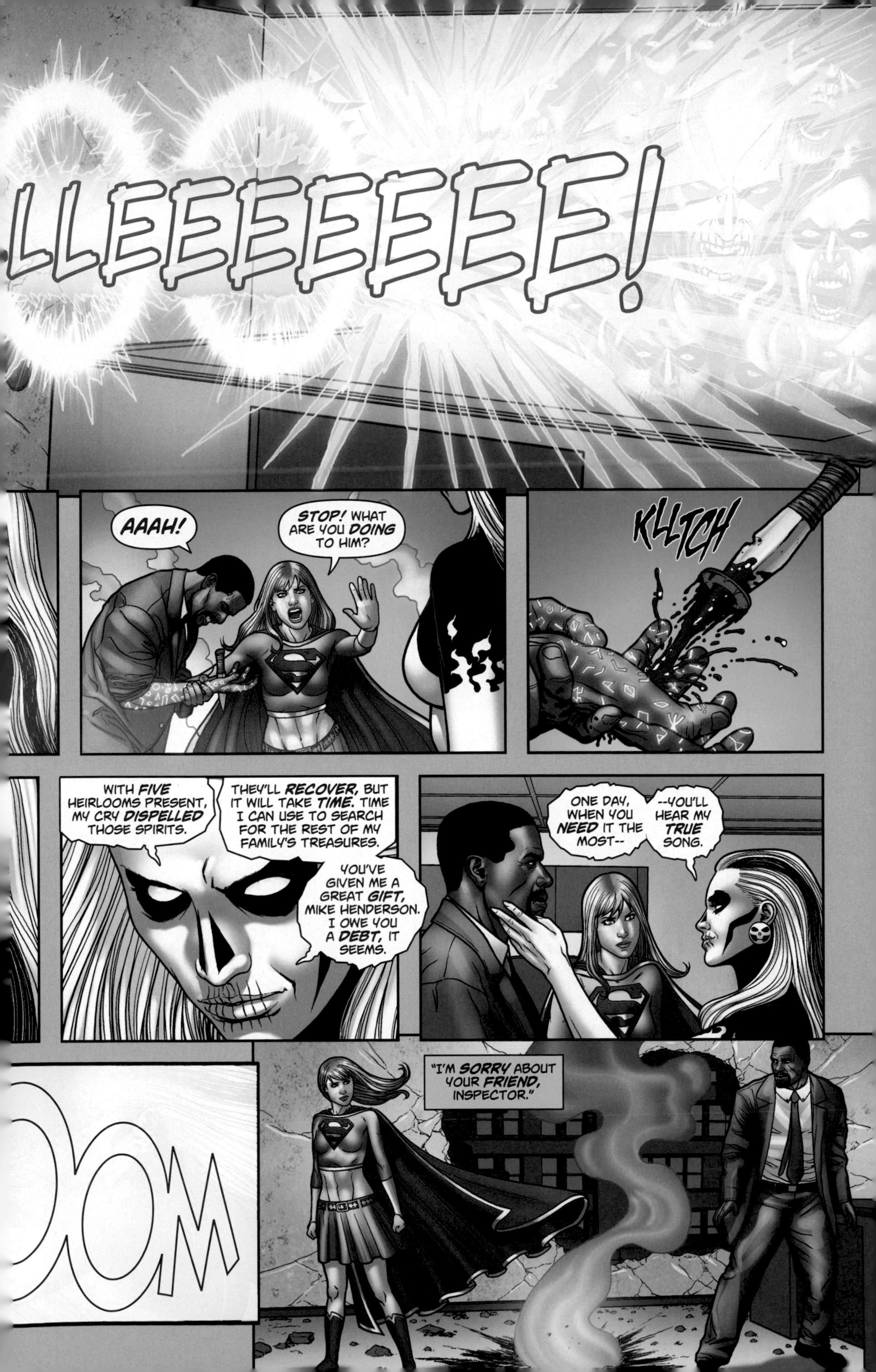

LLEEEEEEE!
AAAH!
STOP! WHAT ARE YOU DOING TO HIM?
KLLTCH
WITH FIVE HEIRLOOMS PRESENT, MY CRY DISPELLED THOSE SPIRITS.
THEY'LL RECOVER, BUT IT WILL TAKE TIME. TIME I CAN USE TO SEARCH FOR THE REST OF MY FAMILY'S TREASURES.
YOU'VE GIVEN ME A GREAT GIFT, MIKE HENDERSON. I OWE YOU A DEBT, IT SEEMS.
ONE DAY, WHEN YOU NEED IT THE MOST--
--YOU'LL HEAR MY TRUE SONG.
OOM
"I'M SORRY ABOUT YOUR FRIEND, INSPECTOR."

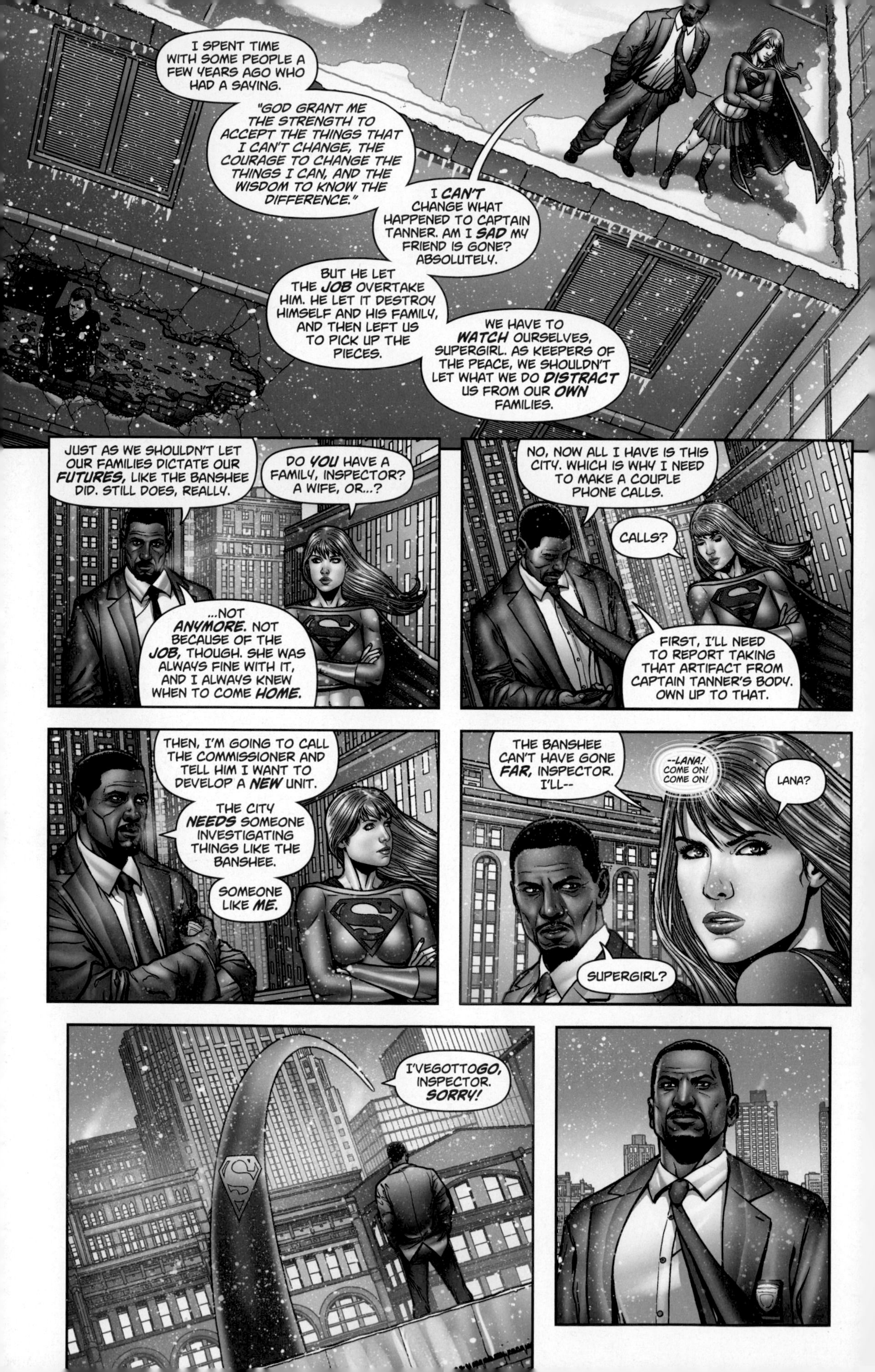
I SPENT TIME WITH SOME PEOPLE A FEW YEARS AGO WHO HAD A SAYING.
"GOD GRANT ME THE STRENGTH TO ACCEPT THE THINGS THAT I CAN'T CHANGE, THE COURAGE TO CHANGE THE THINGS I CAN, AND THE WISDOM TO KNOW THE DIFFERENCE."
I CAN'T CHANGE WHAT HAPPENED TO CAPTAIN TANNER. AM I SAD MY FRIEND IS GONE? ABSOLUTELY.
BUT HE LET THE JOB OVERTAKE HIM. HE LET IT DESTROY HIMSELF AND HIS FAMILY, AND THEN LEFT US TO PICK UP THE PIECES.
WE HAVE TO WATCH OURSELVES, SUPERGIRL. AS KEEPERS OF THE PEACE, WE SHOULDN'T LET WHAT WE DO DISTRACT US FROM OUR OWN FAMILIES.
JUST AS WE SHOULDN'T LET OUR FAMILIES DICTATE OUR FUTURES, LIKE THE BANSHEE DID. STILL DOES, REALLY.
DO YOU HAVE A FAMILY, INSPECTOR? A WIFE, OR...?
...NOT ANYMORE. NOT BECAUSE OF THE JOB, THOUGH. SHE WAS ALWAYS FINE WITH IT, AND I ALWAYS KNEW WHEN TO COME HOME.
NO, NOW ALL I HAVE IS THIS CITY. WHICH IS WHY I NEED TO MAKE A COUPLE PHONE CALLS.
CALLS?
FIRST, I'LL NEED TO REPORT TAKING THAT ARTIFACT FROM CAPTAIN TANNER'S BODY. OWN UP TO THAT.
THEN, I'M GOING TO CALL THE COMMISSIONER AND TELL HIM I WANT TO DEVELOP A NEW UNIT.
THE CITY NEEDS SOMEONE INVESTIGATING THINGS LIKE THE BANSHEE.
SOMEONE LIKE ME.
THE BANSHEE CAN'T HAVE GONE FAR, INSPECTOR. I'LL--
--LANA! COME ON! COME ON!
LANA?
SUPERGIRL?
I'VEGOTTOGO, INSPECTOR. SORRY!

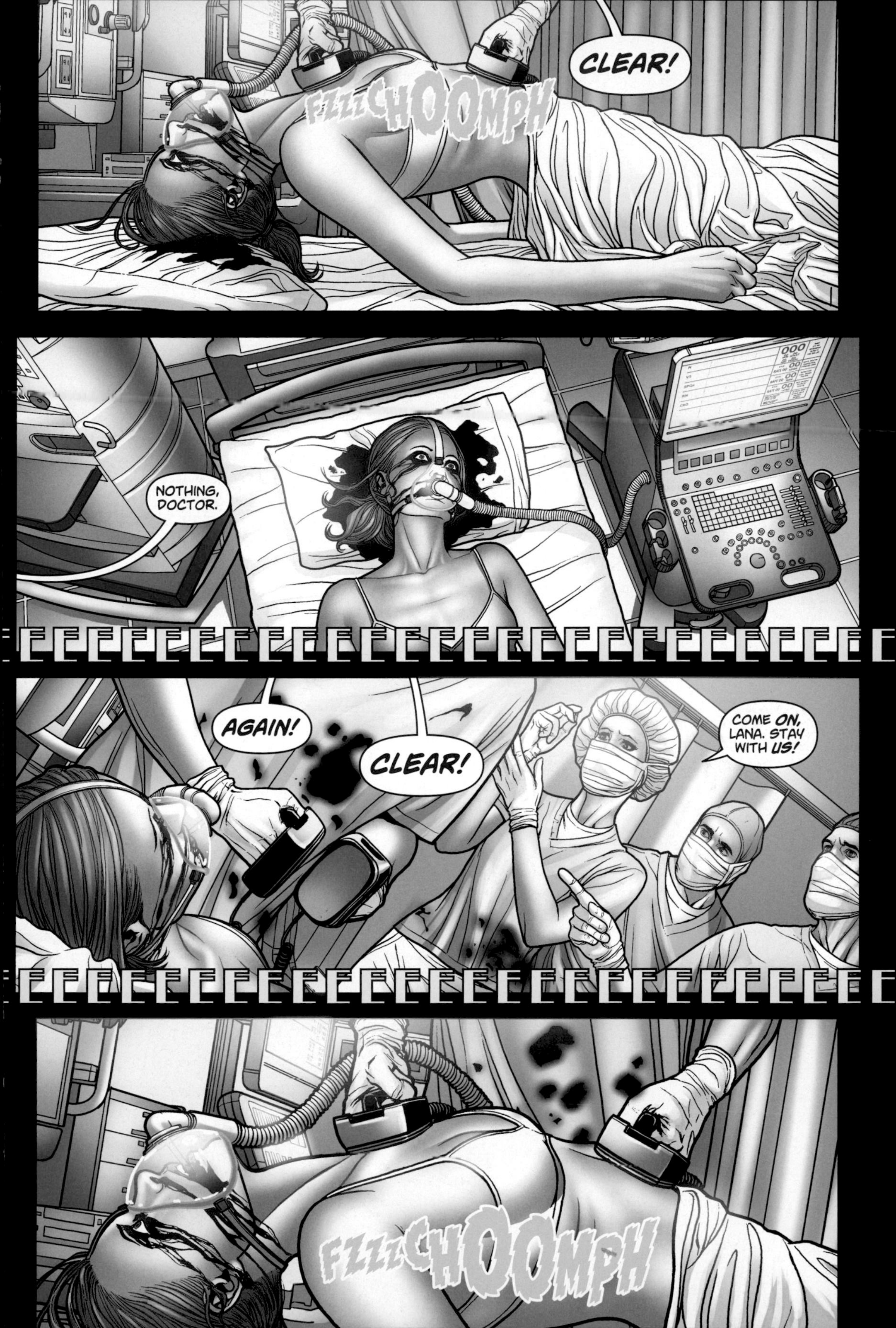

CLEAR!
FZZZCHOOOMPH
NOTHING, DOCTOR.
EEEEEEEEEEEEEEEEEEEEEEEEEEEEEEEEEE
AGAIN!
CLEAR!
COME ON, LANA. STAY WITH US!
EEEEEEEEEEEEEEEEEEEEEEEEEEEEEEEEEE
FZZZCHOOOMPH

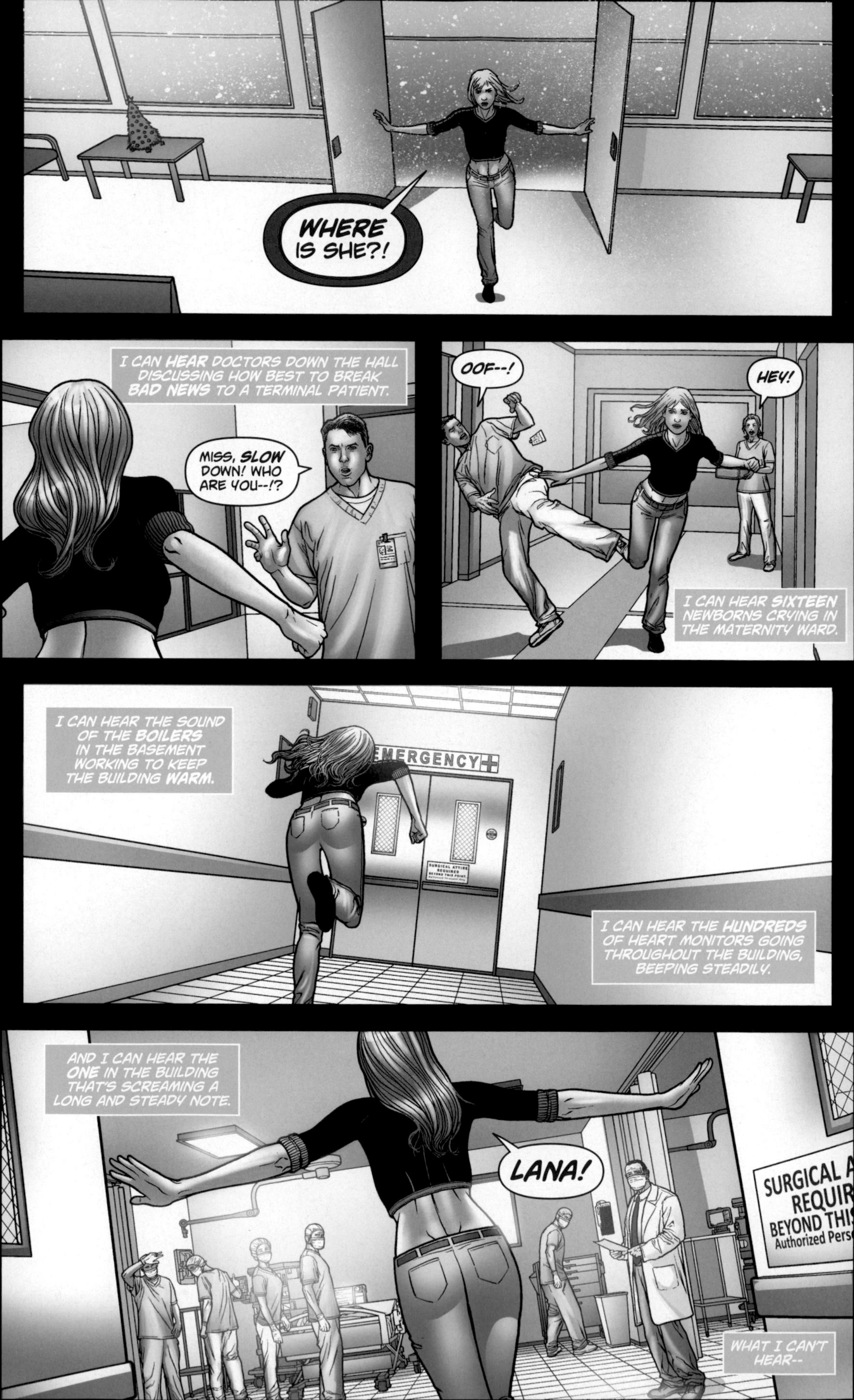
WHERE IS SHE?!
I CAN HEAR DOCTORS DOWN THE HALL DISCUSSING HOW BEST TO BREAK BAD NEWS TO A TERMINAL PATIENT.
MISS, SLOW DOWN! WHO ARE YOU--!?
OOF--!
HEY!
I CAN HEAR SIXTEEN NEWBORNS CRYING IN THE MATERNITY WARD.
I CAN HEAR THE SOUND OF THE BOILERS IN THE BASEMENT WORKING TO KEEP THE BUILDING WARM.
EMERGENCY
SURGICAL ATTIRE REQUIRED BEYOND THIS POINT.
I CAN HEAR THE HUNDREDS OF HEART MONITORS GOING THROUGHOUT THE BUILDING, BEEPING STEADILY.
AND I CAN HEAR THE ONE IN THE BUILDING THAT'S SCREAMING A LONG AND STEADY NOTE.
LANA!
SURGICAL A
REQUI
BEYOND THIS
Authorized Pers
WHAT I CAN'T HEAR--

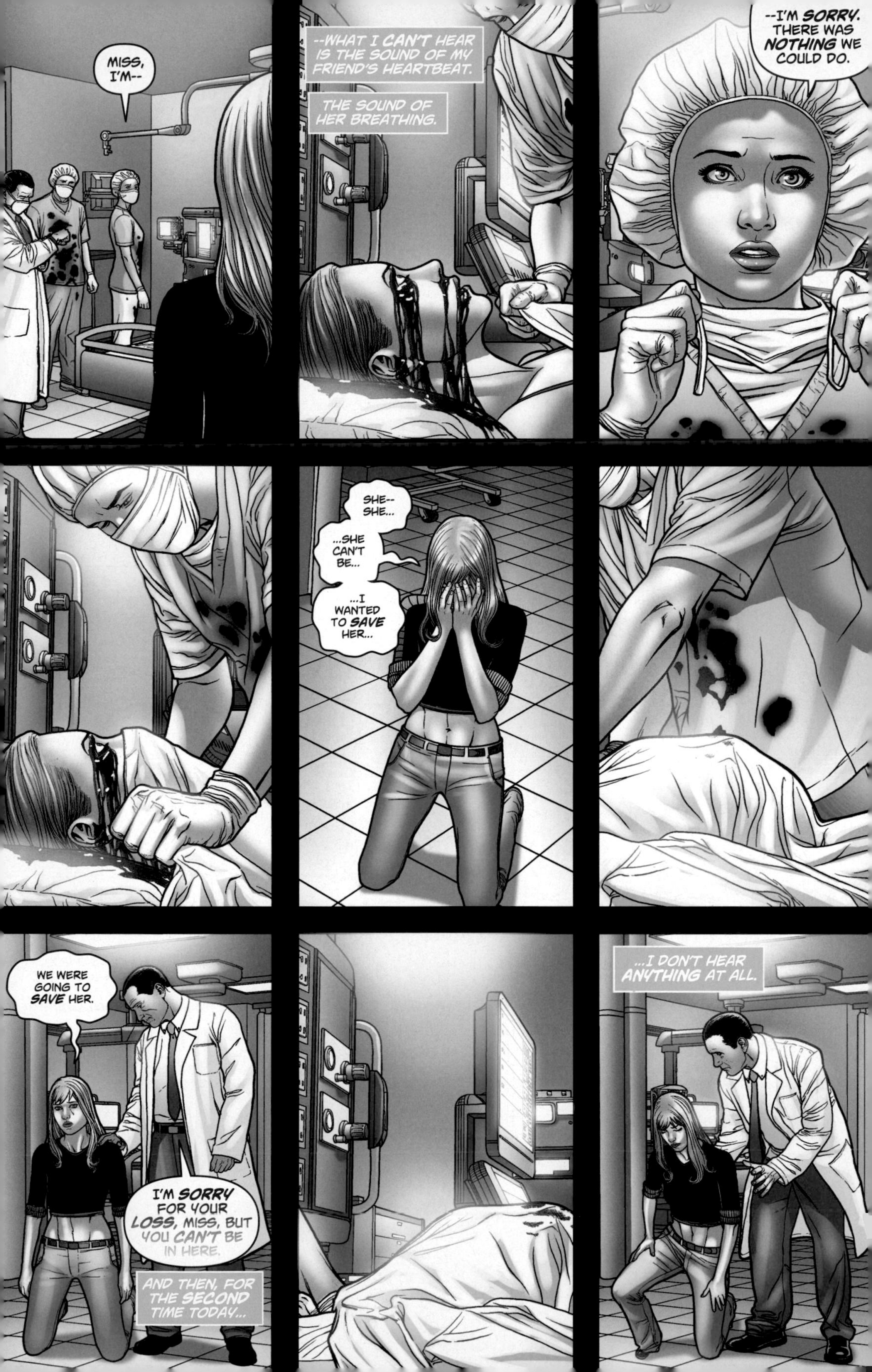
MISS, I'M--
--WHAT I CAN'T HEAR IS THE SOUND OF MY FRIEND'S HEARTBEAT.
THE SOUND OF HER BREATHING.
--I'M SORRY. THERE WAS NOTHING WE COULD DO.
SHE-- SHE...
...SHE CAN'T BE...
...I WANTED TO SAVE HER...
WE WERE GOING TO SAVE HER.
I'M SORRY FOR YOUR LOSS, MISS, BUT YOU CAN'T BE IN HERE.
AND THEN, FOR THE SECOND TIME TODAY...
...I DON'T HEAR ANYTHING AT ALL.

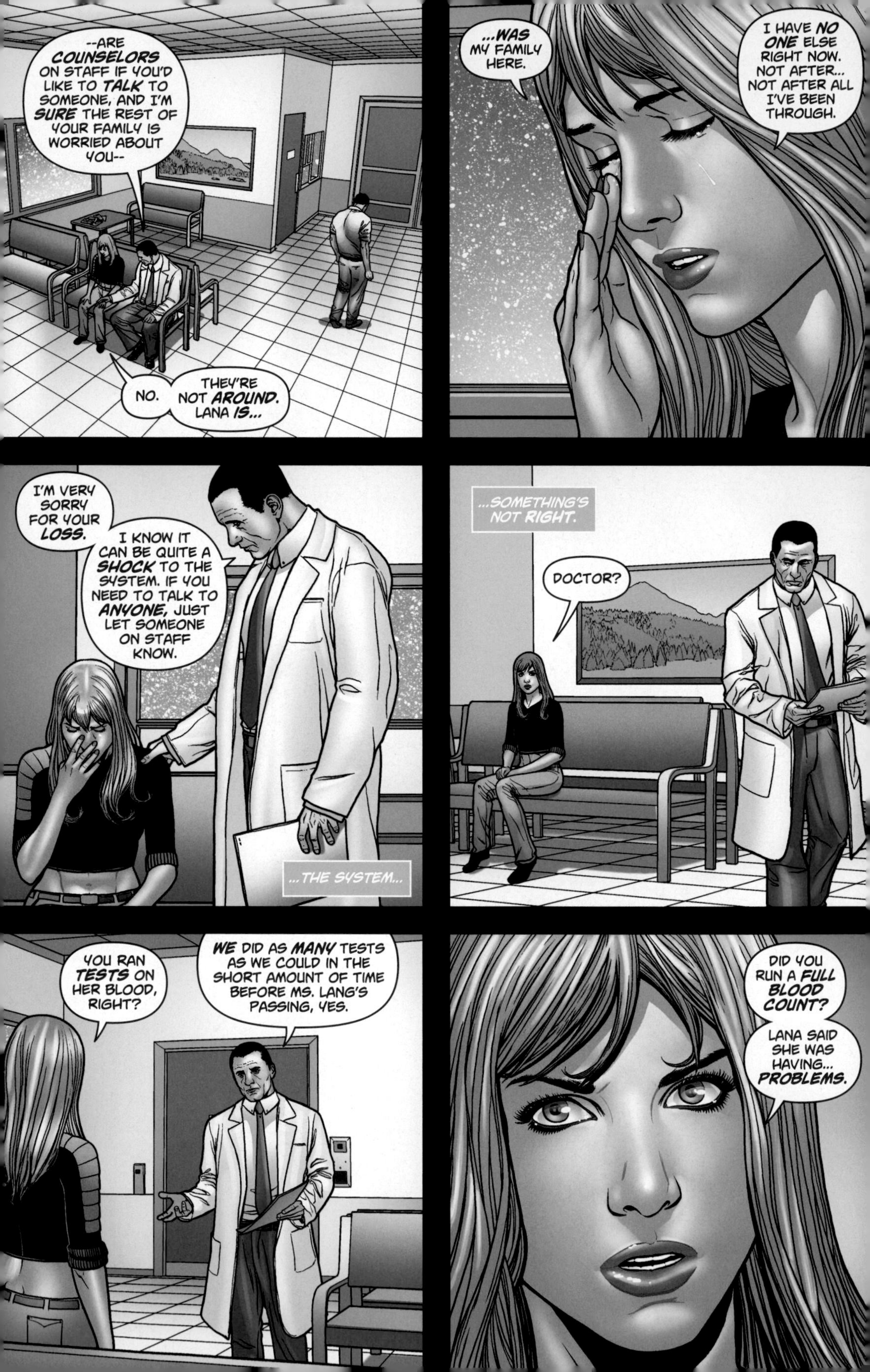
--ARE COUNSELORS ON STAFF IF YOU'D LIKE TO TALK TO SOMEONE, AND I'M SURE THE REST OF YOUR FAMILY IS WORRIED ABOUT YOU--
NO.
THEY'RE NOT AROUND. LANA IS...
...WAS MY FAMILY HERE.
I HAVE NO ONE ELSE RIGHT NOW. NOT AFTER... NOT AFTER ALL I'VE BEEN THROUGH.
I'M VERY SORRY FOR YOUR LOSS.
I KNOW IT CAN BE QUITE A SHOCK TO THE SYSTEM. IF YOU NEED TO TALK TO ANYONE, JUST LET SOMEONE ON STAFF KNOW.
...THE SYSTEM...
...SOMETHING'S NOT RIGHT.
DOCTOR?
YOU RAN TESTS ON HER BLOOD, RIGHT?
WE DID AS MANY TESTS AS WE COULD IN THE SHORT AMOUNT OF TIME BEFORE MS. LANG'S PASSING, YES.
DID YOU RUN A FULL BLOOD COUNT?
LANA SAID SHE WAS HAVING... PROBLEMS.

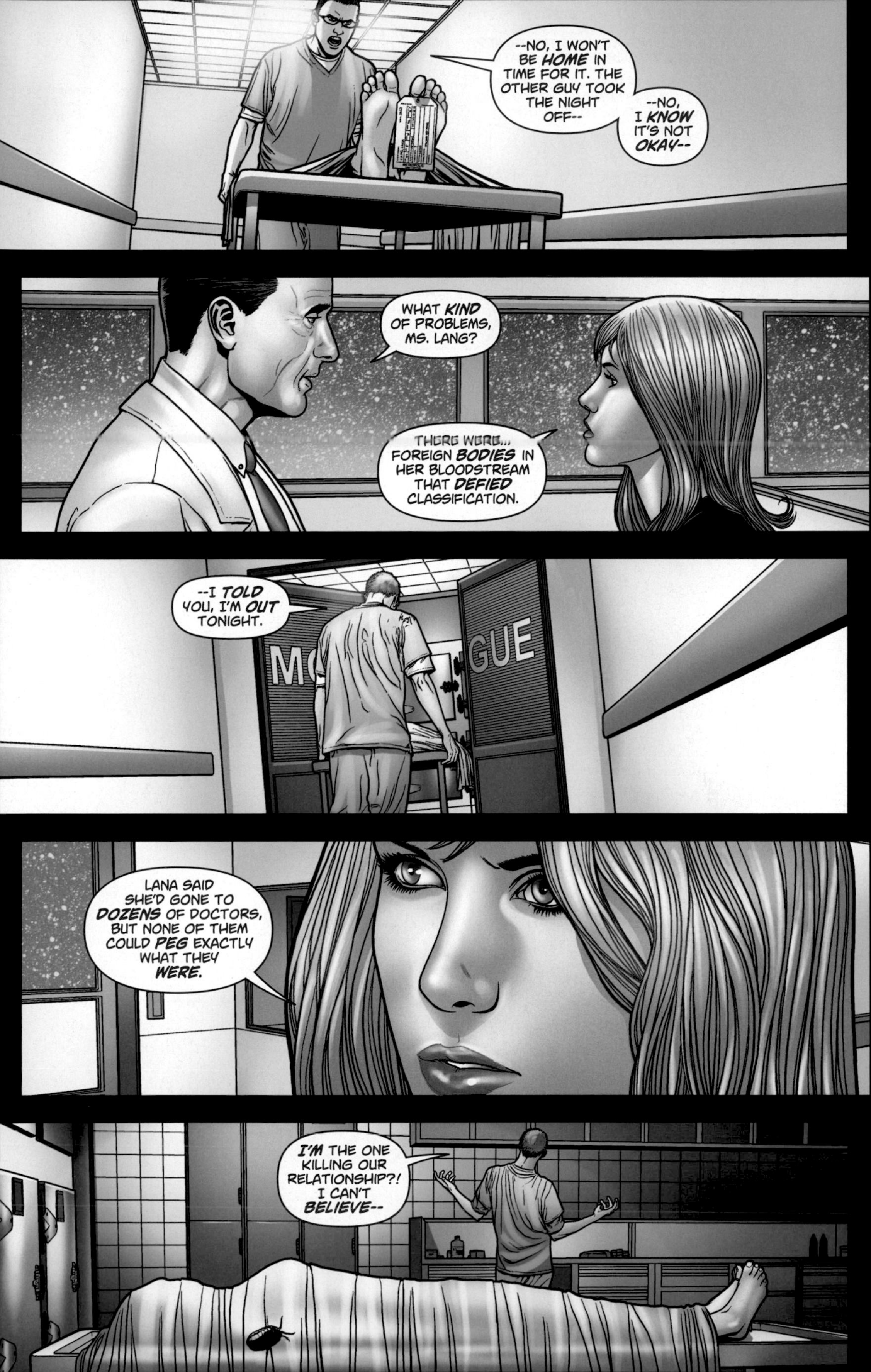
--NO, I WON'T BE HOME IN TIME FOR IT. THE OTHER GUY TOOK THE NIGHT OFF--
--NO, I KNOW IT'S NOT OKAY--
WHAT KIND OF PROBLEMS, MS. LANG?
THERE WERE... FOREIGN BODIES IN HER BLOODSTREAM THAT DEFIED CLASSIFICATION.
--I TOLD YOU, I'M OUT TONIGHT.
MORGUE
LANA SAID SHE'D GONE TO DOZENS OF DOCTORS, BUT NONE OF THEM COULD PEG EXACTLY WHAT THEY WERE.
I'M THE ONE KILLING OUR RELATIONSHIP?! I CAN'T BELIEVE--

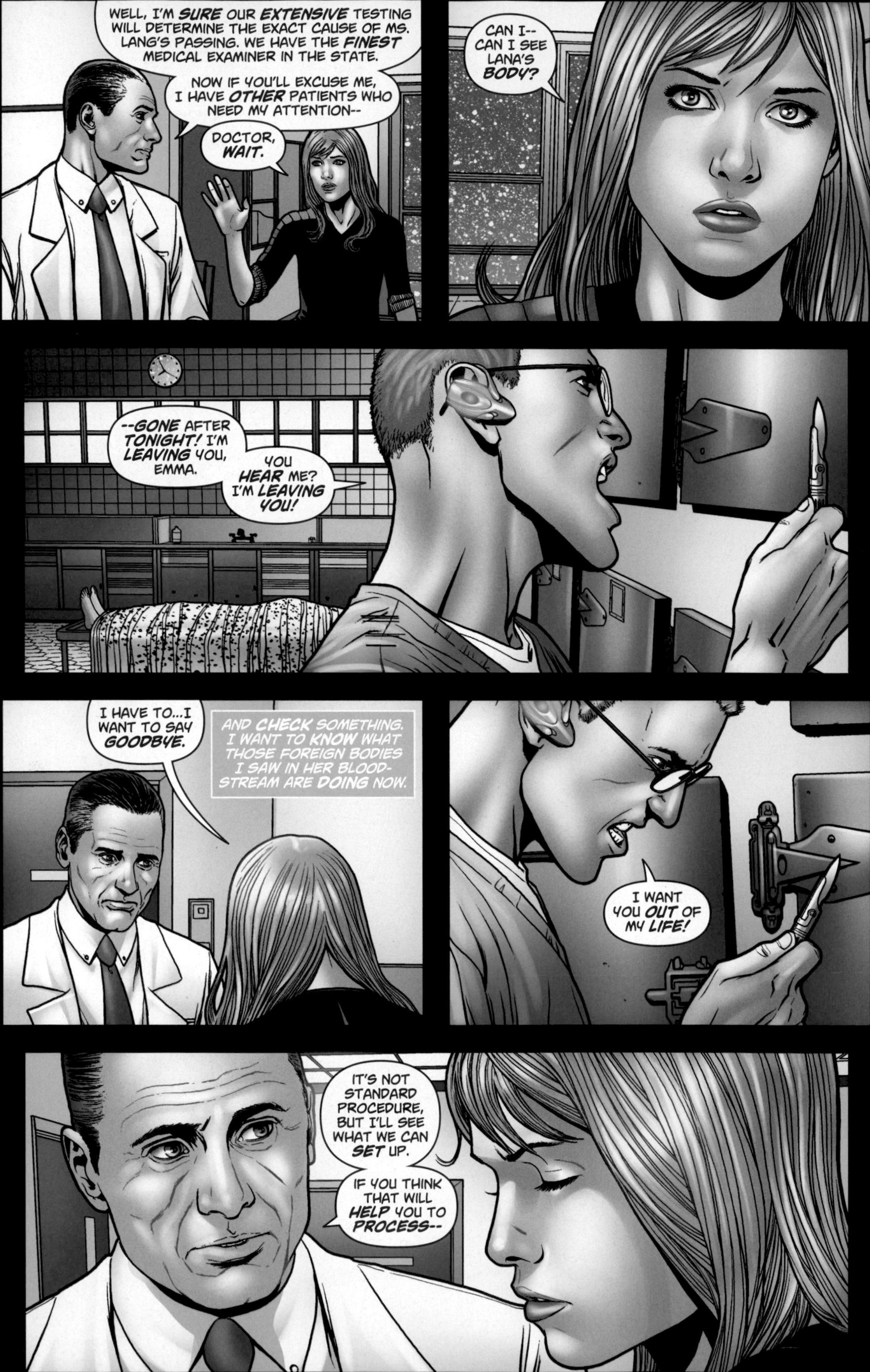
WELL, I'M SURE OUR EXTENSIVE TESTING WILL DETERMINE THE EXACT CAUSE OF MS. LANG'S PASSING. WE HAVE THE FINEST MEDICAL EXAMINER IN THE STATE.
NOW IF YOU'LL EXCUSE ME, I HAVE OTHER PATIENTS WHO NEED MY ATTENTION--
DOCTOR, WAIT.
CAN I-- CAN I SEE LANA'S BODY?
--GONE AFTER TONIGHT! I'M LEAVING YOU, EMMA.
YOU HEAR ME? I'M LEAVING YOU!
I HAVE TO...I WANT TO SAY GOODBYE.
AND CHECK SOMETHING. I WANT TO KNOW WHAT THOSE FOREIGN BODIES I SAW IN HER BLOOD-STREAM ARE DOING NOW.
I WANT YOU OUT OF MY LIFE!
IT'S NOT STANDARD PROCEDURE, BUT I'LL SEE WHAT WE CAN SET UP.
IF YOU THINK THAT WILL HELP YOU TO PROCESS--

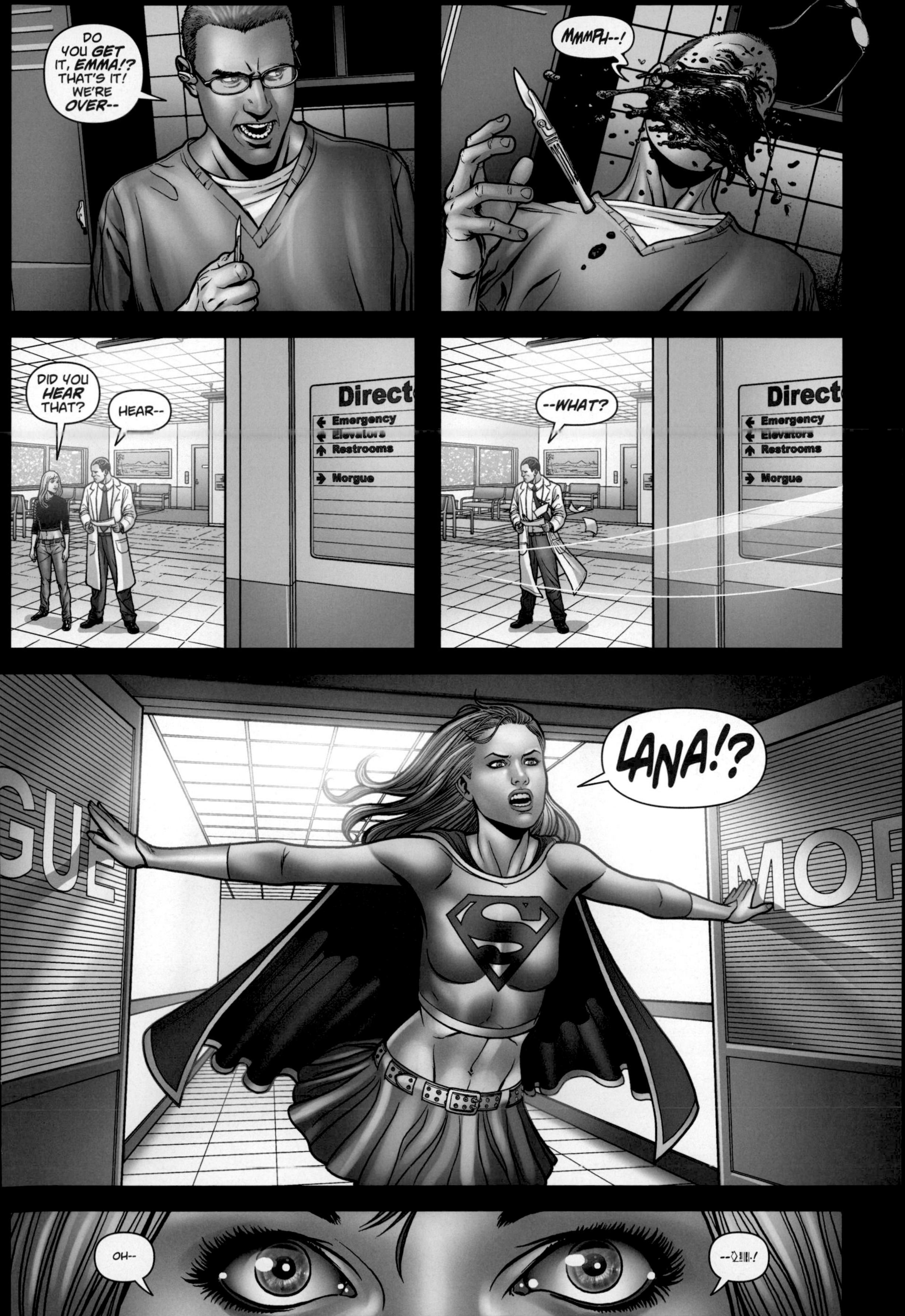
DO YOU GET IT, EMMA!? THAT'S IT! WE'RE OVER--
MMMPH--!
DID YOU HEAR THAT?
HEAR--
Directo
Emergency
Elevators
Restrooms
Morgue
--WHAT?
Directo
Emergency
Elevators
Restrooms
Morgue
GUE
LANA!?
MOR
OH--

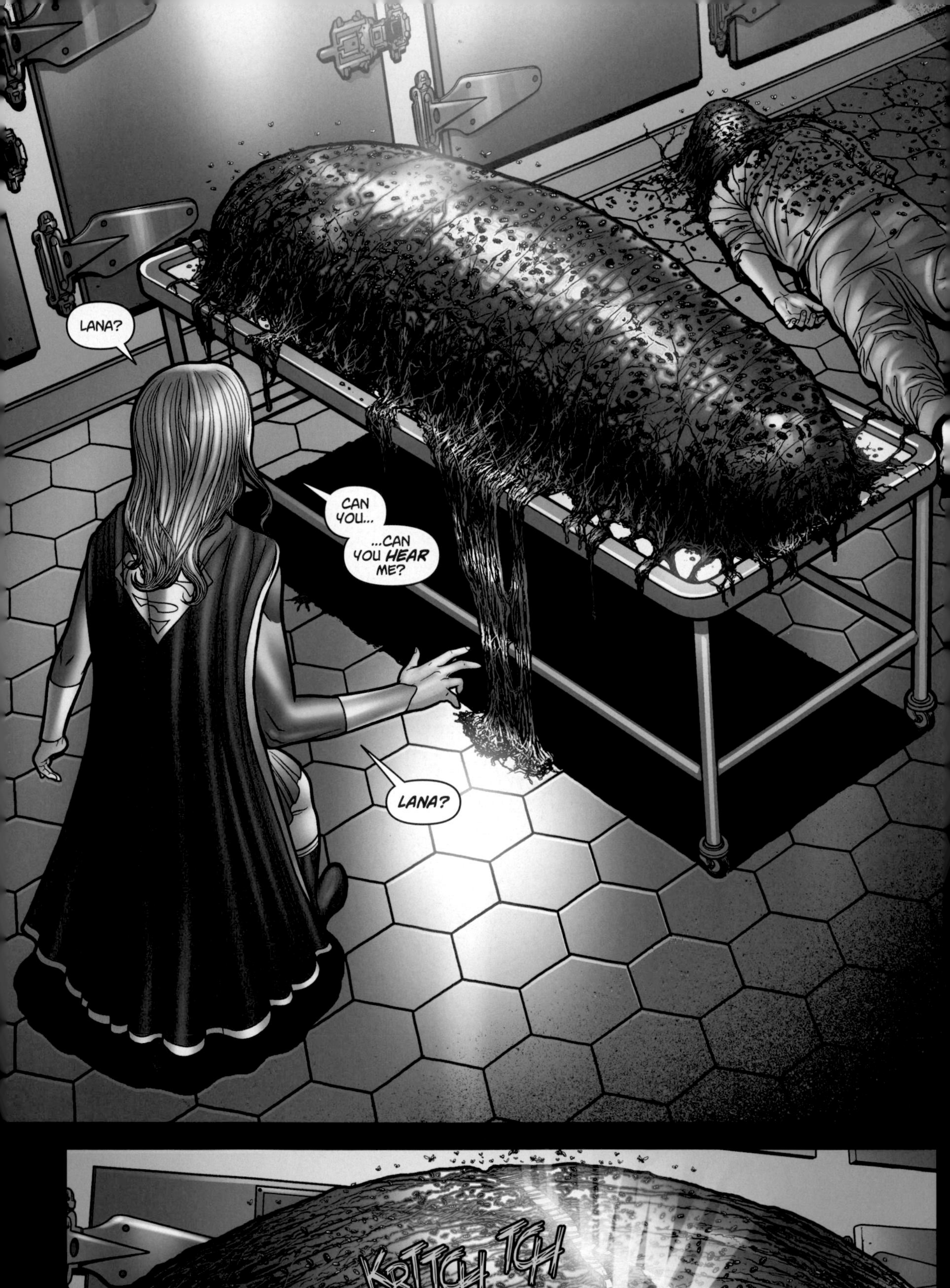
LANA?
CAN YOU...
...CAN YOU HEAR ME?
LANA?

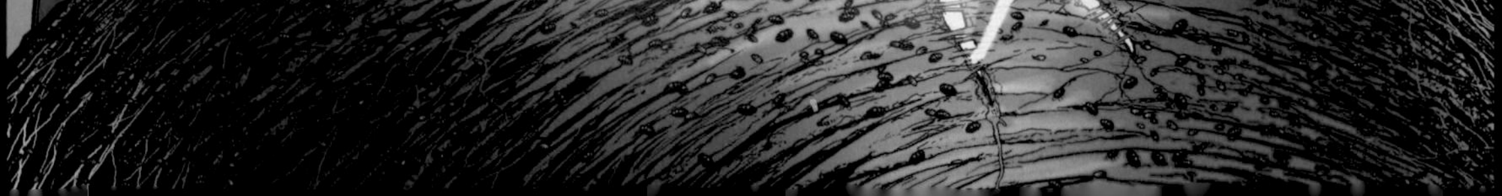
KRITCH TCH

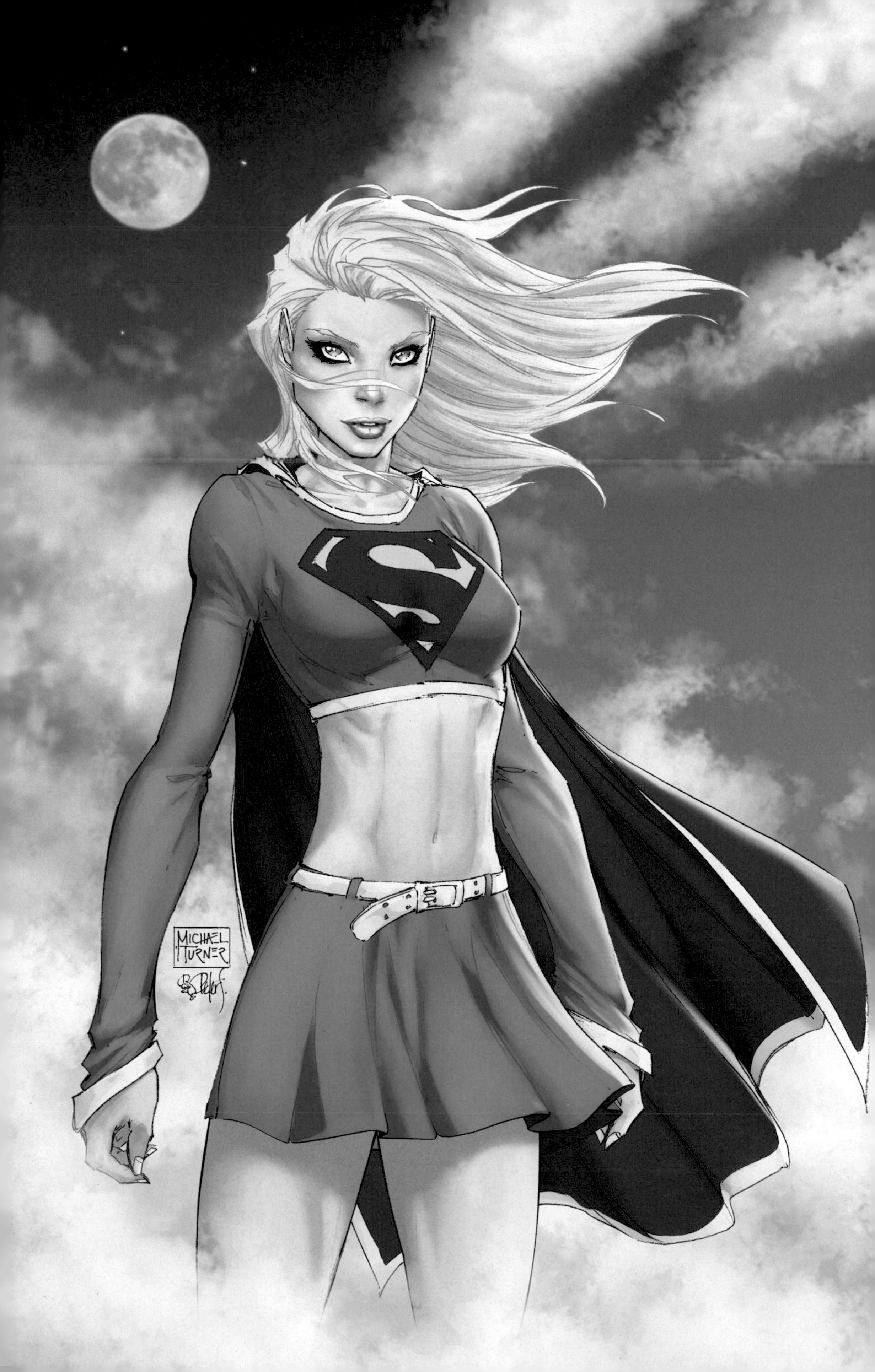
MICHAEL TURNER

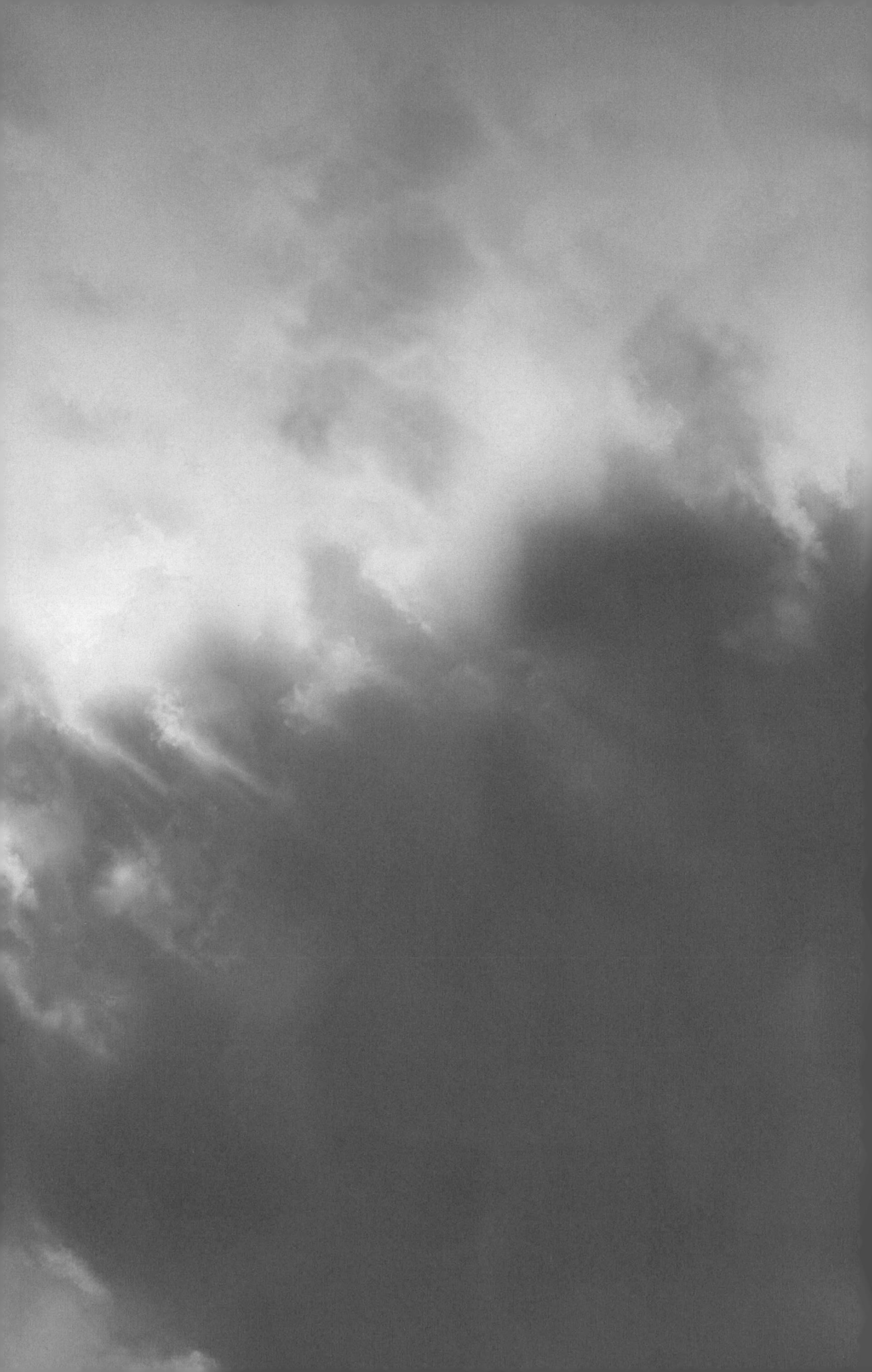

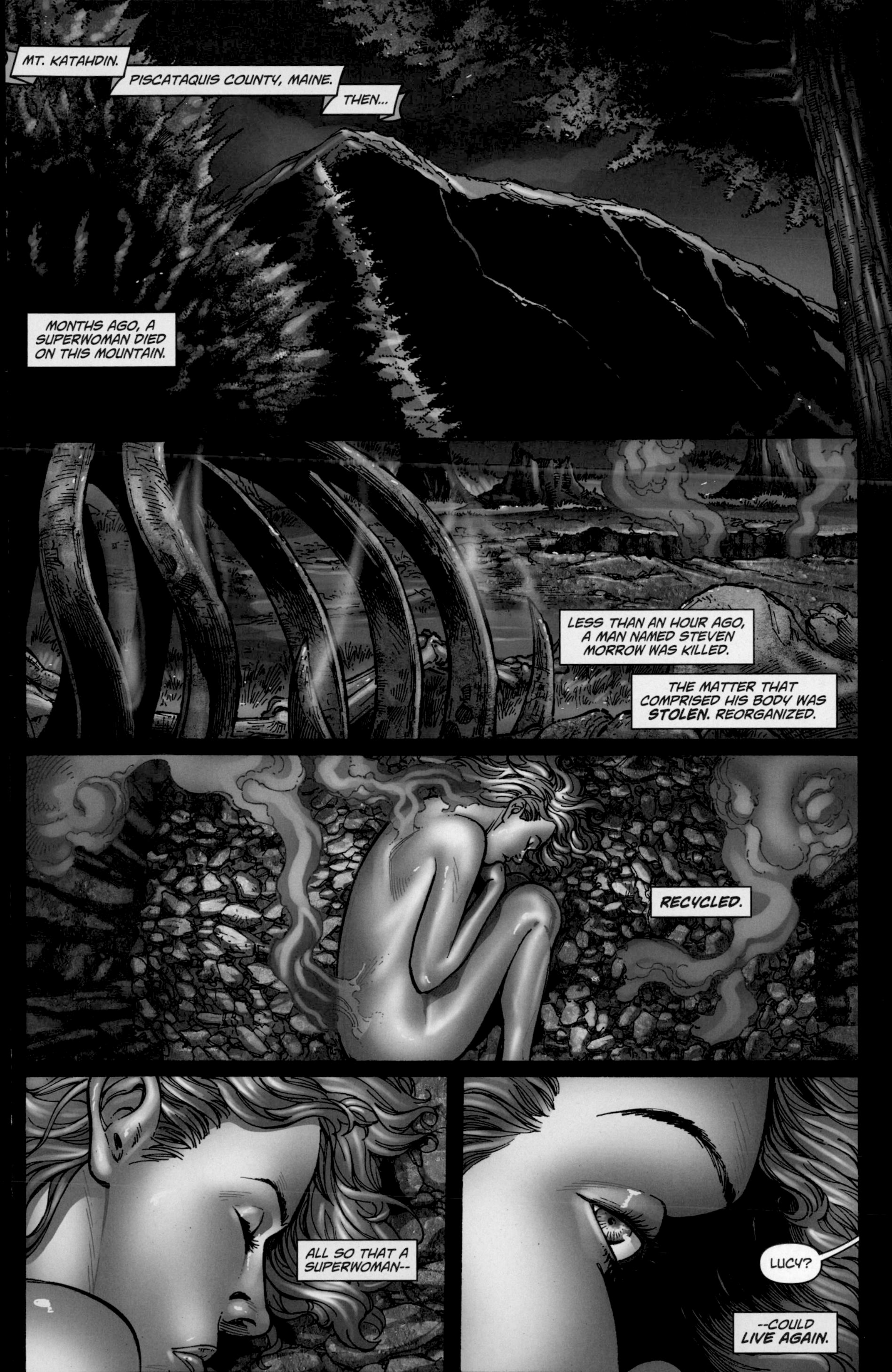
MT. KATAHDIN.
PISCATAQUIS COUNTY, MAINE.
THEN...
MONTHS AGO, A SUPERWOMAN DIED ON THIS MOUNTAIN.
LESS THAN AN HOUR AGO, A MAN NAMED STEVEN MORROW WAS KILLED.
THE MATTER THAT COMPRISED HIS BODY WAS STOLEN. REORGANIZED.
RECYCLED.
ALL SO THAT A SUPERWOMAN--
LUCY?
--COULD LIVE AGAIN.

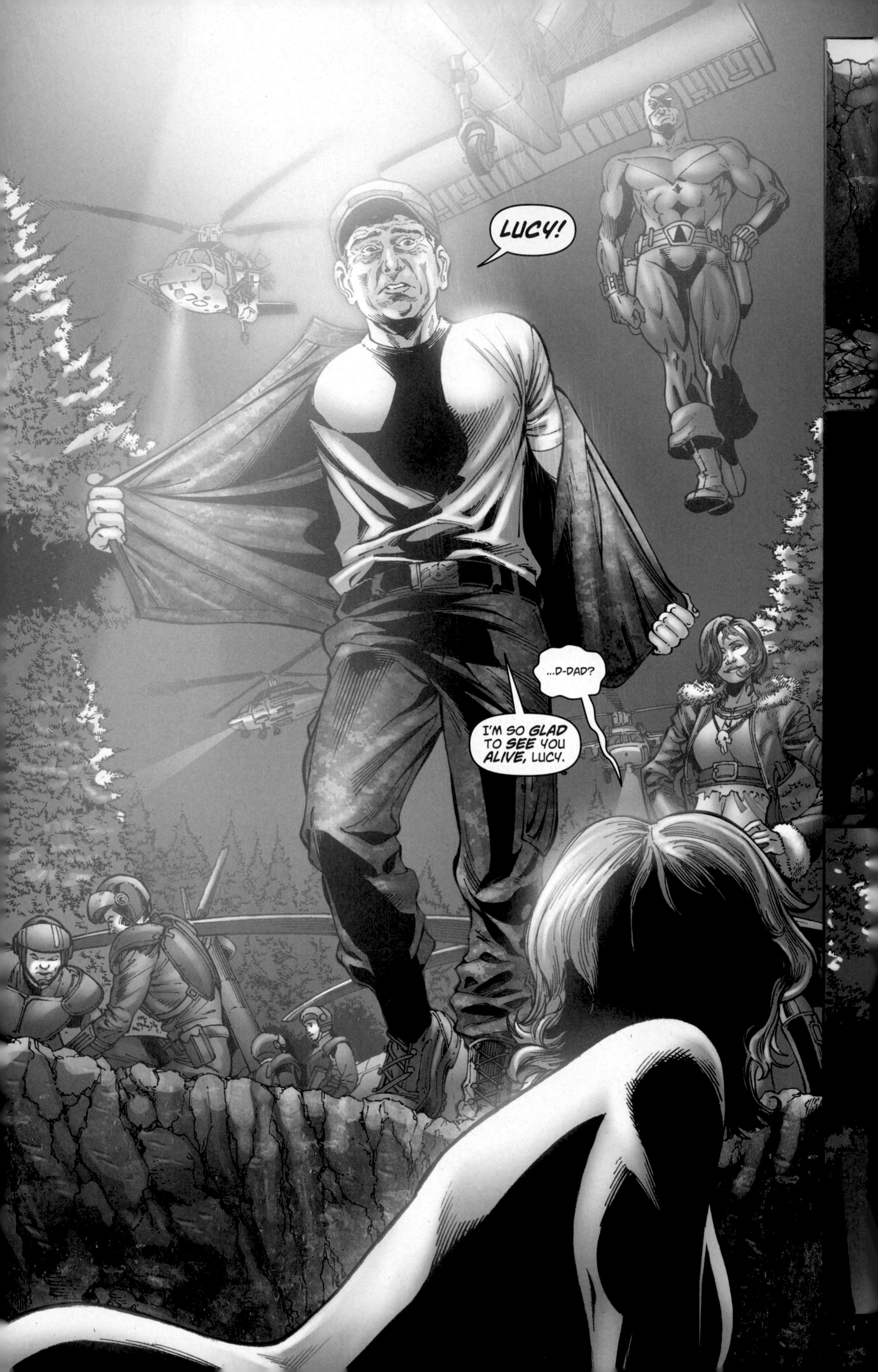
LUCY!
...D-DAD?
I'M SO GLAD TO SEE YOU ALIVE, LUCY.

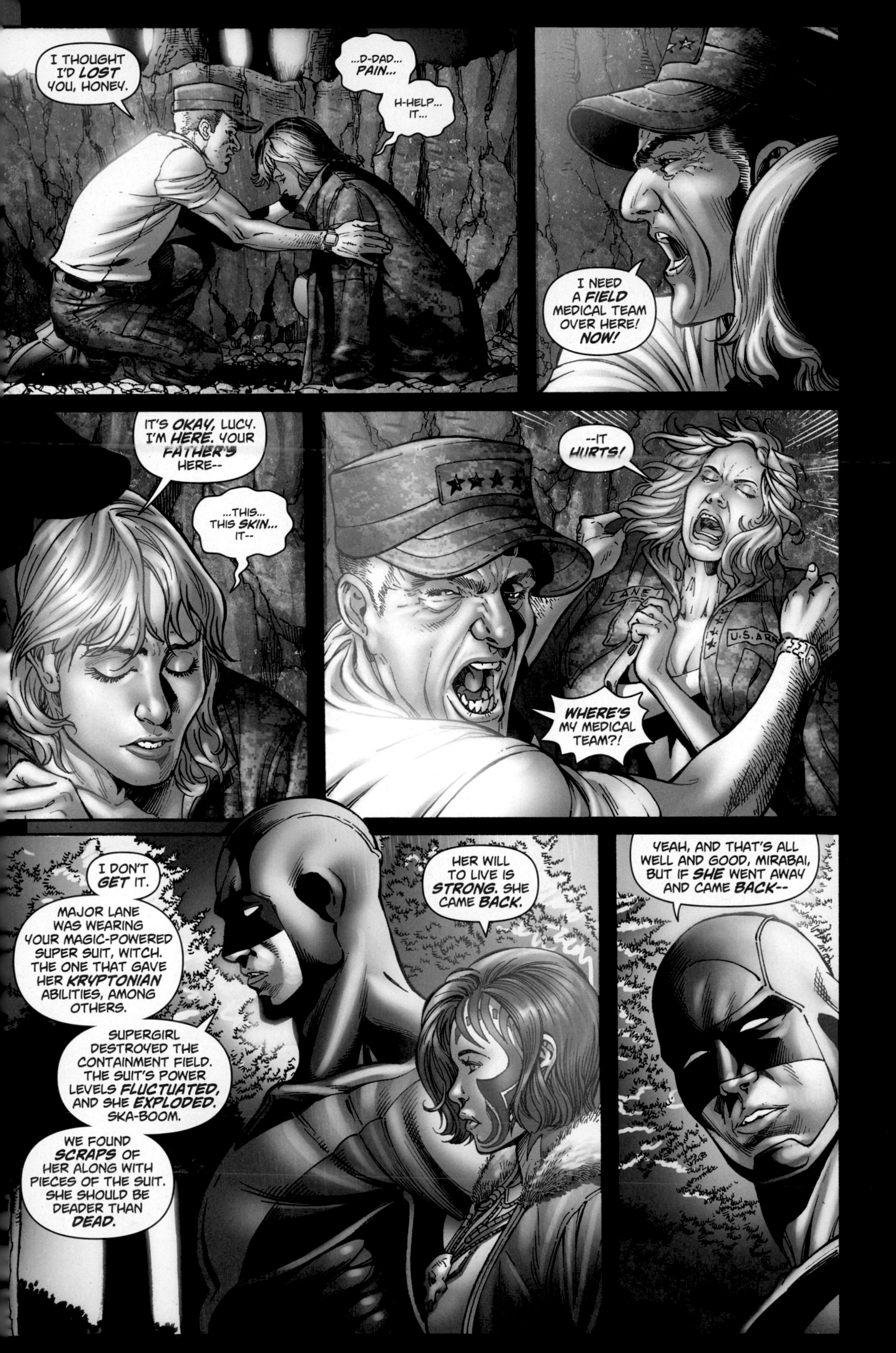
I THOUGHT I'D LOST YOU, HONEY.
...D-DAD... PAIN...
H-HELP... IT...
I NEED A FIELD MEDICAL TEAM OVER HERE! NOW!
IT'S OKAY, LUCY. I'M HERE. YOUR FATHER'S HERE--
...THIS... THIS SKIN... IT--
--IT HURTS!
WHERE'S MY MEDICAL TEAM?!
I DON'T GET IT.
MAJOR LANE WAS WEARING YOUR MAGIC-POWERED SUPER SUIT, WITCH. THE ONE THAT GAVE HER KRYPTONIAN ABILITIES, AMONG OTHERS.
SUPERGIRL DESTROYED THE CONTAINMENT FIELD. THE SUIT'S POWER LEVELS FLUCTUATED, AND SHE EXPLODED. SKA-BOOM.
WE FOUND SCRAPS OF HER ALONG WITH PIECES OF THE SUIT. SHE SHOULD BE DEADER THAN DEAD.
HER WILL TO LIVE IS STRONG. SHE CAME BACK.
YEAH, AND THAT'S ALL WELL AND GOOD, MIRABAI, BUT IF SHE WENT AWAY AND CAME BACK--

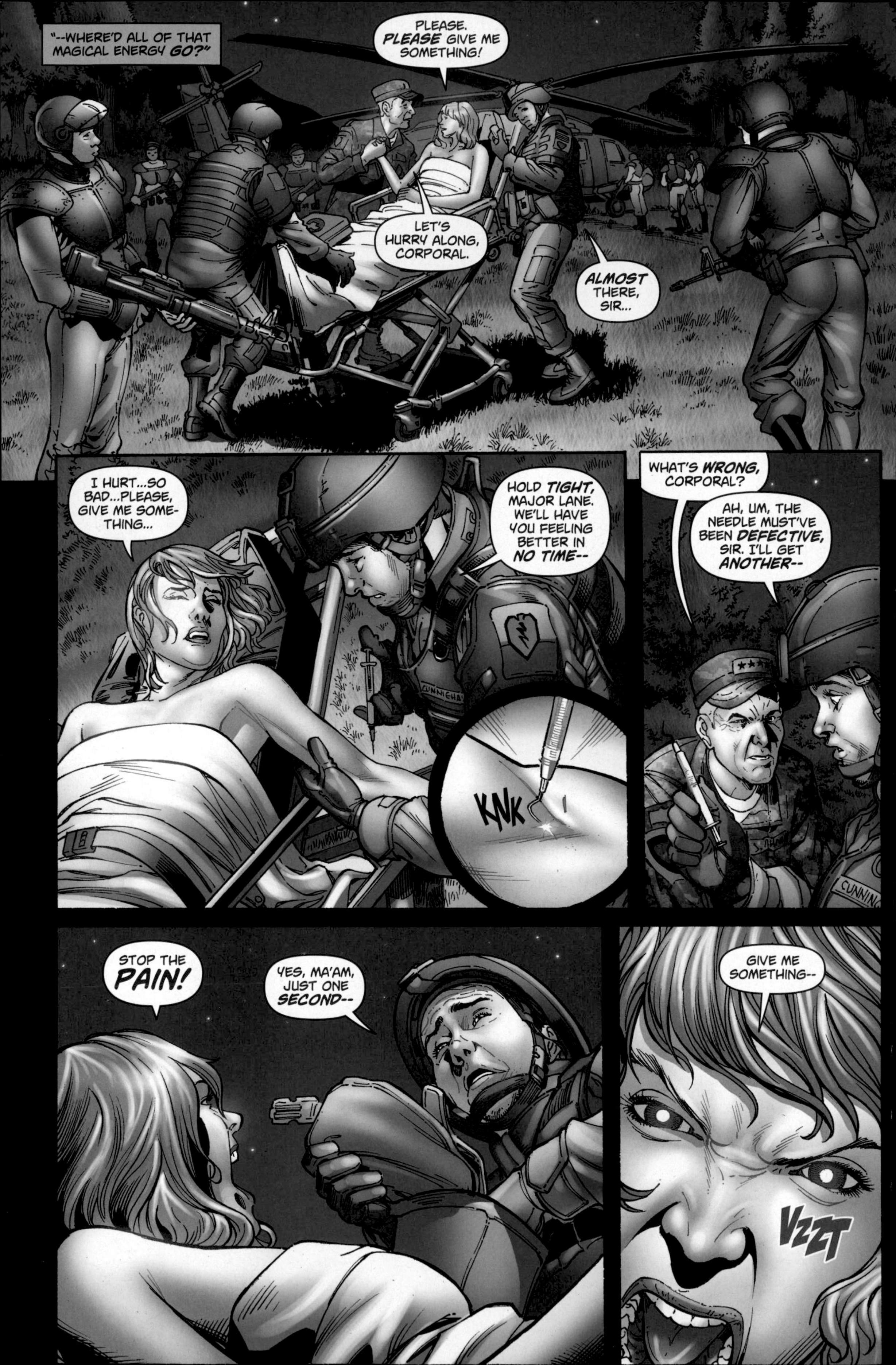
"--WHERE'D ALL OF THAT MAGICAL ENERGY GO?"
PLEASE. PLEASE GIVE ME SOMETHING!
LET'S HURRY ALONG, CORPORAL.
ALMOST THERE, SIR...
I HURT...SO BAD...PLEASE, GIVE ME SOME-THING...
HOLD TIGHT, MAJOR LANE. WE'LL HAVE YOU FEELING BETTER IN NO TIME--
KNK
WHAT'S WRONG, CORPORAL?
AH, UM, THE NEEDLE MUST'VE BEEN DEFECTIVE, SIR. I'LL GET ANOTHER--
STOP THE PAIN!
YES, MA'AM, JUST ONE SECOND--
GIVE ME SOMETHING--
VZZT

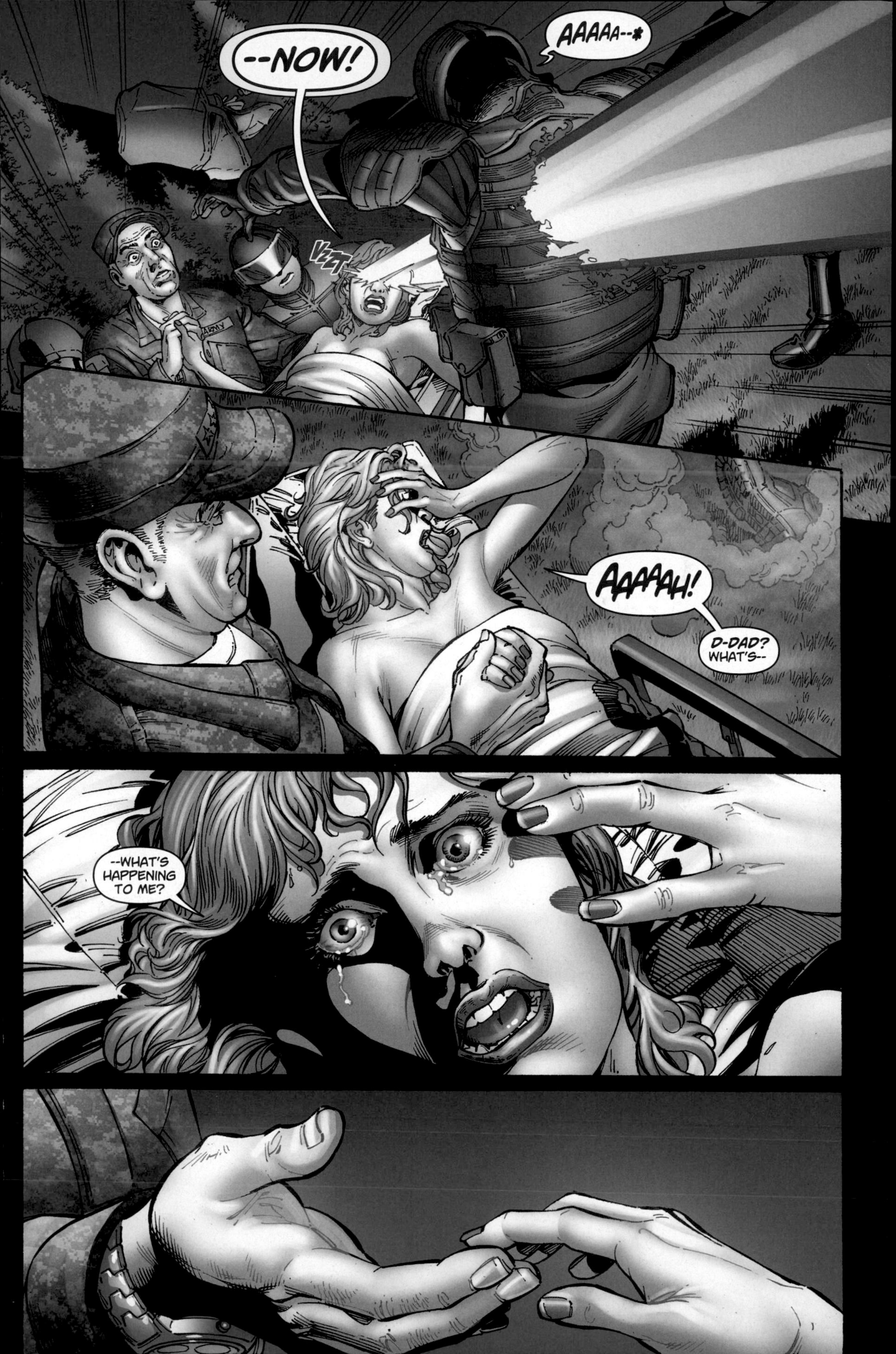
--NOW!
AAAAA--*
VZZT
ARMY
AAAAAH!
D-DAD? WHAT'S--
--WHAT'S HAPPENING TO ME?

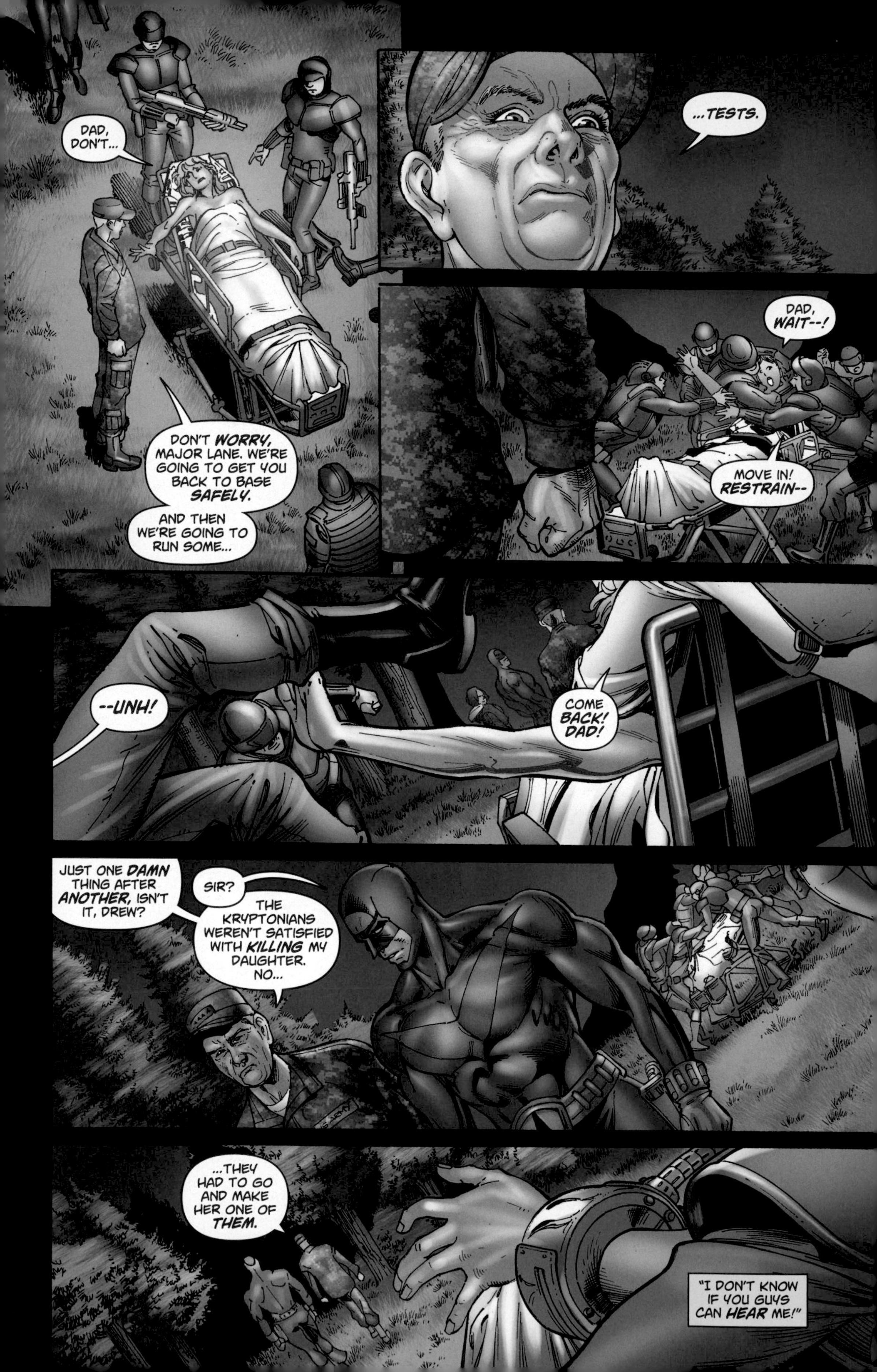
DAD, DON'T...
DON'T WORRY, MAJOR LANE. WE'RE GOING TO GET YOU BACK TO BASE SAFELY.
AND THEN WE'RE GOING TO RUN SOME...
...TESTS.
DAD, WAIT--!
MOVE IN! RESTRAIN--
--UNH!
COME BACK! DAD!
JUST ONE DAMN THING AFTER ANOTHER, ISN'T IT, DREW?
SIR?
THE KRYPTONIANS WEREN'T SATISFIED WITH KILLING MY DAUGHTER. NO...
...THEY HAD TO GO AND MAKE HER ONE OF THEM.
"I DON'T KNOW IF YOU GUYS CAN HEAR ME!"

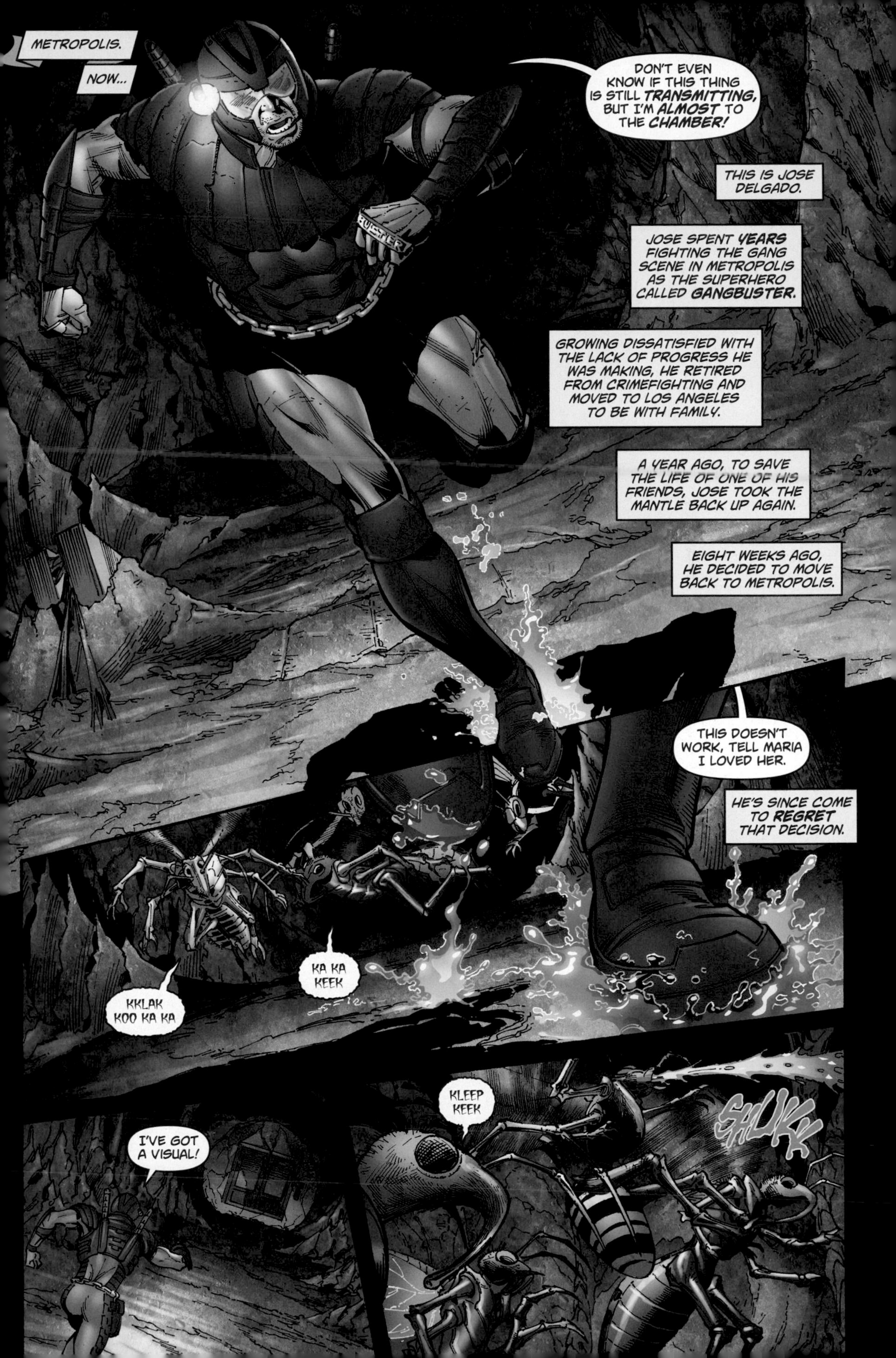
METROPOLIS.
NOW...
DON'T EVEN KNOW IF THIS THING IS STILL TRANSMITTING, BUT I'M ALMOST TO THE CHAMBER!
THIS IS JOSE DELGADO.
JOSE SPENT YEARS FIGHTING THE GANG SCENE IN METROPOLIS AS THE SUPERHERO CALLED GANGBUSTER.
GROWING DISSATISFIED WITH THE LACK OF PROGRESS HE WAS MAKING, HE RETIRED FROM CRIMEFIGHTING AND MOVED TO LOS ANGELES TO BE WITH FAMILY.
A YEAR AGO, TO SAVE THE LIFE OF ONE OF HIS FRIENDS, JOSE TOOK THE MANTLE BACK UP AGAIN.
EIGHT WEEKS AGO, HE DECIDED TO MOVE BACK TO METROPOLIS.
THIS DOESN'T WORK, TELL MARIA I LOVED HER.
HE'S SINCE COME TO REGRET THAT DECISION.
KKLAK KOO KA KA
KA KA KEEK
I'VE GOT A VISUAL!
KLEEP KEEK
SHLIKK

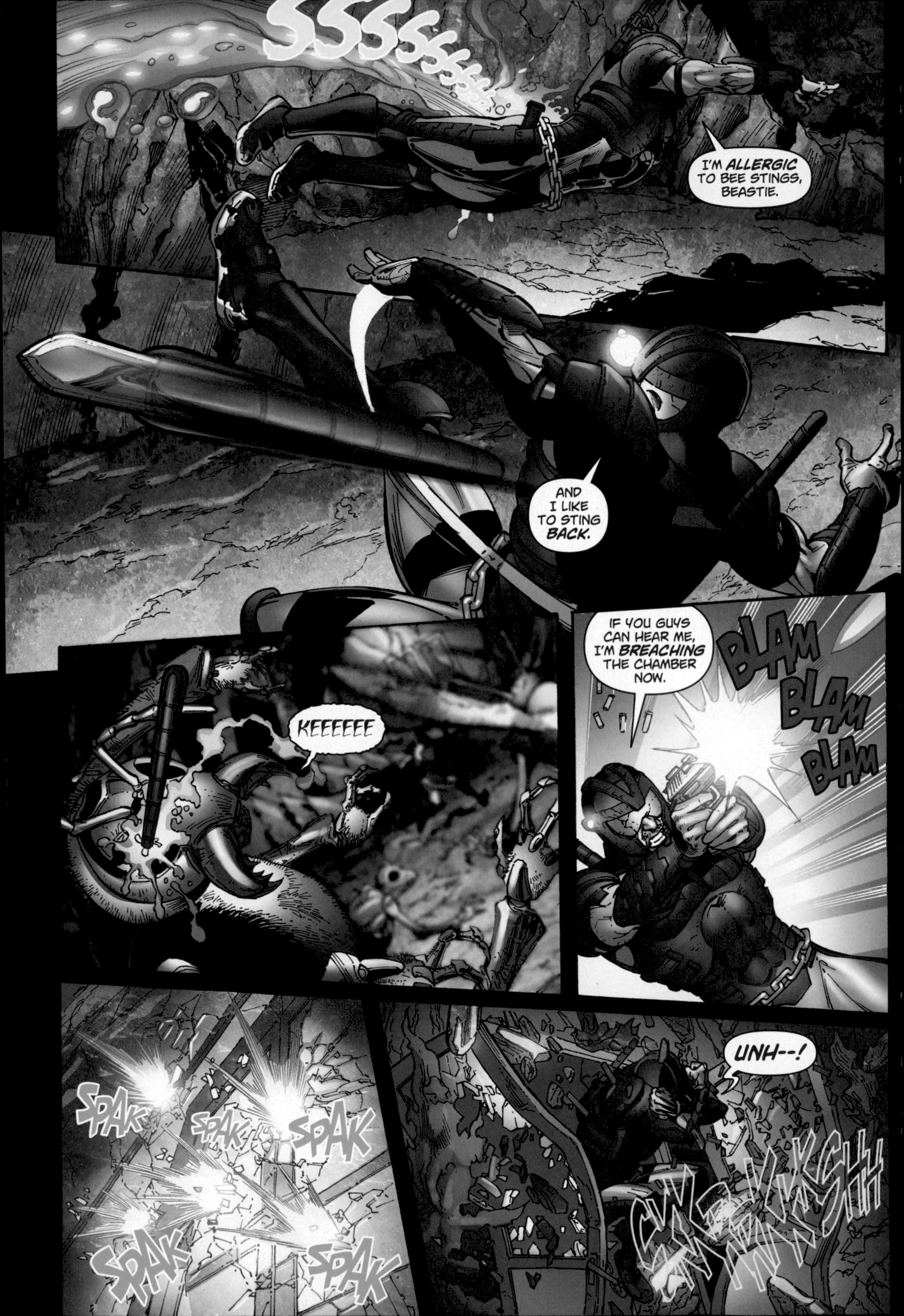
SSSSSSSSS
I'M ALLERGIC TO BEE STINGS, BEASTIE.
AND I LIKE TO STING BACK.
KEEEEEE
IF YOU GUYS CAN HEAR ME, I'M BREACHING THE CHAMBER NOW.
BLAM
BLAM
BLAM
SPAK
SPAK
SPAK
SPAK
SPAK
UNH--!
CHKKKSH

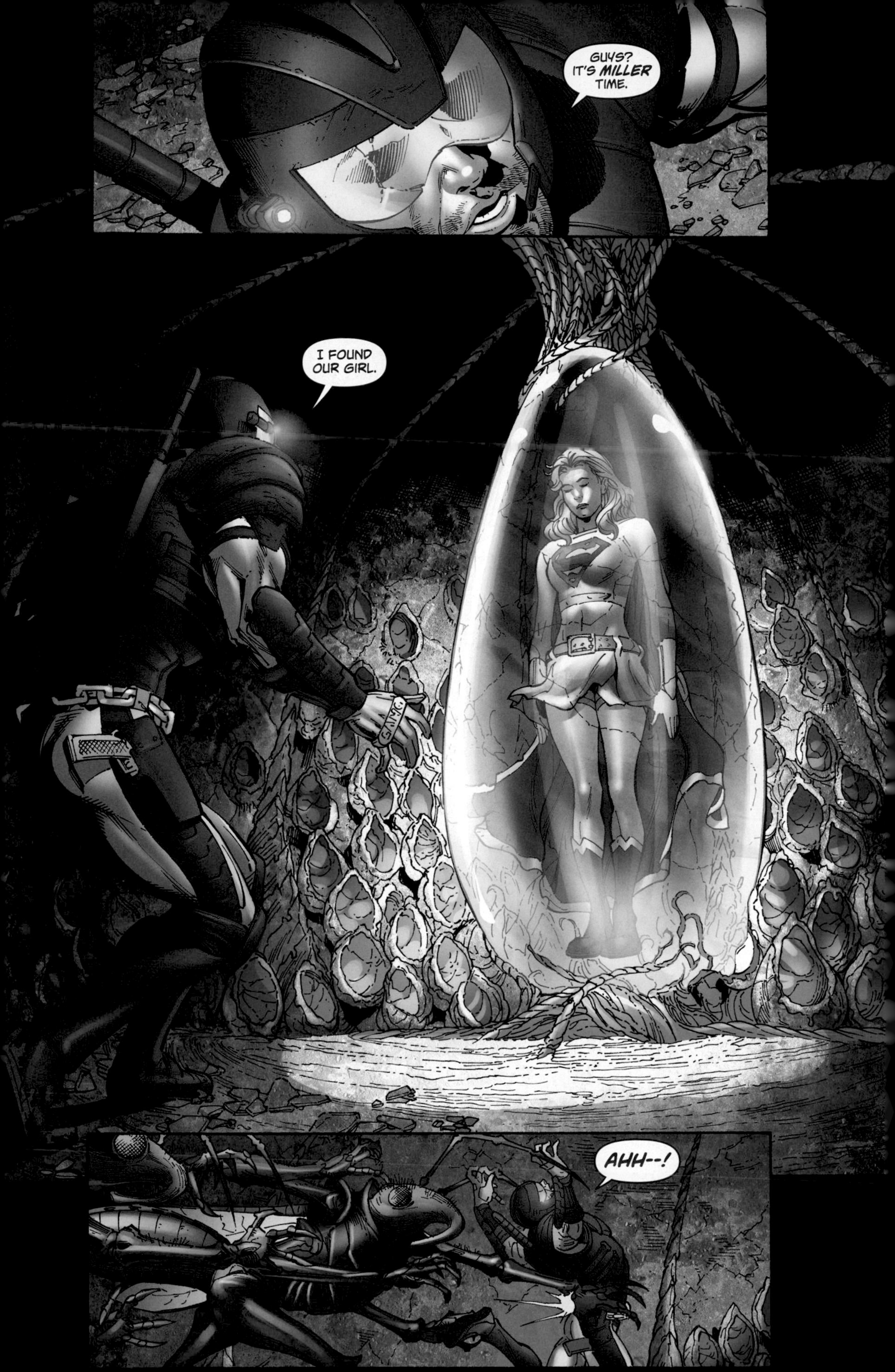
GUYS? IT'S MILLER TIME.
I FOUND OUR GIRL.
AHH--!

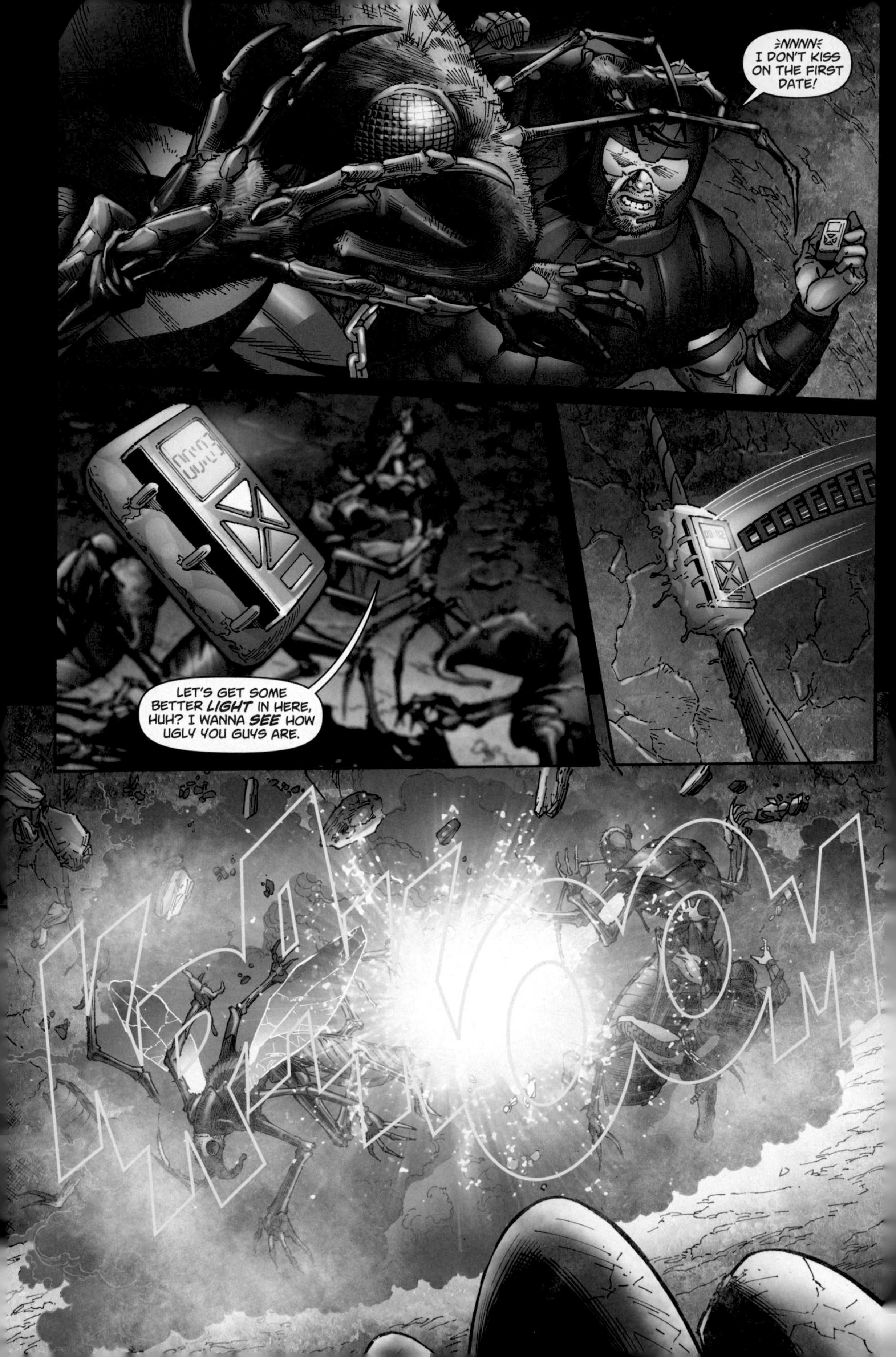
NNNN
I DON'T KISS ON THE FIRST DATE!
LET'S GET SOME BETTER LIGHT IN HERE, HUH? I WANNA SEE HOW UGLY YOU GUYS ARE.
EEEEEEEE
KAWHOOM

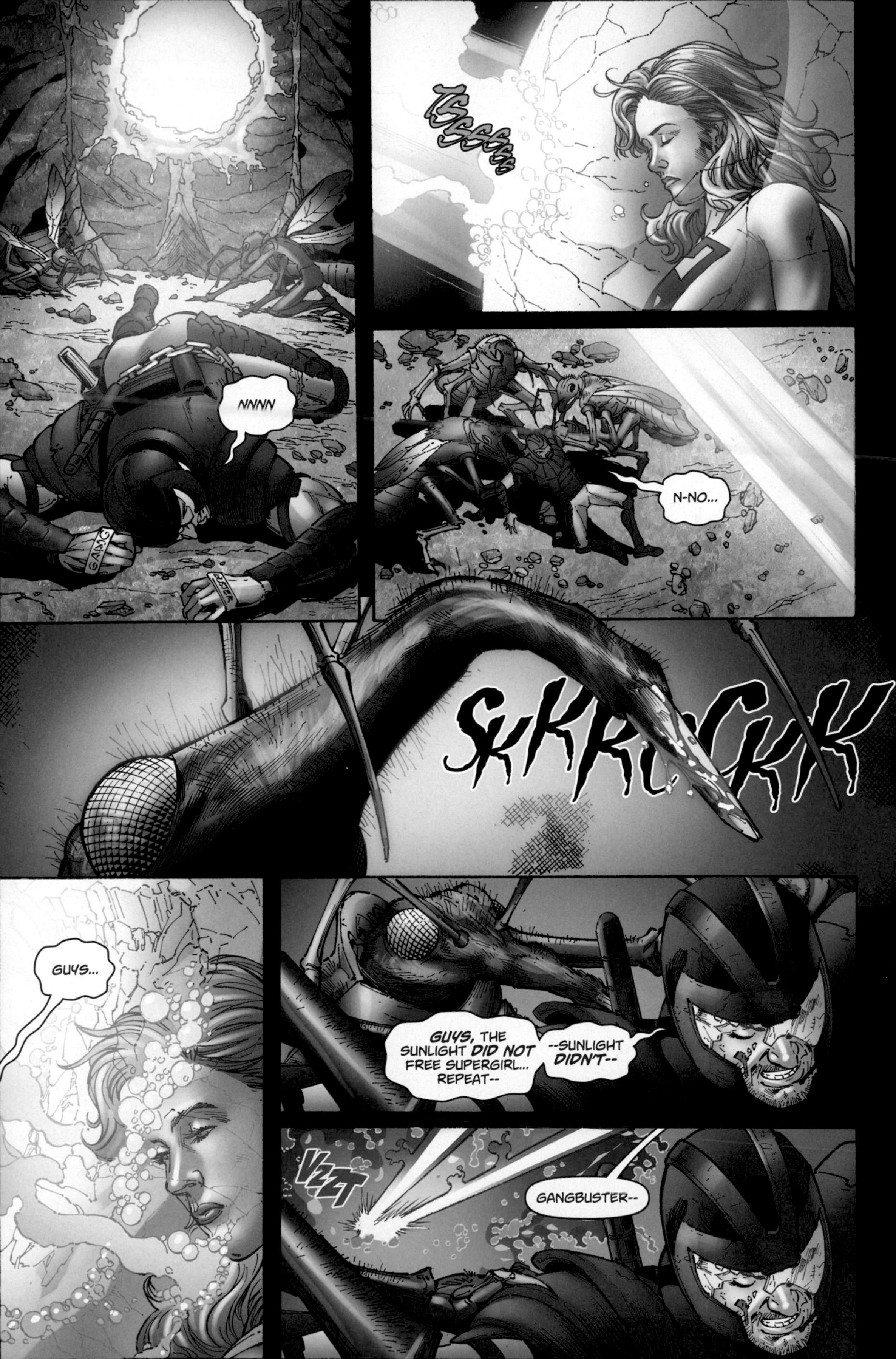
NNNN
TSSSSSS
N-NO...
SKKR CKK
GUYS...
GUYS, THE SUNLIGHT DID NOT FREE SUPERGIRL... REPEAT--
--SUNLIGHT DIDN'T--
VZZT
GANGBUSTER--

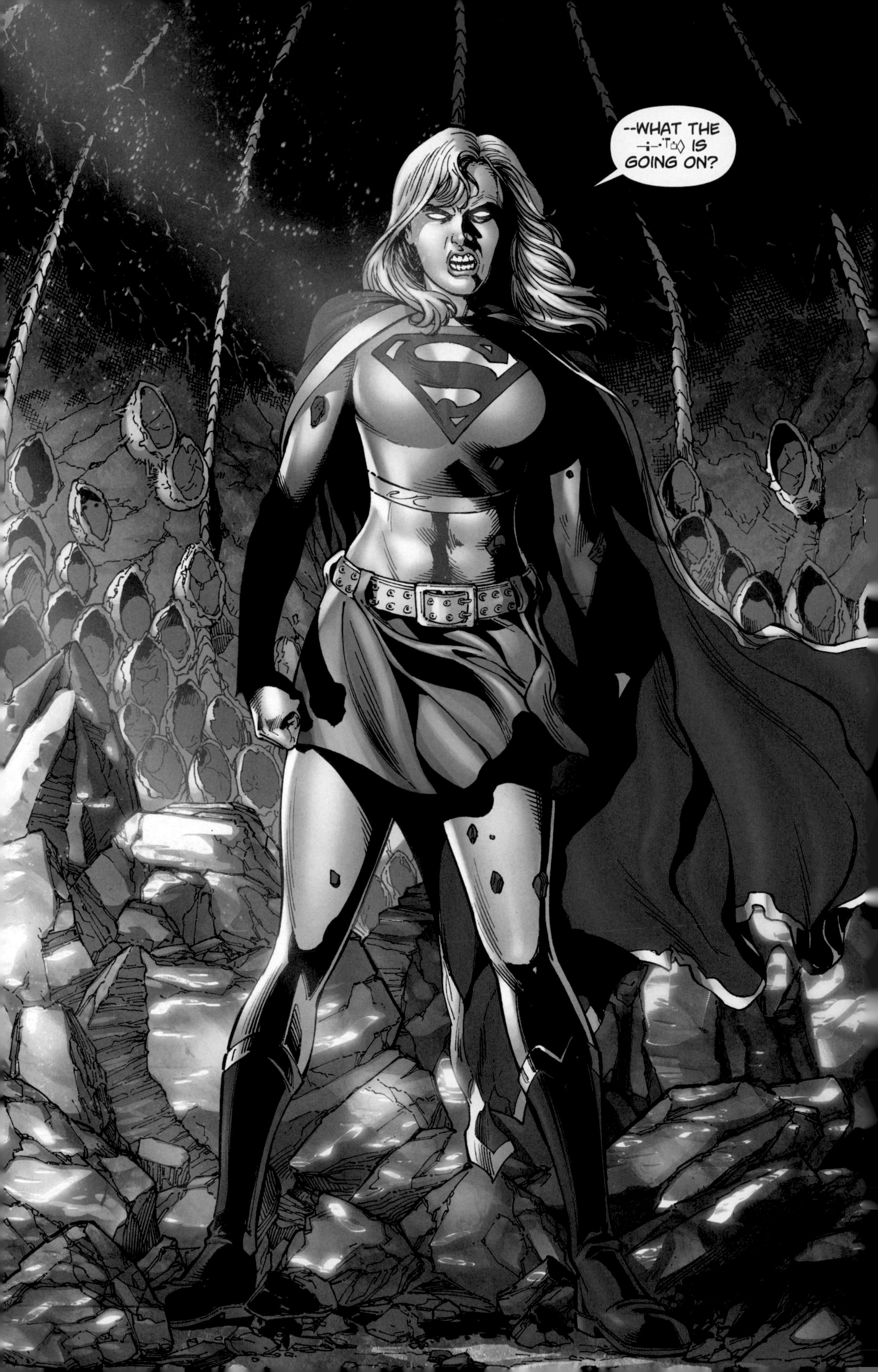
--WHAT THE IS GOING ON?

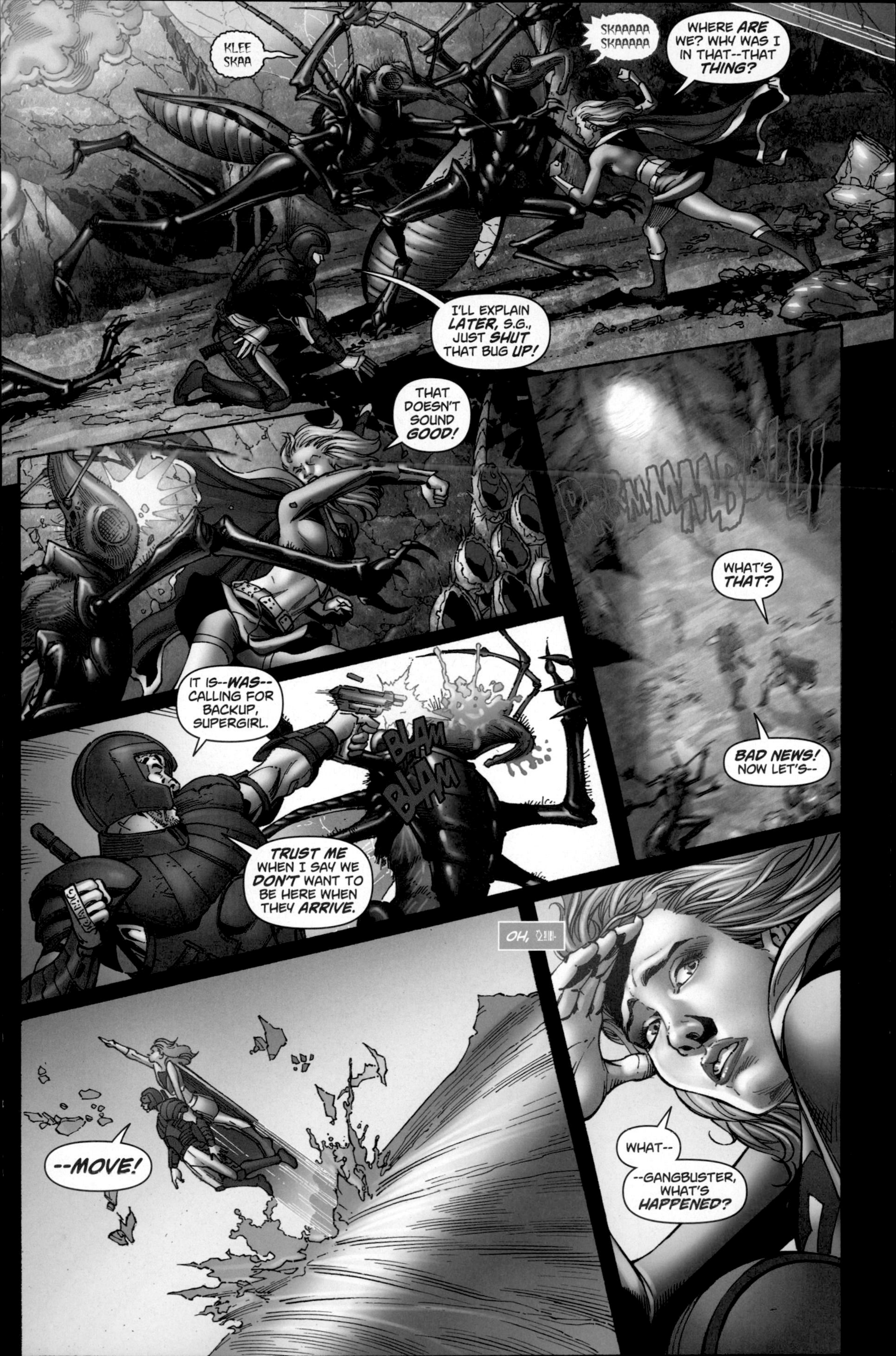
KLEE SKAA
SKAAAAA SKAAAAA
WHERE ARE WE? WHY WAS I IN THAT--THAT THING?
I'LL EXPLAIN LATER, S.G., JUST SHUT THAT BUG UP!
THAT DOESN'T SOUND GOOD!
IT IS--WAS--CALLING FOR BACKUP, SUPERGIRL.
BLAM
BLAM
TRUST ME WHEN I SAY WE DON'T WANT TO BE HERE WHEN THEY ARRIVE.
WHAT'S THAT?
BAD NEWS! NOW LET'S--
--MOVE!
OH,
WHAT--
--GANGBUSTER, WHAT'S HAPPENED?

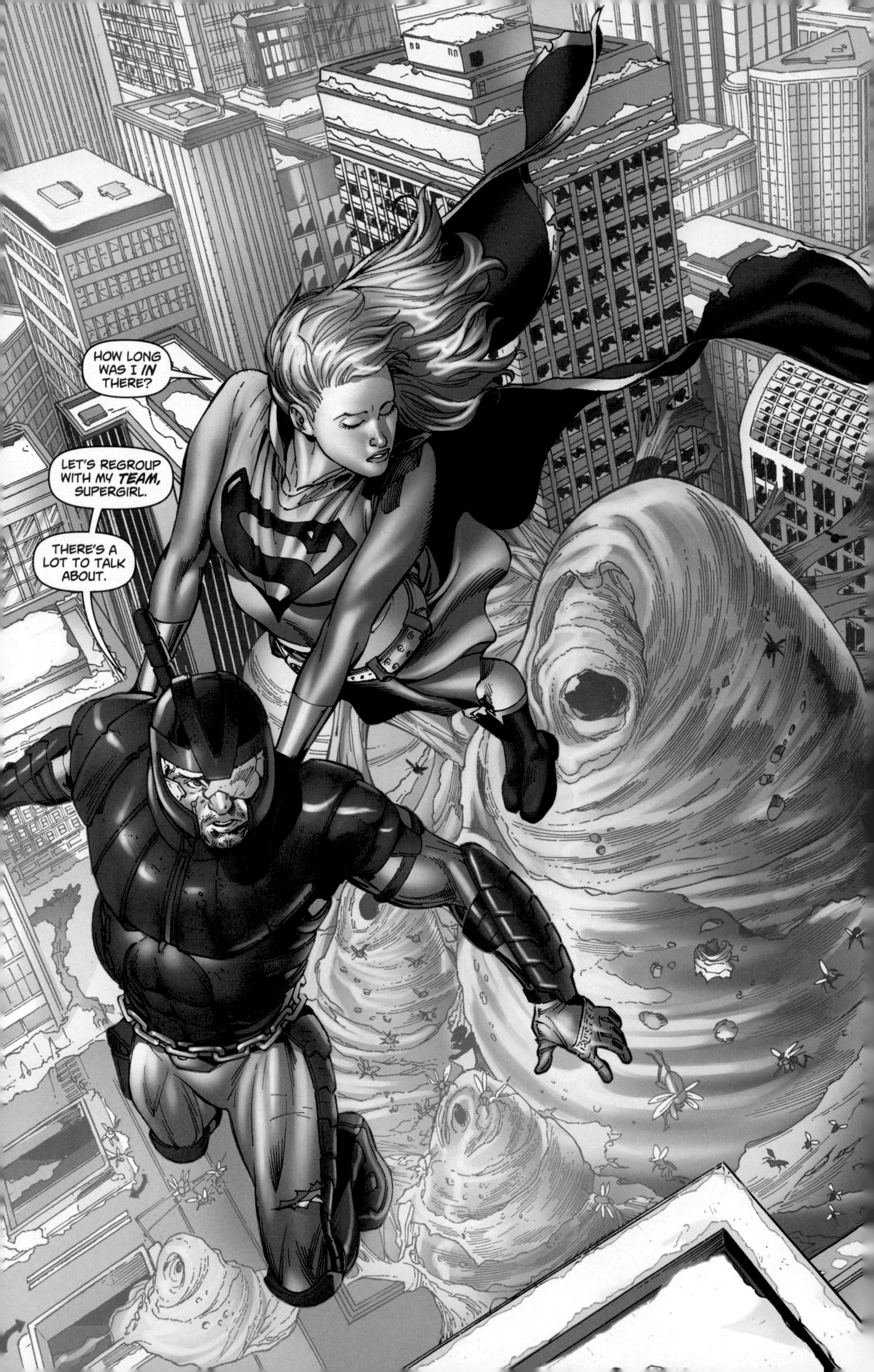
HOW LONG WAS I IN THERE?
LET'S REGROUP WITH MY TEAM, SUPERGIRL.
THERE'S A LOT TO TALK ABOUT.

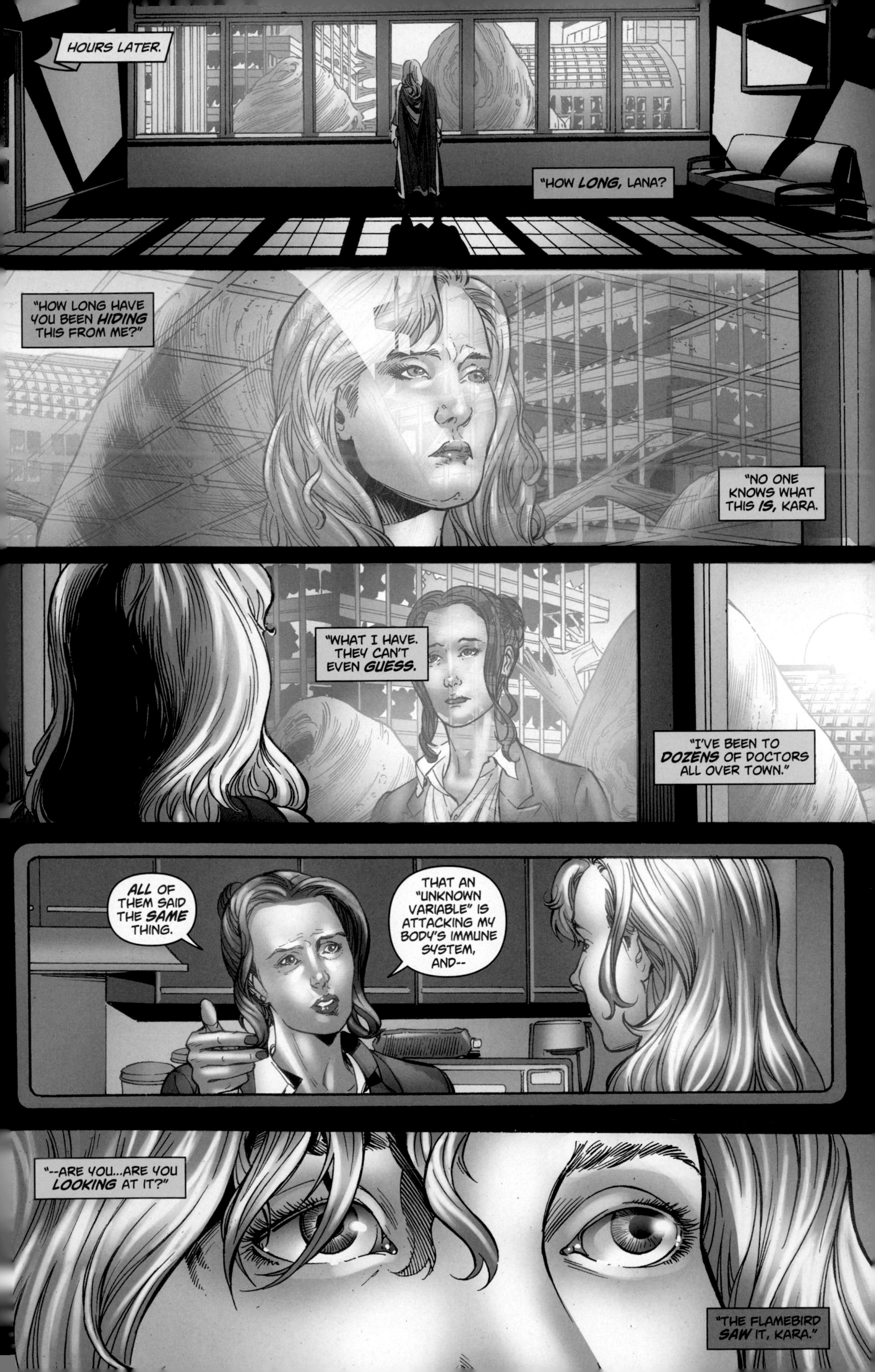
HOURS LATER.
"HOW LONG, LANA?
"HOW LONG HAVE YOU BEEN HIDING THIS FROM ME?"
"NO ONE KNOWS WHAT THIS IS, KARA.
"WHAT I HAVE. THEY CAN'T EVEN GUESS.
"I'VE BEEN TO DOZENS OF DOCTORS ALL OVER TOWN."
ALL OF THEM SAID THE SAME THING.
THAT AN "UNKNOWN VARIABLE" IS ATTACKING MY BODY'S IMMUNE SYSTEM, AND--
"--ARE YOU...ARE YOU LOOKING AT IT?"
"THE FLAMEBIRD SAW IT, KARA."

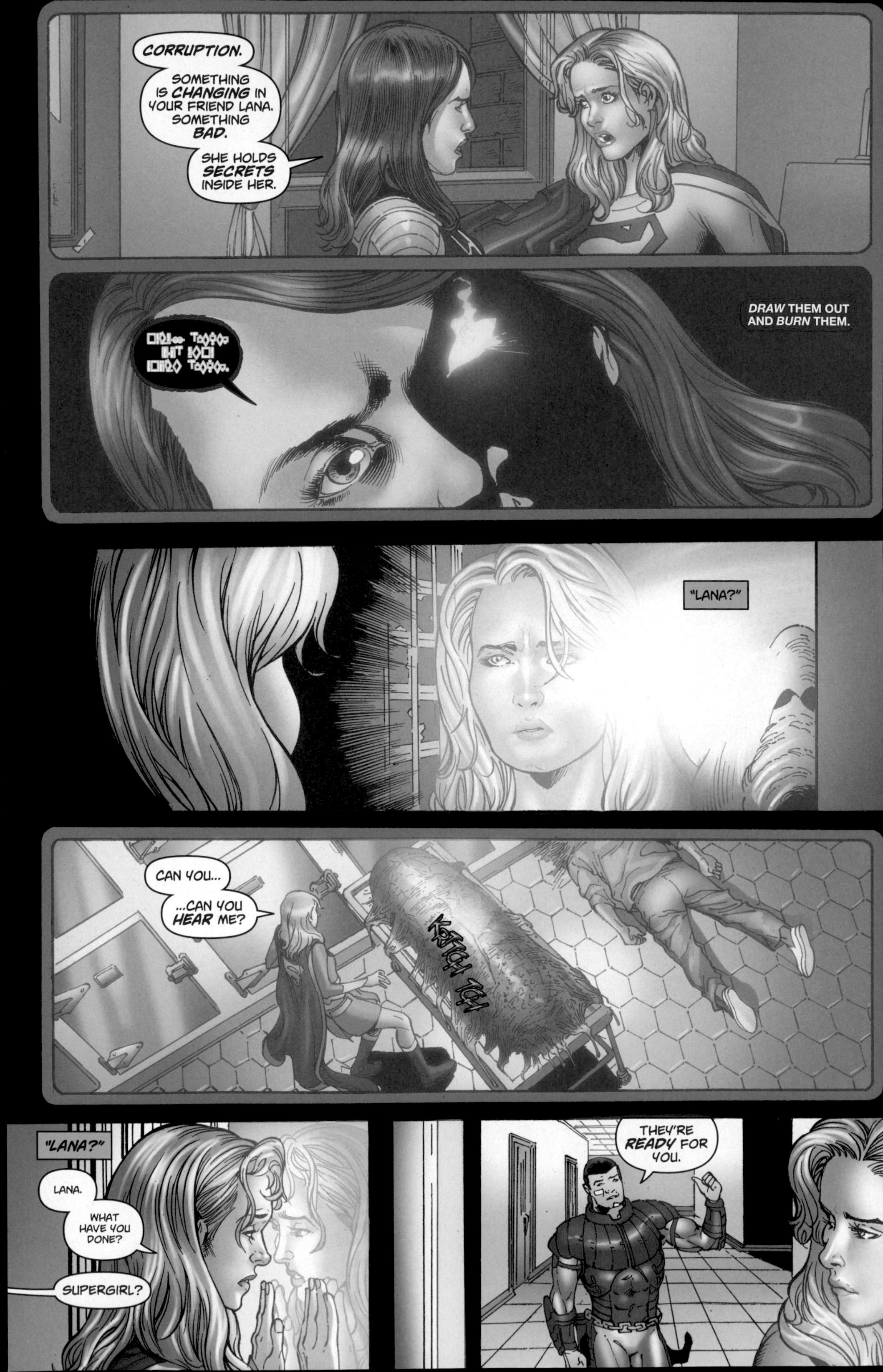
CORRUPTION.
SOMETHING IS CHANGING IN YOUR FRIEND LANA. SOMETHING BAD.
SHE HOLDS SECRETS INSIDE HER.
DRAW THEM OUT AND BURN THEM.
"LANA?"
CAN YOU...
...CAN YOU HEAR ME?
KSSTCH TCH
"LANA?"
LANA.
WHAT HAVE YOU DONE?
SUPERGIRL?
THEY'RE READY FOR YOU.

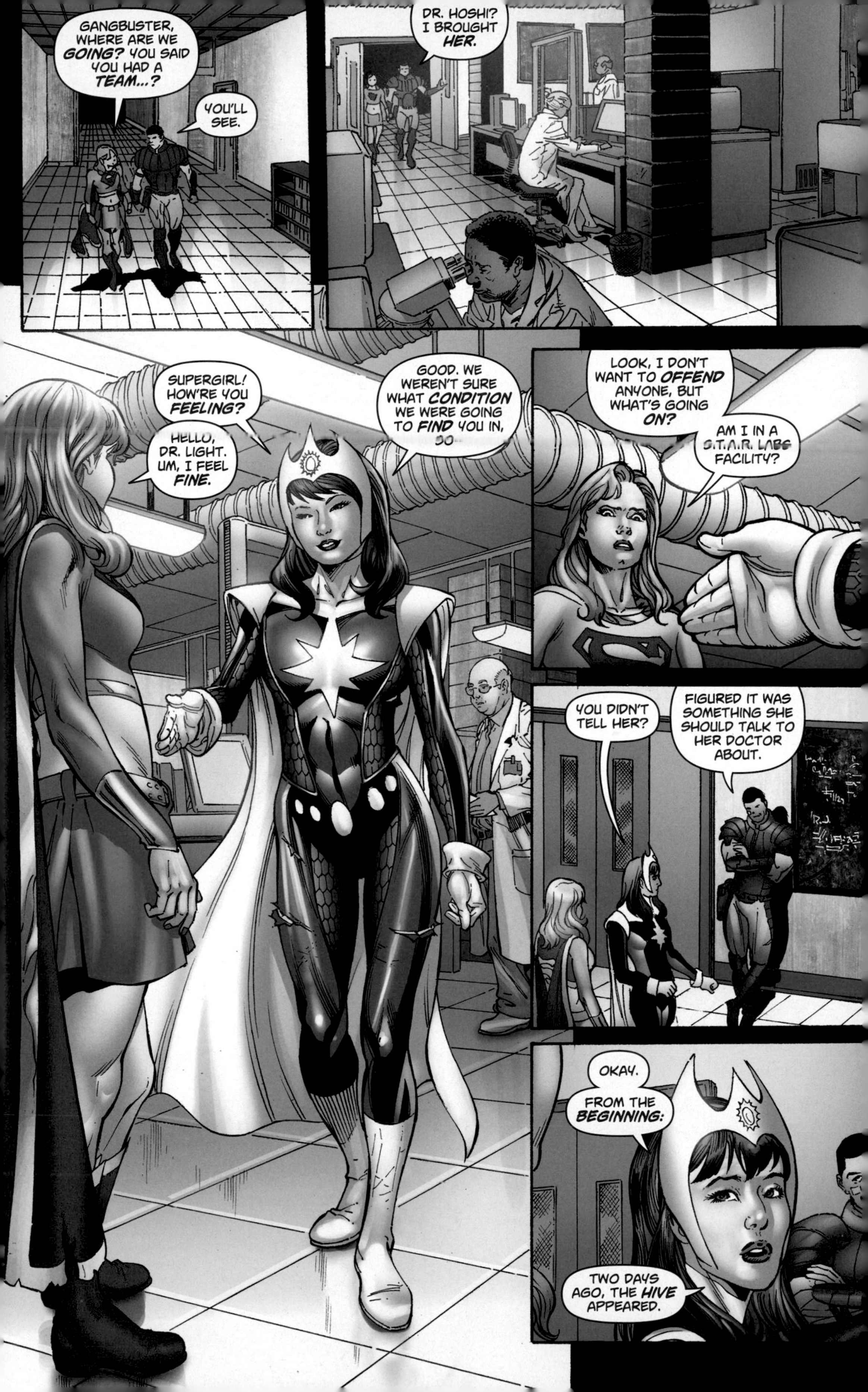
GANGBUSTER, WHERE ARE WE GOING? YOU SAID YOU HAD A TEAM...?
YOU'LL SEE.
DR. HOSHI? I BROUGHT HER.
SUPERGIRL! HOW'RE YOU FEELING?
HELLO, DR. LIGHT. UM, I FEEL FINE.
GOOD. WE WEREN'T SURE WHAT CONDITION WE WERE GOING TO FIND YOU IN, SO
LOOK, I DON'T WANT TO OFFEND ANYONE, BUT WHAT'S GOING ON?
AM I IN A S.T.A.R. LABS FACILITY?
YOU DIDN'T TELL HER?
FIGURED IT WAS SOMETHING SHE SHOULD TALK TO HER DOCTOR ABOUT.
OKAY.
FROM THE BEGINNING:
TWO DAYS AGO, THE HIVE APPEARED.

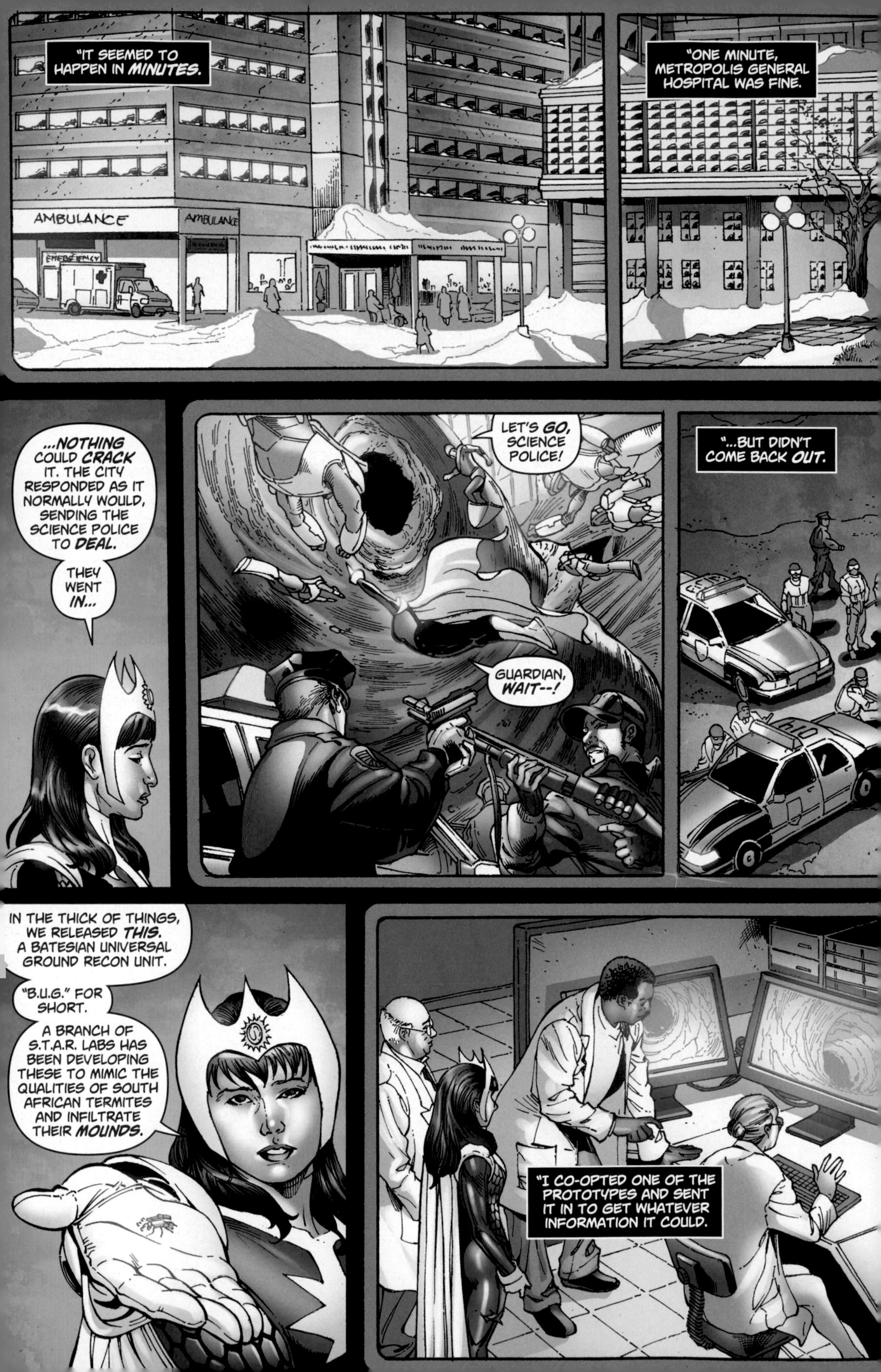
"IT SEEMED TO HAPPEN IN MINUTES.
"ONE MINUTE, METROPOLIS GENERAL HOSPITAL WAS FINE.
AMBULANCE
AMBULANCE
EMERGENCY
...NOTHING COULD CRACK IT. THE CITY RESPONDED AS IT NORMALLY WOULD, SENDING THE SCIENCE POLICE TO DEAL.
THEY WENT IN...
LET'S GO, SCIENCE POLICE!
GUARDIAN, WAIT--!
"...BUT DIDN'T COME BACK OUT.
IN THE THICK OF THINGS, WE RELEASED THIS. A BATESIAN UNIVERSAL GROUND RECON UNIT.
"B.U.G." FOR SHORT.
A BRANCH OF S.T.A.R. LABS HAS BEEN DEVELOPING THESE TO MIMIC THE QUALITIES OF SOUTH AFRICAN TERMITES AND INFILTRATE THEIR MOUNDS.
"I CO-OPTED ONE OF THE PROTOTYPES AND SENT IT IN TO GET WHATEVER INFORMATION IT COULD.

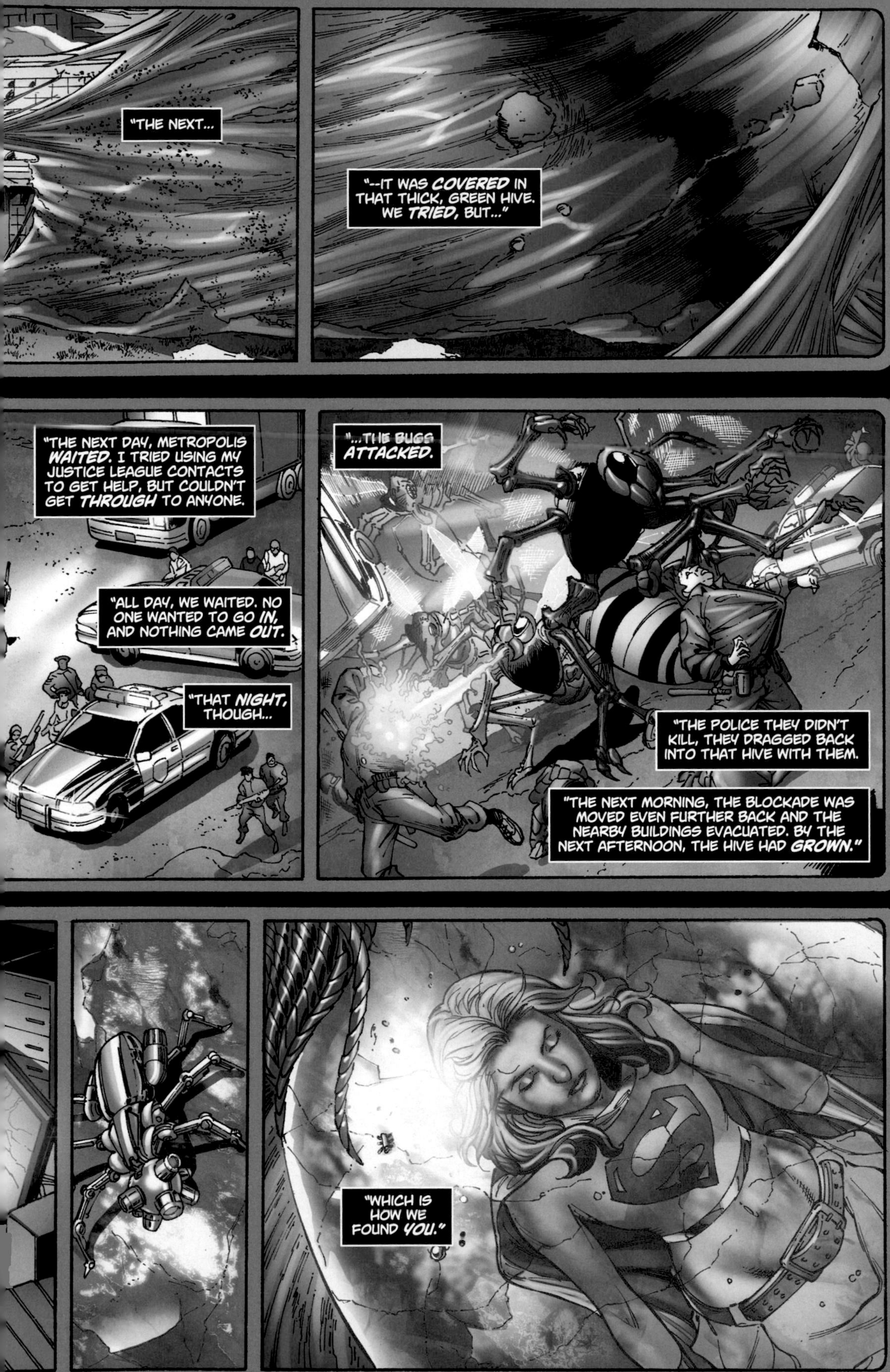
"THE NEXT...
"--IT WAS COVERED IN THAT THICK, GREEN HIVE. WE TRIED, BUT..."
"THE NEXT DAY, METROPOLIS WAITED. I TRIED USING MY JUSTICE LEAGUE CONTACTS TO GET HELP, BUT COULDN'T GET THROUGH TO ANYONE.
"ALL DAY, WE WAITED. NO ONE WANTED TO GO IN, AND NOTHING CAME OUT.
"THAT NIGHT, THOUGH...
"...THE BUGS ATTACKED.
"THE POLICE THEY DIDN'T KILL, THEY DRAGGED BACK INTO THAT HIVE WITH THEM.
"THE NEXT MORNING, THE BLOCKADE WAS MOVED EVEN FURTHER BACK AND THE NEARBY BUILDINGS EVACUATED. BY THE NEXT AFTERNOON, THE HIVE HAD GROWN."
"WHICH IS HOW WE FOUND YOU."

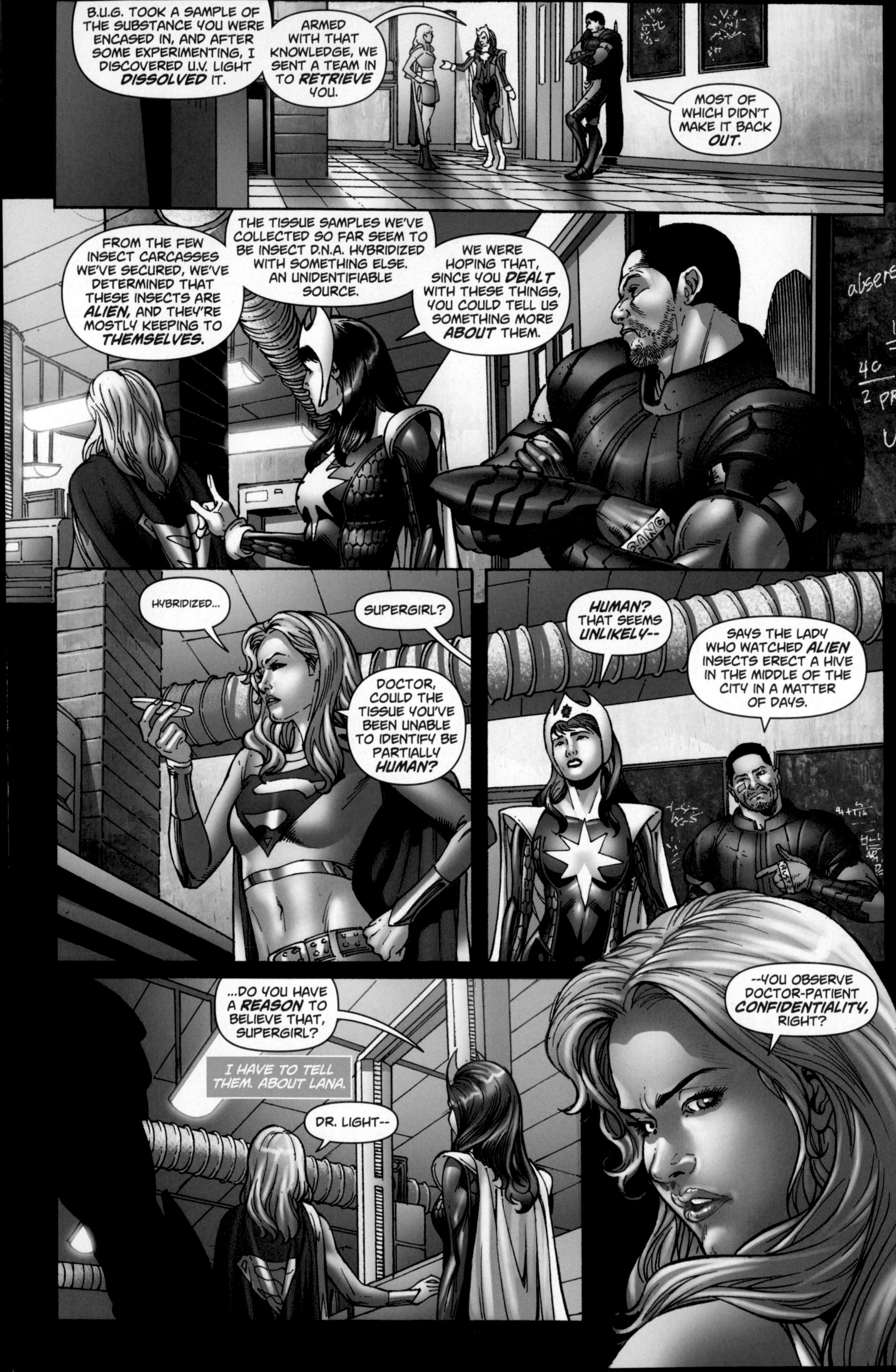
B.U.G. TOOK A SAMPLE OF THE SUBSTANCE YOU WERE ENCASED IN, AND AFTER SOME EXPERIMENTING, I DISCOVERED U.V. LIGHT DISSOLVED IT.
ARMED WITH THAT KNOWLEDGE, WE SENT A TEAM IN TO RETRIEVE YOU.
MOST OF WHICH DIDN'T MAKE IT BACK OUT.
FROM THE FEW INSECT CARCASSES WE'VE SECURED, WE'VE DETERMINED THAT THESE INSECTS ARE ALIEN, AND THEY'RE MOSTLY KEEPING TO THEMSELVES.
THE TISSUE SAMPLES WE'VE COLLECTED SO FAR SEEM TO BE INSECT D.N.A. HYBRIDIZED WITH SOMETHING ELSE. AN UNIDENTIFIABLE SOURCE.
WE WERE HOPING THAT, SINCE YOU DEALT WITH THESE THINGS, YOU COULD TELL US SOMETHING MORE ABOUT THEM.
HYBRIDIZED...
SUPERGIRL?
DOCTOR, COULD THE TISSUE YOU'VE BEEN UNABLE TO IDENTIFY BE PARTIALLY HUMAN?
HUMAN? THAT SEEMS UNLIKELY--
SAYS THE LADY WHO WATCHED ALIEN INSECTS ERECT A HIVE IN THE MIDDLE OF THE CITY IN A MATTER OF DAYS.
...DO YOU HAVE A REASON TO BELIEVE THAT, SUPERGIRL?
I HAVE TO TELL THEM. ABOUT LANA.
DR. LIGHT--
--YOU OBSERVE DOCTOR-PATIENT CONFIDENTIALITY, RIGHT?

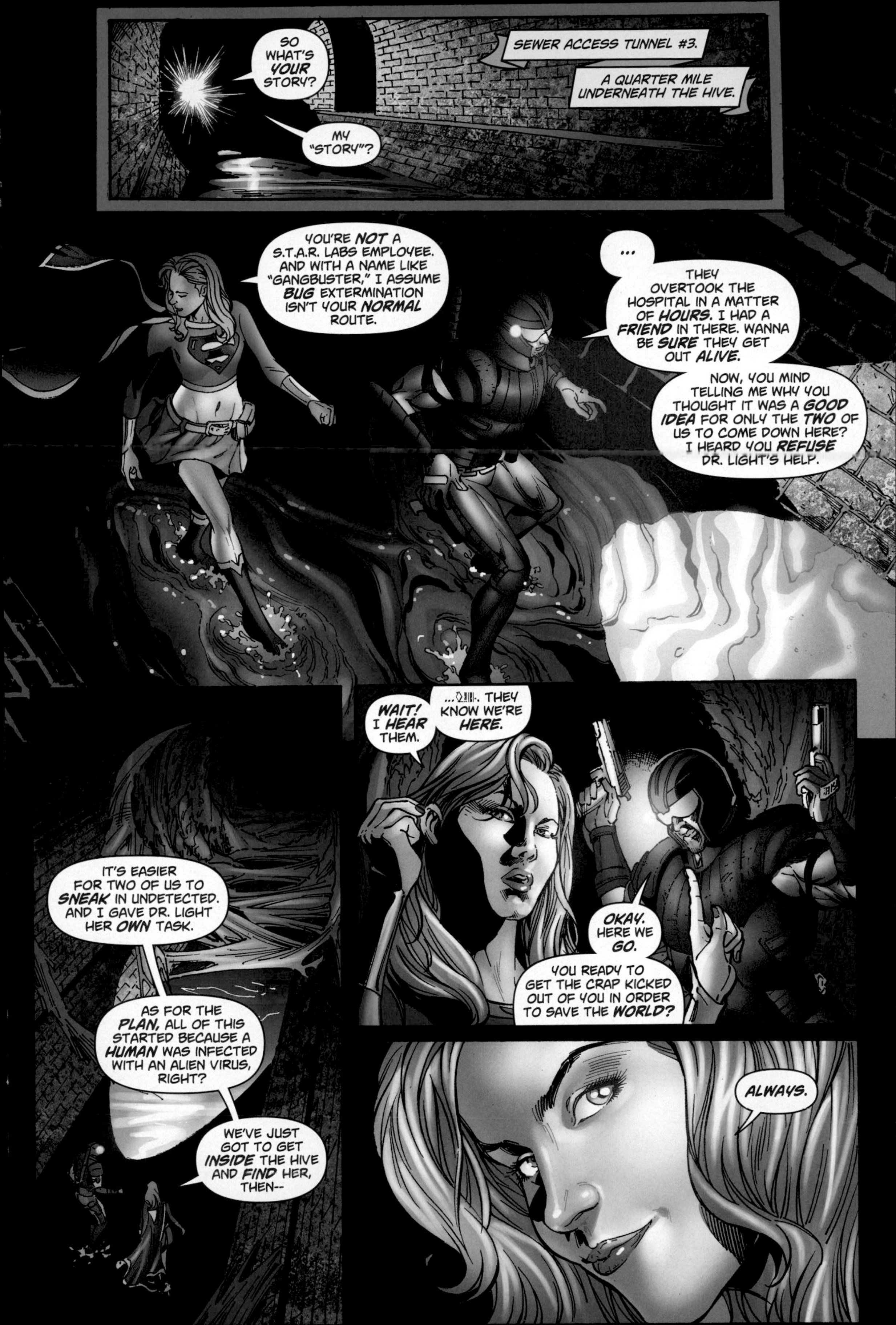
SEWER ACCESS TUNNEL #3.
A QUARTER MILE UNDERNEATH THE HIVE.
SO WHAT'S *YOUR* STORY?
MY "STORY"?
YOU'RE *NOT* A S.T.A.R. LABS EMPLOYEE. AND WITH A NAME LIKE "GANGBUSTER," I ASSUME *BUG* EXTERMINATION ISN'T YOUR *NORMAL* ROUTE.
...
THEY OVERTOOK THE HOSPITAL IN A MATTER OF *HOURS.* I HAD A *FRIEND* IN THERE. WANNA BE *SURE* THEY GET OUT *ALIVE.*
NOW, YOU MIND TELLING ME WHY YOU THOUGHT IT WAS A *GOOD IDEA* FOR ONLY THE *TWO* OF US TO COME DOWN HERE? I HEARD YOU *REFUSE* DR. LIGHT'S HELP.
IT'S EASIER FOR TWO OF US TO *SNEAK* IN UNDETECTED. AND I GAVE DR. LIGHT HER *OWN* TASK.
AS FOR THE *PLAN,* ALL OF THIS STARTED BECAUSE A *HUMAN* WAS INFECTED WITH AN ALIEN VIRUS, RIGHT?
WE'VE JUST GOT TO GET *INSIDE* THE HIVE AND *FIND* HER, THEN--
WAIT! I *HEAR* THEM.
... . THEY KNOW WE'RE *HERE.*
OKAY. HERE WE *GO.*
YOU READY TO GET THE CRAP KICKED OUT OF YOU IN ORDER TO SAVE THE *WORLD?*
ALWAYS.

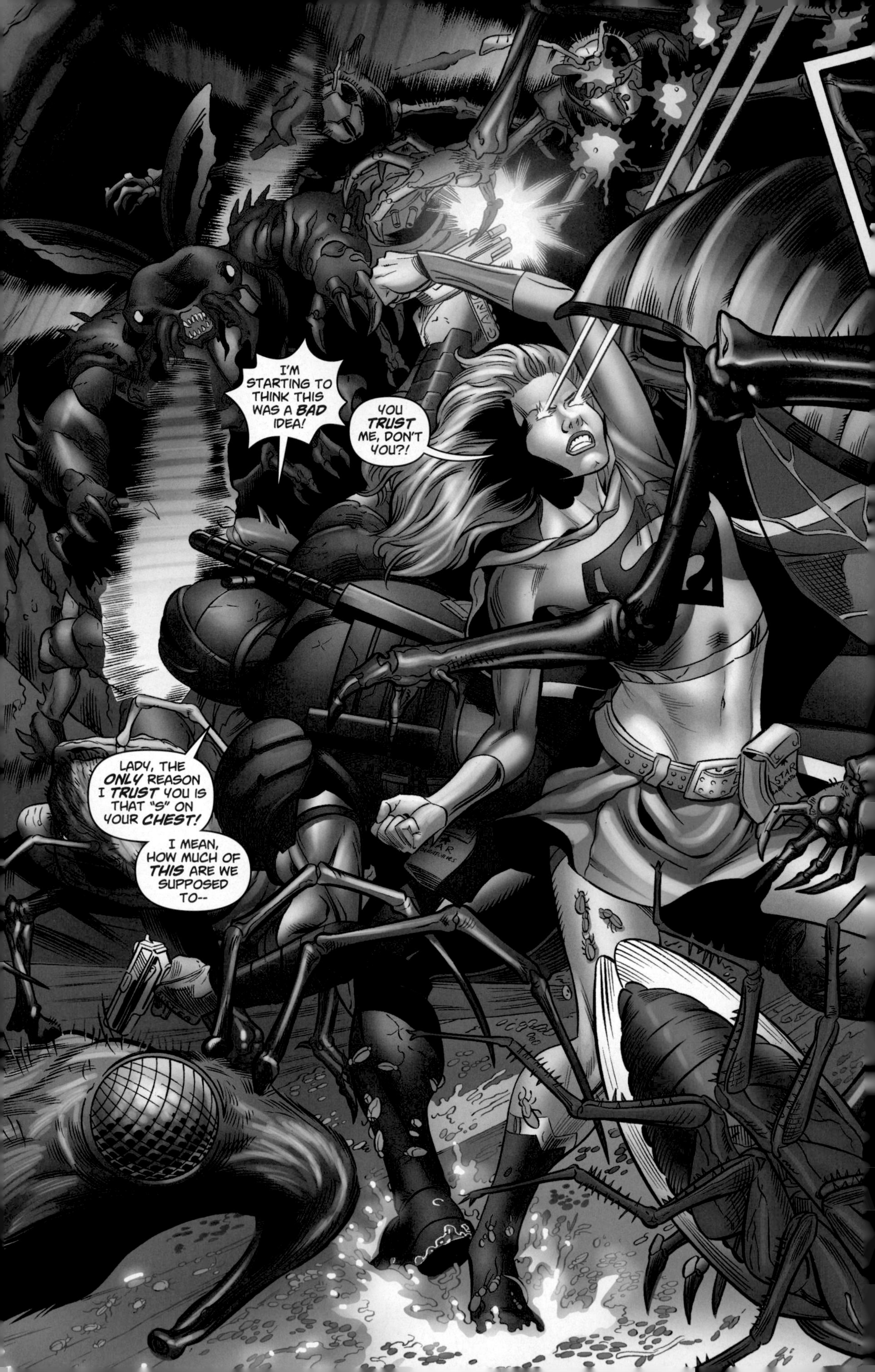

I'M STARTING TO THINK THIS WAS A BAD IDEA!
YOU TRUST ME, DON'T YOU?!
LADY, THE ONLY REASON I TRUST YOU IS THAT "S" ON YOUR CHEST!
I MEAN, HOW MUCH OF THIS ARE WE SUPPOSED TO--

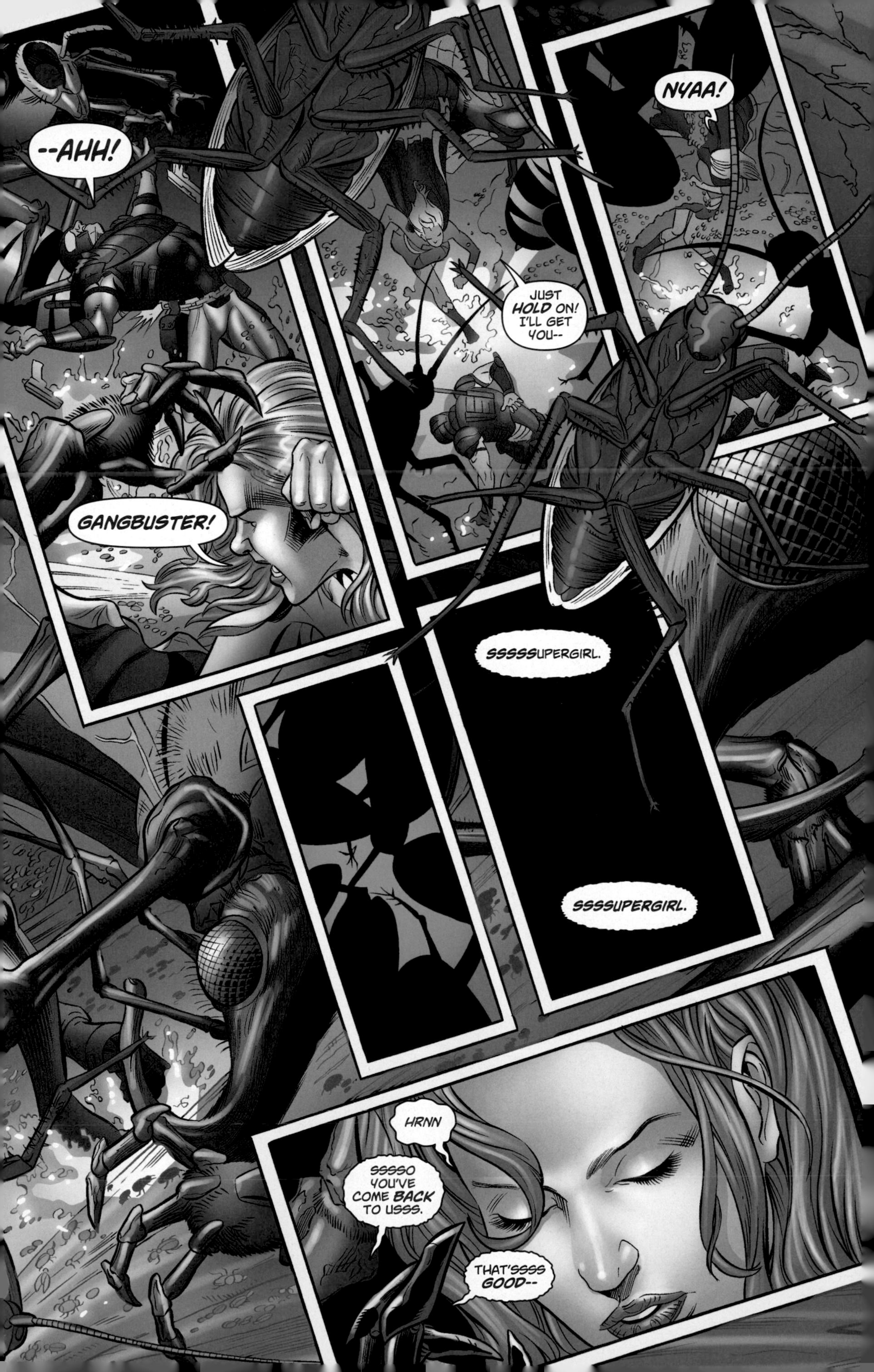
--AHH!
NYAA!
JUST HOLD ON! I'LL GET YOU--
GANGBUSTER!
SSSSSUPERGIRL.
SSSSUPERGIRL.
HRNN
SSSSO YOU'VE COME BACK TO USSS.
THAT'SSSS GOOD--

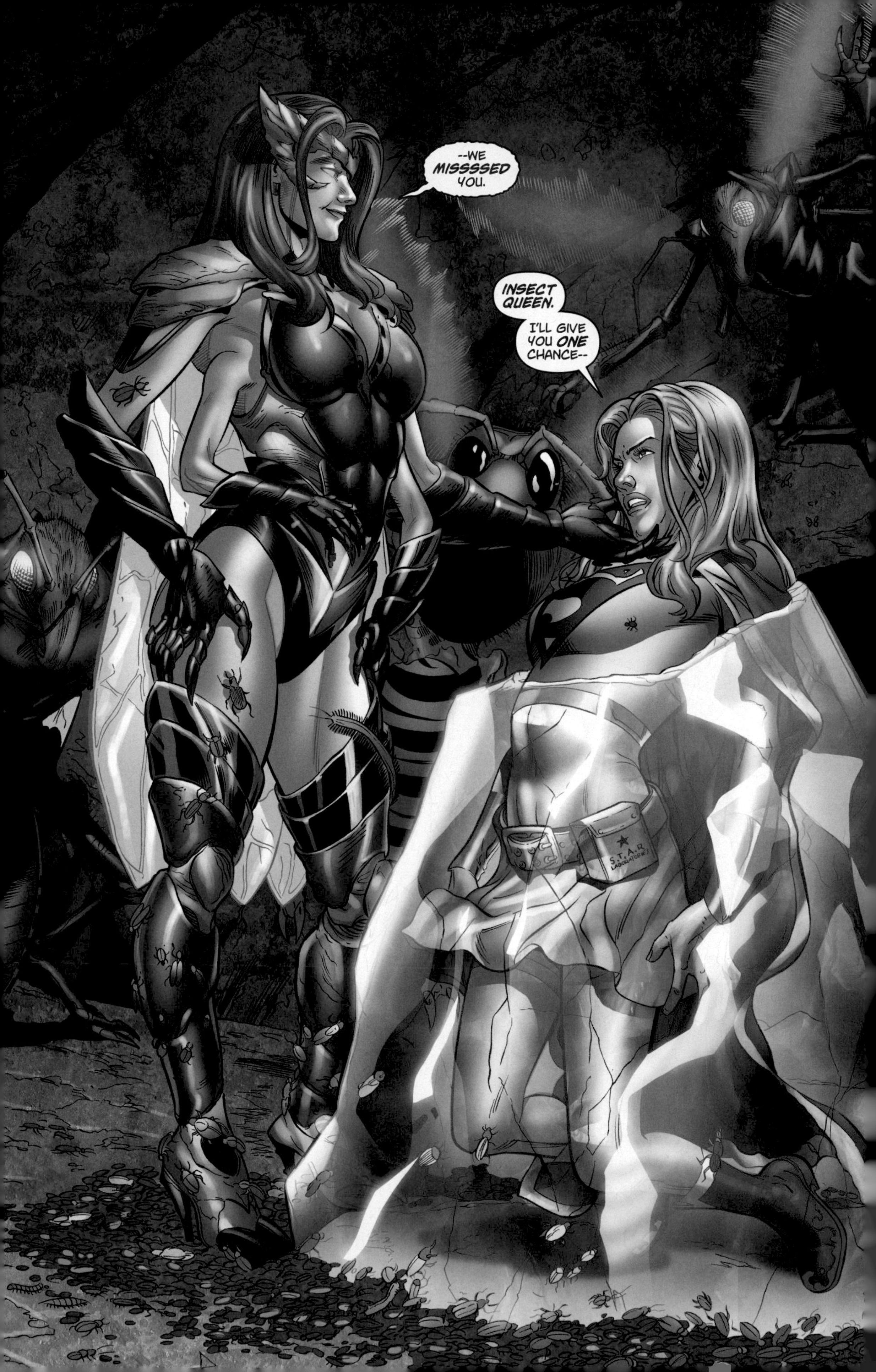
--WE MISSSSED YOU.
INSECT QUEEN.
I'LL GIVE YOU ONE CHANCE--
S.T.A.R. LABORATORIES

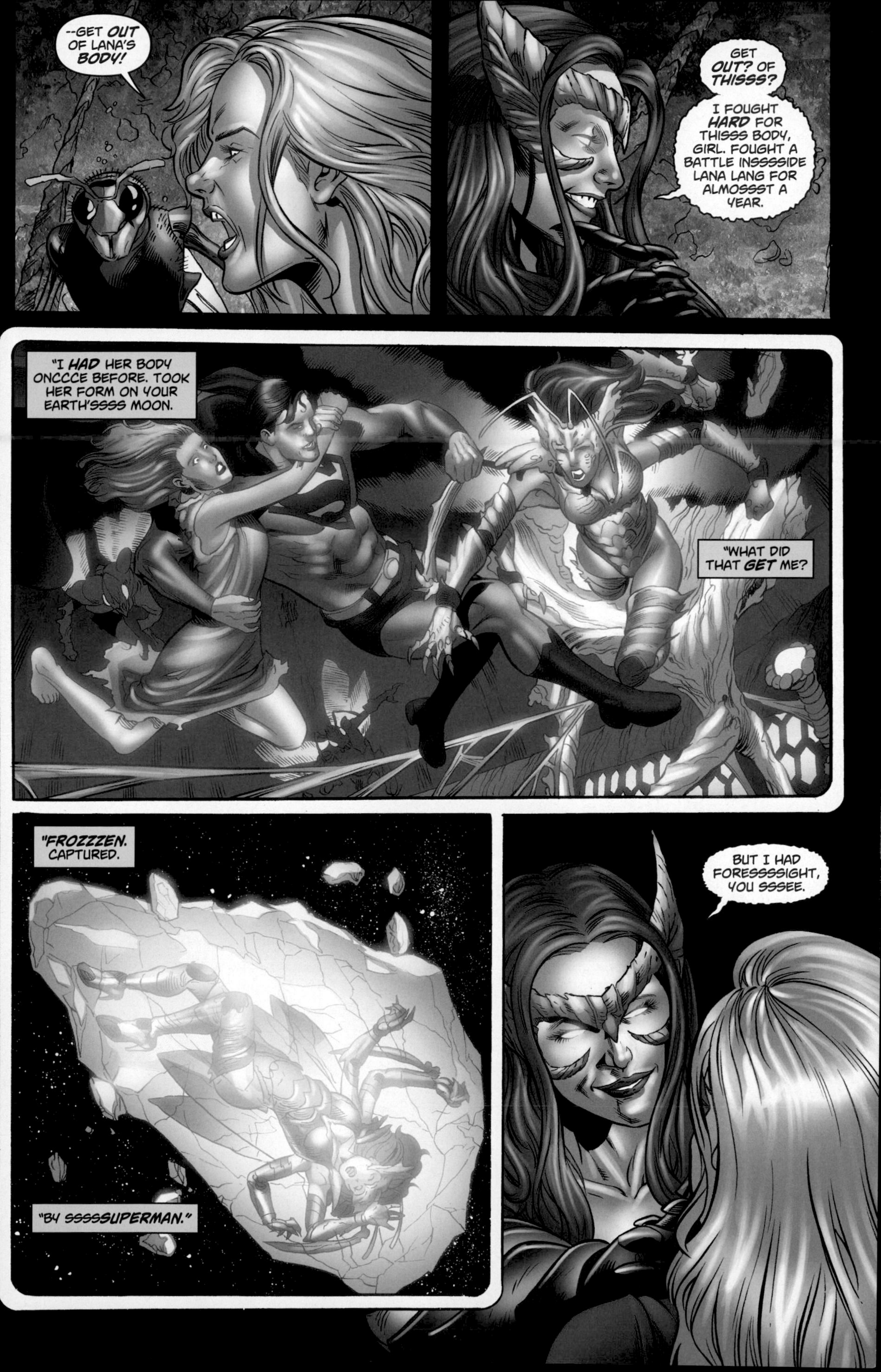
--GET OUT OF LANA'S BODY!
GET OUT? OF THISSS?
I FOUGHT HARD FOR THISSS BODY, GIRL. FOUGHT A BATTLE INSSSSIDE LANA LANG FOR ALMOSSST A YEAR.
"I HAD HER BODY ONCCCE BEFORE. TOOK HER FORM ON YOUR EARTH'SSSS MOON.
"WHAT DID THAT GET ME?
"FROZZZEN. CAPTURED.
"BY SSSSSUPERMAN."
BUT I HAD FORESSSSIGHT, YOU SSSEE.

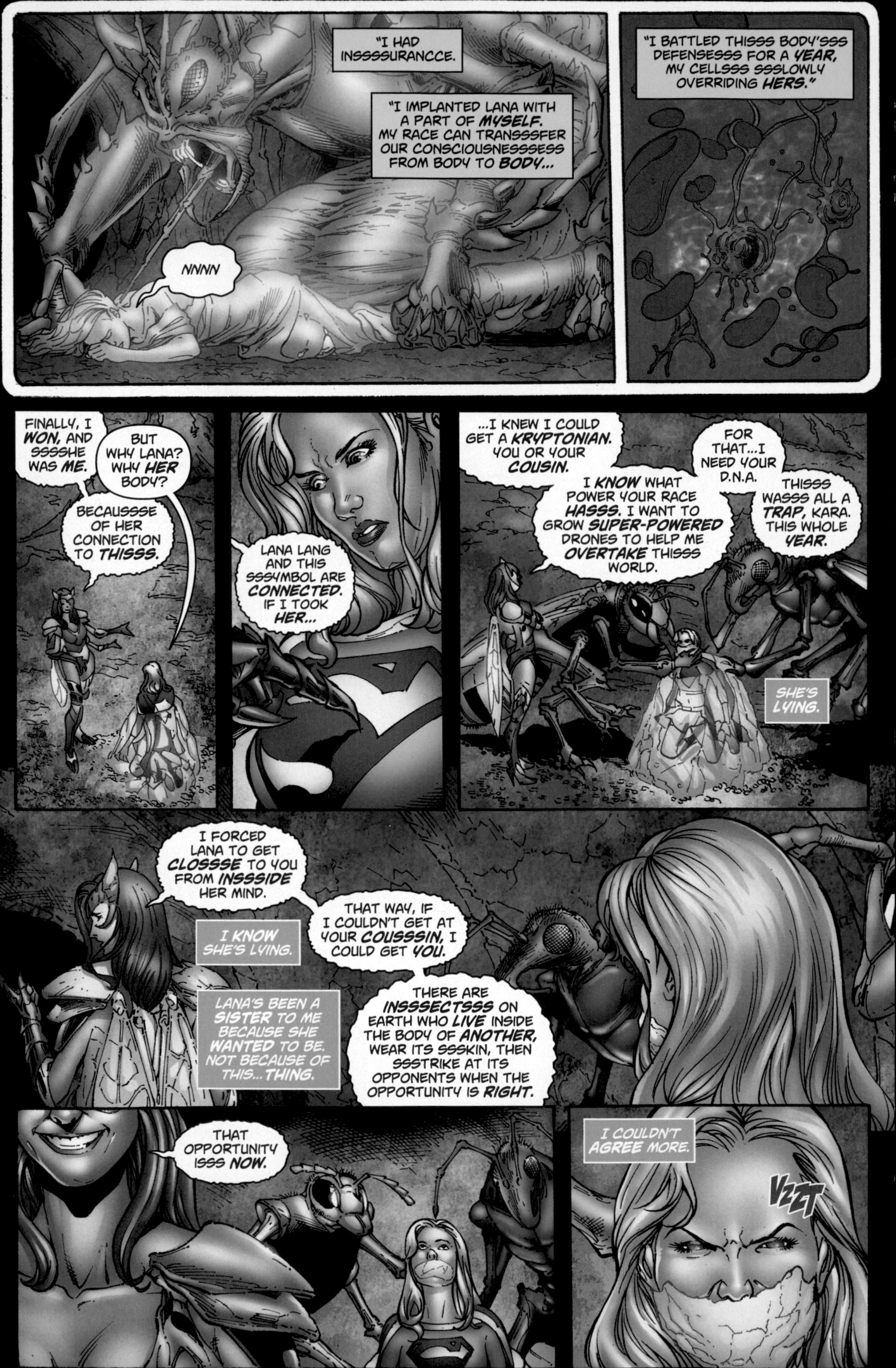

"I HAD INSSSSURANCCE.
"I IMPLANTED LANA WITH A PART OF MYSELF. MY RACE CAN TRANSSSFER OUR CONSCIOUSNESSSESS FROM BODY TO BODY...
NNNN
"I BATTLED THISSS BODY'SSS DEFENSESSS FOR A YEAR, MY CELLSSS SSSLOWLY OVERRIDING HERS."
FINALLY, I WON, AND SSSSHE WAS ME.
BUT WHY LANA? WHY HER BODY?
BECAUSSSE OF HER CONNECTION TO THISSS.
LANA LANG AND THIS SSSYMBOL ARE CONNECTED. IF I TOOK HER...
...I KNEW I COULD GET A KRYPTONIAN. YOU OR YOUR COUSIN.
FOR THAT...I NEED YOUR D.N.A.
I KNOW WHAT POWER YOUR RACE HASSS. I WANT TO GROW SUPER-POWERED DRONES TO HELP ME OVERTAKE THISSS WORLD.
THISSS WASSS ALL A TRAP, KARA. THIS WHOLE YEAR.
SHE'S LYING.
I FORCED LANA TO GET CLOSSSE TO YOU FROM INSSSIDE HER MIND.
I KNOW SHE'S LYING.
THAT WAY, IF I COULDN'T GET AT YOUR COUSSSIN, I COULD GET YOU.
LANA'S BEEN A SISTER TO ME BECAUSE SHE WANTED TO BE. NOT BECAUSE OF THIS...THING.
THERE ARE INSSSECTSSS ON EARTH WHO LIVE INSIDE THE BODY OF ANOTHER, WEAR ITS SSSKIN, THEN SSSTRIKE AT ITS OPPONENTS WHEN THE OPPORTUNITY IS RIGHT.
THAT OPPORTUNITY ISSS NOW.
I COULDN'T AGREE MORE.
VZZT

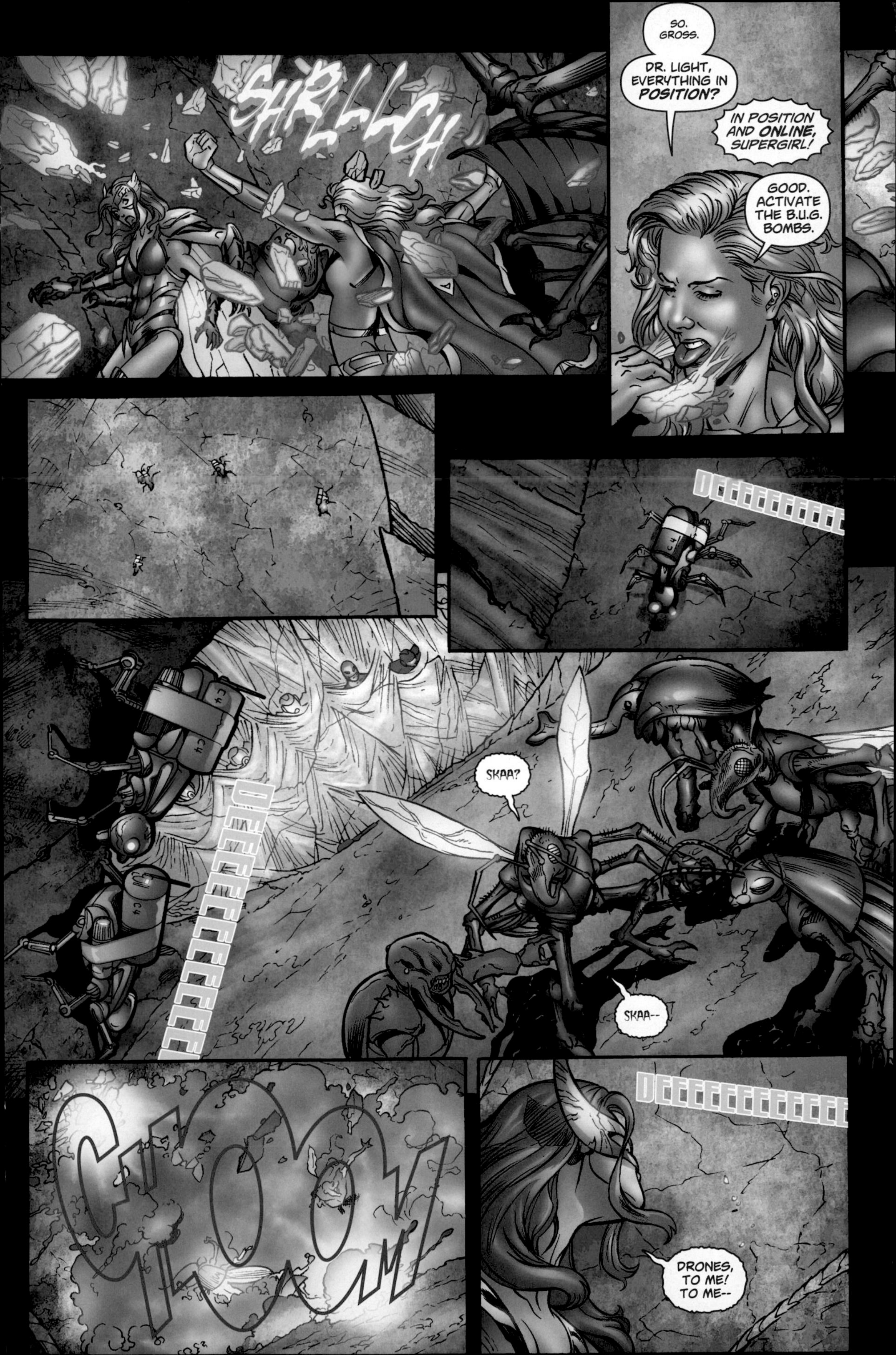
SHRLLLCH
SO. GROSS.
DR. LIGHT, EVERYTHING IN POSITION?
IN POSITION AND ONLINE, SUPERGIRL!
GOOD. ACTIVATE THE B.U.G. BOMBS.
DEEEEEEEEEEEE
DEEEEEEEEEEEEEEE
SKAA?
SKAA--
CHOOOM
DEEEEEEEEEEEEE
DRONES, TO ME! TO ME--

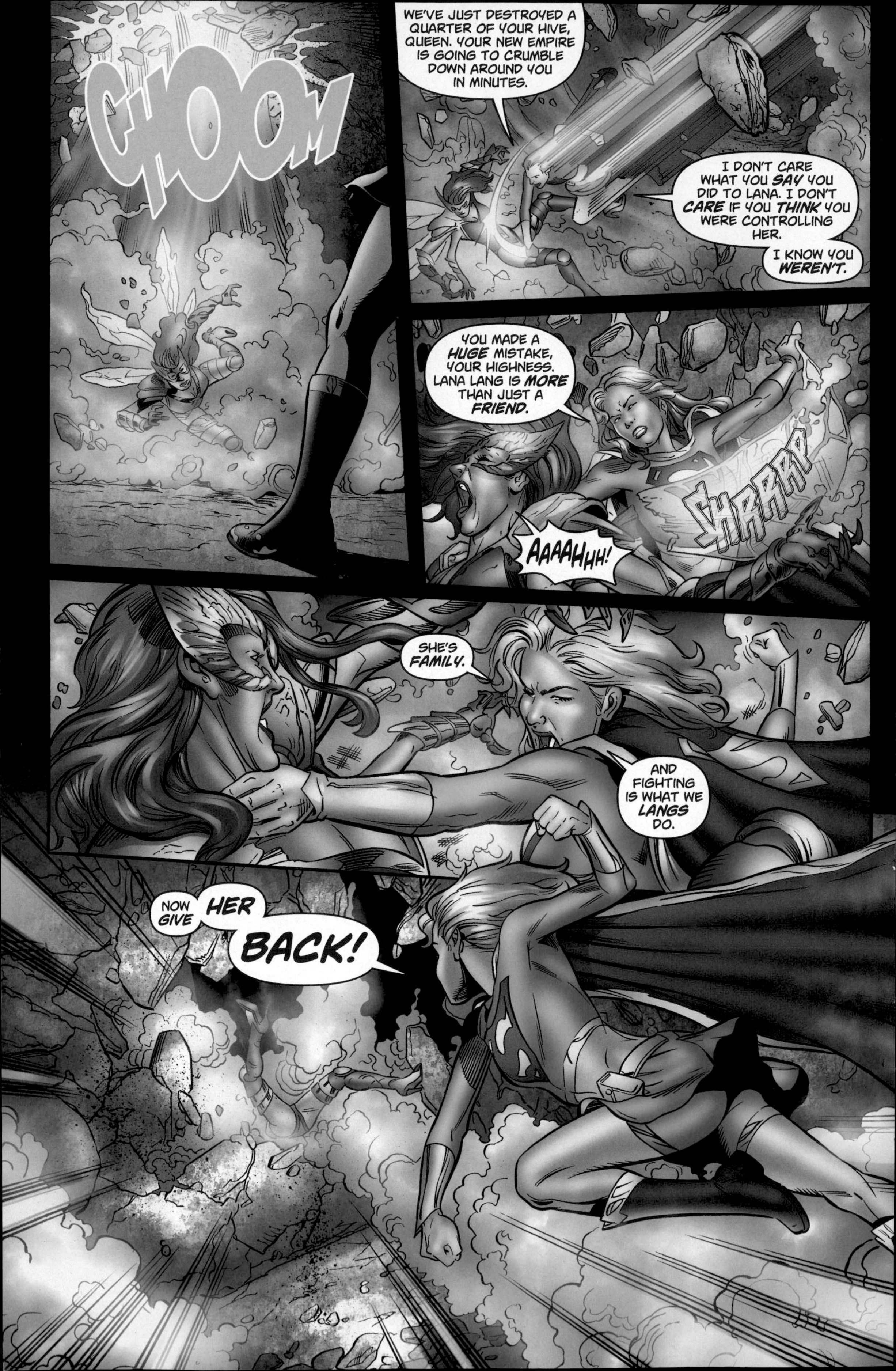
CHOOM
WE'VE JUST DESTROYED A QUARTER OF YOUR HIVE, QUEEN. YOUR NEW EMPIRE IS GOING TO CRUMBLE DOWN AROUND YOU IN MINUTES.
I DON'T CARE WHAT YOU SAY YOU DID TO LANA. I DON'T CARE IF YOU THINK YOU WERE CONTROLLING HER.
I KNOW YOU WEREN'T.
YOU MADE A HUGE MISTAKE, YOUR HIGHNESS. LANA LANG IS MORE THAN JUST A FRIEND.
SHRRRP
AAAAHHH!
SHE'S FAMILY.
AND FIGHTING IS WHAT WE LANGS DO.
NOW GIVE HER
BACK!

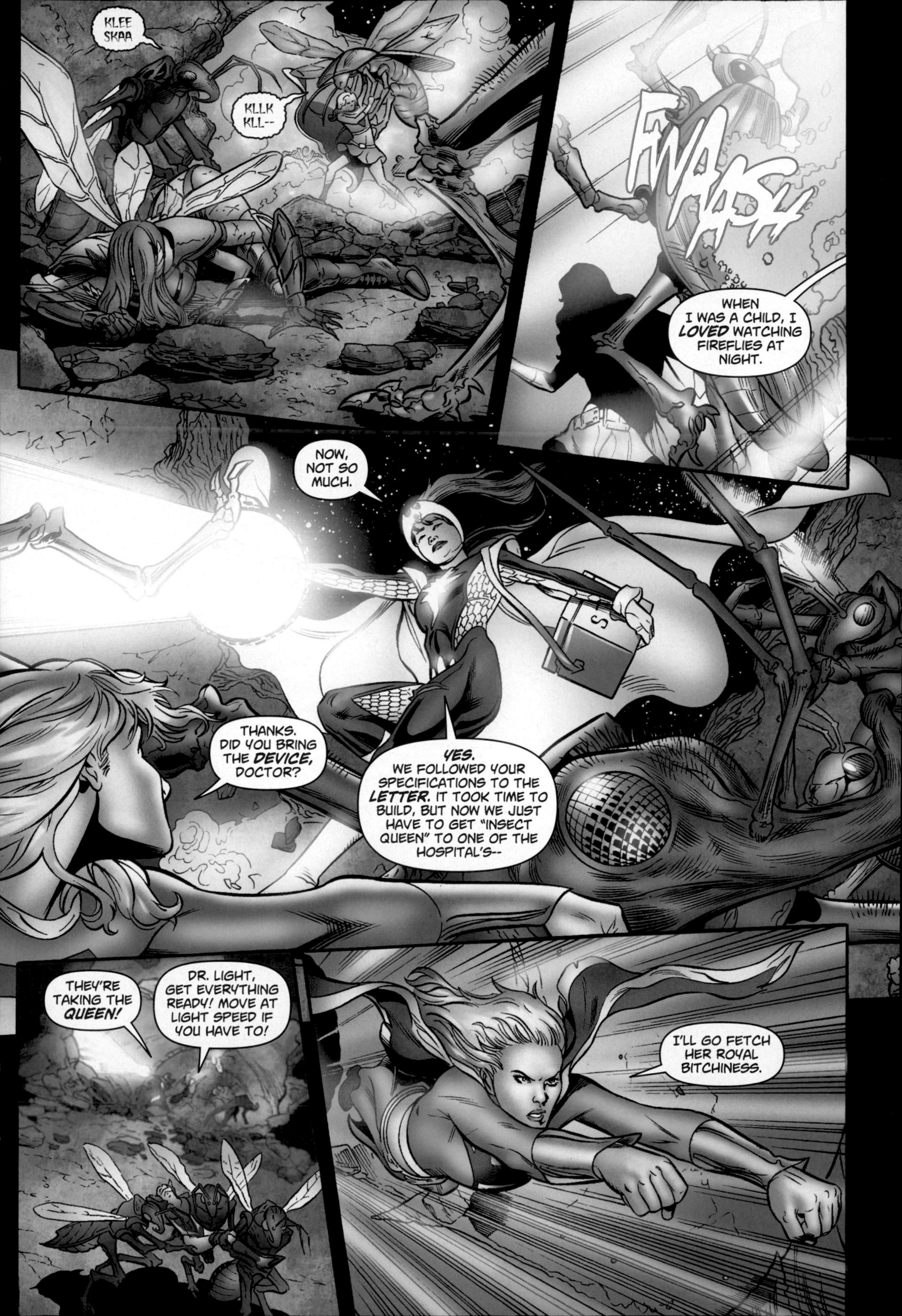

KLEE SKAA
KLLK KLL--
FWASH
WHEN I WAS A CHILD, I *LOVED* WATCHING FIREFLIES AT NIGHT.
NOW, NOT SO MUCH.
THANKS. DID YOU BRING THE *DEVICE*, DOCTOR?
YES. WE FOLLOWED YOUR SPECIFICATIONS TO THE *LETTER*. IT TOOK TIME TO BUILD, BUT NOW WE JUST HAVE TO GET "INSECT QUEEN" TO ONE OF THE HOSPITAL'S--
THEY'RE TAKING THE *QUEEN!*
DR. LIGHT, GET EVERYTHING READY! MOVE AT LIGHT SPEED IF YOU HAVE TO!
I'LL GO FETCH HER ROYAL BITCHINESS.

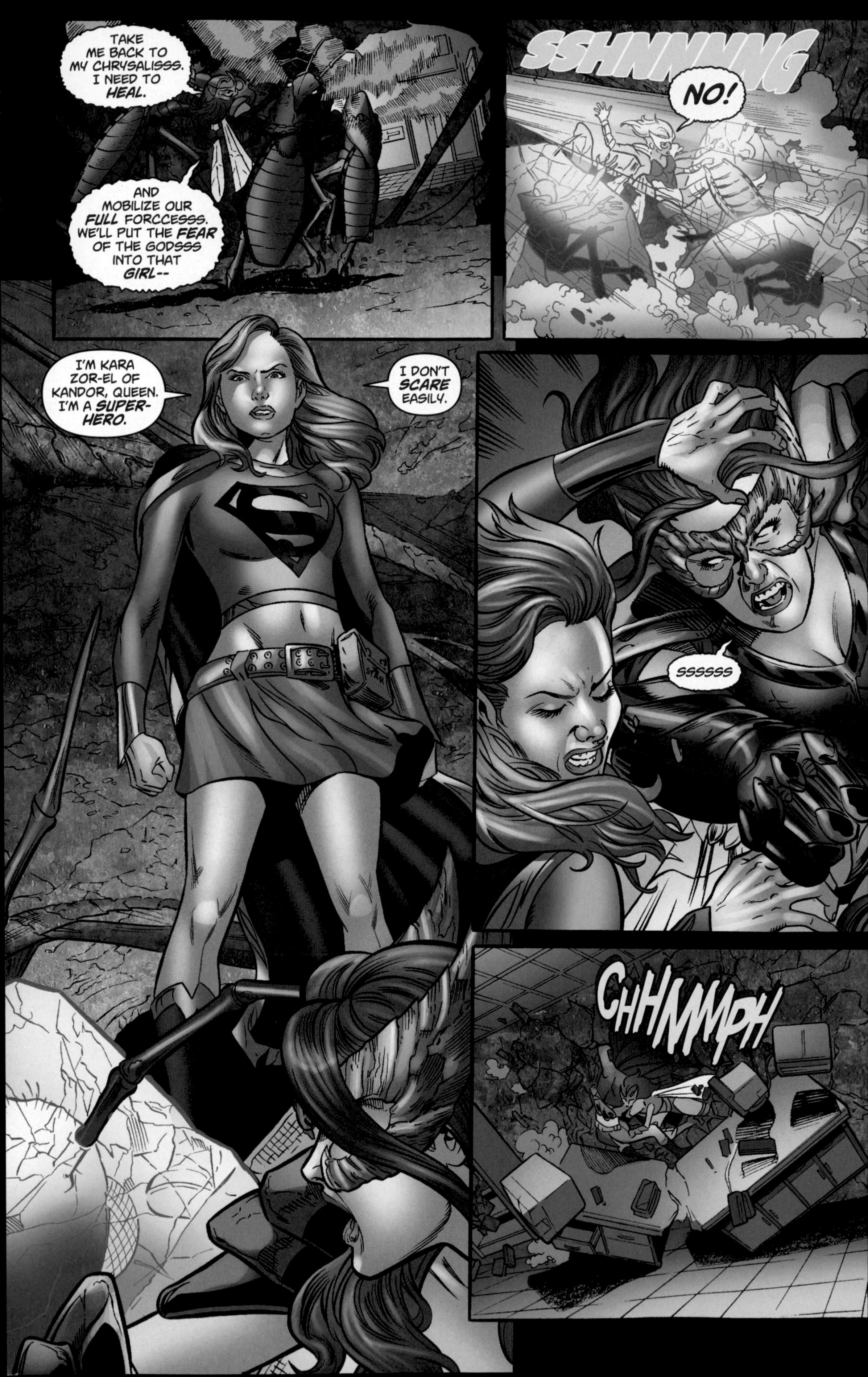
TAKE ME BACK TO MY CHRYSALISSS. I NEED TO HEAL.
AND MOBILIZE OUR FULL FORCCESSS. WE'LL PUT THE FEAR OF THE GODSSS INTO THAT GIRL--
SSHNNNNG
NO!
I'M KARA ZOR-EL OF KANDOR, QUEEN. I'M A SUPER-HERO.
I DON'T SCARE EASILY.
SSSSSS
CHHMMPH

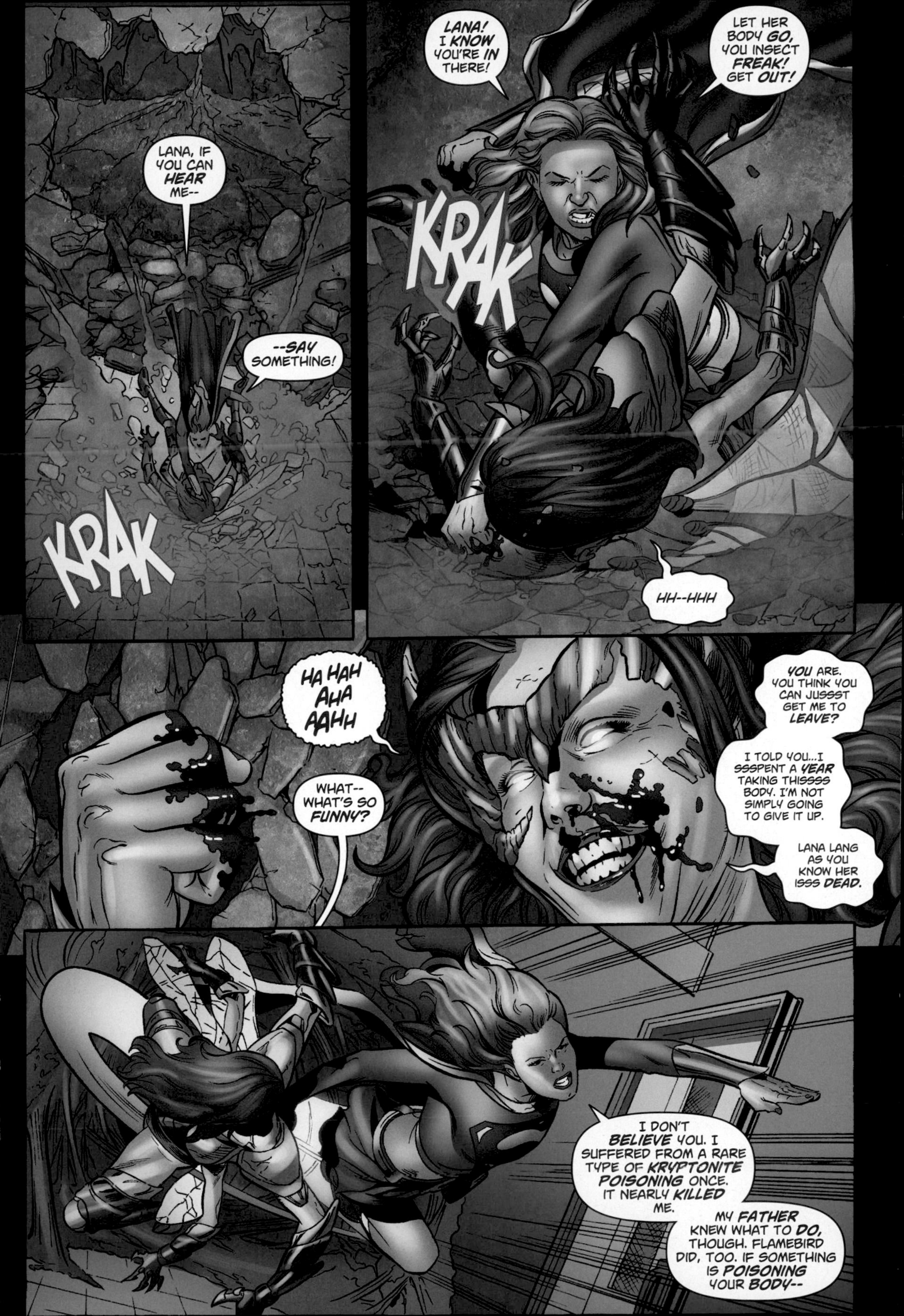
LANA, IF YOU CAN HEAR ME--
--SAY SOMETHING!
KRAK
LANA! I KNOW YOU'RE IN THERE!
LET HER BODY GO, YOU INSECT FREAK! GET OUT!
KRAK
HH--HHH
HA HAH AHA AAHH
WHAT-- WHAT'S SO FUNNY?
YOU ARE. YOU THINK YOU CAN JUSSST GET ME TO LEAVE?
I TOLD YOU...I SSSPENT A YEAR TAKING THISSSS BODY. I'M NOT SIMPLY GOING TO GIVE IT UP.
LANA LANG AS YOU KNOW HER ISSS DEAD.
I DON'T BELIEVE YOU. I SUFFERED FROM A RARE TYPE OF KRYPTONITE POISONING ONCE. IT NEARLY KILLED ME.
MY FATHER KNEW WHAT TO DO, THOUGH. FLAMEBIRD DID, TOO. IF SOMETHING IS POISONING YOUR BODY--

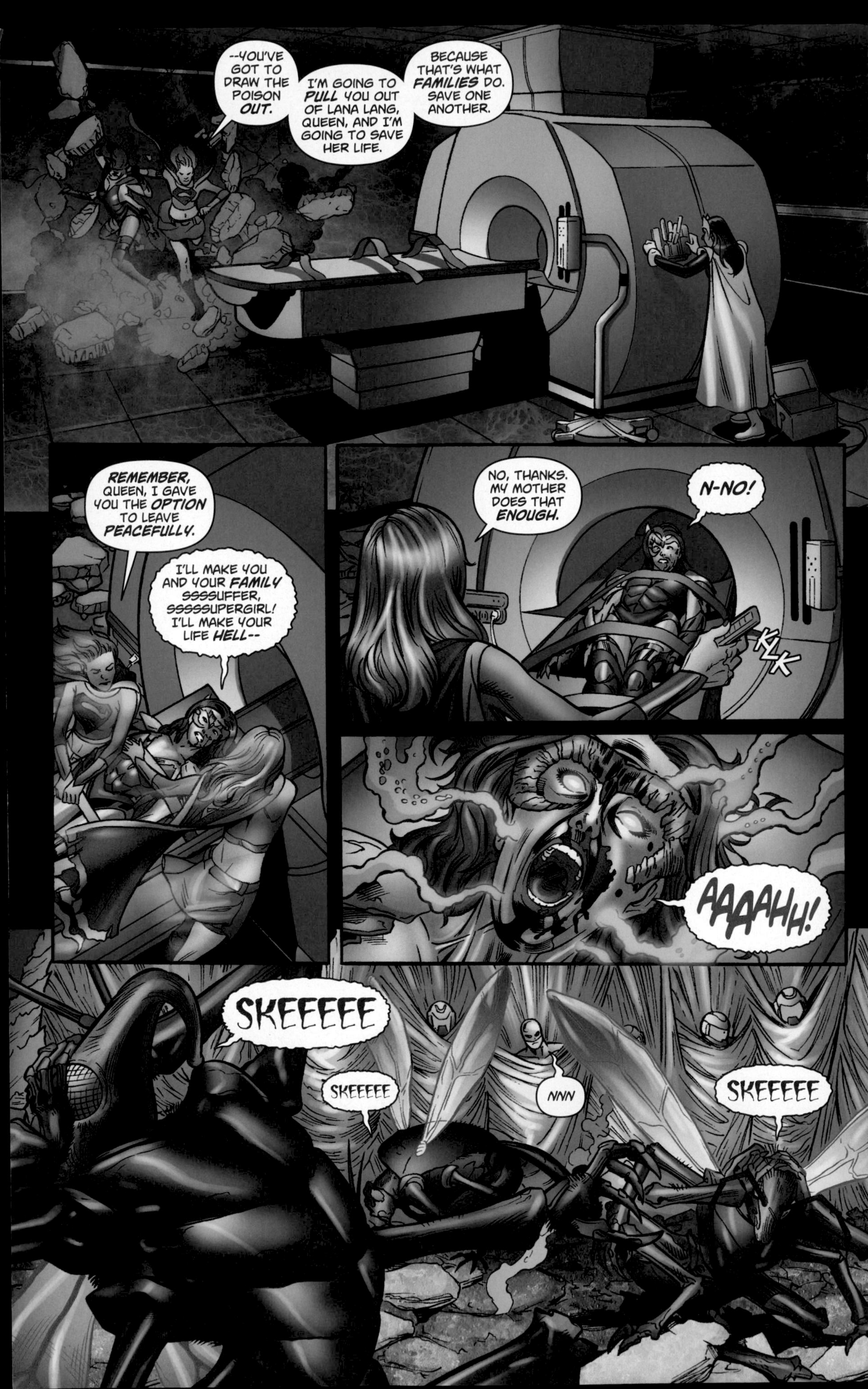
--YOU'VE GOT TO DRAW THE POISON OUT.
I'M GOING TO PULL YOU OUT OF LANA LANG, QUEEN, AND I'M GOING TO SAVE HER LIFE.
BECAUSE THAT'S WHAT FAMILIES DO. SAVE ONE ANOTHER.
REMEMBER, QUEEN, I GAVE YOU THE OPTION TO LEAVE PEACEFULLY.
I'LL MAKE YOU AND YOUR FAMILY SSSSUFFER, SSSSSUPERGIRL! I'LL MAKE YOUR LIFE HELL--
NO, THANKS. MY MOTHER DOES THAT ENOUGH.
N-NO!
KLK
AAAAHH!
SKEEEEE
SKEEEEE
NNN
SKEEEEE

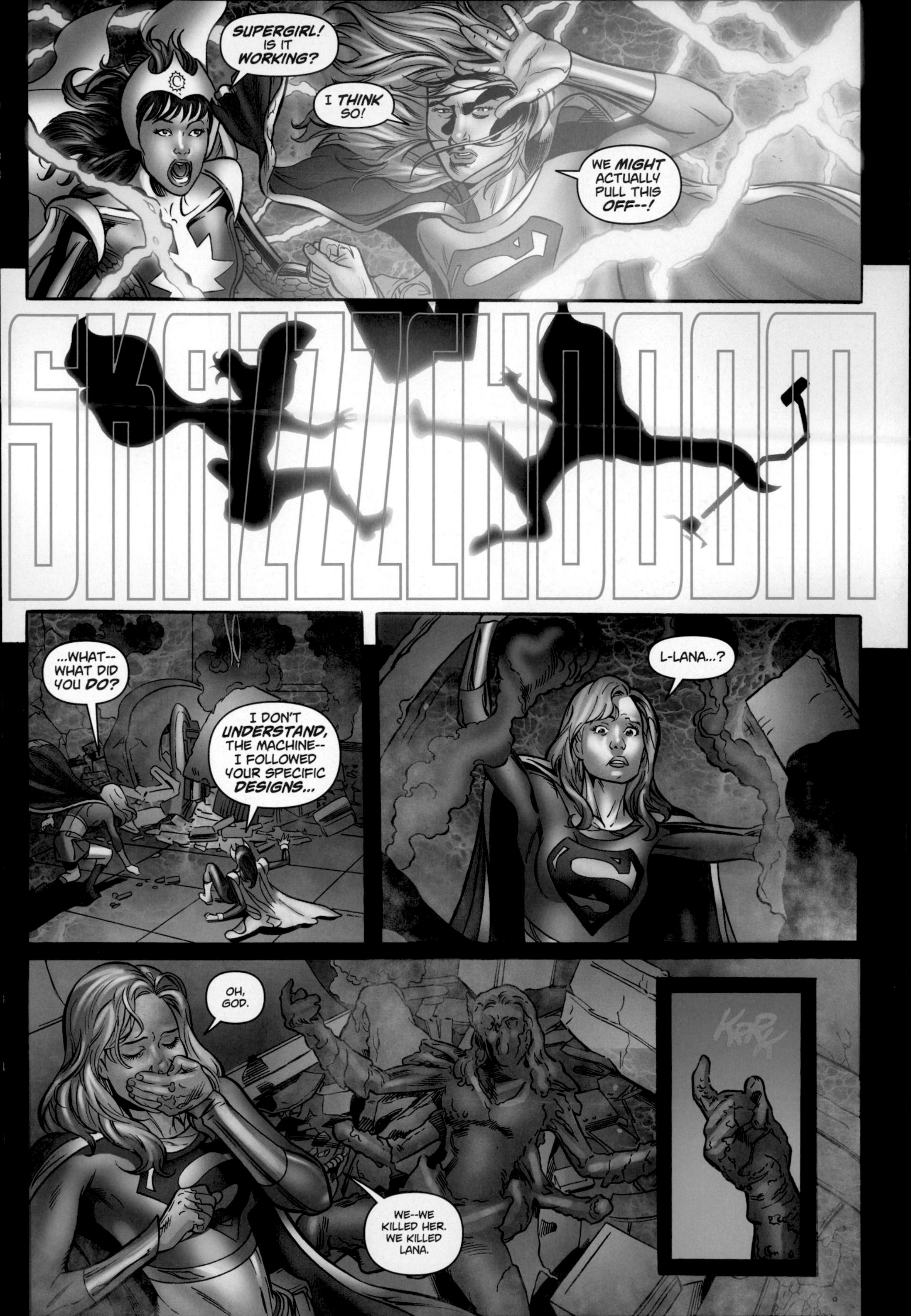
SUPERGIRL! IS IT WORKING?
I THINK SO!
WE MIGHT ACTUALLY PULL THIS OFF--!
SKZZZZCHOOOM
...WHAT-- WHAT DID YOU DO?
I DON'T UNDERSTAND, THE MACHINE-- I FOLLOWED YOUR SPECIFIC DESIGNS...
L-LANA...?
OH, GOD.
WE--WE KILLED HER. WE KILLED LANA.
KERR

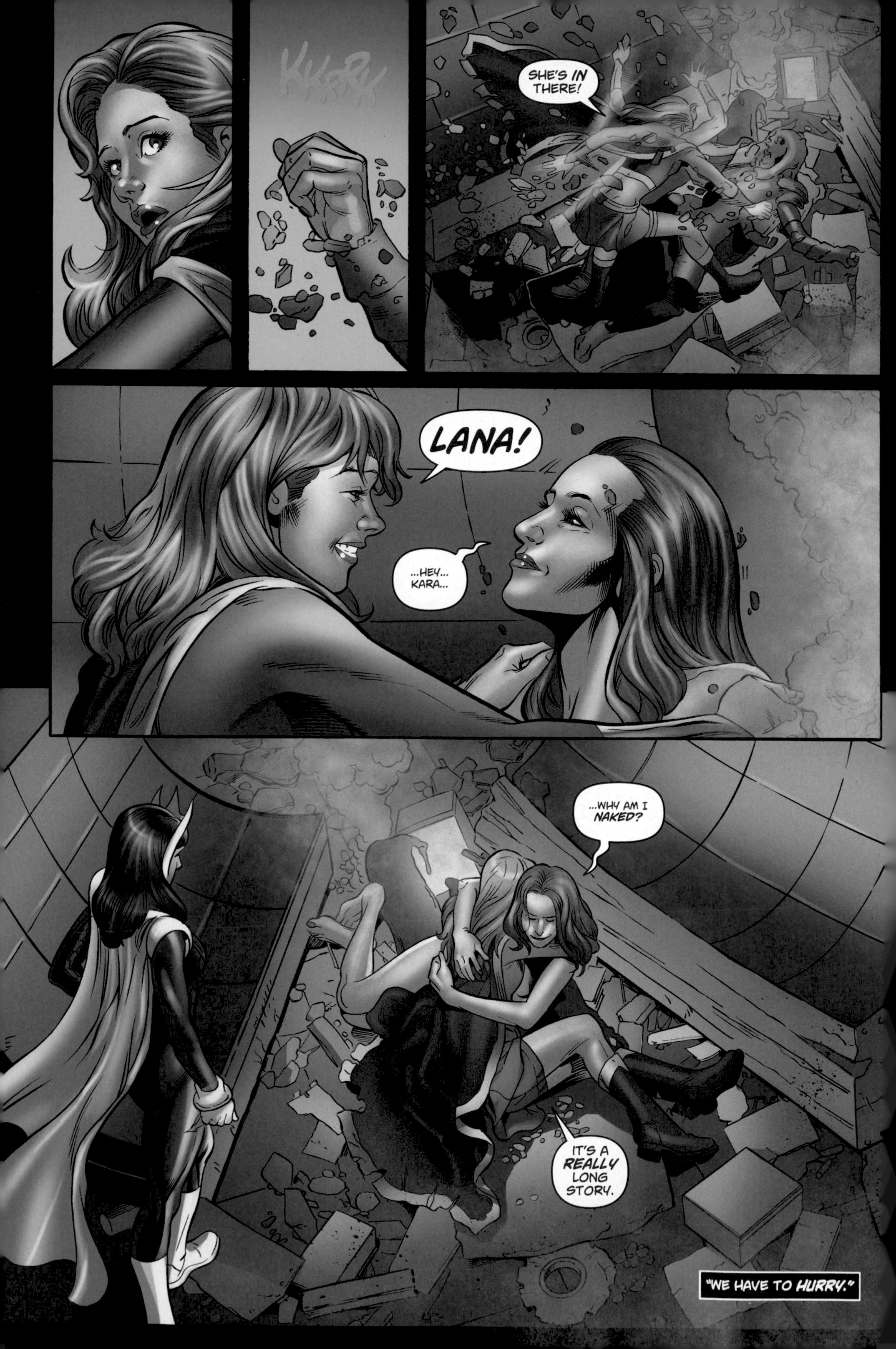
KKRRK
SHE'S IN THERE!
LANA!
...HEY... KARA...
...WHY AM I NAKED?
IT'S A REALLY LONG STORY.
"WE HAVE TO HURRY."

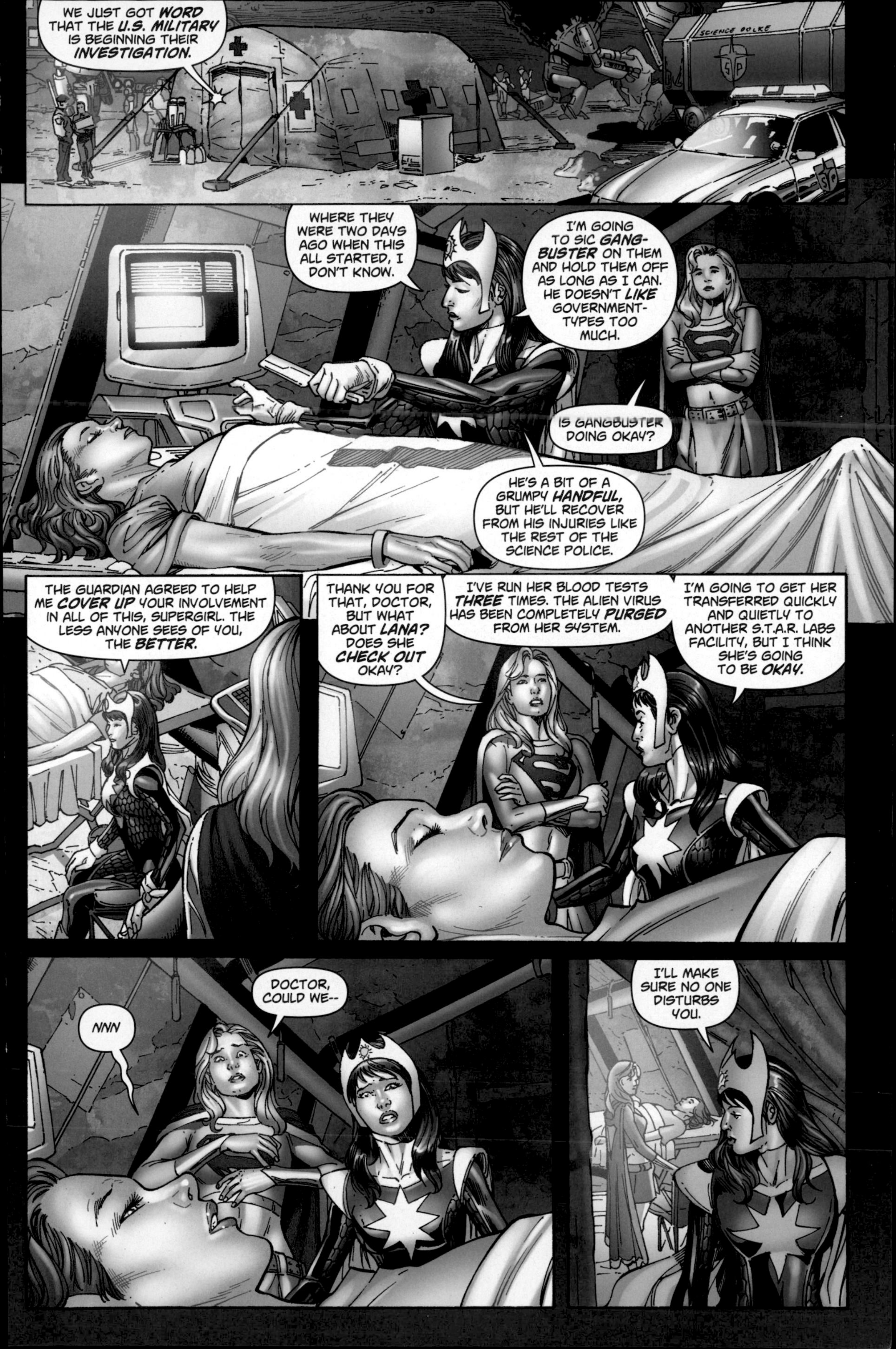
WE JUST GOT WORD THAT THE U.S. MILITARY IS BEGINNING THEIR INVESTIGATION.
SCIENCE POLICE
WHERE THEY WERE TWO DAYS AGO WHEN THIS ALL STARTED, I DON'T KNOW.
I'M GOING TO SIC GANG-BUSTER ON THEM AND HOLD THEM OFF AS LONG AS I CAN. HE DOESN'T LIKE GOVERNMENT-TYPES TOO MUCH.
IS GANGBUSTER DOING OKAY?
HE'S A BIT OF A GRUMPY HANDFUL, BUT HE'LL RECOVER FROM HIS INJURIES LIKE THE REST OF THE SCIENCE POLICE.
THE GUARDIAN AGREED TO HELP ME COVER UP YOUR INVOLVEMENT IN ALL OF THIS, SUPERGIRL. THE LESS ANYONE SEES OF YOU, THE BETTER.
THANK YOU FOR THAT, DOCTOR, BUT WHAT ABOUT LANA? DOES SHE CHECK OUT OKAY?
I'VE RUN HER BLOOD TESTS THREE TIMES. THE ALIEN VIRUS HAS BEEN COMPLETELY PURGED FROM HER SYSTEM.
I'M GOING TO GET HER TRANSFERRED QUICKLY AND QUIETLY TO ANOTHER S.T.A.R. LABS FACILITY, BUT I THINK SHE'S GOING TO BE OKAY.
NNN
DOCTOR, COULD WE--
I'LL MAKE SURE NO ONE DISTURBS YOU.

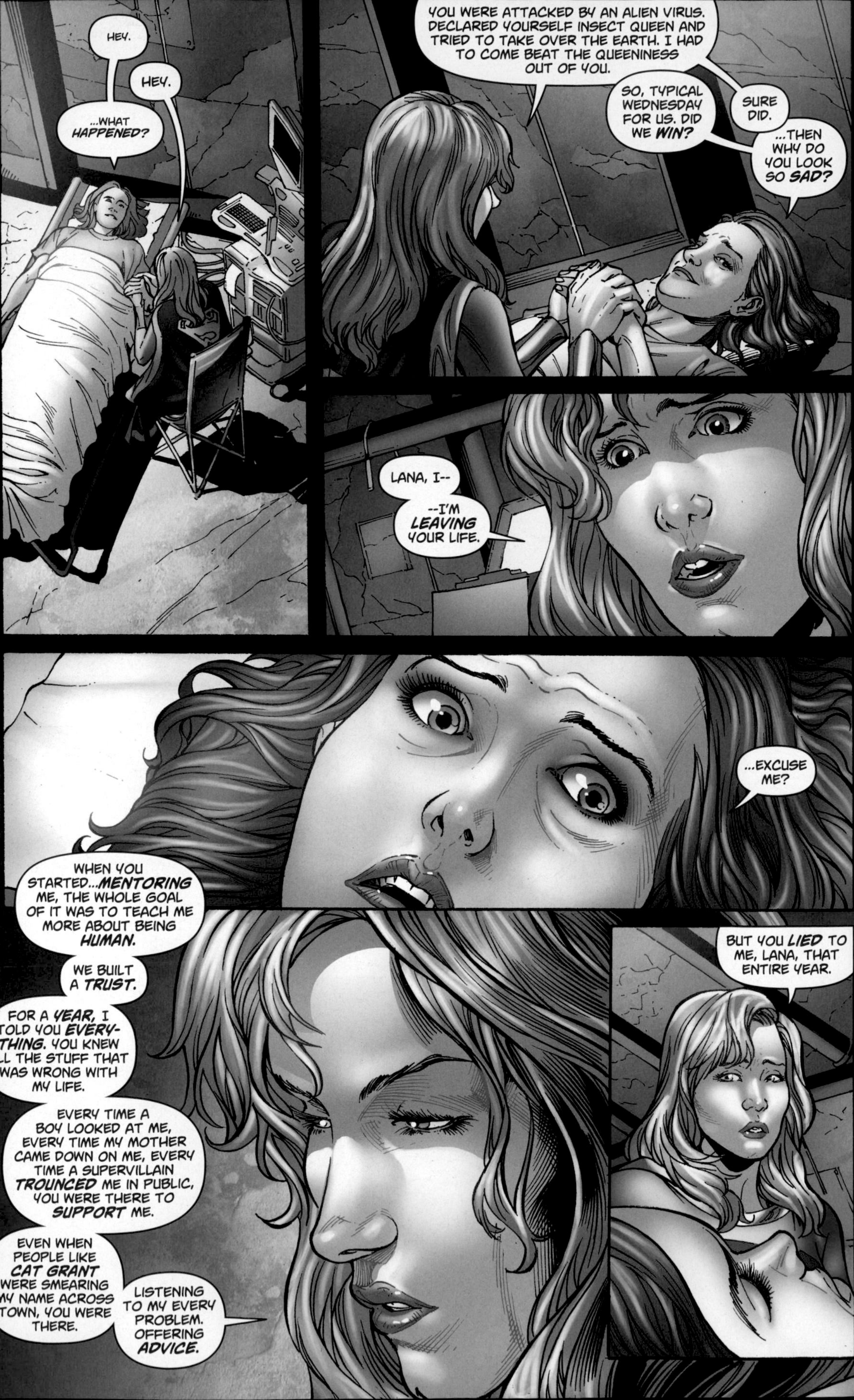
HEY.
HEY.
...WHAT HAPPENED?
YOU WERE ATTACKED BY AN ALIEN VIRUS. DECLARED YOURSELF INSECT QUEEN AND TRIED TO TAKE OVER THE EARTH. I HAD TO COME BEAT THE QUEENINESS OUT OF YOU.
SO, TYPICAL WEDNESDAY FOR US. DID WE WIN?
SURE DID.
...THEN WHY DO YOU LOOK SO SAD?
LANA, I--
--I'M LEAVING YOUR LIFE.
...EXCUSE ME?
WHEN YOU STARTED...MENTORING ME, THE WHOLE GOAL OF IT WAS TO TEACH ME MORE ABOUT BEING HUMAN.
WE BUILT A TRUST.
FOR A YEAR, I TOLD YOU EVERY-THING. YOU KNEW ALL THE STUFF THAT WAS WRONG WITH MY LIFE.
EVERY TIME A BOY LOOKED AT ME, EVERY TIME MY MOTHER CAME DOWN ON ME, EVERY TIME A SUPERVILLAIN TROUNCED ME IN PUBLIC, YOU WERE THERE TO SUPPORT ME.
EVEN WHEN PEOPLE LIKE CAT GRANT WERE SMEARING MY NAME ACROSS TOWN, YOU WERE THERE.
LISTENING TO MY EVERY PROBLEM. OFFERING ADVICE.
BUT YOU LIED TO ME, LANA, THAT ENTIRE YEAR.

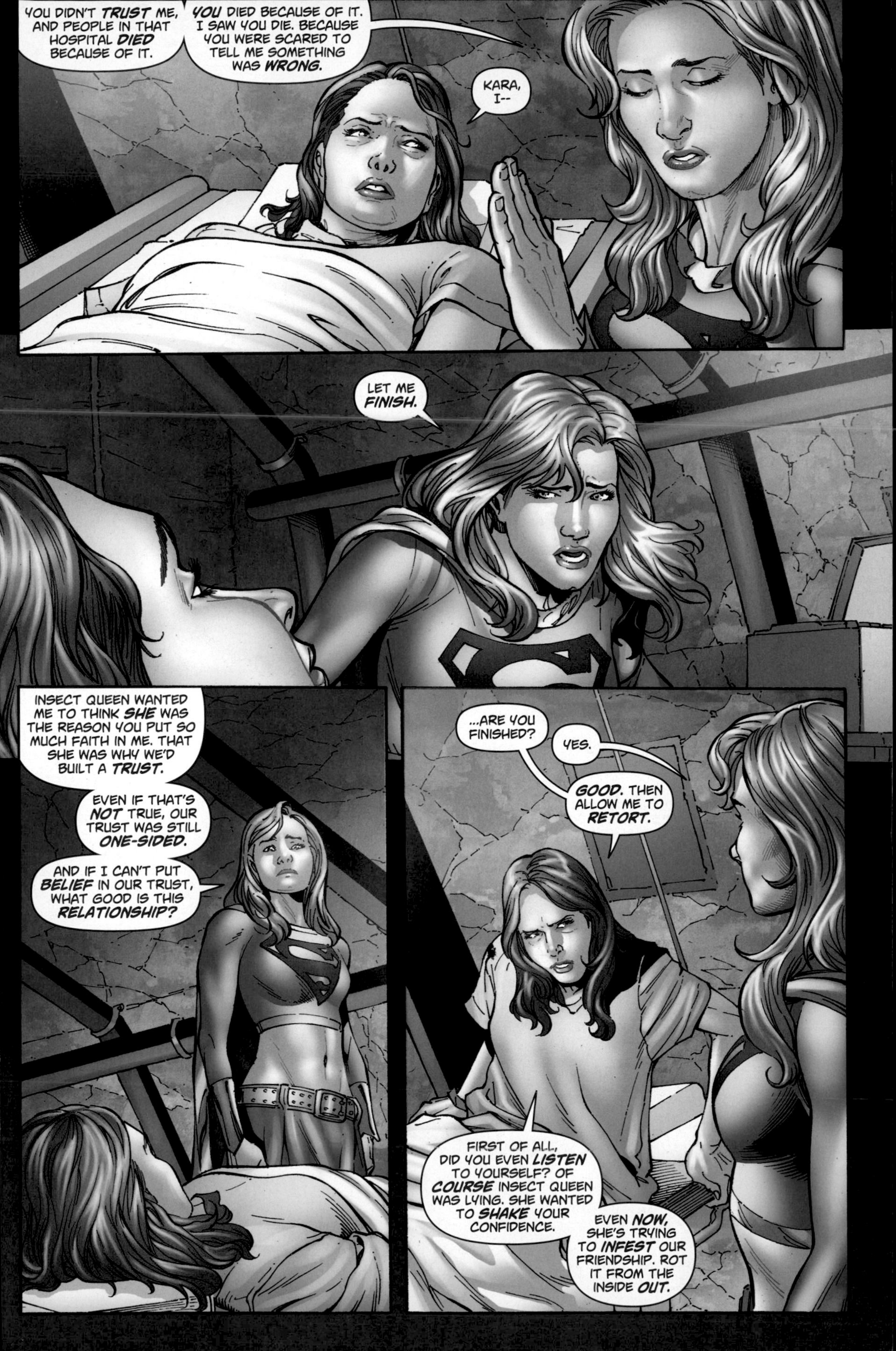
YOU DIDN'T TRUST ME, AND PEOPLE IN THAT HOSPITAL DIED BECAUSE OF IT.
YOU DIED BECAUSE OF IT. I SAW YOU DIE. BECAUSE YOU WERE SCARED TO TELL ME SOMETHING WAS WRONG.
KARA, I--
LET ME FINISH.
INSECT QUEEN WANTED ME TO THINK SHE WAS THE REASON YOU PUT SO MUCH FAITH IN ME. THAT SHE WAS WHY WE'D BUILT A TRUST.
EVEN IF THAT'S NOT TRUE, OUR TRUST WAS STILL ONE-SIDED.
AND IF I CAN'T PUT BELIEF IN OUR TRUST, WHAT GOOD IS THIS RELATIONSHIP?
...ARE YOU FINISHED?
YES.
GOOD. THEN ALLOW ME TO RETORT.
FIRST OF ALL, DID YOU EVEN LISTEN TO YOURSELF? OF COURSE INSECT QUEEN WAS LYING. SHE WANTED TO SHAKE YOUR CONFIDENCE.
EVEN NOW, SHE'S TRYING TO INFEST OUR FRIENDSHIP. ROT IT FROM THE INSIDE OUT.

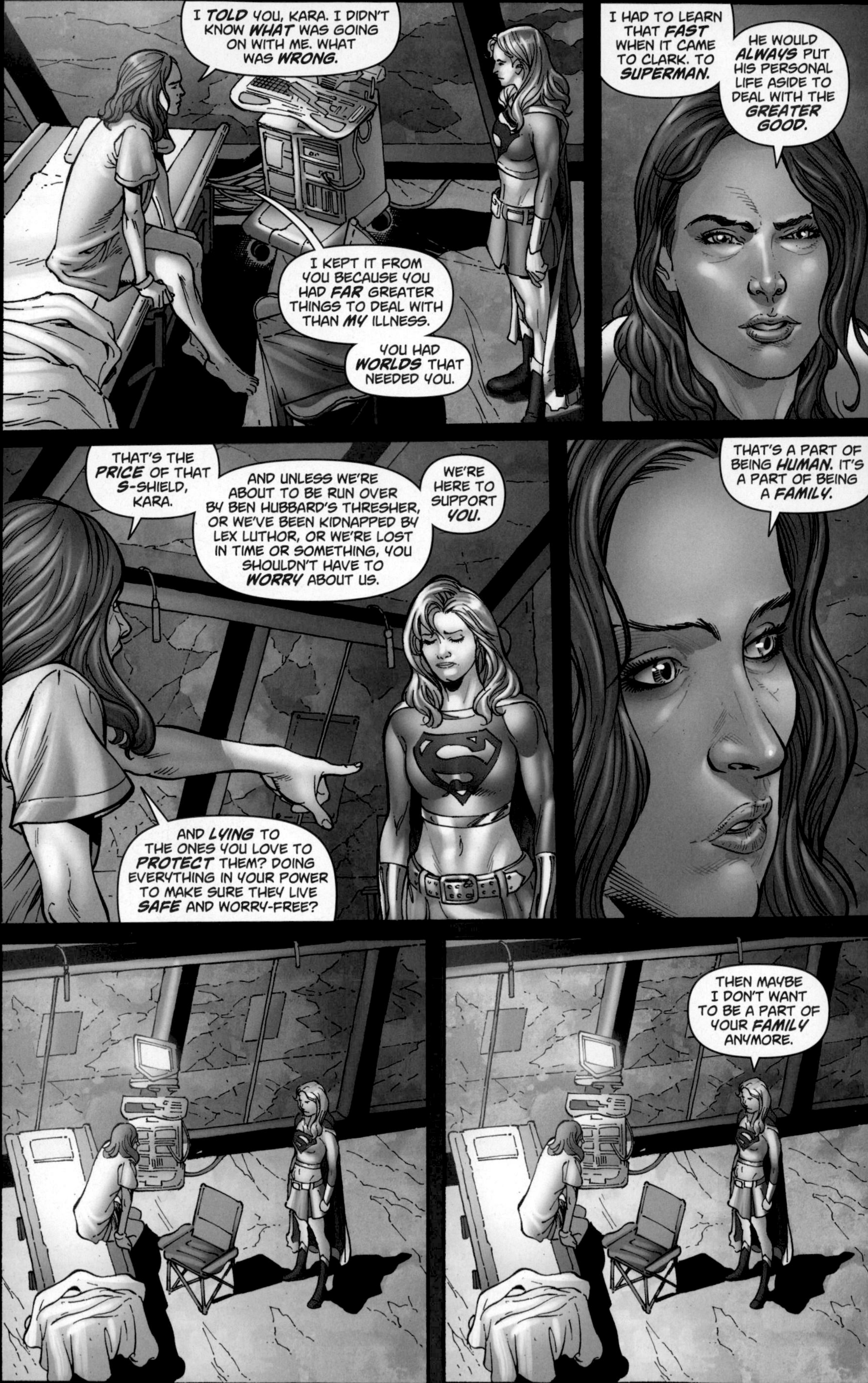
I TOLD YOU, KARA. I DIDN'T KNOW WHAT WAS GOING ON WITH ME. WHAT WAS WRONG.
I KEPT IT FROM YOU BECAUSE YOU HAD FAR GREATER THINGS TO DEAL WITH THAN MY ILLNESS.
YOU HAD WORLDS THAT NEEDED YOU.
I HAD TO LEARN THAT FAST WHEN IT CAME TO CLARK. TO SUPERMAN.
HE WOULD ALWAYS PUT HIS PERSONAL LIFE ASIDE TO DEAL WITH THE GREATER GOOD.
THAT'S THE PRICE OF THAT S-SHIELD, KARA.
AND UNLESS WE'RE ABOUT TO BE RUN OVER BY BEN HUBBARD'S THRESHER, OR WE'VE BEEN KIDNAPPED BY LEX LUTHOR, OR WE'RE LOST IN TIME OR SOMETHING, YOU SHOULDN'T HAVE TO WORRY ABOUT US.
WE'RE HERE TO SUPPORT YOU.
AND LYING TO THE ONES YOU LOVE TO PROTECT THEM? DOING EVERYTHING IN YOUR POWER TO MAKE SURE THEY LIVE SAFE AND WORRY-FREE?
THAT'S A PART OF BEING HUMAN. IT'S A PART OF BEING A FAMILY.
THEN MAYBE I DON'T WANT TO BE A PART OF YOUR FAMILY ANYMORE.

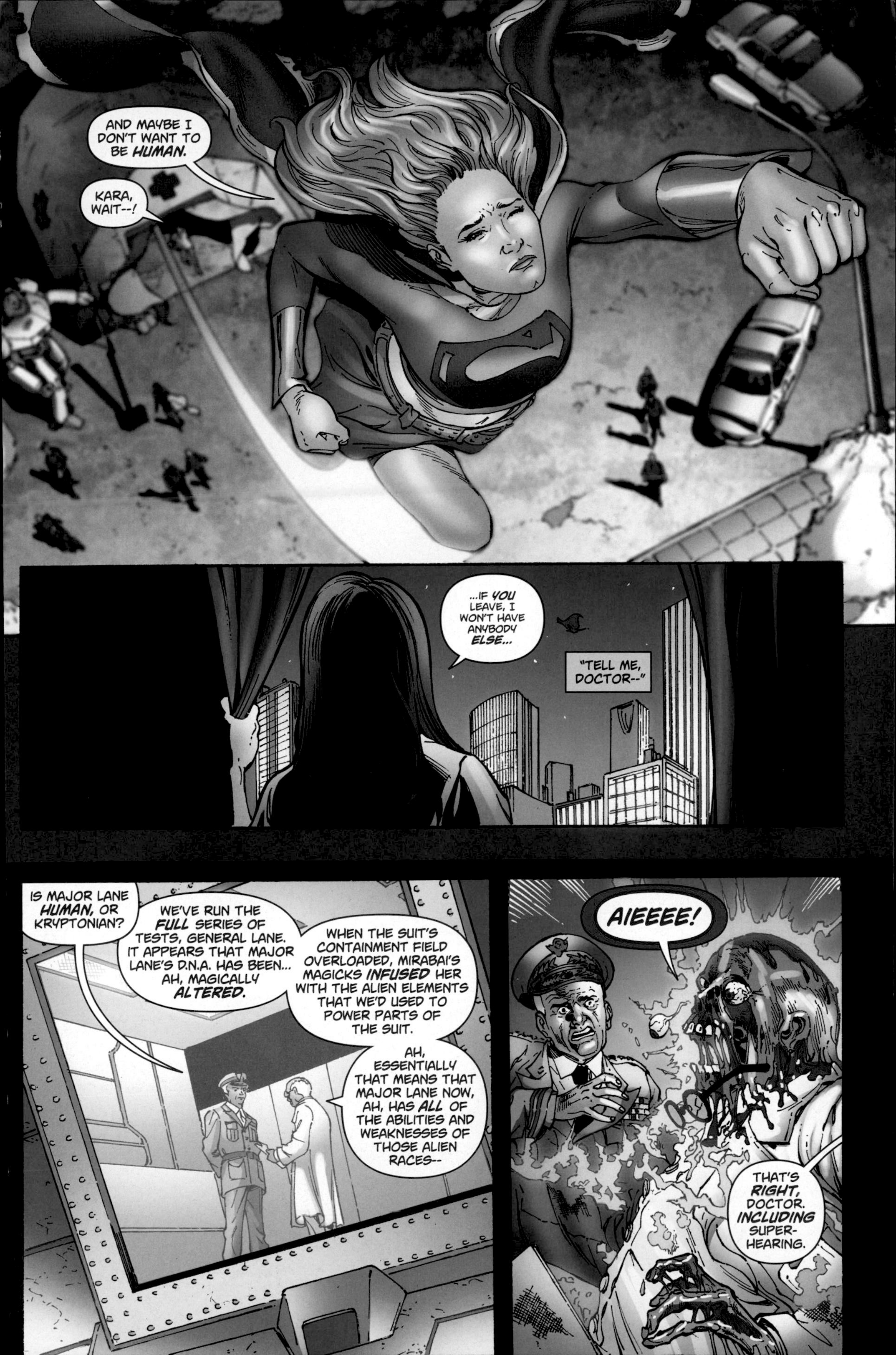
AND MAYBE I DON'T WANT TO BE HUMAN.
KARA, WAIT--!
...IF YOU LEAVE, I WON'T HAVE ANYBODY ELSE...
"TELL ME, DOCTOR--"
IS MAJOR LANE HUMAN, OR KRYPTONIAN?
WE'VE RUN THE FULL SERIES OF TESTS, GENERAL LANE. IT APPEARS THAT MAJOR LANE'S D.N.A. HAS BEEN... AH, MAGICALLY ALTERED.
WHEN THE SUIT'S CONTAINMENT FIELD OVERLOADED, MIRABAI'S MAGICKS INFUSED HER WITH THE ALIEN ELEMENTS THAT WE'D USED TO POWER PARTS OF THE SUIT.
AH, ESSENTIALLY THAT MEANS THAT MAJOR LANE NOW, AH, HAS ALL OF THE ABILITIES AND WEAKNESSES OF THOSE ALIEN RACES--
AIEEEE!
THAT'S RIGHT, DOCTOR. INCLUDING SUPER-HEARING.

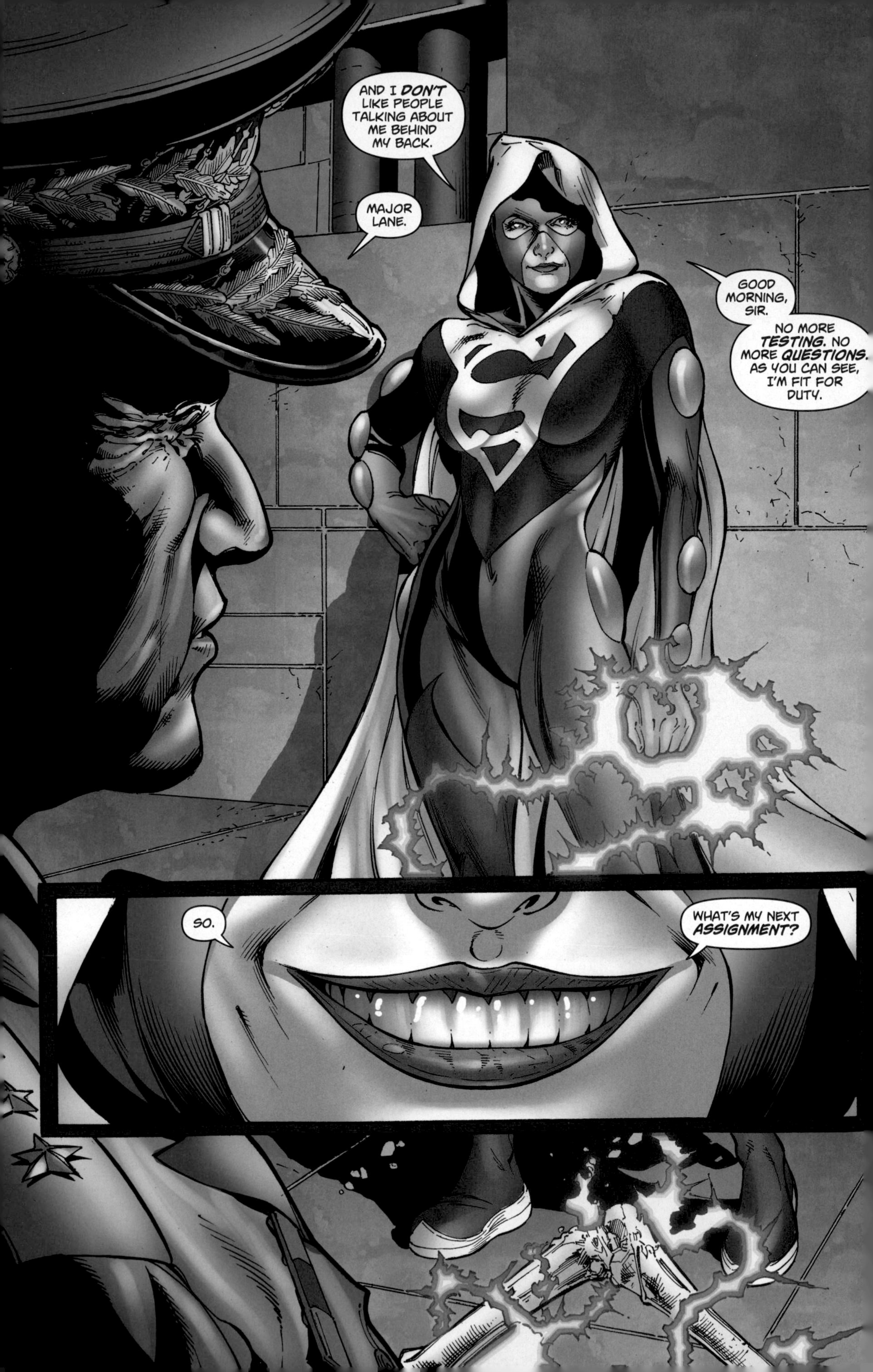
AND I DON'T LIKE PEOPLE TALKING ABOUT ME BEHIND MY BACK.
MAJOR LANE.
GOOD MORNING, SIR.
NO MORE TESTING. NO MORE QUESTIONS. AS YOU CAN SEE, I'M FIT FOR DUTY.
SO.
WHAT'S MY NEXT ASSIGNMENT?

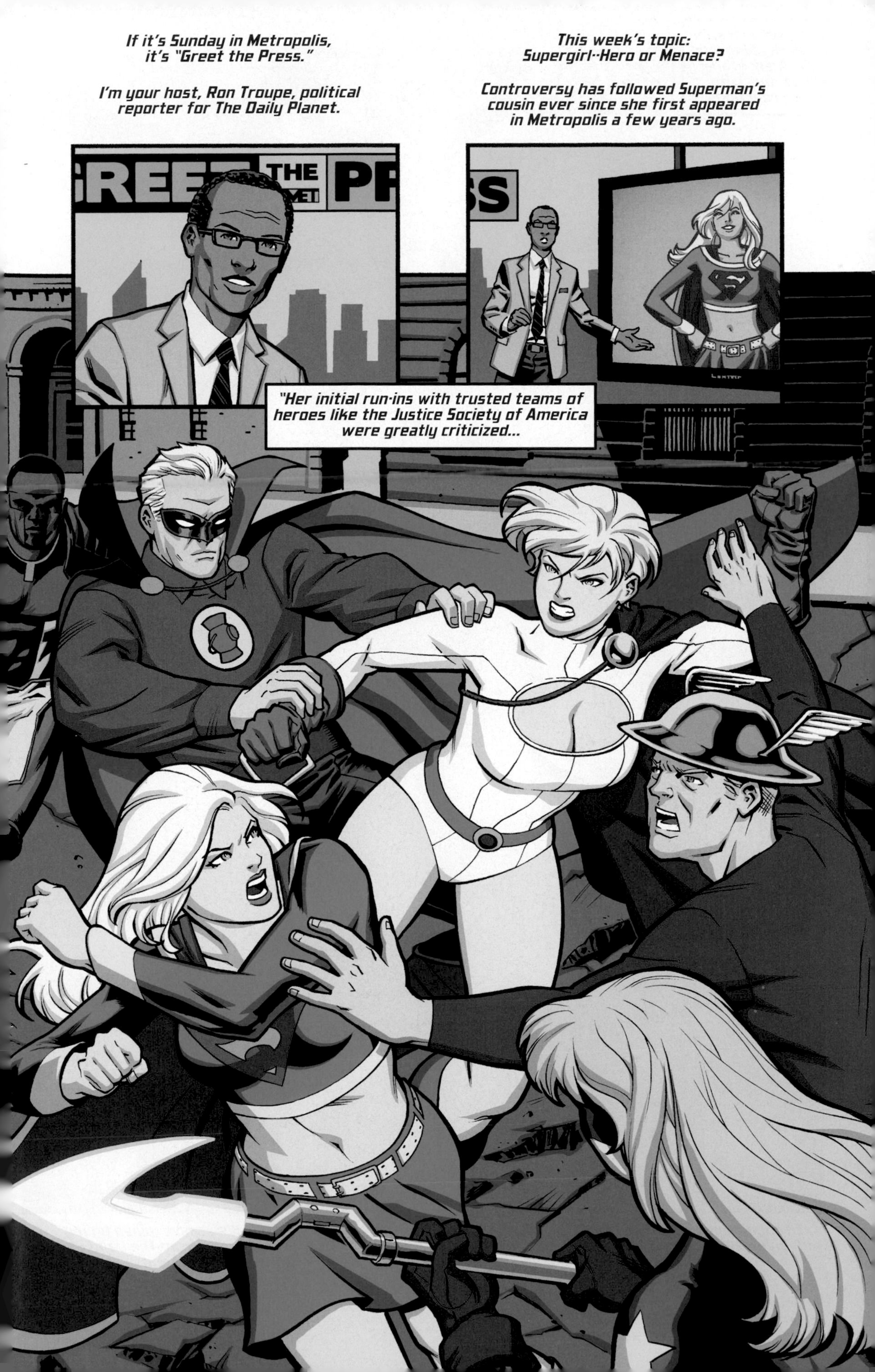

If it's Sunday in Metropolis, it's "Greet the Press."
I'm your host, Ron Troupe, political reporter for The Daily Planet.
This week's topic: Supergirl--Hero or Menace?
Controversy has followed Superman's cousin ever since she first appeared in Metropolis a few years ago.
"Her initial run-ins with trusted teams of heroes like the Justice Society of America were greatly criticized...

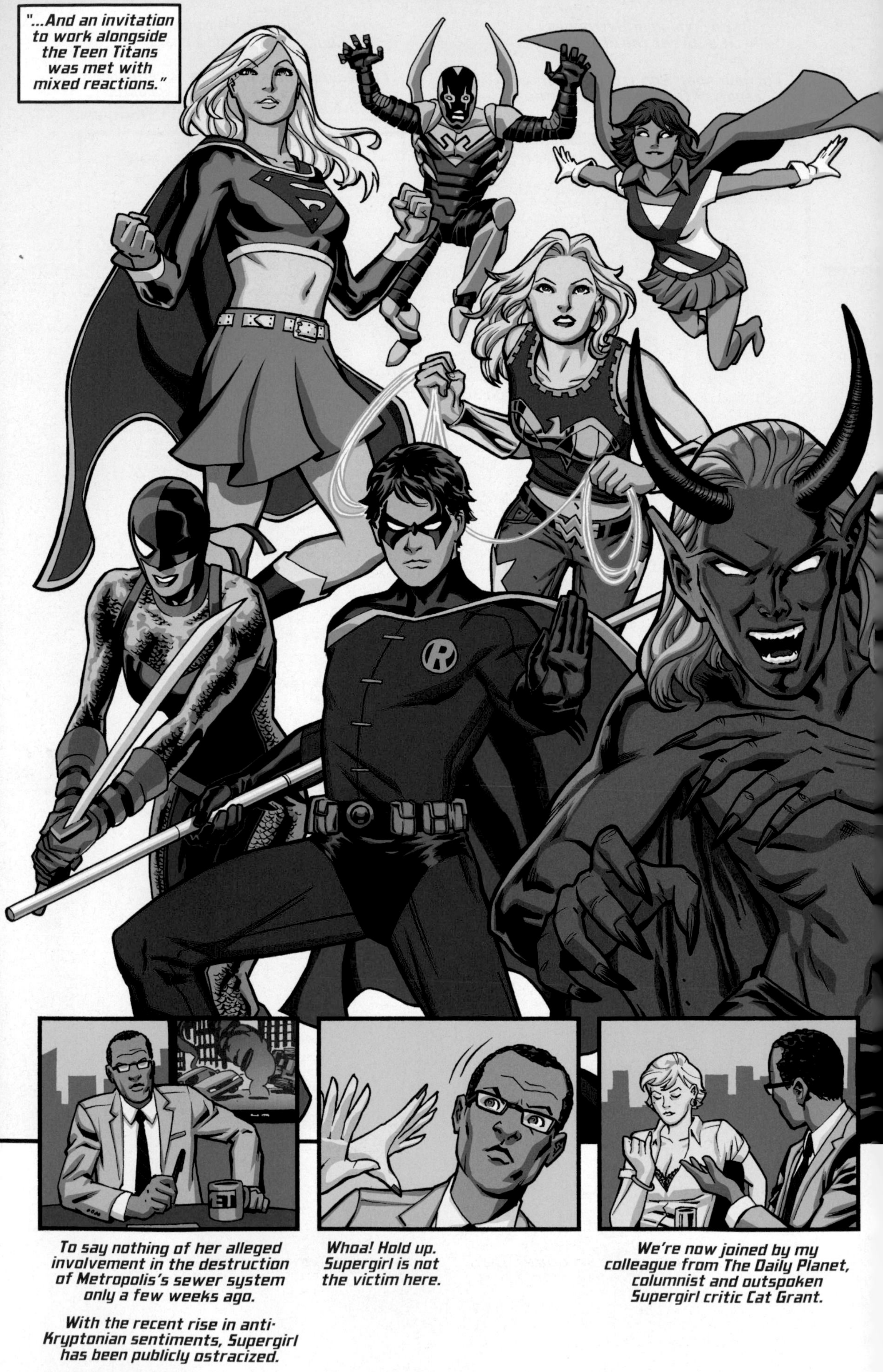
"...And an invitation to work alongside the Teen Titans was met with mixed reactions."
To say nothing of her alleged involvement in the destruction of Metropolis's sewer system only a few weeks ago.
With the recent rise in anti-Kryptonian sentiments, Supergirl has been publicly ostracized.
Whoa! Hold up. Supergirl is not the victim here.
We're now joined by my colleague from The Daily Planet, columnist and outspoken Supergirl critic Cat Grant.

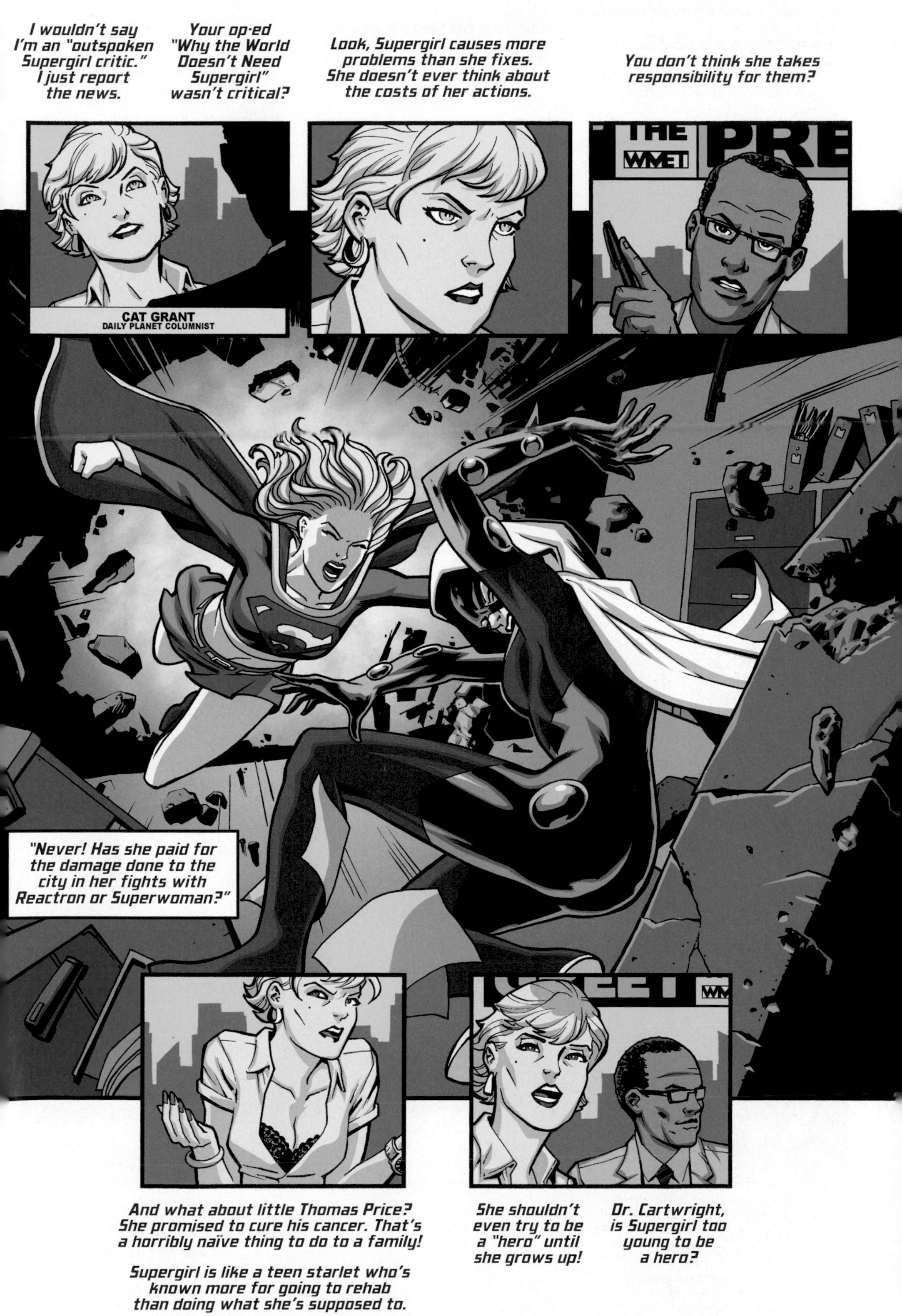
I wouldn't say I'm an "outspoken Supergirl critic." I just report the news.
Your op-ed "Why the World Doesn't Need Supergirl" wasn't critical?
CAT GRANT
DAILY PLANET COLUMNIST
Look, Supergirl causes more problems than she fixes. She doesn't ever think about the costs of her actions.
You don't think she takes responsibility for them?
THE
WMET
PRE
"Never! Has she paid for the damage done to the city in her fights with Reactron or Superwoman?"
And what about little Thomas Price? She promised to cure his cancer. That's a horribly naïve thing to do to a family!
Supergirl is like a teen starlet who's known more for going to rehab than doing what she's supposed to.
She shouldn't even try to be a "hero" until she grows up!
Dr. Cartwright, is Supergirl too young to be a hero?

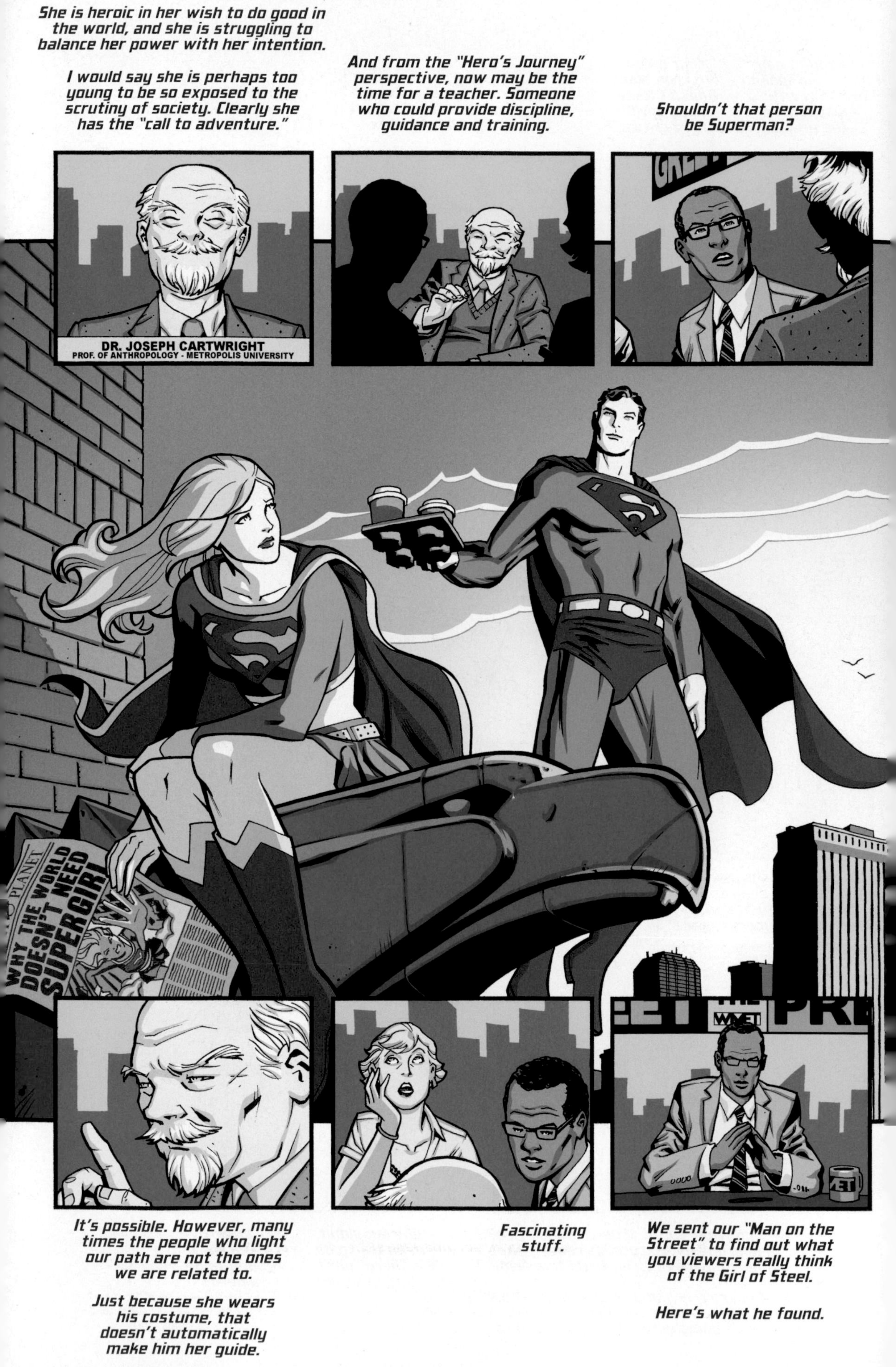
She is heroic in her wish to do good in the world, and she is struggling to balance her power with her intention.
I would say she is perhaps too young to be so exposed to the scrutiny of society. Clearly she has the "call to adventure."
And from the "Hero's Journey" perspective, now may be the time for a teacher. Someone who could provide discipline, guidance and training.
Shouldn't that person be Superman?
DR. JOSEPH CARTWRIGHT
PROF. OF ANTHROPOLOGY - METROPOLIS UNIVERSITY
PLANET
WHY THE WORLD DOESN'T NEED SUPERGIRL
It's possible. However, many times the people who light our path are not the ones we are related to.
Just because she wears his costume, that doesn't automatically make him her guide.
Fascinating stuff.
We sent our "Man on the Street" to find out what you viewers really think of the Girl of Steel.
Here's what he found.

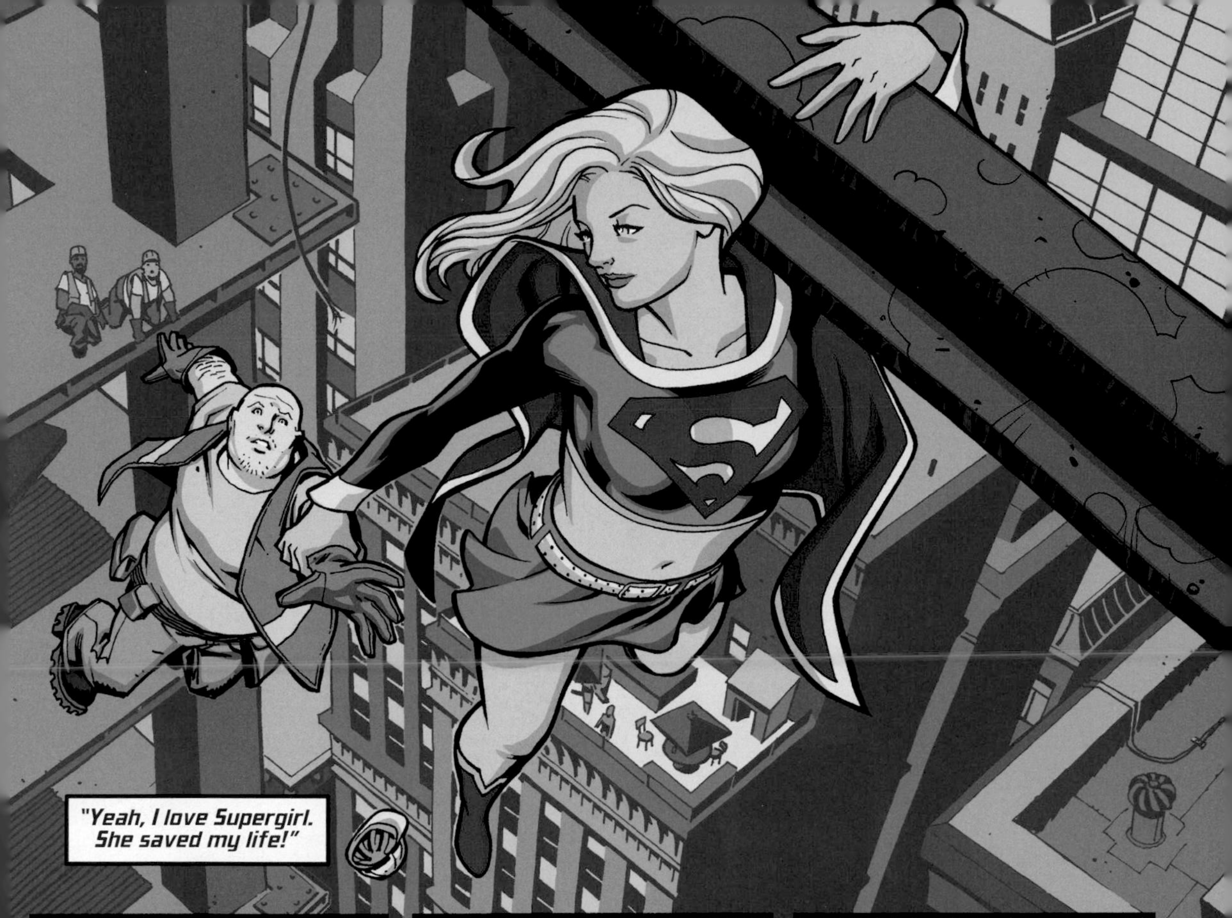
"Yeah, I love Supergirl.
She saved my life!"

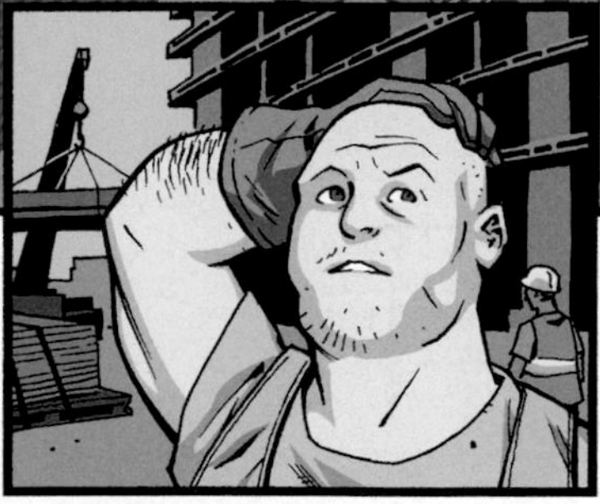

I don't like the Kryptonians any more than the next guy, but you can't judge a person only because of her race!

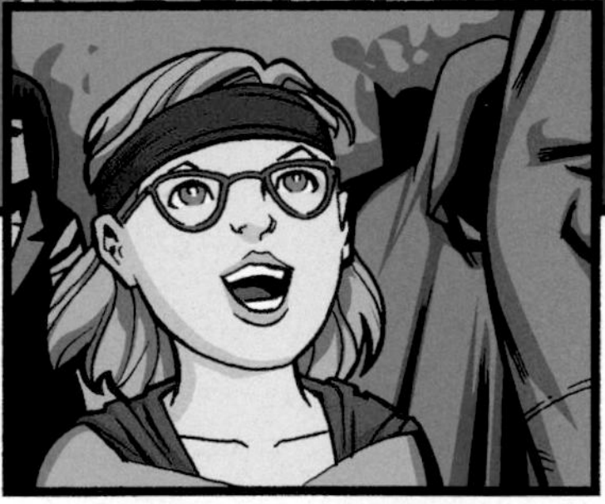

Supergirl brought my daddy back home to my family! She's my hero!

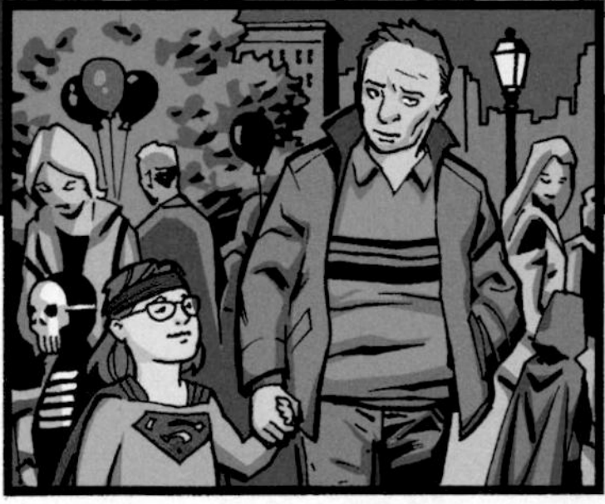

Yeah. She, uh, gave me a new way of looking at life when I'd pretty much hit rock bottom.

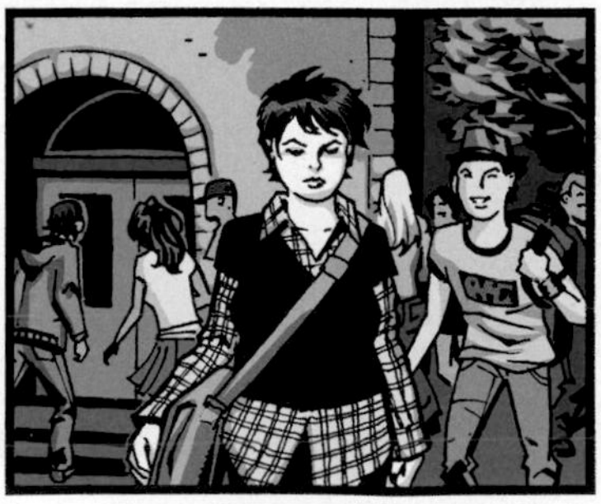

I used to think Supergirl was nothing like me. I mean, c'mon, we're total opposites or whatever.

She's all bright and happy. And I'm not.

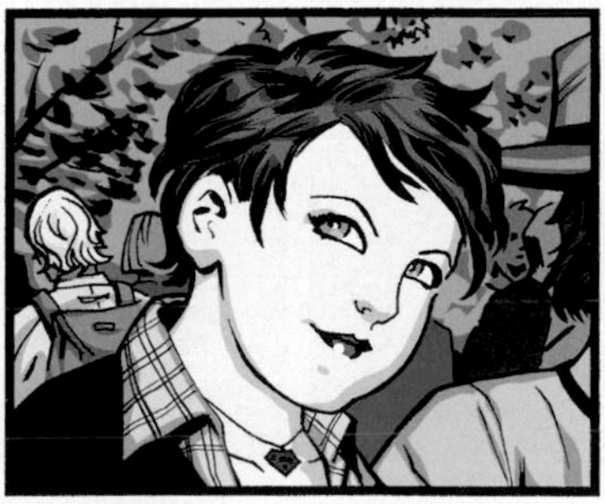

But I saw how tough she was. Seriously independent. I took that from her.

Supergirl made me stronger.

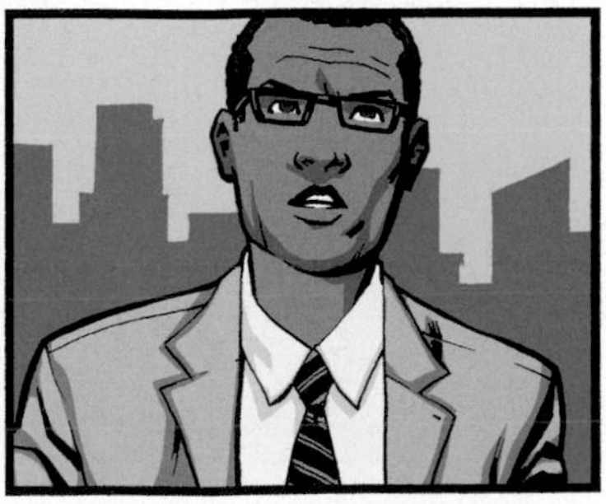

The people of Metropolis are still wary of Supergirl. And that's understandable.

She is, after all, an inexperienced and perhaps undisciplined Kryptonian girl.

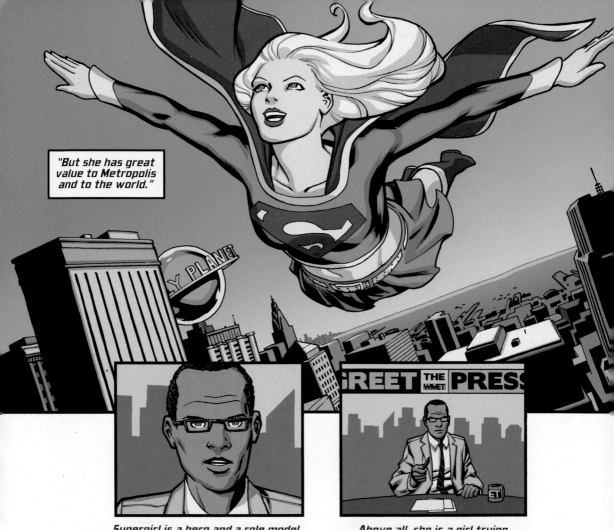

"But she has great value to Metropolis and to the world."
LY PLANET
GREET THE WMET PRESS
Supergirl is a hero and a role model.
Above all, she is a girl trying to find her way in the world. She makes mistakes, but she's growing and developing positively.
THAT'S ALL FOR NOW. WE'LL SEE YOU NEXT WEEK ON WMET'S "GREET THE PRESS."
THANKS FOR STICKING UP FOR ME, RON. AND FOR UNDERSTANDING WHO I REALLY AM.

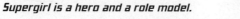

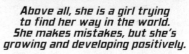

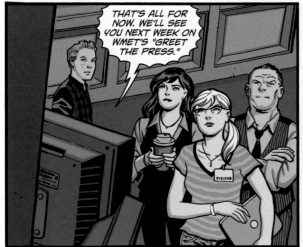

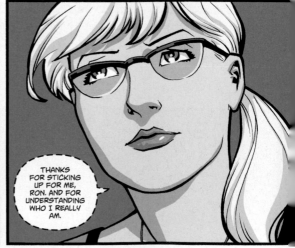